The

European Union

Union

Handbook

Regional Handbooks of Economic Development

The China Handbook
The India Handbook
The Japan Handbook
The CIS Handbook
The Central and Eastern Europe Handbook
The Southeast Asia Handbook

Forthcoming

The South America Handbook

The

European Union

Handbook

Second Edition

Edited by

Jackie Gower

Adviser

Ian Thomson

FITZROY DEARBORN PUBLISHERS

LONDON • CHICAGO

Copyright 2002 by
FITZROY DEARBORN PUBLISHERS

All rights reserved including the right of reproduction in whole or in part in any form. For infor-
mation write to:
FITZROY DEARBORN PUBLISHERS
919 North Michigan Avenue
Chicago, Illinois 60611
USA
or
310 Regent Street
London W1B 3AX
UK

British Library Cataloguing in Publication Data and Library of Congress Cataloging in Publication
Data are available.

ISBN 1-57958-223-0

First published in the USA and UK 2002
Typeset by Florence Production Ltd, Stoodleigh, Devon
Printed by Edwards Brothers, Ann Arbor, Michigan

Contents

Law and Society

External Relations

Contents

Future

Appendices

Editor's Note

The first edition of the *European Union Handbook* was published in 1996 as an authoritative introduction to the EU for the general reader, student or practitioner. It aimed to provide clear and up-to-date factual information on the EU's development, institutions, personalities, and policies in a readily accessible format together with analysis and comment by some of the leading scholars in the field of European integration.

The second edition retains the same objectives and format but has been substantially revised and expanded to incorporate the large number of significant changes that have taken place within the EU over the past five years. Among the most important developments have been the two intergovernmental conferences leading to the Treaties of Amsterdam and Nice, the introduction of the single currency (the euro), the imminent prospect of enlargement to many of the new democracies in central and eastern Europe, the decision to develop a European military capability, and the adoption of a Charter of Fundamental Rights. At the same time, issues concerning democracy and legitimacy in the European Union have been raised in the discourse on the future of European integration and Euroscepticism has become more prevalent across much of the continent. All these topics are covered in newly commissioned chapters together with others considering policy areas that were omitted from the first edition such as the environment, justice and home affairs, and the EU's relations with the Mediterranean, with developing countries, and with Russia.

As many readers may wish to consult just one or two chapters, care has been taken to ensure that each is self-contained although, where appropriate, references are indicated in the text to other relevant material in the book. Each chapter has a guide to further reading which supplements the main bibliography and a comprehensive guide to electronic sources of information on the EU has been compiled by Ian Thomson.

The EU has an extensive (many would say excessive) number of acronyms and specialized terms and these are explained in the Glossary appendix as well as in the text. There are a number of general points that may be helpful to point out at the beginning.

As is now the conventional practice, the terms "the European Union", "the EU" and "the Union" are used to denote the European Union that was established on 1 November 1993 by the Treaty on European Union (or Maastricht Treaty as it is more commonly known). Where it is clear from the context that the author is referring to events prior to this date, the terms "European Community", "European Communities", "EC" or simply "Community" are used as appropriate. However, it is a complex and potentially confusing issue, as the "European Union" consists of three "pillars", one of which is known as "the European Community" and where the decision-making procedures, including the role of the Court of Justice, are very different from those found in the intergovernmental pillars covering the common foreign and security policy and police and judicial cooperation. Therefore where the distinct "Community" methods of decision-making and law enforcement are relevant to the text, the terms "European Community" or "Community" have been used even in the context of developments since 1993.

After the Treaty of Amsterdam had been agreed, a consolidated version of all the treaties was produced and the articles renumbered sequentially, omitting those that had become obsolete and replacing the letters that had been used in the Treaty on European Union (e.g. A–F in the Common Provisions, the "K" articles for Justice and Home Affairs, and the "J" articles for the Common Foreign and Security Policy). Although many people continue to use the old numbering when referring to specific policies or decision-making procedures, the new numbering is becoming increasingly widely used, particularly in official documentation and by younger scholars. It was therefore decided to adopt the new numbering except where referring clearly to a particular period in the past, but to indicate the old number in the text for the benefit of those familiar with the former practice.

The changes to the treaties agreed at the European Council at Nice in December 2000 have been included in the *Handbook*. However, the treaty was still going through the lengthy process of ratification by all 15 member states when the book was published. In the light of the negative vote in the Irish referendum on the treaty in June 2001, a note of caution has been inserted into the text where appropriate.

From 1 January 1999 the ecu was converted into the euro on the basis of one ecu = one euro. Where figures clearly refer to the period before 1999, the ecu has been used, but where figures span the two periods, they have generally been expressed in euros.

A collaborative project on this scale obviously depends entirely on the goodwill, patience and professionalism of the contributors. I was very fortunate that almost all of the authors from the first edition agreed to revise their chapters so that I could concentrate on finding experts to write the new chapters. I am also very grateful to Ian Thomson for his valuable advice. Thanks are also due to Patrick Heenan for his meticulous editing of the text to ensure both clarity and consistency. And finally an enormous "thank you" to Roda Morrison at Fitzroy Dearborn who has managed to combine seemingly inexhaustible patience and good humour with impressive professionalism.

History
and
Context

Chapter One

From a Europe of States to a State of Europe?
An Historical Overview of the Uniting of Western Europe

Derek W. Unwin

One of the most striking historical characteristics of Europe has been its extreme political fragmentation. Across the centuries, numerous intellectuals and political leaders alike have dreamed of bringing order and unity to this mosaic, the latter most obviously through attempts at conquest. There was considerable intellectual agitation for unity in Europe in the 19th century, but almost exclusively by people who were, at best, on the fringes of politics. Their arguments and blueprints held little appeal or relevance for political leaders. However, the century did see a recognition that some form of economic cooperation – a customs union or free trade area – might hold some potential political advantages, but those schemes that did become operative were either short-lived or, like the *Zollverein* (customs union) established among German states in the first half of the 19th century, highly region-specific and protectionist.

The post-World War I peace process, by its emphasis on national self-determination, made the mosaic more complex, thus also making cooperation more urgent and more difficult. After 1918, the hopes that had been invested in, for example, the League of Nations – precursor of the United Nations (UN), the latter founded in 1945 – quickly foundered in a highly charged atmosphere of historic and ethnic rivalries. The Low Countries and the Nordic states did explore possibilities of economic cooperation, but with no significant outcome. A few politicians, most notably perhaps Edouard Herriot and Aristide Briand of France, did raise the idea of political integration, most concretely perhaps through the Briand Memorandum (1930), which presented a proposal for a kind of intergovernmental union, with its own institutional infrastructures, within the League of Nations. Outside political circles, a plethora of associations, headed by the Pan-European Union formed in 1923, expounded cooperation and integration, but failed to achieve any positive results. In the 1930s economic depression and the rise of fascism led countries to look to their own defences; the outbreak of war in 1939 simply confirmed the lack of any advance. The story of western European integration, as it is understood today, therefore essentially begins in 1945.

The Opening Moves

World War II was itself a catalyst for a renewed interest in European unity. It led to the argument that nationalism and nationalist rivalries, by ending in war, had discredited the independent state as the foundation of political organization, and that what was needed was a concerted effort to develop a comprehensive continental community. This argument was found most strongly among the various national resistance movements, many of which demanded that the first postwar priority had to be the immediate establishment of a federal European state. Few activists, however, succeeded in gaining access to government after the first postwar elections, and the new administrations seemed to give European unity a low priority, preferring to concentrate initially on the problems of national economic reconstruction. However, for several reasons arising from the changed political and economic context of Europe, unity was to survive as an item on the political agenda.

The most important factor was the increasingly glacial political climate. The effective division of Europe between East and West after 1945 generated alarm in western Europe and concern about the territorial ambitions of the Soviet Union, and led to a deep involvement by the United States in western European affairs. The consequent Cold War – the ideological, political, and diplomatic conflict between the United States and the Soviet Union, and between western and eastern Europe, that endured until 1991 – created pressures that propelled western Europe towards defining itself as an entity with common interests. This movement was assisted by a general concern over the parlous state of the national economies, with a consequent feeling that economic recovery could only come about through external assistance from the United States, combined with collaboration on development and trade across the states.

The initial moves by governments were limited in scope, with the wartime decision by Belgium, the Netherlands, and Luxembourg to establish the "Benelux" customs union being an exception. While governments were more typically interested primarily in security arrangements, they had done little more than consider mutual aid treaties of the traditional variety. The only formal agreements to emerge were the Treaty of Dunkirk between Britain and France (1947), and its extension in the Treaty of Brussels (1948), which was signed also by the Low Countries and was to serve later as the basis of the Western European Union (WEU). While these two treaties listed economic and cultural cooperation as objectives, these matters remained undeveloped. They

were essentially mutual security pacts, specifically to guard against possible future German aggression, but also with an eye towards possible future Soviet actions. By 1948 the Cold War was in full swing. The final marriage between western Europe and the United States, which alone could provide the desired military security, came with the formation of NATO in 1949. NATO was the conclusion of a programme of US support first outlined in the Truman Doctrine of March 1947, which pledged US support for "free peoples who are resisting subjugation". It provided a protective shield behind which western Europe was free to consider its political and economic options without necessarily having to devote scarce resources to military defence. Equally, the United States, itself a federation, saw nothing inherently evil in closer integration within western Europe, and indeed, also for its own strategic interests, lent its weight after 1947 to proposals for more intensive collaboration.

Against this backdrop, the protagonists of a federal Europe, who could be found across most of western Europe, began to receive endorsement from a significant number of senior politicians from several countries. They continued to press for action on western European integration and union. The issue was no longer whether there should be integration, but what form it should take. Governments and political parties took up positions on the question of whether this should be only intergovernmental collaboration, or something deeper that would embrace an element of supranationality. The first result of the postwar debates was the Congress of Europe, held at The Hague in May 1948. With almost 700 delegates or representatives from 16 countries, as well as observers from Canada and the United States, the Congress itself was too unwieldy to achieve any practical success, but it helped to place integration on the agenda. It was thus a spark that set in motion a process of discussion and debate that culminated in May 1949 in the establishment by ten states of the intergovernmental Council of Europe, the first postwar political organization in western Europe. The Council represents a victory for those who wished only for cooperation, not for integration: its decisions require the consent of all its members and, in any case, it cannot enforce its views on reluctant member states.

These political developments were paralleled by activity on the economic front, through the introduction of the European Recovery Programme, widely known as the Marshall Plan. The US offer of economic aid to western Europe on which this was based was contingent upon the administration of the relief programme being collective, in order to maximize its benefits. The United States further insisted that the European participants in the programme had to decide themselves how aid was to be distributed across the countries involved. These were the basic tasks of the Organization for European Economic Cooperation (OEEC), established in April 1948. The OEEC was primarily concerned with cooperation and coordination. Thus, like the Council of Europe, it was intergovernmental in nature, only able to operate with the consent of all its members. Both organizations, however, had to have some permanent institutions to enable them to perform their allotted functions satisfactorily. While limited in scope and relying very much upon the principle of voluntary cooperation, both bodies nevertheless reflected a realization in western Europe of the interdependency of states: these states, especially against the backdrop of the Cold War, could prosper or fail together. However, both organizations, in terms of degree of integration and of limiting national sovereignty, operated within the broad yet restricting denominator of intergovernmental cooperation (the lowest common denominator), a situation that could not satisfy those who believed in the imperative of union.

If union was to become a practical objective, a different path had to be sought. The radical redirection of effort was provided by a Frenchman, Robert Schuman, who in May 1950 cut through the tangle in the western European debate to propose a pooling of coal and steel resources, specifically between France and the newly established West Germany. The Schuman Plan became the blueprint for the European Coal and Steel Community (ECSC), which was formally established in April 1951 as western Europe's first organization that involved the yielding by member states of some sovereignty to a supranational authority.

Hailed by its drafter, Jean Monnet, as "the first expression of the Europe that is being born", it set in motion a groundswell that, 40 years later, was to result in the EU. While an invitation to join the new body was extended to all western European states, only six countries – Belgium, France, Italy, Luxembourg, the Netherlands, and West Germany – felt able to accept the supranational principle of the ECSC.

The institutional structure adopted by the ECSC, including an assembly of representatives from national legislatures, and a supreme judicial body, was to serve as a model for all future developments. The most significant feature was the divided executive: a High Authority was vested with significant power to represent the supranational principle, while a Council of Ministers represented and protected the interests of the governments of the member states. More generally, the ECSC was to be, for its protagonists, the first step in a process of sectoral integration, whereby, following the arguments advanced by Monnet, the ultimate goal of political union would be built upon an accretion of integrative efforts in a sector-by-sector linkage of specific economic areas and activities that would at some point culminate in a common market (see Chapter 3 for a fuller discussion of the neofunctionalist approach). This inevitably slow process seemed to people who thought like Monnet to be a surer way of achieving union than a sudden imposition of a federal structure on western Europe. The ECSC further served some of the priorities of its two major participants. For West Germany, it demonstrated the country's determination to invest its future and national identity within European structures that would limit its national freedom of action; for France, it represented a means of influencing economic and political policy in West Germany. What it did economically for the other members was to give them better access to a larger market. The Low Countries – already in the Benelux customs union mentioned above, which was to become an economic union in 1960 – were generally in favour of European integration. In Italy, under Prime Minister Alcide De Gasperi, participation in such ventures as the ECSC was seen first as a way of developing the Italian economy, especially its "labour surplus", and secondly as an extra guarantee against possible threats from the country's significant Communist and neo-Fascist movements. The ECSC survived as a separate entity until 1967 and the creation of the European Communities (EC). Its record of economic success was mixed, since it had little or no control over or effect on other economic sectors.

During the ECSC negotiations, the international climate changed for the worse as conflict broke out in Korea. Concerned with a strengthening of NATO, the United States called for a military contribution from West Germany. To avoid the creation of an independent army in West Germany, France proposed a European Defence Community (EDC), modelled upon the ECSC. The EDC would establish a western European army, including units from West Germany, under an integrated western European command structure. Unlike those of the other EDC participants, all West Germany's forces would be within the EDC framework. The EDC was immediately viewed by supporters as a second step towards integration. Further, the question of political control over the EDC soon led to proposals for a European Political Community (EPC), something that could short-circuit sectoral integration through the creation of a comprehensive federation. Only the ECSC countries were willing to explore these developments. Britain declined a specific request to join the EDC process, but stressed that it welcomed and would support the idea of a western European army. The EPC idea remained at the draft treaty stage. It was clear that it depended upon the success or failure of EDC ratification. Ironically, the stumbling block was France, where the idea of a rearmed West Germany, even within the EDC, remained alarming. France had originally wanted and had expected Britain to be part of the new organization, as an extra guarantee against any possible re-emergence of German militarism. In a sense, the French proposal for an EDC had been, for many politicians, a delaying tactic. The speed at which the EDC talks had progressed placed successive French governments, all short-lived, weak, and concerned primarily with survival, in a quandary. Faced

with strong political and popular opposition, all were unable or unwilling to secure a parliamentary majority for its ratification. After four years of stalemate, France rejected the EDC in 1954. Only the ECSC survived the damage to the cause of integration. Even so, there were widespread fears that it too would collapse as a result of the rejection of the EDC.

However, there remained across western Europe a substantial degree of institutional cooperation built up over the previous decade through NATO, the OEEC, the Council of Europe, and the ECSC. Within these networks there was in the "little Europe" of the ECSC Six a commitment to integration. At a meeting of their foreign ministers at Messina in Sicily in June 1955, they launched "a fresh advance towards the building of Europe", agreeing to set in motion plans for the construction of a customs union that would lead to a common market. These developments culminated in March 1957 with the Treaty of Rome, which established the European Economic Community (EEC).

The Derailment of Rome

Because the new organization was to range over an extremely wide area of activity, the provisions of the Treaty of Rome were necessarily complex. The Treaty enjoined its signatories, among other things, to establish a common market, approximate their economic policies, and forge closer relationships among themselves. Although these and other objectives were expressed in economic terms, such as a Common Agricultural Policy (CAP), a political purpose lay behind them. In aiming to create ultimately more than a common market, the Treaty emphasized the principle that the problems of one member state would be the problems of all. It did not possess a limited life span: it was to remain in force for "an unlimited period", meaning essentially that it could not be revoked. The institutional structure was modelled on that of the ECSC, with the quasi-executive and supranational European Commission intended to be the motor force of integration; its authority was to be counterbalanced by that of the Council of Ministers, representing the member states.

Facing these executive bodies were, first, a much weaker Assembly, with no significant decision-making powers, which, having soon adopted the title of "European Parliament" (EP), engaged in a perpetual struggle to enlarge its own authority; and, secondly, a European Court of Justice, which rapidly asserted itself as a major bonding force, notably through the ruling that EEC law took precedence over national law. The less significant European Atomic Energy Community (Euratom) was set up in 1957 by a second Treaty of Rome, and also modelled upon the institutional structure of the ECSC, to promote collaboration on the development of nuclear energy for peaceful economic purposes. Rationalization of the various Communities was completed in 1967 with the merger of the executives of the ECSC, the EEC, and Euratom to form the European Communities (EC).

Under the leadership of a proactive Commission, initial progress towards the goals of Rome was satisfactory. By 1961 internal tariff barriers within the EEC had been substantially reduced and quota restrictions on industrial products had largely been eliminated. Internal trade had flourished. These positive advances raised hopes among those committed to the establishment of a political union that the goal of political cooperation might also be expedited. Indeed, Walter Hallstein, a forceful politician from West Germany who was President of the Commission from 1958 to 1967, informed journalists that he could be regarded as a kind of Prime Minister of western Europe. The optimism, however, proved to be premature. Broadly speaking, the transformation of the EEC into a common market was to be spread over a period of 12 to 15 years, yet by the early 1970s the EEC was seemingly no nearer that goal than it had been a decade earlier. A series of circumstances had led to its derailment.

The difficulties faced by the EEC in the 1960s focused mainly around the French President, Charles de Gaulle. While he was generally supportive of the EEC as a means of retaining French influence in Europe, especially over West Germany – with which France forged a close relationship after 1962 – de Gaulle was suspicious of anything that might

affect both that influence and French sovereignty. Two episodes in particular were significant. First, the immediate economic success of the EEC as a trading bloc after 1958 had led other western European states, which had previously rejected involvement, to revise their opinions and seek membership. The most important of these was Britain, which applied for membership in 1961. In 1963, and again in 1967, de Gaulle, against the wishes of his five partners, vetoed the British application on the grounds that Britain, because of its Commonwealth links and its relationship with the United States, was not sufficiently committed to Europe or to EEC objectives. Secondly, according to the schedule set by the Treaty of Rome, the EEC was expected to move in 1966 to an extension of "qualified majority voting" in the Council of Ministers. As in the EU's Council of Ministers today, each state had an indivisible block of votes within the EEC's Council, roughly proportionate to the size of its population. A qualified majority meant that unanimity on a decision was not necessary: a two-thirds majority would suffice, with the result that a state could be outvoted and unable to veto the decision. The Treaty of Rome had envisaged the steady diminution of the right of member states to exercise vetos. De Gaulle, however, was not prepared to accept the increased risk of France being outvoted in decisions. In 1965 he essentially provoked a crisis that was resolved only by the Luxembourg Compromise of 1966, which allowed states to exercise vetos where they felt that their vital national interests might be adversely affected.

Overall, the results of de Gaulle's actions seemed to indicate that political integration was off the agenda and that the future development of the EEC would be more as an intergovernmental union of independent states – a shift that seemed to be symbolized by Hallstein's resignation from the presidency of the Commission in 1967. To some extent, the early progress made after 1958 had been possible because of a lack of involvement in the EEC by national leaders. If, however, further progress was to be governed by the Luxembourg Compromise, a more positive national input would be required. The way forward was eased by de Gaulle's retirement in 1969. Later that year, at a summit meeting in The Hague, the six heads of government attempted to restore some momentum to the new EC. The summit opened the way for the enlargement of the EC, especially to British membership. It extended the budgetary powers of the EP, called for the implementation of Economic and Monetary Union (EMU) by 1980, reconfirmed political union as the ultimate goal of the EC, and in practice established summit meetings as a new style of EC decision-making. Summitry was to be formalized and placed on a regular basis with the establishment of the European Council in 1974.

These summit objectives were only partially realized. The first enlargement duly occurred in 1973, with the accession of Britain, Denmark, and Ireland. With further enlargements in 1981, 1986, and 1995, Community membership was to grow to 15 over the next two decades, and, with the promise of further expansion into central and eastern Europe around the turn of the century, the adjective "European" has steadily become more meaningful in describing what the Community encompasses. Equally, the EC began to be able to assert a more positive and united presence in international affairs. Represented by the Commission, it spoke with one voice in international trade negotiations and, after the Davignon Report on policy cooperation (1970), the member states, through European Political Cooperation (EPC), developed an impressive and on balance quite successful structure and pattern of collaboration on, and coordination of, foreign policy, with regular meetings of foreign ministers and the issuing of common instructions to their ambassadors in other countries; regular consultations among ambassadors in foreign countries and at the UN; and the adoption of a single EC representation in international forums and conferences, especially in the UN. After the mid-1970s, two structural funds, the European Regional Development Fund and the European Social Fund, began to play important roles in providing aid for economic and employment restructuring. Equally, although the CAP's voracious appetite was beginning to threaten to destroy the EC's budgetary capacity, the CAP could be held up, not so much for what

it had achieved, then at least as a symbol of what commonality meant in a united Community.

While the balance sheet around 1980 therefore showed many positive aspects, these could not disguise the fact that, on the broader front of the objectives of the Treaty of Rome, the EC seemed to be marking time. A common market seemed to be as far away as ever. Further, the major integrative aim of the Hague summit had been EMU. It fitted with the desire to extend the customs union, and monetary union was perhaps the most fundamental policy required for a true economic and political community, for with it would come supranational decisions on fiscal policy, tax harmonization, a single economy, and even a single currency. Yet throughout the 1970s it was thwarted. Up to 1969 the EC had benefited from international monetary stability as a condition for policy coordination. The turbulence that beset the international monetary system after 1970, generating a world of floating currencies, brought the EC's plans for EMU to an abrupt end by the middle of the decade. Its attempts in 1972 to establish a zone of monetary stability (the "Snake") never got off the ground and the structure was already dead when it was abandoned in 1976. The European Monetary System (EMS) of 1979, while successful, was a more modest design and only a first step back on the right road. EMU was not to return to the EC agenda until 1989.

On the broader integrative front, the initiative had passed to the European Council. Its formation in 1974 confirmed the central role of the heads of national governments. More specifically, it brought to an apogee the process of Franco–German collaboration that lay at the core of the EC. While the two states were not always able to impose their will upon their partners, their consent was vital for any progress to be made. Despite the acceptance by both states of the need to use and develop the EC as an instrument of pragmatic integration, the real achievements that were made could not disguise the fact that the EC was not progressing, or at least doing so only minimally, towards the aims of the Treaty of Rome.

Nevertheless, the Council continued to pay lip service to the ideal of political union. From the Tindemans Report (1976), which recommended strengthening the EC institutions and the adoption of more common policies, through to the Solemn Declaration on European Union (1983), the European Council sponsored studies on how to advance the cause of union or rhetorically asserted its faith in the ultimate goal. In 1974, the Council of Ministers eventually agreed that the EP should be elected directly by the national electorates – another delayed implementation of a requirement of the Treaty of Rome – instead of, as had been the case since 1958, being elected by the national parliaments from among their own membership. Direct elections gave the EP a sense of greater legitimacy and the first directly elected EP in 1979 urged rapid movement towards union, issuing a comprehensive Draft Treaty on European Union in 1984. At the end of the day, however, the initiative and commitment had to come from the European Council. To do so, it needed to take on board a growing number of issues that it had tended to shelve or avoid: the EC's budget and national contributions to it; the burgeoning costs and problems of the CAP in particular; the need to consider further common policies; and further enlargement. Before 1980, the Council was more decisive in responding to world problems as they affected the EC. In the 1980s, partly by choice and partly by necessity, Council sessions turned to matters more directly pertaining to the EC: further enlargement, new policies and modifications of existing policies, and institutional and procedural amendments to the EC framework. They contributed to the emergence of a new sense of direction and purpose.

The Revival of Ambition

Perhaps the first important turning point came with the Fontainebleau session of the European Council in 1984. Hosted by the French President, François Mitterrand, it tackled the backlog of issues that had contributed towards the stalling of progress. Most importantly, it reached agreement about funding the EC budget – threatened with bankruptcy because of the growing costs of the CAP – and accepted the principle of imposing limits on CAP expenditure by tying it more clearly to overall EC expenditure. It also reached an acceptable compromise on complaints by Britain about the size of its budget contribution relative to its economic strength and removed French objections to the Iberian enlargement of the EC. The summit also established two committees, which both reported within the year. One, the Committee for a People's Europe, was charged with considering how the EC might develop practical symbols and policies that would help the growth of a Community identity across the national populations, a crucial necessity for integration that had previously barely been touched upon. The other committee, the Dooge Committee, was more directly concerned with political change. It followed a well-trodden path, recommending institutional reforms that would strengthen the coherence and supranationalism of the EC.

All of these issues were considered by the European Council at Milan in 1985. It was the first time that the Council seemed to be prepared to sit down to discuss the details of reform. Because reform was the core issue, the Milan meeting was particularly contentious. Yet, surprisingly, the Council was able to come to some momentous decisions. Despite the objections of some states, it agreed to establish an intergovernmental conference (IGC) to consider the construction of a reform package out of the several reports and initiatives on the EC's future. It further returned to the ideals of the Treaty of Rome, setting the end of 1992 as the completion date for the transformation of the EC into a comprehensive common market. The task of preparing the EC for 1992 was given to the Commission. These decisions coincided with the appointment of a new Commission and in particular a new President, Jacques Delors, a Frenchman with the tenacity and ability to use the greater room for manoeuvre that these decisions had granted the Commission, and thus to re-establish it as a motor force for more intensive union. The Commission rapidly produced a White Paper on the internal market that contained a list of some 300 separate measures relating to physical, fiscal, and technical barriers to trade that would need to be implemented. These were not ranked by priority: for each measure, the paper bluntly gave a strict timetable that would have to be observed if the necessary directives were to be adopted and in place by the end of 1992.

The objective of 1992, according to the Commission, was "a Europe without frontiers". This vision was also, for many, the unwritten item on the agenda of the IGC. Its brief was to study "the institutional conditions in which the completion of the internal market could be achieved within the desired time limit". More specifically, the IGC was asked to consider revision of the Treaty of Rome "with a view to improving the Council's decision-making procedures, strengthening the Commission's executive power, increasing the powers of the European Parliament, and extending common policies to new fields of activity". Although there was some scepticism about, and even hostility towards, the supranational implications of such statements, especially from Britain and Denmark, the IGC was able to construct a package of proposals for consideration by the European Council.

On the basis of the package, the Council accepted in principle a number of texts referring to specific areas of projected action. These were brought together into a Single European Act (SEA) that, subject to ratification by the member states, could be written into the treaties. The SEA was the first major revision of the Treaty of Rome and represented an attempt to secure the latter's goal of a common market. While not drafted as a radical document, it did have revolutionary potential in its clauses on institutional change, new policy objectives, new forms of decision-making and legislative processes, and the extension of the EC to cover foreign policy, and even defence and security. All implied a shift in the balance of power away from the member states towards the supranational institutions. The SEA finally came into force in 1987, providing a further impetus towards, and a weapon for those committed to, closer union.

Maastricht and Beyond

The ratification of the SEA confirmed that 1992 had become a symbol of something significant that all assumed would occur. What that something might be was a matter of interpretation. The fact that the drive towards a more coherent political framework for the EC and a closer degree of union was sustained, seemingly with ever greater intensity, was due to a wide agreement on change across the member states, with the possible exception of Britain. Within that consensus, the major forces were, first, the Franco–German axis at the heart of the EC, which after 1989 was given new urgency by the collapse of European Communism and the impending unification of West and East Germany, and, secondly, the revitalized Commission under the effective and single-minded leadership of Delors.

Between 1987 and 1990 Delors and the Commission took up three major themes necessary for further advancement. A more coherent and rational restructuring of the EC budget was proposed and undertaken. The Social Charter, a programme for a minimum set of workers' and citizens' rights, was accepted, against the lone opposition of Britain. Above all, the EC returned to the theme of monetary policy, something that the logic of the internal market demanded. Responding to a request from the European Council in 1988, Delors produced a report on EMU the following year. It envisaged movement towards EMU in three stages, using the EMS and its Exchange Rate Mechanism (ERM) as the starting point, with completion – including a single currency and single central bank – in place before the end of the century. Events began to accelerate. In December 1989 the European Council agreed to the establishment of an IGC that would discuss and construct an edifice for EMU. The following year a further IGC was established to discuss the issue of political union, to transform the EC "from an entity mainly based on economic integration and political cooperation into a union of a political nature, including a common foreign and security policy".

The two IGCs worked in parallel. Their proposals were due to be considered by the European Council at Maastricht in December 1991. The run-up to the Maastricht summit was affected by the ending of the Cold War, the impending collapse of the Soviet Union, and the changing face of Europe, but these events merely sharpened, rather than altered, the differences of opinion among the member states.

Most importantly, they confirmed the view of the Franco–German axis that the immediate transformation of the EC into a more political entity was an overriding imperative.

The Maastricht summit was contentious and ill-tempered. It had the task of finalizing a radical overhaul of the Treaty of Rome to create a framework for European union that would incorporate political measures and EMU, determine a timetable for implementation of the changes, and launch the EC along a new security dimension. By and large these objectives were achieved, but only after much disagreement and modification. The Treaty on European Union (TEU) set 1999 as the deadline for EMU implementation, but with strict monetary criteria determining the eligibility of member states for participation. It extended EC competence in several policy areas, established a new Cohesion Fund to help the poorer member states to satisfy the conditions for further integration set in the Treaty, and transformed the EC into the EU. The EC and its supranational institutional structure would now be paralleled by two "pillars" of intergovernmental cooperation directed by the European Council, one dealing with a common foreign and security policy (CFSP), the other with justice and home affairs (JHA).

Despite the claims that were made on behalf of the TEU, also widely known as the Maastricht Treaty, the level of general euphoria at the conclusion of the summit was rather muted. Indeed, the ink was barely dry on the TEU before the fledgling EU was beset by problems, leading to fears that Maastricht might be less a major advance on the road to full union than the high-water mark of the integration surge. Popular concerns over some of the sovereignty implications of the Treaty led to ratification problems in several states, and the formal inauguration of the EU, originally intended to coincide with the completion of the single internal market, was delayed until November 1993. The strict criteria for EMU, complemented by downturns in many of the national economies, created severe problems for several states. The capacity of some national economies to meet the criteria did not convince the international money markets, and in 1992–93 intense currency speculation

disrupted the ERM. The debate over whether the 1999 deadline for full EMU was realistic, and whether the criteria should be modified or set aside, continued throughout the decade. Acute differences of opinion persisted over foreign policy issues, and the inability of the EU to handle the series of crises arising from the disintegration of Yugoslavia after 1991 without US and NATO involvement indicated that the EU still had far to travel down the road of common defence and security.

The TEU had thus highlighted once again the gap between those who sought, and those who were wary of, a more intense political integration: neither side was satisfied with the outcome. The TEU, however, was a treaty *on*, not *of*, European union. It was a further advance, not a conclusive outcome. It had been agreed at Maastricht that in 1996 a further IGC would meet to review progress and possible revision of the TEU. The outcome of this process was the Treaty of Amsterdam (1997), essentially a somewhat modest tidying-up exercise that did not address several major institutional and policy issues. It did, however, emphasize the need for the EU to relate more closely with its citizens, reflecting a lesson drawn by political leaders from the Maastricht experience that the drive to integration since the mid-1980s had been too elite-driven, and too prone to ignore popular feelings and concerns. The Amsterdam Treaty also accepted the notion of flexibility, a recognition that some member states might wish to pursue more intensive integration than others in some policy areas, as long as the integrity of the EU and the rights of other member states were not compromised.

Flexibility was a recognition of the fact that there were differing views among member states about the nature and degree of both political and economic integration. While the EU made steady progress on the single internal market, the issue of EMU remained a problem throughout the decade. All member states had difficulties with the criteria, but the final decision on eligibility in 1998 softened or reinterpreted the criteria: all member states except Greece were held to have met the conditions. EMU and a single currency, the euro, were launched on schedule in 1999, with national currencies to be phased out by 2002. However, three eligible member states declined to participate (Denmark, Sweden, and the United Kingdom). The ability to speak with one voice and to act in concert, and the effectiveness of EU institutions, were issues that were kept on the agenda also because of the further enlargement of the EU. Three new members – Austria, Finland, and Sweden – joined in 1995. Between 1994 and 1996 the EU received applications for membership from an array of ex-Communist and new states in central and eastern Europe. In 1998 negotiations for membership began with six applicants that were deemed to have met the necessary criteria, while the door was left open, but with no clear commitment or timetable, for a further six applicants. Partly as a response to a projected membership of over 20 states, in 1997 the Commission issued *Agenda 2000*, an extensive and detailed document that attempted to identify the major challenges of the future – although not all were consequences of enlargement. The *Agenda* indicated that the EU would have to address important questions of policy, budgetary and institutional reform if it wished to remain an effective organization.

The debates, treaties, and policy documents of the 1990s all essentially dealt with and derived from the same issues. Should the EU concentrate on "deepening", on producing a more intensive integration among its existing members, and if so, how much flexibility, or variations of commitment across member states, should be permitted? Or should its first priority be "widening", in order to bring as many countries as possible into the EU family? Either way, there are significant implications for the financing, policies, institutions, and decision-making bodies of the EU. The differences among member states are not only between those that wish to push ahead and those that do not: they also exist between those that are major recipients of EU funding through regional aid and the CAP, and those that are not. A structure designed many years ago for six like-minded countries has remained unchanged in its broad essentials across all the treaties, enlargements, and expansions of policy competences to incorporate a greater number of states with more divergent political and economic patterns: expansion into central and eastern Europe will produce even greater diversity. There is no grand design for the future of the EU, nor any necessary inexorability about its capacity to survive or grow. On the other hand, while differences among – and, of course, within – member states persist about what the EU should be, none has seriously entertained the notion of withdrawal from it. Despite the debates and arguments of the 1990s, progress was maintained on several fronts. EMU and the euro are in place, despite a shaky launch; significant progress towards a more coherent defence and security policy and capability has begun; and collaboration continues to be developed in a wide array of policy areas. While the future nature and efficacy of the EU may be uncertain, it has become, for both the member states and others beyond its boundaries, a fact of life. Some threads have perhaps become too interwoven to be easily unravelled. In that sense, it may be argued, the treaties and other developments of the 1990s should not be classified as either successes or failures. They might more appropriately be regarded as further steps and embellishments in an intricate dance that, over the decades, has locked ever more European states more closely together.

Further Reading

Arter, David, *The Politics of European Integration in the Twentieth Century*, Aldershot: Dartmouth, 1993

A broad historical survey that also considers developments in central and eastern Europe

Burgess, Michael, *Federalism and European Union: The Building of Europe, 1950–2000*, London and New York: Routledge, 2000

A comprehensive review of the role of federalist thinkers, ideas, and strategies in the development of European integration

Church, Clive, and David Phinnemore, *European Union and European Community: A Handbook and Commentary on the Post-Maastricht Treaties*, London and New York: Harvester Wheatsheaf, 1994

A detailed commentary on the provisions of the Treaty on European Union within a broad historical and policy perspective, also indicating the extent to which they amend the Treaty of Rome

Diebold, William, *The Schuman Plan*, New York: Praeger, 1959

A good survey of the origins and workings of the ECSC

Duignan, Peter, and L.H. Gann, *The USA and the New Europe 1945–1993*, Oxford and Cambridge, MA: Blackwell, 1994

A general survey that examines European developments from a US strategic and policy perspective

Fursdon, Edward, *The European Defence Community*, London: Macmillan, and New York: St Martin's Press, 1980

A rigorous and detailed analysis of the EDC proposals, especially from a military perspective

Haas, Ernst B., *The Uniting of Europe: Political, Social and Economic Forces 1950–1957*, Stanford, CA: Stanford University Press, and London: Stevens, 1958

A book presenting a neofunctionalist approach, now rather out of favour, but influential in its day

Hogan, Michael J., *The Marshall Plan*, Cambridge and New York: Cambridge University Press, 1987

One of the more comprehensive studies of the US aid programme and its consequences

Lerner, Daniel, and Raymond Aron (editors), *France Defeats EDC*, New York: Praeger, 1957

A comprehensive account of the difficulties faced by France in seeking to ratify the EDC treaty

Milward, Alan S., *The Reconstruction of Western Europe 1945–51*, London: Methuen, 1984; Berkeley: University of California Press, 1984

A controversial revisionist analysis of the first postwar years that stresses the centrality of national concerns

Milward, Alan S., *The European Rescue of the Nation-State*, London: Routledge, and Berkeley: University of California Press, 1992

An analysis that argues that integration has strengthened, not weakened, the centrality of the national state

Nicholson, Frances, and Roger East, *From the Six to the Twelve: The Enlargement of the European Communities*, London: Longman, 1987

Detailed descriptions of the negotiations leading to each of the first three enlargements of the EC

Pryce, Roy (editor), *The Dynamics of European Union*, London and New York: Croom Helm, 1987

A collection of useful analyses of specific episodes in the history of the EC when political union was on the agenda

Simonian, Haig, *The Privileged Partnership*, Oxford: Clarendon Press, and New York: Oxford University Press, 1985

An outstanding analysis of the Franco–German axis and its impact on the EC

Spierenburg, Dirk, and Raymond Poidevin, *The History of the High Authority of the European Coal and Steel Community*, London: Weidenfeld and Nicolson, 1994

An exhaustive and definitive account of the workings, history, achievements, and failures of the ECSC

Stirk, Peter M., and David Willis (editors), *Shaping Postwar Europe*, London: Pinter, and New York: St Martin's Press, 1991

A collection of useful items on the arguments about the kind of European integration sought from 1945 up to the formation of the EC

Urwin, Derek W., *The Community of Europe: A History of European Integration since 1945*, second revised edition, London and New York: Longman, 1995

A broad introductory survey of the history of European cooperation and integration since 1945

Urwin, Derek W., *A Political History of Western Europe since 1945*, London and New York: Longman, 1997

A broad historical survey in which EC/EU developments are reviewed in parallel with international issues and national politics

Derek W. Urwin is Professor of Politics and International Relations at the University of Aberdeen. Recent publications of his include an *Historical Dictionary of European Organizations* (1994); *The Community of Europe* (1995); *Politics in Western Europe Today* (co-editor, 1990); *A Political History of Western Europe since 1945* (1997); and *Centre–Periphery Structures in Europe* (1987). He was previously co-editor of *Scandinavian Political Studies* and of the *European Journal of Political Research*, and is a former Secretary of the Committee on Political Sociology.

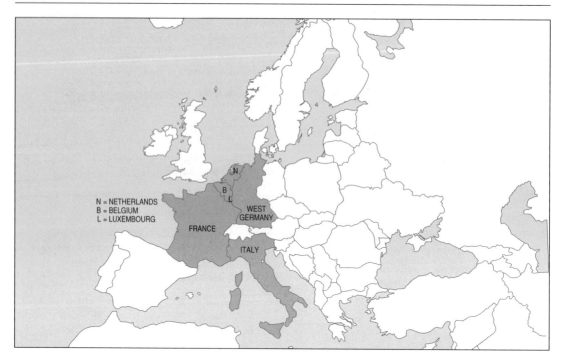

The EC of the Six, 1952–1972

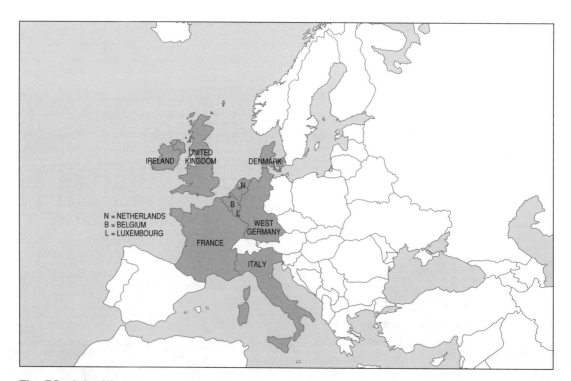

The EC of the Nine
The First Enlargement (Denmark, Ireland, UK) 1973

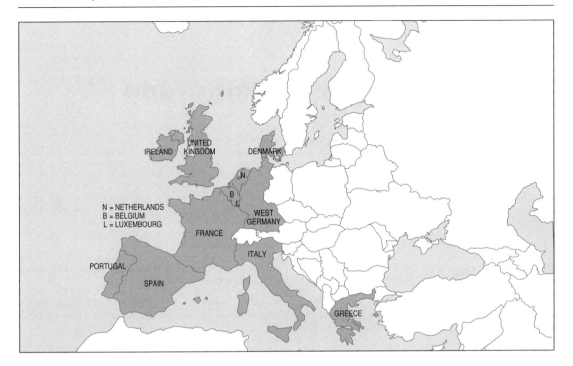

The EC of the Twelve

The Second Enlargement (Greece) 1981
The Third Enlargement (Portugal and Spain) 1986

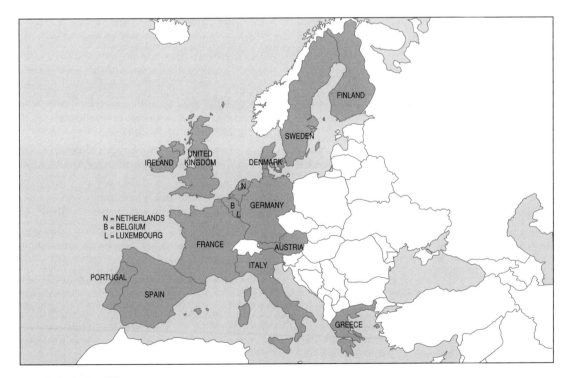

The EU of the Fifteen

The Fourth Enlargement (Austria, Finland, Sweden) 1995

Chapter Two

The Structure, Institutions, and Powers of the EU

Trevor C. Salmon

Founding the EU

The EU came into existence on 1 November 1993. It had a troubled birth. Its gestation had lasted since Robert Schuman's speech of May 1950, which had led to the creation of the European Coal and Steel Community in 1951–52. In 1957–58 the European Economic Community (EEC) and the European Atomic Energy Community (Euratom) had come to life. Of these three it was the EEC that prospered most, and it became known generally as the European Community (EC). It focused on economic integration and by the end of 1992 had not only created a number of policies in key sectors of the economies of the member states but had also moved beyond a customs union to a single market. Arguably it was the very success of this enterprise that persuaded some, such as Jacques Delors, then President of the European Commission, that there needed to be another step in the process of integration, namely Economic and Monetary Union (EMU), particularly but not exclusively the move to a single currency. By 1988 the member states of the EC were beginning to contemplate such a move seriously and began the series of steps that led to the agreement in December 1989 to convene an intergovernmental conference (IGC) on EMU and on changing the founding treaties of the EC in order to accommodate such a development. The IGC was well-prepared and led eventually to agreement at Maastricht, in December 1991, on the steps and the conditions upon which EMU should be created as part of a Treaty on

European Union and thus as an aspect of the new EU.

For many EMU was a logical progression from economic integration. For some it also fitted into the broader political agenda of moving towards more political integration. Because of its economic and monetary features it could be grafted onto the EC, although certain of its organizational features, such as the creation of the independent European Central Bank, mean that its institutions are quite distinct from those of the Community.

Other important aspects of the Maastricht Treaty were products of circumstances, particularly the revolutions in central and eastern Europe in 1989, which also led to the unification of Germany in 1990. The IGC on political union was a response to this upheaval. It was ill-prepared, had no overarching organizing concept, and was almost deluged by the sheer quantity and variety of ideas. It also faced the difficulty that it took place – between December 1990 and December 1991 – at a time of enormous change in the political and security environment of Europe. This was further complicated by the Iraqi invasion of Kuwait in August 1990 and the subsequent war in 1991, and the implosion that was beginning to occur in Yugoslavia. Decision-makers faced a huge workload covering disparate problems. At times the IGC and the putative treaty changes did not receive the attention that they needed. It must also be remembered that every member state has to approve any changes to the treaties, both at the IGC itself and through its own internal procedures for ratification.

Every state therefore had a veto, a factor that was particularly significant given the heterogeneity of national positions. Indeed, the requirement that all existing member states ratify the treaty was nearly its undoing, since in June 1992 the Danes initially voted against it and in September the French approved it by just 51% to 49%. In Britain the treaty was ratified only after being made the subject of a vote of confidence in the government. In Germany, the last member state to ratify, it faced a serious challenge as to its constitutionality before the Federal Constitutional Court. It must also be remembered that, since an IGC is an international negotiation between states, the treaty was the result of bargaining, compromise, and negotiating skill (or the lack of it). It emerged from a tortuous process, with many amendments, caveats and subclauses. The only way that some issues could be resolved was by deliberate, studied ambiguity. Indeed, the treaty itself partially acknowledged that it was not a definitive settlement by providing for another IGC in 1996.

The next IGC resulted in the Treaty of Amsterdam of 1997, which, following ratification, came into effect on 1 May 1999. This treaty did not have the same impact as the treaty of 1992, nor did it contain anything like the structural innovations agreed at Maastricht. Given, however, that it too failed to resolve key issues relating to the decision-making capacity of the EU, there was yet another IGC in 2000, intended to attempt to resolve them. Most initial assessments of the Treaty of Nice, agreed in December 2000, suggest that it too has failed on the major issues, and it had not been ratified by the time this book went to press. Yet again it was agreed that there would be another IGC, in 2004.

The Structure of the EU

The very structure of the EU embodies compromise. Within the three Communities – the ECSC, the EEC, and Euratom – there had evolved the Community "method". Simply put, it was an institutional structure within which the Commission proposed legislation and the governments of the member states, represented in a Council of Ministers, either accepted, rejected or amended the proposal, having taken the advice of the European Parliament (EP). In cases of legal dispute, the European Court of Justice (ECJ) had the determining voice. For all its faults, this system had worked tolerably well and some states wanted it to be transposed to the proposed new areas of EMU, the common foreign and security policy (CFSP), and justice and home affairs (JHA). This became known as the "tree" approach. In effect, advocates of this position took the view that the Community structure should provide the basic model for the new EU, albeit with "branches" sprouting from the trunk to provide for special cases and variations in approach, which were perceived to be necessary in the new areas of competence. This approach was dropped, however, as a number of member states explicitly wished to adopt a more intergovernmental approach to CFSP and JHA, both being regarded as too sensitive to be transferred from national control to that of the Community *per se*, with the key roles that it entrusts to the Commission, the Parliament, and the Court of Justice. The result was the "pillar" structure, with completely different systems of policy- and decision-making in each pillar. Each pillar is different, and the powers of both institutions and member states are different in each, although, confusingly, the names of the institutions have not been changed. Thus the EU consists of three pillars, although it can be argued that, given the distinctiveness of the arrangements for EMU, there are four pillars, or at least three and a half, with EMU being grafted onto the European Community pillar but not identical with it.

The Founding Pillar

Pillar 1 of the EU is the European Community. Pillar 1 comprises five "institutions" – the Commission, the Council, the European Parliament, the Court of Justice, and the Court of Auditors – and three "bodies": the Economic and Social Committee, the Committee of the Regions, and the European Investment Bank. The distinction between "institutions" and "bodies" is based on their respective powers, with the latter having only the power to advise.

The Treaty on European Union states that the EU "shall be founded on the European Communities", and clearly pillar 1 is the central pillar of the EU, given the virtual completion of the single market and the vast *acquis communautaire* built up since its inception in 1958, as well as the distinctive ways and habits of doing business that have evolved over the years. Officially there remain three treaties, founding the three Communities, although the Merger Treaty of 1965 amalgamated their institutions in 1967.

The European Commission

Since January 1995, and the entry of Austria, Finland, and Sweden into the EU, there have been 20 Commissioners, with Britain, France, Germany, Italy, and Spain having two each, and the other ten member states one each. The size of the Commission has been a bone of contention in recent years, both on the grounds that 20 is too large and on the grounds that as the EU enlarges further some action will need to be taken to constrain further growth in its size. Reform became linked to the question of weighted voting in the Council during the 1990s (see below), but the IGC of 1996–97 that culminated in Amsterdam in June 1997 agreed only to return to the issue at a later date. This was done in the IGC during 2000, and at Nice it was agreed, in the "Protocol on the Enlargement of the European Union" (a protocol has legal force), that:

- from 1 January 2005 the Commission that will take office on that date should consist of one member per member state, although there is a clause allowing the Council to waive this provision; and that
- when the EU has 27 member states, the number of Commissioners will be *less* than 27, the members being chosen by a rotation system from among nationals of member states.

The first member of the Commission to be appointed is the President. At the moment the President is nominated by the common accord of the member states (i.e. unanimity), with that nomination being approved by the EP. Once the ratification of the Treaty of Nice has been completed, the President is to be nominated by a qualified majority of the European Council, but the appointment will still require the approval of the EP. This may prove to be a not insignificant change. In 1994 Britain was able to veto the appointment of Jean-Luc Dehaene, on the grounds that he was too "federalist", opting instead, unwisely as it transpired, for Jacques Santer.

Once there is agreement on the Commission President, it is the President and the member states who must agree by common accord on the other members of the Commission. At the moment, this gives the member states the effective right to determine the nominations for their own states. When Nice is ratified this will change: the Council will act by qualified majority and with the accord of the approved President.

In the last ten years or so there has been a movement to strengthen the political and legal position of the Commission President. This can be seen in the President's role, conferred in Amsterdam, to approve or reject the nomination of the other members of the Commission. It can also be seen in the Amsterdam provisions making explicit that the Commission is to work under the political guidance of its President. Following the scandals of 1998–99, when serious accusations were made against the conduct of several members of the Commission, particularly Edith Cresson, the President's position has been further strengthened by the action of Romano Prodi, the incoming President in 1999, who has required that a Commissioner must agree to resign if the President asks him or her to do so, something that Madame Cresson had steadfastly refused to do for Prodi's predecessor, Santer. Prodi's initiative will be regularized, to some extent, once the Treaty of Nice has been ratified, since the treaty makes it clear that "A member of the Commission shall resign if the President so requests, after obtaining the collective approval of the Commission". The President is also given increased powers in the Treaty of Nice to reshuffle portfolios and give direction to the Commission.

Until these changes are completed it will remain difficult to remove a Commissioner.

The ECJ can act on application by either the Council or the Commission itself, but in 1998–99 neither moved against the Commissioners at the centre of the scandals. Alternatively, the EP can force the resignation of the entire Commission, on a motion of censure carried by a two-thirds majority of the votes cast (and including a majority of MEPs, currently 314 out of 626), but it cannot force the removal of an individual Commissioner – a fact that was crucial in 1998–99 when the Parliament refrained from passing a censure motion against the whole Commission.

The Parliament has found that its inability to act in relation to individual Commissioners can cause certain problems, not only as regards removing a Commissioner but also on their appointment. Once the President and the member states have agreed on the other members of the Commission, the whole College of the Commission has to be approved by the EP. In 1994–95 and in 1999 the Parliament held hearings with the individuals who had been nominated to be Commissioners. In 1994–95 it clearly had reservations about three or four proposed individuals, and in 1999 surprise was expressed when four members of the disgraced Santer Commission were renominated. However, the Parliament could not pick and choose, and had to vote for the nominees *en bloc*.

The provisions to vote to approve or reject the Commission *en bloc* are meant to reinforce the collegial aspect of the Commission. The Commissioners are supposed to represent the "European idea". The notion of unity is reflected in the fact that, officially, the Commission speaks and acts with one voice. All the Commissioners are responsible for all aspects of Commission work, and all proposals and decisions are taken in its collective name. If the College has to vote, a simple majority determines the outcome: no Commissioner has a veto and individual Commissioner's votes are not made public.

So far the Commission has been described as a body of 20 Commissioners, but it is in fact a much larger organization, employing another 15,000 staff, one fifth of whom are involved in translating and interpreting. Perhaps another 2,000 individuals are "policy-makers". The Commission is divided into 36 directorates

general (DGs) and services (see Table 2.1). One of the changes made by Prodi in 1999 was to abolish the practice whereby DGs were principally known by their number – for example, DG VI was Agriculture – and to establish the more accessible practice of having them known by their principal activities. Some areas, such as agriculture, have been notoriously influential and powerful in protecting their interests, while other areas have found it more difficult to make an impact. Each Commissioner is responsible for one or more areas of policy but is aided in this task by a director general, a permanent official who heads a particular DG. A Commissioner is also aided by a *"cabinet"* (pronounced as in French, not English), a small group of individually chosen personal staff, usually six in number, who are the eyes and ears of the Commissioner, and help him or her to keep track of what the Commission is doing as a whole, what the DG is doing, and what is going on in the Commissioner's state. While a Commissioner is under an obligation to be independent, to promote the general interest of the Community, and not to take instruction from any government, members of a Commissioner's *cabinet* are not so inhibited, and provide a useful linking function between the Commissioner and his or her home state. While a Commissioner is clearly under an obligation not to follow purely national interests, there are times when it will be expected that a Commissioner can bring a particular perspective to bear, and to be alert to the implications of a putative proposal for his or her particular society.

There are a number of ways of describing the functions of the Commission. Perhaps eight can be taken as encapsulating its responsibilities, although it should be noted that during the existence of the Commission there has been some fluctuation in the importance and skill associated with them:

- as the conscience of the Community and the Union. The Commission has a specific responsibility to embody and promote the European idea and interest, the mystique of the European adventure and vocation, and to be the still small voice that reminds the member states of their specific obligations and general promises.

- as the guardian of the treaties, at least in the first instance. The Commission seeks to make sure that the treaties are respected and their requirements implemented. It was interesting that when doubts grew in the mid-1990s about the feasibility of bringing EMU to fruition, Jacques Santer made it quite clear that, in his view, his responsibility was to see that the provisions of the convergence criteria and timetable were adhered to. Not only must the treaties be observed but so too must all legitimately made Community law, and, although the Court of Justice is the ultimate judge and umpire, the Commission plays a crucial first-stage role in the process.

- as the executive of the Community. The Commission acts with regard to implementing the decisions reached by the Council (see below). These powers have been gradually strengthened as it became clear that the Council by necessity has to confer on the Commission, on an *ad hoc* basis, extensive powers for the implementation of the detail of policy. It must be remembered, however, that these decisions are within the parameters set down by the Council.

- as a body with particular responsibility for applying particular rules, for example in areas such as competition and merger policy, in administering funds, significantly including the disbursement of the structural funds, and in specific cases allowing derogations from Community legislation on the basis of a particular crisis or short-term need of individual member states.

- as the representative of the Community in relation to external economic policy within Community competence, both in third countries and in international organizations.

- as the coordinator of a range of policies, such as on "growth, competitiveness, employment, and sustainable development", to seek to ensure that the left hand of policy knows what the right hand is doing, and that different policies work towards a common objective. The Commission has not always been successful in this but in recent years greater effort has gone towards achieving coherence and strategic planning.

- as an honest broker or diplomat, both in performing the functions mentioned so far, and in its prime function of initiating policy. The Commission has to be able to cajole and persuade, trying to bring together the multifarious interests, concerns, and preoccupations of the member states, pressure groups, and the wider public, as well as trying to promote Community interests.

- as the initiator of Community (pillar 1) law since, except in truly exceptional cases, the Council cannot discuss legislation nor legislate unless there is a Commission proposal. This is the central power of the Commission, and one that it has fought tenaciously to preserve. It has come under some strain from the Council's ability to request the Commission to undertake studies desirable for the attainment of the common objectives of the Community, which is clearly an invitation to submit a proposal, although the nature and shape of the proposal remains that of the Commission. The Treaty on European Union provided that the EP could request the Commission to submit appropriate proposals. These provisions only apply to pillar 1. On CFSP and JHA matters the Commission may submit a proposal to the Council, but so too can member states and the Commission has no special position. It is important to note that in pillar 1 a proposal from the Commission cannot be altered by the Council unless there is unanimity among the Council members, although the Commission can withdraw a proposal and amend it at any time, which again provides it with a strong negotiating position. The real constraint on the Commission is the "anticipation of acceptability", in other words how to frame a proposal so that it has a chance of success, and taking into account the general political and socio-economic environment. This anticipation is clearly eased by the significant increase in the use of qualified majority voting (QMV – see below) over the years in the Council, since it has generally become more difficult for one state to block a decision on a range of issues.

Ideas for legislation come from a variety of sources. The Commission has suggested that 80% of its proposals have originated outside the Commission itself. Ideas are put to it by member states, the EP, and national and EU-wide pressure groups, but the right of formal proposal remains with the Commission itself. The act of legislating the decision, however, is that of the Council. This has led to the adoption of the old and now outdated aphorism: the Commission proposes, the Council disposes.

Before we turn to the Council, it should be noted that the crisis of the Commission in 1998–99 severely damaged the Commission's reputation. The crisis was initiated by the EP's expressions of concern as to whether the Commission had spent the 1996 budget properly, but it spread to allegations of fraud, nepotism, and mismanagement on a fairly wide scale. While a committee of investigation generally exonerated individual Commissioners from direct or personal involvement in fraud and corruption, it damningly noted that Commissioners had admitted that they were not always aware of what went on in their services, and that there was a general failure to take or accept responsibility. While President Romano Prodi and Vice President Neil Kinnock have made the reform of the Commission a major priority, signs remain that thoroughgoing reform will be difficult and protracted.

The Council

Commonly known as the Council of Ministers, in the treaties the central decision-making body is referred to as "the Council". This is important since the Council is a whole system, involving not only the Council of Ministers but also the European Council (the meetings of heads of state or government, two or three times a year) and the subsystem of the Committee of Permanent Representatives (Coreper) and its working groups, frequently composed of staff from the permanent representations who work together on an almost daily basis to seek to bring about agreement between the member states and to move the decision-making process forward. The Council is where all important decisions are made.

Technically there is only one Council, but in practice it meets in different formations. It is composed of the most appropriate minister from each member state, depending on the topic to be discussed, and a representative of the Commission, who can participate but not vote. It is a curious body since it is situated at the interface between the Community and national interests. Those present are clearly expected to defend their national interest, albeit in the expectation that usually a common decision will be regarded as better than no decision at all and that some cognizance should be taken of the general interest. However, it is member states' governments, through the Council, that determine the parameters of Community law and action.

The Council is the central legislative point in the system: broadly speaking, it makes Community law and, as long as it has acted legitimately, its decisions may be binding upon the member states. While this remains fundamentally true, in 1992 the Treaty on European Union introduced a degree of "co-decision" between the Council and the EP (see below under European Parliament for details), and subsequent treaties have steadily increased the number of treaty articles, and thus policy areas, to which this applies. Thus, since 1993 the Council has no longer been the exclusive legislator in pillar 1, although it remains true that the Council must agree to legislation before it becomes law.

Initially, in 1957, it was agreed in the Treaty of Rome that, given the experimental nature of the enterprise, decisions should be taken generally on the basis of unanimity, with a gradual transfer to qualified majority voting (QMV) as various points of progress were achieved. It was always intended that the option offered by a national veto would remain on certain sensitive issues. Since 1957 the areas subject to unanimity have been significantly reduced and concomitantly those subject to QMV have increased. Most recently in Nice in December 2000 this process was taken a stage further, so that the number of issues where there is a legal right to veto will be reduced from about 70 to about half that number once the Treaty of Nice has been ratified. However, it should be borne in mind that, even where the treaty provides for QMV the Council does not rush to vote, and that perhaps in as many as half of the cases where a vote could be taken legally, for political reasons the search for consensus is continued.

Until the Nice reforms come into effect each member state has the following number of votes under QMV:

France, Germany, Italy, and UK	10
Spain	8
Belgium, Greece, the Netherlands, and Portugal	5
Austria and Sweden	4
Denmark, Finland, and Ireland	3
Luxembourg	2

The total number of votes is 87. The majority needed for QMV is 62, but in pillars 2 (CFSP) and 3 (JHA) there is also the requirement that it include votes from at least ten member states. Although the focus might appear to be on what is needed to constitute a qualified majority, at the intergovernmental conferences in 1996–97 and 2000 more attention was focused on what constituted a blocking minority.

The weighting of votes has often been revisited by the member states and it had been hoped that the issue would be resolved by the Treaty of Amsterdam. This proved impossible, and all the heads of state and government could agree in 1997 was that they would revisit the issue before the next enlargement of the EU and that this would take place in connection with the debate about the move to reduce the two Commissioners from the five biggest states to one each. In the event this proved to be one of the most divisive issues at the intergovernmental conference in 2000: it led to a major battle between the "big" and "small" states, which was resolved only after considerable acrimony at Nice itself (see Chapter 4). The debate was further complicated by the fact that they were seeking to resolve the issue not just for the current 15 member states but for up to 27 current and potential members in all. With regard to the 15 it was agreed that from 1 January 2005 each state would have the following votes under QMV:

France, Germany, Italy, and UK	29
Spain	27
the Netherlands	13
Belgium, Greece, and Portugal	12
Austria and Sweden	10
Denmark, Finland, and Ireland	7
Luxembourg	4

The new QMV threshold becomes 169 out of 237, but it is now to be cast by at least a majority of members under pillar 1 and by two thirds when it is QMV under pillars 2 and 3. In addition, however, a new requirement has been inserted, namely that when QMV is invoked the qualified majority must be equivalent to at least 62% of the total population of the EU. The new arrangement means that two large states plus one other constitute a blocking minority, and that large states have the extra weight of their large populations. The proportional weight of the large states in Council decisions has been increased. This was justified by the argument that otherwise decisions could be taken by a coalition of states that did not reflect the majority of the population of the EU.

The Treaty of Nice also allocates votes to the 12 candidate states that were engaged in accession negotiations in 2000 (see Appendix 4). If the EU does expand to contain 27 member states, the new QMV threshold will be 258, with again the requirement that the votes should reflect at least a majority of member states and 62% of the EU's population.

However, as noted above, the issue remains that, even where there is a provision for QMV, there can be a reluctance to invoke it. It is quite clear that for some states the ethos of the *de facto* veto is still strong. Things have clearly moved on since the "empty chair" crisis of 1965–66, when Charles de Gaulle, then President of France, decided that, regardless of what the treaties provided for, it was quite unacceptable that a great power such as France should be outvoted and, to prove his point, absented France from the Council for six months. Nevertheless, states can still play games with the veto, as the British did in May and June 1996. In this case Prime Minister John Major announced that, following a perceived lack of cooperation by Britain's partners over resolving the BSE crisis, which had led to the banning of British beef from most countries in the world, his government would pursue a policy of "noncooperation", invoking its legal veto in 117 cases, even on matters with which it was in agreement. It was thus using the veto as a diplomatic weapon. As the EU enlarges, there are obviously greater possibilities of vetos being used tactically, and the same is true of the myriad compositions of blocking minorities.

The European Council of Heads of State or Government

During the period of relative paralysis in the Community, after the "empty chair" crisis and before the Single European Act, the European Council was invented to provide a sense of momentum, direction, and dynamism. Its members strove, not always successfully, not to become a court of appeal from divided Councils of their ministers. The European Council has had its successes, most notably in the launching of the European Monetary System (EMS) at the end of the 1970s and the Single European Act in the mid-1980s. This role was legally given to the European Council in the Treaty on European Union, which acknowledged that the "European Council shall provide the Union with the necessary impetus for its development and shall define the general political guidelines thereof". This represents an important recognition of its role as bringing together the highest political authorities of the member states. In this capacity, the European Council can enable the member states to be proactive, rather than simply the recipients of Commission initiatives, although the specifics of any proposal are those agreed and put forward by the Commission. There is no question but that the European Council has strengthened the position of the member states, but it is also true that a skilful Commission President, such as Jacques Delors, can use it to back Commission initiatives that, if they had been launched lower down the political hierarchy, might have been blocked. There is nothing to prevent those attending the European Council from transforming themselves into a Council, as long as when they act they respect the procedures proper to the article that contains the powers they wish to exercise. Even heads of state or government must conform to the treaties and EC law.

The European Council meets formally at least twice a year, but in an effort to rekindle the original hope that its meetings could be somewhat intimate discussions of the way ahead ("fireside chats"), there are also "informal" meetings, where there is an attempt to see how the land lies on key issues such as institutional reform (as at Pörtschach in October 1998, which also saw discussions on the possibility of the EU developing a military capability, or at Biarritz in October 2000, which tried to smooth the path for Nice) or financial and policy reform (such as two informal meetings held under the German Presidency in 1999, which were described as "coats off and no grand declarations").

The European Council has also had a rather ambiguous position in the decision-making system of the EU. Article 3 of the Treaty on European Union asserts that the "Union shall be served by a single institutional framework", but is very vague as to what this is. The European Council is the one institution (using the word informally here) that appears to hold the Union of the three pillars together. What is clear is that the European Council's role represents a significant attempt on the part of the member states to take control of the direction in which the EU and its constituent parts are moving. This is epitomized when the European Council doubles as the intergovernmental conference, and when it plays its role in pillars 2 and 3, but it also reflects the general trend towards intergovernmentalism in recent years.

Coreper

Part of the same trend has been the evolution of the Committee of Permanent Representatives (Coreper). Coreper, the parallel Special Committee on Agriculture (SCA), and the working groups under them are at the hub of the pillar 1 system, and now in practice have their parallels in pillars 2 and 3, even if formally business for the Council goes through Coreper. Even Coreper itself has two forms: Coreper I, the meeting of the deputy permanent representatives of the member states to the EU (in effect, deputy ambassadors); and Coreper II, the meeting of the permanent representatives themselves. Coreper II looks after the more politically charged matters. At any one time there are about 300 groups or committees that report to the Council, in its different formations, through the filter of Coreper or the SCA. These groups are involved in the detailed discussion and negotiation of Commission proposals, with a view to identifying and expanding areas of agreement between the member states, isolating and reducing the number of difficult decisions that can be resolved only at Council level, and thus reducing the burden on the ministers. Often agreement can be reached within this system but formally only the Council can take decisions. Therefore, if a decision is reached in the subsystem it is placed on the Council agenda as an "A point", meaning that it invariably goes through without further discussion.

The permanent representations of the member states play a crucial role in liaison between Brussels and national capitals, in helping to prepare national positions, and in making the Community system work. This occasionally gives rise to complaints that too much is agreed by civil servants without ministerial involvement, to which the standard reply is that such officials are operating within agreed national policy parameters and in accordance with the instructions that they have received from their capitals.

The Council Presidency

Another feature of the Council system has been the evolution in the role of the Council Presidency. Representatives of the member states' governments chair the Council, which also means the whole Council system of Coreper I and II, and the myriad working groups, for six-month periods in rotation.

From what was initially a procedural function, the Presidency has become more important as member states have moved to preferring to seek as much control as possible over policy decisions. Increasingly too the Presidency has had to play a representational role in meetings with third countries and in international organizations, although the Amsterdam initiative in creating the High Representative for CFSP has begun to make an impact on that function. It is the Presidency that appears on behalf of the Council in the EP. It also plays a crucial role since it is the Council Presidency, as will be discussed in more detail below (and in Chapters 19 and 22), that largely coordinates and runs pillars 2 and 3, on the CFSP and JHA respectively. In pillar 1 itself, the member states occupying the Presidency have increasingly sought to set specific tones and agendas for their period in office. In 1994 at Ioannina the member states formally recognized that it is the task of the Presidency to seek solutions to outstanding issues and, with the support of the Commission, to undertake initiatives facilitating a wider basis of agreement in the Council. It is aided in these tasks by the General Secretariat of the Council, now numbering some 2,000 staff, of whom about 200 are committee secretaries, with the others providing services for the conference centre.

One of the functions of the Presidency is to convene and chair IGCs. As these have increased in number in the last ten years or so, this task has become pivotal to the operation and the future of the EU. The Presidency is in no position to dictate outcomes, but in seeking to find middle ground among IGC participants and in offering potential ways forward it does have some potential to shape outcomes. It is often caught, however, between fulfilling that role and pursuing its own agenda, a trap that the French Presidency seems to have fallen into during the negotiations that culminated in the Treaty of Nice. Indeed, the test of a "good" Presidency is not usually the headlines made, but the ability to run Council and Union business efficiently. The Presidency is a burdensome task, especially for small states with limited resources, although it is occasionally argued that small states run the best presidencies because they have fewer vested interests at stake.

Any discussion of where power lies in the EU system ought to be focused on the Council and the central role of the member states' governments. It could be argued that, ever since the launch of the experimental ECSC in 1950–52, through the rise of the informal veto, the emergence of the European Council and Coreper, the evolution of the Council Presidency, the provisions for flexibility or closer cooperation, and the creation of the pillar structure, that member states have continually tightened their grip on the system.

The European Parliament

A European Parliament (EP) was not mentioned in the original Monnet–Schuman idea for the ECSC, but was inserted during the negotiations leading to the Treaty of Paris of 1951, in which, perhaps rather ostentatiously, it was referred to as "the Assembly". This title was deliberate and reflected the prevailing view that this body was to be only "advisory and supervisory", and not therefore to play a major part in decision-making. In 1962 the Assembly took to calling itself the European Parliament, but this title was only officially bestowed by the Single European Act of 1986. The title of the body is symbolically important, because it reflects the debates about the standing, roles, functions, and powers of the institution. Since the Assembly first met in 1952, it has continually sought to exert leverage to extend its functions and powers, but this has been a protracted and uphill struggle because fundamental changes can be made only by IGCs and thus by governments of the member states. The pursuit of increased powers is not yet concluded.

Powers have been conferred on the EP grudgingly, although some member states have been more enthusiastic than others about enhancing its position. One significant change occurred in the 1970s when it was given the power to reject the draft budget of the Council. This power was first exercised in December 1979, when the EP rejected the draft 1980 budget, after the first direct elections to the Parliament in June 1979 had increased its legitimacy and thus its authority. Before then Members of the European Parliament (MEPs) had been nominated by their national parliaments, but in June 1979 the electorates of the nine member states voted for their own representatives for the first time. The EP also has the last word over "noncompulsory" expenditure, the proportion of which has steadily grown as a

percentage of the whole budget, and now stands at just under 50%. "Compulsory" expenditure is that necessarily incurred as a result of the treaties and is now primarily the Guarantee Section of the Common Agricultural Policy. The allocation of expenditure to one or other category has been one of the great battlegrounds between the EP and the Council, but since 1988 this has been "demilitarized" by the agreeing of interinstitutional "Financial Perspectives", which seek to set the size of the budget over the medium term, most recently 2000–06. Revenue remains the preserve of the Council (see Chapter 12).

Another budget power of the EP, that of "discharge of the budget", triggered the crisis with the Commission in 1998–99. Early in 1998 the EP's Budget Committee expressed concern over the execution of the 1996 budget and this began the train of events that in the spring of 1999 led to the resignation of the Santer Commission. This crisis also involved the EP's power to censure, that is dismiss, the Commission, although in 1999 that power was not ultimately invoked. Under Article 201 the Parliament can censure the Commission by a two-thirds majority of votes cast and a majority of its total membership (i.e. at least 314 MEPs must support the motion). No censure has ever been successful, and even in January 1999 a motion of censure against the Commission was defeated 232 to 292 (as its authors, supporters of the Socialist Commissioners, had in fact intended). However, three months later it became clear that a censure motion would be passed if it was put forward. This was pre-empted, however, by the Santer Commission's resignation. This power of censure is potentially very powerful, but until the EP gained the right to approve the new Commission President and Commission, it tended to be very wary of the consequences of such an action. The events of 1998–99 showed that it remained cautious, perhaps being concerned about the constitutional and political crisis that might follow such a move. As noted above, the EP does now have the right to approve the nomination of the President and then the whole Commission.

An area that has seen a significant evolution of the Parliament's power is its legislative role.

Here progress has been intermittent and irregular, but the Parliament has moved a long way from its original advisory position. There are now six ways in which it can be involved in legislation or not:

- not consulted;
- consulted for its opinion, but that opinion is not binding on the Council;
- its assent for the legislation is required, such that, while it cannot amend the text, it can kill the proposal by refusing assent; included under this procedure are suspension of a member state, admission of a new member state, certain international agreements, and aspects of the structural funds;
- the "cooperation" procedure introduced by the Single European Act but, after Amsterdam, reserved only for EMU;
- the "co-decision" procedure introduced by the Treaty on European Union of 1992, although the word "co-decision" does not appear in the treaty (discussed below); or
- the budgetary powers already considered.

Since the Treaty of Amsterdam came into effect only assent, co-decision, and the status of joint budgetary authority have been really significant.

Co-decision was an outgrowth of "cooperation" and intimately reflects the battles over the power of the Parliament. It has become the prevailing procedure. A problem with it is that the Parliament is legally given the negative power to say "no", rather than a positive legal power to insist on its point of view. However, the legal power to say "no" has proved to have a corresponding political power to influence the Council. Over a 13-month period in 1998–99, in 17 legislative cases that went to the joint Conciliation Committee of the Council and the Parliament (out of a total of 65 pieces of legislation), the EP claimed to have succeeded in having more than 80% of its amendments accepted. More generally, the Parliament claims that, because this procedure now exists, the Council looks for compromises earlier on in the process, with some 20% of legislation effectively being agreed at first reading and more than 50% at second reading.

In addition to these powers, the Treaty on European Union allowed the EP to appoint an ombudsman to investigate complaints about maladministration in the Community; to set up temporary committees of inquiry on specific issues; and to receive petitions. The most notable committee of inquiry was the inquiry into BSE (1996–97). No less important than such committees, however, are the 17 regular committees of the Parliament, covering all the major areas of Union business (see Table 2.3).

Parliamentary committees are the mainstay of the conduct of the EP's business. Legislation is referred to the relevant functional committee, sometimes with demarcation disputes between committees, and sometimes to more than one committee. Commission officials attend and defend their proposals before the committee, and this is often a key part in the exchanges between the EP and the Commission, with full and frank exchanges of views. This exchange is often much more fruitful than the oral or written questions that may be put at the plenary sessions of the EP either to the Commission or to the Council. The committee reports are drawn up by *rapporteurs* (draftsmen), who are influential in structuring the debate, the final report, and the resolution adopted by the Parliament in plenary session. Indeed, committee reports often become known by the names of the *rapporteurs* in question. This process is part of the informal influence of MEPs, which can be difficult to measure but is nonetheless significant. The informal influence of MEPs was increased by the introduction of direct elections, but the 15% drop in turnout between 1979 and 1999 has had an impact on the legitimacy of MEPs and the authority of the Parliament itself.

After the 1995 enlargement there were 626 MEPs. If the EU increases in size to 27, and the Treaty of Nice is ratified, its membership should be 728. There is no directly proportional relationship to population (see Table 2.2), but the increase in the population of Germany after unification was acknowledged in the Treaty of Amsterdam, and there has long been a view that really small states, such as Luxembourg, Malta or Estonia, need (or will need) to have a plurality of membership so that different strands of opinion can be represented.

However, as with the new votes in the Council, the only explanation for some of the Nice figures is that states such as Luxembourg that are already in the Union have (ab)used their position.

Once elected MEPs do not sit by nationality but rather by political affiliation (see Table 2.3). Usually they also vote in accordance with their group membership, although there tend to be deviations on important national questions. The political groupings have been seen in some theories of integration as being special carriers of integration, and their contribution to forming a European awareness and expressing the political will of the EU's citizens was recognized in the Treaty on European Union. However, elections for the European Parliament since 1979 have overwhelmingly been fought on national issues. The political groups, while very important to the day-to-day organization and functioning of the EP itself, have been of little influence in the wider world. They play a central role in the organization of business in the EP through the Conference of Presidents, which takes the decisions on the organization of the Parliament, the legislative timetable, and related matters. This is an important point because there is no government, as there is in national parliaments, to determine timetables, priorities, or agendas. The groupings have to order and manage the EP among themselves.

The European Court of Justice

The European Court of Justice (ECJ) consists of one judge from each member state, each appointed to serve for a six-year term; the terms are staggered so that there is a partial replacement every three years. The judges are chosen by the common accord of the member states, without the Parliament or the Commission playing any role. Since the ratification of the Single European Act the ECJ has been aided by a Court of First Instance, intended to reduce the workload. The pressure of this workload has been a consistent theme over the years. The Court of First Instance has dealt predominantly with administrative and staff disputes, certain aspects of competition rules, and aspects of the ECSC Treaty. Its role has been expanded somewhat, but all crucial decisions, especially those

involving national governments, are made by the ECJ itself.

The judges can meet either as a full court or in chambers of three or five: there is always an odd number of judges so that if they are divided in opinion there is always a majority. Decisions are made by majority, and only that majority judgement is made public. The Treaty of Nice has added the possibility of the ECJ sitting as a "Grand Chamber", this having a composition of 11 judges, but being able to meet with a minimum of nine. This new Grand Chamber would be invoked if a member state or Community institution that is party to the proceedings so requests. In another attempt to lighten the load on the full 15 judges and ECJ, the Treaty of Nice also provides for the appointment of assistant *rapporteurs* to undertake preparatory inquiries in cases pending before the Court, and to cooperate with the judge acting as *rapporteur*.

In pillar 1 matters the ECJ is the final guardian of the treaties and of the decisions lawfully made. It has established the primacy of Community law in matters covered by the treaties, laying down that Community law is binding and is directly applicable, that EC law prevails over any conflicting national laws, and that the Community constitutes a new legal order for the benefit of which member states have limited their sovereignty in limited fields, that is, in matters covered by the Treaty establishing the European Communities. This latter point is important, since there are many matters that Community law does not touch. The ECJ adjudicates only on matters covered by the treaties. The ECJ interprets Community law and its decisions are final (see also Chapters 17 and 18). The ECJ itself has described its tasks as those that in the legal systems of the member states are carried out by constitutional courts, courts of general jurisdiction, and administrative tribunals.

In the Treaty on European Union the ECJ was given the power on pillar 1 matters, after due process involving the Commission and reasoned opinions, to impose a lump sum or penalty payment on member states that have not taken the necessary measures to comply with its judgement. This was regarded as important at the time, since several member states' governments, particularly the British government, were becoming indignant at the alleged failure of others to comply with or implement fully Community law.

The member states deliberately decided to give the ECJ no standing in pillar 2 (CFSP). The common positions and joint actions adopted by the Council are binding upon member states only under general international law, and not under Community law, it being something of a matter of dispute as to how important the difference is legally – although one important difference is that the ECJ is not involved and another is that general international law is not easily enforceable.

Under the Treaty on European Union the ECJ had only a limited role in pillar 3, JHA matters, which was in interpreting conventions established between some of the member states if they wished it, but it was not given its pillar 1 role of adjudicating in disputes or being the final court of judicial appeal and interpretation. The Treaty of Amsterdam somewhat expanded the role of the ECJ in relation to pillar 3, as regards giving decisions on interpreting pillar 3 conventions and interpreting framework decisions, but this provision applies only in respect of those member states that agree to accept its jurisdiction (see Chapter 19).

Over the years the ECJ has clearly established its authority and primacy, but it has occasionally been challenged. One criticism is that it is guilty of "judicial activism", the claim being that it has gone beyond the letter of Community legislation and interpreted it in the light of its intended – integrationist – effects. A second form of challenge occurred in 1993, when, in allowing the ratification of the Treaty on European Union, the German Federal Constitutional Court in Karlsruhe laid down that it alone was responsible for testing whether certain European decisions overstepped the powers granted to the EU. This challenge has, prudently, not yet been taken any further.

The Court of Auditors

The Treaty on European Union elevated the Court of Auditors to the status of an "institution". The intention was to give a heightened profile both to the Court of Auditors itself and to the issue of financial regularity in the Community. Concern about such matters has steadily risen over the last 20 years, culminating in the crisis of 1998–99. The influence of the Court has steadily increased. In Amsterdam it was given the same power to take proceedings against Community institutions and member states that other institutions and the European Central Bank had been given. In Nice it was again mentioned, this time in a declaration that attempted to lay the foundation for improving cooperation between it and national audit institutions. Its role remains that of examining the Community accounts, determining whether revenue and expenditure have been lawfully raised and spent, and reporting on any irregularity. It reports to the other institutions, but particularly important is its relationship with the Parliament, given the Parliament's powers over discharge of the budget. As noted above, in the late 1990s these arcane procedures had important political consequences. It is worth recording that the Court of Auditors has never yet been able to pronounce its statutory finding that expenditure by the Commission has been free of irregularity.

The Economic and Social Committee, and the Committee of the Regions

Neither of these is designated an "institution" in the treaties, reflecting the fact that they have only the limited power to give advice. Both reflect a belief that democracy and the political process should involve interests within civil society. The Economic and Social Committee (ESC, but also widely known as Ecosoc) was set up by the Treaty of Rome, and the Committee of the Regions by the Maastricht Treaty. The former represents the interests of various economic and social groupings, and the latter those of regional and local authorities. Neither has significant influence, it being made clear in the treaties that each has "advisory" status. There was a brief flurry of expectation, after Maastricht in 1992, that the Committee of the Regions might evolve into some sort of second chamber for the European Parliament, reflecting the apparent growing need to give recognition to subnational political units and authorities such as the German *Länder*, but these committees both remain at the very margins of policy-making.

The European Investment Bank

This has been described as almost but not quite a Community institution, and it dates back to the Treaty of Rome. Fundamentally it is concerned with lending money to less developed regions and to candidates for EU membership. Regional development lies at the heart of its operations, although it also has a function in supporting the development of the common market, and in lending for investment in communications, the environment, energy, and industrial competitiveness.

Another Pillar?

EMU is discussed elsewhere in this volume (see Chapter 10) but it is worth noting here that, although reference is usually made to three pillars of the EU – the EC, the CFSP, and JHA – there is perhaps a case that, since January 1999 and the creation of EMU, with its concomitant creation of the European System of Central Banks (ESCB) and the European Central Bank (ECB), there is another pillar or at least half an additional pillar attached to pillar 1. This argument can be made since, while the new pillars 2 and 3 epitomize intergovernmentalism, the ECB system, by way of stark contrast, is supranational. The Maastricht Treaty and the attached protocols make it clear that the ECB must not seek or take instructions from any member states or Community institutions or any other body, and member states are committed to respecting this principle. This independence was deemed necessary to overcome German apprehensions that EMU might damage monetary stability, one of the great achievements of the German central bank, the Bundesbank. Indeed, the treaty made explicit that the prime objective of the ESCB/ECB is to maintain price stability, and that other tasks, such as defining and implementing monetary policy, conducting foreign exchange operations, maintaining reserves, and ensuring the smooth operation of the payment system, are secondary. All of this is to be done in accordance with maintaining the principle of open market economies with free competition.

The much vaunted independence of the ECB came under great strain in May 1998 in the matter of the appointment of its first President. The favoured candidate was Wim Duisenberg of the Netherlands, chiefly because of the belief that he would maintain that independence. He finally triumphed, but not before President Jacques Chirac of France had fought long and hard for Jean-Claude Trichet of the Banque de France, not so much because Trichet was French as because he was thought to be more amenable to political influence and more likely to take the political dimensions of monetary policy into account. A compromise deal was done that should see Trichet assuming the position at some point in the future. The question of political influence on the ECB is also raised by the creation of the "Euro 12". Not formally a Council, Euro 12, a committee comprising the finance ministers of the states participating in EMU, has sought to become a privileged interlocutor with the ECB, or at least – despite the treaty guarantee of the ECB's autonomy – to put itself in a position to convey its conclusions to the ECB.

The ECB is located in Frankfurt, with its Executive Body deciding on day-to-day matters. The ESCB, bringing together the governors of the central banks of participating states, is rather more of a supervisory board determining overall strategy.

Pillars 2 and 3: Intergovernmentalism

During the negotiations in 1990–91 that led to the Treaty on European Union (TEU), a conscious choice was made not to adopt the traditional Community system for either of the two newly created areas of EU activity: the common foreign and security policy (CFSP), and justice and home affairs (JHA). While CFSP and JHA are discussed more fully elsewhere (see Chapters 22 and 19 respectively), their importance to the structure of the EU and the future of integration is relevant here.

There have been significant developments in both pillar 2 and pillar 3 since they were created by the TEU, but certain points remain valid. In both the EP is not intimately involved. Rather, it is consulted and informed, and allowed to ask questions and hold debates on the issues involved. While it still has no formal powers, it has been given certain leverage, since the administrative expenditures involved in the second and third pillars are charged to the budget of the European Community, and in both cases operational expenditure, in certain circumstances, can also be charged to the Community budget. In these cases it is made clear that the budgetary procedures applying to the Community budget apply to this expenditure too. In practice there is a convention that the two branches of the budgetary authority do not challenge each others' administrative expenditures.

In both pillars the starting position was that the Commission was fully associated with the work in CFSP and JHA, and had a limited but not sole right of initiative, but was not accorded its traditional Community roles and powers.

Exceptionally, and for the first time in the history of the Community/Union, at Amsterdam some matters were transferred from the classically intergovernmental third pillar into the European Community (first pillar): visas, immigration and other policies related to the free movement of persons; external border controls; judicial cooperation in civil matters; actions against fraud affecting the financial interests of the EC; and measures to strengthen customs cooperation (in these latter two cases only insofar as they do not impinge upon criminal law, which remains in the third pillar). Pillar 3 was thus slimmed down and given the new title of "Provisions on police and judicial cooperation in criminal matters". In addition, the Treaty of Amsterdam incorporated the separate Schengen *acquis* on free movement into the European Community.

As noted above, the ECJ has no role in pillar 2 and only a very restricted role in pillar 3. Indeed, the TEU is emphatic that the ECJ has no jurisdiction over member states' police or law enforcement agencies, their law and order provisions, or internal security.

In pillar 2 heavy organizational responsibility is placed on the Council Presidency to represent the Union and to implement CFSP decisions, although it is now aided by the "High

Representative for the Common Foreign and Security Policy" who also heads a policy planning and early warning unit (PPEWU) located within the General Secretariat of the Council. The High Representative is also the Secretary-General of the Council. In June 1999 the European Council announced at Cologne that the first High Representative was to be Javier Solana, then the Secretary General of NATO. Under the Presidency the details of policy are worked out by an intergovernmental system of working groups headed by a Political Committee consisting of the political directors of the member states' departments of foreign affairs. Given the developments in CFSP towards establishing a Common European Security and Defence Policy (CESDP) (see Chapter 23), this has been transformed into the Political and Security Committee. The PSC (commonly referred to by its French acronym COPS) is advised by the EU Military Committee, the EU Military Staff Organization, and the PPEWU. Despite these developments, the security dimension of the EU does not include territorial defence.

The full extent of intergovernmentalism in pillar 2 becomes even clearer when the mechanisms for taking decisions are examined. In essence, the member states have found it difficult to reconcile two conflicting desires: to take decisions expeditiously and efficiently, and to retain the veto. In 1996–1997 the IGC wrestled with this dilemma and finally concluded that key decisions would still require unanimity, but that there could be what came to be known as "constructive abstention", namely, that an abstention was not tantamount to a veto. Further, there was an expectation that member states would not oppose the adoption of decisions by QMV unless there were important reasons of state and national policy for doing so, in which case the veto remained intact. It has been made explicit that there is to be no question of voting on decisions having military or defence implications. Clearly, in areas touching so intimately on the very *raison d'être* of member states and their sovereignty, no risks are to be taken. The experience of the last decade suggests that the member states find it easier to agree on routine matters than on major issues of international relations.

In pillar 3 the Presidency is aided by the Coordinating Committee, but in the post-Amsterdam scheme of things, again given the sensitivity of the matters involved, unanimity is the rule for decisions to be made, except for the adoption of certain measures to implement what has been unanimously agreed.

Conclusion

The structure of the EU, and the distribution of powers between its institutions, and between the Union and the member states are as they are because that is all that the member states could agree at the time. Few would claim that the arrangements amount to the most efficient or transparent way to operate or organize the EU as a whole. Reform has become particularly pressing, for two reasons.

One reason is that there is increasing evidence of EU citizens' apathy or even hostility towards the EU and European integration (see Chapters 5 and 6). Between 1979 and 1999, as we have seen, there was a 15% drop in turnout for direct elections to the EP, and the years 1992 and 2000 saw Danish voters reject (initially) the TEU and then Danish participation in EMU and the single currency. In 1992 ratification of the TEU proved very difficult in France, Germany, and the United Kingdom.

The second reason is that the Community system was constructed 50 years ago, for a European Coal and Steel Community composed of six states. The EU now encompasses a much wider range of activities, has 15 member states, and at Nice tried to make provision for expansion to 27. At the intergovernmental conferences in 1990–91 and 1996–97 the member states failed satisfactorily to address or resolve these problems. The IGC in 2000 seems to have similarly failed and there is a commitment to call a fresh IGC in 2004 to try yet again.

It may be that the real innovation of recent years was the legitimization of "flexibility" by the Treaty of Amsterdam, with some amendments at Nice, notably through the Provisions on Closer Cooperation, which allow groups of states to pursue closer cooperation among themselves, subject to certain restrictions. The establishment and subsequent incorporation of Schengen and EMU may prove to be a model, but then the question arises of what the longer-term implications may be for the EU if x number of states cooperate on one thing, y on another, z on yet another, and so on. That is hardly the "ever closer union" or the "destiny henceforward shared" to which the Treaties of Rome and Paris aspired.

The central question may be whether the member states are all moving in the same direction towards the same objective, but at different speeds; or whether some current (and future) members have no real intention of travelling further down the road to integration. At any rate, it seems that in an expanding EU further integration will, most of the time, take intergovernmental forms.

Further Reading

Dinan, Desmond, *Ever Closer Union: An Introduction to European Integration*, second edition, London: Macmillan, and Boulder, CO: L. Rienner, 1999

This is particularly good on the political evolution of the EU.

Hix, Simon, *The Political System of the European Union*, London: Macmillan, and New York: St Martin's Press, 1999

Hix takes political science concepts as the basis for his analysis, and applies them to the processes and policy-making of the EU in an attempt to enhance understanding of the nature of its system.

Nicoll, Sir William, and Trevor C. Salmon, *Understanding the European Union*, London and New York: Longman, 2001

This has the added advantage of a strong section on the attitudes of the member states.

Nugent, Neill, *The Government and Politics of the European Union*, fourth edition, London: Macmillan, and Durham, NC: Duke University Press, 1999

Very detailed coverage of the institutions, and a good analysis of the origins and working of policy processes within the EU

Peterson, John, and Elizabeth Bomberg, *Decision-making in the European Union*, London: Macmillan, and New York: St Martin's Press, 1999

This book presents the different types of decision-making in the EU, which the authors identify as history-making, policy-making, and policy-shaping, and applies these concepts to policy case-studies.

Wallace, Helen, and William Wallace (editors), *Policy-making in the European Union*, fourth edition, Oxford and New York: Oxford University Press, 2000

There is an excellent introduction on policy-making in the EU, which provides the framework for a large number of very useful case studies.

Weatherill, Stephen, and Paul Beaumont, *EU Law*, third edition, London: Penguin, 1999

A legal perspective on the institutions and an introduction to the main elements of EU law

Trevor C. Salmon is Jean Monnet Professor in European Integration at the University of Aberdeen. He has published extensively on EU institutions and policy-making, in particular the common foreign and security policy.

Table 2.1   The European Commission's Directorates–General and Services

General Services
European Anti-Fraud Office
Eurostat
Press and Communication

Publications Office
Secretariat General

Internal Policy Areas
Agriculture
Competition
Economic and Financial Affairs
Education and Culture
Employment and Social Affairs
Energy and Transport
Enterprise
Environment
Fisheries

Health and Consumer Protection
Information Society
Internal Market
Joint Research Centre
Justice and Home Affairs
Regional Policy
Research
Taxation and Customs Union

External Relations
Development
Enlargement
EuropeAid Cooperation Office

External Relations
Humanitarian Aid Office (ECHO)
Trade

Internal Services
Budget
Financial Control
Joint Interpreting and Conference Service

Legal Service
Personnel and Administration
Translation Service

Table 2.2   Populations and Seats in the European Parliament, of Present Member States (1999–2004) and Prospective Member States (2004 onwards)*

	Population (millions)	Seats EU 15	Seats EU 27
Present Members			
Germany	82.2	99	99
United Kingdom	59.6	87	72
France	58.7	87	72
Italy	57.7	87	72
Spain	39.4	64	50
Netherlands	15.8	31	25
Greece	10.5	25	22
Belgium	10.2	25	22
Portugal	10.0	25	22
Sweden	8.9	22	18
Austria	8.1	21	17
Denmark	5.3	16	13
Finland	5.2	16	13
Ireland	3.8	15	12
Luxembourg	0.44	6	6
Prospective Members			
Poland	38.7		50
Romania	22.5		33
Czech Republic	10.3		20
Hungary	10.1		20
Bulgaria	8.2		17
Slovakia	5.4		13
Lithuania	3.7		12
Latvia	2.4		8
Slovenia	2.0		7
Estonia	1.4		6
Cyprus	0.75		6
Luxembourg	0.44		6
Malta	0.38		5

* Assuming that the Treaty of Nice will have been ratified, the figures for an EU of 27 member states will apply in the European Parliament elected in 2004, subject to a *pro rata* correction if not all the candidate states have signed accession treaties by 1 January 2004, in order to ensure the total membership will be 732 as specified in the Treaty of Nice. Seats will be allocated to new member states only after they have signed accession treaties.

Table 2.3 Committees of the European Parliament, 1999–2004

Foreign Affairs, Human Rights, and Common Security and Defence Policy
Budgets
Budgetary Control
Citizens' Freedoms and Rights, Justice, and Home Affairs
Economic and Monetary Affairs
Legal Affairs and the Internal Market
Industry, External Trade, Research, and Energy
Employment and Social Affairs
Environment, Public Health, and Consumer Policy
Agriculture and Rural Development
Fisheries
Regional Policy, Transport, and Tourism
Culture, Youth, Education, the Media, and Sport
Development and Cooperation
Constitutional Affairs
Women's Rights and Equal Opportunities
Petitions

Table 2.4 Membership of Political Groups in the European Parliament as of 7 April 2001*

	A	*B*	*Den*	*Fin*	*F*	*G*	*Gr*	*Ire*	*I*	*L*	*N*	*P*	*S*	*Sw*	*UK*	*Total*
PPE-DE	7	6	1	5	21	53	9	5	34	2	9	9	28	7	36	232
PSE	7	5	3	3	22	35	9	1	16	2	6	12	24	6	30	181
ELDR		5	6	5				1	8	1	8		3	4	11	52
Verts/ALE	2	7		2	9	5		2	2	1	4		4	2	6	46
GUE/NGL			1	1	11	6	7		6		1	2	4	3		42
UEN			1		3			6	9			2				21
TDI		2			5				12							19
EDD			4		9						3					19
NI	5				7								1			14
Total	21	25	16	16	87	99	25	15	87	6	31	25	64	22	87	**626**

* It should be noted that membership of the groups is rather fluid and there is usually some movement of members between them during the parliamentary term.

PPE-DE   European People's Party (Christian Democrats) and European Democrats
PSE   Party of European Socialists
ELDR   European Liberal, Democrat, and Reform Party
Verts/ALE   Greens/European Free Alliance
GUE/NGL   Confederal Group of the European United Left/Nordic Green Left
UEN   Union for Europe of the Nations
TDI   Technical Group of Independent Members
EDD   Group for a Europe of Democracies and Diversities
NI   Non-attached

Politics

Chapter Three

Theories of Political Integration

Ben Rosamond

The nature of political integration is as much a political issue as it is an intellectual matter. What the EU is and what it should become are matters that exercise politicians and mass publics alike, across the continent. The rival ideas of a European "superstate" or federal state versus a looser, more flexible, community, in which national units remain integral, is the raw stuff of these debates as they are played out in the various member states.

Against this background, "political integration" has been given a variety of definitions. One basic distinction is that between integration as outcome and integration as process. In other words, when references are made to "political integration", it is not always clear whether the reference is to a particular final destination or endpoint – a European federal state, for example – or to a set of continuing dynamic processes that may be driving integration. In the sense of integration as process, there may even be no definite interest in where the process may be leading.

"Integration" is itself a loaded term. Much of the theoretical work done by students of the EU could be said to have very little to do with integration. In recent years, many scholars have been at pains to show that the EU has rather more about it than integration pure and simple. For writers such as Simon Hix (see Hix 1999), the EU is a political system involving various actors pursuing their interests in a classic Lasswellian game of "who gets what, when, and how?". Integration, on this view, is a distant matter of high politics, significant for governmental actors, high-level supranational officials, and journalists, but far removed from the day-to-day realities of the EU.

The equation of "integration" with "what the EU does" is also unhelpful when we come to think about what general lessons about integration can be drawn from studying the EU's experience. It has long been the "holy grail" of integration theory to use the European experience as a laboratory for generating hypotheses about the prospects for regional integration elsewhere. Such comparative analysis remains possible, but the very real specificities of the EU's experience have to be considered seriously. The EU, it is often argued, is the contemporary product of a very particular set of western European circumstances that held 50 years ago. The architects of the European Coal and Steel Community (ECSC) were driven by particular concerns that drove them to design a unique set of institutions with an unusually high level of supranational power. The point for theory is simple and profound: if the EU, the heir to the ECSC, is a unique case, then how can our theoretical efforts be anything more than exercises in dense, descriptive, and ultimately primitive social science?

Classical Definitions of Political Integration

Most starkly, Michael Hodges has defined integration as "the formation of new political systems out of hitherto separate political systems" (Hodges p. 13). Alternatively, Ernst B. Haas, the leading scholar of neofunctionalism, has offered the following definition (Haas 1968 p. 16):

The process whereby actors in several distinct national settings are persuaded to shift their loyalties, expectations and political activities toward a new center, whose institutions possess or demand jurisdiction over pre-existing national states. The end result of a process of political integration is a new political community, superimposed over the pre-existing ones.

In both cases an outcome is envisaged. Haas's definition reminds us that political communities rely on the loyalties of social groups for their integrity and legitimacy. A new European political community will emerge once a transference of mass loyalty has occurred. This idea is also consistent with the idea of state-building, or the transplantation of the features and functions of a political system to the European level.

Others have drawn analogies between the processes of international integration and nation-building. However, in the work of Karl Deutsch and his colleagues this resemblance had more to do with the patterns of social interaction that characterized these processes. Deutsch's own notion of integration was somewhat distinct. His idea of a "security community" was about the containment and gradual withering of particular types of international politics, notably war. Integration in this sense is (Deutsch *et al.* p. 5):

> the attainment within a territory of a "sense of community", and of institutions and practices strong enough and widespread enough to assure, for a "long" time, dependable expectations of "peaceful change" among its population.

Still others have imagined integration to be about the transcendence of traditional forms of politics. This was certainly the message of the functionalists (see below), and it resonates with contemporary writers who grapple with how "governance" is and should be exercised under conditions of globalization.

Clearly, then, different theorists operate with distinct notions of political integration. In technical language, there is a "dependent variable problem": what is it that theories of political integration are trying to explain? This is not to suggest that we should try to narrow the field

to a single working definition, but simply to recognize that intellectual argument is as problematic as the messy business of the politics of integration itself.

Political and Economic Integration

The relationship between economic and political integration is central to much of the deliberation in theoretical work on the EU. Theories of economic integration had predicted a stage-by-stage deepening of the integration process that would follow from the decision of two or more countries to create a free trade area. This logic would culminate in monetary union and *de facto* total economic integration. In such circumstances common policies would emerge from supranational authorities as a matter of the playing out of this rational logic. In other words, economic integration would produce political integration. (As a partial, but significant, aside, it is worth speculating on the extent to which the governments that created the free trade area actually envisaged political integration.) In part this argument suggests that governments are driven by economic logic to solutions that imply political integration. Thus a free trade area cannot become effective without the existence of a common external tariff, otherwise its members could defect from the regime by levying differential tariffs. A working free trade area creates pressures for the wider application of market efficiency to be achieved through the free movement of other factors of production – a single market. The efficiency of a single market, in turn, is best attained through the use of a common unit of account, thereby suggesting a logic towards monetary union, which in turn requires the establishment of common policies administered at the level of the new, *de facto*, single integrated economy.

Another way to think about the relationship between politics and economics is to explore the relationship between state power and market power. Thus, we can think about economic integration as the emergence of a transnational economic space that arises as the consequence of the crossborder activities of private market actors. This is what William Wallace once called "informal integration" (see Wallace) and what has been referred to by others as *de facto* regionalization. This may have two effects. The first is the creation of interdependencies between national economies, such that they can no longer be regarded as discrete spaces. Secondly, they create a set of transnational actors with a particular set of interests that may coincide with the provision of supranational rules. However, the question remains as to why informal integration happens. It may arise in the domain of the market, but we might also point to the deliberate legislative acts of governments that enable transnational economic activity to prosper. Wallace defines this "formal integration" as outcomes that have occurred as a consequence of deliberate political choices. We are faced, therefore, with an interesting "chicken and egg" question that raises not only an issue of how integration happens, but also questions of agency – which actors matter? which actors have power? – as well as profound issues of structure.

These reflections on the nature of political integration in Europe suggest that we are dealing with two issue areas of profound significance. The first – political economy – looks to the relationships between states and markets, and between economic power and political power. Its proponents ask us to think about the long-term political consequences of short-term decisions to engage in economic integration. Political economy also taps into another long-standing issue of integration theory: the extent to which the postwar European experience is comparable with other, more recent, instances of integration. The second issue is the problem of "governance". More specifically, theorizing about the European experience lures us towards a series of questions about the efficacy and future of the nation-state as a capsule for the management of human affairs. Digging deeper, we need to explore what integration means for national governance. If integration entails the "drift" of governance functions to the supranational level, to what extent will the new form of authority be "state-like" in form and function?

"Classical" Theories of Political Integration

These questions are not at all new: in various guises they have been at the heart of debates in the political sciences since their inception. EU studies have been dominated by debates between versions of neofunctionalism and intergovernmentalism, but the effects of earlier currents of debate still linger in contemporary deliberations.

Federalism

We can trace theoretical work on integration back a long way in the annals of political thought. Schemes for universal and lasting peace emerged from the 18th century in the writings of Immanuel Kant and others. Twentieth-century variants of this idea appeared in the aftermath of the unprecedented violence of World War I and as the discipline of international relations was developing its founding debates. The idea of creating a European federation, which was present, if largely marginal, in the 1920s and 1930s, found its most famous and compelling articulation in Count Richard Coudenhove-Calerghi's book *Pan Europa* (1926). He argued that "Europe" possesses a cultural cohesiveness that has been undermined by the centrifugal and conflictual logic of the nation-state system. The founders of international relations, meanwhile, were grappling with the great issues of war and peace: is war avoidable? is the nation-states system the most ethical or efficacious way to organize human affairs? can institutions and bodies of law be created above the nation-state to ameliorate the worst consequences of international conflict?

There is no single coherent body of federalist theory as applied to European integration (but see Burgess). Federalists have tended to regard the "realist" prognosis of the inevitability and timelessness of the nation-states system as pessimistic. They have put their faith in the capacity to devise constitutional solutions to political problems, in particular those that derive from diversity among territorial units. Thus, a federal political order would distribute authority between different levels of government, without sacrificing the diversity of national units. In the federalist view, this would be an optimal way both of governing complex modern societies and of ensuring that conflict does not arise between those national units. Further, the federalist formula disallows hegemony by any of its component units and thereby helps to ameliorate a potential source of conflict. Moreover, an integrated federal entity would become a stronger unit in the face of external threat. Therefore, whether arising from enlightened and rapid constitutional design, or through the gradual actions of social groups "from below", a federal Europe would be a state-like entity, albeit writ rather larger than any existing European nation-state.

Functionalism

For some critics, federalists were too wedded to conventional notions of politics, as revealed by their advocacy of a state-like institutional order for "Europe" (however they defined "Europe"). In contrast, functionalists took the view that normal politics could and should be transcended. Aside from producing conflict and war, conventional politics – that is, politics driven by ideological or nationalistic credos – is, they argued, a deeply irrational way to deliver governance. Functionalists such as David Mitrany, writing in the 1940s (see Mitrany), suggested that governance should be a rational activity geared to the fulfilment of human welfare needs. Not all human needs arise within the neat capsule of national territory and thus, by definition, nation-states cannot be rational maximizers of public welfare in all instances. This technocratic vision of politics saw the state as by no means a necessarily permanent feature of the political landscape. As such, functionalism represented a challenge to most orthodox ways of thinking about politics and international relations, both of which were characterized by a state-fixation. Defenders of the nation-state and advocates of world government were equally subjected to withering critiques by Mitrany.

"Form follows function" was the functionalist mantra. Human needs change over time and vary across space, so the design of institutions had to be an open-minded and flexible process. In some cases, but not all, transnational institutions would be the optimal providers of human welfare. The successful creation of such bodies would induce a transfer of loyalty away from the nation-state. As states became residual, so the likelihood of international conflict would be drastically diminished. The functionalist vision was of a cobweb of diverse and overlapping institutions of governance, differing in form as functions varied.

This meant, of course, that regional integration schemes such as the European Communities infringed the basic precepts of functionalism. To Mitrany's way of thinking, regional integration imposed territorial limits on human needs, while integration schemes tended to be devised with an express political purpose rather than a commitment to meet human welfare needs.

Transactionalism

The proponents of transactionalism (alternatively labelled the pluralist or communications approach) thought about integration quite differently. By and large, theorists such as Deutsch, who was a pioneer of a more rigorous and "scientific" approach to the study of politics, thought about integration as the achievement of stable peaceful relations between states. There was less emphasis on either the transcendence of the states system or the creation of "superstates". At the same time, those who adopted this approach drew analogies with the processes of nation-building, and specifically the role of human interaction therein.

In *Political Community and the North Atlantic Area* (1957), Deutsch and his colleagues developed an account of the development of "security communities" in which the expectation of the peaceful resolution of conflicts prevailed. These could be achieved through formal institutional fusion, in the case of "amalgamated security communities", but Deutsch's clear preference was for what he labelled "pluralistic security communities". These arose when the component units (states) shared major values and when key political groups were able to respond to each other's stimuli without violence. Transactionalists held that a sense of community among states was a function of the level of communication between states. Political integration would be the product of networks of mutual transactions, which in turn would be facilitated by advances in communications and transport technology. Transaction flows would need to be accompanied by what Deutsch called "mutual responsiveness", the willingness and capacity of state and societal actors to interact.

Deutsch focused less on Europe than other integration theorists and to this day the idea of "security communities" might have better purchase as a general theory of integration, because its focal point is the transformation of international relations and intersocietal exchange, rather than the development of supranational institutions and the demise of state sovereignty (see Adler and Barnett).

Neofunctionalism

Neofunctionalism is by far the most salient theory of European political integration. It is much criticized, but the heirs of the neofunctionalists of the 1950s and 1960s retain a significant voice in EU studies. In its earliest manifestations neofunctionalism drew inspiration from the three theories described above. It shared with functionalism a concern with technocratic notions of politics. From federalism it drew a concern with postnational solutions to political problems. Like transactionalists, neofunctionalists were in the vanguard of modern social science. Their project was one of analysis, explanation, and prediction, rather than normative advocacy. At the core of the work of writers such as Ernst Haas (see Haas 1968) was an interest in the role of social groups in political change.

A striking feature of neofunctionalism was its close relationship to the strategies of the founding figures of postwar European integration. The Schuman Declaration of 1950, which laid the basis for the ECSC, proposed an incremental, technocratic, and economic strategy for greater political ends. The choices to initiate integration in strategically important economic sectors and to create supranational institutions to oversee the integration process were clearly designed to create deeper and wider economic integration, and to promote the drift of governance capacity away from the nation-state.

Neofunctionalists placed an emphasis on the interplay of key self-interested actors, notably social groups and supranational sponsors of integration. They suggested that, where two or more countries agree to an act of economic integration in an economic sector, they are likely to be persuaded of the efficacy of setting up a supranational bureaucracy to oversee the project. The full advantages of integration in the chosen sector are not likely to be realized without integration in cognate sectors. Cognate sectors become involved in any case, because of perceptions among producer groups of the benefits of integration. In addition, the transnationalization of group activity that accompanies integration begins to transform the interests of various economic actors, so that their loyalties tend to be directed to the new integrated economic space and the forms of authority that oversee it. In the meantime, the supranational authority has a vested interest in acting as an advocate of further integration and the expansion of supranational authoritative capacity. Its interactions with producer groups will therefore be vital in developing a consensus about the real functional linkages that exist between integrated and nonintegrated sectors, and about the utility of regional interest associations. The net effect of these exchanges is growing societal support for integration and thus greater pressure on state actors to negotiate integrative agreements.

The key concept used by neofunctionalists to describe these processes was "spillover". In part, "spillover" recalls the idea mentioned above that integration has a built-in logic that deepens the formal interdependence of economies, and institutionalizes and "politicizes" the whole process. The foundation of a customs union would create pressures for that union to evolve into a common market, which in turn would require the development of supranational regulatory capacity. "Spillover" also describes the pressures to join an integration scheme that are placed on related parts of the economy following an act of integration in a particular economic sector. These processes have an inbuilt logic and, while they are "rational", they do not necessarily occur automatically. Spillover in economics therefore requires a degree of political activism. Most obviously, this comes from supranational institutions, such as the Commission, but, as their material circumstances shift, various social groups such as business associations could become advocates of deeper integration.

Intergovernmentalism

Intergovernmentalism has often been misunderstood as the outcome of a backlash among international relations "realists" against their institutionalist-idealist rivals, the neofunctionalists. Intergovernmentalism is indeed resolutely centred on states, but to label it as "realist" is to misconstrue some of its central insights and, especially in the contemporary context, to misunderstand the underlying debates among international relations scholars that spill over into EU studies. For their part, realists have had little to say about the EU. In part this is because European integration is read in realist terms as a classic alliance between states, which may dissolve once the conditions for its creation have been superseded, and which in any case is largely secondary to the "real" issues of security that, hitherto, have been played out in other forums in Europe.

Intergovernmentalist critiques of neofunctionalism were led by Stanley Hoffmann in an often quoted article written in 1966. Hoffmann drew ammunition from the empirical record of the time, notably the rise of Charles de Gaulle in France and its impact on the Community. Hoffmann characterized this as the reappearance of nationalist sentiment, providing an emphatic reminder of the continuing importance of governments, as well as evidence for a shift in the balance of forces within the Community, away from the classic balance between intergovernmentalism and supranationalism that had characterized the Monnet model, towards a more decidedly intergovernmentalist style of policy-making. Hoffmann's conclusion was that Haas and his colleagues had radically misunderstood the residual capacities of the European nation-state. On the intergovernmentalist view, integration – and thus neofunctionalists' explanations of integra-

tion – works in technocratic areas of "low politics", such as the removal of barriers to the operation of markets, but areas of "high politics" are much more immune to integrative impulses. Areas where vital national interests are deemed to be at stake cannot be penetrated by neofunctionalist logic. Moreover, states are self-interested actors, and this could lead to divergence as much as it could to convergence. In other words, there is a constant dialectic between what Hoffmann called the "logic of integration" on the one hand and the "logic of diversity" on the other.

States' interests may be explained by reference to two sources. The first is domestic politics: as many intergovernmentalists have suggested, national governments can be thought of as "gatekeepers" at the junction of national and international politics. This means that integration is mediated in domestic politics by national governments. At the same time, an emphasis on domestic politics as the source of governmental preferences reminds us that national polities are diverse arenas, representing very different sources of group, cultural and institutional pressure upon governments. The second source of a state's interests is its orientation towards the international system. For instance, the various member states of the European Communities had very different relationships with powerful external actors, such as the United States. For Hoffmann, the wider international system is inherently diverse and thus the differential location of states in the global political economy can ultimately produce tensions in the project of European integration, particularly as member states would be unable to agree on the place of their Community within the global system. States matter, therefore, because of the twin pulls of the domestic and the global. In any international system, Hoffmann argued, diversity and dissensus would arise out of both the natural plurality of domestic imperatives faced by governments and the fact that every state's situation within that system would be distinct.

Others built on Hoffmann's critique to argue that, even in areas of "low politics", integration was most likely to occur as the consequence of deliberate state-led cooperative acts, rather than as the product of social forces. For instance, Roger Hansen reasoned that the neofunctionalist assumptions about "spillover" drastically underestimated the capacity of complex pluralistic societies to contain the sort of crisis that might lead to the sort of transfer of loyalty necessary to propel political integration. Integration should rather be seen as the product of states acting in concert to achieve positive-sum economic gains, not as the outcome of a mixture of supranational activism and pressure from social groups.

Alongside these expressly theoretical interventions from scholars in political science and international relations, there emerged an intergovernmentalist position that largely eschewed the whole idea of "theory". A collection of historians around Alan Milward argued that the concern with theory had led many scholars of integration away from the real dynamics of European reconstruction and integration in the postwar period (see Milward *et al.*). While their contempt for theory and theorists is sometimes withering, the view adopted by Milward and his colleagues is interesting for what it suggests about state behaviour and, specifically, why it is that states in Europe have engaged in the seemingly counterintuitive act of surrendering elements of their authority or sovereignty.

The Milward hypothesis, simply stated, is that governments in western Europe chose to engage in a cooperative and integrative process as a means to secure better management of the complex demands emerging from their societies in the 1940s. The successful delivery of such policy programmes to domestic publics was crucial to the survival both of office-seeking politicians and of nation-states as the primary units of governance. Thus the neofunctionalist idea of integration as a progressive transfer of power away from the nation-state, managed by emerging supranational elites, has little appeal to this view. What is particularly interesting is the claim that to a very large extent, integration amounts to what Milward has called the "rescue of the nation-state", the preservation of executive capacity at the national level rather than its erosion. This is an idea that has crept into several contemporary intergovernmentalist accounts.

Old Themes Revisited

Intergovernmentalism and neofunctionalism have supplied the foundations of much of the scholarly debate on integration (if not the broader political and public debate) since the 1960s. Much contemporary academic discussion is premised on an effort to escape the dichotomous terms of debate that these two rival accounts are thought to spawn. At the same time, the discussion between neofunctionalists and intergovernmentalists offers an entry point to thinking theoretically about the EU. After all, they give us two quite distinct accounts of the integration process. Neofunctionalists explain integration with reference to the changing preferences of social groups, the compulsive functional logic of economic integration, and the politics of activist supranational institutional actors. Intergovernmentalists, by contrast, see integration as the product of bargains between governments. Moreover, they explain lapses in or retreats from integration in terms of the lack of incentives for states to engage in positive-sum bargaining. However, neither offers a static theoretical prospectus and both schools have developed significant contemporary variants.

The Neofunctionalist Revival and Supranational Governance

Writing in the mid-1970s, Ernst Haas described integration theory, for which read "neofunctionalism" as "obsolescent" (see Haas 1975). By this he meant not only that a dissonance had developed between neofunctionalist predictions and events in the real world, but also that it would be more productive to study integration as a subset of broader discussions developing in the field of international relations studies around the idea of interdependence.

Neofunctionalism underwent a small-scale revival from the mid-1980s, when events in western Europe seemed to bear a striking resemblance to some of the theory's core ideas. The radical deepening of integration represented by the Single European Act, with its aim of facilitating the completion of the Community's internal market, was sponsored by an activist Commission under the leadership of

Jacques Delors: clearly, there was potential for "spillover". The "negative" integration associated with the removal of barriers to the free movement of goods, services, and persons required extensive legal harmonization, the growth of decision-making and regulatory capacity at the supranational level, and the incursion of interstate cooperation into new areas such as policing. Moreover, functional spillover potential was also evident in the claims that market liberalization would be best achieved with the development of a single currency and that Community social programmes might offer the most effective way of ameliorating the worst effects of adjustments prompted by the single market. Finally, supranational activism was evident not simply in the actions of the Commission but also through the jurisprudence of the European Court of Justice.

Supranational activism sat at the core of studies by scholars who addressed the political economy of integration from the 1980s. For Wayne Sandholtz and John Zysman, it was the interaction between supranational bureaucrats and social groups with an interest in market harmonization that was vital in building a persuasive alliance in favour of integration that the governments of member states could not ignore (see Sandholz and Zysman). This way of thinking has more recently been fashioned into a more formal theoretical statement (see Sandholtz and Stone Sweet). They argue that supranational governance – a version of "political integration" – is the consequence of the interaction of actors demanding the provision of supranational rules with supranational actors willing to supply those rules. The former are economic actors who, through their private market actions, have begun to fashion a transnational economic space but are not able to optimize their position in this *de facto* economy without a rule-bound order. The willingness of supranational bureaucrats, in the shape of the Commission, to supply these rules makes for a compelling and powerful alliance.

Contemporary Intergovernmentalism

Sandholtz and Stone Sweet's explanation of supranational governance was designed as a counterweight to the influential liberal inter-governmentalist theory of Andrew Moravcsik. This was a direct descendant of Hoffmann's intergovernmentalism, but it also owed much to the growth of liberal institutionalism within the discipline of international relations in the United States.

Moravcsik also uses the metaphor of supply and demand. In his work, the demands for integration arise in the domestic politics of member states and national governments are the principal suppliers of integration outcomes. Governments are engaged, therefore, in a permanent two-level game: their preferences are derived from processes of domestic politics; these preferences are bargained in the intergovernmental forums of the EU. These intergovernmental settings are not venues for classical diplomacy. Rather, they are institutionalized and "information rich", which makes positive-sum bargaining possible. The outputs of these deliberations feed back into domestic politics.

The "game" of integration in Moravcsik's account is centred around national executives rather than supranational institutions and nonstate actors. But this is a state-centrism that recognizes the significance of domestic politics and the institutional mediation provided by European-level bargaining. One of his most striking conclusions is that governments can use bargaining at the "European" level to enhance their positions domestically. In this view, integration actually strengthens the state.

Intergovernmentalists have to deal with the paradox of why states voluntarily cede parts of their authority. Moravcsik provides one explanation. Considerable emphasis in this regard has also been placed upon institutions. Specifically, some writers have tried to describe how states use the complex institutional fabric of the EU. For example, Geoffrey Garrett and George Tsebelis have pointed out that the outputs of intergovernmental bargains have as much to do with the specifics of decision rules as with strategic interaction between states (see Garrett and Tsebelis). This suggests the importance of institutionalist perspectives (see below). Finally, approaches centred on the state need not imply an attachment to rigid models of the unitary nation-state. This is especially notable in Wolfgang Wessels's "fusion hypothesis", which treats integration as the way in which governments seek to solve common problems: these problems reflect changed priorities that arise in the context of the welfare state, and the net outcome is a transformation of the patterns of governance within as well as between states (see Wessels).

New Frontiers of Integration Theory

The story of integration theory is a subplot in the history of the discipline of international relations after the World War II. Intergovernmentalism and neofunctionalism represented quite distinct views about the workings of the international system, and the prospects for change therein; yet the EU is viewed increasingly as a polity or a political system. From this vantage point, it may be seen as a novel phenomenon, but one that nevertheless has discernible cleavage structures, embedded games, and actors pursuing their interests. "Integration" is not central to the everyday deliberations of actors working within this polity. This observation has led writers such as Hix to reject international relations as a suitable parent discipline for EU studies, on the grounds that its core problematic disables it from asking the key questions about European policy-making and governance. Where international relations has a function, it would be to explain the role of the external, global system and its impact upon actors within the EU polity.

This is a complex debate, but defenders of international relations claim that it remains a fertile breeding ground for a number of useful ideas, such as forms of institutional analysis and constructivism (see below). Moreover, they argue, international relations is not locked in age-old debates about states, war, and peace. Indeed, areas such as international political economy are concerned with the blurring of boundaries between the domestic and the international, the emergence of powerful transnational actors operating in new transnational spaces, and the growth of a world order built around regional integration schemes (of which the EU may be an instance) in the context of globalization.

Institutionalism

A case in point is the proliferation of institutionalist perspectives. The institutionalist "turn" has been one of the major developments in political science during the past 20 years, but it also has had an equally significant impact on studies of international relations. Indeed, particular versions of institutionalism are at the core of Moravcsik's liberal intergovernmentalism (see above).

The basic claim of all institutionalists is that "institutions matter". Whether formal and constitutionalized, or informal (collections of established practices and ongoing norms of interaction), institutions have an impact upon both political behaviour and political outcomes. They act as intervening variables between the preferences of actors and the outcomes of those actors' deliberations. In particular, institutions are said to provide information-rich venues in which transparency and thus trust may be high. This facilitates a high proportion of positive-sum bargains (see Schneider and Aspinwall).

The connections to the EU, with its dense array of formal and informal institutional venues, are obvious. Most accounts identify three variants of the institutionalist hypothesis. The first, "rational choice institutionalism", conceptualizes actors as rational and self-interested, and institutions as largely formal entities with clear decision rules. Decision rules, such as the voting schemes in the Council of Ministers, influence the strategic calculus of actors. Those working within this variant also present institutions primarily as the rational creation of states seeking to reduce the transaction costs of bargaining.

Alternatively, "historical institutionalism" focuses on two attributes of institutions: the circumstances of their creation, and their capacity to embed interests and agendas. The conditions under which institutions are devised tend to be very particular. A case in point would be the sets of calculations that led European elites to create the ECSC in 1951. While the specific historical circumstances that produced the ECSC have faded, the legacy of this institutional choice has not. Thus purposeful institutions with discernible and continuing interests have been created. In this view, institutions "structure" the political situations in which actors find themselves.

In both of these versions of institutionalism, the preferences of actors are exogenous; that is, they exist prior to institutional interaction. In the third variant, "sociological institutionalism", interests tend to be endogenous to institutions. This means that institutions provide venues for learning and socialization. Institutions are thus thought of as carriers of beliefs, knowledge, understandings, and values. Institutional cultures exert key influences upon the ways in which actors behave. This can apply equally to established patterns of interaction between governmental actors and to formal institutions such as the directorates-general of the European Commission.

Constructivism

Constructivism emerged as a major movement in international relations in the 1990s. Its core insight emerges from the claim that the structures of politics are social rather than material. This places it in opposition to the "rationalist" mainstream of integration theory, which tends to assume the presence of rational self-seeking actors (this is a shared assumption of both neofunctionalism and intergovernmentalism). Constructivists see interests as "socially constructed", that is, as derivatives of processes of social and linguistic interaction (various constructivist-inspired approaches are discussed in Jørgensen, and in Christiansen, Jørgensen, and Wiener).

The focus of constructivism is on the role of symbols, norms, discourses, and belief systems in the processes of integration and EU governance. The identities of actors, such as states, are not materially given. Rather, they are contingent and founded upon the achievement of mutual understandings both of "self" and of context. Thus, in the EU context, constructivism draws attention to the operation of norms – ongoing, self-perpetuating practices and rules – and the role of institutions as venues for communication and socialization, as opposed to instrumental rationality (see Risse-Kappen). Also, given that identities are socially constructed, constructivists are interested in how European notions of community

emerge through social and linguistic interaction. Much of this work remains in its infancy, but constructivism may well have a fruitful future in the study of the EU.

Multilevel Governance

The political sciences have become increasingly concerned with "governance". Governance is generally defined as being about the organization, steering, and coordination of social systems. The authoritative structures and processes that are normally associated with government may be one way in which governance occurs. Therefore, the literature on governance tends to deal with the recalibration of state authority, the emergence of alternative (nonstate) forms of authority, and the appearance of policy networks.

These issues are particularly salient in the context of the EU, and the governance "turn" in EU studies is associated with the breakdown of dichotomous discussions of political integration as polarized between ideas of "nation state" and "superstate". This brings into the analysis of the EU various analytical tools such as policy network analysis, but it also begins to use the EU as a laboratory for the exploration of possible transformations in policy-making on a much wider scale.

One popular recent image in the literature is of the EU as a system of "multilevel governance" (see Marks, Hooghe, and Blank). This metaphor suggests that the EU is a polity in which authority has been dispersed between levels of governance and political actors are mobile between the different levels. Levels of integration are also asymmetrical. Thus, the essence of political integration is not easily captured by this approach and for many this way of thinking signals an end to grand theorizing about the EU. For some, however, different kinds of theories can be used at different levels of analysis (see Peterson and Bomberg).

Conclusions

Theoretical debates about political integration remain lively within EU studies. The vibrancy of these discussions is influenced in part by the continuing ambiguity of what "political integration" means in the European context. This in turn raises issues of the extent to which the theoretical toolkit of EU studies is generally applicable to other instances of regional integration. If integration theory relies too heavily on the institutional architecture of the EU, then it runs the risk of accounting only for the integration of the European economy and the emergence of supranational governance capacity there.

The abandonment of a quest for a general theory of integration may be no bad thing, however. Perhaps the future of European integration studies lies with the development of mid-range accounts that explain the specificities of the European experience. On the other hand, debates about both governance and political economy suggest that the study of the EU might have helpful things to say about how economic governance can be delivered under conditions of globalization and how the private actions of market agents may be related to the deliberate decisions of formal authoritative actors.

Further Reading

Adler, Emanuel, and Michael Barnett (editors), *Security Communities*, Cambridge and New York: Cambridge University Press, 1998

An interesting selection of essays seeking to update the idea of "security communities", associated most with Karl Deutsch and the transactionalist school of integration theory

Burgess, Michael, *Federalism and European Union: the Building of Europe, 1950–2000*, London and New York: Routledge, 2000

An elegant contemporary attempt to develop a federalist account of the origins and development of the EU

Christiansen, Thomas, Knud Erik Jørgensen, and Antje Wiener (editors), *Constructing Europe*, London and New York: Sage, 2001

A selection of constructivist-inspired analyses of European integration along with contributions from critics. This book is notable, in particular, for a rare recent intervention in the debate by Ernst Haas, comparing neofunctionalism and constructivism.

Coudenhove-Calerghi, Richard N., *Pan-Europa*, New York: Knopf, 1926

Probably the most influential example of interwar federalist ideas designed to secure European unity and (thus) peace

Deutsch, Karl, *et al.*, *Political Community and the North Atlantic Area: International Organization in the Light of Historical Experience*, Princeton, NJ: Princeton University Press, 1957

The classic text for the transactionalist approach to integration

Garrett, Geoffrey, and George Tsebelis, "An Institutional Critique of Intergovernmentalism", in *International Organization*, 46/2, 1996, pp. 533–60

An elegant example of "rational choice institutionalism" that engages significantly with liberal intergovernmentalism

Haas, Ernst B., *The Uniting of Europe: Political, Economic and Social Forces, 1950–1957*, second edition, Stanford, CA: Stanford University Press, 1968

The classic founding statement of neofunctionalism. The second edition contains an extended preface in which Haas begins to engage with his intergovernmentalist critics.

Haas, Ernst B., *The Obsolescence of Regional Integration Theory*, Berkeley, CA: Institute of International Studies Working Paper, 1975

Notable for its self-critique of the integration theory project

Hansen, Roger D., "European Integration: Reflections on a Decade of Theoretical Efforts", in *World Politics*, 21/2, 1969, pp. 242–71

A notable critique of neofunctionalism from a writer of intergovernmentalist persuasions

Hix, Simon, "The Study of the European Community: the Challenge to Comparative Politics", in *West European Politics*, 17/1, 1994, pp. 1–30

An influential critical review of the integration theory literature that makes a strong case for the deployment of the tools of comparative political science, as opposed to international relations, in EU studies

Hix, Simon, *The Political System of the European Union*, London: Macmillan, and New York: St Martin's Press, 1999

A landmark text, premised on the idea of applying the classical tools of political science to the EU

Hodges, Michael, "Introduction", in Michael Hodges (editor), *European Integration*, Harmondsworth and Baltimore, MD: Penguin, 1972

A critical introduction to a collection of some of the earlier statements of integration theory

Hoffmann, Stanley, "Obstinate or Obsolete? The Fate of the Nation-State and the Case of Western Europe", in *Daedalus*, 95/3, 1966, pp. 862–915

A statement of position for intergovernmentalists, written as a critique of neofunctionalism in the light of the Gaullist turn in the European Communities at the time

Jørgensen, Knud Erik (editor), *Reflective Approaches to European Governance*, London: Macmillan, and New York: St. Martin's Press, 1997

A collection of early constructivist contributions to thinking about European integration and EU governance

Marks, Gary, Liesbet Hooghe, and Kermit Blank, "European Integration from the 1980s: State-Centric v. Multi-Level Governance", in *Journal of Common Market Studies*, 34/3, 1996, pp. 341–78

A discussion of the "multilevel governance" approach to the EU

Milward, Alan S., *et al.*, *The Frontier of National Sovereignty: History and Theory 1945–1992*, London and New York: Routledge, 1993

A collection of forthright, largely state-centric contributions to the debate from economic historians

Mitrany, David, *A Working Peace System*, Chicago: Quadrangle Books, 1966 (orginally published 1943)

The classic statement of functionalist integration theory

Moravcsik, Andrew, *The Choice for Europe: Social Purpose and State Power from Messina to Maastricht*, Ithaca, NY: Cornell University Press, 1998; London: UCL Press, 1999

An exposition of the "liberal intergovernmentalist" theory of integration

Peterson, John, and Elizabeth Bomberg, *Decision-making in the European Union*, London: Macmillan, and New York: St Martin's Press, 1999

A recent text on EU policy-making that argues for a "levels of analysis" approach to theorizing, so that different sorts of theoretical work are used to analyze different aspects of the EU's operation

Risse-Kappen, Thomas, "Explaining the Nature of the Beast: International Relations and Comparative Policy Analysis Meet the EU", in *Journal of Common Market Studies*, 34/1, 1996, pp. 53–80

This article discusses the usefulness of "communicative action" and "sociological institutionalist" perspectives for the study of the EU.

Rosamond, Ben, *Theories of European Integration*, London: Macmillan, and New York: St Martin's Press, 2000

A survey of classical and contemporary theoretical work on political integration and EU governance

Sandholtz, Wayne, and John Zysman, "1992: Recasting the European Bargain", in *World Politics*, 27/4, 1989, pp. 95–128

An important article that seeks to explain the rebirth of integration in the 1980s through the strategic interaction of supranational institutions and transnational business

Sandholtz, Wayne, and Alec Stone Sweet (editors), *European Integration and Supranational Governance*, Oxford and New York: Oxford University Press, 1998

A presentation of a theory that challenges Moravcsik's liberal intergovernmentalism by emphasizing the significance of nonstate transnational actors and supranational institutions, and that draws on both neofunctionalism and transactionalism

Schneider, Gerald, and Mark Aspinwall, *The Rules of Integration: Institutionalist Approaches to the Study of Europe*, Manchester: Manchester University Press, 2001

A state-of-the-art collection surveying the contributions of various institutionalist approaches to the EU

Wallace, William, "Introduction", in William Wallace (editor), *The Dynamics of European Integration*, London and New York: Pinter and Royal Institute of International Affairs, 1990

A broadranging discussion of the political economy of integration that makes a useful distinction between "formal" and "informal" integration

Wessels, Wolfgang, "An Ever Closer Fusion: A Dynamic Macropolitical View on Integration Processes", in *Journal of Common Market Studies*, 35/2, 1997, pp. 267–99

A recent contribution highlighting the importance of states in the integration process, but
accepting at the same time that the nature of
statehood is undergoing significant change

Dr Ben Rosamund is Senior Research Fellow in the
Centre for the Study of Globalisation and
Regionalisation at the University of Warwick. In
1999 he was Marshall–Monnet Visiting Professor of
EU Studies at the European Union Centre of New
York. He was the editor of *Politics*, a journal of the
Political Studies Association of the United
Kingdom, from 1994 to 2000.

Chapter Four

The Evolving Union: The Treaties of Amsterdam and Nice

Clive H. Church

The European Union as we know it today is the product of a long history of change. This history is continuing and not only is change continuous in the Union, but it can be more formative than change in nation states. Because the EU is a new body, without a clear and agreed final destination, some changes can alter its very nature, leading to talk of the inherent instability of the Union.

"Change" can, of course, mean many things, especially in the context of the EU. One key element is alterations in patterns of governance or in what can be called constitutional questions. Most of these come about through formal amendments to the Union's treaties, negotiated through the special mechanism of intergovernmental conferences (IGCs). The IGC leading to the Treaty of Nice was at least the seventh overall and certainly the fifth in 11 years. Because of this acceleration, even the massive and controversial changes made under the Maastricht Treaty (1992) did not bring real stability. Not merely have there been two further IGCs in less than four years – leading at Amsterdam to significant revisions of the Maastricht arrangements and at Nice to alterations in decision-making to try and enable the EU to deal with the implications of enlargement – but the Union now faces further changes. Thus the IGC in 2000 opened up the question of the Union's long-term future with a formal commitment to a new public constitutional consideration, ending with a further IGC in 2004.

All this has alarmed Eurosceptics, who see the Union turning into a "superstate" and threatening the autonomous identity of the member states. Conversely, the process has not satisfied those who are in favour of a more radical restructuring of the Union. They see growing fragmentation and diminishing powers for the institutions. Hence, there has been a developing debate about the longer-term destination and shape of the Union. As in 2000, this could overshadow the actual negotiations, if not the treaty changes themselves. Nonetheless, the treaties and the way in which they are actually negotiated are crucial to an understanding of the evolution and politics of the Union. It is through the treaties that the states constitute and amend the Union's structures and operations.

The Mechanics of Intergovernmental Conferences

The process by which treaties are negotiated plays a significant part in shaping substantive changes. To an extent, the intensity of treaty revision has bypassed the formal provisions of Article 48 of the Treaty on European Union (TEU). This allows the Commission or a member state to suggest treaty changes to the Council, which, after consultation, can decide whether or not to agree. In fact, since Maastricht the norm has been for one treaty to ordain the calling of the next IGC, as did Nice.

Over the last few years the IGC process has become increasingly institutionalized. Indeed, the term "IGC" is somewhat of a misnomer for, while they remain highly political affairs, being dependent on the agreement of all participating states, they are not single conferences in the sense of specific one-off meetings to decide on constitutional questions. They are more drawn out, multilevelled, and routinized than this. To begin with, they are a series of gatherings, often taking place over many months, 15 in the case of Amsterdam and nine for Nice. Secondly, they exist on several levels, from agenda-setting "reflection groups", through the preparatory panel of officials and junior ministers, where the bulk of the negotiations take place, to the monthly meetings of foreign ministers, which are the IGC proper. The latter simply add IGC matters to their normal agenda. As a result, the IGC process is not as detached from the normal workings of the Union as might be supposed. The habit has now developed of consulting the European Parliament on the negotiations, whether through a formal exchange before ministerial meetings or through representation at the lower-level sessions, as in 2000. The IGC can also call on the services of other experts, sometimes known as the "friends of the presidency", for technical studies, such as those of the European Court of Justice before Nice.

Finally, since the early 1990s the heads of government have been brought in to provide the finishing touches to the process. This reflects both the increasing importance and sensitivity of EU affairs, and the way in which the media have helped to personalize government. Only heads of government now have the weight and standing to take key decisions, something that was made very clear in the run-up to Nice. They also have the chance both to demonstrate their machismo and to feed in ideas, which might help them at home, thus intensifying the fragmentary and "garbage can" nature of the IGC process.

All the questions left unanswered by officials and ministers have to be resolved by the presidents and prime ministers. Unfortunately, they have to do this in a very short time, while also trying to deal with other, sometimes more pressing matters. Nice was unusual in that the summit clearly divided its routine side from its IGC concerns. The heads of government also have to negotiate without real access to their officials and this isolation can affect the

outcome, since it is very hard to negotiate complex technical agreements in such "pressure cooker" circumstances, particularly in the early hours of the morning, when the, usually, middle-aged leaders are tired. It can also lead, as both Amsterdam and Nice showed, to sloppy and doubtful treaty texts.

The Treaty of Amsterdam

The IGC in 1996 was the first to be convoked by a previous treaty. It also had a large and sprawling agenda, but one that, because of the British problem, achieved a breakthrough only right at the end of its life, in the run-up to the Amsterdam summit. Nonetheless, the eventual Treaty of Amsterdam led to many significant changes in the way in which the Union is organized. At the same time, it also restyled the treaties in an innovative way, so it has a dual character, as an amending and as a rationalizing treaty.

The Travails of the Amsterdam IGC

In a way the Amsterdam IGC was an unwanted negotiation. It was called because the TEU required that it should be, listing several minor questions that should be considered by a new IGC in 1996. It was assumed that, by then, the TEU would have "bedded down", and that it would be possible to tidy up such things as the pillar structure, questions of the common foreign and security policy (CFSP), the co-decision procedures, the hierarchy of acts, and three new policy areas. In other words, it was intended to be a routine matter of readjustment, not a search for new economic or policy imperatives.

However, the public crisis over ratification of the TEU both delayed its implementation until November 1993 and revealed deep political differences about how, given growing public alienation, the Union could best be developed. The member states would probably have preferred not to risk a possibly destabilizing new attempt at treaty amendment. However, they were condemned to go ahead, not merely because of the requirement of the Maastricht Treaty itself, but because they hoped that clarifying the treaties and refocusing the Union on matters of relevance to ordinary people might help to restore its wider appeal. There was also a need to remedy some of the failings of Maastricht, notably where foreign policy, enlargement, and the institutions were concerned.

Hence new items were added to the IGC's shopping list at various summits: institutional questions, subsidiarity, and, especially, enlargement, which had not been considered at Maastricht. This meant, paradoxically, that although the IGC in 1996 was a "negotiation in search of a purpose", it ended with a very wide agenda. Because of this it was agreed at Corfu in 1994 to prepare the way through a reflection group, which could sift the possibilities and indicate where agreement might be possible. It was assisted by another innovation, a set of reports from the institutions on the way in which Maastricht had actually worked in its short life.

Unfortunately, the reflection group, chaired by Carlos Westendorp of Spain, did little sifting. States merely stated their positions, refusing concessions. Because there was so little consensus, the idea of flexible arrangements, which would allow some states to integrate more deeply, emerged as a way of solving the impasse. Nonetheless, in its final report to the Madrid meeting of the European Council the group picked out three themes: making the treaties work better, in order to facilitate enlargement; reinforcing the Union's international identity; and bringing the Union closer to its citizens.

The lack of consensus became all too evident when the IGC proper began work in March 1996. Some of the Maastricht ideas were set aside, creating pessimism about prospects. Nonetheless, outside forces, including the Commission and the Parliament, continued to press for a much more radical restructuring of the Union. In the event, in December 1996 the Irish Presidency produced an innovative treaty draft that sought to explain to the world why they were suggesting the changes they did. There were large gaps, notably on institutions and enlargement.

Many of the ideas in the draft were taken up by the incoming Dutch Presidency. However, this had to proceed very carefully, partly in order to avoid upsetting things, as a Dutch presidency had in 1991, and partly because the imminence of a general election in Britain (legally due by, and in fact held in, May 1997) made agreement even harder to achieve. Even though the Dutch speeded things up as the summer approached, there were real fears that a deal might not be done. Even flexibility became a subject of discord rather than a way of finessing it.

The Amsterdam Settlement

Labour's victory in the British election led to an immediate breaking of the deadlock, notably on social policy and the incorporation of the Schengen arrangements on border controls into the Community pillar. Nonetheless, negotiations were still difficult. Reservations in other countries were exposed once the British ceased to block everything. The way in which protocols and declarations were flying about reflected the level of distrust among negotiators, who felt that they had to spell everything out to ensure that they got what they wanted.

Despite the new tempo, many questions were left to the European Council to resolve. Yet the Amsterdam summit actually found it hard to do this. Arguments over the Stability Pact inspired by Lionel Jospin's new left-centre coalition government in France combined with enhanced media pressures to make it difficult for leaders to concentrate on the treaty or to make potentially unpopular compromises. The lack of agreement between France and Germany also reduced pressures for change, especially as Chancellor Helmut Kohl, harassed by the *Länder* (the 16 German states), sought to resist increases in the use of qualified majority voting (QMV). Although the summit was due to end early on the afternoon of Tuesday 17 June, it dragged on until 4 am on the Wednesday, held up by arguments over the CFSP and institutional reform. This meant that, at the end, a number of items were "nodded through while people nodded off". Many observers commented unfavourably on the "chaos" of the final sessions. The final text was unclear and some delegations felt that things were included that had not actually been agreed.

In fact, simply getting an agreement at all, in such circumstances, was an achievement. The deal, published as the Treaty of Amsterdam immediately after the European Council, presented the initial results of the IGC in a distinctive way, as Table 4.1 shows. The 100-plus changes were not initially presented as consecutive amendments to the treaties, but were grouped into six thematic packages, in the hope of making the new treaty more attractive to the public.

All told, these changes were more significant than was often appreciated at the time. Under the first heading, the treaty provided two things: new commitments to human rights and democracy, including a procedure for suspending states felt to be offending against them; and secondly, a series of measures to guarantee the rights of citizens against the abuse of free movement, whether through asylum, immigration or visa policy. Hence, elements of the existing Justice and Home Affairs (JHA) pillar were communitized via insertion into the EC Treaty, while provision was made for the Schengen system to be incorporated into EU practice and into legislation that was to be enacted allowing Britain and Ireland a special status because they are connected islands. Cooperation among customs services, judiciaries, and police was also enhanced within the now restricted Third Pillar.

The second heading was slightly misleading, given the diverse content. It included provisions for the encouragement and monitoring of employment policies, and the transfer of most of the Social Charter to the Community proper. There were also minor clarifications of policies on citizenship, consumer protection, the environment, fraud, public health, and subsidiarity. It was hoped that such things would have a popular appeal.

External affairs, and especially the CFSP, made up the third package. This was retained as a separate pillar, but was reorganized so as to give it more consistency and efficacy, and, it was hoped, a higher profile. This involved a new procedure known as "constructive abstention", by which doubting states would stand aside to let external actions go ahead. Institutionally, a new High Representative, backed by a policy planning unit, was introduced to lead the CFSP. The treaty also brought the so-called "Petersberg" tasks into the remit of the CFSP, which means that military instruments could be used in humanitarian intervention. It also left it open to the European Council to merge the Western European Union (WEU) with the Union, and to create an EU defence policy and force.

Where institutions were concerned, the negotiators failed to agree on the key changes necessary for enlargement, conceding merely the possibility of a process of adjusting the size of the Commission as enlargement got under way. Yet, despite this, the Treaty did produce a large number of minor institutional changes, which, cumulatively, are likely to have a real impact. Many of these are related to the Parliament, the size of which was capped but which had its legislative role increased through the extension (and simplification) of co-decision. Changes were also made to Council practice, to the remit of the European Court of Justice, and to the standing of the Commission President. The consultative organs were also given more rights of consultation, while the role and status of the European Council were strengthened.

Finally, the IGC agreed a complicated set of provisions on "closer cooperation", initially known as "flexibility". These were aimed at allowing impatient groups of states to integrate more deeply. However, there were strict general conditions about using the provisions so as to preserve the *acquis communautaire* and prevent exclusion. Special constraints for the First and Third Pillars also figured. As with constructive abstention, there was the possibility of unhappy states being able to appeal upwards to the European Council, partially restoring the Luxembourg veto.

The Aftermath

Despite the extent of these changes, initial reactions were muted. This was partly because the Amsterdam process ended in a rush amid relief that a deal had been done without a crisis. It was also because the many detailed changes pointed in different directions and created no clear identity. Those who called it a dog's dinner of a treaty could be forgiven for doing so.

Hence, few euphoric defences were offered at the time. Trenchant views were few and far between, and totally contradictory. Robin Cook, the Foreign Secretary in the new British government, hailed it as "federalism in retreat", a view supported, paradoxically, by many federalists, who lamented the fact that Amsterdam did not mark the great breakthrough that they had expected, and that it seemed to fragment the Union. They saw its gains as illusory window-dressing, offering rhetorical promises with no guarantee of action. Indeed, in the eyes of some, it was a classic example of the member states safeguarding their control of the Union's development.

Conversely, British Tories, as well as some French Gaullists, saw it as threatening national sovereignty through the extension of the powers of the European Court of Justice as much as through the increased use of QMV. They were also alarmed about the implications of the new human rights provisions. All of them tended to agree with a Danish MEP, Jens-Peter Bonde, who saw Amsterdam as taking the Union into deeper "superstate" waters. Both Britain and France saw unsuccessful demands for a referendum on Amsterdam.

Over the summer, innovative work on the treaties continued with experts, notably "friends of the presidency" and the Committee of Permanent Representatives, working on the precise texts of the treaty. Hence, when the treaty came back in the early autumn it had been given a new form. Gone was the thematic presentation. Instead, as Table 4.2 shows, there was a classic three-part treaty with 15 articles. In making this change Amsterdam surrendered its initial identity. It now had no real preamble and contained almost no items that do not constitute amendments to other treaties. Only those provisions concerning simplification actually have a life of their own. Moreover, all protocols are attached to one or more existing treaties, as are most of the declarations. As a result, all that is really seen through the window of the new articles is the landscape of other treaties. Amsterdam is therefore technically a "disappearing treaty".

As well as transferring the June changes to the Treaty establishing the European Community (Rome) and the Treaty on European Union (Maastricht), the revisers also acted on the hint in the sixth heading of the June draft, and simplified both these earlier treaties. They eliminated out-of-date material, filled the resulting gaps, and renumbered the restructured treaties. This led to the production of two clear, consolidated documents. Although their authority derives from the original treaties, which remain legally effective, they have increasingly become the texts used in the Union's day-to-day life. The revisers also went on to produce two experimental codifications of the various treaties into a single document, something that was to influence the decision at Nice to consider further simplifications of the treaties. This rationalization helped to unify the treaty base and give it a more constitutional appearance, a development often overlooked.

This may have helped to change opinions of the Treaty of Amsterdam and avoid any real crises during ratification. The European Parliament grudgingly gave its approval and ratification followed surely, if slowly, even though two fifths of those in Denmark and Ireland voted against it. Ratification was held up mainly by local constitutional problems in Belgium and France. In the latter, a constitutional amendment was necessary, and this was only effected in January 1999. In France, as in Greece, there was some opposition both from the far left and from rightwing Eurosceptics. In the end the treaty became operative on 1 May 1999. Well before then, of course, preparations for implementation were well-advanced.

The Treaty of Nice

Amsterdam left the way open to a new IGC, but, even though its agenda was to be relatively limited, negotiating was still difficult. In the end a deal was cut, but only just. It was to prove both contested and divisive, and there had to be a "post-Nice" process as well.

From Amsterdam to a new IGC

The IGC in 1996–97 had been meant to prepare the way for enlargement by making the Union more efficient, but, because there was no real agreement on how to do this, the Treaty of Amsterdam did no more than hold out the hope that this could be tackled in the future. The relevant protocol stated that, at the next enlargement, the Commission might move to a basis of one Commissioner for each member state, provided that those states that would lose their second seats in the College of Commissioners were compensated by increased weighting in Council voting. Assuming that this was done, there could be a comprehensive review ahead of enlargement to more than 20 states, a proposition that worried those candidate states that did not expect to be amongst the first five admissions.

In the event, things were to move ahead more rapidly than this and without really respecting the staged process set out in the protocol. This was due, first, to the feeling of the governments of Belgium and France that Amsterdam was totally unsatisfactory. In a declaration tacked on to the treaty, they implicitly threatened to veto enlargement unless substantial institutional changes were put in hand. They were supported by the European Parliament and outside forces, such as the European Movement. These began to call for a constitutional process to replace the existing treaties, and for a Charter of Rights.

Secondly, the situation regarding enlargement itself began to change. While talks with a first, select group, started in March 1998, the Kosovo crisis raised the question of what to do with the next group of applicants, notably those in southeastern Europe, that supported NATO. This development, and the resolution of the thorny questions of funding and the CAP in the light of Agenda 2000, opened the way to a broader approach to enlargement. This was confirmed by the Helsinki summit, which agreed to start talks with all candidates (see Chapter 7).

As the EU ceased to think in terms of distinct waves of new entrants, it became increasingly apparent that a coherent, unified solution had to be found, as quickly as possible, for the institutional questions. At Luxembourg in December 1997 the European Council recognized that improved institutional efficiency was indispensable for enlargement, while it agreed at Cardiff to take an early decision on an IGC once Amsterdam had been ratified. Partly thanks to Kosovo, this was done at Cologne in June 1999, when a new IGC was called for 2000, not just to resolve the question of the Commission and weighting of votes, but also to look at other issues related to enlargement that had been left over from Amsterdam, notably the extension of QMV.

The narrowness of the proposed agenda and timetable was much criticized by those who had been calling for a more "federationist" overhaul of the Union. The Commission itself came out in favour of a wider agenda that autumn, as did the Parliament. They regretted the fact that the process of treaty revision was not going to be made more open, community-based, and constitutional. In fact, the member states ruled out a preparatory group and took no notice of informal expert reports, such as that from the Dehaene Group set up by Romano Prodi.

As the Finnish Presidency reported to the Helsinki European Council in 1999, the member states preferred to keep matters in their own hands. This included the agenda, although they agreed that it might be extended to a fourth group of organizational issues related to enlargement, focusing on the size of the institutions. Broader issues, such as flexibility, and splitting the treaties into principles and policies, were set aside, whereas the possibility of writing into the treaties the bilateral defence arrangements then under discussion was not ruled out. No decision was taken on the sensitive question of the legal status of the Charter of Rights then being negotiated (see Chapter 20).

These stances were confirmed by the European Council itself, opening the way for the formal IGC process to begin in January 2000. The European Council agreed that the European Parliament would now be involved in detailed IGC discussions. However, it also agreed that the IGC must finish by the end of the year, at the Nice summit, and be restricted to discussing "institutional adaptation", especially key decision-making rules in the Council of Ministers, related both to QMV and to the weighting of national votes. The last was linked directly to the size and composition of the Commission, which in turn was connected to more general questions of reforming the Commission, including the power of the Presidency and the personal liability of individual Commissioners. Working out how to implement caps on the sizes of the various institutions, notably the Parliament, and how far to go in extending co-decision also had to be addressed. Resolution of these issues was seen as essential for ensuring that an EU of up to 30 states could function acceptably. In other words, the IGC was seen as a matter of an oil can and a few new parts, not as the launch of a new model.

The IGC Process

The actual negotiations in 2000 conformed to the existing pattern, although the timetable was shorter than in 1996. From the beginning it was clear that the heads of state and government, rather than ministers and officials, would take the key decisions. Unusually, two MEPs participated alongside the latter and were given a status equal to that of national delegates. A "friends of the presidency" group also helped with judicial reform. More significantly, the conference published all its position papers on the worldwide web. Nor were objections raised to the Parliament's representatives, and the Commission, briefing the public on progress. Equally, the candidate countries were brought more closely into the process than before.

For a long while, negotiations went very slowly, because the very divided states were not inclined to engage in real negotiations so far ahead of Nice. The Portuguese Presidency was largely a period of stalemate although it was agreed at Fiera that flexibility would be added to the agenda. This was encouraged by French and German proposals on the subject, and by controversial talk, sparked by President Jacques Chirac of France and by Joschka Fischer, Foreign Minister of Germany, about a "core group" of states moving ahead towards a distinct future based on a written constitution. Fiera also ruled out any move to QMV on constitutional questions, although leaving open the question of changes to Article 7, made more relevant by the opposition to the way in which Austria was treated after the Freedom Party entered the government there.

When they took over the Presidency, for the second half of 2000, the French hoped to push on more rapidly and emphatically towards an agenda that suited them. This did not materialize and the French often had to retreat, despite talk of new methods. They began to talk of aborting the process if it did not lead to a substantial deal, while the Parliament threatened to block enlargement for the same reasons. Even a ministerial conclave ahead of the informal Biarritz summit did little more than reveal underlying difficulties. The resurgence of intergovernmentalism was contrasted with the progress being made by the convention on the Charter of Fundamental Rights.

The informal Biarritz summit was expected to move things on but it proved a disappointment. It was notable for blunt talking by the Presidency, directed mainly against the smaller states. While it was said that this cleared the air and established a new willingness to get the talks back on track, the "spirit of Biarritz" proved ineffective. It neither speeded up negotiations nor reassured the smaller states. There was growing criticism of the French Presidency's abrasive style and its refusal either to give up unanimity or to narrow down the options open to the IGC. Some feared that the Presidency was risking the kind of crisis created by the Dutch at Maastricht. The fact that the Italians and Germans put in a new paper on flexibility suggested that blockage was still possible.

On 3 November the French presented a progress report: a listing of treaty articles where QMV might be introduced, including taxation, much to the anger of the British. However, the French made no formal proposals about the composition of the Commission and Council weightings. The smaller states were also offended by some proposals and renewed their attack on the Presidency's failure to play the honest broker. Even though there was some progress on matters such as the Court of Justice, the impression developed that reducing the size of the Commission would be long delayed. There was even talk of extending or reconvening Nice. The Commission's President, Romano Prodi, felt that the chances of a deal were no better than 50–50.

The French tried to answer some of the criticisms with a second progress report in late November. This was more like the final draft, although it still aroused many doubts. Indeed,

Germany then raised the stakes by asking for a representation greater than that of the other large states, to reflect its increased population as a result of unification, leaving the smaller states increasingly unhappy. Hence, the last ministerial "conclave" before Nice did not even broach many of the critical issues.

Because of this, the actual summit was a more than lively affair. This was despite prior agreement on a certain number of uncontentious issues. The sensitive issues of power remained almost as open as they had been at the start of the process. However, Nice was unusual, not merely because of the level of street protest that surrounded its opening, but for the fact that it did not formally start to function as an IGC until the Friday evening. This was given over to what proved abortive bilateral discussions between the Presidency and the other participants. It was only on the Saturday that treaty drafts appeared. However, these were felt to be too close to France's own position, and it was left to Tony Blair of the United Kingdom and Gerhard Schroeder of Germany to help things forward.

Even though a third draft, circulated on the Sunday morning, was more acceptable, divisions over weighting continued to run deep, notably amongst the smaller states. QMV by then was a secondary issue, especially when it became clear that neither the United Kingdom nor France would allow their red lines in the sand to be breached. There was talk both of walkouts and of the abandoning of the conference. In the end, President Chirac was persuaded both to keep going into the early hours of Monday morning and to make crucial concessions to the small states, as well as to Germany. In return for agreement on a new IGC, Germany dropped its demand for an increase in votes. With further adjustments to satisfy the recalcitrant Belgians, a deal was finally struck at 4.30 on the Monday morning, even though elements of the final chaotic bargaining were at variance with what had been agreed earlier in the summit.

The Outcome of the Nice Summit

It is very hard to describe and characterize what emerged from this chaos. Although the agenda had remained focused on decision-making and institutional adjustment, it still touched many other aspects of the Union. Hence, the initial draft treaty contained more than 90 separate items. Many of these were treaty amendments, mainly to the TEC, each with a handy title, and with declarations attached in some cases. In all there were 21 declarations and one "unilateral statement". Four protocols also figured, notably one "On the Enlargement of the European Union". This covered all the summit's main themes: seats in the Parliament, Council weightings, and the size of the Commission, mainly referring to the period up to enlargement, plus declarations on the size of institutions in the enlarging Union (of up to 27 members) and on the future of the Union. Like some of the language used, this proliferation of changes and declarations added to the complexity of the treaties, although the negotiators did try to copy Amsterdam and prevent the new treaty from cluttering up the treaty base. The Treaty of Nice is, then, a purely amending treaty, and its changes will be absorbed into the consolidated TEU and TEC, leaving little separate behind them.

Nonetheless, even the institutions have found it hard to sum up the contents of the treaty. The preamble refers to encouraging the reunification of Europe, making precise changes to facilitate the resulting enlargement, and arranging necessary adjustments to the working of the Union. The treaty then does all this, beginning with clear symbolic encouragement to enlargement through the rest of the preamble, the protocol, and the Declaration on the Future of the Union. All this is important.

The precise changes, however, are complex, and were not always motivated by concern for enlargement. Thus, the Treaty of Nice does provide for the lifting of unanimity in 39 instances, so as to make decision-making easier in an enlarged Union. The issues no longer requiring unanimity include appointment of Union officials, enhanced cooperation, and some ten separate policy areas. For internal reasons, these were hedged around with conditions, excluding parts of policies, delaying their introduction, and requiring much higher levels of support for getting majorities. After 2005 QMV decisions will be easier to block because, as well as requiring a minimum number of states, the support of states with virtually 75% of the available votes will be needed. Also, a decision can be challenged if the states in favour do not account for more than 62% of the Union's population. The complex new weightings, which go from a range of 2–10 to one of 3–29, with an eventual maximum of 258 (out of 345) votes for a majority and a blocking majority of only 91, may actually make reaching decisions harder (see Appendix 4 for the voting figures).

Where the size of institutions in the enlarged Union is concerned, a better solution has been found. The memberships of the Committee of the Regions and the Economic and Social Committee have been capped, although, paradoxically, the European Parliament has seen its numbers increased, both in total and while fitting new states in (see Appendix 4). The increase to 732 was necessary to allow Germany to keep its existing allocation of 99 seats. The 732 can be exceeded, however, in order to allow acceding states to send MEPs before the next elections.

Equally, the European Central Bank now has greater flexibility to alter the size of its governing council once new entrants have signed up to EMU. Similar arrangements are made for the two courts and for the Commission. The Declaration on the Future of the Union also makes some allowance for the consequences of enlargement by opening the possibility that successful candidate countries can take part in the elections for the European Parliament and the IGC both due in 2004. The IGC will be part of the "post-Nice" process of constitutional thinking about the shape of the enlarged Union.

The changes made to the Commission, enhanced cooperation, and the Parliament also seem to involve gestures both to enlargement and to other, more immediate considerations. Where the Commission is concerned, the decision was taken to reduce it to one member for each member state after 2005, but to cap its size only after the Union has 27 members. Thereafter there will be some form of equitable rationing. At the same time the President has gained extra powers to manage the structures, and to dismiss, promote or transfer other Commissioners. As for what is now called

"enhanced cooperation", rather than "closer cooperation", the effect of the Treaty of Nice is a substantial rewriting of the existing, unused, provisions. These are now easier to use, they have been extended to non-defence areas of the CFSP, and they have been made more accessible to later entrants. The Parliament gains new rights in flexibility, as well as before the European Court of Justice, and a limited extension of co-decision to five previously unanimous areas. The importance of political parties is also recognized. All this has to be set against the fact that the states have used the Parliament as a means of compensating states for losses elsewhere.

Finally, other adjustments were made in six areas, not directly linked to enlargement but responding to perceived weaknesses in existing provisions or to new events. Thus, the WEU was partly eliminated from the TEU, leaving the Political Committee to take over humanitarian operations (see Chapter 23). There were also other changes to external relations, most of which seem to have strengthened the position of the member states. These include a revised form of negotiation, led by the Presidency; a move towards allowing the Commission to negotiate in the field of services; and a new title on technical cooperation with developing countries.

The last title makes human rights an issue, in line with Nice's general stress on values. An early warning system has been introduced for states in which offences against human rights and democracy may be suspected, following the furore over the ostracism of Austria. There were also moves to ensure further protection and rights for ordinary citizens. The people are also offered a new concern for "social protection" through the creation of a new transnational committee (see Chapter 15). On the judicial front, there have been major changes to the operation of both the Court of First Instance and the European Court of Justice. The former becomes very much the first port of call, while both are given more freedom to organize their own proceedings so as to cope with the ever increasing burden of cases (see Chapter 17). At Nice the decision was also taken to write into the treaty the transnational linkages of judges and legal officers known as Eurojust and

European Judicial Network, so as to help the fight against organized crime (see Chapter 19).

Assessment

By the time that it was signed, on 26 February 2001, Nice had taken on a more conventional treaty form, as Table 4.3 shows. Although formally a separate treaty, it consists almost wholly of amendments. Articles 7–10 simply note the repeal of the old statute of the European Court of Justice and the implications that this has for the European Coal and Steel Community. The last three articles provide for unlimited validity, ratification and entry into force, and language. Assuming that it is ratified, the Treaty of Nice will, like the Treaty of Amsterdam before it, be absorbed, probably unnoticed, into the treaty base. However, this does not help to make sense of the treaty, or the reactions to it.

Clearly, the Nice process did not involve major new projects, such as the single market, monetary union, or political union. Unusually, it was an attempt to adjust to something that is almost certainly bound to happen in the future: enlargement of the Union to the east. This it achieved, giving enlargement just enough encouragement and agreeing the changes in decision-making procedures needed, always assuming that they work as hoped. It also brought about major changes in the judicial system and elsewhere, which were not directly linked to enlargement. At the same time, although Nice managed to avoid a breakdown in doing this, it has also led to a political rebalancing. The Commission and the Parliament have gained less than the increasingly divided member states. This too is significant.

Nice, in other words, continues the revival of the influence of member states that began, uncertainly, in 1991. This can be seen in the way in which the Union is given importance above that of the Community, which is symbolized both by the change in the name of the *Official Journal* – now of the EU rather than the EC – and the talk of "Union" institutions, policies, and principles. The way in which the enhanced cooperation provisions, and guidance to the European Court of Justice, have now

become parts of the TEU reinforces the point. At the same time, the member states have gained in other ways: through the enhanced role of the European Council, through the delays in implementing changes in QMV, and through the way in which the concessions on voting were extracted.

However, the member states emerged from Nice increasingly diversified, not to say antagonistic. Not only were they split between smaller and larger states, but they differed over values, over their alliances, and over the future of the Union. There was a particular irony in the quarrel between Belgium and France, given that it had been their joint initiative that had ensured that the Amsterdam compromise was re-examined. Moreover, the new flexibility provisions open the way to further fragmentation.

On the other hand, it is probably too much to say, as some have done, that Nice marks the end of the "federal dream" and the imposition of an absolute ceiling on "deepening". For one thing, it is clearly not seen in this light by many Eurosceptics. They see it as leading not just to further transfers of power to Brussels in the here and now, but also to future exploitation of references to the "precautionary principle". Nevertheless, treaties have not in the past been successful in determining how they are interpreted and, with the Parliament in particular seeking to exploit all its possibilities and joining the many voices who wish to see more integration, there will clearly be a continuing struggle. Indeed, the European Parliament has already effectively made progress in the post-Nice phase a prerequisite for approving the Treaty of Nice itself. It is determined to try and remedy the lack of democratization and efficiency that, in the view of most of its members, still marks the outcome of the Nice summit.

Both views seem a little exaggerated. There has been development as well as stagnation. The deal seems politically acceptable, since many member states, in particular Germany, Spain, and the United Kingdom, are all relatively satisfied. As with previous outcomes of IGCs, the complexity of the deal means that quite varying interpretations can all have a certain justification. Like the EU itself, the Treaty of Nice is a messy mixture of intergovernmentalism and supranationalism.

Further Treaty Revision or a New Model of Reform?

Although the negotiators refused to consider it at Nice, the treaty does also provide for further consideration of the shape of the Union. The Declaration on the Future of the Union calls on the Swedish and Belgian Presidencies (2001) to encourage wideranging discussions, drawing in public opinion in the existing member states as well as the candidate countries. A preliminary report will be made to the Gothenburg Council and a final decision will be made at Laeken/Brussels on initiatives to carry forward the process towards the IGC in 2004.

Whether this has been thought through is not at all clear, and whether it will lead to a more effective form of treaty reform is not guaranteed. The details of the process are extremely vague, and there are doubts both about the various modes of treaty amendment and the willingness of the IGC to act on what comes out of the debate, especially if it goes beyond the items specified. These are: the division of responsibilities between member states and EU institutions within the framework of subsidiarity; the status of the Charter of Fundamental Rights; the simplification of the treaties, to make them more comprehensible without changing their content; and the role of national parliaments in the Union's new architecture. None of these is to be a barrier to enlargement, although only those countries that have agreed entry terms by 2004 will be allowed to play a full part in the IGC that year: the others will simply be observers. It could be that the post-Nice process will prove to be no more than a slightly more public form of "reflection group". In any case, the issues themselves are fraught with difficulty.

Thus, while this process, which has its roots in the thinking aloud started by Fischer and Chirac, may at first sight seem to promise a real clarification of the modes of treaty revision, and of the Union's nature in the medium and long term, it is far from sure that such clarification will result. This is not merely because of the technical limitations of the post-Nice process, but also because it rests on two contradictory responses. It reflects both the desire of those who want to go further, and the wish of the German *Länder* and some British opinion to prevent further loss of autonomy by enshrining a (restrictive) list of EU powers. This suggests that getting agreement, whether on method or outcome, will not be easy. The two are, of course, closely related in the minds of both federalists and Eurosceptics, and further fierce argument is likely.

What is clear, nonetheless, is that Nice will not be the end of the evolution of the Union. To begin with, there is a chance that the deal may unravel at some stage, always providing that it is ratified in the first place. Moreover, change in the EU will not be restricted to constitutional processes. Flexibility, external events, and internal dynamics will all no doubt help to ensure that things do not stay as they are. Challenges from popular alienation (and from organized Euroscepticism – see Chapter 6), as well as from enlargement, are likely to play a major part. While the Declaration on the Future of the Union refers optimistically to changing the treaties and the Union in ways that strengthen its popular legitimacy, proximity, and transparency, we do not know whether this will be yet another abortive attempt to bring the EU closer to its citizens, just as legitimation by social policy and treaty readability failed after Amsterdam. The future is far from settled or certain, and the likely future shape of the Union, always assuming that it ever reaches a plane of stability, is still to be decided by those whom Westlake (cited below) has called its blind watchmakers.

Further Reading

Christiansen, Thomas, and Knud Erik Jørgensen, "The Amsterdam Process: A Structurationist Perspective on EU Treaty Reform", in *European Integration Online Papers*, 15 January 1999, available on http://eiop.or.at/eiop

This paper advances the argument that, essentially, IGCs mostly ratify what is already happening inside the Community.

Church, Clive, and David Phinnemore, *European Union and European Community: A Handbook and Commentary on the Post-Maastricht Treaties*, London and New York: Harvester Wheatsheaf, 1994

This provides one of the few commentaries on the treaties as a whole, setting them in a wider context.

Devuyst, Youri, "Treaty Reform in the EU: The Amsterdam Process", in *Journal of European Public Policy*, 5/4, 1998, pp. 615–31

A subtle analysis of the Amsterdam IGC, covering both national and international politics

Dinan, Desmond, "Treaty Change in the EU: The Amsterdam Experience", in Laura Cram *et al.* (editors), *Developments in the European Union*, London: Macmillan, and New York: St Martin's Press, 1999

A useful narrative of the process that suggests that the Treaty of Amsterdam would represent the last major treaty revision

Edwards, Geoffrey, and Alfred Pijpers (editors), *The Politics of European Treaty Reform: The 1996 Intergovernmental Conference and Beyond*, London and Washington, DC: Pinter, 1997

Offers a series of analyses of various forces and issues involved in the early stages of the IGC in 1996, but ends well before the Amsterdam summit itself

Galloway, David, *The Treaty of Nice and Beyond: Realities and Illusions of Power in the EU*, Sheffield: Sheffield Academic Press/UACES, 2001

A very comprehensive analysis of the outcomes of the Nice negotiations and their implications for the future

Gray, Mark, "Negotiating EU Treaties", in Edward Best, *et al.* (editors), *Rethinking the EU*, Maastricht: European Institute of Public Administration, 2000

Provides the best listing of the IGCs, together with some sensible suggestions for reforming the process

Moravcsik, Andrew and Kalypso Nicolaïdis, "Explaining the Treaty of Amsterdam: Interests, Influence, Institutions", in *Journal of Common Market Studies*, 37/1, 1999, pp. 59–85

Argues the case for IGCs, and the EU, being driven by the preferences of the member states

Morhold, H., "Change of Method in European Integration", in *The Federalist*, 1998, pp. 177–84

A plea for a more constitutional approach to treaty revision

Sverdrup, Ulf, "Precedent and Present Events", in Karlheinz Neunreither and Antje Wiener (editors), *European Integration After Amsterdam: Institutional Dynamics and Prospects for Democracy*, Oxford and New York: Oxford University Press, 2000

A theoretical examination of the internal dynamics of the 1996 process

Westlake, Martin, "The EU's Blind Watchmakers", in Martin Westlake (editor), *The European Union Beyond Amsterdam: New Concepts of European Integration*, London and New York: Routledge, 1998

Suggests that although treaty amendments look chaotic there is an underlying dynamic, so that they usually succeed

The Treaties of Amsterdam and Nice can be found at:

http://europa.eu.int/abc/treaties_en.htm

These are the official texts without commentary.

Clive H. Church is Jean Monnet Professor of European Studies at the University of Kent at Canterbury and Director of the Kent Centre for Europe. He has written widely on the treaties and the Maastricht, Amsterdam, and Nice IGCs, and is presently working with David Phinnemore on a focused revision of their commentary, to appear as *The Penguin Guide to the European Treaties* in 2002.

Table 4.1   The Headings for the Initial Version of the Treaty of Amsterdam, June 1996

1. An Area of Freedom, Security and Justice
2. The Union and the Citizen
3. An Effective and Coherent External Policy
4. The Union's Institutions
5. Closer Cooperation/Flexibility
6. Simplification and Consolidation of the Treaties

Source: Council: *Intergovernmental Conference. Amsterdam European Council. Draft Treaty.* EC, 1997

Table 4.2   Table of Contents of the Final Version of the Treaty of Amsterdam, October 1996

Preamble
Part One: Substantive Amendments
Article 1 –   Amendments to the Maastricht Treaty on European Union
Article 2 –   Amendments to the Rome Treaty establishing the European Community
Article 3 –   Amendments to the European Coal and Steel Community Treaty
Article 4 –   Amendments to the Euratom Treaty
Article 5 –   Amendments to the 1976 Act on European Parliament Elections

Part Two: Simplification
Article 6 –   Changes to the Rome Treaty establishing the European Community
Article 7 –   Changes to the European Coal and Steel Community Treaty
Article 8 –   Changes to the Euratom Treaty
Article 9 –   Changes in Other Acts
Article 10 – Continuing Legal Force and Unchanged Effects of Old Treaties
Article 11 – Responsibilities of the European Court of Justice

Part Three: General and Final Provisions
Article 12 – Renumbering of the Treaties on European Union and the European Community
Article 13 – The Treaty concluded for an unlimited period
Article 14 – Ratification and Entry into Effect
Article 15 – Authenticity of texts
Annex –   Tables of Equivalences between the old and new versions of the Treaties on European Union and the European Community
Protocols
Final Act
Declarations

Source: Council: Treaty of Amsterdam amending the Treaty on European Union and the Treaty establishing the European Communities and certain related acts: *Official Journal,* C340, 10.11.97

Table 4.3   Table of Contents of the Treaty of Nice Amending the Treaty On European Union, The Treaties Establishing The European Communities, and Certain Related Acts, 26 February 2001

Preamble

Part One: Substantive Amendments
> Article 1:   Changes to the Treaty on European Union (1-15)
> Article 2:   Changes to the Treaty establishing the European Community (1-47)
> Article 3:   Changes to the Euratom Treaty (1-25)
> Article 4:   Changes to the European Coal and Steel Community Treaty (1-19)
> Article 5:   Protocol on the Statute of the European System of Central Banks/European Central Bank
> Article 6:   Protocol on the Privileges and Immunities of the European Communities

Part Two: Transitional and Final Provisions
Articles 7–13

Protocols
> On the Enlargement of the European Union
> On the Statute of the Court of Justice
> On the Financial Consequences of the Expiry of the European Coal and Steel Community Treaty and the Research Fund for Coal and Steel
> On Article 67 of the Treaty establishing the European Community

Final Act

Declarations Adopted by the Conference

Declarations of Which the Conference Took Note

Source: Council: Treaty of Nice amending the Treaty on European Union and the Treaty establishing the European Communities and certain related acts: *Official Journal*, C80, 10.03.2001

Chapter Five

Legitimacy and Democracy in the EU

Julie Smith

At the start of the 21st century, several leading European politicians began to discuss the future direction of the EU, noting in particular a need to ensure its democratic legitimacy in the light of future enlargement. It is indicative of the EU's unique position in international affairs, as more than an intergovernmental organization, but less than a sovereign state, that so much time is devoted to the issues of whether it is sufficiently democratic and whether it is legitimate. No one discusses the democratic underpinnings of the UN or NATO and, if they are concerned about the legitimacy of such bodies, it is the legitimacy of their actions, such as NATO's bombardment of Serbia in 1999, that is at issue, not the legitimacy of these organizations *per se*. In recent years, however, the democratic credentials of the EU have repeatedly been brought into question, as academics, politicians, and a host of others have begun to express concern that there is a "democratic deficit" in European decision-making and that the EU lacks legitimacy.

In the early years of integration, there was little question about the legitimacy of the European enterprise. Citizens in the founding member states were perceived to be at least as supportive of European cooperation as the elites. Thus, political leaders felt able to move ahead, secure in the knowledge that their voters were in tune with the ideals of peace, prosperity, and security that integration was assumed to offer. Although there was little clear evidence of widespread enthusiasm for integration in the late 1950s and early 1960s, there was assumed to be, in the words of Leon Lindberg and Stuart Scheingold, a "permissive consensus" (Lindberg and Scheingold p. 41). Thus, the European Community (EC), as it was then known, enjoyed a certain social legitimacy, in part engendered by the fact that it seemed to serve the interests of the people.

Moreover, the institutional framework of European integration did – and still does – enjoy "legal–rational" legitimacy (in the sense developed by Max Weber). Each member state signed the founding treaties or, in the case of latecomers, treaties of accession, in accordance with their standard legislative practices. The founding countries accepted the treaties by normal parliamentary methods, as did the United Kingdom when it joined in 1973. Other states, including Denmark, Ireland, Spain, Austria, and Finland, asked their citizens directly whether they should enter the EC in referenda preceding accession. Thus, membership of the EC/EU has legal legitimacy in all member states.

Similarly, any reform of the founding treaties has to be accepted by each member state according to its own national procedures. For many, this is by way of approval by their parliament. However, some members, notably Denmark and Ireland, have held referenda each time the treaties have been revised. Thus, there has been scope for citizens to reject the institutional arrangements that their leaders have signed up to, again offering an even greater opportunity to ensure that the nature of the EU has the support of the people, as well as legal legitimacy. In June 1992, the Danish "No" to the Maastricht Treaty highlighted the fact that popular support could not simply be assumed: citizens need to be persuaded of the benefits of European integration.

Although a second Danish referendum in May 1993 saw a "Yes" vote that ensured that Maastricht came into effect, any assumption of a permissive consensus had to be reconsidered. The French had also accepted the treaty by only the narrowest of margins, in a referendum held in September 1992. Admittedly, domestic factors had contributed to the narrow vote in France; nevertheless, European elites began to realize that they could no longer merely assume that voters were in favour of further integration. Moreover, even if the framework for European decision-making has been agreed by domestically legitimated methods, it is less certain that this is the case for secondary legislation, on which member states can be outvoted and where the role of parliaments, national and European, is often limited. Gradually, the legitimacy of the integration process and the democratic credentials of its decision-making processes have come into question. What challenges are there to the legitimacy of the EU and what can be done about it? Is a failure of democracy at fault?

The Electoral Dimension

As early as the late 1940s there were attempts to ensure that European cooperation was based on democratic foundations. Many of those present at the Congress of Europe, held in The Hague in May 1948, which led to the creation of the Council of Europe, were active federalists, who favoured an elected parliament. Yet there was some concern even among the federalists that it was, perhaps, too soon to consider such a body. In the event, British and Scandinavian opposition ensured that the Council of Europe Assembly that was set up was but a pale shadow of the parliament the federalists sought. Nevertheless, the idea of an elected assembly was not abandoned, re-emerging in the 1950s, first with the negotiations that led to the European Coal and Steel Community (ECSC), and later with the Spaak Committee, which led to the Treaties of Rome, and the creation of the European Economic Community (EEC) and the European Atomic Energy Community (Euratom).

The founders of the EC themselves fell into at least three camps: the federalists, who believed that the emerging European Community should resemble a federal state and thus should have the trappings of democracy, notably periodic, free elections, ideally to a legislative assembly; the intergovernmentalists or Gaullists, who could see no legitimacy for such assemblies beyond the nation state; and the pragmatists or rational technocrats, such as Jean Monnet, who favoured a strong role for rational technocrats like themselves. This last group was less concerned about the need for democracy at the European level than about the promotion of efficiency. However, they were gradually convinced of the need to introduce a parliamentary body in the face of the supranational High Authority, which enjoyed certain sovereign powers ceded to it by the member states. Thus, the Treaty of Paris established a "Common Assembly" for the ECSC, which had the right to "supervise" or, more precisely, scrutinize, the work of the High Authority. The Assembly could throw out the High Authority by a two-thirds majority of the votes cast, representing an absolute majority of its members. Apart from that significant power, the Assembly's role was very limited. The members of the Assembly were nominated members of national parliaments, who clearly represented national rather than European interests. Despite this, right from the start there was a move towards transnational cooperation, as members sat with colleagues from sister parties in the Communities, not with other members from their own countries.

The Treaties of Rome went a stage further, providing for a European Parliamentary Assembly, an enlarged version of the Common Assembly, which was to be directly elected. However, because the negotiators could not agree on the form that the elections should take, it was decided to leave the arrangements for direct elections to the incoming members of the Assembly.

Although the Assembly began to be called the "European Parliament" as early as 1962, the name was not formally changed until the Single European Act, ratified in 1987. Nevertheless, the new body rapidly began to draw up proposals for direct elections, exercising one of its few powers under the founding treaties, and its only right of legislative initiative. A working group was set up under the chairmanship of Fernand Dehousse to consider the introduction of elections by "direct, universal suffrage in accordance with a uniform procedure", as specified in the Treaty of Rome, Article 138 (3). However, members of the Assembly were no better able than national negotiators had been to come up with a common electoral system. While members all agreed that direct elections under a common system represented a good idea in principle, they all tended to feel that their own national systems were preferable. The proposals put forward in 1960 in the final report of the working group therefore argued that "uniformity was not synonymous with identity", suggesting that each member state should be allowed to draft its own rules for European elections, provided that they ensured "universal, free, equal and secret elections" (Dehousse Report, para. 18). This liberal view of uniformity was adopted when elections were finally introduced in 1979.

That it took more than 20 years to introduce direct elections was in part a reflection of reluctance on the part of member states. National parliaments were unwilling to see their powers undermined as the Assembly gained legitimacy via elections and, perhaps, therefore more powers. Nor, by and large, were national governments clearly supportive of an elected body: an assembly of delegates could scarcely be a threat to their decision-making functions within the European Communities, but directly elected politicians wielding their own European mandates might be. Since elections could only be introduced if the Council of Ministers agreed to the Assembly's proposals, the Dehousse Report was left to gather dust. Only when members of the Assembly threatened to take the Council to the European Court of Justice, in 1969, did member states remember their Treaty obligations. Even then, despite a statement by the heads of state and government in a communiqué issued at their Hague summit in December 1969 that "the problem of direct elections will continue to be studied by the Council of Ministers", progress remained slow.

In some ways, the delay in introducing direct elections was understandable. For many it seemed unrealistic and undesirable to hold elections for a virtually powerless body: who would vote for such an institution? One logical response to this concern was to grant the institution more powers. Yet this fell foul of another anxiety: could one give powers to an unelected body? There therefore seemed to be a circular problem, to which the introduction of direct elections alone could certainly not be the answer. However, the final issue could be circumvented by the argument that members had indeed been elected, even if they did have national, not European mandates. Gradually, therefore, the Assembly saw an accretion in its powers, starting in 1970 with powers in the budgetary sphere.

Nevertheless, despite the Assembly's role in the budgetary sphere, by the time the heads of state and government finally decided, in 1974, to introduce direct elections, it remained a weak institution. Over the years since then, the Assembly/Parliament has accrued a considerable amount of power and influence, in part as a result of an expansion of policy-making at the Community or Union level, in part as an indirect result of becoming directly elected. From 1979, members of the Assembly – or MEPs, as they quickly became known – were able to claim a direct mandate and, hence, a degree of legitimacy that they had not previously enjoyed. Thus, as the member states agreed to further integration under the Single European Act and later the Treaty on European Union (TEU) which entailed a loss of parliamentary accountability at the national level, the Assembly, now the European Parliament (EP), was seen as the logical repository for such powers. Gradually the EP began to wield significant power and influence.

Despite the EP's growing role, the anxieties of those worried that voters would not bother to participate in elections to a powerless institution seem to have been borne out in the years since 1979, as voters and politicians appeared reluctant to participate actively in the elections. The aim of direct elections to the European Parliament was to introduce an element of democracy into the integration process, and to confer legitimacy on the EP in particular and on the EU as a whole. European integration began as a profoundly elitist process, in which the support of the citizens was simply assumed. By the mid-1970s, however, it had become clear to some, such as the Belgian Prime Minister, Leo Tindemans, that popular support for the integration process was waning. Direct elections could be a way of rekindling citizens' interest in the Community. Such elections have certainly allowed public participation in the selection of members of the EP. However, since individual MEPs play such a small role in EU decision-making, the level of representation is very dilute compared with elections in nation states and can scarcely be considered as permitting "self-government". Perhaps for this reason, direct elections seem, if anything, to highlight the failure to engage the people in the integration process and to cast a shadow over the legitimacy of the integration process – quite the reverse of what was expected.

The five sets of elections that have been held since 1979 have been characterized by national election campaigns, with national politicians and national issues taking centre stage, and average turnout has been low and declining. Although transnational parties have been established by the main party families – the Social Democrats, the Christian Democrats, and the Liberals and their allies – progress towards the creation of stable, coherent parties has been very limited, with national parties continuing to play the key role in voter identification. On the face of it, this seems to suggest a sad indictment of democracy at the European level: Europe has the trappings of democracy, but democratic practice, at least as measured by elections, seems to be fragile. Several issues need to be taken into consideration, however. Compared with national parties in western Europe, the weak, fragmented parties in the European Parliament, and the focus on national politicians and national issues during EP election campaigns, might seem to indicate a failure in the system. Yet compared with parties in the United States, for example, the parties in the EP are not so unusual. Similarly, while turnout might be low in comparison with the average in national elections in western Europe, it is not low when compared with elections in the United States or Switzerland. One might therefore argue that low turnout is not a symptom of a lack of legitimacy, but rather a sign of contentment with the system. However, as has been noted, in the case of the European Parliament it is not appropriate to take such a relaxed attitude (Corbett, Jacobs and Shackleton p. 53).

Data from public opinion surveys suggest that the citizens of the EU are not interested in EU politics or institutions, and that their support for the integration process is declining. The dramatic decline in turnout between the elections for the EP in 1994 and those in 1999 seems to reflect a general sense of frustration with the EU, and a belief that the institutions are self-serving and may even be corrupt. The resignations of Jacques Santer and the rest of the Commission in March 1999, amid allegations of cronyism and mismanagement, meant that many voters saw the whole Union as being tarred with the same brush, even though MEPs had played a vital role in ensuring the departure of the Commission.

Moreover, despite its enhanced role in decision-making, voters do not perceive the European Parliament to be a particularly important institution and generally assume that it has fewer powers than it actually has. Indeed, ignorance about the workings of the EU is one of the major problems for democracy within it. The complexity of the decision-making system, its lack of transparency, and the absence of any EU-wide media dedicated to covering EU affairs have resulted in a situation in which citizens formally have the right to participate in the decision-making process, yet feel themselves to be under-represented or not represented at all. They enjoy the trappings of democracy, but are not convinced about what lies underneath. What, then, does lie underneath?

Decision-making Processes

The nature of EU decision-making differs markedly from that in any nation state or international organization, and this has created many difficulties for theorists and practitioners alike. If the EU resembled a nation state we might expect it to conform to standard practices of representative democracy; if it was a traditional international organization, its decisions would be on the basis of unanimity, with each state having an equal voice in decisions.

In practice, the EU is something of a hybrid, with decisions relying on national and supranational institutions. Nor does it look likely to begin to become any easier to categorize in the near future.

In the early years, the process was relatively straightforward: the Commission proposed legislation, the Assembly/Parliament was consulted, and the Council of Ministers decided. Thus, the crucial legislative body was not the European Parliament, whose opinions mattered little, but the Council of Ministers, comprising representatives of national governments. Since decisions were taken on the basis of unanimity, no member state could be outvoted, hence each national parliament could hold its ministers responsible for the outcome of decisions taken by the Council. Decisions were made behind closed doors, but if the result went against a country's perceived national interest it was clear that the minister had accepted those decisions and s/he could be held to account. Hence decision-making could be seen to be legitimate and democratic.

All this was to change with the introduction of qualified majority voting (QMV). Although the Treaty of Rome had provided for QMV after a transitional period, this was rendered a dead-letter by the Luxembourg Compromise of 1966 and unanimity remained the norm in Council decision-making. This had begun to change slightly by the mid-1980s, but it was the Single European Act of 1986 that fundamentally altered the nature of decision-making in the EU. In order to facilitate the passage of legislation relating to the introduction of the "1992" internal market programme, member states agreed to use QMV. However, this made it difficult for national parliaments to keep their ministers accountable: any minister could claim that s/he had tried to act according to the national interest or the will of their parliament, but had been outvoted, and there was nothing a national parliament could do to gainsay this. To overcome this reduction in accountability at the national level, it was decided that the newly renamed European Parliament should be granted further powers, under the "cooperation procedure".

The cooperation procedure gave MEPs the power to amend Community legislation, initially only in the area of the internal market. The Treaty on European Union (TEU) extended this power into several other policy areas where Council decisions are made by QMV and also introduced a veto power through the "negative assent" or "co-decision" procedure. Subsequent reforms, embodied in the Treaty of Amsterdam of 1997, saw a further expansion of QMV and of the co-decision procedure, with the cooperation procedure remaining in place for only a limited number of policy areas. Thus, over the years the EP has gone from being a virtually powerless institution to one with the power to co-legislate with the Council in budgetary matters and in many policy areas, primarily as a result of the need to ensure parliamentary scrutiny of EU legislation.

As more powers have been passed from member states to the EU, members of national parliaments have become increasingly concerned at the accretion of executive power. Issues that they would previously have tackled are increasingly being shifted to the EU level, where it is members of the Council, representing national governments, not MEPs, who have decided on Community legislation. Increasing the powers of the EP was designed to overcome this problem. Ironically, the increase in its powers has not been met by increased popular support. The attempts by the Council to ensure greater democratic accountability have in practice been met with growing public resentment about the integration process. Indeed, it was just at the time that the member states were beginning to augment the powers of the EP via the Single European Act that serious concerns were voiced about the "democratic deficit". Although MEPs had considered this problem in the past, it was only the extension of QMV that brought it to the fore in popular discussions.

Ironically, although the cooperation procedure was introduced to overcome concerns about the democratic deficit, it was at this time that the deficit was suddenly perceived to be of major importance. Similarly, Danish voters initially rejected the TEU, which had been designed in part to enhance the EU's democratic profile, partly because they objected to the creation of EU citizenship, which they feared would undermine Danish citizenship. Thus, one of the innovations introduced at Maastricht to try to make Europe more meaningful for its citizens backfired. How then might the EU's problems of legitimacy and democracy be effectively overcome?

MEPs' preferred solution to the apparent democratic deficit has generally been to claim more powers for the institution they belong to. Is granting the EP ever more powers the way to overcome the deficit? One immediate answer from a sceptical perspective would be that the EP has quite enough powers already, and would be better engaged in demonstrating that it can use them responsibly and effectively. This is a somewhat harsh response, however. MEPs certainly have accrued a considerable range of powers, including the right to veto legislation, the power to accept or reject the Community budget, and the possibility of throwing out the entire European Commission. Yet they have become far more responsible since they have acquired more powers. That the media have not covered their activities to any large extent is not the MEPs' fault (nor is it for their lack of trying).

A second response might be to suggest that the EP and national parliaments should work together in a spirit of greater cooperation (Smith 1994 p. 3). In the past they have tended to view each other as rivals, whereas they could have complementary roles, with national parliamentarians holding national politicians to account, and MEPs scrutinizing legislation from the EU perspective. This could certainly help overcome some aspects of the "democratic deficit": parliamentarians would still not be initiating legislation, but via the EP's right of co-decision and joint scrutinizing powers they could wield considerable influence over the whole process.

The Legitimacy of the EU

Ensuring greater activity by the EP and/or the national parliaments cannot by itself overcome the EU's problems of democracy or legitimacy. As the British Prime Minister Tony Blair pointed out in a speech delivered in Warsaw in November 2000:

The problem Europe's citizens have with Europe arises when Europe's priorities aren't theirs. No amount of institutional change – most of which passes them by completely – will change that . . . Reforming Europe to give it direction and momentum around the people's priorities will. The citizens of Europe must feel that they own Europe, not that Europe owns them.

If reform resulted in even more complex decision-making it could have the negative impact of further alienating people who already feel unable to comprehend the system.

The widespread sense of detachment from the system is one of the biggest challenges facing the EU. The fact that voters are so far removed from the EU's decision-making processes means that they frequently feel they are unable to influence the process at all, and this can lead to resentment and a lack of social legitimacy. Over the years, however, voters in many states have begun to question the benefits of EU membership and, with it, support for the EU itself. Legally, as we have seen, EU membership remains legitimate, but the EU has not won over the hearts and minds of its citizens. The absence of social legitimacy in turn makes it harder to win voters over to the integration process.

In the early years of integration the problem of legitimacy was far less profound. The assumption of a "permissive consensus" was one that seemed to be borne out in popular attitudes towards integration. The fact that integration did contribute to peace and stability in western Europe, coupled with rising economic prosperity, meant that the Community was generally viewed in a favourable light. Indeed, there was almost a western form of the "legitimation by consumption" that has been attributed to János Kádár's reform-Communist regime in Hungary: as the EU ensured prosperity, peace, and security, the fact that it was not particularly democratic did not seem to matter. Moreover, voters in the 1950s and 1960s were, arguably, considerably more deferential than those in the 1990s and the 21st century: if their leaders claimed that something was in their national interest, they were more likely to believe it. In recent years, however, voters have become more sceptical about integration. After all, peace seems to be guaranteed and the economic benefits of integration do not perhaps seem so obvious. In addition, the process of integration has become more clearly political than in the past.

For many of the founders, the aims of European integration were always inherently political, although the methods were economic. In the six founding member states, the distinction mattered relatively little, for citizens desired the economic and political benefits of integration. Indeed, most Italians and most Germans have traditionally been more favourable than the average citizens of other member states to the idea of a "federal" Europe. Newer member states, by contrast, have tended to be far less wedded to the ideal of a political Europe. Voters in Denmark and the United Kingdom were "sold" EC membership largely on the basis of the economic benefits it would bring. Relatively few politicians, certainly among those supporting membership, were willing to discuss the political aspects.

Over the years, however, the political dimension has become more pronounced, leading to a sense of frustration and disillusionment on the part of many British and Danish citizens, who feel that they were misled. This was only partially true: the future path of integration could not have been predicted with certainty in the early 1970s, and the fall of the Berlin Wall and the subsequent unification of Germany played a large and unforeseeable part in the subsequent development of the EU. Nevertheless, some of the runes could have been read and a sense of betrayal, justified or not, does exist. The three former members of EFTA that joined the EU in 1995 – Austria, Finland, and Sweden – had held out against membership in part precisely because they did not want to join a political enterprise. Gradually, however, membership came to seem inevitable for economic reasons. Yet in Austria and Sweden, in particular, commitment to the *finalité politique* remains muted. Thus, by the year 2000 it had become clear that, even if the member states were formally committed to the same goal of "ever closer union", they had different views about what its end-state should look like.

Moreover, as the EU prepared itself for further enlargement, new questions emerged concerning democratic legitimacy in an enlarged EU. In the early 1990s, the newly emerging democracies in central and eastern Europe saw membership of the EU and NATO as a way to ensure their "European" credentials. Geography was not enough: the security guarantees provided by NATO, and the political and economic credibility provided by the EU, were seen as vital to their return to the comity of western nations. A first wave of NATO expansion to embrace Poland, Hungary, and the Czech Republic has taken place, but the EU has been rather slower to enlarge. This is in large part due to the complexity of the EU, which makes the conditions of membership far harder for candidates from former Communist states to meet. Nevertheless, the apparent unwillingness of the existing member states to press ahead with enlargement is contributing to a decline in popular support in many of the candidate countries, with potentially harmful consequences for legitimacy and democracy in an enlarged EU.

In particular, there is a tension between enlarging before introducing serious institutional reform, on the one hand, and reforming before enlarging, on the other. Arguably it is in the interests of all member states, new and old alike, to be in an effective EU, and this in part entails efficient and democratic decision-making. The intergovernmental conference that culminated with the Treaty of Amsterdam in 1997 fudged the institutional issues necessary for enlargement, and another such conference had to be convened in 2000. However, the Nice conference covered only the more technical, albeit highly sensitive, aspects of reform: reducing the number of commissioners, reweighting votes in the Council, extending the scope of QMV, and introducing an element of flexibility or "enhanced cooperation" into the EU. It did not tackle the broader questions associated with making the EU more legitimate or more democratic. These issues must be left until yet another such conference, which is scheduled to be convened in 2004. Such a conference will have the advantage that new member states that have completed accession negotiations by then will be able to participate in the decisions affecting their future. This would at least enhance the legitimacy of any such changes in the eyes of their citizens and help to reduce the potentially negative impact of an enlargement that brings in a set of countries that are disaffected even before they have crossed the threshold of the European house.

Enhancing Legitimacy and Democracy in the EU

As already argued, the EU is legally legitimate, yet it lacks social legitimacy. In large part this seems to result from the absence of a clearcut "European" identity and also from the fact that citizens seem able to exert very little influence over the process of integration. Yet it is not at all clear that voters can expect to be able to affect decisions at the EU level in the way they can affect matters in their home country. For some observers, such as Robert Dahl, the matter is quite simple: people can have a large amount of influence on fairly trivial issues close to home, or a very small amount of influence on major issues of international importance. The former situation is closer to Athenian city-state democracy, which did offer citizens the chance of self-government. The nearest modern analogies are citizens' initiatives in Switzerland and local government in some countries. The second option reflects the possible nature of "democracy" in an interdependent world: it does not allow "self-government", in the sense of pure democracy or even representative democracy as we have come to know it in modern nation states, but it does represent the best options that citizens can have of affecting transnational decisions. Indeed, the problem facing elites and citizens in the EU is twofold: the very size of the EU renders traditional forms of democracy unworkable, but this is in part due to the challenges of globalization, it is not merely the result of European integration. Thus, ways of introducing new sorts of democracy must be found that allow for some participation by citizens and that they themselves believe to be legitimate.

In order to enhance its legitimacy in the eyes of its citizens, the EU needs to appear both effective and accountable. The former may

have little to do with democracy; the latter, by contrast, is intimately linked with it. Efficient decision-making may well be achieved behind closed doors, but it is difficult to "sell" the results to voters: if the EU seems to be unaccountable they will inevitably become alienated. However, problems arise because the different member states do not all have the same views of the type of governance appropriate to the EU.

For some, the obvious way ahead is to grant more powers to the central institutions. This approach, long favoured by the most integrationist states, the Commission, and the European Parliament, has gradually become less popular, as member states have begun to favour the principle of subsidiarity, whereby powers are devolved to lower levels, whether nation-states, regions or municipalities. The idea of a directly elected Commission or Commission President, floated by the German Foreign Minister, Joschka Fischer, speaking in a personal capacity at the Humboldt University, Berlin, in 2000, has found few supporters. Rather, member states now seem to prefer mechanisms that would enhance the role of national parliaments in the integration process.

In marked contrast to this federalist approach to integration, Tony Blair has asserted (in the speech already quoted above) that

we can spend hours on end trying to devise a perfect form of European democracy, and get nowhere. The truth is [that] the primary sources of democratic accountability in Europe are the directly elected and representative institutions of the nations of Europe – national parliaments and governments.

Thus, Blair advocates the creation of a second chamber for the European Parliament, comprising members of national parliaments. This would certainly ensure that national politicians were brought into the integration process, thus gaining a better understanding of the EU, the ability to represent their constituents at the EU level, and the opportunity to scrutinize EU legislation more effectively than national parliamentarians are currently able to do. However, such an arrangement would also create considerable problems. The dual mandate would put considerable pressure on members, who would be expected to be present in both their national parliaments and the European Parliament, making high levels of absenteeism inevitable. Moreover, as the British journalist Hugo Young has pointed out, this idea is "not very *communautaire*". It is therefore unlikely that such a proposal would win support from many of Blair's EU partners.

In practice, what is needed is a way of making citizens believe that they are "European" and that the EU matters for them. The former could, perhaps, be achieved by education, just as national identities were frequently fostered by national educational systems promoting official languages and (somewhat more ominously) official histories (see, for example Eugen Weber's *Peasants into Frenchmen*). The latter might be brought about by effective EU-wide media coverage, following elections in all member states and covering activities in the European Parliament. Proactive leadership by national politicians could also play a part. Inevitably, however, competing interests mean that it is unlikely that any of this will happen in the near future. Thus, the only way to ensure the more positive attitudes towards integration vital to the legitimacy of the EU is for the EU to provide economic, political or security benefits to citizens, who will then perceive a real interest in supporting integration.

Further Reading

Blair, Tony, Speech to the Polish Stock Exchange, Warsaw, 6 October 2000, available at www.fco.gov.uk/news/speechtext.asp?4913

Chirac, Jacques, Speech to the Bundestag, Berlin, 27 June 2000, published as "Our Europe", Federal Trust Essay No. 9, London: The Federal Trust, 2000

Corbett, Richard, Francis Jacobs, and Michael Shackleton, *The European Parliament*, fourth edition, London: John Harper, 2000

Dahl, Robert A., "A Democratic Dilemma: System Effectiveness versus Citizen Participation", in *Political Science Quarterly*, 109/1, 1994, pp. 23–34

Featherstone, Kevin, "Jean Monnet and the 'Democratic Deficit' in the European Union", in *Journal of Common Market Studies*, 32/2, 1994, pp. 140–70

Fischer, Joschka, "From Confederation to Federation – Thoughts on the Finality of European Integration", Federal Trust Essay No. 8, London: The Federal Trust, 2000

Lindberg, Leon N., and Stuart A. Scheingold, *Europe's Would-be Polity: Patterns of Change in the European Community*, Englewood Cliffs, NJ: Prentice-Hall, 1970

Smith, Julie, *Citizens' Europe: The European Elections and the Role of the European Parliament*, London: Royal Institute of International Affairs, 1994

Smith, Julie, *Europe's Elected Parliament*, Sheffield: Sheffield Academic Press/UACES, 1999

Smith, Julie, "The European Parliament and Democracy in the European Union" in Roland Axtmann (editor), *Balancing Democracy*, London and New York: Continuum, 2001

Wallace, William, and Julie Smith, "Democracy versus Technocracy: European Integration and the Problem of Popular Consent", in *West European Politics*, 18/3, 1995, pp. 137–57

Weber, Eugen, *Peasants into Frenchmen: The Modernisation of Rural France, 1870–1914*, London: Chatto and Windus, and Stanford, CA: Stanford University Press, 1976

Weiler, Joseph H.H., "After Maastricht: Community Legitimacy in Post-1992 Europe", in William James Adams (editor), *Singular Europe*, Ann Arbor: University of Michigan Press, 1992

Young, Hugo, "Can a Touch of Pragmatism Bring Europe into New Focus?", in *The Guardian*, 7 October 2000

Dr Julie Smith is Head of the European Programme at the Royal Institute of International Affairs, Assistant Director of Studies at the Centre of International Studies of the University of Cambridge, and a Fellow of Robinson College, Cambridge. Her recent publications, in addition to those listed above, include *A Sense of Liberty: A Short History of the Liberal International 1947–1997* (1997), and *Democracy in the New Europe*, coedited with Elizabeth Teague (1999).

Chapter Six

The Challenge of Euroscepticism

Christopher Flood

The Issue

The concept of Euroscepticism carries the meaning of doubt and distrust on the subject of European integration. It is the most widely used of a number of related terms that became current in British political discourse during the 1990s as shorthand labels for positions adopted in public debates concerning the EU. It has come to designate a transnational phenomenon since it refers not only to a feature of the British political landscape but also to its counterparts in other European countries. There are different degrees and kinds of Euroscepticism, but if the concept is to have any analytical value, its meaning should not be extended too far. Eurosceptic positions should be distinguished from reformist positions that involve criticism of particular aspects of the EU and a corresponding desire for improvement, but are sufficiently sympathetic towards the aims and achievements of integration thus far to accept that the process should legitimately continue in the future.

At its most moderate, Euroscepticism covers the standpoints of those who argue that European integration has gone as far as it should go and that, in principle, further extensions of the process should be resisted. Harder versions of Euroscepticism are encapsulated in revisionist positions, according to which the political and/or economic integration of the EU has already gone too far and should be reversed to an anterior state, usually the stage reached before the Maastricht Treaty. At the extreme, Euroscepticism amounts to outright rejection of membership of the EU, implying withdrawal if the Eurosceptic's country is already a member or refusal of the idea of joining if it is not.

It need hardly be said that there are no watertight compartments as far as these positions are concerned. Today's moderate Eurosceptic might evolve towards qualified support for further integration. Alternatively, his/her attitudes might harden towards revisionism. Equally, a revisionist frustrated by the continuing advance of integration might turn in due course to outright Europhobic rejectionism.

Euroscepticism is more than a mere attitude. It has an ideological dimension. Like other ideological phenomena, it is communicated in many forms and on varying levels of sophistication, ranging from everyday exchanges of opinions between individuals of any social class to the production of articles, interviews, broadcasts, pamphlets, and books by politicians, intellectuals, journalists, and other publicists. It has given rise to single-issue pressure groups, think-tanks, and protest parties, as well as contributing to the policy platforms of other parties, or to the positions of Eurosceptic factions within parties that are officially Europhile. It can be found in leftwing as well as rightwing versions, especially at the extremes, and it can cut across traditional divisions, creating paradoxical affinities. Although it is often driven primarily by concern for the future of the Eurosceptics' own countries, the possibility of making common cause is represented in the European Parliament by two groups, the Union for a Europe of Nations and Europe of Democracies and Diversities, although these loose, ideologically diverse alliances do not include all of the Eurosceptic parties. The potential for making common cause is even symbolized in cyberspace by a transnational internet ring linking the sites of a number of Eurosceptic organizations around Europe.

73

The Eurosceptic attitude did not originate in the 1990s. Some member states, including Britain, Denmark, and Greece, had previously been the scene of deep divisions over the advantages and disadvantages of membership, both before and after they joined the Community. Nevertheless, the debates over the Maastricht Treaty focused public attention on the extent to which member states were in the process of transferring what had formerly been considered sovereign national powers to the supranational level. This produced a crystallization of opposition to further political integration and to other aspects of integration, including European Monetary Union, which were taken to underpin the political. Whereas the 1980s had been marked by rising popular support for the EU after the uncertainties of the 1970s, the period from 1992 to the time of writing has been marked by lower support.

In some member states, such as Ireland, Luxembourg, the Netherlands, Spain, and Portugal, Euroscepticism has had little purchase on political elites or among the wider public, but at various times in other states it has been a key item on the political agenda, with varying effects in different member states. For example, it has been a major constraint on government policy in Britain, under both Conservative and Labour governments. It forced changes of government policy in Denmark after the negative majorities in the referenda on Maastricht in 1992 and on participation in the single currency in 2000. In France, it contributed to the fragmentation of the mainstream right and, to a lesser extent, the mainstream left at the time of the referendum on Maastricht ratification in 1992, and in the European Parliament elections of 1994 and 1999. Its increasing potency in Austria was a factor in prompting withdrawal of the EU sanctions imposed after the extreme rightwing Freedom Party entered government with the conservative People's Party following elections in 1999. It is a significant force outside the EU in Norway and Switzerland, which might have been expected to be member states by now if it had not been for the weight of public opinion opposed to joining. It also exists to some extent within the states in central and eastern Europe that are candidates for accession.

The identification of Euroscepticism as a significant phenomenon holding potential dangers for the future of EU integration has fed into academic as well as political debates. It has given rise to claims of a legitimacy crisis in the EU, with optimistic or pessimistic assessments of its likely resolution. It has coloured different, sometimes competing analyses of the importance of the democratic deficit, including issues of the transparency and accountability of decision-making processes, the appropriate balance between intergovernmental and supranational competencies, the respective spheres of EU, national, and subnational governance, the impact of European issues on domestic politics and national party systems, and questions of collective identity (see, for example, Banchoff and Mitchell, Beetham and Lord, Hedetoft, Hix 1998, and Schmitt and Thomassen). It is likely to remain an issue of concern for those who wish to see integration actively endorsed by citizens of the EU.

Euroscepticism as Popular Dissatisfaction

The principal sources for examining public opinion concerning the EU are the twice-yearly Eurobarometer surveys deriving data from all member states. These and other sources give some indication of the strength of popular Euroscepticism. On the one hand, public attitudes can be measured in terms of raw percentages based on those giving responses that reflect negative perceptions of the integration process and/or of their country's place in it. On the other hand, by convention a crude index of the net weight of opinion for and against integration can be gained by setting the negative responses against the positive, normally excluding those who give neutral responses of the "neither good nor bad" type, as many questions allow, or those whose response is that they do not know – even though neutrality, acquiescence, lack of knowledge or lack of interest are obviously significant in themselves. The information clearly needs to be treated with caution.

As has often been pointed out, "European public opinion" consists of different national public opinions, reflecting differing national contexts, cultures, and domestic economic and political circumstances and preoccupations. Levels of affective attachment to the idea of European unity can change slowly within a single country over time, while utilitarian perceptions of the material costs and benefits of integration can shift more rapidly (see Gabel 1998). Therefore generalizations have to be made with extreme caution and always subject to qualifications, given the immense complexity of the political, economic, and cultural demography of the EU. For example, it has been argued that an effect of acculturation has occurred among the publics of the six founding member states, so that their levels of support for integration are higher than those in countries that joined later. However, political and economic factors can cut across the cultural dimension to produce contrary effects. Since 1990 French support for membership has merely followed the EU average and there has been only one year since 1992 when German support has not been below the average. Conversely, some of the states that joined later show very different patterns, with Ireland, which joined in 1973, consistently far above the average throughout the 1990s, whereas Spain and Portugal, which both joined in 1987, after falling significantly below the average during the first half of the 1990s, have climbed and remained substantially higher since that time. Nevertheless, observation of crossnational tendencies and trends on the basis of aggregated percentages for the EU as a whole can still have some indicative value.

The study of public attitudes is one of the areas in which it is particularly important to bear in mind the distinction between Eurosceptics, on the one hand, and, on the other, frustrated supporters of integration who are critical of aspects of the EU's performance but wish to see integration taking place more rapidly or more effectively in particular respects. For example, a major survey of opinion carried out during December 2000 in eight member states (France, Germany, Greece, Italy, Luxembourg, Netherlands, Spain, and the United Kingdom) suggested that 56% of respondents were not satisfied with the way in which the EU was evolving at that time, whereas only 38% expressed satisfaction (as reported in *The Guardian*, 15 January 2001). However, the level of dissatisfaction could obviously have different causes among different sets of respondents in different countries, including those who were not so much Eurosceptics as frustrated Europhiles, or those who considered some dimensions of integration desirable and others undesirable. The three countries showing the highest levels of negative responses to the general question on the evolution of integration were France (61%), Germany (61%), and Greece (65%), but majorities in all three favoured a directly elected EU presidency, harmonization of member states' legal systems, and creation of a common European army.

The *Eurobarometer 53* survey published in October 2000 (the latest available in full at the time of writing) showed an EU average of 14% responding that they considered their country's membership of the EU to be a bad thing. The percentage was small compared with the 49% who considered their country's membership to be a good thing and the acquiescent 28% who regarded it as neither good nor bad. Having declined during the 1980s while positive support for the European Community rose, the lowest percentage of hostile responses had been reached in 1990, before rising to 1996, then falling somewhat in the later 1990s, only to rise again, although to a lesser extent, at the end of the decade (see Figure 6.1). Contingent factors, including the coincidence of economic problems and high unemployment with the debates over the Maastricht Treaty, had no doubt helped to break the rising trend in support for the EU, which had characterized the 1980s. Among the factors that have been cited as contributing to waning enthusiasm and rising unease are the wars in the former Yugoslavia, to which the EU's response was neither coherent nor effective; the vociferous presence of Eurosceptic groups in some member states for the European elections of 1994; the accession of Austria, Sweden and Finland, each with significant Eurosceptic sections of national opinion, in 1995 (while a majority of Norway's voters rejected membership in the 1994 referendum); and the onset of the BSE crisis in 1996. Nevertheless, amid improving economic conditions, support for the EU and for the impending European Monetary Union made a recovery until autumn 1998, while hostility diminished. However, among other factors, the controversy leading to the resignation of the Commission in March 1999 fed into increased scepticism and lower active support – also evident in the record level of abstentions in the European elections in June – from which the EU has yet to recover fully. The pattern of negative perceptions is repeated more strongly in *Eurobarometer 53* on the question of whether or not respondents consider that their country has benefited from EU membership (see Figure 6.2).

The rankings of member states showing the most consistently high levels of negative perceptions on a range of key issues inevitably vary to some extent from one question to another, reflecting different preoccupations within different member states and among different sections of the public within those states. Still, the countries that figure most frequently among the most negative five include the three most recent entrants, Sweden, Austria, and Finland, alongside the United Kingdom and Denmark, which have been members since 1973 (see Table 6.1). This pattern has been broadly consistent since the mid-1990s, or earlier in the case of the United Kingdom and Denmark, both of which had seen a rise in Euroscepticism since the time of the debates on the ratification of the Maastricht Treaty. Germany, one of the six founding states, also shows relatively high levels of dissatisfaction on a number of issues. The United Kingdom, Sweden, Finland, and Austria also have majorities of respondents professing to feel a sense of national identity only, as opposed to "national and European", which accounted for by far the largest number of responses across the EU as a whole, "European and national", or "European" only.

Where the publics of this group differ markedly is on the question of support for EU enlargement, on which the United Kingdom, Austria, and Germany are among the least enthusiastic, whereas the Scandinavian states are among the most positive. Views on enlargement obviously do not correlate in any straightforward way with Euroscepticism. The debates on widening and/or deepening contain so many variables that they allow for the coexistence of Europhiles and Eurosceptics on both sides in relation to the accession of any one or more candidate states. However, there is a more revealing difference within the group on the question of self-perceived knowledge of the EU. In *Eurobarometer 53* Austria, Denmark, Germany, and Finland, in that order, were the member states with the highest proportions considering themselves well-informed, and Sweden ranked seventh. Only the United Kingdom figures among the five with the lowest levels of self-perceived knowledge. This marked progress for the newest member states since the time of accession in the mid-1990s, and a decline for the United Kingdom in the same period. Indeed, the United Kingdom now showed the lowest level among all the member states, an indicator that correlated with the very high levels of "don't know" responses to some other questions to convey an impression that there were large numbers of British people who did not *want* to know about the EU.

Within the EU as a whole levels of support across age groups do not vary significantly, except that there is lower support for the EU among those aged 55 and over. However, polls have regularly shown that there are substantial differences depending on ages of leaving education, such that the lower the level of education, the higher the percentage of Eurosceptics. *Eurobarometer 53* illustrated this pattern, with hostility to the EU showing at 16% among those who had left education aged less than 15 or between the ages of 16 and 19, whereas the level was 11% among those who had left education aged over 20, and 8% among those who were current students. Using Eurobarometer's very broad socioeconomic categories, lower levels of support are typically found among the retired, the unemployed, and manual workers than among white-collar workers, the self-employed, and managers.

Broadly speaking, then, there is a correlation between socioeconomic level, educational level, and level of support for the EU, with the more disadvantaged or dependant socioeconomic groups more likely to lack confidence in the EU and more inclined to think of their own identities in exclusively national terms. Nevertheless, this does not necessarily mean that a utilitarian calculation of relative personal advantage or disadvantage is invariably the key, particularly when combined with narrow cultural horizons arising from low educational levels. Clearly, the perception of advantage or disadvantage will vary between economic sectors, which cut across the Eurobarometer categories and require more sophisticated analysis of the type offered by Matthew Gabel (1998) and Simon Hix (1999a), but in any case some

Eurosceptics remain sceptical regardless of their perception of personal economic advantage. Hence, in *Eurobarometer 53*, of those who considered EU membership a bad thing, 7% responded that they thought that they had themselves gained more advantages than disadvantages from their country's membership and 28% considered that they had gained as many advantages as disadvantages.

Euroscepticism as Ideology and Mythology

Unlike nationalism, of which it is often, but not always, a vehicle, Euroscepticism is a purely negative concept, like anticapitalism, antimilitarism or anti-Semitism. In the discourse of political and economic elites and intellectuals it can involve more or less coherent, highly elaborated arguments, expressing sets of ideas, beliefs, and attitudes relating to the ordering of society, but it obviously does not constitute a fullblown ideology in its own right, since it does not offer a comprehensive, potentially universalizable view of man and society. It focuses only on particular dimensions of a particular set of societies insofar as they are bound together in the EU. It might perhaps be considered as a partial ideology, but it is more usefully viewed relationally, as a component of other ideologies. Variation between different versions of Euroscepticism, as well as between the arrangements offered as preferable alternatives to the integration of the EU, depends on the wider ideological framework in which Euroscepticism is embedded. There are characteristic areas of difference between leftwing and rightwing perspectives. There are also differences within the broad left and the broad right. Further, different national traditions and contexts generate further variations of focus or emphasis: for example, there are significant distinctions between the positions of the French left or right (analysed in Benoit) and those of their British counterparts (see Daniels, as well as Flood). Nevertheless, there are areas of common ground. Some of the most widely aired arguments, which recur across the ideological spectrum, can be summarized as follows:

- The EU is on the way to being a centralized superstate, absorbing the independence of its member states. This is an outdated and unacceptable goal. The self-destruction of Yugoslavia shows what happens when diverse peoples are bound together too tightly without adequate expression of their national identities and aspirations.

- The EU is undemocratic, bureaucratic, inefficient and largely unaccountable to the peoples of its member states, but democratizing it by increasing the powers of the European Parliament in its current form is not the answer, since that would involve further transfer of sovereignty to a remote body having little connection with the citizens of member states.

- European Monetary Union and the operation of the European Central Bank will not only be economically ruinous but will further consolidate the movement towards a centralized political system by effectively removing member states' control of their finances, taxation, and national economies.

- It is unacceptable that European laws should have primacy over national laws. Moreover, the European Court of Justice has far too much power and misuses it by reinterpreting the treaties and other European legal instruments in a federalist direction.

- To base a common foreign and security policy on qualified majority voting is unacceptable and can only lead to division, given the vital national interests and the lives of nationals of member states involved in these fields. It is equally undesirable that the Western European Union (WEU) should be subsumed as the integrated defence arm of the EU.

- The obsession with deepening integration increases the difficulty of widening to include the nations of central and eastern Europe, since the entry conditions become increasingly rigorous. The risk is that these states will dissolve into economic, ethnic, and political chaos without the support that they need from the West.

- Instead of developing further in its present direction, Europe should become a community of free, independent nations engaging in cooperative intergovernmental relationships with each other and with the rest of the world.

Euroscepticism creates strange bedfellows by crosscutting traditional ideological divisions. For instance, when translated into revisionist party platforms, it produces a paradoxical degree of commonality in France between the socialist Citizens Movement led by Jean-Pierre Chevènement and the national-populist, extreme rightwing National Front, led by Jean-Marie Le Pen, or the National Republican Movement led by Le Pen's former deputy Bruno Mégret. Still, beyond the more or less shared positions lie characteristic differences along several axes.

Notwithstanding differences of emphasis in the formulation of criticisms of the EU, and despite more fundamental differences in positive alternatives (for example, between anti-productivist and productivist conceptions of economic organization), there is a high degree of convergence between Green new-left critiques of the EU and those of the traditional socialist and communist left. Euroscepticism of the left attacks the EU on the grounds of its commitment to liberal capitalism, deregulation, free trade, and globalization, which are viewed as inimical to the interests of disadvantaged sections of European societies and of other societies throughout the world. Just as it is hostile to US economic power and the EU's acquiescence in a neoliberal world order, it also opposes what it sees as the EU's excessive subservience towards NATO and towards US military domination of the planet, although the antimilitarist stance of the new left and most of the traditional left equally discourages support for European defence cooperation except for strictly limited purposes of UN-sanctioned peacekeeping.

On the right and the extreme right, objections to the EU focus heavily on defence of national sovereignty and of intergovernmentalism. In the economic sphere, whereas the left attacks the EU's excessive liberalism, the right, except some neocorporatist groups on the neofascist ultraright, denounces its insufficient liberalism, its excessive regulation and intervention coupled with inordinate budgetary demands to sustain the costs of redistributive programmes including the structural funds, the Cohesion Fund, and the Common Agricultural Policy. The Schengen Treaty and the opening of internal borders are attacked as a recipe for massive influxes of economic migrants claiming to be asylum seekers: the prospect of immigration policy passing under the control of the Commission, as stated in the Treaty of Amsterdam, compounds the perceived threat, which is not viewed only in terms of disruption of domestic labour markets, but also in terms of demands on the welfare state, problems of integration, and the dilution of national culture. Defence of national identities against EU homogenization is seen as vital. At the same time, there are differences on the right between the strongly free-trading, pro-NATO, Atlanticist positions of Conservative Eurosceptics in Britain or the national populists of the Danish People's Party, for instance, and the anti-American, Euro- or national-protectionist, anti-NATO positions of many of their French counterparts, for example.

Besides giving rise to critical arguments aimed against particular features of the EU, or even against the whole principle of the EU, Euroscepticism has generated a rich mythology. That is to say, it has produced myths both in the popular sense of false stories about the EU, often alleging threats of apparently absurd regulative excesses on the part of the Commission, but also in the more technical sense of narratives that are ideologically coloured in their selection and/or interpretation of past, present, and predicted events, whether or not the facts recounted are more or less accurate. Again, there are leftwing and rightwing Eurosceptic mythologies coloured by the values, beliefs, and preoccupations of different ideological currents in the member states, but there is also common ground. Conspiracy myths offer negative accounts of the integration process as a whole or of particular aspects of it, often including dire predictions of the future if the process is not reversed. The activity of specific groups of EU actors – and especially of the Commission with its retinue of Brussels bureaucrats – are depicted as agencies of damage to the interests of EU member states or, more specifically, the interests of the state with which the purveyor of the account identifies. Negative stereotypes of individual member states feed into such stories, as in the example of British rightwing Eurosceptic representations of collusion between France and Germany in the EU's drive to undermine British sovereignty. Ironically,

French Eurosceptic myths are often no less anti-German than their British counterparts, but the other major threat for the French often takes the form of the hegemonic United States, outside the EU but seeking to dominate it, with the British as its lapdogs but also with the connivance of the globalist, Atlanticist free-traders of the Commission. On the right, a second major class of narratives corresponds to variant forms of traditional nationalistic, exceptionalist, and often xenophobic mythology based on deterministic notions of a permanent, unique national character that the teller attributes to his/her own country. The essential virtues and qualities of that people are presented in contrast to the lesser qualities of other European nations, accompanied by claims that the continuation of the heritage requires resistance to absorption within the stifling mediocrity of an all-embracing EU superstate.

Britain constitutes a particularly striking case of this type of mythmaking, with a prolific output of Eurosceptic publications produced by politicians and other publicists, particularly from the right. The titles often convey the melodramatic, doomladen flavour of the content in works such as *The Castle of Lies* (Booker and North), *The Tainted Source* (Laughland), *Treason at Maastricht* (Atkinson and McWhirter), *The Rotten Heart of Europe* (Connolly), and *Britain Held Hostage: The Coming Euro-Dictatorship* (Jenkins). A similar outlook is conveyed in two futuristic novels, *The Aachen Memorandum* by the historian Andrew Roberts and Terry Palmer's *Euroslavia*, which is set in the corrupt European superstate of the mid-21st century. It permeates much of the commentary in the rightwing press, ranging from the upmarket *Times* and *Telegraph* to the middle-market *Mail* to the lowbrow *Sun*, not to mention the *Spectator* magazine and the supposedly apolitical heritage magazine, *This England*, which promotes a virulent Europhobia under the banner "Don't Let Europe Rule Britannia".

Euroscepticism and Party Politics

The impact of Euroscepticism on party politics since the early 1990s has varied widely from country to country. Its effect is difficult to assess because of the extent to which EU issues, though increasingly salient, remain second-order concerns for electorates in comparison with domestic issues. This is not only true in national elections. European Parliament elections, and even referenda on European issues, are coloured by domestic political considerations such as the popularity or unpopularity of governments. For example, a major opinion poll conducted in five EU countries (France, Germany, Italy, Belgium, and Britain) three weeks before the European Parliament elections in 1999 showed 59% of respondents stating that they would be primarily motivated by the problems of their own countries, while only 29% said that they would vote mainly in the light of European issues (as reported in *L'Express*, 10 June 1999).

In many member states Euroscepticism has had a negligible influence on party politics because the strength of Eurosceptic opinion has been very slight, but even in states where there are relatively high levels of popular scepticism towards the EU this is not necessarily reflected clearly in party platforms. While the general ideological frameworks of leftwing or rightwing parties impart their particular colourings to different versions of Euroscepticism – just as they do to the different versions of support for integration – there is no automatic correlation between a party's membership of a particular ideological family and its position in favour of, or against, EU integration. Ideologies are not normally rigid or immutable, least of all in a changing environment of inter- and intraparty competition, and this is all the more true when the sheer complexity of the EU in all its ramified, evolving aspects makes its signification infinitely open to reinterpretation. Thus, ideology is a factor of variable importance in shaping party positions on the EU and it is constrained by other factors, including parties' locations within the national systems of which they are parts.

By the 1990s, whether or not they had once been associated with opposition to integration, most of the mainstream parties of the social-democratic centre-left, the liberal centre, and the Christian Democratic or conservative centre-right had increasingly converged on positions of moderate support for EU integration. Competition between them did not occur along the axis of national independence versus supranationalism, but rather on lines of traditional left–right cleavage extending to the EU level (see Hix 1999b, Marks and Wilson, and Taggart). The centre-left and centre overlapped in their concern for democratization, transparency, accountability, and the protection of citizens' rights on the political level, while diverging on socioeconomic questions of intervention, regulation, planning, welfare, and redistribution, on which parties of the centre were closer to the neoliberal, anti-interventionist, deregulatory, free-market concerns of the centre-right. Although the reasons vary from one national context to another, the tendency for parties to move away from radical, rejectionist Euroscepticism towards a nuanced stance of reformist engagement has continued. In the course of the 1990s a number of Green and Red/Green parties that had previously been opposed to EU membership moved in this direction That was the case, for example, with the Socialist People's Party in Denmark from 1999 onwards, or with the British Green Party, which now belongs to the reformist Green Group in the European Parliament. However, while most mainstream parties do not advocate rejectionist or even radically revisionist Eurosceptic positions, they may contain factions that are Eurosceptic to a greater or lesser degree. Most parties may not be deeply divided internally (see Ray), but some are: for example, there are substantial Eurosceptic factions within the Social Democrats, the Conservatives, and the Centre Party in Sweden, the Danish Social Democrats, the Centre Party and the Left-Wing Alliance in Finland, and the British Conservative Party.

Mainstream parties, and other, more marginal parties that have evolved away from rejectionism, can therefore pose a dilemma for Eurosceptic voters, between party loyalty and/or preference based on traditional left–right choices, on the one hand, and Eurosceptic concerns left unanswered by the party's official platform, on the other hand. In the case of parties that have realigned themselves by shedding earlier Eurosceptic positions as they moved into, or returned to, the mainstream, the division between party elites and grassroots activists or voters poses a potential electoral threat. In Britain that is a problem that faces the Labour Party, and that the Conservative leadership has sought to exploit – albeit at the risk of deepening divisions within its own party – by means of a calculatedly ambiguous rhetoric carrying increasingly heavy undertones of Euroscepticism notwithstanding a professed commitment to constructive engagement. Its impact thus far has been limited. It was certainly not enough to save the Conservatives from defeat in the general election in either 1997 or 2001. Nevertheless, it has been argued that the EU is becoming the basis of a new cleavage in British electoral politics and potentially in other member states as well (see Evans, as well as Gabel 2000).

Rejectionist or radically revisionist Euroscepticism is mainly found among two types of organization competing for public support. Anti-establishment parties of the extreme right and left frequently – though by no means invariably – propagate Eurosceptic positions as part of their wider agendas for fundamental reform. This is the case with some national populist parties of the radical right, such as the rejectionist Danish People's Party, the revisionist National Front, and the National Republican Movement in France, or the Austrian Freedom Party (which has somewhat softened its line while in government with the People's Party). It appears on the new and the old left, as in the examples of the Green Party and the Left Party in Sweden, or the surviving former Communist Parties of many other member states. In addition, there are single-issue organizations of various forms, some of them campaigning as parties, such as the United Kingdom Independence Party, the Movement for France, and the Gathering for France; others operating as crossparty movements, such as the June Movement and the People's Movement in Denmark; and a plethora of pressure groups that campaign mainly by lobbying politicians, pamphleteering, maintaining internet sites, and organizing meetings. Britain has a particularly large number of pressure groups, some of them more or less spanning right and left, such as the Bruges Group, but the majority being clearly on the right and in many instances led by Conservative politicians or party activists who also campaign as members of ginger groups within the Conservative Party itself. In the right political circumstances anti-establishment parties and single-issue parties campaigning on Eurosceptic platforms can achieve respectable scores in European Parliament elections. For example, 29% of the votes cast in France in 1999 went to Eurosceptic lists on the right or the extreme right. However, in view of the fact that many voters cast their ballots primarily on the basis of domestic concerns even in these contests, it is unsurprising that EU issues do not yet figure large in most voters' motivations for their choices in national elections.

Conclusion

Euroscepticism has become a significant factor in the politics of the EU. In some member states it is shared to a greater or less degree by substantial minorities of the population. The debates over ratification of the Maastricht Treaty, and then the showing of Eurosceptic parties in European Parliament elections and the Danish EMU referendum in 2000, were some of the more obvious pointers to the fact that integrationist elites can no longer take the acquiescence of the wider public for granted. The EU's democratic authority and the extent of its regulative powers have become a matter of controversy in some member states, giving rise to debates as to the nature of the EU as a political system, its likely evolution in the future, and the criteria according to which its legitimacy as well as its efficacy should be judged. Although the incidence of Euroscepticism in some countries is very low, these countries may not be immune to its influence at some later date if events occur to destabilize the EU or to give the impression that it is incapable of assuring the well-being and security of its citizens in ways in which the nation-state cannot.

At the same time, the importance of Euroscepticism should not be exaggerated. It is a diffuse, ill-defined phenomenon corresponding to a multitude of different shades and viewpoints. It is not strongly represented within party systems at national level, nor is it a powerful force in the European Parliament. On the contrary, it is politically marginal if considered across the EU as a whole. Even in the cases of individual member states with relatively high

levels of popular Euroscepticism, the effects have so far been limited to imposing a brake or caution on government policy. Three of the member states in which it has been most widespread are those that joined most recently and have therefore had the least length of time for political acculturation of the public. Of course, the United Kingdom and Denmark have been members for much longer, and Germany was a founding member. Yet the United Kingdom is a very particular case, given the historic strength of its extra-European relations and the fact that its political, economic, and cultural links with the United States were reinforced during the 1980s and 1990s by the increased ideological affinities of the British Conservative and "New" Labour leaderships with their US counterparts. Germany has been in the extraordinary situation of digesting reunification, and the new set of relationships in central and eastern Europe, while facing the prospect of losing its currency, which held enormous symbolic as well as economic importance for the country. Denmark, though home to one of the largest national percentages of Eurosceptics, is also a country that has an above-average percentage of Europhiles who see membership as a good thing, and one of the higher percentages of respondents who see their country as having derived benefit from membership. Still, Euroscepticism undoubtedly warrants further theoretical and empirical research, as part of the wider study of the evolving European political space. It clearly needs to be taken into account by EU policymakers in the pursuit of further institutional integration, not merely as a negative constraint but also as the expression of legitimate concerns that need to be addressed.

Further Reading

Atkinson, Rodney, and Norris McWhirter, *Treason at Maastricht: The Destruction of the Nation State*, second edition, Newcastle-upon-Tyne: Compuprint, 1995

Banchoff, Thomas, and Mitchell P. Smith (editors), *Legitimacy and the European Union: The Contested Polity*, London and New York: Routledge, 1999

Beetham, David, and Christopher Lord, *Legitimacy and the European Union*, London and New York: Longman, 1998

Benoit, Bertrand, *Social Nationalism: An Anatomy of French Euroscepticism*, Aldershot: Ashgate, 1997

Booker, Christopher, and Richard North, *The Castle of Lies: Why Britain Must Get out of Europe*, London: Duckworth, 1996

Connolly, Bernard, *The Rotten Heart of Europe: the Dirty War for Europe's Money*, London and Boston: Faber, 1995

Daniels, Philip, "From Hostility to 'Constructive Engagement': The Europeanization of the Labour Party", in *West European Politics*, 21/1, 1998, pp. 72–96

European Commission, *Eurobarometer: Public Opinion in the European Union, Report Number 53*, 2000, available at http://europa.eu.int/comm/dg10/epo/

euro-sceptic.org

The search engine at this website is a useful starting point for the websites of Eurosceptic parties, pressure groups, and think tanks, which offer a vast repository of material (often including sections in English, whatever the main language of the site).

Evans, Geoffrey, "Is the European Union the Basis of a New Cleavage in British Electoral Politics?", in Bruno Cautrès and Dominique Reynié (editors), *L'Opinion européenne*, Paris: Presses de Sciences Po, 2000

Flood, Christopher, "Euroscepticism in the Ideology of the British Right", in Noel Parker and Bill Armstrong (editors), *Margins in European Integration*, London: Macmillan, and New York: St Martin's Press, 2000

Gabel, Matthew, *Interests and Integration: Market Liberalization, Public Opinion and European Union*, Ann Arbor: University of Michigan Press, 1998

Gabel, Matthew, "European Integration, Voters and National Politics", in *West European Politics*, 23/4, 2000, pp. 52–72

Gaffney, John (editor), *Political Parties and the European Union*, London and New York: Routledge, 1996

Hedetoft, Ulf (editor), *Political Symbols, Symbolic Politics: European Identities in Transformation*, Aldershot: Ashgate, 1998

Hix, Simon, "Elections, Parties and Institutional Design: A Comparative Perspective on European Union Democracy", in *West European Politics*, 21/3, 1998, pp. 19–52

Hix, Simon, *The Political System of the European Union*, London: Macmillan, and New York: St Martin's Press, 1999 (referenced as 1999a in the text)

Hix, Simon, "Dimensions and Alignments in European Union Politics: Cognitive Constraints and Partisan Responses", in *European Journal of Political Research*, 35/1, 1999, pp. 69–106 (referenced as 1999b in the text)

Holmes, Martin (editor), *The Eurosceptical Reader*, London: Macmillan, and New York: St Martin's Press, 1996

A useful selection of primary sources

Jenkins, Lindsay, *Britain Held Hostage: The Coming Euro-Dictatorship*, Washington, DC: Orange State Press, 1997

Laughland, John, *The Tainted Source: The Undemocratic Origins of the European Idea*, London: Little Brown, 1997

Marks, Gary, and Carole Wilson, "National Parties and the Contestation of Europe", in Banchoff and Smith (editors), cited above

Palmer, Terry, *Euroslavia: Can You Escape it?*, Brentford: Pallas, 1997

Ray, Leonard, "Measuring Party Orientations towards European Integration: Results from an Expert Survey", in *European Journal of Political Research*, 36/2, 1999, pp. 283–306

Roberts, Andrew, *The Aachen Memorandum*, London: Weidenfeld and Nicolson, 1995

Schmitt, Hermann, and Jacques Thomassen (editors), *Political Representation and Legitimacy in the European Union*, Oxford and New York: Oxford University Press, 1999

Taggart, Paul, "A Touchstone of Dissent: Euroscepticism in Contemporary Western European Party Systems", in *European Journal of Political Research*, 33/3, 1998, pp. 363–88

Christopher Flood is Professor of European Studies at the University of Surrey. His research has focused particularly on questions of ideology and political mythology in Europe, especially France. He is co-editor of the *European Horizons* series with University of Nebraska Press.

Figure 6.1   Support for EU Membership, 1981–2000, average

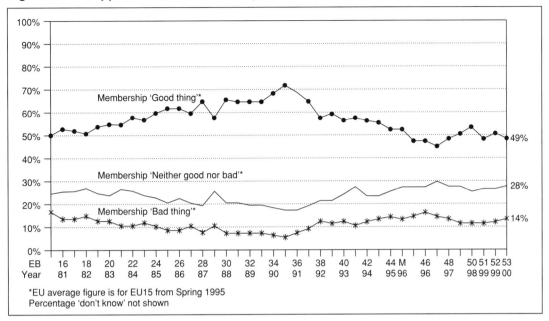

Source: European Commission, *Eurobarometer: Public Opinion in the European Union, Report No. 53*, 2000

Figure 6.2   Benefit from EU Membership, 1983–2000, average

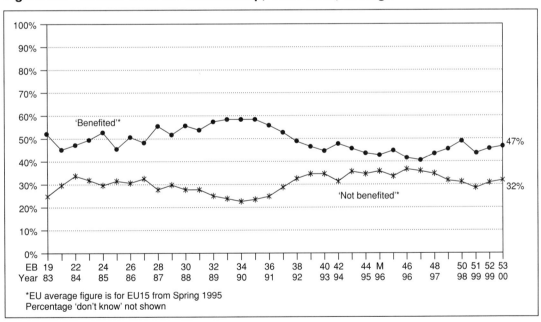

Source: EC Commission, *Eurobarometer: Public Opinion in the European Union, Report No. 53*, 2000

Table 6.1   Public Opinion in the Most Eurosceptic EU Member States, 2000 (% except as shown)

Against membership

EU	14	(−35)
Sweden	38	(4)
Austria	25	(−8)
UK	24	(−1)
Denmark	24	(−29)
Finland	22	(−18)

No benefit for country

EU	32	(−15)
Sweden	56	(30)
Austria	48	(14)
UK	44	(19)
Germany	42	(5)

Negative image of EU

EU	19	(−24)
Sweden	43	(17)
Austria	36	(13)
UK	35	(15)
Denmark	32	(3)
Finland	28	(−4)

Personal disadvantage

EU	17	(−12)
Sweden	27	(8)
UK	26	(6)
Austria	24	(0)
Germany	22	(−3)
Finland	18	(−11)

Desire lesser role in daily life five years from now

EU	15	(−29)
Sweden	31	(−5)
Denmark	30	(2)
UK	25	(3)
Finland	21	(−5)
Austria	21	(−6)

Lowest median of trust in nine EU institutions

EU	38
UK	18
Germany	34
Sweden	34
Austria	38
Denmark	39
Greece	39

Reject euro

EU	33	(−25)
UK	61	(39)
Sweden	54	(−16)
Denmark	51	(11)
Finland	48	(−1)
Germany	39	(−11)

Dissatisfied with EU democracy

EU	37	(−6)
Sweden	61	(36)
Austria	59	(29)
Denmark	57	(22)
Finland	45	(4)
Germany	44	(5)

National identity only

EU	41	(−16)
UK	64	(31)
Sweden	60	(20)
Ireland	56	(13)
Finland	55	(10)
Austria	53	(8)

Low support for enlargement (average in favour of 13 applicant countries)

EU	38
France	26
Austria	30
Germany	34
Luxembourg	34
UK	35

Self-perceived level of knowledge of EU (ten-point scale)

EU	4.26
UK	3.49
Portugal	3.63
Spain	3.9
Ireland	3.93
France	4.24

Note 1: Figures in brackets represent the percentage by which anti-integration responses exceed or are exceeded by pro-integration responses. Where anti-integration responses exceed pro-integration responses, the difference is shown as a positive number. Conversely, where pro-integration responses exceed anti-integration responses, the difference is shown as a negative number. This reverses the convention used in Eurobarometer surveys, but is consistent with the aim of ranking countries positively by strength of Eurosceptic responses. It maintains the practice of excluding quasi-neutral evaluations (e.g. "neither good nor bad"), responses supporting the status quo for questions measuring attitudes to change, and "don't know" responses.

Note 2: The figures in brackets for the question on identity measure the percentage of respondents claiming to feel "national identity only" against the combined total of the alternatives, "national and European", "European and national", and "European only".

Source: Derived from *Eurobarometer 53 Annexes*, Tables 2.1a, 2.2a, 2.3a, 2.4a, 2.11a, 2.8, 3.4a, 6.2a, 6.3a, 3.7, and *Eurobarometer 53 Report*, Fig. 5.6, respectively

Chapter Seven

Preparing for Enlargement

David Phinnemore

There can be little doubt that the largest challenge facing the EU over the next ten years is enlargement. The governments of a whole variety of countries are intent on joining. If the EU admits them this will result in a doubling of its membership, and significant changes to its character and dynamics. Before then reforms have to be introduced to prepare the EU for its new members. These reforms, however, are far from complete and are being introduced very slowly. Likewise, accession negotiations with the candidate countries are not proceeding as swiftly as many want them to. All the same, enlargement of the EU is approaching.

The Applicants

In total there are 13 countries officially seeking membership of the EU (see Table 7.1). Ten of them are in what is termed central and eastern Europe, essentially that part of Europe that was dominated for much of the second half of the 20th century, until 1989, by the Soviet Union. The remaining three applicants border on or are in the Mediterranean: they are Turkey, and the two islands of Cyprus and Malta.

Of these countries, the first to seek membership of the EU was Turkey, in 1987. The application signalled a strong desire on the part of the government of the day to further the western orientation and economic modernization of the country. It also came against a background of notionally close yet politically strained relations with the EU, dating back to the early 1960s and the signing of an association agreement (in 1963). This had provided the basis for freer trade and economic cooperation, yet it had failed to provide the basis for

the development of a meaningful and mutually satisfying relationship. Turkey's enthusiasm for membership was not shared by the EU and, as the list of applicants rapidly lengthened, the country soon found itself languishing half-forgotten at the bottom.

Turkey's application was soon followed by the first of five applications from members of EFTA. The first to signal its desire to join was Austria, in 1989; it was followed by Sweden two years later. There then came a spate of applications in 1992 from Finland, Switzerland, and Norway. In among these applications were those submitted by Cyprus and Malta in 1990. As in the case of Turkey, these did not represent a first step in the development of relations between the two Mediterranean islands and the EU. Both Cyprus and Malta had signed association agreements in the early 1970s, providing for free trade in industrial goods as well as economic cooperation. Once again, these agreements had not led to wholly satisfactory relationships. This was due in no small part to the domestic situation in each country. Maltese governments had generally turned their backs on the agreement until 1987, while the division of Cyprus since 1973 had resulted in the EU demanding a resolution to the situation as a prerequisite for the development of ties. There were, however, significant external considerations behind the applications, not least the collapse of Soviet power in central and eastern Europe. This and the increasing likelihood of applications from more EFTA countries threatened to divert the EU's attention away from the Mediterranean. In submitting membership applications, in July 1990, the Cypriot and Maltese governments therefore sought to ensure that they would not fall too far down the list of EU priorities, especially if enlargement were to emerge as a key item on the EU's agenda.

Enlargement became a major concern for the EU in the 1990s, initially with regard to the EFTA applicants, and later with regard primarily to countries in central and eastern Europe. Before it had completed enlargement to the former in 1995, applications from the latter began to come in. The first of the ex-Communist countries to apply was Hungary, in spring 1994, followed shortly after by Poland. That these two countries should apply came as little surprise to the EU. Governments in both countries had expressed a strong wish to see their countries accede to the EU. Moreover, Hungary and Poland were the first two countries in central and eastern Europe to conclude "Europe agreements", the EU's new purpose-designed vehicles for relationships with countries in central and eastern Europe. Such agreements recognized the countries' respective membership aspirations and had recently come into force. A membership application appeared the logical next step in the development of ties with the EU.

In the light of these applications, the EU began to address the prospect of enlargement to the East. Conscious of this, and with their Europe Agreements now signed and in some cases entering into force, other countries in the region soon submitted their own membership applications. In 1995, the EU received applications from Romania, Slovakia, Latvia, Estonia, Lithuania, and Bulgaria. The Czech Republic and Slovenia followed in 1996. Thus, within little more than two years ten ex-Communist countries had applied for membership of the EU, and by mid-June 1996 the EU had 13 applicants knocking on its door. Never had the EU been faced with so many countries wishing to become members; never had it been forced to face such challenges as those posed by the prospect of admitting these countries.

The Challenges Posed by Enlargement

Highlighting a few of the characteristics of these countries helps to explain some of the challenges raised by enlargement. First of all, there is the sheer number of applicants. In the past, the EU has dealt with no more than four applications in any one enlargement. Henceforth, it would have to deal with a larger number at any one time if it wished to avoid differentiation, and counter fears on the part of certain applicants of being left out and marginalized. Moreover, there is a significant challenge posed by admitting all applicants: will the EU be able to continue taking decisions on the basis of unanimity or will enlargement to 28 member states lead to a paralysis of decision-making?

Secondly, there is the question of the size of the applicant countries (see Table 7.2), which range in population from Malta, which has 300,000 inhabitants and is therefore smaller than Luxembourg, to Turkey, with a population of 63.5 million. In between, there are a further four countries that are smaller than the EU's second smallest member state, Ireland. Of the remainder, all except Poland (38,300,000 inhabitants) and Romania (22,800,000 inhabitants) are small to medium-sized countries. Admitting the smallest raises crucial questions about the allocation of votes within the Council. Should Malta or Cyprus be allocated two votes when Germany, a member state more than 100 times the size of either, has traditionally been allocated only ten votes? Can the smallest countries be expected to assume the costs and other difficulties of holding the presidency of the Council when their turn comes round? With so many more small to medium-sized countries as members, can the existing decision-making mechanisms, which already favour such countries, be justified, even as they further weaken the positions of the larger member states?

Thirdly, there is the challenge of extending policies to such a large number of states. Of particular significance here is the size of the agricultural labour force and the contribution that agriculture makes to GDP in each country. Can the EU afford to extend the Common Agricultural Policy to the likes of Poland and Romania? Further, all the applicant countries are poorer than the existing EU member states. This raises two related questions. Can the EU afford financially to extend its policies designed to promote economic and social cohesion to all new members? If not, can it afford politically to redirect financial assistance away from existing recipients to those joining the EU?

Such questions clearly need to be addressed if the EU is to admit any of the current applicants, let alone all of them. They would also need to be revisited if the list of applications lengthens, a prospect that should not be ruled out, for several other countries have indicated their desire to become members. One of these, Switzerland, submitted a membership application back in May 1992, although it was effectively frozen seven months later when Swiss voters used a referendum to reject closer ties with the EU. The Swiss government remains committed, however, to eventual accession to the EU. Voices advocating membership can also be heard in official circles in Norway, where governments have twice completed membership negotiations, in 1972 and in 1994, only to see the electorate vote against accession. A third application cannot be ruled out. Similarly, the EU is likely one day to receive requests for membership from other countries in eastern Europe. These may well include, in the short to medium term, Croatia, where the government has optimistically set 2005 as its target year for entry, and Albania. The governments of other countries, such as Macedonia, Ukraine, Moldova, and Georgia, have also indicated a desire to join the EU albeit within a much longer timeframe. Hence, even if the EU does complete its current plans for enlargement, there will be other applicants to deal with. Indeed, the list could get even longer: the Icelandic government has in the past considered an application and could well respond to a further Norwegian application by submitting one of its own, while Bosnia–Herzegovina, Serbia, and/or Montenegro may also make applications.

From Copenhagen to Helsinki: The EU's Approach to Enlargement

Ever since the EU's forerunner, the European Economic Community, was established in 1958, priority has almost always been given to the "deepening" of integration over the "widening" of the membership. Only rarely has the Community or the EU looked upon the prospect of enlargement with particular relish. Its tendency has been to delay the admission of new members, and the response to the desire of the current candidates to join its ranks has been no exception.

The Customs Union with Turkey

When Turkey submitted its membership application in 1987, the EU duly responded by acknowledging the country's "European vocation". It argued nevertheless that Turkey was ill-prepared to accede to the EU and that membership should be considered only as a long-term option. Hence, for much of the 1990s relations were focused on reviving and bolstering the existing association agreement (mentioned above) that linked Turkey with the EU. To this end, and despite a backdrop of often acrimonious relations and trenchant criticism within the European Parliament of the Turkish government's human rights record, a customs union agreement was signed in 1995. This committed the Turkish government to aligning much of its domestic legislation governing trade to that of the EU and saw the establishment of new bilateral institutions. In the eyes of Turkish governments, the customs union was seen as a precursor to EU membership. For most of the 1990s, the EU viewed the upgrading of relations differently, as was apparent in the way in which Turkey was excluded from emerging plans on how the EU was going to approach enlargement.

The Enlargement of 1995

Despite the EU's determination to give priority to its own internal development in the early 1990s, it soon found itself having to deal with the large number of applications for membership noted above. The EU's initial response to these applications was to defer any accession negotiations until after 1992, and the completion of the internal market, and then until the newly negotiated Treaty on European Union, the so-called Maastricht Treaty, had come into force. It then declared in 1993 that Cyprus and

Malta were as yet insufficiently prepared for membership. Hence, with Switzerland freezing its application (as described above), the first set of enlargement negotiations in the 1990s was restricted to four affluent states that seemed to present few problems and to demand minimal adjustments. Negotiations were completed in 1994 and on 1 January 1995 the membership of the EU was enlarged to 15 with the accession of Austria, Finland, and Sweden (Norway, as mentioned, having decided again not to join). With this relatively straightforward enlargement complete, the EU found itself facing some more challenging prospects.

Applications from Central and Eastern Europe

An attempt had already been made to address the growing demands for membership. Against a backdrop of widespread criticism of its responses to the initial aspirations of countries in central and eastern Europe, in June 1993 the EU declared its position with regard to eastward enlargement. At its meeting in Copenhagen, the European Council issued a commitment to admitting countries from the region, announcing that "the associated countries of central and eastern Europe that so desire shall become members of the European Union". Membership would, however, be conditional on individual countries meeting the "Copenhagen Criteria":

> Membership requires that the candidate country has achieved stability of institutions guaranteeing democracy, the rule of law, human rights and respect for and protection of minorities; the existence of a functioning market economy as well as the capacity to cope with competitive pressure and market forces within the Union. Membership presupposes the candidate's ability to take on the obligations of membership including adherence to the aims of political, economic and monetary union.

The outcome of the Copenhagen Council was welcomed by the governments of the countries hoping to join, although they still had concerns about when and how accession would be achieved. The commitment to admit new member states boosted confidence in the EU's intentions but, as critics were quick to point out, no dates for eastward enlargement had been mentioned, let alone fixed. Also, what did the criteria mean? No attempt had been made to provide clear definitions of what exactly the EU understood by "guaranteeing democracy", "respect for and protection of minorities", and "a functioning market economy". Moreover, criteria lacking definition could be reinterpreted in the future by the EU. There were also concerns about the rather onesided nature of what was being proposed: the countries in question were being required to adjust to the EU, while no obligations were being placed on the EU other than ensuring that it had the capacity to absorb new members and to maintain the momentum of integration.

The welcome commitment to admitting at least some ex-Communist countries, and the announcement of the criteria for accession, were clearly insufficient to bring about eastward enlargement. The countries of central and eastern Europe needed guidance on the criteria and support in achieving them. Europe Agreements, establishing free trade, political dialogue, and cooperation with these countries, were being signed, but these did not spell out what needed to be done if the Copenhagen criteria were to be met. In late 1994, the EU moved to remedy the situation by launching a "pre-accession strategy" for the ten applicants in the region. In part, this simply brought together aspects of existing relations under a more focused and politically more appealing umbrella. It did, however, see a further opening of EU markets to goods from the region and the expansion of multilateral dialogue within the framework of the "structured relationship" that had been launched at Copenhagen. More significantly, the pre-accession strategy was to involve integration into the internal market as a precursor to membership. The Commission was charged with providing guidelines on how this would be achieved and in May 1995 it published a White Paper detailing the measures that needed to be adopted. The clear emphasis was on legal approximation with the *acquis communautaire* – the body of EU law and policy already "acquired" since 1958 – although applicant governments were left to devise their own timetables for implementation. Regarding the White Paper as setting out concrete steps towards membership, the applicant governments responded positively and were soon adopting national strategies for implementing legislative harmonization.

At the same time as the EU launched the pre-accession strategy, it was only a matter of weeks away from admitting Austria, Finland, and Sweden on 1 January 1995. With the fourth enlargement complete, it turned its attention to preparations for the next increase in its membership. Clearly, Cyprus and Malta could not be excluded from any plans. This was confirmed in spring 1995, when the EU declared that negotiations with both countries would begin six months after the conclusion of the intergovernmental conference (IGC) scheduled for 1996, which was to prepare the EU institutionally for further enlargement. The need for institutional reform was widely recognized but there was no guarantee that the IGC would deliver. Indeed, the Treaty of Amsterdam that emerged from the conference failed to include more than modest reforms. The weighting of votes within the Council remained unaltered, the extension of qualified majority voting was limited, and the membership of the Commission stayed at 20. Another IGC would have to be held before enlargement could take place (see Chapter 4 for details).

The failure of the member state governments to agree on the necessary institutional reforms at Nice clearly disappointed those who sought early enlargement of the EU. Yet the conclusion of the IGC was welcomed, nevertheless, since it cleared the way for accession negotiations to begin, not just with Cyprus and Malta but also with sufficiently prepared countries in central and eastern Europe. In December 1995, as the "pre-accession strategy" was being implemented, the European Council announced at Madrid that the start of their accession negotiations could coincide with those between the EU and Cyprus and Malta. The European Council also called on the Commission to expedite preparation of its

formal "opinions" (often referred to as *avis*) on the membership applications. By this point, eight countries in central and eastern Europe had applied, and the Czech Republic and Slovenia soon followed suit in 1996. Only when the Commission's opinions had been issued could the Council decide on the launch of negotiations.

Agenda 2000

The opinions were published in July 1997 as part of a broader study of enlargement optimistically and misleadingly titled *Agenda 2000*. In this document the Commission set out its blueprint for enlargement, which included proposals for the reform of EU policies, the individual country-specific opinions, and a strategy for dealing with enlargement. As far as the latter was concerned, the Commission recommended that accession negotiations should be opened in early 1998 with Cyprus and five other applicants: Estonia, the Czech Republic, Hungary, Poland, and Slovenia. These were all deemed to have met the political criteria laid down at Copenhagen, to be able to meet the economic criteria in the medium term, and to be capable of withstanding the competitive pressure and market forces of the EU. As for the other applicants, the Commission argued that Slovakia did not meet the political criteria for membership, while Bulgaria, Latvia, Lithuania, and Romania were deemed to be lagging behind the others in moving towards fully functioning market economies. The Commission therefore recommended that their positions be reviewed at a later date. For the time being, accession negotiations should not be opened.

This left the applications of Malta and Turkey unresolved. The former was barely mentioned in *Agenda 2000*, since a change of government in October 1996 had resulted in the membership application being frozen. The possibility of Maltese accession to the EU was therefore off the agenda for the time being. The Commission did, however, discuss Turkey's position within the context of enlargement, recommending the further development of relations. Turkey was not, however, recommended for accession negotiations, on the grounds that it did not yet meet the democratic criteria for membership.

The Luxembourg Strategy

Although *Agenda 2000* was significant for providing a first comprehensive study of EU enlargement beyond 15 member states, it was nevertheless the work of the Commission and therefore amounted to no more than a set of proposals. The actual decisions on how the EU should proceed in dealing with all the applications on the table rested with the Council. This was just as well, since several member states, as well as those applicants not recommended for negotiations, were keen to see the adoption of a more inclusive approach to enlargement. They objected to the differentiation that the Commission was seeking to introduce into the enlargement process. Hence, as a result of their pressure on the other member states, the European Council, meeting in Luxembourg in December 1997, avoided strict adherence to the Commission's proposals. Instead it was agreed that an inclusive "accession process" would be launched, involving all ten applicant countries in central and eastern Europe, plus Cyprus. Turkey was not included. Instead, the European Council called on the Commission to propose a new strategy for integrating Turkey into the EU. Returning to the 11 states now involved in the accession process, the European Council declared that each was "destined" to join the EU. Differentiation would, however, characterize the accession negotiations. The European Council followed the Commission's recommendation and agreed to open formal negotiations with only six countries, which quickly became known as the "ins". The remaining five other applicants were diplomatically if clumsily referred to as the "pre-ins".

Following the Luxembourg Council, the EU set about launching the accession process, in which all "ins" and "pre-ins" alike would negotiate "accession partnerships", bringing together existing means of assistance, and detailing the precise measures that the applicants needed to adopt in the short, medium and long term if they were to meet the Copenhagen criteria in full. The accession partnerships were of great importance for the "pre-ins", since compliance with the obligations agreed appeared to be a prerequisite for accession negotiations. A second aspect of the accession process launched in 1998 was the European Conference. Ostensibly introduced as a mechanism in which Turkey could play a role, this replaced the existing multilateral "structured relationship" between the EU and the applicants in central and eastern Europe, and was designed to provide an annual forum in which matters of common concern and interest could be discussed. Thirdly, the launch of the accession process led to an increase in the number of EU programmes in which applicant states participated. These were primarily concerned with education, training, the environment, small and medium-sized enterprises (SMEs), research, and energy. Finally, as part of the accession process the EU was committed to a regular review of each applicant's progress in meeting the accession criteria. Regular reports on these reviews would be published each autumn. Before the first set of reports was compiled, however, the EU turned its attention to opening formal negotiations with the "ins".

The Accession Negotiations

Negotiations began on 31 March 1998 and were expected to last at least three years. This was very much a reflection of the complexity of negotiating accession. In all, 31 "chapters" covering all aspects of the EU's *acquis communautaire* would have to be negotiated, and negotiations would take place, not with the EU as a body, but within bilateral intergovernmental conferences involving negotiators from the applicant country as well as from all the EU member states. The positions of the 16 states in each of these sets of negotiations would have to converge. Before substantive negotiations could take place, each of the applicants would go through a "screening" process, in which the Commission and the applicant state would identify issues that were likely to arise in the negotiations. In the case of the "ins", these were essentially completed by July 1998. In each case, the Commission then proposed a negotiating position for the member states, while the applicant government prepared and submitted its position. Negotiations proper could then begin.

Following the "screening" exercise, substantive negotiations with the "ins" were opened on 10 November 1998 on seven chapters covering such relatively uncontroversial matters as education and training. Then, in the second half of 1999, negotiations were extended to a further eight chapters. By June 2000, all except two chapters – those concerning the "institutions" and "miscellaneous" issues – had been opened. Cyprus had made most progress, having provisionally closed negotiations in 16 chapters. Of the remaining "ins", Estonia and the Czech Republic had each closed 13 chapters, Slovenia 12 chapters, and Hungary and Poland 11 chapters each. Evidently, significant progress still had to be made before enlargement could take place.

During the first two years of negotiations, the "pre-ins" had little option but to negotiate and implement their accession partnerships, adopt complementary "national programmes for the adoption of the *acquis*", and watch as the "ins" gradually proceeded with negotiations and moved closer to EU membership. The clear differentiation within the accession process was, however, becoming increasingly difficult to stomach, particularly since certain "pre-ins" were making significant advances in remedying the deficiencies in their economies and, in the case of Slovakia, political development noted in the opinions issued by the Commission in 1997. Meanwhile, some of the "ins" appeared to be slipping in their efforts to fulfil the economic criteria for membership. This was clear from the content of the first regular reports published by the Commission in 1998. Latvia was singled out for promising progress with economic reform, and the victory of democratic forces in elections in Slovakia in September 1998 was also noted, with the implication that, if the new government could swiftly remedy the deficiencies in the political system, it would be eligible for negotiations. In addition, there was Malta, which in September 1998 re-elected the pro-EU Nationalist Party to government: it soon reactivated the country's application for membership.

Such developments did not convince the EU to begin negotiations with any more states in 1999. By the time the second regular reports

had been published, in October that year, the situation had changed. The EU was well aware that some states had increased their eligibility for membership. It also wanted to reduce the much-criticized differentiation within the accession process. Moreover, the EU was eager to reinforce its commitment to the countries of central and eastern Europe in the light of the Kosovo conflict earlier that year. Hence, the Commission proposed that negotiations be opened in 2000 with all five "pre-ins", as well as Malta. Concern over economic developments in Romania and Bulgaria meant that some conditions were attached. These were soon overlooked, however, as the European Council, meeting in Helsinki in December 1999, endorsed the Commission's proposal, and announced the launch of negotiations with Bulgaria, Latvia, Lithuania, Malta, Romania, and Slovakia. In another significant move, the European Council signalled the inclusion of Turkey in the "accession process", by declaring that it too was now "destined to join the European Union". Finally, in an attempt to reinforce its commitment to enlargement, the member states agreed to drop the term "applicant country" from discussions and documents related to enlargement. Instead, the 13 states involved in the accession process are referred to as "candidate countries".

The decisions taken at Helsinki were soon followed, on 15 February 2000, by the opening of negotiations with the five remaining central and east European candidate countries and Malta. Screening with regard to the *acquis communautaire* adopted up to 31 December 1998 had already been completed as part of the pre-accession process and up to eight chapters were swiftly opened. Negotiations did not, however, proceed at a uniform pace. Fewer chapters were opened with Bulgaria and, in particular, Romania, thus giving credence to the view that the European Council's decisions at Helsinki were, for at least some of the candidate countries, essentially symbolic and rather lacking in substance. Progress with negotiations developed very much in line with the extent to which candidates were meeting the accession criteria: hence, differentiation was maintained. Moreover, progress was effectively conditional on efforts made by candidate countries to transpose the *acquis communautaire* into national law and to implement it.

This emphasis on conditionality was underlined by the Commission in the third set of regular reports, issued in October 2000. These concluded that Cyprus and Malta were best prepared for membership, and that Estonia, Hungary, and Poland headed the list of likely first entrants in central and eastern Europe, with the Czech Republic and Slovenia not far behind. The generally favourable reports that these countries and the other candidates received – albeit with the possible exceptions of Bulgaria and Romania – generated optimism about the prospects for accession. These were strengthened by the Commission's proposed "road map" for enlargement, subsequently endorsed by the Council. Accordingly, priorities for negotiations over the next 18 months were established, with the EU setting itself the goal of concluding accession negotiations with some candidate countries by the end of 2002. The reports of October 2000 and the Commission's accompanying "strategy paper" confirmed the view that enlargement was now firmly on its way.

Preparing the Candidates: From PHARE to Accession Partnerships

The progress that the EU has made towards launching accession negotiations, and ultimately admitting countries in central and eastern Europe to membership, has seemed to many observers to be often slow and rather hesitant. Nevertheless, it reflects the publicly stated commitment of the existing 15 member states to enlarge the EU eastwards. The promise of membership may have been grudgingly conceded at Copenhagen in 1993 and the prospect of accession may still be a distant prospect for some candidate countries, but an authentic enlargement process has been launched. Moreover, since *Agenda 2000* the EU has become more proactive in supporting the efforts of candidate countries to meet the accession criteria and in promoting preparations for membership. The situation in 2001 is a great improvement on that of the early 1990s and underlines the extent to which enlargement has

become a key focus of the EU's attention.

The EU's support for the integration efforts of the candidate countries dates back to the launch of the PHARE programme of western (not just EU) assistance for economic restructuring, originally targeted at Poland and Hungary in 1989. "PHARE" originally stood for "Pologne, Hongrie – Assistance à la Réstructuration Economique", but, more significantly and lastingly, it means "lighthouse" in French. The programme was soon extended to other central and east European countries as they committed themselves to democratic principles and the introduction of market-based economies (see Tables 7.3 and 7.4). At the time, and up to the late 1990s, the PHARE programme was used to promote the restructuring and privatization of state-owned enterprises, the development of SMEs, the modernization of financial systems, the development of services such as tourism, and the consolidation of liberal democracy. None of this was linked to meeting the Copenhagen criteria. Since 1997, however, there has been a reorientation of PHARE spending towards accession. Hence, 70% of its annual budget of €1 billion is now used to assist in the adaptation of national legislation to the *acquis communautaire*, while the remaining 30% is being directed at reinforcing candidate countries' administrative and judicial capacities. Spending on the latter is vital for the candidate countries, given the increasing emphasis that the Commission is placing in its regular reports on their capacity, not only to adapt to EU legislation, but also to ensure its effective implementation and enforcement.

In addition to PHARE, the EU's financial assistance for candidate countries comes in the form of the pre-accession aid announced in *Agenda 2000*. This has been made available since the beginning of 2000 and is divided between two "instruments". The first is the Instrument for Structural Policies for Pre-Accession (ISPA), which is worth €1.040 billion a year, and is used to help candidate countries develop their environmental and transport infrastructures, and align them with those of the EU. The second instrument, the Special Accession Programme for Agriculture and Rural Development (SAPARD), is focused on providing assistance for structural adjustments in agriculture and rural areas, as well as the implementation of the *acquis* governing the Common Agricultural Policy. The European Investment Bank is also active in providing loans for priority investments designed to facilitate the adoption of the *acquis* and to strengthen integration with the EU. Loans are usually made available for infrastructure projects and regional development.

Beyond direct financial support, the accession process has seen the introduction of "twinning", designed to assist candidate countries in developing modern and efficient domestic administrations. In this process, advisers from the member states are seconded to candidate countries on a long-term basis to work alongside their counterparts on projects involving the transposition, enforcement, and implementation of a specific part of the *acquis communautaire*. Initial priority sectors included agriculture, the environment, finance, and justice and home affairs.

Preparing the EU: The Need for Reform

Preparing the candidate countries for accession is clearly important if enlargement is to take place and the acceding countries are to take on successfully the obligations of membership on joining the EU. However, enlargement also requires preparations on the part of the EU, since adding new members has an impact, not only on the size and functioning of institutions, but also on the sustainability of policies in their existing forms, particularly where they consume large proportions of the budget and enlargement involves the admission of relatively poor countries. The need for the EU to prepare itself for any enlargement has long been recognized. In the past, enlargements have been relatively small, involving no more than three new members at a time, and the financial costs have been affordable. In the case of what is primarily eastward enlargement, however, the number of candidate countries is much greater and they are generally much poorer. Hence, the need for preparations is much greater. There are two main areas in which preparations are necessary.

The first area comprises the EU's institutions and its decision-making processes. Admitting more members will mean more Commissioners, more representatives speaking and voting in the Council, and more seats in the European Parliament. It will also mean greater difficulty in agreeing matters where unanimity is required. There are also issues concerning the balance of power between small and large member states, as well as the rotation of the Council presidency to include the smallest member states. It is widely acknowledged that such issues have to be addressed if the EU is to retain a credible and functioning capacity for making decisions and formulating policies. Hence, reforms have long been proposed, often focusing on increased majority voting in some form, the reduction of unanimous voting to an absolute minimum, and the capping of the size of the Commission and the European Parliament. The history of the EU's efforts to prepare itself for enlargement has, however, been characterized by general failure to agree vital reforms. As already noted, the IGC of 1996 failed to address them, deferring discussion to the 2000 IGC, which led to the Treaty of Nice (2001). As noted in Chapter 4, although the latter conference has been heavily criticized for the limited progress made with regard to institutional reform, it did restate the EU's commitment to enlargement and introduce sufficient reforms to pave the way for at least some candidate countries to join the EU. Yet the reform process is far from over. A further IGC scheduled for 2004, could remedy Nice's shortcomings and thus genuinely prepare the EU for the substantially increased membership, accommodating both candidate states already in negotiation and other countries beyond those likely to be admitted by 2005 (see below).

Some progress has also been made with regard to the second area where preparations for enlargement is needed: the reform of the EU's largest redistributive mechanisms, namely the Common Agricultural Policy (CAP) and the Structural Funds (see Chapters 13 and 14). With relatively poor countries about to join the EU, either more money would have to be found to pay for their full participation in these areas or the policies themselves would have to undergo substantial, if not radical, reform. Given the reluctance of existing member states, notably Germany, to increase their contributions to the EU budget, the latter course of action was the only one available. This the Commission recognized in *Agenda 2000*, in which it outlined proposals for the reform of both the CAP and the Structural Funds. During the course of 1997–98 these were developed further and formally presented to the member states for approval. Following often heated discussion and debate, reforms were finally adopted once the European Council, meeting in Berlin in March 1999, had agreed a new Financial Perspective for 2000–06 (see Chapter 12). Opposition to anything more than minimal reform meant that the outcome with regard to the CAP was far less radical than the Commission had originally proposed. This opened up the possibility that the policy would require further reform before enlargement (see Chapter 13). Preparing itself for the admission of new member states has proved to be a major challenge for the EU. It is a challenge to which it has risen reluctantly and not always successfully.

The Challenges Ahead

Assuming that the Treaty of Nice is ratified and that accession negotiations are successfully concluded, a first group of candidate countries should start joining the EU in 2003–04. Indeed, the Treaty of Nice envisages some countries that are now candidates participating in the elections for the European Parliament in 2004. In addition, enlargement-related changes in the weighting of votes in the Council and the size of Commission enter into force on 1 January 2005. Other candidate countries should then follow once they are in a position to assume the obligations of membership.

This at least is how the enlargement process has been conceived. However, in recent years it has become increasingly evident that enlargement may not proceed so smoothly. The EU has already experienced considerable difficulties in adopting policy and institutional reform. The piecemeal approach followed to date means that similar difficulties will have to be faced in the future, as the EU seeks to prepare itself for the admission of more states. Beyond these issues, there are other challenges that seem increasingly likely to have an impact on the speed and extent of enlargement.

A first challenge involves maintaining support for enlargement among member states and in the EP. Several have shown limited enthusiasm for admitting new members, particularly if this is perceived to threaten the possibilities for closer integration, or to result in a decline in financial transfers. The Spanish government in particular has often indicated that it might oppose enlargement if it feels that it is, in effect, having to pay for enlargement through lower receipts from the Structural Funds. In addition, there are bilateral issues that have the potential to derail the enlargement process. The Austrian government is reluctant to see the Czech Republic admitted to the EU unless it can guarantee the safety of the Temelin nuclear power plant. Greece threatens to veto eastward enlargement unless Cyprus is admitted to the EU. Finally, it should be noted that a candidate country can only join the EU once the EP has approved its accession treaty. In the past, the EP has indicated that it might oppose a country's accession where there is concern over its human rights record and/or over the impact of enlargement on the prospects for integration within the EU. Although the EP has tended to be a major advocate of enlargement in recent years, this could change.

The second challenge involves ensuring popular support for the admission of new members. Enlargement has aroused little interest among electorates within the EU. The voters who have counted have been those in the applicant countries, where referenda have often taken place to decide whether the terms of accession should be accepted. Except twice in the case of Norway, voters have endorsed membership. Opinion polls within the current candidate countries generally show consistently solid levels of support for the EU (see Table 7.5) and there is little reason to doubt at this stage that governments will succeed in convincing electorates to approve the outcome of accession negotiations when the time arrives. All the same, opposition to membership is growing in some candidate countries, notably Poland, where dissatisfaction with the speed of negotiations is causing frustration and farmers express fears of increased competition with producers in western Europe as a consequence of accession. All the same, the big challenge for the EU does not really lie in projecting a positive image so that voters in candidate countries approve membership. Rather, it lies in convincing electorates in the existing member states that enlargement is a worthwhile process that can benefit all.

That electorates need convincing reflects, first, the fact that support for enlargement is generally low. Surveys conducted for *Eurobarometer* in the autumn of 2000 suggest that on average only 44% of people within the EU are in favour of enlargement (see Figure 7.1), while opposition stands on average at 35%. Such figures do not reflect the often significantly different levels of support both for individual candidate countries and within individual member states. In Austria, for example, there is almost majority support for admitting Hungary, yet much less support for admitting Romania. Indeed, within the EU opposition to the admission of countries such as Romania, Slovenia, and Turkey clearly outweighs support. Interestingly, the only countries for which there is overwhelming support are Switzerland and Norway, neither of which are candidates at present.

The need to convince electorates of the benefits of enlargement has also been affected by the possibility that some member states' governments could subject decisions on which countries join the EU to referenda. Constitutionally, no member state is obliged to hold a referendum on enlargement, but since the early 1990s the use of referenda in Europe has increased as popular votes have been seen as a means of involving the people more fully in decision-making. Many referenda have focused on EU-related matters, notably treaty reform. This trend seems likely to continue as politicians promote referenda in an attempt to reduce the democratic deficit within the EU and to allow the people to express their views. In some cases, too, where domestic opposition to enlargement is high, member states' governments appear willing to let the people decide rather than impose unpopular decisions. Hence, Austria could well hold a referendum on enlargement and Germans too could be asked to vote on which candidate countries should be admitted if plans to reintroduce referenda, announced in 2000, are agreed.

A third challenge facing the EU in enlarging involves maintaining the momentum for enlargement. At present, there appears to be little prospect of the EU's failing to enlarge to include up to six candidate countries by 2005, but it remains unclear what the impact of an initial enlargement will be on the prospects for more candidate countries to be admitted. For example, the difficulties experienced in accommodating new members may deter the EU from proceeding swiftly to further enlargement. Further, newly admitted member states will not necessarily support plans for more candidates to be admitted. It would be inadvisable to assume that enlargement will be a smooth and continuous process.

Finally, the EU's insistence that accession is conditional on applicants' capacity to meet the Copenhagen criteria means that enlargement will depend as much on successful progress with economic and political reform within candidate countries as on the EU's preparations for coping with more new members. If reform processes falter then this is likely to lead to a candidate's membership prospects worsening and, by implication, to enlargement being limited to fewer countries. Simply starting accession negotiations does not guarantee that they will be concluded and that accession will ensue.

Conclusion

The prevailing view is that an initial round or wave of enlargement will take place some time between 2003 and 2005. Much will depend on the accession negotiations with the "ins" being successfully concluded and the treaties of accession ratified. Moreover, existing member states will have to ratify the Treaty of Nice. Without the institutional reforms detailed therein, the EU is unlikely to be able to function effectively with an enlarged membership. It is almost inconceivable, however, that enlargement will not go ahead. The political pressure on the EU is considerable and, given its publicly stated commitment to enlargement, not to admit new members by 2005 would entail a considerable loss of face.

Enlargement will not be an easy or unproblematic experience for the EU. Much progress has been made in helping the candidate countries to prepare for membership and further issues will be addressed before the first wave of countries is admitted. Yet enlargement involves much more than simply preparing the candidates and readying the EU. It creates new dynamics that will have an impact on how the EU continues to accommodate the aspirations both of the remaining candidate countries and of those that have yet to signal formally their intention to join. Enlargement now poses the single most important set of challenges for the EU. It can be expected to retain its prominent position on its agenda for many years to come.

Further Reading

Avery, Graham, and Fraser Cameron, *The Enlargement of the European Union*, Sheffield: Sheffield Academic Press/UACES, 1998

Written by Commission officials, this provides an overview of *Agenda 2000* and of initial reactions to the Commission's proposals.

Baun, Michael J., *A Wider Europe: The Process and Politics of European Union Enlargement*, Lanham, MD: Rowman and Littlefield, 2000

A detailed presentation of the EU's approach to eastward enlargement in the 1990s

Brabant, Jozef M. van (editor), *Remaking Europe: The European Union and the Transition Economies*, Lanham, MD: Rowman and Littlefield, 1999

A solid collection of essays examining the contrast between the EU's handling of enlargement and the central and east European countries' aspirations and expectations. The volume also explores the complexity of accession negotiations.

Croft, Stuart, *et al.*, *The Enlargement of Europe*, Manchester: Manchester University Press, 1999

A welcome comparison of various European organizations' attempts to deal with the increasing number of applications for membership since 1990

EC Commission, *Enlargement Homepage*, via europa. eu.int/comm/enlargement/

The Commission's website on enlargement, with links to all major reports and other documents

Grabbe, Heather, and Kirsty Hughes, *Enlarging the EU Eastwards*, London: Royal Institute of International Affairs, 1998

An analysis of the progress made in promoting integration between the EU and the countries of central and eastern Europe, and of the challenges faced by the EU in enlarging eastwards

Henderson, Karen (editor), *Back to Europe: Central and Eastern Europe and the European Union*, London: UCL Press, 1999

An accessible collection of essays on various aspects of the EU's relations with central and eastern Europe, including some chapters on specific candidate countries and policy areas

Mayhew, Alan, *Recreating Europe: The European Union's Policy Towards Central and Eastern Europe*, Cambridge and New York: Cambridge University Press, 1998

A detailed and highly informative examination by someone involved in the process of the EU's evolving relationship with countries in central and eastern Europe during the 1990s

Phinnemore, David, *Association: Stepping-Stone or Alternative to EU Membership*, Sheffield: Sheffield Academic Press/UACES, 1999

An introductory analysis of association, the main mechanism for European non-member states' relations with the EU short of membership

Preston, Christopher, *Enlargement and Integration in the European Union*, London and New York: Routledge, 1997

Based on an analysis of previous enlargements, this widely cited text assesses the appropriateness of established EU approaches to enlargement for the challenges faced by the EU in admitting the current candidate countries.

Dr David Phinnemore is a Lecturer in the Institute of European Studies at the Queen's University, Belfast. His publications, in addition to the book listed above, include (as editor) *Post-Communist Romania: Coming to Terms with Transition* (2001); and (as co-editor) *European Union and European Community* (with Clive H. Church, 1995) and *Post-Communist Romania: Geographical Perspectives* (2000).

Table 7.1   Dates of Applications for EU Membership, 1987–96

Turkey	14 April 1987
Cyprus	4 July 1990
Malta	16 July 1990
Hungary	31 March 1994
Poland	5 April 1994
Romania	22 June 1995
Slovakia	22 June 1995
Latvia	13 October 1995
Estonia	24 November 1995
Lithuania	8 December 1995
Bulgaria	14 December 1995
Czech Republic	17 January 1996
Slovenia	10 June 1996

Table 7.2   Selected Data on Applicant Countries, various dates

	Population (millions), 1998	Surface area (thousands of square kilometres)	Agriculture (% of employment), 1993	GDP per capita at purchasing power parity (% of EU average), 1998	GDP growth (%), 1998	Inflation rate (%) 1998
Bulgaria	8.3	111	23.2	23	3.4	22.3
Czech Republic	10.3	79	6.3	60	−2.3	10.7
Estonia	1.4	45	13.1	36	4.0	8.2
Hungary	10.1	93	8.0	49	5.1	14.3
Latvia	2.4	65	18.5	27	3.6	4.7
Lithuania	3.7	65	23.8	31	5.1	5.1
Poland	38.7	313	26.9	39	5.0	11.8
Romania	22.5	238	34.4	27	−7.3	59.1
Slovakia	5.4	49	9.7	46	4.4	6.7
Slovenia	2.0	20	7.1	68	3.9	7.9
Cyprus	0.7	9.2	n.a.	77*	5.0	2.2
Malta	0.4	0.3	n.a.	n.a.	4.1	2.4
Turkey	63.4	775	n.a.	32	2.8	84.6

* 1997

Source: Eurostat

Table 7.3   PHARE Commitments, by Country, 1990–97

	€ millions	Proportion of total PHARE funds (%)
Albania	450.6	5.8
Bosnia–Herzegovina	250.3	3.3
Bulgaria	604.3	7.8
Czech Republic (since1993)	344.0	4.5
Czechoslovakia (to1993)	232.7	3.0
Estonia	134.3	1.7
Hungary	771.6	9.9
Latvia	174.1	2.3
Lithuania	228.2	3.0
Macedonia	142.4	1.8
Poland	1,536.3	19.8
Romania	824.4	10.6
Slovakia (since1993)	173.5	2.2
Slovenia	115.3	1.5
Multi-country	781.7	10.0
Other programmes	992.4	12.8
Total	7,756.1	100.0

Source: PHARE Website (http://europa.eu.int/comm/enlargement/pas/phare/wip/budget.htm)

Table 7.4   PHARE Commitments, by Sector, 1990–98

	€ millions
Public health	106
Social development and health	273
Integrated regional measures	340
Private sector, restructuring, SMEs	1,156
Consumer protection	13
Approximation of laws	84
Infrastructure	2,146
Humanitarian aid	533
Financial sector	269
Environment and nuclear safety	753
Education, training, and research	1,012
Civil society	105
Agriculture	563
Administration and public institutions	761
Other	778
Total	8,892

Source: EC Commission, *European Union Enlargement: An Historic Opportunity*, Brussels: EC Commission, 2000

Table 7.5	Net Difference Between "Yes" Votes and "No" Votes in Reported Voting Intentions in a Referendum on EU Membership in Candidate Countries in Central and Eastern Europe	
Hungary	+ 47	
Poland	+ 54	
Romania	+ 65	
Slovakia	+ 54	
Latvia	+ 27	
Estonia	+ 21	
Lithuania	+ 27	
Bulgaria	+ 53	
Czech Republic	+ 36	
Slovenia	+ 39	

Source: EC Commission, *Central and Eastern Eurobarometer 8*, Brussels: EC Commission, 1998

Figure 7.1 Support for Enlargement in EU Member States in Autumn 2000

Reported responses to the question "What is your opinion of the following statement: the European Union should be enlarged and include new countries. Please tell me whether you are for or against it?"

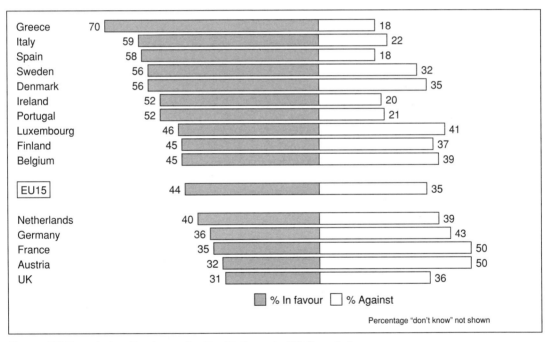

Source: EC Commission, *Eurobarometer No. 54*, Brussels: EC Commission

**Figure 7.2   Position on the Accession Negotiations with the Candidate States
in June 2001**

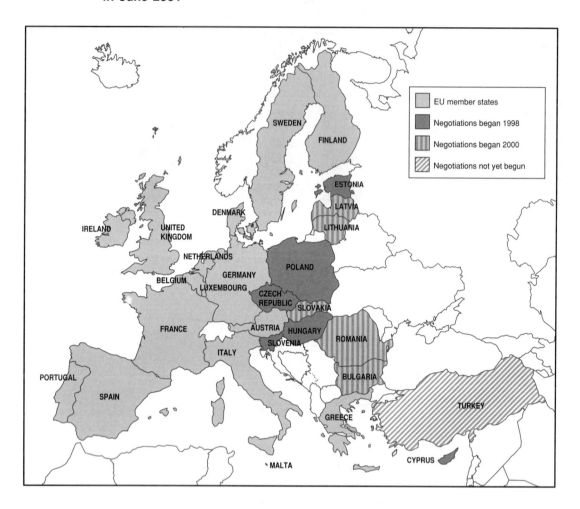

Economics
and
Policies

Chapter Eight

Theories of Regional Economic Integration and the Global Economy

Andrew Scott

Economic integration describes the process whereby the economies of independent nation states unify progressively in response to the removal of barriers both to trade in goods and services (product markets), and to the movement of factors of production (factor markets). The degree of economic integration achieved between two or more countries is, therefore, directly linked to the extent to which restrictions to the free flow of goods, services, capital, and labour (the "four freedoms") are eliminated, and national product and factor markets are opened to international competition. The theory of international economic integration examines the economic effects that result from these measures. The crucial difference between the economic theory of integration on the one hand, and general international trade theory on the other, is that integration theory deals with situations in which national product and factor markets concessions are restricted to a specific group of countries, rather than being available to all trading partners. Its starting point, therefore, is the analysis of preferential trading arrangements in which a number of countries agree to eliminate obstacles to trade and factor flows between themselves, but also agree to retain restrictions against such flows originating outside the area. As the removal of national barriers to the "four freedoms" proceeds, the process of economic integration gathers pace until, in the final instance, national product and factor markets effectively combine to become a single market. One of the main sets of questions that the economic theory of integration addresses concerns the impact that these arrangements have on global economic welfare. In other words, assuming that global free trade results in the optimal allocation of productive resources and maximizes global economic welfare, what will be the impact on global economic welfare from a move to free trade that involves a limited number of countries under the guise of a preferential trading area? Is this likely to increase welfare or reduce it?

The EU is undeniably the most advanced model of economic integration in the world. Beginning as a preferential trading area in 1958, it has evolved into a single market in which goods, services, capital, and labour have the right to move between its 15 member states virtually without restriction. Yet the EU is much more than a single market. Alongside the elimination of barriers to the "four freedoms", the EU has developed an extensive range of "common" economic policies within a complex structure of governance that combines elements of interstate bargaining (intergovernmentalism) with constitutionally empowered transnational decision-making bodies (supranationalism). However, although unique in many senses, the EU is by no means a curiosity in the international economy. Indeed, one of the dominant features of contemporary global economic developments is the upsurge in the number of preferential trading arrangements being established. Moreover, because they almost always involve countries in close geographical proximity to each other, their increase is, at the same time, constitutive of an increase in *regional* trading arrangements. In turn, the more ambitious the free movement provisions within these regional trading arrangements, the higher the degree of regional economic integration – or "regionalism" – that will result. This raises another important question for students of international economics: what implications does this trend towards "regionalism" triggered by preferential trading arrangements hold for international economic relations generally and, specifically, for conventional channels of international commercial diplomacy? Does the proliferation of regional trading arrangements threaten to undermine the role of the World Trade Organization (WTO) as the guardian of the multilateral trading system? Indeed, does it challenge the existence of the form of multilateral trade negotiations that has delivered considerable gains since 1945?

In a review of regionalism, Jagdish Bhagwati (1993) has identified two periods during which regional trade arrangements flourished. The first occurred during the 1960s and followed the creation of the European Economic Community in 1958 – indeed, it was a reaction to that event. However, by the end of the decade only the EEC and the European Free Trade Area (EFTA) continued to function effectively as regional trading arrangements. Beyond western Europe, attempts at forming preferential trading arrangements, especially between developing countries, foundered, and there was little interest in these arrangements elsewhere in the industrialized world. The second wave of "regionalism", which Bhagwati anticipated lasting much longer, began in the early 1980s. In fact, not only has this second wave persisted, but since the mid-1990s it has intensified. The distinguishing feature of this "second wave" of integration, which in part accounts for its longevity, has been the conversion of the United States to the cause of regional trading arrangements, first with the Canada–US Trade Agreement (CUSTA) and subsequently through the creation of the North American Free Trade Area (NAFTA). The interest of the United States in regional trading arrangements shows no signs of abating, with the government engaged in ongoing discussions with its trading partners in Latin America and the Caribbean over the viability of establishing a "hemispheric" free trade area.

The reawakening of interest in regional economic integration during the 1980s has met with a mixed response. On the one hand, there are those who welcome this development as furthering the interests of global free trade and who regard preferential trading arrangements as an alternative – indeed a complementary – mechanism to multilateralism in securing progress along this road. Advocates of regional trading arrangements see them as pioneering developments that allow the limitations of multilateral trade negotiations to be overcome and point the direction that the multilateral trading system must take if further progress towards global free trade is to be achieved. On the other hand, there are critics who view regional trading arrangements as harbingers of a new era of discrimination in international commercial diplomacy, and, consequently, view them as being fundamentally at odds with stability and harmony in the international economic order. Critics stress the essentially discriminatory nature of their trade policies, and point to the economic power that a small number of these global "regions" command, which, in their view, can be used as a highly effective bargaining counter in global trade negotiations. They question where this trend leaves many of the world's weaker nations in vital discussions on trade policy, and what it implies for the future of the entire multilateral system.

The Stages of Integration

The phrase "economic integration" is used to describe a process in which the economies of independent countries are progressively unified as a result of the removal of barriers to trade. The theory of regional economic integration is a branch of international trade theory, which focuses on the economic gains and losses accruing to countries as barriers to trade and factor mobility are removed. Orthodox trade theory has to be modified in recognition of the fact that, in the case of regional economic integration, we are discussing an arrangement that involves preferential liberalization between a limited number of countries within the international community. As we discuss later, unlike moves towards universal free trade, under certain circumstances regional economic integration may impose welfare losses upon individual participating countries.

According to Bela Balassa (1961), economic integration can take one of five forms, each of which differs from the other in terms of the degree of integration involved: a free trade area, a customs union, a common market, an economic union, or total economic integration.

Free Trade Area

A free trade area describes a situation in which all barriers to trade in goods and services between participating countries are eliminated. Consequently, consumers will have access to the lowest-cost source of supply across the area as a whole and, as a result, will benefit from the welfare-enhancing gains from trade. As there is no requirement for members of a free trade area to harmonize their trade policies towards non-member countries, intra-area customs posts must be retained to avoid "trade deflection". Trade deflection occurs when a country that is not a member of the free trade area can circumvent import restrictions imposed by one of its members by exporting to that country via another member country that has a less restrictive import regime. Border posts provide an opportunity for ensuring that goods entering one country from another in the free trade area in fact originate in that partner country.

Customs Union

A customs union is equivalent to a free trade area, but in addition provides for the introduction of a common commercial policy with respect to non-member countries. Consequently, the problem of trade deflection does not arise in a custom union; a good or service imported into a customs union faces identical conditions of entry, regardless of the country through which it enters the area. In the absence of a potential for trade deflection, the economic rationale for border posts fades as the common commercial policy is established. As the central element in a country's commercial policy is its external tariff, the first step towards a common commercial policy is to establish a common external tariff. Thereafter, attention turns to harmonising all other, non-tariff measures of international commercial policy. Experience has shown that this latter stage is extremely difficult to achieve.

Common Market

A common market represents a customs union along with provision being made for the free movement of labour and capital. With the creation of a common market, therefore, the "four freedoms" are established: the free movement of goods, services, capital, and labour. A common market is sometimes described as an area in which there is integration between the national product and factor markets of the member countries.

Economic Union

An economic union goes beyond a common market in that it involves a degree of harmonization in economic policies within member states, to the extent required for the proper functioning of the common market. The distinction between a common market and an economic union is a fine one, and revolves around the implications for national economic policy associated with the economic union that are not apparent when constructing a common market. As Jacques Pelkmans (1980) pointed out, the first three stages of integration implicitly assume away a role for government. Integration proceeds through market liberalization – that is, by governments desisting from practices that discriminate against partner country imports solely on grounds of nationality. This phase is typically referred to as "negative" integration. However, when we turn to economic union, suddenly we are confronted with a wide range of economic policies devised and implemented by governments, many of which, by their nature, constitute obstacles to trade. These policies must be harmonized if the four freedoms are to be realized, bearing in mind that these policies themselves reflect an unwillingness of government to accept the outcomes generated by the unfettered operation of market forces. This is the much more complicated stage referred to as "positive" integration.

(See, for instance, Holland 1980 or Taylor 1983.)

Total Economic Integration

In the final stage of total economic integration, national economies effectively merge into one another to be supplanted by a single, unified "economy". A supranational authority decides all matters pertaining to economic policy – including fiscal and monetary policies – although a significant degree of policy autonomy can be retained at lower levels within the hierarchy of governance. (The literature on fiscal federalism sets criteria for the assignment of economic policies within a multilayered structure of governance: see Volume 2 of the MacDougall Report (CEC, 1977) for a comprehensive review of this literature. Scott *et al.* (1994) develop an approach, informed by this general literature, to the principle of subsidiarity, the EU equivalent on which there is debate at present.) The area is likely to be a currency union in which a single currency circulates and where all aspects of monetary policy are conducted by a common central bank.

Technically a group of countries can adopt any one of these five distinctive arrangements. For instance, the Treaty of Rome initially set the objective of achieving a common market, although with the ratification of the Treaty on European Union (the Maastricht Treaty) the EU aimed to become a monetary union. This objective was partially achieved on 1 January 1999, when 11 of the 15 member states adopted the euro as a common currency and control over monetary policy in those 11 countries was transferred to the European Central Bank. Greece joined the euro area on 1 January 2001, leaving only the United Kingdom, Denmark, and Sweden outside it. On the other hand, both EFTA and NAFTA are examples of free trade areas, and, in the case of NAFTA, there is a firm determination on the part of the United States that it should not proceed to any higher rung on the integration ladder. However, in practice it may be difficult to arrest the process of integration at a particular stage. Integration may well have an inherent dynamic that propels countries beyond their initial aims. This dynamic is likely to be more compelling the higher the stage of integration that is being sought. For instance, the harmonization of the many instruments of external commercial policy necessary to create a customs union must result in a greater erosion of national policy autonomy (and thus sovereignty) than will be the case in a free trade area. Similarly, the shift from a customs union to a common market necessarily means that national autonomy over a wider range of economic policy instruments will be compromised. For example, controls on the movement of capital are not compatible with the "four freedoms" that define a common market. If capital controls are there to protect the exchange rate, their removal will necessitate closer approximation of monetary policies between the participating countries if the objective of exchange rate stability (which explains the use of capital controls) is to be maintained. This is the idea of "functional spillover", which was central to the neofunctionalist account of the building of political integration from economic foundations (see Chapter 3 and Moravscik (1993) for a critical review of the processes involved). The specific issue of monetary unification in the EU as an example of functional spillover was dealt with at length in the report by a group of experts under the chairmanship of Tomaso Padoa-Schioppa (see Padoa-Schioppa *et al.*).

Integration and Economic Efficiency

The Static Effects of International Integration

The orthodox economic analysis of international integration originated in the work of Jacob Viner (1950). Until then, the general assumption was that regional economic integration must, by definition, always be beneficial as it serves to move the world closer to the optimum situation of universal free trade – and it is a commonplace that efficiency in the allocation of global resources can only be maximized under free trade. Viner, however, established that the static (or impact) effects of international integration – the once-and-for-all gains or losses, as opposed to recurring "dynamic" effects – could in fact be either welfare-enhancing or, under certain conditions, welfare-reducing. The welfare-enhancing effects derive from trade creation, while the welfare-reducing effects result from trade diversion.

Trade creation arises when, upon membership of a customs union, consumers in the home country switch from a high-cost domestic supplier to a lower-cost source of supply in a partner country. This switch in consumption patterns results from the change in the relative price of imports from the partner country *vis-à-vis* home produce following the elimination of intra-area tariffs. By definition, therefore, trade creation leads to greater efficiency in the allocation of resources within the customs union and increases economic welfare accordingly. Trade diversion, on the other hand, reduces economic welfare as it involves a switch in consumption away from a low-cost supplier outside the customs union to a higher-cost source of supply in a partner country. In that case, resources within the customs union are diverted to produce an increased supply of a product that can be produced more efficiently outside it. This results in a less efficient allocation of union-wide resources and reduces welfare accordingly. Trade diversion will arise when, upon membership of a customs union, a country increases its protection against imports from non-member countries beyond the level prevailing prior to membership of the customs union (see Swann for a comprehensive analysis of customs union theory).

Typically, the formation of a customs union will involve elements of both trade creation and trade diversion, with the net effect on economic welfare being determined by the relative magnitudes of each. In practice, economists have found the magnitudes of these static effects to be relatively small. In the most studied case, that of the EU, trade creation has been estimated at less than 1% of the EU's aggregate GDP, while the magnitude of trade diversion has been significantly below this level. Further, the static effects of economic integration are nonrecurring: they are once-and-for-all effects and must be set against the considerably more important dynamic effects of integration, which are not captured by Viner's comparative static approach.

The Dynamic Effects of International Integration

A common criticism of Viner's contribution to the theory of international integration is that economic integration has important dynamic effects that are not captured in the comparative static framework that he developed. Consequently, that approach would inevitably underestimate the overall welfare effects arising from the creation of a customs union. The dynamic effects of integration are those that influence the rate of economic growth of the members of that union. These are, therefore, recurring effects and will have an impact upon the underlying rate of economic growth for the area. The dynamic effects are expected to be positive for the customs union as a whole, although not necessarily for every member of that union. There are two principal sources of dynamic gain.

The first is economies of scale in production. Scale economies describe a situation in which long-run unit costs of production decrease as the scale of production increases. Economies of scale are directly related to market size. Where the available market becomes larger, following the creation of a common market, firms will be able to increase output and exploit opportunities for cost savings in production. Assuming competitive conditions are maintained, as average unit cost of production falls, consumers will benefit through the resulting decline in product price. Moreover, the decline in price will result in an increase in both internal and external demand, which will stimulate investment activity and, consequently, raise the rate of economic growth for the union as a whole.

The second dynamic gain associated with a customs union directly derives from the intensification of competition between firms following the elimination of barriers to trade. As domestic firms find that their hitherto protected national market is being increasingly contested by partner-country rivals, managerial and organizational inefficiencies will be eliminated, with consequent benefits to consumers. In the literature, this dynamic gain is commonly called the "cold shower" thesis, although formally it involves the expulsion of X-inefficiencies – that category of losses attributable to managerial, and related, underperformance.

Some authorities add a third form of dynamic gains, those arising from an improvement in research and technological development following the creation of a customs union. The argument here is that a firm may react to intensified competition by devoting a greater volume of resources to factors that enhance the non-price competitiveness of their products. Both process and product technologies fall into this category. To the extent that this effect does occur, we would anticipate that creating a customs union would increase the pace of technological change for the area as a whole. Further, the pace of technological development might increase if the customs union leads to an increase in the average size of firms, to the extent that larger firms devote a greater volume of resources to research and development than smaller firms do. In practice, however, researchers have found difficulty in drawing clear conclusions concerning any link between economic integration and the pace of technological change (for a full discussion of this in relation to European integration, see Emerson *et al.* pp. 157–62).

Each of these three sources of dynamic gain from economic integration has considerable intuitive appeal. However, each is essentially unmeasurable, principally because it is not possible to attribute any change in efficiency, or intensified research and development activity, directly to the creation of a customs union. Consequently, the literature tends simply to assume that the dynamic effects of economic integration are positive from the perspective of the union as a whole and that, for any particular member state, any static loss attributable to trade diversion is more than fully compensated by dynamic benefits.

Negative and Positive Integration

To conceptualize the practical process of economic integration, we need to extend the analysis beyond the confines of international trade theory. This is because economic integration is, in the final instance, a policy-related – and so a political – process. Moreover, the "higher" the stage of integration that is sought, the more

the integration process will spill over into the sphere of economic policy, and thus into domestic politics, raising the prospect of conflicts arising between different domestic constituencies. At the same time, differences in policy preferences between the countries participating in the integration arrangement are likely to emerge as common approaches to particular policy issues are considered, this being necessary to achieve the "four freedoms". In that event, much will depend upon the procedures for decision-making and dispute-settlement that have been devised to facilitate and promote the integration process. The EU has the most sophisticated institutions of any regional integration scheme, which include, among others, a common policy-making process over a significant range of matters of mutual concern, including external trade policy, and an independent Court of Justice, which upholds the legal order of the EU.

The explicitly political dimension to economic integration arises initially from the need to adjust national economic policies in order that a "common market" can be established. As we have discussed previously, the case for harmonizing national policies to achieve a common market is most obvious in, for example, the case of external commercial policy or competition policy. Yet policy harmonization typically extends over a much wider range of economic policy instruments, ultimately embracing all those policies that may favour producers in one country over their competitors elsewhere in the common market. Indirect taxation, regulations governing conditions of employment, and social policy are all examples of policy instruments of this type. Generally, the more interventionist governments are, the greater is the need for harmonization of policies between the participating countries. Political problems arise, however, when governments, in adjusting national policies to conform to the agreed common position, find that harmonization can be secured only at the expense of domestic objectives. At that stage domestic political debate will intensify and opponents of the integration are likely to assert that integration necessarily involves an unacceptable loss of national sovereignty.

Within the literature this problem is captured by positing a dichotomy between "negative integration" and "positive integration". "Negative integration" describes the removal of impediments to the free movement of goods, services, capital and labour: that is, it refers to the process of dismantling the obstacles to the establishment of a common market. It has been referred to as a set of "thou shalt not" rules (Holland pp. 10–14) The term is also used to describe changes in public policy that liberalize the operation of market forces in pursuance of economic integration: governments may have to abandon specific policy instruments as these are incompatible with membership of the common market. Negative integration is generally relatively uncontroversial among economists as, by strengthening the role of market forces, it holds out the prospect of gains in economic welfare through improved resource allocation.

The process of negative integration alone will be insufficient to create a common market. Real economies are governed by a vast array of rules, regulations, and other public policies that, collectively, represent a significant obstacle to international economic integration: national health and safety regulations, preferential public procurement, industrial policies, antimonopoly regulations, and a range of domestic tax and subsidy arrangements. The need to harmonize these policies and to develop a common approach arises because otherwise they would undermine free and fair competition within the customs union, even though claims may be made to the contrary. This is "positive integration": a set of agreed "thou shalt do" rules (see Holland). "Positive integration" describes that stage in the integration process at which the harmonization of the relevant national policies is necessary in order that the common market can function effectively.

The negative–positive dichotomy itself offers no insight as to the mechanism of policy harmonization. This will be determined by the institutional arrangements within the particular example of integration under consideration. Nor does it explain the nature or aims of the common policies ultimately adopted. Positive integration simply describes that phase

in the process of economic integration when the limit to integration by "negative" means is encountered, and a common "positive" policy response is required. It also represents the moment in the process when governments will be confronted with erosion of their constitutional sovereignty. No longer will a government be free unilaterally to introduce public policies without considering their impact on the integration process. Thereafter, the joint interests of all the members of the customs union will shape national policy in areas where it has been agreed that a common policy approach is necessary.

Considering international integration in terms of the "negative" and "positive" dimensions of the process facilitates a clearer appreciation of the substantive political issues that accompany integration. For instance, although the Treaty of Rome set out the conditions required for a common market to be established, it was not until the end of 1992, some 34 years later, that a truly unified market was realized. In part, the delay was attributable to the unwillingness of member states to adjust domestic policies to the extent required for the creation of a common market. In turn, this reluctance demonstrates the influence that national interests play in the domestic political arena.

Consequently, the pace at which integration proceeds is determined, in part, by the political realities of the participating countries themselves. Of course, the political realities confronting member states can change over time, and this will influence the pace of integration. For example, in the early part of the 1980s concerns about the decline in the competitive position of European Community producers in global markets was directly responsible for changing national attitudes about the importance of achieving comprehensive market integration within the Community. Member state governments came to explain the erosion of the global competitiveness of domestic firms as being the result of the fragmentation of the Community's internal market, a fragmentation caused by the large number of nontariff barriers preventing intra-Community trade. If these barriers were removed, producers would be able to enjoy the dynamic gains from integration, and this would, in turn, enhance corporate competitiveness, and lead to job creation and faster economic growth. The case for liberalizing the internal market from government restrictions was restated, was found by decision-makers to be persuasive, and culminated in the presentation of the single European market programme. In that sense, the single market programme represented a revival in "negative integration" rather than continuing with attempts at "positive integration". The limits to negative integration had been rolled back.

Regional Economic Integration and the Global Economy

As we noted at the beginning of this chapter, the creation of preferential trading agreements on a regional basis has been one of the dominant features of the international economy in recent years. In 2000, the WTO reported that some 214 regional agreements for trade in goods or services had been notified to it, of which 90 had been implemented since 1995 alone. Clearly, the formation of regional trading arrangements is an increasing force in the organization of global trade. In fact, by now nearly all of the WTO's 136 member countries are involved in at least one regional trading arrangement, and each member is on average involved in five such arrangements. The value of trade among countries participating in regional trade arrangements currently accounts for more than 50% of total world trade. It is not only the rising incidence of regional trading agreements that makes them a significant development. In addition, the terms of many of these agreements go beyond the creation of local free trade arrangements and include provisions for intra-area cooperation on trade-related issues, for example on national public procurement policies, investment, environmental standards, competition policy, and state aid to industry. These are key matters, which so far have been excluded from (or not fully discussed in) multilateral trade diplomacy and, therefore, lie outside the ambit of the WTO.

The recent proliferation of regional trade agreements, in conjunction with the trend for them to include rules on trade-related policies and internal dispute resolution procedures, has led to a broader debate on their impact on the prevailing arrangements of multilateral commercial diplomacy, at the heart of which stands the WTO. One view is that regional trade arrangements are to be regarded as the "building blocks" of an emerging international system in which there is greater liberalization of international trade. This argues that regional trade arrangements are able to move towards trade liberalization faster than the multilateral trading system, and finds support from WTO studies showing there has been a definite trend toward broader as well as faster liberalization of market access, through the removal of nontariff barriers, under regional rather than WTO arrangements. In other words, the aims of regional trade agreements are regarded as being consistent with the WTO, and indeed strengthen the multilateral trading system. Critics of this view instead view regional trading arrangements as "stumbling blocks" to greater liberalization of trade. Because these arrangements are essentially discriminatory towards third countries, they are liable to generate international disputes, which will be to the detriment of the continued growth of world trade. Further, the recent dramatic growth in the numbers of regional trade arrangements, along with the extent to which countries increasingly are members of a number of them, is creating significant complexities over issues such as rules of origin and national policies on trade-related matters, which is also likely to have negative effects on world trade.

The "Threat" from Regional Trade Agreements

There are a number of interlinked arguments, advanced both by international trade theorists and by policy-makers, that collectively portray regional trade agreements as being inimical to the long-term viability of the orthodox multilateral trading system overseen by the WTO. It is important to understand why *preferential* trading arrangements (regional trade agreements) can arise within a system of commercial diplomacy that has, since the signing in 1947 of the General Agreement on Tariffs and Trade

(GATT), developed on the basis of the principle of nondiscrimination in trade policy between participating countries. This principle remains at the core of the WTO, which replaced the GATT in 1995 following the conclusion of the Uruguay Trade Round. In the immediate postwar era, the primary aim of international commercial diplomacy was the elimination of physical barriers to trade, that is, of tariffs and quotas. To this end the first Article of the GATT elaborated the "most favoured nation" principle of trade policy to which all signatories to the GATT were required to conform. This states that a signatory (contracting party) to the GATT must extend to all other signatories the same treatment with respect to tariffs and quotas that it extends to its most favoured trading partner. The sole exception to the most favoured nation principle at that time was under the provisions of Article 24, which allowed two or more countries to establish a local free trade area, that is, a preferential trading area, without extending this zero-tariff to other GATT members (otherwise no country would have opted to participate in a free trade area). Article 24 reflected the conventional wisdom of the time that local free trade agreements were desirable as they represented a move (albeit limited) towards global free trade (see Finger for a full discussion of Article 24). Later, a further exemption to the most favoured nation principle was introduced to enable developed economies to extend trade preferences to imports of certain produce from less developed countries. One leading trade theorist, Jagdish Bhagwati, has commented that although Article 24 makes regional trade agreements and thus regional economic integration schemes "GATT-consistent", ultimately such schemes "may be considered threatening to GATT's basic conception of the world trading system" (Bhagwati 1991 p. 58). The source of this perceived threat is the essentially discriminatory nature of regional trade agreements and their implications for the future of international commercial diplomacy.

The thrust of the attack on economic integration can be easily summarized (see Lal for a good exposition of this argument). The fear is that regional trade arrangements undermine the core method of multilateral commercial diplomacy that has delivered enormous advances in trade liberalization throughout the postwar era. At the heart of that method is reciprocity in trade liberalization and observance of a common, rule-based regime in which "trade rules extend without discrimination to all members of the trading regime . . ." (Bhagwati 1992 p. 443). Regionalism is viewed as antithetical to this multilateral trading system for four reasons. First, regional trading agreements create large trading blocs that are likely to be protectionist and thus put at risk the continued development of free trade and the position of the WTO. Secondly, trading blocs are likely to spawn yet more trading blocs as countries react strategically to prevent the possible accretion of economic power to a particular region. Thirdly, regional trading blocks are less likely to use WTO machinery in trade negotiations and dispute settlement, preferring instead direct bilateral contact, which heightens the risk of confrontation between blocs and carries with it the attendant danger of periodic trade wars between blocs at the expense of global economic welfare. Finally, as regional trade arrangements proliferate, there will be an incentive for every country to participate in one or more schemes because they fear that the multilateral trading system is no longer effective in representing their interests.

Together these arguments combine to present a powerful indictment of regional trade arrangements. Is this an accurate portrayal of their effects? Following Bhagwati (1993 p. 33), we can divide these four criticisms into two groups. First is the straightforward claim that regional trade arrangements are discriminatory to third countries and result in trade diversion that lowers global economic welfare. Secondly, regional trade arrangements generate an unstable trajectory for the development of international trade policy and, crucially, undermine the authority of the WTO. In that way they put the future of the multilateral trading system in jeopardy.

However, it is not self-evident that a regional trade arrangement serves to reduce economic welfare. This is an empirical question that can only be answered by comparing the degree to which new trade is created and existing trade diverted as a consequence of a regional trade arrangement being established or a current arrangement being enlarged. Article 24 of the GATT sought to insure against the latter by requiring that the common external tariff, and "other regulations of commerce", consequent upon the formation of a customs union, "shall not on the whole be higher or more restrictive than the general incidence of ... [those] applicable in the constituent territories prior to the formation of ... or the adoption of such interim agreement" (cited in Finger p. 131).

Indeed, as noted by Sapir (1993), the empirical record from the European experience suggests that – excepting trade in foodstuffs – the static effects of integration have been positive: that is, welfare-enhancing trade creation in industrial goods has exceeded welfare-reducing trade diversion in agricultural products for the EU as a whole. More generally, Richard E. Baldwin has noted that "almost all empirical studies of European and North American [regional trade agreements] find positive impacts on members' living standards and inconsequential impacts on non-members' living standards". Nonetheless, some critics insist that, given the nontransparent nature of contemporary trade policy instruments – such as antidumping duties and voluntary export restraints – regional trade agreements are likely to be trade-diverting in their overall impact. In his critique of such agreements, and the use of "new protectionist" instruments such as antidumping actions and voluntary export restraints, Bhagwati asserts (Bhagwati 1993 pp. 36–37) that:

> countries today have access to selective and elastic instruments of protection. Given this reality, even the modification of Article 24, to ensure that external (explicit and implicit) tariff barriers come down as a price for customs unions to be allowed under the GATT rules, will leave open a big, gaping hole that would be tantamount to an open invitation to trade diversion by these preferential arrangements ... [i]t is well-known that the EC has used antidumping actions and voluntary export restraints profusely to erect Fortress Europe against the Far East.

Bhagwati's second line of attack on preferential trade arrangements raises a different question, namely, to what extent is the trend to more, and increasingly complex, regional trade agreements a more or less viable method of advancing the cause of trade liberalization than is a reinvigoration of multilateral commercial diplomacy within the framework of the WTO. On a very basic level this argument appeared to have lost some of its potency simply because the WTO was successfully established with the conclusion of the Uruguay Trade Round. The WTO served precisely to reinvigorate the framework of the multilateral trading system, with multilateral trade diplomacy being extended into new areas of trade, especially trade in services, and of trade-related policy, while the dispute settlement powers of the WTO are considerably stronger than those that were available under the GATT. In that sense the claims that "regionalism" was undermining "multilateralism" were clearly exaggerated.

Yet this has not silenced the critics, who have been alarmed by the significant acceleration in the number of regional trade arrangements formed since 1995. Indeed, concern over their impact led the WTO in 1996 to establish a Committee on Regional Trade Agreements (CRTA), with a remit to examine the consistency of regional trade agreements with WTO rules, and to look at how they might affect the multilateral trading system and what the relationship between these two arrangements might be. If we consider the first issue, the chief problems revolve around the number and complexity of regional trade arrangements, and the lack of transparency with regard to the impact that their trade and other policies are having on third countries, especially the world's poorer ones. With the upsurge in the number of new agreements, and given the trend for countries to sign more and more separate bilateral ones, the coordination of global trade policy becomes highly problematic and the risk of systemic confusion increases. Further, although all regional trade agreements have to be notified to the WTO and observe the requirement of Article 24 of the GATT (and, since 1995, Article 5 of the General Agreement on Trade in Services, or GATS), it has become virtually impossible to assess whether or not all those notified are compatible with WTO rules, and whether they continue to be as membership of a regional trade agreement changes (for example, through the enlargement of the EU).

On the second issue, the relationship between regional trade agreement rules and WTO rules is unclear. With the multiplication of regional trade arrangements and the growth in overlapping membership, a trend has emerged for their networks to become increasingly "constitutionalized" – that is, based on rules that can be enforced by binding judicial arrangements, and that, implicitly or explicitly, take precedence over WTO rules and dispute settlement procedures. In this environment there is no clear understanding of exactly how regional trade arrangements interact with the multilateral trading system.

The "Opportunities" of Regional Economic Integration

The persuasiveness of the view that "regionalism" presents a threat to the liberalization of global trade derives in part from the appeal that it makes to the central tenets of orthodox international trade theory. Accordingly, while it is possible to conceive of a customs union that is not welfare-reducing either for participating or non-participating countries (see Kemp and Wan), it is at the same time also possible to show that welfare for any country participating in a regional trade agreement will be higher if, instead of granting trade preferences to a few countries, it engaged in a policy of *nonpreferential* trade liberalization within the multilateral trading system (see Ethier and Horn). Consequently, as regional trade arrangements are held to lack a robust theoretical justification, it is unsurprising that the trend towards greater regionalism has been viewed by some as driven by ulterior, usually protectionist motives. However, going beyond the theoretical debate, the most potent argument favouring multilateral commercial diplomacy rather than regional trade agreements is the enormous success that multilateralism has had, first under the GATT and now under the WTO, in dismantling obstacles to international trade. However, it is with the assertion that regional economic integra-

tion necessarily is inferior to, and incompatible with, the multilateral trading system that many "non-critics" of regionalism take issue. A number of less extreme positions can be detected within the literature (for a thorough review of the arguments see Cable and Henderson).

One argument regards regional economic integration as a mechanism for eliminating, on a limited geographic scale, a wide range of trade barriers that the WTO simply is unable to tackle. This is especially true in the case of many nontariff barriers to trade in both goods and services, such as those taking the form of divergent national rules, product standards, or procurement practices. A good example of this is the EU's single market programme, which aimed at eliminating all intra-EU obstacles to the free movement of goods, services, capital, and persons by 31 December 1992. The objective was indeed achieved, albeit with a few notable exceptions. Although the success of the single market programme can be attributed to a number of factors, undoubtedly one of these is the collective nature of EU decision-making and the role assigned to the European Court of Justice, which is to uphold and enforce Community law in each member state. Certainly, the single market programme improved the level of economic welfare for EU member states, and was compatible with the aims of the multilateral trading system. In this vein, Woolcock concluded that "the EC and multilateral *acquis* have, on balance, been mutually supportive" (Woolcock p. 540). At the same time, however, international trade theory is unable to explain why an individual country should opt for membership of a regional trade agreement, rather than eliminate nontariff barriers to trade in a multilateral forum. This accounts for the view some critics took of the single market programme, that it was intended to create a protectionist "Fortress Europe". Accordingly, the distinction made by Vincent Cable (1994) between "open" and "closed" variants of regionalism is undoubtedly a highly significant one in this debate, where "open" regionalism is supportive to the multilateral trading system and the latter inimical to it. Armed with that distinction, at least two further explanations can be advanced to explain the attraction of regional trade arrangements.

First, members of a regional trade arrangement might well find it easier to introduce legally binding dispute settlement procedures within the arrangement than would be possible within the broad multilateral trading system. Consequently, the process of regional liberalization of trade would be faster than within its multilateral counterpart. For instance, the European Court of Justice (ECJ) arbitrates in instances of dispute between EU member states and its decisions are binding upon them all, even where the ECJ decision conflicts with domestic law. Under this arrangement, the influence of domestic pressure groups, which may be hostile to trade policy reforms, is likely to be considerably reduced. While no other regional trade arrangement has an arbitration procedure comparable to the EU's, many of them do incorporate dispute settlement procedures that are more effective than those available to the WTO.

Secondly, regional integration may be a consequence simply of economic geography rather than a strategic move designed to effect a change in the global distribution of economic activity. That is, countries that are neighbours tend to trade with each other more intensively than non-neighbours do and, consequently, encounter the limits inherent to the multilateral trading system sooner than non-neighbouring trading partners do. The potential (local) economic gains from overcoming these limits may be considerable. For example, transport costs or shared cultural characteristics are both factors explaining why trade might grow more rapidly between neighbouring countries than between non-neighbours (see Krugman, and also Thomsen, for fuller discussions of this point). Where the limits to the multilateral trading rules are encountered, regional trade agreements can be seen as a device to facilitate the further development of "neighbourly" trade by providing for the elimination of the types of impediments to trade that are not addressed so effectively by the multilateral trading system. Moreover, regional agreements may be preferred to multilateralism because they can include financial mechanisms that compensate those parts of the total area damaged by the liberalization of trade. The EU's structural funds play precisely such a role.

Compensation at the global level would not be feasible.

Conclusions

The current debate surrounding the proliferation of preferential trading arrangements and regional integration schemes continues to dominate many of the learned journals. However, with the successful conclusion of the Uruguay Round of multilateral trade talks and the establishment of the WTO, it seems that at least some of the dangers seen to be associated with regionalism have been avoided. Indeed, in the current environment it is more likely that regional arrangements are capable of providing approaches and models that could usefully be imitated by global agencies as they continue to promote the liberalization of international trade. In 1995 a study conducted by the WTO concluded that: "To a much greater extent than is often acknowledged, regional and multilateral integration initiatives are complements rather than alternatives in the pursuit of more open trade".

In the present international environment, in which we observe a rapid expansion in the numbers and complexities of regional trade arrangements, it may be time for this subject to be re-examined. As Jagdish Bhagwati has recently pointed out, the sheer confusion caused by the explosion in regional trade agreements bears most heavily on the world's poorest countries. One is left puzzling over the answer to the question he has posed (see Bhagwati 2001):

Can anyone really be confident that today's massive and ongoing fragmentation of the world's trading system into bilateral preferential agreements can become the building blocks of tomorrow's global free trade? Blocks with such a disparity could never be of any use.

Further Reading

Balassa, Bela, *The Theory of Economic Integration*, Homewood, IL: Irwin, 1961; London: Allen and Unwin, 1962

The seminal work on the various stages of economic integration

Baldwin, Richard E., "The Causes of Regionalism", in *The World Economy*, 20/7, pp. 865–88

A useful recent article

Bhagwati, Jagdish, *The World Trading System at Risk*, Hemel Hempstead: Harvester Wheatsheaf, and Princeton, NJ: Princeton University Press, 1991

In this book, as well as in the three items cited below, this author presents a critical view of regional economic arrangements and the threat that some authors argue they pose to multilateralism.

Bhagwati, Jagdish, "Regionalism Versus Multilateralism", in *The World Economy*, 15/5, 1992, pp. 535–56

Bhagwati, Jagdish, "Regionalism and Multilateralism: An Overview", in Jaime de Melo and Arvind Panagariya (editors), *New Dimensions in Regional Integration*, Cambridge and New York: Cambridge University Press, 1993

Bhagwati, Jagdish, "A Costly Pursuit of Free Trade", in *Financial Times*, 6 March 2001

Cable, Vincent, and David Henderson (editors), *Trade Blocs? The Future of Regional Integration*, London: Royal Institute of International Affairs, 1994

An important collection of papers on regional economic integration, notably including Steven Thomsen's "Regional Integration and Multinational Production"

Emerson, Michael, *et al.*, *The Economics of 1992*, Oxford and New York: Oxford University Press, 1988

An economic assessment of the impact of the completion of the single European market

Ethier, W., and H. Horn, "A New Look at Economic Integration", reprinted in Alexis Jacquemin and André Sapir (editors), *The European Internal Market: Trade and Competition*, Oxford and New York: Oxford University Press, 1989

A relatively technical treatment of the theory of customs union

Finger, J. Michael, "GATT's Influence on Regional Arrangements" in Jaime de Melo and Arvind Panagariya (editors), *New Dimensions in Regional Integration*, Cambridge and New York: Cambridge University Press, 1993

Holland, Stuart, *UnCommon Market: Capital, Class and Power in the European Community*, London: Macmillan, and New York: St Martin's Press, 1980

A view of the process of integration from what was then the left of the British Labour Party

Kemp, M.C., and H. Wan, "An Elementary Proposition Concerning the Formation of a Customs Union", in *Journal of International Economics*, 6, 1976, pp. 95–97

Another technical treatment of the theory of customs unions

Krugman, Paul, *Geography and Trade*, Leuven: Leuven University Press, and Cambridge, MA: MIT Press, 1991

An accessible account of the theoretical analysis of customs unions

Lal, Deepak, "Trade Blocs and Multilateral Free Trade", in *Journal of Common Market Studies*, 31/3, 1993, pp. 349–58

Another broadly critical discussion of regional economic organizations and their impact on multilateral arrangements

Moravcsik, Andrew, "Preferences and Power in the European Community: A Liberal Intergovernmentalist Approach", in *Journal of Common Market Studies*, 31/4, 1993, pp. 473–524

A useful discussion of the broader theoretical debate on European integration

Padoa-Schioppa, Tommaso, *et al.*, *Efficiency, Stability, and Equity*, Oxford and New York: Oxford University Press, 1987

This volume also addresses the broader theoretical debate on European integration.

Pelkmans, Jacques, "Economic Theories of Integration Revisited", in *Journal of Common Market Studies*, 18/4, 1980, pp. 333–54

Another accessible account of the theoretical analysis of customs unions

Swann, Dennis, *The Economics of Europe: From Common Market to European Union*, London: Penguin, 2000

The most recent of several available accounts of the theory of customs unions

Taylor, Paul, *The Limits of European Integration*, London: Croom Helm, and New York: Columbia University Press, 1983

A survey of the debate on European integration

Thomsen, Steven, "Regional Integration and Multi-national Production" in Cable and Henderson (editors), cited above

Viner, Jacob, *The Customs Union Issue*, New York: Carnegie Endowment for International Peace, and London: Stevens, 1950

Viner sets out the analytical framework that economists still use for assessing the economic consequences of integration.

Woolcock, Stephen, "The Acquis and Multinational Trade Rules: Are they Compatible?" in *Journal of Common Market Studies*, 31, 1993

Dr Andrew Scott is Jean Monnet Senior Lecturer in the Economics of the European Union at the Europa Institute, University of Edinburgh.

Chapter Nine

The Single Market

Keith Hartley and John Suckling

The "single market" programme was designed to complete the internal market among member states of the European Community, now the EU. In 1985, the European Council agreed to the creation of a single European market by the end of 1992 and this commitment was reflected in the Single European Act of 1987. The single market programme was widely referred to simply as "1992": its aim was to create a single market by removing the remaining nontariff barriers to trade among the member states.

It was claimed at the time that the failure to achieve a single market had resulted in costs of "non-Europe", reflected in red tape, protectionism, nationalism, and other barriers to the free mobility of capital and labour, and to crossborder trade among member states. Completion of the single market was expected to provide major economic benefits to member states, in the form of enhanced growth, more jobs, and improved competitiveness, or, as Lord Cockfield put it, "in short, the prospect of significant inflation-free growth and millions of new jobs" (Cockfield pp. xiii–xiv).

These are impressive claims, which, if valid, would rank the single market programme as one of the most important economic policy measures of recent times. Yet questions have to be asked as to the impact and effectiveness of the programme: principally, have the expected economic benefits been achieved? Answers to this question depend upon the underlying economic model for the single market, the methods used originally to estimate the size of its economic benefits, and the available evidence; and the search for the answer

provides an opportunity to compare theory and reality. Inevitably, all policy changes involve gainers and losers, and the potential losers will oppose change and seek to thwart efforts to exploit fully the economic benefits of a single market.

The Economic Model of the Single Market

The single market programme aimed to achieve a better allocation of resources by removing nontariff barriers to trade, thereby promoting free trade in goods and services, and free mobility of capital and labour among member states of the Community. Tariff barriers among member states had been abolished and a common external tariff had been introduced with the creation of the original European "common market" (the European Economic Community), but there remained nontariff barriers, which came to be classified as physical, technical, or fiscal. As a result, the Community consisted of fragmented national markets separated by frontier controls, varying public procurement practices, and different product and technical standards, all of which hindered trade in goods and services among member states. Similarly, there were barriers to labour mobility, such as requirements for educational qualifications that were not transferable between countries, or the system of transfer fees for footballers. The aim was to remove these various barriers and so create a single market by the target date of the end of 1992.

"Physical" barriers comprised frontier controls, which caused stoppages, delays, administrative burdens, and associated paperwork ("red tape"). "Technical" barriers resulted from different national product standards, technical regulations, and business laws. In addition, national public procurement markets were characterized by preferential purchasing, government protectionism, and support for "national champions": hence the aim of liberalizing and opening up such markets. "Fiscal" barriers existed in different rates of value-added tax (VAT) and excise duties, and in varying degrees of subsidization. Differences in tax-subsidy policies among member states created the prospect of harmful tax-subsidy competition, with implications for the movement of goods, services, labour, and capital throughout the Community. For example, some countries used very specific and highly distortionary tax and subsidy incentives in order to attract firms to favoured locations: hence the emphasis on the need for the harmonization of tax rates and, ultimately, a common fiscal policy.

The single market initiative was thus basically a competition programme. It aimed to open up national markets in member states by reducing entry barriers. The result was expected to provide economic gains from five sources:

- cheaper goods and services supplied from other member states (the "import effect");
- competition inducing firms to improve efficiency if they are to survive (the "competition effect");
- the removal of monopolies in national markets (another form of the "competition effect");
- the exploitation of economies of scale, leading to further reductions in unit costs (the "scale effect"); and
- dynamic gains as the single market stimulates innovation, new products, and new processes ("dynamic effects").

These economic gains were expected to lead to lower costs and reduced profit margins, with the results reflected in lower prices for consumers, as well as better quality and improved product choice. Overall, economic welfare was expected to improve; but what was the size of the expected economic benefits from creating the single market?

The Estimated Benefits

The benefits from completing the single market were estimated by Paolo Cecchini and others to exceed ECU200 billion, equivalent to between 4.3% and 6.4% of the Community's GDP in 1988. Table 9.1 outlines the estimated contributions of the different sources of economic gain to the overall total. It can be seen that economies of scale were estimated as being likely to make the greatest single contribution to the total gains, at almost 30% of the total. However, Table 9.1 does not include any estimates of the longer-term dynamic benefits of the single market.

Further supporting arguments for the likely gains from the single market were based on observed price differences among member states for given products. In 1985, the general price variation from the Community average (before tax) was 15.2% for consumer goods and 12.4% for capital equipment. These broad averages concealed much greater variations in the prices for specific products and services (see Cecchini p. 79), such as books (49%), boiler-making equipment (22%), or telegraph and telephone services (50%). Such price differences were used to estimate the potential gains from the single market.

The predicted benefits of the single market were also expressed in terms of its macroeconomic effects. With this approach, it was estimated that the 1992 programme would lead to a once-and-for-all increase in total Community output of 4.5%; the creation of 1.8 million new jobs, thereby reducing the unemployment rate by 1.5 percentage points; and the lowering of inflation by some 6% (Cecchini p. 97). It was expected that these gains would be achieved in the medium term, taken to be a period of up to five years.

An Example: Liberalizing Public Procurement

Economists usually focus on anticompetitive behaviour by suppliers. In contrast, public procurement highlights the possibilities and opportunities for anticompetitive behaviour by governments acting as buyers. The Community directives seeking to liberalize public procurement in the single market can be regarded as regulatory requirements designed to change and constrain the behaviour of public buyers. Preferential public purchasing is likely to arise where the government is a major buyer able to use its buying power to influence the size, structure (e.g. mergers and entry conditions), conduct, and performance of an industry. Sectors likely to be protected by public procurement include defence, high technology industries, and state-owned industries.

Efforts to liberalize or open up public procurement markets provide a good example of how the single market initiative was implemented. Government protectionism in public procurement markets was seen as forming one of the barriers to the successful completion of the single market. Research in the 1980s found preferential public purchasing reflected in support for national champions and discriminatory practices favouring domestic over foreign suppliers: this meant that public procurement agencies were failing to exploit the benefits from wider competition. Generally, only part of public purchasing was put out to tender; restricted or negotiated tenders were preferred to open competitions; tenders were not advertised in the *Official Journal* of the European Communities; bidders from other member states were excluded; governments subsidized some activities; there were widely differing national or exclusive standards; and discrimination occurred in assessing the technical and financial capabilities of the bidders (see Cecchini, Emerson *et al.*, and Martin and Hartley).

The research done in the 1980s also found that public purchasing was concentrated in construction (building and civil engineering), energy products (electricity, oil, coal), transport equipment, and market services. High-technology areas, such as telecommunications, power generation, railway equipment, and defence equipment, were also characterized by dominant public buyers, few suppliers, and little trade among member states (see Cecchini). One indication of protectionism in public procurement markets was the fact that the level of imports for public contracts was considerably lower than the general level of import penetration for the Community. For example, in 1987 imports represented less than 2% of public purchasing, compared with 22% at the level of the whole economy; and for UK defence equipment in 1992, imports were less than 10% of equipment purchases, compared with import penetration for the UK economy of 20%. Similarly, in 1991, for a sample of technically comparable products, it was found that public sector purchasers in the Community were paying prices that varied by as much as 150% compared with the lowest price (see Bohan and Redonnet).

Estimates showed that liberalizing or opening up public procurement markets would lead to substantial savings, in the region of 0.5% of Community GDP, over the medium to long term, and the creation of some 350,000 jobs. If defence procurement was included, the estimated savings rose to 0.6% of Community GDP, equivalent to more than 22 billion Ecu at 1989 prices (see Cecchini, and Emerson *et al.*). According to the official studies, these savings would arise from three sources. First, opening national markets would enable public procurement agencies to buy from the cheapest (often foreign) suppliers (the "static trade effect"). Secondly, increased competition would mean that domestic firms in previously protected national markets would reduce prices in order to compete with foreign rivals entering the market (the "competition effect"). Thirdly, in the longer term increased competition would mean that industries were rationalized and restructured, enabling the surviving firms to obtain economies of scale and learning (the "restructuring effect"). The relative contribution of each of these three sources to the estimated savings were, respectively 32%, 16%, and 52%. In other words, it was predicted that the long-term restructuring effect would account for about one half of the estimated savings, which implied that the aggregate savings would be long-term, and would therefore be sensitive to assumptions about industrial rationalization and the associated economies of scale. In the short term, the benefits of liberalizing public procurement markets would be reflected in the competition effect. Assuming that it was possible to identify separately and estimate static trade and competition effects – thus avoiding double counting – then increased competition would, it was estimated, account for some 16% of the total savings that would represent the more immediate benefits of liberalized public procurement. Throughout these estimates, it was assumed that reductions in costs and profits were fully reflected in price reductions: in reality, however, such full forward shifting to lower consumer prices is unlikely.

The Rules for Opening Public Markets

The task of opening up public procurement markets is an example of the problems of translating economic models into a set of legally enforceable rules. Problems arise with economists' traditional interpretation of competition, which starts with the simple model of competitive markets, assuming large numbers of suppliers, free entry, and firms unable to fix prices. This approach fails to recognize a possible role for the threat of entry (contestability); the role of uncertainty and markets in continuous change (tending towards, but never achieving, equilibrium); and recent developments that incorporate considerations of economies of scale and oligopolistic markets. Generally, problems arise because buyers and sellers in public procurement markets have greater opportunities for pursuing self-interest, subject to any constraints imposed on their behaviour: they will actively seek to thwart the aims of legislation and regulations.

The single market legislation aimed to create open, liberalized public procurement markets, often expressed in terms of nondiscriminatory purchasing and a "level playing field" (see Arrowsmith 1993). However, Community rules affecting public procurement were not new. During the 1970s, the Community had adopted specific directives, including requirements for purchasing organizations to advertise contracts above specific thresholds on a Community-wide basis. However, these initiatives had had limitations, all of which created opportunities for ignoring or thwarting the rules. Further, there was little in the way of legal penalties to force compliance and there were a number of excluded sectors, namely water, energy, transport, and telecommunications (see Cox).

Next came the single market directives of the late 1980s, which aimed to remove the remaining barriers to open public procurement markets for civil goods and services. These directives embraced public works (such as the building of hospitals or schools); public supply (of physical goods and equipment such as office equipment, furniture or computers); utilities (energy, transport, telecommunications, water); and public services (such as accounting, advertising, architectural, financial, insurance, maintenance and repair, and computer services). The directives specify:

- contract thresholds, above which all contracts must be advertised on an EU-wide basis in the *Official Journal*;
- awards procedures, comprising "open", "restricted", and "negotiated" procedures, among which the norm is expected to be open or restricted tendering, with negotiated tendering regarded as exceptional;
- technical standards, the aim being to apply EU-wide technical standards where possible, so reducing opportunities for using special national standards that might be discriminatory;
- transparency and time limits, requiring contracting authorities to indicate their future contract awards by estimated value and to provide minimum time periods for firms to respond to advertised contracts, so ensuring proper and fair competition (a "level playing field");
- awards criteria, specifying that contracts must normally (but not necessarily) be awarded to the lowest-priced or "most economically advantageous tender", so allowing consideration to be given to such non-price factors as artistic and technical merit, delivery dates, running costs, and after-sales service, and providing obvious opportunities for public buyers to exercise discretion in their procurement choices; and
- reporting and monitoring requirements, mandating member states to inform the Commission annually of any regional and other preferential schemes, and to provide annual statistical reports on contract awards (covering, among other items, the

number and value of contracts above the threshold mentioned above, the procedures used, the nationalities of the contractors, and the products purchased).

Compliance with the directives is achieved through procedures under the Remedies Directives. These can be enforced through two routes. First, the European Commission can take a member state to the European Court of Justice for infringement of the Community rules on public procurement. Secondly, an aggrieved party in the public procurement process can take legal action against the offending authority through the national courts (private parties cannot bring an action before the European Court of Justice, since this option is open only to the Commission and to the governments of member states). Typical public procurement cases that have been brought to the European Court of Justice have covered failure to advertise in the *Official Journal*; failure to implement the relevant directives within the specified time period; and disputes about awards criteria, contract specifications, the financial and economic standing of eligible contractors, and criteria for contractor selection (e.g. requiring contractors to allocate work to the long-term unemployed). In such cases, action might be taken to suspend a contract already concluded, to require an authority to reopen the awards procedure, to require the amendment of national regulations, or to award damages. In the case of damages, it can be difficult for a firm to prove that it would have won a contract and to assess the monetary estimates of any loss. For example, courts have to estimate lost profits, namely, what the profits would have been, allowing for the risks and uncertainties of specific industries; and whether tendering costs should be included in any estimate of damages (see Arrowsmith 1992, 1993, and 2000 for detailed analysis and examples).

Evidence on the Impact of the Single Market

In 1996, the European Commission published the results of a major study of the impact and effectiveness of the single market programme (see Bohan and Redonnet). The study found that the single market was beginning to have a positive and favourable effect on the EU's economic performance, but had yet to achieve its full potential. It was estimated that by 1994 the single market had created up to 900,000 more jobs, added 1.1% to 1.5% to Community income, lowered inflation rates by 1.1% to 1.5% and boosted trade among member states by 20–30%. There was also evidence of growing competition, both in manufacturing and in services; an accelerated pace of industrial restructuring; and a broadening of the range of products and services available at lower prices to retail, public sector, and industrial consumers.

The study also concluded that there was greater mobility among member states, both for workers and for those not economically active; and that the removal of border controls on goods had resulted in faster and cheaper crossborder deliveries. Price-cost margins were estimated to be 0.5% lower. It was claimed that, in manufacturing, real labour productivity had risen by 14% in the five years after the launch of the single market, compared with a growth rate of 6.6% before the programme. Significantly, there was said to be no evidence of an increase in the size of firms in sectors sensitive to the single market, suggesting that the anticipated exploitation of economies of scale has not been a major source of efficiency benefits (about one third of the estimated benefits, as discussed above and shown in Table 9.1). However, a true single market for energy had still not been achieved and a single market for pharmaceuticals was far from complete, mainly because the governments of member states retained exclusive or near-exclusive responsibility for health care and for prices, in order to control health costs. In sectors where there were no EU-wide standards, the governments of member states continued to impose specific national product requirements, as, for example, in building and construction, foodstuffs, and telecommunications in Austria, Germany, and the Netherlands.

Evidence on the Impact of the Public Procurement Rules

By 1995–96 evidence on the impact of the single market directives on public procurement suggested the following broad conclusions (see Bohan and Redonnet).

First, more than 70% of companies (in manufacturing and services) regarded the legislation as having had no effect, and procurement markets remained the preserve of larger companies. However, it was also reported that in the construction industry the single market programme had resulted in greater competitive pressure.

Secondly, there was greater transparency by public purchasers, with an increasing number of calls for tenders being published and a shift towards greater use of the *Official Journal*, but this was not perceived to generate significant tangible benefits. This was a significant result, since it suggests the limitations of some statistical measures of performance such as the number of tender invitations advertised in the *Official Journal* (see Martin and Hartley). In addition, apart from utility purchasers, the majority of public purchasers reported no change in the nationality of firms submitting tenders.

Thirdly, there was an absence of price savings, despite an increase in the number of firms submitting tenders: either firms were not competing on price or competition was not being stimulated by the increasing number of bidders.

Fourthly, concerns about threats of legal action by suppliers appeared to have resulted in public purchasers adopting a defensive and bureaucratic approach to the implementation of the procurement rules. Nevertheless, the proportion of public purchases of nondomestic origin had increased from 6% of total public sector purchases in 1987 to 10% in 1994, and the liberalization of procurement had resulted in some substantial price reductions in some sectors, including reductions by 30–40% in power generation and distribution equipment, and reductions by 20–30% for rail rolling stock.

Fifthly, since optimal plant size had decreased in many sectors, smaller operations had become more viable, reducing the incentive to concentrate production on a smaller number of sites and calling the "scale effect" (see above) into question.

Finally, various indicators of market integration, such as price dispersion or concentration ratios, all pointed in the direction of increased crossborder competition.

The general conclusion was that the procurement legislation had not yet achieved a significant change in the degree of crossborder procurement of supplies: in the words of Niall Bohan and Denis Redonnet, "on the basis of impact observed to date, commentators may be inclined to portray [the] procurement legislation as the mountain which gave birth to a molehill" (Bohan and Redonnet p. 165).

Questions then arose as to the extent to which the shortfall between initial expectations and the observed impact was due to deficiencies in the framework of legislation and enforcement, or to "structural rigidities", whether on the demand side (public buyers), on the supply side (tendering companies), or on both. For example, risk-averse public purchasers might prefer known firms that seemed to them to be "tried and tested"; potential suppliers still had to incur substantial costs in entering a new market; and there were always incentives for collusion.

What Happened to the Estimated Benefits?

There are various explanations for the differences between the estimated benefits of the single market and the realized benefits as reported by various observers. The official view in the late 1990s was that, it was still too early to make an accurate assessment of the economic benefits of the single market; and that the benefits would have been greater if member states had been more diligent in applying the measures already agreed. By mid-2000, the Commission's *Internal Market Scorecard* was reporting a slowdown in member states' efforts to implement the legislation, with Greece, France, Portugal, and Luxembourg together accounting for more than 40% of the reported delays (see European Commission). At the Community level, it has also been recognized that further policy initiatives are needed in a few key areas, such as the abolition of border controls on people, taxation issues (such as a common origin-based VAT system), the creation of a European company law system, and the need to remove unnecessary ambiguities and complexities in existing single market legislation.

Other reasons might explain the differences between the expected benefits and the realized benefits of the single market. In particular, there are at least five general areas of concern about the economic model and the supporting evidence.

First, the model used by the Commission and most other observers assumes competitive markets, so that lower costs are passed on to consumers in the form of lower prices. This is particularly so with the expected gains from economies of scale yet to be realized. However, the price of efficient scale might be EU oligopolies or monopolies, with the possibility of higher prices, higher profits, poorer product quality, greater inefficiency, and reduced innovation. Public procurement and private markets do not correspond to the perfectly competitive model. As a result, there is a need for an active EU competition policy.

Secondly, as Michael Emerson pointed out soon after the launch of the single market programme, estimates of the effects of such a complex policy change "are extremely difficult to make, especially as regards some of the more speculative and long-term effects" (Emerson *et al.* p. 3). Estimates are needed of demand and cost conditions, and of the extent of inefficiencies among firms; and care is needed to avoid double counting. Other influences also make it difficult to identify the impact of the single market programme, notably globalization and technical change.

Thirdly, the estimated savings could reflect efforts by the European Commission to obtain the largest possible budget and more staff; hence, it would have every incentive to exaggerate the benefits and underestimate or ignore the costs of the single market, notably by emphasizing optimistic estimates and predictions.

Fourthly, creating the single market, with its greater competition and industrial restructuring effects, involves losers as well as gainers. Some firms and their workforces will be losers. Reallocating resources to alternative uses takes time and involves adjustment costs, in the form of unemployment and the underemployment of resources. On this basis, the single market resembles an investment process involving short-term costs in return for expected greater long-term benefits. Yet not all investments are successful: some fail. Questions have to be asked about the size of the short-term costs and the time period required to achieve a successful reallocation of resources.

Finally, the potential losers from the single market are likely to oppose change, and to create barriers and obstacles designed to thwart its aims. For example, uncompetitive firms might demand generous subsidies to allow them time to adjust to the change; or governments might continue to award contracts to their "national champions" where they provide the "most economically advantageous tender" or meet specific national technical requirements; and oligopolies might lead to collusive tendering.

Future Prospects: A Single Market for Defence Equipment?

Defence procurement is one sector that is not part of the single market. Europe is characterized by inefficient defence markets. Within the EU, support for national defence industries, which is costly, is allowed under Article 296 (previously Article 223) of the EC Treaty. Costly research and development programmes are duplicated, and there are relatively short production runs, so that there is a failure to obtain economies of scale and learning. For example, at the time of writing member states are developing three different advanced combat aircraft, namely the Gripen (Sweden), the Rafale (France), and the Eurofighter (United Kingdom, Germany, Italy, and Spain). The total development costs for the Eurofighter alone have been estimated at some £14 billion. Production orders have been estimated at 620 units for the Eurofighter, almost 300 units for the Rafale, and some 200 units for the Gripen. If these separate orders were combined into an order for more than 1,100 units of one type, there would be savings in unit production costs of 10–20% – a substantial sum on unit production costs of £41.7 million per aircraft for the Eurofighter (at 1999–2000 prices).

Extending the single European market to defence equipment may secure some major economic benefits, resulting from greater competition, following the opening up of national defence markets; reduced duplication of equipment, leading to savings in research and development costs; and savings in production costs, due to the economies of longer production runs. Thus, the economic case for a single market for defence equipment is similar to the case presented for the internal market for civil goods and services (especially the liberalization of public procurement markets). Experience in the United Kingdom suggests that greater competition in defence markets could lead to cost savings of at least 10%, and that longer production runs could reduce unit costs by some 10% for each doubling of output.

However, creating a single market for defence equipment would not be without its difficulties. There would be problems in creating a "level playing field"; maintaining competition when the long-term trend is towards a smaller number of large defence companies; catering for different national interests; and coping with the inevitable pressure to create a "Fortress Europe" characterized by protectionism, cartels, and the inefficiency of *juste retour* (work-sharing arrangements on European collaborative projects).

By the end of 2000, three developments were affecting European defence policy. First, the emergence of a "European security and defence identity" (or ESDI), which is "separable but not separate" from NATO, had raised the prospect of the creation of a European rapid reaction force of 50,000 to 60,000 troops for peacekeeping and crisis management operations, with the EU taking on the functions of the Western European Union (see Chapter 23 for more details). Secondly, there were possible bases for the formation of a European armaments agency, both in the Organisation Conjointe de Coopération pour l'Armament (OCCAR), an armaments agency formed by France, Germany, Italy, and the United Kingdom in 1996 with the aim of improving the efficiency and effectiveness of collaborative ventures (see Sandler and Hartley); and in a framework agreement signed in July 2000 by these four countries, plus Spain and Sweden, supporting specific measures for improved cooperation on security of supply, export procedures, handling of classified information, research and technology, and the harmonization of military requirements. Thirdly, EU-based defence companies were responding to the threat of competition from the US defence giants Boeing, Lockheed Martin, and Raytheon by undertaking mergers and restructuring. In addition to European industrial consolidation in helicopters and missiles, three major European groups had been created:

- the European Aeronautic, Defence and Space Company (EADS), a merger of Aerospatiale–Matra (France), Daimler–Chrysler Aerospace (or DASA, Germany), and CASA (Spain), and a joint venture with Finmeccanica (Alenia Aeronautics, Italy);
- BAE Systems, a UK company formed after the acquisition of GEC–Marconi Electronics Systems by British Aerospace; and
- Thomson–Racal, created after Thomson-CSF of France acquired the British Racal Group, including Racal Defence Electronics.

Conclusion

The completion of the single market will require vigilance and supporting policy measures. At the level of the EU, policy-makers need to be careful to ensure that national governments implement and enforce the rules for the single market, and that their producers abide by the rules. National governments and their producers might seek to thwart the rules: after all, it is not unknown for governments to be influenced by producer groups and for such groups to capture regulatory agencies. Firms can also acquire rivals in other member states. All these considerations highlight the importance of an effective EU competition policy, designed to control EU monopolies, mergers, restrictive practices, and anticompetitive behaviour, and to provide for a "level playing field" by addressing issues such as subsidies and differences between state-owned and privately owned companies (see Chapter 11).

While the benefits of the single market may appear impressive, it is likely that they will not be as large as was originally predicted. Nor should the costs and distributional implications of change, adjustment, and resource reallocation be ignored. Given the opposition to change and the ability of economic systems to thwart "good intentions", it is likely that it will take longer than expected before the full benefits of the single market are realized.

Future challenges include defence and enlargement. In defence, the United States achieves its competitive advantage by providing its contractors with a large home market based on a single US Army, Navy, and Air Force: any EU equivalent would require a United States of Europe. Future enlargement of the EU, meanwhile, raises questions about its ideal size and whether there are any limits to its size. For economists, assessments of the wisdom of further expansion of the EU would have to be based on an assessment of the benefits and costs of enlargement, both for existing member states and for new members.

Further Reading

Arrowsmith, Sue, *A Guide to the Procurement Cases of the Court of Justice*, Winteringham: Earlsgate Press, 1992

For both lawyers and non-lawyers, an account of the case law of the European Court of Justice on public procurement

Arrowsmith, Sue (editor), *Remedies for Enforcing the Public Procurement Rules*, Winteringham: Earlsgate Press, 1993

A guide to the legal rules governing remedies across the Community

Arrowsmith, Sue, "EC Procurement Rules in the UK Courts: An Analysis of the Harmon Case: Part II", in *Public Procurement Law Review*, 4, 2000, pp. 135–47

A case study of the remedies available in the UK courts to enforce the procurement rules

Bohan, Niall, and Denis Redonnet, "EU Procurement Legislation: Does the Emperor Have Clothes? An Examination of the New Empirical Evidence", in *Public Procurement Law Review*, 4, 1997, pp. 141–73

While the focus is on public procurement, an annex reports overall findings on the impact and effectiveness of the single market programme

Cecchini, Paolo, *The European Challenge 1992: The Benefits of a Single Market*, London: Wildwood House, 1988

A nontechnical description of the prospective economics of the single market

Cockfield, Lord, Foreword, to Cecchini, as cited above

A brief official view of the case for the single market, presented by a British politician who was a member of the European Commission at the time

Cox, Andrew, *The Single Market Rules and the Enforcement Regime after 1992*, Winteringham: Earlsgate Press, 1993

A guide to the rules for public procurement in the single market and the remedies for infringements of the rules

Emerson, Michael, *et al.*, *The Economics of 1992*, Oxford and New York: Oxford University Press, 1988

A technical account of the economic theory and evidence for the benefits of the single market

European Commission, *Internal Market Scorecard*, available at europa.eu.int/comm./internal_market/en/update/score

This official publication provides updates on the member states' record in the transposition of single market directives into national law and the number of recent infringement proceedings that have been launched against them.

Martin, Stephen and Keith Hartley, "Public Procurement in the European Union: Issues and Policies", in *Public Procurement Law Review*, 2, 1997, pp. 92–113

An empirical survey reporting the effects of the single market programme on public procurement tendering behaviour

Sandler, Todd and Keith Hartley, *The Political Economy of NATO: Past, Present and into the 21st Century*, Cambridge and New York: Cambridge University Press, 1999

An economic analysis of NATO and its future prospects

Keith Hartley is Professor of Economics and Director of the Centre for Defence Economics at the University of York. He is the Editor of the *Journal of Defence and Peace Economics*, and has published extensively on defence economics and public procurement issues. *John Suckling* is a Lecturer in Economics at the University of York.

Table 9.1   The Economic Benefits of 1992

Source of gain	ECU billions	Percentage of EC GDP
1. Gains from removal of barriers affecting trade	8–9	0.2–0.3
2. Gains from removal of barriers affecting overall production	57–71	2.0–2.4
Subtotal: gains from removing barriers	*65–80*	*2.2–2.7*
3. Gains from exploiting economies of scale	61	2.1
4. Gains from greater competition reducing firm inefficiencies and monopoly profits	46	1.6
*Subtotal: gains from market integration**	*62–107*	*2.1–3.7*
Total		
– for 7 member states at 1985 prices	127–187	4.3–6.4
– for 12 member states at 1988 prices	174–258	4.3–6.4
– average	216	5.3

Note: *This estimated subtotal cannot be derived from the sum of subtotals 3 and 4.

Source: Cecchini, Paolo, *The European Challenge 1992: The Benefits of a Single Market,* 1988, p. 84

Chapter Ten

Economic and Monetary Union

Brian Ardy

When the euro was launched on 1 January 1999 economic governance in the euro zone made a decisive shift to the EU level. Economic and Monetary Union (EMU) represents a profound increment in the political power of the EU, with a new EU institution, the European Central Bank (ECB), controlling the money supply, interest rates, and the exchange rate between the monetary union and the rest of the world. The exchange rates between member countries' currencies were permanently fixed and the euro became an electronic currency. EMU members also accept considerable limitations on their national fiscal policy as a result of the provisions of the Treaty on European Union (TEU – the Maastricht Treaty), which have been reinforced in the Stability and Growth Pact (SGP). The importance of EMU was magnified by its large membership, which was wider than anticipated. At its launch it encompassed 11 of the EU's 15 member states, the "outs" being Denmark, Greece, Sweden, and the United Kingdom. Membership widened further when Greece joined on 1 January 2001. Powerful symbols of national sovereignty will cease to exist when euro notes and coins replace the national currencies of these countries in 2002.

The Creation of EMU

The goal of monetary union had been a long-standing one for the European Community. In 1970 agreement was reached to achieve it by 1980. Subsequent economic instability, related to the first oil crisis (1973–74) and the collapse of the international monetary system based on fixed exchange rates meant that this goal was not achieved. The system of fixed exchange rates set up within the Community under this initiative, known as "the snake", gradually collapsed into a limited Deutschmark zone. In 1979 monetary integration was chosen as the area in which the Community was to try to restore momentum to the process of integration after the doldrums of the 1970s. Thus, the European Monetary System (EMS) established a zone of monetary stability in Europe by maintaining a grid of fixed exchange rates, the Exchange Rate Mechanism (ERM), among member states' currencies. All the members of the Community were members of the EMS, but not all were members of the ERM. Despite the instability of the period 1979–83, the EMS was successful in stabilizing exchange rates. From then on, ERM exchange rates became increasingly stable. This stability was helpful for the process of integration and for the operation of the Community economy, but it also exacted a price. Countries within the ERM found that they had ceded economic sovereignty to the central bank of what was then West Germany, the Bundesbank, which effectively determined the monetary policy of the ERM. Since the Bundesbank's monetary policy was based on conditions in West Germany, it did not necessarily suit the other ERM members. Gradually other ERM countries, especially France, began to appreciate that only in a monetary union could a share of pooled sovereignty over monetary policy be achieved. Moreover, a single currency would significantly enhance the effectiveness of the single market. Thus, in 1988 an expert group under the chairmanship of the President of the Commission, Jacques Delors, was established by the European Council to assess the viability of monetary union. The Delors Report was published in 1989 and formed the basis of the EMU provisions of the TEU agreed at Maastricht in 1991.

Despite exchange rate turmoil in 1992 and 1993, and severe criticisms both of the design of EMU and of the provisions for the transition to EMU, the procedures in the TEU were followed and EMU was launched in accordance with the agreed deadline. The establishment of a monetary union involving such large and diversified countries was a technical triumph. Monetary policy and techniques of monetary control have functioned smoothly, and the euro zone now operates as a single monetary area. The experience of the EMS was essential in fostering the techniques and experience of cooperation between national central banks, which is vital for the operation of EMU.

Membership of EMU is based on pre-entry convergence: only countries with similar levels of economic performance are allowed to join. Given the very disparate levels of economic performance at the start of the process, a remarkable degree of convergence was achieved. The convergence process and the operation of EMU have been enhanced by a convergence of government views on what constitutes sensible macroeconomic policies. Thus, conservative policies of independent central banks, low government borrowing, and flexibility in the economy have become fashionable. The convergence process remains relevant to the three EU member states, Denmark, Sweden, and the United Kingdom, that are not members of EMU, and to any new EU member states. To become EMU members, these states will have to satisfy the same four convergence criteria as the existing member states:

- an average rate of inflation for one year that does not exceed by more than 1.5% that of the three best performing member states;
- a government deficit of less than 3% of GDP and government debt amounting to less than 60% of GDP;
- participation in the ERM and observance of its normal fluctuation margins for at least two years without devaluing; and

- long-term interest rates that do not exceed by more than 2% those in the three best-performing member states for one year.

There was some flexibility in the interpretation of these conditions in relation to the level of debt for Italy and Belgium, and for ERM membership in the case of Finland. When Finland was accepted for membership it had not been in the ERM for two years, but it had completed its two years of membership by 31 December 1998.

With the rejection of EMU membership in the Danish referendum of October 2000, early entry looks increasingly unlikely for Sweden and the United Kingdom as well. This is because the referendum result may well harden public opinion against EMU and reduce the potency of arguments about being disadvantaged and isolated outside.

The Euro-Zone Economy

The euro zone is an enormous economic entity: in 1998 its population exceeded that of all other industrial market economies (see Table 10.1). Its aggregate GNP is smaller than the GNP of the United States, but much larger than that of Japan. Thus, the euro zone is one of the three major pillars of the world economy; the United States, the euro zone, and Japan together accounted in 1998 for 64.7% of the world's aggregate GNP, with the euro zone alone accounting for 23.1%. With a larger population and a smaller aggregate GNP than the United States, the productivity of labour is lower than in the United States. This productivity gap is currently widening but the euro zone is still one of the world's most productive economies. This is reflected in the level of income per capita, which is 456% of the world average.

The euro zone plays a major role in the world economy (see Table 10.2) Excluding intra-EU trade, it is the world's second largest exporter and importer of goods. The euro zone is also the world's largest single source of, and a major destination for, foreign direct investment (FDI). The euro zone, the United States, and Japan are the most important players in the international economy, accounting for 42% of the world's merchandise exports and imports. Together, they are the sources of 77% of the world's FDI and the recipients of 52% of this investment.

While the euro zone is comparable in size to the United States, it differs from all national economies because it is more heterogeneous and less integrated. Heterogeneity is most obvious in language and culture, which have implications for economic integration. It also extends to the economic sphere, with greater differences in income levels: only 33 of the 62 regions in the euro zone have a GDP per capita between 75 and 125% of the average for the 12 countries in the zone, compared with 44 out of the 50 states in the United States (see Table 10.3; but note that Washington, DC, which has a GDP per head 327% of the US average, is a special case and is excluded from the table). Other economic differences within the euro zone occur in sectoral structures of employment and output, the importance of trade, trade partners, and the commodity composition of trade. There are also large variations in the public sectors of the 12 countries, not just in overall government expenditure but also in particular services such as social security, health, and defence, and in the degree of decentralization of government. Lower degrees of economic integration are manifested in the lesser extent of trade, the smaller flows of labour and capital, the lower level of capital stock invested in other countries, and the smaller degree of industrial specialization.

Institutions and Decision-making in EMU

The European Central Bank

The ECB is the most important example of the current vogue in economic policy-making for the establishment of independent central banks. The economic justification for the creation of an independent central bank rests upon the view that there is an inflationary bias to discretionary policy-making by political actors. Although it may not be possible to raise the long-run rate of growth of output and employment, the short-time horizons within which politicians work mean that a temporary boost to output and employment, and its accom-

panying unexpected inflation, may be in the government's interest. The problem is that economic agents such as companies, unions, and the financial markets will factor inflation into their expectations. Thus, at each level of output and employment, inflation will be higher than if expectations of inflation were lower. This is the "inflation bias" of the system. One solution is to delegate monetary policy to a "conservative" central bank that has long time horizons and is committed to controlling inflation. Such a central bank should be credible, that is, economic actors should believe that it will meet its avowed aim of achieving low inflation. Thus, replacing barely credible or even incredible national government control of monetary policy with credible independent central control could reduce the costs of disinflation, because economic actors' expectations will be adjusted downwards to a lower level of expected inflation.

The difficulty lies in developing the credibility of an existing institution, or in the case of the ECB, a new institution. The effectiveness of a central bank's independence in moderating inflation may be related to the wider institutional and social setting within which it is located. To establish credibility and effectiveness it is also important that the central bank has legitimacy: the belief among the public that the institution is the correct one to carry out the functions assigned to it. Legitimacy can be established by clear democratic accountability, or by embedding it in the shared values of the polity. Thus, success in controlling inflation, in a culture that valued this achievement, could establish a central bank's legitimacy. Within EMU the approach to these issues has primarily been to make the ECB exceptionally independent and to model it upon the Bundesbank, in the hope that it can inherit its credibility and legitimacy.

The ECB has legal personality and it is independent. To be independent the ECB must be in a position when making decisions to ignore pressure from other institutions and individuals. Thus, the Maastricht Treaty specifies legal requirements covering the ECB's institutional and financial situation so as to guarantee its independence. Institutionally, neither the ECB nor any member of its decision-making bodies shall seek or take instructions from Community institutions or bodies, from any government of a member state, or from any other body. This applies to the Executive Board of the ECB, which comprises its President, its Vice President, and four other members who are appointed by common accord of the member states, as well as to the governors of the national central banks of the states in EMU. The ECB has its own budget, to ensure that financial pressure cannot be put on it.

The TEU provides for the establishment of a European System of Central Banks (ESCB), which comprises the ECB and the national central banks of all EU member states – whether they are members of EMU or not. The General Council of the ESCB is composed of the President and Vice-President of the ECB and the national central bank governors of all EU member states, and its primary responsibility is to provide advice on preparations for membership of EMU.

Since three EU member states are not members of EMU, the "Eurosystem" has been created, comprising the ECB and the national central banks of the 12 states in the euro zone. Decision-making in the Eurosystem is undertaken by the Governing Council, which consists of the 12 governors of the national central banks and the six members of the Executive Board of the ECB. It is the Governing Council that is the principal decision-making body of the Eurosystem, deciding monetary policy (for example, setting interest rates), authorizing the issue of euro banknotes and coins, adopting regulations to ensure the smooth operation of payments systems, and fulfilling the advisory role of the ECB. The Executive Board is responsible for day-to-day operations and for the administration of the ECB. The General Council and the Executive Board take decisions on the basis of a simple majority of their members.

The ECB's primary objective is price stability. It is required to contribute to the achievement of other objectives of the Community, such as noninflationary growth and a high level of employment, but only to the extent that doing so does not compromise the primary objective of price stability.

The credibility and legitimacy of the ECB also requires that it be both accountable (held responsible for its actions) and transparent (able to explain the reasons for its actions). Accountability is achieved in various ways through legal requirements for the publication of an annual report, and for the attendance of the ECB's President and other members of its Executive Board at competent committees of the European Parliament. The presiding member of the Economic and Finance Council (Ecofin) and a member of the Commission may attend meetings of the Governing Council without having the right to vote. So far, at least, the presiding member of Ecofin has seldom exercised this right. In addition to these legal requirements, the President of the ECB gives press conferences every month as well as after interest rate changes; the ECB publishes a monthly bulletin; and the European Parliament holds regular hearings with members of the ECB's board.

In comparison with other central banks, the ECB enjoys considerable independence, as is shown by the legislative provisions governing its constitution and operation. The governor is appointed for a minimum renewable term of office of five years and members of the Executive Board have a relatively long nonrenewable term of eight years. They are appointed by common accord of the member states and are fully independent, acting strictly in a personal capacity. The governors of the national central banks within the euro zone are similarly required to be independent. The Eurosystem is given an overriding primary objective of achieving price stability and the final authority over monetary policy. However, it can be argued that, since the primary objective is rather vaguely defined, it has rather more independence than might appear. Indeed, it enjoys considerable "goal independence", in deciding what the objective of policy should be, as well as "instrument independence", the ability to decide how to use policy instruments to achieve this objective. The ECB's independence is reinforced by the absence of a counterweight in the form of a European government. Political leverage over the Eurosystem is also limited by its decentralized nature and the use of "one member, one vote" and simple majority voting.

However, the governors of the national central banks are powerful within the system.

There are 12 of them, as compared with six members of the ECB's Executive Board, and they have considerable standing and resources. The ECB has only 500 employees, compared with 20,000 at the Bundesbank or 16,000 at the Banque de France. The importance of these 12 governors in the system could be regarded as a problem, leading to an over-emphasis on individual nations rather than the euro zone as a whole. However, this seems dubious, since any individual governor is only one among 18 on the Governing Council. In any case, these governors are likely to be cautious and to take decisions in the interests of the euro zone as a whole, and this development is being fostered by the ECB's collegiate approach to decision-making, with a preference for consensus. There is perhaps a short-term problem caused by the fact that most of the governors of the national central banks have no experience of operating a major currency like the euro, and this could have contributed to a lack of consistency and decisiveness in the ECB's policy. The Eurosystem reflects the political realities of the EU: it is a decentralized system, characterized by strong nation states and a comparatively weak centre.

The ECB has established *ex post* transparency, that is, it comments on decisions *after* they have been made and is judged on whether goals have been met. In contrast, the Bank of England, for example, has *ex ante* transparency, since it explains how it intends to achieve its goal by publishing forecasts and descriptions of various possible outcomes of policy. The ECB started publishing projections in December 2000, but their usefulness as an *ex ante* guide to ECB thinking is limited because of the wide range of possibilities presented. The US Federal Reserve stands between these two extremes: it does not publish its own forecasts but it does publish the forecasts of the individual reserve banks that are affiliated to it. The ECB's *ex post* approach could undermine the attempt to establish the credibility of this new institution by making it more difficult for markets to understand its actions. The ECB's transparency is also limited by its system of collective accountability, which means that only the decisions of the Governing Council are known, while differences of opinion and voting records are not publicized. In contrast, the Federal Reserve and the Bank of England both publish unattributed views and individual voting records. The collective accountability of the ECB seems desirable, given the high degree of decentralization of the ECB and the possibility that interests will diverge along national lines. However, although there are good reasons for these policies and they do reinforce the independence of the ECB, they also make it potentially vulnerable to being held responsible for the economic performance of the euro zone as a whole, and not just for inflation.

The Operation of the ECB

In deriving its policy strategy the ECB had a difficult task. It sought to inherit the anti-inflation credibility of the Bundesbank, while also being inclusive of the traditions of the other national central banks in the euro zone and responding to the new situation represented by EMU. However, it is clear that the Bundesbank inheritance is the most important of these elements, and this is reflected in the "one target and two pillars" strategy agreed in October 1998. The target is price stability, defined as a year-on-year increase in the harmonized index of consumer prices of less than 2%. The first of the two "pillars" is a reference value for the annual growth of the broad monetary aggregate (M3) set at 4.5% and the second pillar is a broadly based assessment of the outlook for future price developments.

The two-pillar approach, especially when one of the pillars is so vague, gives considerable discretion to the ECB in its decisions on monetary policy. Yet this discretion makes it more difficult for the ECB to communicate the reasons for its decisions and to convince the markets that it is following its declared intentions. This creates special difficulties for a new institution such as the ECB, which has to establish its credibility. Even the monetary targeting part of the Bundesbank's strategy was far from precise. In retrospect it was probably a mistake simply to inherit the Bundesbank's strategy, since its effectiveness was at least partly due to the fact that it was the Bundesbank that was implementing it. These difficulties compound the problems of transparency and accountability considered above.

Economic Policy in the Euro Zone

There are two essential elements in the making of macroeconomic policy in the euro zone. While there is a clear central authority for monetary policy in EMU, the situation is much less clear for fiscal policy – that is, the control of the balance between the overall level of public expenditure and taxation to try to influence the level of aggregate demand and output of the economy. Unusually for a monetary union, in the euro zone public expenditure and taxation remain overwhelmingly decentralized under the control of national governments. National budgetary discipline is necessary to protect the credibility of the ECB, by removing the possibility of national government defaults and bailouts. Monetary policy will also operate more effectively in a stable fiscal environment where there is consistency between the policies. Since it is difficult in practice to make rapid changes to government expenditure and revenue, it can be argued that fiscal policy should be the subject of longer-term planning and that monetary policy should be used for short-term adjustments.

Coordination of economic policy is based on three interrelated mechanisms: broad guidelines for economic policy; multilateral surveillance; and the excessive deficit procedure. The broad guidelines for economic policy are contained in an annual report adopted by the European Council, addressing such issues as the overall macroeconomic situation, public finances, structural reforms, employment, and growth. Coordination is sought through advice and peer pressure, as no sanctions are involved. Outcomes are not very precisely defined, although there is perhaps some tightening over time.

The guidelines most directly seek to influence outcomes through multilateral surveillance. The Commission and Ecofin evaluate the annual updates of member states' five-year stability programmes, which detail their budgetary positions. The objective of multilateral surveillance is to ensure that national economic policy is broadly consistent with the guidelines and thus with the proper functioning of EMU. However, compliance is again achieved largely by peer pressure, because the only sanction is a recommendation to a member state that it modify its policy.

Fiscal policy is more tightly controlled by the excessive deficit procedure introduced by the Stability and Growth Pact agreed at the Dublin Council in 1996. When a country's budgetary deficit exceeds 3% of GDP, Ecofin can decide by a qualified majority that an excessive deficit exists, make recommendations for its correction, and impose penalties if the member state fails to remedy the situation. The only exemption is where the excess is exceptional and temporary. The restrictions on government debt are looser: this should be less than 60% of GDP unless it is diminishing towards the reference value at a satisfactory pace. Sanctions against excessive deficits are the requirement to make deposits with the EU of up to 0.5% of GDP in any year. The penalty is that interest would not be paid on such deposits and if the excessive deficit persists, these deposits could be forfeited as fines. These procedures are geared to the achievement of medium-term budgetary positions close to balance or in surplus. Fiscal policy acts as an automatic stabilizer: the public sector deficit will expand in a recession, due to rising social security expenditure and falling tax revenue, and this will tend to boost economic activity, offsetting the effects of the recession. For this effect to operate, there must be sufficient headroom, with the 3% deficit ceiling, for the public sector deficit to expand in a recession, hence the aim for the medium term of balance or close to surplus.

The Economic and Financial Committee (EFC) plays an important role in this coordination process. This committee has 34 members, two appointed by the Commission, two by the ECB, and two by each member state. It is an advisory body to the Council (akin to the Committee of Permanent Representatives, or Coreper), but, because it includes the Commission and representatives of the ECB, it provides a forum for dialogue over economic policy. The EFC has several other functions, including giving its opinion on excessive deficits; if its opinion differs from that of the Commission, then the Council has to arbitrate. Given the preponderance of member state representatives on the EFC, this perhaps reinforces the power of member states over these processes.

The Council takes decisions on recommendations in relation to surveillance and excessive deficits on the basis of qualified majority voting. The European Parliament has a very limited role in these procedures, being informed by the Council's President of the broad economic policy guidelines, receiving a report from the Commission and the Council on multilateral surveillance, and being informed of recommendations and the use of the excessive deficit procedure. These arrangements clearly establish the coordination of economic policy as an intergovernmental matter.

The economic policy mechanisms so far described were developed on the basis of the TEU's vision of EMU. There were concerns that EMU was preoccupied with the control of inflation and largely ignored the real side of the economy. Accordingly, a title on employment policy was included in the Treaty of Amsterdam (1997). This provides, however, only for a coordinated strategy that member states can be encouraged to follow by limited incentives, recommendations, example, and peer pressure. Employment policy is important because, in the absence of a system for fiscal transfers between states, the labour market is going to take a lot of the adjustment pressures that previously could have been coped with by changes in the exchange rate and in national monetary or fiscal policy. Employment policy is thus seeking to develop the ability of national labour markets to absorb shocks.

The European Councils at Luxembourg (1997), Cardiff (1998), and Cologne (1999) developed a European Employment Pact, which seeks to coordinate strategy on unemployment, structural and economic reform, and to establish macroeconomic dialogue. The Commission and the Council produce a joint report and guidelines on employment. Member states submit annual reports on the implementation of these guidelines and, where there are problems with national implementation, a recommendation can be issued. The annual assessment of structural and economic reform is incorporated in the broad guidelines on economic policy, permitting coordination with EMU. Macroeconomic dialogue is even less formal, but involves the important actors in economic policy-making: the ECB, the Council, the Commission, and representatives of the "social partners", namely the trade unions and employ-

ers' organizations. It is a forum for an exchange of views, not for the establishment of policy.

The overall constitution of EMU is a curious mixture of national and supranational elements, like the EU itself. The ECB is a supranational institution determining monetary policy in the euro-zone states, and they have no direct influence over it. Fiscal policy has a mixture of supranational and intergovernmental elements. Employment policy is purely intergovernmental and has characteristics in common with other new elements of EU policy, such as justice and home affairs, that have been termed "intensive transgovernmentalism".

The Performance of the Euro-Zone Economy

The ultimate test of EMU is its impact on economic performance. However, it is difficult to identify an "EMU effect" separate from other influences on economic performance and it is too early to form a definitive judgement on the operation of EMU. Accepting these qualifications, the economic performance of the euro-zone economies has been good (see Table 10.4). Economic growth has accelerated, with aggregate GDP growing considerably faster than the average for the period 1992–98, while employment creation has dramatically improved. This improved real economic performance has been achieved with considerable economic stability. Inflation has remained low and the balance of payments current account is in surplus. There was a minor increase in inflation in 2000, caused by higher oil prices and the falling external value of the euro, but core inflation remained very low. However, the economic performance of the euro zone suffers by its comparison with the United States, where there has been spectacular growth in both GDP and employment. The sustainability of this high rate of US growth might be questioned, given the inflation pressures, which are being held in check by an overvalued exchange rate and an unsustainably large current account deficit, and strains were already appearing in early 2001.

The Euro Exchange Rate

The optimistic aggregate situation for the euro zone is marred by the falling exchange rate of the euro and the significant differences in economic performance that have arisen between the 12 countries in the euro zone. The euro has depreciated substantially in value relative to other currencies since its launch. The depreciation has been most spectacular against the yen and the US dollar, but its trade-weighted index fell more than 15% in nominal terms and just under 15% in real terms in the first two years after its launch. (A trade-weighted index has to be used since most countries have floating exchange rates: overall exchange rate movements can be calculated only as an index against other currencies, with their weighting depending upon their importance as trade partners.) This fall in the value of the euro is particularly worrying at this early stage in its development because it is undermining public confidence in the currency.

Large fluctuations in currency values have been the norm since currencies were floated in 1973. Although the fall in the value of the euro is unusual, it is not unprecedented. While any calculation of euro exchange rates before 1999 would of course be artificial, as it was only introduced in that year, it is worth noting that the value of the Deutschmark, which may be taken as a proxy for the euro, was significantly above current levels for the whole of the 1990s, but its value was much lower against the US dollar in the mid-1980s (see Figure 10.1).

Most estimates suggest that the euro is now substantially undervalued but the question remains, why did it fall to such low levels in the first place? As can be seen in Figure 10.1, the euro's slide seems to predate 1999. Its value appreciated in the run-up to its launch and thus it commenced with a relatively high value, so some initial depreciation was perhaps to be expected. This was to be reinforced by a number of factors. The unexpected continuation of strong US growth and some revival in Japan encouraged purchases of these countries' currencies. The growth potential of the US economy and of US companies was increasingly seen as having been enhanced by the "new economy" effect of information technology. This, together with higher interest rates in the United States, encouraged large outflows of direct and portfolio investment from the euro zone.

These external factors were reinforced by a lack of market confidence engendered by apparent disagreements over economic policy. This is an obvious potential problem with a decentralized system. It is not unusual to have regional representatives on the board of a central bank, but the weight given to the opinions of the governors of the national central banks within the Eurosystem is unusual. What is unique about the Eurosystem is that comments from governments come not only from Ecofin but also from the 12 separate national governments. The problem might also have been reinforced by worries about the ambiguity over responsibility for the overall orientation of the euro's exchange rate, which is a joint responsibility of the ECB and Ecofin. There is apparently an internal agreement resolving this particular issue. There was also concern over the perceived slow pace of structural reform in the euro-zone economies.

The fact that the US Federal Reserve, the Nippon Ginkō (Bank of Japan), and the Bank of England intervened together with the ECB to support the euro in October 2000 indicates that the currency is fundamentally undervalued, and that there will be an upward correction in the future. An appreciating euro is also likely to dispel many of the criticisms that have been levelled against the operation of the ECB and economic policy in the euro zone.

Differences between Member States of EMU

There remain substantial differences in economic performance within EMU (see Table 10.5). In 1999, growth in GDP varied from 9.9% in Ireland to 1.4 % in Italy, although in most of the other euro-zone states it fell within the range from 2% to 4%. Unemployment in 1999 ranged from 3.2% in the Netherlands to 15.9% in Spain, with the member states seeming to divide into those with low unemployment and those with high unemployment. Inflation also varied substantially in 1999, from 6.2% in Ireland to 0.3% in France, with the poorer member states generally having higher rates of inflation. Balance of payments current account balances also differed considerably, ranging from a surplus of 5.7% of GDP in the

Netherlands to a deficit of 8.8% of GDP in Portugal.

Of course, variations in economic performance occur even within long-established monetary unions, so it is not surprising that there are quite large differences in the current period of adjustment to EMU. It is also to be expected that the poorer member states will register more rapid rates of GDP growth and of inflation. Higher growth is the result of improvements in productivity achieved by catching up with best practice. Higher inflation, on the other hand, is due to the "Balassa–Samuelson effect": poorer countries generally have lower prices for nontraded goods and services, but as productivity improves in the traded sectors wages generally rise and the prices of nontraded goods and services also rise, increasing inflation but not reducing competitiveness. It is also likely that the poorer member states will run balance of payments deficits because they may be importing capital. Differences in unemployment rates seem to stem from differences in medium-term growth and differing degrees of success in implementing structural reform.

Whether these differences in national economic performance present problems for EMU is difficult to judge. The higher growth and inflation in the poorer member states is likely to persist, and, provided that the divergences do not become too large, they should not present significant difficulties. For other countries it is only persistent divergence of economic performance that will be problematic, and it is still too early to judge whether this is the case.

Economic Adjustment to EMU

The process of economic adjustment to EMU began with the convergence process for membership. This required the maintenance of fixed exchange rates in the EMS, an inflation rate close to the best, and the control of government deficits and debt. The measures put in place to achieve convergence largely remain, but EMU has led to reinforcement and additional measures, especially in relation to deficits and debt. The ability of governments to meet the 3% deficit rule over the economic cycle is seen to require, on average, a situation of close to balance or even surplus in the government's finances. In the longer term the need to finance increased pensions as populations age, and the need to reduce the high levels of debt, will put further pressure on public finances.

The convergence requirements for deficits were met mainly by increasing taxes, but, given resistance from taxpayers and the perceived need to avoid disincentives, further improvements in government finances must come largely from reductions in expenditure. Some countries, such as Germany, seem to be making genuine progress in this direction. In other countries, notably France, progress seems to have slowed, with tax cuts being based on current favourable government finances, not on the long-term fundamentals.

Structural reform is occurring in the euro zone, but since this involves technical legislative changes to taxation, social security, industrial relations, and the behaviour of companies and other organizations it is difficult to gauge its extent. One visible indicator of change has been the growth of mergers and acquisitions within the EU, the value of which totalled more than one trillion US dollars in 1999, catching up with the US market. With the reform of German corporate taxation agreed in July 2000, the unwinding of financial and other organizations' shareholdings should further invigorate the market for corporate control in the euro zone. Access to venture capital for start-ups and small enterprises is another area of change in Europe. The deepening of the single market resulting from EMU is acting as a further fillip to structural change in the EU. The single market is being reinforced by reductions in government subsidies to industry, liberalization, and privatization, especially in finance and telecommunications. France, Belgium, and Spain have reduced social security contributions in order to reduce the cost of taking on workers, especially the low-paid. There has been a considerable use of temporary and part-time contracts to increase flexibility. Thus there is considerable structural change occurring in the EU, some of it driven by EMU, some of it by the new processes accompanying EMU, and some simply by the desire to increase economic growth and reduce unemployment.

Conclusion

EMU is a major achievement for the EU, and represents a major advance in political and economic integration. Despite severe doubts about the feasibility and design of EMU, it has operated very successfully in its first two years, being associated with a major improvement in the EU's overall economic performance. The major problem in this period, the falling euro exchange rate, has undermined confidence in the Eurosystem, but it has had a generally positive impact on economic performance. The launch of the euro took place in comparatively benign economic conditions and undoubtedly there will be more testing times ahead. On the basis of the performance so far, however, the EU can look forward with reasonable confidence in the ability of EMU to cope with this potentially more difficult future.

Further Reading

Crouch, Colin (editor), *After the Euro: Shaping Institutions for Governance in the Wake of European Monetary Union*, Oxford and New York: Oxford University Press, 2000

De Grauwe, Paul, *Economics of Monetary Union*, Oxford and New York: Oxford University Press, 2000

The best basic text on the economics of EMU

Eijffinger, Sylvester C.W., and Jakob de Haan, *European Monetary and Fiscal Policy*, Oxford and New York: Oxford University Press, 2000

A close second to de Grauwe and particularly good on institutional aspects of EMU

European Commission, "Annual Economic Report for 1999", in *European Economy*, 68, 1999

Favero, Carlo, Xavier Freixas, Torsten Persson, and Charles Wyplosz, *One Money, Many Countries: Monitoring the European Central Bank 2*, London: Centre for Economic Policy Research, 2000

Federal Reserve, *Downloadable Statistics*, at www.federalreserve.gov/releases/

Gros, Daniel, Olivier Davanne, Michael Emerson, Tomas Mayer, Guido Tabellini, and Niels Thygesen, *Quo Vadis Euro: The Cost of Muddling Through*, Second Macroeconomic Policy Report from the Macroeconomic Policy Group, Brussels: Centre for European Policy Studies, 2000

This and Favero *et al.* are the best available surveys of the operation of EMU, so far with Gros *et al.* being a little more up to date.

Gros, Daniel, and Niels Thygesen, *European Monetary Integration: From the European Monetary System to European Monetary Union*, second edition, London and New York: Longman, 1998

Excellent on the development of EMU and very comprehensive on the economics of EMU

IMF, *World Economic Outlook*, October 2000, at www.imf.org

Levitt, Malcolm, and Christopher Lord, *The Political Economy of Monetary Union*, London: Macmillan, and New York: St Martin's Press, 2000

Provides an up-to-date survey of the politics of EMU

OECD, *EMU: Facts, Challenges and Policies*, Paris: OECD, 1999; *EMU: One Year on*, Paris: OECD, 2000

These two volumes from the OECD provide a comprehensive survey of the theory and practice of EMU.

OECD, *A Statistical Window on OECD Countries' Government Sectors*, www.oecd.org/puma/stats/

UN Commission on Trade and Development, *World Invest Report 1999*, Geneva: UN, 2000

World Bank, *World Development Report 1999/2000: Entering the 21st Century*, 2000, at www.worldbank.org/wdr/2000/index.html

World Trade Organization, *Downloadable Statistics*, 2000, at www.wto.org/english/res_e/statis_e.htm

Websites

Bureau of Economic Analysis: www.bea.doc.gov/bea/regional/data.htm

European Central Bank: www.ecb.int

Eurostat: www.europa.eu.int/comm/eurostat/

Brian Ardy is Research Fellow at the European Institute, South Bank University, London, where he is engaged in research projects on economic and monetary union. Research for this chapter was supported by award no. L213252034 from the One Europe or Several? programme of the Economic and Social Research Council. He is review editor (with Jackie Gower) for the *Journal of Common Market Studies*, and has published widely on both EMU and the economics of EU enlargement.

Table 10.1 **Main Economic Indicators for the EU, the Prospective Euro Zone, the United States, and Japan, 1998**

	GNP (US$ billions)	Share of world GNP (%)	Population (millions)	Share of world population (%)	GNP per capita (% of world average)
Euro 11[1]	6,488.1	22.5	291	4.9	456
Euro 12[2]	6,611	22.9	301.5	5.1	448
EU 15	8,278.1	28.7	374.9	6.4	452
United States	7,921.3	27.4	268.8	4.6	600
Japan	4,089.9	14.2	126.5	2.1	662

[1] EU 15 excluding nonmembers of EMU as of 1999 (Denmark, Greece, Sweden, and UK)
[2] Euro 11 plus Greece, which became a member of EMU on 1 January 2001

Source: World Bank, *World Development Report 1999/2000: Entering the 21st Century*, 2000

Table 10.2 **Major Economies' Share of World Trade and FDI 1998 (%)**

	Shares of world merchandise trade[1]		Shares of world foreign direct investment[2]	
	Exports	Imports	Outflows	Inflows
Euro 11	15.7	13.6	37.7	21.8
Euro 12	15.8	13.8	37.8	21.9
EU 15	19.9	18.0	59.5	35.7
United States	16.9	21.9	35.9	30.0
Japan	9.6	6.5	3.7	0.5

[1] Excluding trade within the EU
[2] Including foreign direct investment within the EU

Sources: European Commission, "Annual Economic Report for 1999", in *European Economy*, 68, 1999; UN Commission on Trade and Development, *World Invest Report 1999*, Geneva: UN, 2000; World Trade Organization, *Downloadable Statistics*, 2000

Table 10.3 **Regional Differences in Incomes in the United States and within the Prospective Euro Zone, 1997**

Regional income (% of national/Euro zone average)	Number of US states	Number of regions in prospective euro zone
200–224		1
174–199		1
150–174		4
125–150	3	4
100–124	16	17
75–99	28	16
50–74	3	12
25–49		7

Sources: Bureau of Economic Analysis, at www.bea.doc.gov/bea/regional/data.htm; Eurostat, at www.europa. eu.int/comm/eurostat/

Table 10.4   Economic Performance of the Euro zone

	1992–98	*1999*	*2000 (estimate)*	*2001 (projection)*
	Growth of real GDP per capita %			
Advanced economies	2.0	3.4	4.2	3.2
United States	2.5	4.2	5.2	3.2
Euro zone	1.5	2.4	3.5	3.4
	Growth of employment %			
Advanced economies	0.8	1.3	1.3	0.9
United States	1.6	1.5	1.2	0.6
Euro zone	0.1	1.9	1.9	1.4
	Change in consumer prices %			
Advanced economies	2.5	1.4	2.3	2.1
United States	2.7	2.2	3.2	2.6
Euro zone	2.7	1.2	2.1	1.7
	Balance of payments current account as proportion of GDP			
United States	−1.6	−3.6	−4.2	−4.2
Euro zone	0.7	0.5	0.7	1.0

Source: IMF, *World Economic Outlook*, October 2000

Table 10.5   Selected Economic Indicators for States in the Euro Zone

Euro zone states[1]	*Growth of real GDP %*			*Unemployment %*			*Inflation[2] %*			*Balance of payments current account as proportion of GDP*		
	1992– 98	*1999*	*2000[3]*	*1992– 98*	*1999*	*2000[3]*	*1992– 98*	*1999*	*2000[3]*	*1992– 98*	*1999*	*2000[3]*
Germany	**1.3**	1.6	2.9	**8.2**	8.3	7.9	**2.3**	0.9	0.4	**4.1**	−0.9	−0.2
Austria	**1.7**	2.2	3.5	**4.1**	4.4	3.5	**2.2**	0.6	1.5	**2.5**	−2.8	−2.0
Finland	**2.4**	4.0	5.0	**14.1**	10.3	9.0	**2.0**	0.7	1.6	**4.7**	5.2	5.6
Belgium	**1.8**	2.5	3.9	**9.2**	9.0	8.3	**2.1**	0.9	0.9	**4.3**	4.4	4.4
Netherlands	**2.7**	3.6	3.9	**6.1**	3.2	2.3	**1.9**	1.3	3.1	**2.4**	5.7	6.2
France	**1.5**	2.9	3.5	**11.8**	11.3	9.8	**1.6**	0.3	0.6	**4.7**	2.7	2.7
Ireland	**6.9**	9.9	8.7	**12.2**	5.6	4.5	**3.4**	6.2	5.5	**4.8**	0.3	−0.6
Italy	**1.3**	1.4	3.1	**11.2**	11.4	10.7	**3.9**	1.7	1.7	**5.8**	0.7	1.0
Spain	**2.1**	3.7	4.1	**21.4**	15.9	14.0	**3.9**	3.1	3.4	**7.9**	−2.2	−2.2
Greece	**1.8**	3.5	3.5	**9.6**	11.7	11.5	**10.1**	2.9	3.1	**7.6**	−4.1	−4.9
Portugal	**2.4**	3.0	3.4	**6.1**	4.4	4.1	**6.0**	3.2	2.2	**3.8**	−8.8	−10.4

[1]   States are listed in descending order of their GDP per capita
[2]   Inflation is measured by the GDP deflator rather than the consumer price index
[3]   Estimate

Source: IMF, *World Economic Outlook*, October 2000

Figure 10.1   Exchange Rate against the US Dollar of the Deutschmark (1973–99) and the Euro (1999–2001)

Source: US Federal Reserve, *Downloadable Statistics*, 2001

Chapter Eleven

Competition Policy

Jeffrey Harrop

Competition policy is of great importance to the EU, and has particular interest for economists and lawyers (although the main focus in this chapter is on the economic rather than the legal aspects). Competition policy has been a preoccupation of microeconomists for a long time, and a strong policy is generally favoured because it is believed to be conducive to an optimal allocation of resources and efficiency. In the past policy in this area would have been referred to as antimonopoly policy, instead of by the more recent term "competition policy". The two terms will be treated synonymously, although the newer term is favoured.

The Case for a Pro-Competition Policy

Historically, most economists since the days of Adam Smith have taken the view that monopolists represent a conspiracy against the public. They abuse their power by exploiting the consumer, with prices being higher and output lower than in a perfectly competitive market. In the latter, firms charge prices that are equal to marginal (incremental) costs and in the long run can make only normal profits. By contrast, monopolists are able to charge prices above marginal costs; also, they are able to enjoy supernormal profits that persist from the short term into the long term. In addition, monopolists, unlike firms in perfect competition, are able to engage in price discrimination, charging consumers different prices for the same product. By separating their markets, they can charge higher prices in those parts of the market where demand is more inelastic.

Therefore, in terms of static analysis (ignoring changes that may occur over time), monopolists have been condemned for their inefficiency. While restrictive practices are more clearly undesirable, since they offer no economies of scale, when one examines monopoly in terms of dynamic analysis (with long-term growth over time) the assessment is ambivalent. This is because there are two main benefits that can be derived by monopolists. The first is that they are able, through their size, to enjoy the benefits from economies of scale. This means that the average and marginal cost curve of the monopolist is likely to be lower than that of the smaller supplier in a competitive market. Internal economies of scale apply both to larger plants and to larger firms, with the range of economies varying between different industries, but they tend to be particularly high in industries such as aerospace, chemicals or the motor vehicle industry.

Secondly, it has been argued, particularly by the Austrian and later US economist Joseph A. Schumpeter, that large firms would be able to spend more on research and development, and that their propensity to innovate would therefore be greater. Hence competition is not just about price competition but also other important dimensions, such as the ability to develop new products through innovation. These are the source of what Schumpeter called "creative destruction", by which only the fittest and healthiest firms survive through innovatory change and cost-cutting.

A critical assessment of these potential benefits indicates that economies of scale, and research and development, are both of growing importance in many industries. However, they do not automatically swing the balance in favour of monopolists. This is because, though economies of scale may create lower costs per unit of production, the benefits are unlikely to be passed on to consumers in the form of lower prices. Also, any increased productive efficiency may be offset by "X inefficiency", or "slack", on the part of managers and workers, arising from the lack of competitive pressure. Further considerations also weigh against monopoly, such as the degree to which there are diseconomies of scale arising from more difficult managerial control and increasing costs; also the extent to which in some industries technology is favouring small and medium-sized enterprises (SMEs), in industries such as textiles and engineering.

The issues of research and development, and the claimed consequences for innovation, need careful examination. Invention is different from innovation and historically many inventions have come from lone individuals or SMEs, rather than from larger firms. However, the latter may be better able to finance commercial production and are increasingly important in many industries, such as chemicals and pharmaceuticals. Monopolies have the resources to finance innovation, but often fail to do so because of the absence of competitive pressures. Hence there is a need to assess how far high profits have arisen from monopoly power or from monopoly high spending on past research and development, and how far high profits are necessary in the future to maintain and reward successful research and development.

It can be seen, therefore, that economic theory has moved from an automatic and dogmatic condemnation of monopolies, based on static analysis, to a more pragmatic position that takes dynamic considerations into account. Meanwhile, empirical evidence of the welfare losses from monopolies spans a wide range of estimates, from 0.1% of GNP to welfare losses of one half of monopoly profits (see Kemp pp. 97–99).

It appears, therefore, that economic theory does not offer a clearcut position. While most economists focusing on the EU still start off from a suspicious view of monopoly, they are generally prepared to assess and evaluate each case on its merits. In this respect the mainstream tendency in western Europe differs from the more clearcut "antitrust" (antimonopoly) position that underpins policy-making in the United States. With its large unified market, the United States has been able to take a stronger line, breaking up monopolies but still having sufficient producers to reap economies of scale and maintain competition. For example, in 2000 Microsoft was condemned for overexploiting the interlinkages between its Windows system and its software, which made it difficult for other software companies to compete. It was recommended that the company should be broken up into two separate parts. In contrast, each national market in the EU has been too small to combine effective anti-monopoly measures with the reaping of sufficient economies of scale. This is why the single European market is so important in giving the EU a market of a size comparable to that of the United States, offering both economies of scale and competitive benefits, even though the market is very different in character because of the diversity of history, culture, and languages among member states. It also underpins the growing importance and linkage between single market policies, industrial policy, and competition policy.

Monopoly Power and its Abuse

In economic theory, monopolies are defined as single firms that dominate markets. However, in practice most markets are not dominated 100% by a single firm. In other words, there are usually many markets that are oligopolistic, with a few large firms – or, in the case of a duopoly, two firms – dominating the market. Further, oligopolies can choose either to collude or to compete, with the former being most likely to occur where there are fewer firms and greater product homogeneity. Where there is completely free entry into and exit from an industry, it is defined as perfectly contestable.

The basic approach and starting point from which to view the relative power of monopolies is that of market dominance. The more narrowly the market is defined, the greater is the degree of monopoly power, as, for example, in regional or national markets of member states compared with the whole EU market, which has grown enormously from the original six to 15 members. Hence the monopoly problem is a lesser one within the EU market as a whole than it is within any national market.

The shares of the largest firms in particular industries in the EU market are shown in Table 11.1 below. (Market share depends upon just how few firms are chosen; the table shows the top five firms.) It can be seen that the most concentrated industries are aerospace, motor vehicles, and computers/office equipment, in which the top five firms account for nearly two thirds of total output. However, this structural indicator can provide only a guide to policy-makers, since in these industries economies of scale are high and the EU needs firms of sufficient size in these key industries to compete with those in the United States and Japan. It should also be noted that the EU market itself is dominated by foreign multinationals in some industries, such as IBM in electronics.

An analysis of the share of the largest firms in total sales of manufacturing industry in the EU, compared with the United States and Japan, has shown the EU share is quite closely comparable with Japan's, while both the EU and Japan have less concentration of manufacturing share by the largest companies than the United States has.

The Herfindahl index (H) is often considered to be more revealing than the market shares held by the largest firms, since it reflects the distribution of the market shares of all firms. To obtain the index as a whole number, the squares of the market shares expressed as fractions are multiplied by 10,000. In the case of a monopoly with one firm holding 100% of the market, H is therefore 10,000. Where the industry is composed of n firms of equal size, H is 10,000 divided by n.

While industrial concentration provides an important guide to monopoly policy, it is also necessary to go beyond this to include conduct and performance in assessing the situation. In the United Kingdom, for example, national policy starts from a clear structural definition of a "dominant firm" as accounting for 25% or more of the market. National and EU policies remain separate, however, with the latter being used where intra-EU trade is likely

to be adversely affected. For the EU as a whole, under Article 82 (formerly Article 86) of the EC Treaty, while the undertaking must be in a "dominant" position (usually meaning, in this case, having more than 40% of the market share), the focus is far more upon the abuse of this position. Concern about abuse by dominant firms goes back to the early days of the European Coal and Steel Community (ECSC), when France was fearful of any renewed concentration in the German coal and steel industries.

Article 82 of the Treaty has been used to tackle different types of abuse by dominant firms. Adverse effects include charging unfair prices – not just high prices that exploit consumers, but also excessively low prices intended to drive out competitors. Dominant firms that have been examined and acted against over the years include manufacturers such as Commercial Solvents, which controlled materials and refused to supply them freely to other firms, and Hoffmann–La Roche, which dominated the market for vitamins, charging different prices in various markets and also giving "fidelity rebates" that were aggregated across all products.

Merger Policy

Mergers are driven by increasing the value of two businesses, whereby one plus one increases beyond the mathematical value of two. Growth by acquisition is quicker than internal growth, offering immediate and less risky entry into a new product market. A full legal merger fuses the assets and liabilities of two or more companies into a single new or existing company. In the EU, there have been widespread legal obstacles to such mergers, and instead the most common type of merger has involved a takeover of one company by another, with both companies continuing to exist as legal entities. Another looser link that falls well short of a legal merger includes a joint venture, where companies agree to cooperate together on a particular project.

Mergers between firms may occur at different levels in the chain of production. While horizontal integration takes place between businesses at the same level of production, vertical integration may develop either backwards, to sources of supply, or forwards, into the marketplace. The other type of merger to mention is the forming of a conglomerate, which brings together businesses to produce a disparate range of products, but in which a merger offers financial benefits. Stock markets can play a significant role in encouraging mergers when a company's share price drops to such an extent that it becomes vulnerable to a takeover bid. This possibility is generally said to serve as a spur to maintain company efficiency.

It might be argued that mergers offer significant potential benefits to companies. These include better management, reduced transaction costs, rationalization, and the opportunities to exploit greater economies of scale. Furthermore, one of the main aims of the single European market is to allow companies to reorganize their operations in order to compete more effectively. However, the results of many mergers in the past have been disappointing. The mergers contributed little to increased profitability or sales and did not lead to lower prices for consumers. The latter point is of particular importance, since it suggests that a significant adverse cost was the reinforcement of monopoly power (see *European Economy*, May 1989, Chapter 2).

Since mergers have increased in number, it is important to examine them closely, looking at sources of mergers and the sizes of the companies involved. While most mergers have been national ones, there has been an increasing and continuing trend in merger activity involving companies from different EU countries, and also companies from EU and non-EU countries combined. Historically the majority of mergers were national, but globalization has led to more crossborder mergers. Mergers can involve companies of all sizes, but there has been a rapid growth of mergers between very large companies, which provide a greater threat to competition than mergers between SMEs.

As mergers may result in varying mixtures of both costs and benefits, it is necessary for policy-makers to have some guidance about the sectors in which mergers may be beneficial or not. Mergers need to be scrutinized very closely in sectors that tend to be mature or declining

and in which there is limited competition from imports. These are shown in Table 11.2, being divided into four categories. In group 1, mergers offer few benefits. Mergers are less inappropriate in group 2, though they may not constitute the most effective strategy. The industries in group 3 are more appropriate to mergers since they provide potential gains in efficiency without a danger of reducing competition. Finally, in group 4, European mergers since the implementation of the single market have led to rationalization and gains in efficiency, but there is a danger of reducing competition.

There is no problem in allowing mergers that raise efficiency without reducing competition, nor in banning mergers that offer no efficiency gains and reduce competition. More careful and delicate assessment is necessary when mergers result in efficiency gains but do reduce competition. Mergers will be more tolerable when one has contestable markets, in which there is complete freedom of entry and exit into the market.

The European Community's policy on mergers was initially weak: it was only invoked where it was involved under Articles 85 and 86 (now 81 and 82) of the Treaty of Rome, concerning restrictive practices and abuse of a dominant position. With a spate of mergers sparked off by the single market programme, a European Merger Control Regulation was introduced in 1990. The Commission investigates and controls mergers above a given sales turnover threshold. This measure is used since turnover figures are readily available and provide legal certainty about when the merger regulation will be applied. The Merger Task Force for the Directorate General on Competition (DG IV) has examined mergers with a Community dimension where the following two turnover thresholds have applied:

- an aggregate worldwide turnover of all those involved in excess of ECU5 billion;
- an aggregate Community turnover for at least two of the firms involved of more than ECU250 million.

It should be noted that when each of the firms involved has two thirds or more of its turnover within one member state the merger regulation does not apply. A stronger Commission role in controlling mergers would emerge if the turnover thresholds were to be lowered further in the future, as was suggested in a Commission Green Paper in 1996. Some favour this proposal in order to ensure that countries with few or no merger rules, such as Greece, Denmark or Italy, could be constrained from leniently supporting domestic mergers to create "national champions".

Mergers that meet the two turnover criteria above have to be notified to the Commission, which then investigates them. The Commission also examines agreements that lead to an increase in industrial concentration, but with no economic benefits. Such potential mergers are put before the Merger Task Force, which decides, within one month of notification, whether to act on the case and, if so, reaches its final decision within another four months.

Despite the theoretical independence of the Commission, some see it as being open to national political pressures. Such concerns were raised, for example, in connection with the merger in 1988 between two Dutch coffee companies, Douwe Egbert and Van Nelle, which created a near monopoly in the Benelux market. Many would prefer a completely independent agency, modelled perhaps on the German *Kartellamt* (Cartel Office).

The majority of the mergers dealt with have been allowed to proceed: of some 140 merger proposals up to the end of March 1993 only 11 resulted in serious doubts. In those where problems existed, conditions were imposed before the mergers were allowed to occur. In one key industry, aerospace, there have been two interesting cases. The merger between Aérospatiale and Messerschmitt–Bölkow–Blohm was approved because sufficient competition existed to prevent a dominant position – in this case, in helicopters – from arising. However, in the case of turboprop aircraft, a proposed merger between Aérospatiale, Alenia, and De Havilland was prohibited, in a controversial decision, since it would have resulted in the firm having a dominant position controlling well over half the world market.

The Commission in phase I gets a formal undertaking from the companies, thus reduc-

ing the number of more detailed phase II investigations. In 1998 there were nine phase II cases decided (see European Commission 1999 p. 212). Five involved clearances subject to formal undertakings, while three were approved without undertakings. In the case of a merger between two accountancy firms, Price Waterhouse and Coopers and Lybrand, the conclusion was that there was no risk of a dominant position, following the abandonment of a proposed merger between KPMG and Ernst and Young. The case of Enso/Stora in newsprint in Scandinavia was cleared because major buyers, including firms such as Tetra Pak, were considered to have countervailing power. In the third of these cases, ITS/Signode Titon, the Commission approved the merger in spite of the high share of steel strappings because there was competition from plastic strappings. New technology featured in the single important prohibition of the proposed mergers of Bertelsmann–Kirch–Premiere and Deutsche Telecom/Betaresearch. The Commission was determined to avoid the creation or strengthening of dominant positions in digital television services.

Restrictive Practices

As with monopoly legislation, so with restrictive practices: national and Community legislation apply with minor differences and in separate situations. In the United Kingdom, restrictive practices legislation is again more tightly defined in its legal form, whereas Community policy focuses more on the adverse effects of such restrictions. Article 81 of the EC Treaty covers agreements or concerted practices between two or more enterprises that distort competition and are likely to affect trade among member states. This applies not just to current trade but also to future trade. Also, all firms operating in the EU are affected, whatever their nationality. The term "agreements" covers written or oral agreements, as well as the consequences of membership of a trade association (even including its recommendations) and loose concerted practices where there is common action, such as aligning price changes.

"Horizontal" agreements that are prohibited include price-fixing and market or production sharing (for example, sharing sources of supply, quotas, or sales). While cartels may at times offer superficial gains in reducing surplus capacity, they hamper the most efficient businesses and in practice, according to Dennis Swann, "virtually no cartel with significant market power has been exempted" (Swann p. 120). Also prohibited are discriminatory practices; collective boycotts (forcing potential competitors out, or preventing market entry); and agreements that tie the sales of several products together. Other agreements that may pose some problems include joint purchasing agreements; joint selling agreements; sales promotion; exchange of information; trade association/market foreclosure; and noncompetition clauses connected with the sale of an undertaking.

"Vertical" agreements that may adversely affect competition include simple distribution agreements; exclusive distribution agreements; selective purchasing agreements; and selective distribution. Exceptions are made for simple single distribution agreements where the distribution is by the manufacturer itself, a branch office, or a local subsidiary, or under a true agency agreement. Where distribution is improved by exclusive distribution, a group exemption exists, but otherwise exclusive distribution agreements go too far when they have adverse effects on competition, particularly when no parallel imports are possible.

Exclusive purchasing agreements occur when a seller is obliged to buy supplies exclusively from a stated manufacturer or other supplier. Group exemption was allowed from January 1984, but the maximum duration of the exclusive purchasing obligation was limited to five years (renewable) and the products in the range concerned had to be related to each other. For example, this applied to beer and other drinks, but for beer alone, or for petrol, the maximum duration of the exclusive tie was ten years (and for long tenancy agreements may be even longer). The tie does not extend to products other than petroleum-based motor vehicle fuels and lubricants or beer and other drinks (so it does not extend to crisps, fruit machines, and other such specified items).

Selective distribution ensures that many products are sold by selected and properly techni-cally qualified dealers. Hence, in the motor vehicle industry a block exemption applies. However, concern about excessively high car prices in some national markets, as a result of firms partitioning the market, has led to firmer EU policy. For example, in 1998 the EU imposed its largest ever fine on a single company – ECU102 million on Volkswagen – since the company's dealers in Italy refused to sell Volkswagen and Audi cars to foreign buyers, especially from Germany and Austria. The level of fine reflects the severity of the infringement, past action, and the degree to which the company has been uncooperative. In relation to car prices, the Commission also publishes a twice-yearly report to try to increase competition.

Franchising similarly has a block exemption since it offers positive benefits in improving distribution by accelerating the entry of new competitors. Industrial property rights cover patents, copyrights, trademarks, performing rights, registered designs, and models. Group exemptions exist to recognize the beneficial effects of patents. However, industrial property rights have to be consistent with the free movement of goods across the national boundaries within the EU.

Where restrictive practices exist, such as those covered in this section, the parties must notify them to the Commission. The Commission may decide that some of these are safe and can be allowed to continue through negative clearance. Also, agreements of minor importance covering SMEs are normally permitted (under the *de minimis* rule); for example, where they cover less than 5% of market share and have a low turnover of less than €200 million (see European Commission March 1989 p. 16). Other exemptions exist in relation to particular cooperation agreements, and in relation to research and development. Various agreements are allowed if the harmful effects of a restrictive agreement are offset by benefits, such as improved production or distribution of goods, or promotion of technical and economic progress, and a fair share of the benefits go to consumers. Exemptions may be granted on an individual basis or on a group basis. For example, in January 2000 the Commission approved an exemption for washing machine producers to stop producing and importing the least energy-efficient machines on environmental grounds. This was also said to offer consumers benefits by reducing electricity bills (Competition Directorate General pp. 13–14).

Where companies are in doubt about the adverse effects of restrictive practices, particularly on trade, they are best advised to notify the Commission, otherwise they are liable to fines. Notification to the Commission is done on an official form and the information submitted should be accurate, since otherwise fines of up to €5,000 may be imposed. The Commission also obtains information from other sources, such as complaints from the governments of member states, companies or trade associations. The Commission is obliged to examine all formal complaints. It also has the power to carry out enquiries on its own initiative. It may make written requests for information, with daily fines of up to €1,000 for failure to respond and fines of up to €5,000 for incorrect or incomplete information. The Commission can also conduct its own investigations, sending in its own officials, sometimes unannounced, to prevent firms having forewarning and giving them the possibility of destroying incriminating evidence, as in the case of the raid on AstraZeneca in May 2000 to examine its activities in relation to a particular patented drug.

The Commission is responsible for enforcing competition policy, backed up by the European Court of Justice. The outcomes are either negative clearance, exemptions, or decisions that order the termination of restrictive practices. The cases are presented in the *Official Journal* so that interested parties can react. There is also consultation with the authorities in the member states, which have representatives on the Advisory Committee on Restrictive Practices and Dominant Positions. When the Commission seeks to terminate an infringement, the parties involved are informed and given time to respond; they can also request an oral hearing organized by the Directorate General for Competition and conducted by the Hearing Officer. The Commission has the power to impose fines of up to €1 million or 10% of the world annual turnover of the undertaking in the previous business year, whichever of the two

is greater. The fines are heaviest and most punitive where the restrictive practices have existed for a long time and are similar to those that have been penalized in the past under Commission case law. Since Commission action may be lengthy in complex cases, interim measures are taken immediately to stamp out objectionable behaviour. The majority of cases are concluded with an informal settlement in which the undertakings sweep away the restrictive practices. The European Court of Justice has the power to review and vary all formal decisions of the Commission, and to confirm, reduce, cancel or increase the Commission's fines and penalty payments.

Proposed reforms by the Commission in a White Paper include abolition of the notification and authorization system for restrictive practices, leaving it to undertakings themselves to decide whether their agreements comply with the ban on restrictive practices. This could create more uncertainty, but it would provide the national authorities and the courts with greater roles to play in the application of competition rules, especially in the case of disputes.

State Aids

The term "state aids" covers any actions by any member state that distort or threaten to distort competition by favouring certain national undertakings and adversely affecting trade with other nations. State aids have been defined by the European Court of Justice as applying when firms would not be able to obtain the finance from private capital markets, or, if they could do so, only on less favourable terms. There is a wide range of state aids going beyond government grants, cheap loans, and interest subsidies, such as tax concessions, public guarantees of company borrowing, provision of goods and services on preferential terms, and, in certain circumstances, the acquisition of public shareholdings in businesses. These are all condemned unless they fall into the limited categories of state aids that are deemed to be compatible with the development of the common market. The EU has made it clear that state aids have to be scrutinized closely where they are specific and offer unfair advantage to certain firms or goods compared with others.

In a first best analysis or ideal world, where perfectly competitive markets provide the most efficient allocation of resources, subsidies would reduce economic welfare. However, when ass⸺ ⸺ ⸺re relaxed to consider external fac⸺ ⸺⸺⸺⸺ng returns to sc⸺ it⸺ su⸺ si⸺ r⸺

electronics, and ⸺.

Both the Treaty of Paris and the Treaty of Rome conferred powers to control state aids on, respectively, the High Authority of the ECSC and the Commission of the European Economic Community. Article 4 of the Treaty of Paris declared subsidies and state aids to be generally incompatible with the common mar-

ket in coal and steel. Similarly, Articles 87 and 88 (formerly 92 and 93) of the EC Treaty still forbid state aids that affect trade and competition within the European Community. This can be interpreted to extend not just to firms that export from, but also to those that are ⸺ffe⸺ted by imports into, home markets. The ⸺⸺rnments of member states have to notify ⸺ Commission before introducing new aid ⸺mes or altering existing ones. If the Com⸺ sion decides that a scheme is problematic, ⸺ invites comment from all those affected ⸺ the publication of a notice in the *Official* ⸺urnal. If any member state government dis⸺grees with the Commission's conclusion, it has ⸺o months in which to demand a judicial ⸺eview by the European Court of Justice. The ⸺ommission can order a member state government to recover from the recipient any illegal aid that has been given.

The basic principle is that state aids must not distort competition among firms in the EU, but that derogations are permissible in particular limited cases, for example, to promote regional development for Objective 1 regions to which investment aid of up to 75% of "net grant equivalent" (NGE) of the investment cost may be given. The term "NGE" is used in order to standardize the different types of assistance given. Other areas are also eligible for state aids. For example, where GDP is 15% below the national average or unemployment at least 10% higher than the national average, then the ceiling is normally up to 30% of NGE. (For further explanation, see *European Economy*, September 1991 pp. 58–59.) Apart from regional aid schemes, the Commission has a block exemption for other acceptable types of state aid, such as SMEs, research and development, environmental protection, employment, and training. Also, it may adopt a regulation in connection with the *de minimis* rule. It checks that measures conform, so as to ensure, for example, that research and development is not too close to the marketplace, or that training measures are general and not specific to particular firms. The Commission concentrates on the more important cases. A new regulation adopted in 1999 codified and speeded up its procedures (to take no more than 18 months), and enables immediate provisional

recovery of unlawful aid from the original beneficiary. It also provides for on-site monitoring
visits; enables examination of state aids over the
past ten years; and extends to unfair state aids
in tax schemes – for example, Ireland's preferential tax treatment of manufacturing has been
declared an unauthorized state aid.

State aid that falls foul of the following four
tests is illegal: it confers an advantage to a firm
or firms; it is granted by the states or through
state resources; it is granted selectively to certain undertakings or to the production of
certain goods and thus distorts competition;
finally, it affects trade among member states
(see European Commission 1999 pp. 81–110).

The Commission assesses whether the benefits of state aids outweigh the disadvantages,
particularly the potential trade distortion.
Since the growth in state aids to help depressed
industries in the 1980s, the Commission has
taken a stronger line against them in recent
years, on the grounds that the single market
cannot bring about the projected gains if state
aids grow and replace other barriers that have
been removed. In addition, in view of the aims
of the Maastricht Treaty and EMU, the countries with significant state aids, especially those
in southern Europe, had budgetary deficits that
infringed the Maastricht fiscal criteria. The EU
also wishes to ensure that richer countries are
not giving their own state aids that merely
offset the benefits that poorer countries are
deriving from EU structural funding.

The EU has started to look closely at general
investment aid schemes lacking a specific sectoral or regional objective and approved years
ago. These were discretionary national state
aids, which the EU now wants to abolish. It
also wishes to move from national support of
industrial "champions" towards the creation
of EU champions. Article 86 (formerly 90) of
the EC Treaty states that public enterprises
should also be subject to competition rules, but
these tend not to be as transparent as those in
the private sector. Large public enterprises
have to show government transfers clearly in
their financial accounts. Further, with the current vogue for the privatization of such industries, steps have been taken to ensure that they
are sold to the private sector at more realistic prices that do not involve a subsidy to

the private sector purchaser. Privatization often
occurs by selling not on the open market but
by private sales, with great uncertainty in
setting correct market values since these are
dependent on future profits. Where governments still perceive some economic and political gains from an underpriced sale, it would
be useful for the EU to have an independent
consultant's view of valuation. Otherwise it will
be difficult for EU policy makers to control
national governments, showing that hopes and
reality are hard to match.

The scope of EU competition policy has
grown, especially when led from the top by a
strong Competition Commissioner. Policy has
become much tougher in liberalizing public
sector monopolies and in limiting state aids.
Unfortunately, the Commission has been constrained in exercising its power fully by its
growing case load, some unclear Treaty articles, and particular interest groups including
those of some member states. State aid should
mainly be confined to cases such as restructuring, with more negative decisions in other
cases, plus an attempt to shame those who
persistently infringe competition policy.

Further Reading

European Commission, *EEC Competition Policy in the
   Single Market*, second edition, Luxembourg: Commission of the European Communities, March
   1989

   This explains the objectives and rules of competition policy so that companies can understand
   how they operate, and whether they are affected
   by them.

European Commission, "Horizontal Mergers and
   Competition Policy in the European Community", in *European Economy*, 40, May 1989

   This paper analyzes the costs and benefits of
   mergers in the EC, providing a basis for merger
   control regulation.

European Commission, "Fair Competition in the
   Internal Market: Community State Aid Policy",
   in *European Economy*, 48, September 1991

   This focuses in particular on the economic rationale for subsidy control; trends and problems of
   state aid; and the application of competition
   policy in tightening up on state aids.

European Commission, *XXVIIIth Report on Competi-*

tion Policy, 1998, Luxembourg: Commission of the European Communities, 1999

This edition of an annual publication that covers all aspects of competition policy in depth, with illustrations and details of cases, includes a foreword by Karel Van Miert, arguing the case for more multilateral cooperation to ensure fair trade, and to deal with globalization and the threat posed by anticompetitive practices.

European Commission Directorate-General for Competition, *Competition Policy Newsletter*, February 2000

This is one issue of a series published three times a year that covers antimonopoly rules, mergers, and state aids through short articles, statements of opinion, and comments.

Kemp, John, "The Competition Policy of the European Union", in Frank McDonald and Stephen Dearden (editors), *European Economic Integration*, second edition, London and New York: Longman, 1994

Kemp provides both theoretical and empirical coverage of the case for competition policy in the United Kingdom and the EU.

Swann, Dennis, *The Economics of the Common Market*, seventh edition, Harmondsworth and New York: Penguin, 1992

Chapter 5 covers nontariff barriers in the customs union. It provides examples of many cases in which the Commission and the European Court of Justice have taken action against companies involved in restrictive practices and dominant firm abuse.

Jeffrey Harrop is Lecturer in Economics in the Department of European Studies at the University of Bradford. He is the author of *Structural Funding and Employment in the European Union* (1996) and *The Political Economy of Integration in the European Union* (third edition, 2000).

Table 11.1   Share of Largest Firms in Output of Selected EC Industries

Industry	Share of top five firms in total output %	
Tobacco	43.7	
Textiles	6.4	(top 3 firms)
Chemicals	41.5	
Rubber	17.4	(top 3 firms)
Construction materials	22.3	
Iron and steel	27.5	
Metal goods	6.9	
Electronics	42.2	
Motor vehicles	65.5	
Aerospace	65.6	
Pharmaceuticals	28.7	
Computers, office equipment	65.3	
Industrial and agricultural machinery	13.7	
Drink	34.1	
Food	13.5	
Printing and publishing	12.1	

Source: Commission services DGII, cited in Commission, "Horizontal Mergers and Competition Policy in the European Community", *European Economy*, No. 40, May 1989, p. 41.

Table 11.2 Illustration of Classification of Industries for Merger Control Purposes

Group Industry	Characteristics	Implications
1 Building materials Metal goods Paints and varnishes Furniture Paper goods Rubber goods Tobacco	● Declining or mature industries ● Markets closed to international trade ● Not technology-intensive or only slowly changing technologically ● Economies of scale limited or acting as entry barriers	In these industries mergers offer little prospect of efficiency gains and present a danger of a reduction of competition
2 Steel Industrial and agricultural machinery Leather and leather goods Fur Clothing and textiles Sawn and processed wood and related products Pulp, paper and board Jewellery, toys, musical instruments	● Declining or mature industries ● Fairly open to imports from inside and outside the EC ● In some industries, strong competition from low-wage countries ● Economies of scale limited or already exploited ● Not technology-intensive or with technology known throughout the world ● Some industries highly fragmented (toys, furs)	Less danger of reduction of competition because of high import penetration and the fragmentation of some industries. But growth by merger is no longer an appropriate strategy for European firms. Instead, they should set out to specialize in top-of-the-range products, requiring modern and flexible production facilities
3 Advanced materials Chemicals/pharmaceuticals Computers/offces automa-tion Telecommunications Electronics Motor vehicles Aerospace Instruments	● Growth industries ● Open to international trade ● Strong competition from American and Japanese products ● Large economies of scale ● R&D very important, fast-changing technology	Less danger of monopolization and prospects of substantial efficiency gains from mergers. In these industries, link-ups between European firms would allow them to internationalize their operations from a solid European base
4 Boilermaking Cables and heavy electrical plant Railway equipment Shipbuilding Some food industries (confectionery, chocolate, flour, pasta) Beer	● Mature industries ● Little intra-Community trade and competition, restricted by seg-mentation of public procurement markets or differences in standards and regulations ● Not technology-intensive (food and drink industries) or only moderately so ● Large economies of scale	In these industries the removal of barriers with the single market programme will lead to ration-alization and European-scale mergers. These may produce efficiency gains but there is also a danger of reduction of competition

Source: Commission services, cited in Commission, "Horizontal Mergers and Competition Policy in the European Community", *European Economy*, No. 40, May 1989, p. 32.

Table 11.3 New Cases of State Aid Registered in 1998

	Notified aids	Non-notified aids	Existing aids	Total
Agriculture	276	32	0	308
Transport	34	10	0	44
Fisheries	45	7	0	52
Coal	6	0	0	6
Other	342	97	5	444
Total	703	146	5	854

Source: Commission of the European Communities, *XXVIIIth Report on Competition Policy, 1998*, Luxembourg: Commission of the European Communities, 1999

Chapter Twelve

The EU Budget

Roger Levy

It may seem perverse to characterize the EU's plannned budget of more than €93 billion for the financial year 2001 as relatively small. Yet it represents little more than 1% of the total GNP of the 15 member states, or about 2% of their aggregate public expenditure. The EU budget would barely cover one fifth of annual total public spending in Britain. On the other hand, because of the specific policy areas that are financed by the EU and their differential incidence across the member states, EU spending can have a big impact, for example on the agricultural sector and the less developed member states.

Five policy domains account for the overwhelming bulk of the budget. These include the Common Agricultural Policy (CAP), structural policy, research and technological development (RTD), cooperation and development with third countries, and the European Development Fund (EDF) – although it should be noted that the EDF has a separate budget. As might be expected in the EU's multi-level system, budgetary decision-making and financial management processes are complex and sometimes cumbersome. As in any budgetary context, planned spending can differ from actual spending and revenue sources have changed over time.

Expenditure Trends, 1977–98

The levels of expenditure by the European Community/EU have been driven by three main variables: the scope of policy competences, the limits on available resources, and the number of member states. Between 1977

and the present, there has been substantial change in all three. The number of member states has risen from nine to 15, and the total population base has increased by about one third, from 270 million to 360 million. Thus, if spending levels had simply remained constant, we could have expected a real increase of about one third just to keep pace with changes in population. If a generous average economic growth rate of 2.5% a year was also to be factored in, we might have expected an increase of about 123%.

In fact, spending rose by more than 200% (or threefold) in real terms, and by almost nine times in nominal terms, between 1977 and 1998. The scope and extent of policy competences in the areas of structural funding, RTD, and cooperation aid to third countries have grown beyond recognition, and revenue sources have been expanded to meet this increase. Table 12.1 shows both a huge nominal increase of around 775% (or 8.75 times the total in 1977) and a real increase (adjusted for inflation) in the order of 200% (a threefold increase). While some of the largest increases did take place around the time of the accession of new member states (Greece in 1981, Spain and Portugal in 1986, and Austria, Sweden, and Finland in 1995), there were some very large increases in other years too, for example in 1978, 1988, and 1991. It is notable that the real figures fluctuated quite sharply, with decreases in some years followed by huge increases in others.

A further general characteristic worth noting is the cyclical nature of the data. While peaks and troughs were more pronounced in some areas compared to others (see below), the wave pattern is evident throughout the totals. As we have argued, peaks have sometimes coincided with enlargement, but this is not the whole story. Generalized five-year budgetary planning was introduced in 1988, and it is perhaps significant that big increases seem to have occurred both in 1988–89 and in 1992–93. This seems to be repeating itself. The smallest ever nominal increases occurred in the last two financial years for which figures are available, representing a stage in the cycle where real decline also took place (in 1997–98). As we shall see below (Table 12.3), a large increase in real spending was projected for the first year of the new five-year cycle (2000), while projections for subsequent years show a steady if modest decline.

The figures can be further broken down into specific programme area budgets, some of which have grown much faster than others since 1977, so changing their relativities. In order to make a comparison, we have rebased real expenditure totals for all five sectors at 100 for 1977. As Table 12.2 shows, while spending in one sector, the EDF, had increased by 73% in real terms in 1998 compared to 1977, real spending on the structural funds grew by more than 1,500% over the same period. It may be argued that 1977 was a particularly low base point for structural spending, but even if 1977 and 1978 are taken as an aggregate starting base, the real increase would still have been in excess of tenfold. Although not increasing as rapidly, spending on RTD and on cooperation with third countries, also notched up very large real increases, to end up in 1998 at roughly six and seven times the original figures. The aggregate figure of 306 is largely accounted for by the relatively slower growth in spending on the CAP guarantee fund (the European Agricultural Guidance and Guarantee Fund, or EAGGF, more usually known by its French acronym FEOGA), which perennially bulks large in the overall budget. Between 1977 and 1998 CAP spending roughly doubled in real terms. It has been showing some significant real declines from its peak in 1995, although even in 1998 CAP guarantees still constituted just under half of total spending. It is nevertheless an incontrovertible fact that spending

on the CAP has grown at roughly one fifth the rate of the growth in spending on structural actions, RTD and cooperation combined. The slowest-growing programme overall has been the EDF: although it was well ahead of the average until 1992, it has since declined relatively, and in some years absolutely.

These relativities are both interesting and revealing. At one level, they epitomize the changing composition of the Community itself and the redefined priorities of the member states. Thus, while spending on the CAP has continued to grow, the relative decline of the farm sector in all member states, the addition of countries with declining industrial areas, and the spread of those problems within the core group of member states have led to the creation of a vast new range of structural policies, which have grown much more rapidly. Ironically, these have perhaps an even longer provenance than the CAP, insofar as their origins can be traced back to the European Coal and Steel Community, but the scope and ambition of the European Social Fund, the European Regional Development Fund, the Cohesion Fund, and other Community initiatives are of a completely different magnitude to any of the early measures (on the structural funds, see Chapter 14).

At another level, the changes can be seen as embodying policy responses to the changing external environment. In the case of spending on RTD, one stimulus has been external competition in a range of strategic sectors such as pharmaceuticals and electronics, from other industrial countries, principally the United States and Japan. Spending in the area of cooperation has also grown rapidly, especially since the collapse of the Soviet bloc starting in 1989, reflecting the growing importance of countries outside the African, Caribbean and Pacific (ACP) group of states, and the EU's role as a global aid donor. EU development programmes have long ceased to be narrowly focused on former colonies of the member states. Nevertheless, the slower growth in real resources going to the EDF may occasion some surprise. What is most striking is the cyclical nature of EDF spending in comparison with some other areas. For example, at the high point of 1992 EDF spending was respectably ahead of the average, but by 1996 it had sunk back to the same level as in 1977, although it has since recovered somewhat.

Leaving aside changing policy priorities, occasioned by whichever driving force, the pattern of EDF spending may indicate particular types of managerial problems that may be less pronounced in, say, the CAP guarantee system (although, conversely, the nature of CAP guarantees creates its own managerial idiosyncrasies). However, there may be something about the life cycle of policies that the EDF may presage for other areas, particularly structural spending. It is interesting, therefore, that the EU's "financial perspective" for 2000–06 (see Table 12.3) foresees a real reduction of 10% in the structural funds (excluding the Cohesion Fund).

The "perspective" is the financial expression of the *Agenda 2000* programme of priorities to which the EU committed itself in 1997. In order of significance, the CAP will still account for the largest share of expenditure, at around 45% of the total, followed by structural spending (around one third), internal policies (mostly RTD), and then external actions, at around 6–7%. However, if pre-accession aid to candidate countries is added into the figure for external actions, then the share for this area goes up to about 10%. Administration costs remain stable, at roughly 5% of the total.

The figures suggest that real spending will be at about the same level in 2006 as it is in 2000, with a bulge in the intervening years. In fact, there is a rebalancing of priorities, with the reduction in structural funding signifying a radical departure from the previous two perspectives. On the other hand, spending on the CAP is actually planned to increase over the period to 2006. Although it is to peak in 2002, after which it will fall slightly, it will nevertheless be higher in real terms in 2006 than it is in 2000. Given the focus on enlargement of the EU into central and eastern Europe, it is not surprising that other areas of growth include external and internal policies (aid and cooperation, and RTD), which are projected to grow by 10%. Starting in 2002, substantial sums will be available to assist agriculture and other sectors in the accession countries, assuming that there are any. These have been set at €4,140 million initially, rising

rapidly to €14,220 million in 2006, and represent at least a statement of intent that the enlargement process will start sooner rather than later. These sums represent substantial increases over the budget for the existing 15 member states.

In addition to the changing programmatic composition of the budget, the other issue that preoccupies decision-makers is the incidence of revenue and expenditure on individual member states. Historically, net beneficiary member states have tended to outnumber net contributors, so creating a coalition for increased spending. It can be argued that this has been redistributive, insofar as German and, to a lesser extent, British taxpayers have subsidized poorer member states on the periphery of the Community/EU. Yet this is a more complex issue than balancing total revenues paid against expenditure made, nor can it be reduced simply to a question of whether the UK is "entitled" to a budget rebate or not.

If we look at this issue in very crude terms, it becomes clear that there are a number of clear "winners" and "losers". At the present time, the former group includes Greece, Ireland, Portugal, Spain, and Denmark, while the latter includes Germany, the UK, the Netherlands, Belgium, and Sweden (see Begg and Grimwade). Most of these states have been perennially in one category, some have changed over – most notably the Netherlands, now the highest net contributor per capita – and others, France and Italy for example, have alternated between the two.

It will immediately be apparent that the effects are not entirely redistributive, as one of the richest member states, Denmark, has been a perennial net beneficiary, and one of the poorer member states (the UK), has been a perennial net contributor. It is also clear that in any member state some groups benefit disproportionately from EU spending at the expense of others, irrespective of the overall balance. Thus, it can be argued, for example, that although Greece is a substantial net beneficiary of EU funds, the money goes disproportionately to farmers while the general population pays higher food prices as a result of the CAP. This benefits not only Greek agriculture, but agriculture in the richer member states more generally. Moreover, the internal single market and the common external tariff on other products provide disproportionate benefits to the richer industrialized member states. That said, net inflows of EU funds have made a substantial positive difference to the economic growth of poorer countries, Ireland and Portugal in particular.

Sources of Revenue

The EU's revenues are known as "own resources", and are currently made up of four elements. These are agricultural duties and sugar and isoglucose levies; customs duties on imports from third countries; a proportion of member states' revenues from value-added tax (VAT), fixed at 1% for 1999; and a fourth resource calculated on the basis of the GNP of each member state. The Luxembourg Agreement of 1970 identified the first three of these elements as constituting the system of own resources, replacing the previous arrangement of national contributions. In practice, the duties and levies have been in place since 1971, and the VAT resource since 1979. The fourth resource was added in 1988. As can be seen in Table 12.3, total own resources have been fixed at a maximum level of 1.27% of the EU's aggregate GNP for the next planning period (2001–06), although roughly 10% of this figure is earmarked for emergencies and contingencies. Assuming there are no such circumstances, the ceiling varies between 1.12% and 1.18% of aggregate GNP. The detailed revenue figures for 1999 (in Table 12.4) show that VAT and the GNP-based element are now the two most important components, contributing 38% and 45% respectively to the total. Customs duties are the only other significant source (16%). Looking at the national origins of the total revenues, it is apparent that Germany, France, the UK, and Italy are respectively the largest individual sources. The lowest totals originate from, respectively, Luxembourg, Ireland, Portugal, and Finland.

From about 1985, revenues coming from VAT were by far the biggest single source, but these have now been overtaken by the GNP-based element. In the context of inter-national agreements on agricultural and customs duties, it is evident that these sources could never provide sufficient revenues to finance the growing level of Community expenditure from the 1970s onwards, as Ian Begg and Nigel Grimwade have shown. The VAT resource was agreed in principle in 1967, but because of difficulties in establishing a uniform VAT base across the member states it did not become fully operational until 1979. Thus, the current formula not only fixes a percentage take but also specifies a maximum relationship between each national VAT base and GNP (set at 50% for 1999). In addition to variations in VAT rates and coverage across member states, it is also complicated by arrangements for the UK's budget rebate, which give special consideration to the German share. All these factors serve to fracture the uniformity of national contributions from VAT. There are also collection and administration problems that have been exacerbated by the open borders of the single market. This has made "diversion fraud", where goods are ostensibly being exported but are then diverted to the home market, much easier to perpetrate.

Irrespective of the impasse over the harmonization of rates, the problem was that by the late 1980s VAT revenues had become insufficient too, although the option to increase the Community take was always there. However, as VAT is basically a regressive tax, which falls on expenditure rather than income, such a strategy would have disproportionately affected the poorer member states with lower savings and lower levels of public expenditure. As a result of the budget crisis of 1988 and the first interinstitutional agreement that same year, a new resource element based on GNP was introduced. In being based on the ability to pay, the GNP element is supposed to provide a degree of redistribution from wealthier to poorer member states, avoiding the pitfalls of VAT-derived revenues. The contributions from VAT revenues have been reduced from 1.4% to 1% since its introduction.

The fourth resource can be seen as a return, in part, to the model that the Community abandoned in 1970, namely a system of national contributions based on GNP. It has been adopted because of the unpalatable nature, in the view of some or all of the member states, of the other alternatives. Nevertheless, it has many critics. The European Parliament, for example, has been concerned by any movement away from a VAT-centred system, as it considers this to provide the most direct link between taxpayers and policy-makers. The Commission made a proposal for a fifth resource in 1992 and carried out a further review of the financing system in 1998. The study by Begg and Grimwade, conducted for the European Parliament in 1997, noted that there was a distinct lack of enthusiasm for any new resource, and it is interesting that a GNP-based resource was not included among the eight possible sources they considered. The result of their own evaluation was that a "modulated" VAT system, the option favoured by the Parliament's Budget Committee, would provide the most benefits at least cost, and was likely to meet with least resistance from member states. Looking at the other options they appraised – including income and corporation taxes, energy and communication taxes, and alcohol and tobacco duties – it is not difficult to see why.

The evidence suggests that the member states are moving in the opposite direction from a VAT-centred model. The European Council meeting held in Berlin in March 1999 decided to reduce the contribution from VAT revenues still further, to 0.75% in 2002–03, and to 0.5% from 2004 onwards, as well as allowing member states to retain more of the income from customs duties and levies. In the absence of any new revenue source, the inevitable result will be to increase the share of own resources accruing from the GNP element.

Budget-making

Since 1988 the annual budget-making cycle has taken place within the context of a five-year financial perspective agreed between the Council, the Commission, and the European Parliament. The most recent "interinstitutional agreement", as it is known, was signed in May 1999, during the German Presidency, and covers the period 2000–06. As Table 12.3 shows, this agreement sets the total spending levels, the relative allocations between the major programme areas, the revenue sources, and the revenue limits as percentages of the EU's aggregate GNP. However, even a cursory reading of the figures suggests that the agreements are very broadbrush statements, without much evidence of detailed planning. Round numbers, nominal changes, and steady-rate projections make up much of the data. This is in complete contrast to the annual budget document, which, over more than 1,500 pages, includes details of all planned expenditure lines.

The five-year perspective is the pinnacle of "high politics" within the budgetary process, in which the heads of state and government, and the Commissioners, play the leading roles. Within this group, the President of the Commission and the member state holding the Council Presidency at the time are perhaps the most significant players. The Commission generally holds the right of proposal and one of its former presidents, Jacques Delors, was proactive in asserting that role in the first two agreements, putting forward the "Delors I" and "Delors II" budget packages in 1988 and 1992. The agreement in 1992 showed the way in which the Council Presidency, held by the UK at that time, can attempt to pursue a different agenda, but also has to mediate between competing claims from member states and others for future resources. It is apparent from the latest agreement that future members of the EU constitute an added ingredient to be taken account of, and, like the 1992 package, the final outcome of the 1999 agreement was rather different from the Commission's proposals (within the *Agenda 2000* programme).

As can be imagined, the lobbying and manoeuvring on the financial perspective now starts years in advance. This gives the annual budget decisions an added strategic importance, as they are factored into the Commission's next five-year perspective. Thus, while the annual budget is a much more detailed affair bound by complex procedures and rules, it still represents an important political process. At more than 1,500 pages, it is both a policy statement and a management document. As Brigid Laffan has observed, budget-making is at the fulcrum of the power struggle between the Commission, the Council, and the Parliament. Authority was shared between the

Council and the Commission until the Budget Treaty of 1975, as a result of which the Parliament gained significant powers to reject the budget entirely, to grant discharge to the budget, and to alter "noncompulsory" expenditure (spending not arising directly from the treaties). After the first direct elections to the Parliament in 1979, it started to exercise these powers, and so conciliation mechanisms have been developed within the framework of the interinstitutional agreements and other instruments to smooth the process along.

However, the first stage of the annual budget-making process properly begins in the Commission. It is responsible for drawing up the preliminary draft budget within the framework of the financial perspective for that year, according to the principles of annuality, equilibrium, and universality laid down in Articles 268–78 of the TEC (formerly numbered 199–209). This process is managed by the Directorate General for Budgets, which issues guidelines to, and receives bids from, the spending directorates general. After the conclusion of negotiations within the Commission, some of which may be considered by the whole college of Commissioners, the preliminary draft budget is passed on to the Council for discussion and revision, initially in the Committee of Permanent Representatives (Coreper) and ultimately by Ministers. Within the Council, member states must negotiate with each other and collectively with the Commission, while the Parliament's Budget Committee consults the policy committees and the Commission while it awaits the Council's decisions. The Parliament receives a draft budget from the Council in the autumn, which it must then try and reconcile with its own aspirations. It may propose amendments to the Council's draft, which the Council is obliged to consider. If the Council rejects these proposals by majority vote, the Parliament has the option of rejecting the draft budget by securing a two-thirds majority against it.

It is not difficult to see that the scope for disagreement and divergence is already enormous within the Parliament, within the Council of Ministers, and variously between the Council, the Parliament, and the Commission – hence the need for a conciliation procedure. The "trialogue" between the Commission, the Council, and the Parliament starts very early in the process, and involves senior figures from each institution: the President of the Budget Council, the convenor of the Parliament's Budget Committee, and the Commissioner responsible for budgets. The latest interinstitutional agreement specifies that the first meeting between the parties is to be convened before the Commission has decided on the preliminary draft budget, in order to discuss the budget priorities for that year. It is significant that all expenditure – both compulsory and noncompulsory – is now included in these discussions, reflecting the enhanced role of the Parliament in decision-making. A further meeting is held before the Parliament's first reading of the budget, in order to identify those areas where further conciliation is needed, and this process continues after the first reading has taken place and until outstanding issues have been resolved.

Managing Expenditure

The basic responsibilities are laid down in the treaties, regulations governing particular sectors, and the Financial Regulation (1977, 1990, and 1995) covering all expenditure. Article 274 of the TEC (formerly 205) states that "the Commission shall implement the budget". In fact, once the budget has been decided, the management of expenditure is shared among a great variety of local, national, and Community agencies and bodies. At the end of the process the Court of Auditors provides an annual report and a declaration of assurance, and, acting on this information, the Parliament, via its Budgetary Control Committee, decides whether or not to grant "discharge" to the budget. This in effect is a vote of confidence, or otherwise, on the Commission's management of the funds, and has been refused on two occasions. Rather than using this "nuclear" option, the Parliament is usually inclined to issue a lengthy discharge decision that requires the Commission to take action on scores of specific financial management issues, the implementation of which can be checked up on during the following year.

There is no one single model of financial management as between the Commission and the implementing agencies in the field, because of the varied nature of the spending programmes. However, the principle of subsidiarity, as now set out in Article 5 of the TEC is supposed to govern the allocation of managerial responsibilities between national and Community levels. Daniel Strasser has identified three basic types of management: "direct", "decentralized", and "shared". He concluded that most programmes fall into one or other of the latter two categories. "Direct" management refers to all parts of the budget managed solely by the Commission, including its own administrative expenditure and the joint research centres (for example at Ispra and Petten). Under "decentralized" management, the Commission delegates frontline implementation to national and local agencies, supervising them through programme-specific regulations and directives.

In the case of the CAP, the Commission manages the system of intervention spending through approved national paying agencies, of which there are currently more than 90. Because of the highly detailed regulation of market intervention and product specification, there is relatively little local discretion, which is not to say that the quality of financial management and control is also uniform – far from it. While the Commission has tried to specify minimum standards for checking and data quality, for example, enforcement practices vary from state to state.

Another variant of decentralized management takes the form of ten new regulatory agencies established by the EU in 1993. Dispersed throughout the EU, the agencies are nevertheless "arm's length" satellites of the Commission, charged with implementing certain policy areas, for example, environment and training. Closer to "shared" management are the systems used for the EDF, and for aid programmes such as PHARE and TACIS. In these cases, the Commission manages its programmes through local EU delegations in the recipient countries, which work with national agencies and other donors, including non-governmental organizations such as Oxfam and international agencies such as the World Bank. The more partners there are the more difficult financial control becomes, as elements of shared management are introduced. The most

clearly defined examples of the latter subsist within the structural programmes, including the European Regional Development Fund and the European Social Fund. As these programmes are jointly funded with national governments, local implementation is carried out by field agencies and private providers in the member states, under the supervision of programme management committees that liaise directly with desk officers in the Commission and contain Commission representatives. Within the framework of an individual programme located in one area of a member state, there can be literally hundreds of projects running at any one time. Expenditure on RTD is more difficult to classify because the Commission deals directly with recipient organizations, but via panels of peer-selected scientific experts who evaluate proposals beforehand and monitor results afterwards. The recipient organizations manage the projects once they have been approved.

Irrespective of the application of the subsidiarity principle, from the point of view of practicality it is evident that the Commission in its present form can have only a very limited role in financial management in the field. Historically, the Commission has focused on policy-making and it is still the case that relatively few officials are involved in financial management. Until recently, the Directorate General for Financial Control was the only part of the Commission dedicated to this function, although there were internal audit units within the spending directorates general too, and the Directorate General for Budgets has taken a close interest in audit and evaluation issues. In effect, the Commission's role has been confined to authorizing expenditure (the visa) destined for the implementing agencies, checking and monitoring expenditure (or more likely, checking the systems in place locally to do this), and internal and external auditing. Through the financial regulation (1995 and earlier versions), it also has a role in securing value for money via cost benefit analysis and other cost effectiveness techniques (under Article 2).

The distribution of these tasks within the Commission has been subject to sustained criticism over the years, particularly the arrogation by the Directorate General for Financial

Control of both the authorization and audit functions to itself. As a result of the resignation of the Santer Commission in 1999 and the Committee of Independent Experts' reports of the same year, reforms have now been put in place. An Internal Audit Service to manage internal audits and a Central Finance Service within the Budget Directorate General to manage financial management relations with the member states have been created. The visa function has been decentralized to designated financial controllers in the spending directorates general. In the spirit of the new emphasis on financial control, the latter are supposed to move over to a system of activity-based management for all their programmes. In addition, the anti-fraud office (OLAF) has been strengthened, although it has no independent legal powers to prosecute fraudsters.

While these reforms may well result in an improvement of financial management within the Commission, they do not directly address the operational problems within the member states, nor are they based on a scientific long-term appraisal of the Commission's management performance. They also do nothing to solve the structural weaknesses inherent in many Community policies. It is significant that the Court of Auditors has focused increasing attention in its annual and special reports on local management difficulties, most of which are extremely basic. In an external appraisal of EU programme management covering 20 years, management information deficiencies at all levels have emerged as the consistently most important area of weakness: while spending on RTD had been relatively well-managed, the CAP and foreign aid programmes have fared much less positively (see Levy). It may be thought that programme management is dull, uninteresting, and relatively unimportant, but it is well to remember that the one and only occasion on which the Commission has resigned was for reasons of management failure.

As the ultimate oversight bodies, the Court of Auditors and the Parliament are the last line of defence for the EU's taxpayers in securing probity and value for money. Indeed, the Court's special and annual reports are fundamental for an understanding of how well or badly EU programmes are managed. The Court's relationship with the Commission has often been tense because of disputes over just how far the Court's jurisdiction extends, and it was not until the Treaty on European Union was agreed at Maastricht that the Court was granted the status of an official EU institution. Working with the Parliament, not always harmoniously, via the Budgetary Control Committee and the discharge process, has been the main avenue for the Court to make its influence felt.

Issues for the Future

At the level of "high" politics, there is the problem of adjusting agricultural and structural policies to accommodate the candidate countries, while fitting the budgetary envelope agreed at the Berlin summit in 1999. This can be achieved so long as economic growth in the present 15 member states remains strong while increases in spending remain low to nonexistent. In this case, the growth in revenues will allow for rises in spending without breaking the agreed ceiling on the EU's "own resources". One consequence of this model is that the fastest-growing economies, such as Ireland, will be paying in relatively more, thus narrowing their net benefits, or in the case of net contributors, such as the Netherlands, widening net contributions. However, such a strategy implies a much less generous regime for structural and agricultural support after the new applicants enter, or a radical shift of resources away from existing member states towards the new entrants. In less favourable circumstances, spending can only be revised upwards if there is an agreement to increase existing own resources beyond planned levels, or to introduce a new resource. There are options on the table, but neither the Commission nor the Council seems keen to pursue any of them.

There is a very large agenda also on the management and accountability side. The reforms sketched out by the Commission for itself in its White Paper of March 2000 will necessitate internal cultural and structural changes of unprecedented proportions. While the conditions for such changes have perhaps never been more auspicious, earlier attempts at reform, most notably by Jacques Santer, met with only limited success. It does look more serious this time, but it will need a sustained effort over a period of years to be successful. Working practices, and staff recruitment and training policies, will have to change radically. Moreover, reform limited to rearranging the furniture at the centre will fail, just as it has in the past. The most pressing needs are at the local and field levels, which strongly suggests that an even more radical strategy of "decentralization" of the Commission will have to be contemplated. It can be argued that this need will be all the greater with the accession of states in central and eastern Europe.

The irony of such a development would be that it would make it even harder for the Parliament and the Court to audit and control expenditure effectively. At the moment, the Commission serves both as a convenient whipping post and as an ally against the Council when things go awry. If a dispersal of Commission staff to member state agencies took place, both would become more difficult.

Finally, there is the issue of how to deal with fraud on the EU budget. The Commission has been arguing for independent legal powers of prosecution for some time now, but this raises fundamental questions about parallel European authorities and enforcement mechanisms in the criminal law. Given member states' reluctance to relinquish control over taxation, the more mundane alternatives of better "fraud-proofing" of EU legislation and improving cooperation between member states are more likely in the medium term.

Further Reading

Begg, Ian, and Nigel Grimwade (editors), *Paying for Europe*, Sheffield: Sheffield Academic Press/ UACES, 1998

Based on a study commissioned by the European Parliament, this is an excellent and up-to-date survey of the "own resources" system, and of the arguments for and against possible new sources of revenue.

European Commission, *White Paper: Reforming the Commission Parts I and II*, Communication from Neil Kinnock, Brussels, 1 March 2000

This is the Kinnock plan for the internal reform of the Commission, which has been under way since early 2000.

European Court of Auditors, "Annual Report" concerning the financial year 1998, in *Official Journal* C349, 3 December 1999; and for 1999, in *Official Journal* C342, 1 December 2000

As with all the Court's annual reports, these provide invaluable qualitative and quantitative evidence on budget implementation and management. Such reports are published towards the end of every year on the previous year's budget.

Laffan, Brigid, *The Finances of the European Union*, London: Macmillan, and New York: St Martin's Press, 1997

The most comprehensive recent general survey of the politics of the budgetary process available in English from an academic commentator

Levy, Roger, *Implementing European Union Public Policy*, Cheltenham: Edward Elgar, 2000

Using data from the Court of Auditors' reports, this study provides an empirical analysis of the performance of EU programme management in the five main spending areas between 1977 and 1996.

Middlelhoek, André, Inga-Britt Ahlenius, Pierre Lelong, Antoni Tizzano, and Walter van Gerven, *Second Report on Reform of the Commission: Analysis of Current Practice and Proposals for Tackling Mismanagement, Irregularities and Fraud*, Brussels: Committee of Independent Experts, 1999

A landmark document on the Commission's current management practices, with many themes taken from the Court of Auditors' reports over the years

Strasser, Daniel, *The Finances of Europe*, Luxembourg: Office for the Official Publications of the European Communities, third English edition, 1992

Still the standard work by a practitioner on the nuts and bolts of financial management, although it is now largely out of date

---

Roger Levy is Professor and Head of the Division of Management in the Caledonian Business School at Glasgow Caledonian University. His recent research and publications have been on the EU budget, and the auditing and management of EU programmes.

Table 12.1   EU General Budget: Total Estimated Expenditure in Nominal and Real Terms (ECU millions and %), 1977–98

Year	Nominal expenditure (ECU millions)	Change in nominal expenditure (%)	Inflation rate (%)[1]	Real growth (%)	Real expenditure (1977 prices)[2]
1977	9,584.3	na	9.8	na	9,584.3
1978	12,362.7	29.0	8.5	20.5	11,549.1
1979	14,447.0	16.9	9.3	7.6	12,426.8
1980	16,182.5	12.0	10.8	1.2	12,575.9
1981	18,434.0	13.9	9.0	4.9	13,192.2
1982	21,984.4	19.3	10.7	8.6	14,326.7
1983	25,061.1	14.0	8.4	5.6	15,129.0
1984	27,248.6	8.7	7.2	1.5	15,356.0
1985	28,433.2	4.3	6.1	−1.8	15,079.6
1986	35,174.1	23.7	3.5	20.2	18,125.6
1987	36,168.4	2.8	3.2	−0.4	18,053.1
1988	43,820.4	21.2	3.6	17.6	21,230.5
1989	44,840.6	2.3	5.1	−2.8	20,636.0
1990	46,928.2	4.7	5.7	−1.0	20,429.6
1991	56,085.4	19.5	5.1	14.4	23,371.5
1992	61,096.8	8.9	4.2	4.7	24,470.0
1993	66,857.9	9.4	3.3	6.1	25,962.6
1994	68,446.0	2.4	3.1	−0.7	25,780.9
1995	75,468.8	10.3	3.1	7.2	27,637.1
1996	81,989.0	8.6	2.5	6.1	29,323.0
1997	82,422.7	0.5	1.3	−0.8	29,088.4
1998	83,833.7	1.7	0.9	0.8	29,321.1

[1] For the European Community of 10 member states, 1977–81; for the European Community of 12 member states, 1982–94; for the EU of 15 member states 1995–98
[2] With 1977 as the base year

Sources: European Court of Auditors, Annual Reports, 1977–99; *Eurostat Review*, 1972–81; Eurostat, Basic Statistics of the EC/EU (various) and Eurostat Yearbook (1999).

Table 12.2   Rebased Growth in Real Expenditure on All Areas of the EU's Budget, 1977–98 (1977=100)

Year	General	EAGGF	Structural Funds	RTD	Cooperation	EDF
1977	100	100	100	100	100	100
1978	121	114	194	99	141	155
1979	130	126	154	116	170	166
1980	131	125	148	154	195	154
1981	138	115	192	112	231	198
1982	149	119	439	147	210	172
1983	156	132	389	475	239	177
1984	160	141	280	207	200	160
1985	157	148	303	195	220	149
1986	189	158	444	200	234	176
1987	188	159	449	239	234	168
1988	222	185	510	285	182	247
1989	215	171	615	344	200	242
1990	213	159	697	405	261	220
1991	244	187	840	335	467	198
1992	255	183	1,033	422	484	314
1993	271	195	1,187	454	480	209
1994	269	186	1,148	516	514	268
1995	288	217	1,255	554	640	200
1996	306	209	1,416	634	702	99
1997	303	204	1,428	594	720	147
1998	306	197	1,523	614	680	173

EAGGF: European Agricultural Guidance and Guarantee Fund
RTD: Research and Technological Development
EDF: European Development Fund
Cooperation: external action in relation to third countries

Source: Derived from data in the European Court of Auditors Annual Reports, 1977–99

Table 12.3   Financial Perspective for the EU of 15 Member States, 2000–06 (€millions at 1999 prices)

Commitment Appropriations	2000	2001	2002	2003	2004	2005	2006
Agriculture	40,920	42,800	43,900	43,770	42,760	41,930	41,660
EAGGF guarantee	36,620	38,480	39,570	39,430	38,410	37,570	37,290
Rural development	4,300	4,320	4,330	4,340	4,350	4,360	4,370
Structural operations	32,045	31,455	30,865	30,285	29,595	29,595	29,170
Structural funds	29,430	28,840	28,250	27,760	27,080	27,080	26,660
Cohesion Fund	2,615	2,615	2,615	2,615	2,515	2,515	2,510
Internal policies	5,930	6,040	6,150	6,260	6,370	6,480	6,600
External action	4,550	4,560	4,570	4,580	4,900	5,000	5,100
Administration	4,560	4,600	4,570	4,580	4,590	4,600	4,610
Reserves	900	900	650	400	400	400	400
Monetary	500	500	250	0	0	0	0
Emergency aid	200	200	200	200	200	200	200
Loan guarantee	200	200	200	200	200	200	200
Pre-accession aid	3,120	3,120	3,120	3,120	3,120	3,120	3,120
Agriculture	520	520	520	520	520	520	520
Structural instruments	1,040	1,040	1,040	1,040	1,040	1,040	1,040
PHARE (candidate countries)	1,560	1,560	1,560	1,560	1,560	1,560	1,560
Total commitment appropriations	92,025	93,475	93,955	93,215	91,735	91,125	90,660
Total payment appropriations	89,600	91,110	94,220	94,880	90,910	90,160	89,620
(% of GNP)	1.13	1.12	1.13	1.11	1.05	1.00	0.97
Available for accession			4,140	6,710	8,890	11,440	14,220
Agriculture			1,600	2,030	2,450	2,930	3,400
Other expenditure			2,540	4,680	6,440	8,510	10,820
Ceiling on payment appropriations	89,600	91,110	98,360	101,590	100,800	101,600	103,840
Ceiling (% of GNP)	1.13	1.12	1.18	1.19	1.15	1.13	1.13
Margin for unforseen expenditure (%)	0.14	0.15	0.09	0.08	0.12	0.14	0.14
Own resources ceiling (% of GNP)	1.27	1.27	1.27	1.27	1.27	1.27	1.27

Source: European Parliament, Council and Commission, Interinstitutional Agreement of 6 May 1999, *Official Journal*, C172, 12–13

Table 12.4 "Own Resources" – Actual Revenues for Financial Year 1999, by Member State, including Corrections (€millions)

	Agricultural levies	Sugar and isoglucose levies	Customs duties	VAT	GNP resource	Budgetary corrections	Total own resources[1]
Austria	13.8	34.3	223.7	775.6	928.5	104.9	2,053.6
Belgium	38.1	72.3	1,115.1	827.9	1,121.7	143.5	3,196.0
Denmark	8.5	42.0	278.9	543.4	722.5	93.9	1,656.3
Finland	7.1	8.5	126.9	448.2	567.9	66.4	1,210.8
France	60.5	334.9	1,256.1	5,457.1	6,269.3	781.3	13,994.1
Germany	167.8	347.9	3,026.6	7,864.3	9,318.3	698.3	21,069.0
Greece	10.9	11.9	185.9	524.2	565.4	73.4	1,350.8
Ireland	2.0	12.1	180.1	406.8	430.2	47.8	1,059.6
Italy	81.0	126.5	1,213.0	3,689.5	5,115.9	681.8	10,765.6
Luxembourg	0.6	–	22.0	76.1	86.1	11.6	194.1
Netherlands	192.9	67.5	1,530.8	1,566.8	1,704.0	208.6	5,091.5
Portugal	43.4	3.2	158.6	469.6	511.0	62.4	1,227.7
Spain	57.4	47.3	805.1	2,462.2	2,620.8	329.5	6,231.3
Sweden	19.8	22.4	352.9	831.6	1057.7	104.0	2,348.9
UK	483.5	72.7	2,530.8	5,389.0	6,492.7	–3,576.6	11,083.4
Totals	1,187.3	1,203.5	13,006.5	31,332.3	37,512.0	169.2	82,532.7

1 Total includes deductions for costs incurred in collecting own resources.

Source: European Court of Auditors, Annual Report for 1999, Official Journal C342/01, 1 December 2000

Chapter Thirteen

The Common Agricultural Policy

Alan Swinbank

The Treaty of Rome explicitly states that "the common market shall extend to agriculture and trade in agricultural products", and that "the operation and development of the common market for agricultural products must be accompanied by the establishment of a common agricultural policy among the member states" (Article 33, formerly Article 38). For France in particular, it seemed important in 1957 that its agricultural goods should have access to a wider European market if its own market was to be opened up to manufactured products from other member states.

In the late 1950s agriculture was of major electoral and economic importance. In France more than 20% of the working population, and in Italy more than 30%, were engaged in agriculture (see Table 13.1), and many city dwellers had close family ties with the land. Farms were small, fragmented, and inefficient. Furthermore, in the aftermath of the World War II food shortages had been common and starvation had presented a real threat. Consequently, it is not surprising that all states in western Europe pursued agricultural policies to protect their farm sectors and to reassure their citizens that "food security" was of national concern. However, the pursuit of national agricultural policies was inconsistent with the inclusion of agriculture within the free-trading provisions of the common market. It followed that a Common Agricultural Policy (CAP) would have to be developed to displace national policies.

Article 33 (formerly 39) of the Treaty of Rome, which remains unaltered by the Single European Act, the Maastricht Treaty on European Union, or the Treaties of Amsterdam and Nice, sets out the objectives of the CAP as follows:

- to increase agricultural productivity, by promoting technical progress and by ensuring the rational development of agricultural production, and the optimum utilization of the factors of production, in particular labour;
- thus to ensure a fair standard of living for the agricultural community, in particular by increasing the individual earnings of persons engaged in agriculture;
- to stabilize markets;
- to assure the availability of supplies; and
- to ensure that supplies reach consumers at reasonable prices.

There is not space here for a full appraisal of these objectives, but the concern with both farm incomes and food security might be noted. For "persons engaged in agriculture", a "fair" standard of living was to be achieved by the pursuit of economic efficiency in agricultural production. Over the years, the farm income objective has dominated this list, yet it has always been unclear what is meant by the word "fair", and who the "persons engaged in agriculture" are. For example, part-time farming is common in many parts of the EU, and it is often difficult to differentiate between "hobby farmers" and those struggling to eke a living from inadequate resources. Paid employees now account for more than 30% of the agricultural workforce in Denmark, Germany,

Spain, Italy, the Netherlands, and the United Kingdom, but there is little evidence to suggest that the CAP has been deployed on behalf of farm workers. By contrast, where the landlord–tenant system is common – for example, in the United Kingdom – much of the largesse of CAP support has been captured by landlords, in the form of higher rents and land prices.

Policy-makers around the world face a dilemma with respect to agriculture. Beyond a certain level of income, our capacity to eat more food is limited. At relatively low incomes we might shift our purchases to meats from grains; at higher incomes we buy higher-quality foods, incorporating an enhanced service component supplied by the food processing and distribution industries, but very little additional volume. Thus, with limited population growth western Europe's farmers have faced static markets. However, they have access to new technologies and managerial techniques that are capable of generating impressive gains in productivity. Consequently, a progressively smaller resource base in agriculture is capable of supplying the food and fibre requirements of the population. In particular, fewer farmers, and larger farms, are required. At best, agricultural policies attempt to facilitate the adjustment process and to cushion its impact on those least able to change. At worst, agricultural policies attempt to thwart what are, arguably, inexorable economic trends. Nonetheless, as is clear from Table 13.1, the farming industry in all the countries that now form the EU has declined in importance over the last 40 years.

The "Old" CAP

In the 1960s it was intended that there should be two complementary strands to the CAP. First, a series of "common market organizations" (CMOs), covering virtually all agricultural products, determined the framework within which those products were marketed and, in the main, ensured that market prices exceeded those prevailing on world markets, thus protecting the Community's producers, who were largely uncompetitive on world markets. This was the mechanism by which, it was

hoped, the farm income objective would be achieved in the short term. However, the longer-term objective of improved economic performance was conditional on the implementation of a structural policy that would encourage rationalization and amalgamation of farms, and the retirement of redundant farmers, and would, it was further hoped, ultimately render the price support policy redundant. The Community therefore established a European Agricultural Guidance and Guarantee Fund (EAGGF, more usually known by its French acronym FEOGA), with a guidance section concerned with structural policy, and a guarantee section to fund price and income support.

In practice it proved much easier to establish a price and income support policy than a structural policy, and by 1968 market imbalances, particularly in milk, were evident. If agricultural product prices are maintained at artificially high levels, in the hope that an increase in farm revenues will be reflected in an increase in farm incomes, farmers will be encouraged to increase output beyond the market's absorptive capacity. In the ill-fated Mansholt Plan, the Commission urged adoption of a set of structural policy measures that would enable farmers to retire, retrain, or adapt their holdings into modern agricultural enterprises. In 1975, following the adoption of the Directive on Less Favoured Areas, the Community introduced a regional dimension into the CAP, with the payment of additional subsidies to farmers in regions suffering from natural physical handicaps. As structural policy has subsequently progressed, the original emphasis on aiding the development of commercially viable holdings has lessened, and an increasing attention to regional and environmental concerns has become apparent.

Price Policy

Although there are considerable differences between one product group and another, the price support mechanisms that were applied for cereals (until May 1992 – see below) were characteristic of the "old", unreformed CAP, and, indeed, of the CAP as a whole. Figure

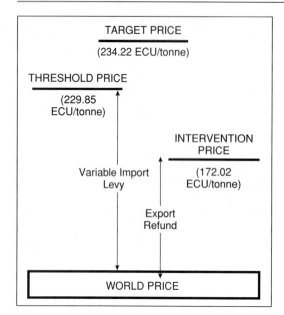

Figure 13.1   The "Old" CAP: Price Support for Wheat

July 1990 prices, before the introduction of MacSharry Reforms [agreed May 1992] or the implementation of the GATT Agreement [in force from 1 July 1995]

13.1 illustrates the main features of the "old" CAP, in contrast to the "new" CAP (discussed below), which followed the MacSharry and *Agenda 2000* reforms, and the Agreement on Agriculture overseen by the World Trade Organization (WTO).

The Council and the Commission fixed various support prices on an annual basis: these were known as "target", "threshold" and "intervention" prices. The target price indicated the price level that should be received by farmers delivering grain in that region of the Community showing the greatest deficit. In theory, if not in practice, it was the price that was required to deliver the CAP's "fair" income objective. The threshold price, valid along all of the Community's external frontiers, was actually calculated for the port of Rotterdam. Provided that imports through Rotterdam did not undercut the threshold price, they could not be sold in the area of greatest deficit at less than the target price unless the trader incurred a financial loss.

To ensure that imports into the Community did not undercut the threshold price, they were taxed. This tax was known as a variable import levy, and for cereals it was determined daily as the arithmetical difference between a variable world market price and the fixed threshold price. Except for brief periods of high world market prices, in particular for sugar, the CAP has typically imposed significant taxes on imports of agricultural goods and, despite the WTO Agreement, this will remain the case for the foreseeable future.

If the Community, now the EU, was less than self-sufficient in cereals, then import taxes alone would ensure that EU market prices remained above world market prices. However, with self-sufficiency approaching or exceeding 100%, market prices would fall. In this instance, the EU's intervention agencies can buy products from farmers, or more usually traders, at the intervention price, thus helping to maintain EU market prices. This is the origin of the "wine lakes" and "butter mountains" that have fired the popular imagination. The intervention price is valid throughout the EU. For cereals it was derived from the target price by deducting transport costs from Orléans in France (the area of greatest surplus) to Duisburg, and a marketing margin.

If surpluses are only temporary, intervention stocks can later be sold back onto the market. However, if EU production regularly exceeds consumption, then intervention stocks would continuously increase unless disposed of at a loss on international markets. Alternatively, traders can be paid an export subsidy, known as an export refund, when EU products are sold in approved export destinations. Thus, with self-sufficiency ratios above 100%, the surplus can either be added to intervention stocks, or dumped on world markets. In practice, the European Commission has been given considerable discretion to fix export refunds and generally manage the market, and it does so with a number of objectives in mind. These include the comparative short- and long-term budget costs of the two alternatives; the balance between supply and demand within the EU; and the EU's international commitments in the WTO.

Three principles that underpin the price support policy are often cited. These are market unity, or common pricing; "Community preference"; and "financial solidarity". (They can also be illustrated by reference to Figure 13.1.) A common market implies that there are no barriers to trade among the participating states. This is only feasible if support prices under the CAP are the same throughout the EU, for otherwise products would be moved to the member state with the highest support. "Community preference" has two connotations. First, it implies that the price received by EU producers is in excess of world market prices. Secondly, and more usually, it is reflected in the gap between the threshold and intervention prices evident in Figure 13.1. If this gap is sufficiently large, the buyers in deficit regions in the EU will obtain their requirements from EU producers rather than on the world market. If the gap is too small, it will be cheaper to buy on the world market and pay the import tax.

The CAP could be likened to a seamless web: intervention and market support activities undertaken in any one member state help to maintain market prices throughout the EU. Thus, it is argued, the financial consequences of a common policy must be borne collectively: if a member state was itself responsible for funding intervention activities on its territory it would be less willing to maintain open borders *vis-à-vis* its partners. The "Rotterdam effect" is also cited to justify financial solidarity: consumers throughout the EU pay the taxes that are levied on goods imported into the EU through Rotterdam (and other ports). Thus it is argued that the revenues accruing from this common policy should be treated as the EU's own resources, rather than those of the Dutch (or other national) authorities.

Financial solidarity does, however, lead to what economists call "moral hazard". Consider a group of colleagues in a restaurant who have agreed to share the bill equally among themselves. The incentive to economize is blunted: why choose a plain omelette if you can have lobster with all the trimmings, with your colleagues being forced to pay the bulk of the additional bill?

Problems Associated with the CAP Price Policy

Many of the problems associated with the CAP's price support policies have been alluded to already. They involve major economic inefficiencies, in that resources are wastefully deployed to produce foodstuffs at costs in excess of their value on world markets. The following points in particular should be noted.

First, it is doubtful that a lasting increase in farm incomes can be achieved through price support, although it is probable that land and other asset values will be enhanced, and that the input supply industries will enjoy larger sales. Further, because, in the main, support is not targeted at small-scale farmers and all marketed produce benefits from higher market prices, the bulk of the benefit is captured by a minority of large-scale, and usually prosperous, farmers and landowners.

Secondly, as a result of higher land prices the environmental impact of the CAP has been adverse. High land prices have encouraged an undesirable intensification of agricultural production, with otherwise unproductive land, such as ponds, copses or heaths, being drawn into agricultural use, and heavier applications of fertilizers and agrochemicals being made in attempts to increase yields.

Thirdly, the CAP, by maintaining high prices for farm products, necessarily raises the raw material costs faced by the food industries. If they are to compete in the market, they must be protected from food companies that have access to agricultural raw materials priced on world markets. Thus EU import taxes and export subsidies apply on lemonade as well as on sugar, and on pasta as well as on wheat. Some of the benefits of the CAP price support will nonetheless have been captured by the food industries, most notably by companies providing cold-stores and other services to the intervention agencies.

Fourthly, the costs of the CAP, in the form of higher food prices, bear more heavily on low-income groups. Estimates of the costs to consumers vary, depending upon movements in world market prices and the particular assumptions made. Nonetheless, the British Ministry of Agriculture, Fisheries, and Food estimated that in 1993, for example, the total cost of the CAP to consumers was some 55 billion ecu, or almost 160 ecu for each of the EU's citizens (see MAFF). However, it should be remembered that the farmer's share of retail food prices is typically less than 50%, reflecting the costs of processing, storing, and distributing food. In addition, as production has responded to high support prices and new technologies, surpluses have accumulated, giving rise to an escalating budgetary cost borne by the EU's taxpayers.

Fifthly, stemming from the implementation of the single market and the principle of financial solidarity, the CAP has generated significant financial transfers among member states. Those that are net importers of food obtain their supplies from other member states at CAP prices, not world prices, and make a net contribution to the EU budget. Thus the CAP benefits food-exporting member states, and penalizes the net importers. For countries such as Ireland, the transfers can be important (as can be seen from Table 13.2).

It follows that, given a large gap between EU and world prices, and the sizeable aids paid to farmers and food-processing companies, there are significant incentives to "milk" the CAP. At worst this involves fraud, and the possibilities are legion. At best, it validates the employment of armies of CAP experts, whose purpose is to ensure that their employers maximize returns from the CAP while remaining on the right side of the law. Worryingly, member states wishing to maximize their national receipts from the EU budget perceive fewer incentives to minimize fraud than would be the case if their own taxpayers' funds were directly at risk.

Finally, the CAP itself has a major impact on world prices. As EU production has expanded, other suppliers have seen their markets within the EU contract and have then faced unfair competition from subsidized EU exports on world markets. Thus world market prices are lower than they otherwise would be and efficient agricultural exporters have seen their export revenues fall. Furthermore, the CAP's pursuit of price stability within the EU has increased the instability of prices on the world market. While it would be unfair to blame the CAP for all the disarray evident in world food

markets in the past four decades, it is a major culprit. Consequently, CAP reform was a particular objective of the EU's trading partners in the Uruguay Round of multilateral trade negotiations.

The "New" CAP

The CAP has, of course, changed over the years, but, despite the introduction of milk quotas in 1984, the rhetoric of "prudent pricing" and "budget stabilizers" in the 1980s, the weakening of intervention mechanisms, and the increased emphasis placed on structural reform and regional assistance programmes, by 1990 the CAP was fundamentally unchanged from the 1970s. However, the CAP of the late 1990s was rather different, perhaps justifying the adjective "new", even if it almost certainly represented the outcome of a transitional phase, with further reforms to come in the early years of the new millennium. In particular, two interlinked decisions were taken in the period 1991–93. The first was a switch in the system of CAP price support for cereal and beef producers, known as the MacSharry reforms after the then Commissioner for Agriculture, Ray MacSharry. The second was the conclusion, in December 1993, of the Uruguay Round of negotiations under the General Agreement on Tariffs and Trade (GATT) system, the predecessor of the WTO.

The MacSharry Reforms and *Agenda 2000*

The Commission first presented proposals for a major reform of the CAP in February 1991. It pointed out that agricultural production was expanding at 2% a year, whereas increases in consumption were limited to 0.5% a year, leading to surplus production of food and other products, which could be sold on world markets only with the aid of export subsidies at increasing budgetary cost; it also noted that "80% of the support . . . is devoted to 20% of farms" (see European Commission 1991). Press comment had suggested that the proposals were "budget-driven internal reforms" that had "very little to do with the current GATT negotiations" (*Agra*

Europe 11 January 1991). In fact, they were intimately linked with the GATT negotiations and, as adopted in May 1992, proved extremely costly to the Community's budget.

The MacSharry reforms centred on cereals. Over three years, covering the harvests of 1993–95, intervention prices were significantly reduced, bringing them much closer to world market prices. This encouraged the use of cereals in animal feeds, displacing substitutes such as manioc (providing the carbohydrate) and maize gluten feed or soybean meal (providing the protein), which had enjoyed an artificial price advantage in the Community because of the CAP. Associated with the reduction in support prices, farmers became entitled to claim "area payments" on eligible arable land, which, broadly speaking, were designed to maintain farm revenues. However, beyond a certain size threshold, receipt of area payments was conditional on farmers setting aside a proportion of their eligible land, that is, taking it out of agricultural production. Initially, on a rotational basis, this was fixed at 15% of the farmer's total "set-aside" and cropped area. An enhanced area payment was, however, paid on the set-aside land. This outcome represented a major negotiating success for larger-scale farmers, predominantly but not exclusively located in the United Kingdom, as the Commission had originally proposed a system of "modulation", under which larger-scale farmers would have been compensated only in part for the reduction in price support. The Commission's original proposal would have been less costly to the budget and would have helped redress the 80% to 20% imbalance between large-scale and small-scale farmers referred to above.

MacSharry attempted to change the policy mechanisms for milk, but, like most of his predecessors, failed. Sugar, wine, fruit and vegetables, and olive oil were left untouched by the reform package. Beef producers suffered a fall in market price support, but were compensated by a series of headage payments on eligible animals, which were in effect limited by quotas. Headage payments for sheep were also restricted by quotas.

The CAP reforms agreed in *Agenda 2000* in March 1999 deepened, extended, and consolidated the MacSharry reforms. Thus further cuts to intervention prices for cereals and beef were agreed, offset, at least in part, by increases in the area and headage payments, which had become permanent features of the CAP. They were originally introduced in 1992 to compensate farmers for the change in policy, but there is as yet no commitment to phase out these direct payments. Understandably, farmers in the applicant states in central and eastern Europe have expectations that they too will receive these subsidies in due course.

The *Agenda 2000* agreement also rolled over the milk quota regime to 2008, but with a review scheduled for 2003. Intervention prices for butter and skimmed-milk powder are to be cut by 15% over the period 2005–08, but, offsetting this, farmers will become entitled to a new subsidy linked to their quota holdings.

The WTO Agreement on Agriculture

The Uruguay Round of GATT negotiations, which culminated in the establishment of the WTO, was the first in which the EU had agreed to discuss the policy mechanisms of the CAP, although the agriculture ministers of several member states remained extremely hostile to WTO-imposed constraints to the bitter end. The Agreement on Agriculture that emerged from these negotiations constrains all WTO signatories, not just the EU. However, it should be recognized that the CAP was the focus of much of the negotiations. The new constraints have been progressively applied over six years, beginning in 1995.

The Agreement introduced a new vocabulary, notably the term "tariffication". This refers to the conversion of nontariff barriers into conventional import tariffs. This, in theory, has resulted in the abolition of the variable import levy mechanism, so characteristic of the "old" CAP, and its replacement with a bound import duty that has been progressively reduced over the implementation period. Across all tariff lines, the reduction had to average 36%. However, derogations to tariffication, and the prohibitively high level of tariffs initially set, meant that for most products the tariff reductions did not result in increased imports. Import competition will become a more potent constraint to the excesses of the CAP after the next round of multilateral trade negotiations, if a further reduction in tariff rates is then agreed and imposed.

The WTO's requirement that the overall level of farm support be reduced by 20% had already been achieved by the EU, largely as a result of the MacSharry reforms. This is because the area and headage payments introduced in the MacSharry package are deemed to be "decoupled", and hence are not included in the computed level of support. Decoupling refers to the breaking of any formal link between production and entitlement to aid: thus a decoupled payment would be made regardless of the level of farm output or farm income. The total level of support on an annual basis (an "aggregate measurement of support", or AMS) had to be computed for the farm sector for the base period 1986–88, preceding the MacSharry reforms. Thus the base period AMS includes support to cereal and livestock producers under the "old" CAP. It is this AMS that has had to be reduced by 20% over the implementation period – but the AMS of the "new" CAP has easily achieved this target.

It is the export constraints of the Agreement that were expected, and have proven, to be most problematic for the CAP. Compared to a base period of 1986–90, expenditure on export subsidies had to be cut by 36%, and the volume of subsidized exports by 21%. One fear, expressed strongly by the government of France at the time, was that the area of set-aside would have to be increased substantially to meet the targets for wheat and other cereals. In the event, favourable developments on world markets in the intervening years restrained that threat, but underlying the Commission's quest for CAP reform in *Agenda 2000* was the fear that the export constraints inspired by the WTO could necessitate an increase in intervention stocks, and/or a tightening of supply controls, unless CAP support prices were brought more into line with those prevailing on world markets. Indeed, by 2000 significant problems had emerged for the EU's food-processing industry, for the WTO constraints meant that export subsidies on

processed foods could no longer be paid on the volume of goods that the industry wished to export.

A Widening of Policy Objectives?

In recent years the rhetoric, if not the practice, of the CAP has undoubtedly changed. For its supporters, its central purpose has always been social, with the aim of succouring disadvantaged small-scale farmers. According to its detractors, however, it has stifled the pursuit of economic efficiency and generated market imbalance. For many years a number of critics suggested that the CAP should be recast as a Common Food Policy, without always articulating clearly how such a policy would differ from a CAP. Increasingly the environmental effects of farming, both positive and negative, have been recognized, and the environmental lobby has suggested that agricultural subsidies should be made conditional upon the achievement of minimal environmental conditions on the farm (a form of "cross-compliance"), and that there should be a redirection of agricultural subsidies to payments made for the delivery of specified environmental services. Indeed, in *Agenda 2000* cross-compliance was incorporated into the CAP, and member states are now obliged to introduce schemes that insist that farmers meet minimum environmental standards if they are to receive in full the area and headage payments to which they would otherwise be entitled.

In the Cork Declaration of November 1996, a European Conference on Rural Development, convened by the Irish government when it held the EU Presidency, proposed a ten-point rural development programme for the EU. However, although Franz Fischler then restyled himself the Commissioner for Agriculture and Rural Development, the Council of Agriculture Ministers failed to endorse the Cork Declaration. Nonetheless, there is widespread concern that modern agriculture has been shedding labour at an unprecedented rate, leading to depopulation in some (but not all) remote rural regions, and this is coupled with a fear that radical reform of the CAP could lead to the abandonment of vast tracts of poor-quality land in remote regions, with implications for landscape, wildlife habits, and the viability of rural communities. *Agenda 2000*, in addition to the changes in the commodity support regimes outlined above, did repackage the CAP's structural policy measures. These were relaunched as a new rural development policy, which is now referred to by officials in Brussels as the "second pillar" of the CAP. Cynics suggest nonetheless that, fundamentally, the CAP remains a policy for supporting prices and farm incomes, reflecting the long-standing if misplaced belief that without such support a "fair" income for the agricultural community could not be secured, with just a few "add-ons" to recognize concerns about the environment and rural development. Allan Buckwell and his colleagues are not alone in suggesting that the CAP should be recast: in their case, they suggest redeploying existing CAP expenditure to fund a common agricultural and rural policy for Europe (see Buckwell *et al.*).

During the *Agenda 2000* debate and the preparations for the ill-fated WTO Ministerial Meeting in Seattle in December 1999, still more new concepts entered the specialist CAP vocabulary. The Commission asserted that there is a "European model for agriculture" that is not the same as that pursued by the EU's major competitors:

> The fundamental difference lies in the multi-functional nature of Europe's agriculture, and the part it plays in the economy and the environment, in society, and in preserving the landscape, whence the need to maintain farming throughout Europe and to safe-guard farmer's incomes (see European Commission 1998).

The EU's attempts to have its concept of "multifunctionality" accepted in the WTO as legitimate grounds for a continuation of its systems of CAP support have so far been rejected by its major trading partners; although the concept has been adopted enthusiastically by Norway, South Korea, and some other individual countries.

The Future of the CAP

Earlier in this chapter I suggested that the "new" CAP is perhaps a transient phenomenon and that further reform of the CAP is to be expected in the first decade of the new century. There are a number of related pressures that prompt this prediction, but two considerations in particular have dominated the policy discussion at the turn of the century. They are, first, the prospect of further CAP reforms being forced on the EU by the WTO process; and, secondly, the challenges to the CAP implicit in the prospective eastward enlargement of the EU.

The EU's quest for a satisfactory conclusion to the Uruguay Round undoubtedly prompted its search for compromise on agriculture and triggered the MacSharry reforms of 1992. However, as a result of the 1992 reforms and the rather generous "bindings" built into the Agreement on Agriculture, the impact of the Agreement on the CAP over the period 1995–2000 was modest. Nonetheless, the Agreement did provide (in Article 20) for a new round of negotiations to begin in 2000 and, although the WTO Ministerial Meeting in Seattle failed to launch a new, "millennium" round of trade negotiations, the mandated negotiations on agriculture did begin at the WTO's headquarters in Geneva. Further, in the Agreement's "Peace Clause" export subsidies and domestic support programmes provided for in the Agreement are protected from the full rigour of the WTO's otherwise overriding rules on subsidies. However, the Peace Clause expires at the end of 2003, and it is widely assumed that the EU's need to have its effectiveness extended will force major changes to the CAP, in the form of improved market access and further constraints on the use of export subsidies. If there are to be further cutbacks in subsidized exports from, say, 2004, then the *Agenda 2000* reforms to the dairy industry – which do not begin until 2005 – are clearly inadequate.

The accession to the EU of several countries in central and eastern Europe is likely to impose further pressure on the CAP. The enlarged EU would certainly be more "agricultural" in orientation. It has been estimated, on the basis of data from 1998, that if all 10 candidate states in that region were to join, the EU's farmed area would increase by 50% and the number of people engaged in agriculture would increase by more than 130% (see the Agriculture Directorate-General's website). Fears have been expressed that, given their agricultural potential, the extension of the present CAP to these countries would result in a major increase in output and a fall in consumption, and hence a burgeoning of budget expenditure. In fact, it is the prospective extension of the area and headage payments, introduced by the MacSharry reforms and consolidated in *Agenda 2000*, that would most inflate the budget. However, apart from the imposition of a quota regime on milk producers in 1984, budget pressures in the past have failed to trigger fundamental reform of the CAP. A more potent concern is that extension of the CAP to the applicant states would rupture the WTO's constraints on export subsidies. The candidate states in central and eastern Europe have entered into commitments involving modest levels of farm support and export subsidies. If these commitments are added to those of the EU of 15 member states, they do not allow the existing CAP to be applied in an enlarged EU.

The genesis of *Agenda 2000* lay in the perceived need to adapt the EU's institutions and policies to the challenges of enlargement. In practice, the Commission's proposals for CAP reform were conditioned more by the need to ensure that the existing EU was able to respect the export constraints imposed by the Uruguay Round Agreements. In the event, the weakened package agreed by the European Council in Berlin in March 1999 most probably will not achieve even that limited objective. Another "reform" of the CAP will be needed if enlargement is to proceed without a massive escalation of budget expenditure, notably on area and headage payments, and if the WTO negotiations are be successfully concluded.

Tradeable Bonds

Not only is the CAP in its present form unsuited for an enlarged EU and vulnerable

within the WTO, but it is little better than the "old" CAP in terms of economic efficiency. The area payments are only partially decoupled. Farmers still have to plough and plant their land. Thus alternative land uses will not readily compete with cereals unless comparable levels of support are offered, and area payments will inevitably affect the value of arable land. New purchasers and tenants have to pay inflated entry prices that their businesses can justify only on the basis of a continuation of the area payments. Ironically, the 1992 legislation introducing these payments referred to the need "to compensate the loss of income caused by the reduction of institutional prices" (Council Regulation (EEC) No. 1762/92). What is in place, in fact, is a system of revenue support, apparently forever, for anyone who cares to become a cereal farmer; and it is therefore difficult to see how farmers in the applicant states could be denied these payments after accession.

Agricultural economists have long advocated a more market-based approach to farming. If, for political reasons, this means that compensation has to be paid to individuals who have made investment decisions in the past on the basis of information that the new policy renders invalid, then such payments should compensate only those who suffered the loss, and they should be truly decoupled. The MacSharry and *Agenda 2000* reforms represented only small steps in this direction. It has been suggested that, in order to complete the process, farmers' entitlements to area and headage payments (and all other CAP price support) should be recast as compensation or adjustment payments, and converted into tradeable bonds. In year 1, the total compensation payment received by a farmer on a tradeable bond would be identical to that received under the existing CAP, but over ten or 15 years the payments would be progressively reduced and then eliminated. Thus the budgetary cost of the policy would gradually decline, but many existing businesses would be saved from bankruptcy. Farmers in the applicant states could have no legitimate expectation of receiving these payments, provided that the change is effected before levels of price and income support in the applicant states are increased to match those of today's CAP.

Farmers would no longer have to produce cereals or other products, or even remain in farming, to qualify for the compensation payments. Thus the payments would be truly decoupled and acceptable to the WTO, in that they would have no relevance for production decisions. Indeed, if they wished, farmers could sell their entitlement to receive future payments, and the discounted value of these future payments (guaranteed by the EU or national governments) would be reflected in the market value of the bond. Other asset prices, such as those of arable land or milk quotas, would fall, but new entrants into the industry could base their investment and farming decisions on the new, lower levels of asset and farm output prices.

The main problem with this proposal lies in the fall in land prices, as future support payments would instead be capitalized into the price of bonds. This is because landowners and farmers are not necessarily the same individuals, and landowners experiencing a fall in asset values would wish to secure their "share" of the value of the bonds from their tenants. At least, however, such a scheme would expose the myth that CAP price support is all about the support of farm incomes.

Further Reading

Ackrill, Robert W., "CAP Reform 1999: A Crisis in the Making?", in *Journal of Common Market Studies*, 38/2, 2000, pp. 343–53

A discussion of the *Agenda 2000* reforms

Buckwell, Allan, *et al.*, "Towards a Common Agricultural and Rural Policy for Europe", in *European Economy*, Reports and Studies no. 5, Luxembourg: Office for Official Publications of the European Communities, 1997

The authors outline an alternative approach to reform of the CAP.

Cork Declaration, November 1996, at europa.eu. int/comm/dg06/rur/cork_en.htm

Directorate-General on Agriculture, official website

The homepage for this website, which contains useful briefings and statistics, is at europa.eu. int/comm/dgs/agriculture/index_en.htm

European Commission, *The Development of the CAP*, COM(91)100, Brussels: Commission of the European Communities, 1991

European Commission, *Explanatory Memorandum. The Future for European Agriculture*, Brussels: Commission of the European Communities, 1998

European Commission, *The Agricultural Situation in the European Union*, Luxembourg: Office for Official Publications of the European Communities, various years

An annual report containing up-to-date statistics and a briefing on significant developments in the industry

Fennell, Rosemary, *The Common Agricultural Policy: Continuity and Change*, Oxford: Clarendon Press, and New York: Oxford University Press, 1997

A history of the CAP, focusing in particular on the thwarted attempts to develop a structural and social dimension to match the expansion in market intervention

Grant, Wyn, *The Common Agricultural Policy*, London: Macmillan, and New York: St Martin's Press, 1997

A discussion of aspects of the "new" CAP

Harris, Simon, Alan Swinbank, and Guy Wilkinson, *The Food and Farm Policies of the European Community*, Chichester and New York: Wiley, 1983

An account of the "old" CAP

MAFF, *European Agriculture: The Case for Radical Reform*, Conclusions of the Minister's CAP Review Group, London: Ministry of Agriculture, Fisheries, and Food, 1995

Marsh, John, *et al.*, *The Changing Role of the Common Agricultural Policy: The Future of Farming in Europe*, London: Belhaven, 1991; New York: Halsted Press, 1992

A wideranging study that includes a proposal for transferable bonds

Ritson, Christopher, and David R. Harvey (editors), *The Common Agricultural Policy*, second edition, Wallingford: CAB International, 1997

A discussion of aspects of the "new" CAP

Swinbank, Alan, "CAP Reform, 1992", in *Journal of Common Market Studies*, 31/3, 1993, pp. 359–72

An overview of the MacSharry reforms of 1992

Swinbank, Alan, "CAP Reform and the WTO: Compatibility and Developments", in *European Review of Agricultural Economics*, 26/3, 1999, 389–407

A paper on the *Agenda 2000* reforms

Swinbank, Alan, and Carolyn Tanner, *Farm Policy and Trade Conflict: The Uruguay Round and CAP Reform*, Ann Arbor: University of Michigan Press

A review of the linkages between CAP reform and the Uruguay Round negotiations

Tracy, Michael, *Government and Agriculture in Western Europe 1880–1988*, third edition, London: Harvester Wheatsheaf, and New York: New York University Press, 1989

A history of state protection of agriculture in western Europe

Periodicals

The weekly Agra Europe is published by Agra Europe (London) Ltd; there are many other trade papers. The academic journals in which papers are to be found include the *Journal of Agricultural Economics*, the *European Review of Agricultural Economics*, *Food Policy*, and the *Journal of Common Market Studies*.

Professor Alan Swinbank is a member of the Department of Agricultural and Food Economics at the University of Reading. He has written, lectured and advised extensively on the CAP. The financial support of a Leverhulme Trust Research Fellowship during the preparation of this text is gratefully acknowledged.

Table 13.1   Agricultural Employment in EU Member States as a Proportion of Total Civilian Employment, selected years 1960–98 (%)

	1960	1970	1980	1990	1998
Belgium	8.7	5.0	3.2	2.7	2.2
France	22.5	13.5	8.5	5.6	4.4
Germany[1]	13.8	8.6	5.3	3.7	2.8
Italy	32.6	20.2	14.3	8.8	6.4
Luxembourg	16.6	9.7	5.5	3.3	2.9
Netherlands	9.8	6.3	4.9	4.6	3.5
Denmark	18.2	11.5	8.1	5.7	3.7
Ireland	37.3	27.1	18.3	15.0	10.9
UK	4.8	3.2	2.4	2.2	1.7
Greece	57.1	40.8	30.3	23.9	17.7
Spain	42.3	29.5	19.3	11.8	7.9
Portugal	43.9	30.0	28.6	18.0	13.7
EU–12	21.1	13.8	9.5	6.5	n.a.
Austria	na	18.7	10.6	7.9	6.5
Finland	na	24.4	13.5	8.4	7.1
Sweden	na	8.1	5.1	3.4	3.1
EU–15	na	na	na	na	5.0[2]

1 West Germany up to and including 1990
2 Figures for 1997

Source: Adapted from Table 3.5.1.3 of European Commission, *The Agricultural Situation in the European Union, 1999 Report*, available on the website of the Directorate-General on Agriculture (address given above), and earlier printed versions of this annual publication

Table 13.2   National Gains and Losses Stemming from the CAP in 1993

	Net transfers between the Member States stemming from the CAP, expressed as a % of GDP
Belgium	0
Denmark	+0.8
France	+0.3
Germany	−0.3
Greece	+2.8
Ireland	+4.4
Italy	−0.3
Luxembourg	0
Netherlands	+0.3
Portugal	−0.5
Spain	+0.3
United Kingdom	−0.2

This table reports the British Ministry of Agriculture, Fisheries, and Food's computations of the budget transfers, and the transfers implicit in trading at EU rather than world prices. It does not include the economic efficiency losses suffered by all member states as a result of the CAP.

Source: MAFF, *European Agriculture: The Case for Radical Reform*, Conclusions of the Minister's CAP Review Group, London: Ministry of Agriculture, Fisheries, and Food, 1995, Annex II

Chapter Fourteen

Cohesion Policy

Iain Begg

Regional disparities in the EU are substantial and represent one of the main challenges to its cohesiveness. Indeed, "economic and social cohesion" is identified in Article 2 of the Treaty on European Union as one of the fundamental objectives of the EU. Regional policy, however, was not initially a formal competence of the Community tier of government, but this changed in 1975 with the establishment of the European Regional Development Fund (ERDF). Spending on structural policies has increased progressively since then as greater attention has been paid to the need to go beyond the common market that was the original *raison d'être* of the European Community.

Building a genuine Union is now recognized to require that there be a sufficient degree of cohesiveness between different regions and common policies to achieve these ends. European regions are defined in a hierarchical classification known as "NUTS" – the acronym of the French title of the classification. This has differing levels of aggregation based, loosely, on the sizes of regions. The first level of the classification below member states is known as Level 1. In the case of the United Kingdom, for example, this refers to the standard regions delineated by the national government; in Germany it refers to the federal states, the *Länder*. For smaller member states, such as Ireland or Luxembourg, the entire country initially counted as a Level 1 region, although a revision in 1999 led to Ireland being split into two, a change that ensured that the country's phenomenal economic growth did not prevent its poorer areas from continuing to benefit from the ERDF and the other "structural funds" discussed here.

Although the small size of the EU's budget relative to GDP inevitably limits the capacity of the Community tier of government to advance cohesion, the EU nevertheless has a range of policy instruments at its disposal. These include controls on "state aids" (subsidies), to ensure that richer areas do not use them to obtain unfair advantages for their companies; loan finance from the European Investment Bank; and various technology and infrastructure programmes designed to upgrade the economies of less favoured regions.

The main contribution of the EU towards cohesion comes, however, from its "structural actions", especially the structural funds. The two main structural funds are the ERDF and the European Social Fund (ESF); the latter was established under the original Treaty of Rome. These are administered by separate Directorates-General of the European Commission, each headed by one of the Commissioners. The "guidance" component of the European Agricultural Guidance and Guarantee Fund (EAGGF or FEOGA), the fund that finances the Common Agricultural Policy (as mentioned in Chapter 13), provides further support aimed at restructuring in agriculture, and is administered by the Agriculture Directorate-General. There is also the Cohesion Fund, an outcome of the intergovernmental deal struck at the Edinburgh European Council in December 1992. This fund is targeted specifically at the poorest member states of the EU, those with per-capita GNP below 90% of the EU average, that is, Greece, Ireland, Portugal, and Spain. The Cohesion Fund was intended primarily to support economic development through improvements in infrastructure, with the aim of preparing countries for monetary union, but the Fund has been renewed for the period 2000–06 even though all the recipients will have adopted the euro by the beginning of 2001. A review of eligibility, which is likely to see Ireland disqualified, will take place in 2003.

The budget for the "structural actions" was set for 2000–06 at the European Council in Berlin in March 1999. A total of €260 billion (at 1999 prices) will be spent on all structural measures, roughly a third of the EU budget and 0.4% of the EU GDP. Of this total, €195 billion has been allocated to the structural funds and €18 billion to the Cohesion Fund. The balance has been set aside and ringfenced for the countries that are candidates for membership of the EU. Initially, the aid to candidate countries will be distributed under a new "Instrument for Structural Policies for Pre-Accession" (ISPA).

Regional Disparities: Extent and Causes

A variety of indicators can be used to monitor the well-being of regions, although the most commonly used are GDP per capita (as a proxy for income) in relation to the EU average, and the unemployment rate. Both measures have widely acknowledged shortcomings. GDP figures are a measure of production rather than income, and thus ignore net transfers: Ireland exemplifies the problem, as its GNP is some 10% lower than its GDP because of remittances paid abroad. Unemployment rates are difficult to measure consistently across regions, especially where there is a substantial amount of undeclared employment, and they do not always correlate closely with relative prosperity. Despite these methodological caveats, the gaps revealed by both types of indicator are sufficiently large to be persuasive. Thus, according to the European Commission's latest *Periodic Report* (1999) on the EU's regions, the ten most prosperous regions have a GDP per capita three times as high as that of the ten least prosperous.

These disparities in income are mirrored in other indicators of standard of living, such as possession of consumer goods or access to care services. It is important to note, however, that the extent of regional disparities increased substantially as a result of the accession of the three Mediterranean member states (Greece, Spain, and Portugal) in the 1980s, all with levels of income per capita substantially below the then Community average. Accession of much poorer countries in central and eastern Europe would inevitably widen the disparities again. During the 1990s, the least favoured members states did well: Portugal and Greece progressed from around half the EU average (expressed in the "purchasing power standard", a measure that makes allowance for differences in price levels) to two thirds, while Ireland has grown so rapidly that its GDP per capita now exceeds the EU average.

Unemployment disparities are also great, with particularly high rates of unemployment in the South and West of Spain, in southern Italy, and in the eastern *Länder* of Germany. In Greece and Portugal, by contrast, unemployment is much less severe, although it is difficult to compare like with like. Comparing the US states with the EU regions at an equivalent level of territorial breakdown, there is a considerably greater spread of unemployment in the EU than in the United States. Explanations for this include the much higher labour mobility in the United States, which tends to equalize unemployment rates, the generally lower level of unemployment in the United States, and the fact that there is greater social protection in much of the EU, which reduces pressure to migrate in search of work.

Regional disparities in the EU stem from a variety of causes, an observation that is often overlooked in the search for an appropriate policy response. Most of the "less favoured" regions are on the periphery of the EU, suggesting that this, in itself, is part of the explanation. The notion of peripherality as a matter of geographical distance from an economic "core" implies that transport costs are the main obstacle, but it may be more accurate to analyze peripherality in terms of marginalization in a wider sense. It is also important to note that there are many relatively prosperous regions (Grampian or North Yorkshire in the United Kingdom, Bavaria in Germany) in ostensibly remote locations, whereas some of the less favoured regions, such as Hainaut in Belgium or the Saarland, could scarcely be more centrally located.

An altogether different category of regional problem arises from lack of economic development. In much of southern Europe until very recently, agriculture remained the dominant industry and there was relatively little industrialization. Regional differences in the growth of labour supply are another important phenomenon. High "natural" rates of labour force growth (that is, where the entry of younger people into the labour market is substantially higher than the retirement of older workers) have traditionally characterized much of southern Europe, as well as Ireland, and have led to a steady emigration of individuals of working age from these regions. Advances in agricultural productivity have meant that fewer workers can be supported by farming, with the result that in such regions there has been a drift of population towards urban centres. This pattern of a shakeout in agriculture is likely to be repeated in many of the countries of central and eastern Europe that are candidates for accession to the EU.

In northern Europe, where the decline of agricultural employment occurred at an earlier stage, regional problems are associated mainly with the decline of staple industries, especially coal-mining, steel-making, textiles, and shipbuilding. More recently, some regions have been adversely affected by the relative decline of newer manufacturing industries, such as motor vehicles – the West Midlands of England being a prime example – and it is apparent that "sunrise" industries, such as computer software or biotechnology, are drawn to different sorts of locations. For most of the regions affected by industrial decline, adjustment has proved to be slow and painful, instead of happening as quickly as was predicted by the more sanguine economic theorists. In addition, and in contrast to the experience in southern Europe, there has been something of a drift away from large conurbations as both residents and businesses have found it more attractive to relocate to smaller cities and more rural areas.

Insofar as they signal a lack of competitiveness, there is a common thread to these problems, but this does not mean that they are necessarily amenable to common solutions. In some regions, there are manifestly still some shortcomings in much of the basic infrastructure of roads, telecommunications, and other services. Elsewhere, the problem may have more to do with training, while in other regions it is the promotion of small business and rates of innovation that is most urgent. Faced with such diverse demands, the structural funds have to try to respond.

The Structural Funds

The aims, operation, and scale of the structural funds have evolved considerably over the 25 years since the ERDF was established. The ERDF was originally intended to support member states in regional policy, just as the ESF was intended to provide such support in the field of social policy. During the 1990s, however, flows of money from the Commission came to represent sizeable proportions of regional policy assistance and the influence of the Commission in shaping programmes grew. There was an effective doubling in real terms of the budget between 1988 and 1993, taking it to 0.3% of the Community's GDP, and annual spending on the funds increased further from ECU21.2 billion in 1993 to ECU30 billion in 1999 (at 1992 prices in both cases), taking it to around 0.4% of the EU's GDP. In anticipation of demands on the budget from the countries of central and eastern Europe, the resources for the funds will, however, fall slightly from the rates applying at the end of the 1990s under the current *Financial Perspective* (see Chapter 12), between 2000 and 2006.

In principle, the structural funds aim to concentrate efforts on regions and groups in society most in need. As agreed at the European Council in Berlin in 1999, the structural funds have three objectives for 2000–06 (reduced from six under the previous regulations).

Under Objective 1, the funds are to be used to promote the development and structural adjustment of regions where development is lagging behind. For regions to be eligible for Objective 1 they have to have GDP per capita of less than 75% of the EU average. Most of the regions designated in this way are in the southern periphery, but half of Ireland, much of eastern Germany, and small parts of other member states, such as Cornwall and the Isles of Scilly, West Wales and the Valleys, Merseyside, and South Yorkshire in the United Kingdom, or Burgenland in Austria, are also covered, as are the remote regions of Sweden and Finland (previously designated as Objective 6 regions). In a classic EU compromise, the 1999 agreement provided for those regions due to lose Objective 1 status to have an extended transitional period designed to give them a "soft landing" from the withdrawal of support. The Objective 1 regions receive the bulk of the money allocated under the structural funds and will be further favoured in the coming years, with their share rising to 69.7% (of which 4.3% will go on transitional support) between 2000 and 2006, giving them a total of €135.9 billion.

Objective 2 requires the funds to support the economic and social conversion of areas facing structural difficulties. Most of these Objective 2 regions are either traditional industrial areas in the northern member states, such as the Franco–Belgian coalfield, Northeast England, or the Saarland in Germany, or rural regions, for example Southwest France (previously designated under Objective 5b).

Objective 3 is to support the adaptation and modernization of policies and systems of education, training, and employment. In particular, it aims to combat long-term and youth unemployment, and to facilitate the integration into working life of those exposed to exclusion from the labour market. The funds are to try to achieve this objective by providing training schemes and by a variety of initiatives to promote the employability of unemployed individuals. Objective 3 brings together what were previously two labour market objectives.

Objectives 1 and 2 are explicitly spatial, in that only designated regions are eligible for them. Objective 3, by contrast, is open to regions throughout the EU other than those that are designated under Objective 1. In total, the spatially targeted areas have been reduced from regions covering just over 50% of the population of the EU in 1994–99 to some 40%. Although this does represent a better con-

centration of support, in line with one of the principles governing the structural funds, the coverage is still open to the criticism that it is far too thinly spread and that it cannot, consequently, make a meaningful difference. However, for many of the Objective 1 regions the flows of resources from the structural funds represent sizeable proportions of GDP, as much as 6% for those that receive the most. In relation to national or regional budgets for public investment, on which much of the money from the ERDF is spent, EU aid makes a substantial difference.

The second principle on which the funds operate is "programming": in order to obtain funding from the structural funds, member states are required to elaborate plans, known as Community Support Frameworks (CSFs), or to produce Single Programming Documents (SPDs). These are agreed between the government of a given member state and the Commission, and comprise a series of linked programmes to promote the development of the region. In addition, the structural funds include a number of "Community initiatives", which are intended to transcend national boundaries and thus to support EU-wide objectives. These proliferated between 1994 and 1999, but in response to criticism that they were too piecemeal, they were pruned sharply to just four schemes in 1999 and had their share of the structural funds cut from 9% to 5.4% of the total.

A third focus in the allocation of the funds is on "partnership", which is, in part, about cooperation between the Commission, on the one hand, and both national and subnational tiers of government, on the other. There has also, however, been a growing emphasis on involving other agencies and the "social partners" in the process. A further stipulation concerns "additionality", the requirement that EU money should add to, rather than substitute for, member state funding. This has been the source of considerable friction, especially in relation to the United Kingdom, where the Treasury believes that it, rather than the European Commission, should have the final say on how public expenditure is allocated.

In the current set of regulations governing structural actions (see European Commission

2000) "efficiency" is given a higher profile than hitherto. Concern about fraud and misman-agement, culminating in the resignation of the Santer Commission early in 1999, helps to explain this change, but it can also be attrib-uted to a form of "institutional learning", as the various actors have sought to draw on the experience gained since the reform of the structural funds in 1988. More weight is given to monitoring and evaluation, and the forms of financial control are simultaneously being tightened and adapted to assure more stream-lined procedures for decision-making.

The EU has been much more tentative about developing a specifically urban policy, partly because of the risk that urban and regional pol-icy could pull in different directions. The nature of these conflicts can be illustrated by reference to London, which, although it is situated in one of the more prosperous British regions, the Southeast, and consequently is not eligible for EU help, does nevertheless contain boroughs with some of the most deprived populations in the United Kingdom. In fact, in the current round of the structural funds some small areas of London, such as the Lea Valley in Northeast London, have been designated under Object-ive 2, and much of the territory covered else-where is, in practice, urban, examples being Sheffield, Newcastle upon Tyne, or the cities of the Ruhr Valley in Germany. In addition, one of the Community initiatives that has survived from the previous period, entitled URBAN, is intended to offer support, albeit on a modest scale, for economic development in selected urban localities.

Related Policy Instruments

The Cohesion Fund, as its name implies, is intended to promote the cohesiveness of the EU by assisting the least favoured economies to improve their relative levels of income, thereby achieving "real" convergence. Despite this shared intention, the Cohesion Fund dif-fers from the structural funds in a number of critical respects. First, it is targeted at member states rather than regions, with the result that it can be used for projects in regions not eligible for ERDF support. This consideration has been especially important for Spain. Secondly,

it is confined to a narrower range of areas, supporting transport infrastructure and pro-jects to improve the environment. Thirdly, there are conditions that have to be met by eligible member states, principally to do with adhering to "convergence plans" linked to economic and monetary union. In addition, the scale of funds is comparatively modest, at less than 10% of the money allocated to the structural funds. This is not to belittle the sig-nificance of the Cohesion Fund for the recipi-ents, but it does put it in perspective.

Additional assistance for economic develop-ment comes from the European Investment Bank (EIB), which has a remit similar to that of the World Bank. It provides loans for pro-jects aimed at improving infrastructure or other-wise supporting economic development. The Channel Tunnel was one project that obtained such a loan, while the Trans-European Net-works (TENs) have been notable beneficiaries. In eligible regions, the EIB is also able to pro-vide support for small businesses. Its loans are always on commercial terms, rather than being at subsidized rates, but EIB loans are, never-theless, advantageous in two respects. First, the interest rates charged do not, typically, include the sort of risk premium that the money mar-kets tend to levy on less favoured borrowers, so that the cost to the borrowing region is lower than it would be if it tried to borrow directly from the markets. Secondly, because the EIB conducts a careful evaluation of proposed pro-jects, the fact that they are accorded a loan is generally interpreted as a favourable signal by other potential lenders or investors.

Commission support for research and technological development (RTD) also gives some priority access to less favoured regions, although this does little more than offset the advantages of more favoured regions in secur-ing RTD funding. On the whole, CAP spend-ing also now goes disproportionately to the less favoured member states, although this is not strictly aimed at economic development.

The Way Forward for the Structural Funds

Evaluating the effectiveness of the structural funds and the related instruments discussed above is far from easy. In the first place, it is extremely difficult to devise a research methodology capable of separating their effects from other determinants of economic performance. Even if there is no discernible improvement in a region's economy, policy may still have had a beneficial impact if it prevents a relative deterioration. Economic development is, moreover, a complex process in which a variety of policy initiatives have to come together in a mutually reinforcing manner. Evaluation is further complicated by the fact that the transformation of a region typically requires decades rather than months. Critics of the structural funds nevertheless argue that they tend to be ineffective because they often support inappropriate projects, are poorly managed, and/or are too narrowly focused. Supporters point to the substantial levels of investment stimulated or made by the funds in the EU's least favoured regions, and argue that this at least creates some of the conditions necessary for economic development, which seem to be bearing fruit.

This raises the rather awkward question of whether the European Commission should continue to have such a prominent role in structural policies. There are, inevitably, conflicting views on this matter. "Regional" policy is essentially about supply-side measures aimed at boosting the competitiveness of less favoured regions and should therefore be seen as providing measures to improve the *future* economic performance of assisted regions. This needs to be distinguished in principle, even if it cannot always be distinguished in practice, from measures intended to redistribute current income from more prosperous to poorer regions. The latter is best achieved by transfers for income support. One point of view is that, because the funds are spread rather thinly across all 15 member states, notwithstanding the aim of concentration, they are simply too small in scale to have much impact on the supply side. Certainly, the level of spending by member states on state aids is significantly higher, especially in Italy, and this often conflicts with the EU's efforts to upgrade the least favoured regions.

Equally, the fact that the four "cohesion" countries do receive substantial net inflows of investment funding not only helps their development, but also provides a macroeconomic stimulus. The latter, however, could be achieved by a straight fiscal transfer, without the European Commission dictating how the money be spent. It is therefore pertinent to ask whether a case can be made for intervention by the supranational tier to promote the development of regions, rather than a simple fiscal transfer. The argument for the European Commission exercising some control is reasonably persuasive where it is an entire country that is the net recipient of assistance from the structural funds. In these circumstances, "donors" must be convinced that their money is being well spent and is not simply used to bolster current consumption. Ensuring both that additionality is observed and that projects add to productive potential will never be easy, but it would be difficult to retain political support without them. This, arguably, implies that the Commission needs to improve its monitoring of the outcomes of structural funds spending.

In the case of Objectives 2 and 3, the arguments for Commission involvement are less compelling and there may eventually need to be a reassessment of these components of the structural funds as more countries accede. The circular flow of money from member states (via their budget contributions) to the Commission and back again must be open to question, especially when the total sums involved are relatively limited. This should not preclude the Commission from providing appropriate technical assistance, possibly by promoting sharing of experience. However, the case for Commission involvement in actually administering programmes is of more doubtful value, since national administrations and, often, regional or local governments generally have a better appreciation of what needs to be done. The irony is, however, that the structural funds provide one of the main channels through which those countries that believe that they pay excessive net contributions to the EU recoup some of their outlays. Indeed, some of the payments agreed in the Berlin deal on the structural funds take this to an extreme: thus, "to take account of the particular characteristics of labour market participation in the Netherlands, an additional amount of €500 million is allocated to Objective 3". One can only speculate on what these unique characteristics of the Dutch labour market might be.

In the past, the bulk of the support from the ERDF was channelled towards infrastructure development. This, arguably, gave it too narrow a focus, in that it addressed only one component of competitiveness when others, such as low innovation rates or skill shortages, may be more telling. To their credit, the decision-makers have broadened the coverage of the structural funds in recent years, although more efforts on technology diffusion and on boosting rates of innovation in less favoured regions still seem to be warranted. Indeed, the establishment of a technology-related objective for the funds might be an interesting experiment.

The prospect of enlargement of the EU evokes mixed feelings in the less favoured regions of the existing member states. On the one hand, the accession of significantly less well-off members could be expected to give a new impetus to cohesion policy and could trigger fresh debate on the scale of regional transfers. On the other hand, many regions fear that the support that they currently receive will be cut to support transfers to the new members. The outcome of the negotiations in Berlin in 1999 was an artful compromise, which provided for the prospective new members while keeping the disbursements from the structural funds broadly at the same level as before. However, it is open to question how much longer this approach can endure: the artful compromise may represent nothing more than a postponement of hard decisions.

The issue of redistribution through transfers for income support is one that the EU has been reluctant to contemplate. It is, nevertheless, at the heart of what the concept of "Union" means. To some extent, the structural funds are already seen as a form of tacit income support, even though their intention is to promote economic development. This is especially true where flows from the funds are inadequately monitored and where little effort is made to evaluate their effectiveness. Structural measures, by definition, are not an appropriate means of achieving redistribution and it would be wrong for them to be appraised in such a manner. Yet it is clear that some regions and/or member states – the United Kingdom, for one, often

appears to take this view – regard the structural funds primarily as a source of public funding that comes with tiresome rules and conditions attached. This contradicts their purpose and suggests that a more precise assignment of instruments to targets within the EU would be helpful.

More generally, this raises the question of whether the EU's role in structural policies should increasingly be to set the rules, rather than to continue funding and implementing programmes directly. One area to which the supranational tier is manifestly best suited is mediating between member states on the use of state aids. Spatial planning of the EU territory is another area where the Commission has latterly shown increasing interest, notably with the publication of the European Spatial Planning Perspective, which set out ideas under a number of headings for the physical planning of the EU territory. These and related aspects of the administration of spatial and social cohesion may come more into prominence as the EU becomes more closely integrated.

Further Reading

Armstrong, Harvey, and Jim Taylor, *Regional Economics and Policy*, third edition, Oxford and Malden, MA: Blackwell, 1999

  A respected textbook on regional economics that pays particular attention to policy issues

Bachtler, John, and Ivan Turok (editors), *The Coherence of EU Regional Policy: Contrasting Perspectives on the Structural Funds*, London: Jessica Kingsley, 1997

  A collection of chapters looking at how well the structural funds have functioned

Begg, Iain (guest editor), "Special Issue: The Reform of the Structural Funds", *European Planning Studies*, 1998

  An introductory article and five specialist contributions on the future of the structural funds

European Commission, *Sixth Periodic Report on the Social and Economic Situation and Development of the Regions in the Community*, Luxembourg: Office for Official Publications of the European Communities, 1999

  This is the latest of the Commission's regular, general reports on the regions, which provide a wealth of statistical material and analysis of developments. The Commission also publishes occasional studies on specific issues, including numbers 29, *Economic and Social Cohesion in the European Union: the Impact of Member States' own Policies*; 35, *The Impact of Economic and Monetary Union on Cohesion*; and 36, *Spatial Perspectives for the Enlargement of the European Union.*

European Commission, *Structural Actions 2000– 2006: Commentary and Regulations*, Luxembourg: Office for Official Publications of the European Communities, 2000

This publication provides a summary of the key features of the structural funds and contains the official text of the regulations concerning them.

European Commission, *Unity, Solidarity, Diversity for Europe, its People and its Territory: Second Report on Economic and Social Cohesion*, volumes 1 and 2, Luxembourg: Office for Official Publications of the European Commission, 2001

This contains an update of the Sixth Periodic Report (see above) and an analysis of cohesion policy in the context of enlargement.

Heinelt, Hubert, and Randall Smith, *Policy Networks and European Structural Funds*, Aldershot: Avebury, 1996

A useful collection of papers on the politics of the structural funds

Hervé, Yves, and Robert Holzmann, *Fiscal Transfers and Economic Convergence in the EU: An Analysis of Absorption Problems and an Evaluation of the Literature*, Baden-Baden: Nomos, 1998

This book takes a somewhat sceptical look at the philosophy behind the structural funds and comments on the implications for enlargement.

Honohan, Patrick (editor), *EU Structural Funds in Ireland: A Mid-term Evaluation of the CSF 1994–99*, Policy Research Series Paper 31, Dublin: Economic and Social Research Institute, 1997

This study, one of the few published evaluations of how the funds have operated, shows how they have been integrated into public investment plans in Ireland.

Inforegio, website at www.inforegio.org

The material available here includes listings of designated regions, reports produced by the Commission or under its auspices, information sheets, proceedings of conference, and speeches. The site is linked to the ERDF.

Oxford Review of Economic Policy, Summer 1995

A special issue containing a series of articles on regional policy and focusing particularly on European Commission policy

Regional Policy Directorate of the European Commission, website at europa.eu.int/comm/ regional_policy/index_en.htm

This site presents a substantial amount of information about the regulations governing the structural funds and the Cohesion Fund.

Yuill, Douglas, John Bachtler, and Fiona Wishlade (editors), *European Regional Incentives 1999–2000*, London: Bowker-Saur, 1999

This book, updated regularly by specialists at the European Policies Research Centre of the University of Strathclyde, provides a comprehensive guide to regional incentives available in EU countries.

Iain Begg is Professor of International Economics at South Bank University, London. His recent publications on the regional and social consequences of European integration include "Factor Mobility and Regional Disparities in the EU", in the *Oxford Review of Economic Policy*, 1995; "Reform of the Structural Funds after 1999", in *European Planning Studies*, 1997; "Previsiones sobre convergencia regional en la Unión Europea", in *Papeles de Economia Española*, 1999; and, with Dermot Hodson, "Regional Adjustment Mechanisms under EMU", in *Tijdschrift voor Economische en Sociale Geografie*, 2000. He is co-editor with John Peterson of the *Journal of Common Market Studies*.

Figure 14.1   Regional Unemployment Disparities US States + DC (1992) and EU Level-1 Regions (1993)

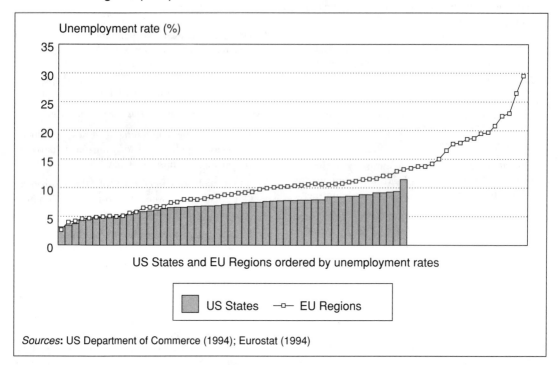

Sources: US Department of Commerce (1994); Eurostat (1994)

Chapter Fifteen

Debates on Social Policy

Caitríona A. Carter

Like other economic systems engaged in intensifying patterns of international trade, the EU has increasingly been faced with a number of emergent dilemmas over social policy. Perhaps the most important of these concern the turning of economic growth into employment growth, the balancing of labour market flexibility with job security, and the promotion of social inclusion. A question that has consistently dogged the member states since the inception of the European Community is whether they should adopt some form of collective response, at the level of the Community, and thus develop a common social policy, or whether social policy decisions, including settlements with redistributive consequences, should remain the preserve of the nation state.

The development of a common policy is problematic both constitutionally and politically. From a constitutional perspective, national social welfare policy is premised on the notion of forging a social consensus for the redistribution of the resources of a nation. National welfare systems have historically provided a link between the nation state and civil society, and have been promoted as valuable sources of legitimacy for a political system. (This is not to imply that the welfare state is a "neutral" institution, since national social systems are subject to criticism of their redistributive decisions and of their conceptualization of what social citizenry is: rather, it suggests that there is an underlying bargain whereby welfare systems protect "their" citizens.) The European Community/EU, as a system of governance beyond the state, lacks such a state apparatus,

and indeed a "European" society, yet it has frequently been argued that these would be necessary to legitimize and sustain programmes at the level of the Community. From a political perspective, the different models of social welfare and labour market systems deployed by the member states have been presented as obstacles to the forging of a common response. Consequently, as we move into the 21st century it is uncertain whether a convergence of social systems within the EU is either feasible or, from the point of view of implementing policies effectively and legitimately, desirable.

Against this background, the Community/ EU has struggled to devise the "best" responses to persistent social challenges: structural unemployment, social exclusion, the ageing society, and new employment trends. These responses have involved both arrangements for governance and choices between policies. A central element of this process has been a rethinking of the concept of a "common" social policy. This rethinking has been manifest in the marked shift in approach to the question of policy convergence, with proposals for harmonization of social policy in the 1980s giving way to new proposals for coordination, or what has been defined as "policy transfer" (Peterson and Bomberg p. 264). The impact of this rethinking can also be seen in the high-level political argument that emerged in the 1990s, expressed by both the European Commission and the member states within the European Council, that the EU has indeed adopted an approach to social policy that is distinct from the approaches of its competitors, such as the

United States or Japan. This "common" approach is said to be the application of the "European social model". Notwithstanding certain differences between national systems, it is argued, all member states' national policies fall within the rubric of a model with "common" salient national elements: a system of industrial relations, a welfare state, and the principle of social partnership. In this view, what is required to achieve a "common" substantive response to social policy challenges is a collective coordinated "modernization" of the European social model, while its core components are preserved.

Treaty Developments

Free Market, Social Welfare, and EEC Treaty Models

After the establishment of the European Coal and Steel Community (ECSC) in 1952, political discussions between France, West Germany (as it then was), Italy, and the Benelux countries centred on the creation of further institutional arrangements for the purposes of increased integration. In 1955, ECSC foreign ministers meeting in Messina decided to establish an intergovernmental committee to give consideration to various methods of integration. The committee, presided over by the Belgian Foreign Minister Paul-Henri Spaak, published a report in 1956 (the Spaak Report), which was to lay the foundations for the Treaty of Rome.

According to the Spaak Report, the main feature of Community integration would be the creation of a common market, requiring the elimination of all obstacles to the free movement of goods, services, capital, and labour. Beyond this, however, it was agreed that the effective functioning of a common market would involve a degree of policy harmonization between individual member states, otherwise competition within the common market would be undermined by different national programmes. This has since become familiar as the notion of creating a "level playing field". A corollary to this was the introduction of an element of supranationalism to the process of economic integration, a common approach

to key policies being necessary to ensure the establishment of a truly competitive system within the common market (Collins 1975 p. 9). For the most part, the suggested areas of common policy were those in which national intervention was the norm, made necessary to correct instances of market failure or externality – for example, competition policy concerned with preventing monopoly control of resources, agricultural policy, and so on. However, a common social policy was not considered essential to ensure the success of the common market. Instead, it was argued that "redistributive benefits used as an instrument of social policy should remain entirely a matter for member states" (Collins 1975 p. 9). This original constitutional decision to leave redistributive policies to the national systems was premised on the understanding of the link between the social welfare state and the nation state. Socially redistributive or market-correcting policies were delivered at the national level within the institutional framework of the social welfare state and were seen as important legitimating devices, not only for the national political system, but also for the process of economic integration on which the nation state had embarked (see Carter). Social policy, understood in a redistributive sense, was thought to be irrelevant to the sphere of production, although it might play a significant role in the national politics of redistribution.

The Spaak Report also considered the effect of the costs of national legislation for social welfare and employment protection on competition within the common market, and, in particular, whether such costs jeopardized free and fair competition. The Report suggested that specific distortions caused by differences in social provisions could exist, for example in direct or indirect taxation, or working conditions such as equal pay policies, overtime, and paid holidays, but, in the main, there was a lack of certainty over the exact relationship between social charges and future trading patterns (Collins 1975 pp. 37–38). Such uncertainty in the Report reflected a difference of opinion between France, West Germany, and Italy: the French experts were keen to ensure that free and fair competition should not be distorted as a result of high French social security charges imposed by national legislation, while the experts from West Germany and Italy were keen to promote the establishment of a common market on the basis of a liberal capitalist or free market system, reflecting their own market systems, with harmonization of social policy only if it was certain that social costs gave rise to distortions of competition (Collins 1975 pp. 4–7). It was suggested in the Report that the Commission of the proposed European Economic Community (EEC) would be responsible for considering, at some future date, whether or not such costs were distorting competition. In fact, the "social dumping" arguments of the 1980s stemmed from the Commission looking into this very question (these arguments are explored in detail below). The other main consideration of social policy issues in the Spaak Report related to the future Community's financial arrangements. A European Social Fund would need to be established to finance programmes in pursuance of Community objectives, increasing worker mobility and enabling workers to find employment in the new common market. This Fund would also serve to compensate for job losses brought about by the restructuring of industry, this being a corollary of the removal of all obstacles to free trade in goods and services (Collins 1975 p. 10). As a result, what emerged as social policy in the formative years of the EEC was a policy aimed at improving the functioning of labour markets, with a view to enhancing the economic prospects for individuals from the integration process itself.

The provisions of the Treaty of Rome, which established the EEC, to a great extent reflected the proposals made in the Spaak Report. The founding treaty contained a Social Policy Title, Title III – later to become part of Title XI of what is now called the Treaty establishing the European Community (TEC) – which is divided into two chapters. One deals with social provisions (Articles 117–22 EEC, later 136–45 TEC): key among these was Article 119, which established the principle that men and women should receive equal pay for equal work. The other deals with the European Social Fund (Articles 123–28 EEC, later Articles 146–50 TEC). Article 117 EEC, in its

original form, set out the main objective of social policy insofar as this was to be conducted at the Community level:

> Member States agree upon the need to promote improved working conditions and an improved standard of living for workers, so as to make possible their harmonization while improvement is being maintained.
>
> They believe that such a development will ensue not only from the functioning of the common market, which will favour the harmonization of social systems, but also from the procedures provided for in this Treaty and from the approximation of provisions laid down by law, regulation or administrative action.

As Doreen Collins (1994) notes, the wording of Article 117 was intended, in part, to reassure member states that common activity would not extend to certain aspects of social policy, such as direct welfare provision or retirement pensions. However, at the same time the notion of harmonizing social systems did introduce an element of ambiguity on the question of whether the Community was competent to regulate in the area of social policy. Additionally, no timetable was set out for the harmonization of social systems: it was left up to the member states and the Commission to decide upon this at some future point (Collins 1975 p. 22).

All in all, an indefinite message was given by the Treaty of Rome on the relationship between social policy and economic integration. Indeed, precisely this ambiguity lay at the heart of the social policy debate as it first emerged. The lack of certainty meant that it was possible in the first instance to interpret the treaty either as a liberal capitalist manifesto or as a mandate for the promotion of social welfare concerns, suggesting visions of the role of social policy, in relation to the economic system, that were diametrically opposed to one another.

Conventional economic orthodoxy suggested that the provision of enhanced social welfare would inevitably result in losses in economic efficiency and thus would impair the capacity of the economy as a whole to maximize its rate of economic growth. In turn, this would result in lower levels of employment and income than otherwise would be the case. This conclusion contrasts sharply with the welfarist model. According to this vision, social policy did not have a direct impact on economic processes and enhanced social welfare would not necessarily result in a loss of economic efficiency. The aim of social policy was to correct instances of market failure in the allocation of resources to activities from which benefits to society as a whole accrued, resources that, if the market was left to itself, would fail to be supplied in their entirety or would be delivered in less than socially desirable quantities (for example, health care, education, and the eradication of extremes of poverty).

In fact, neither of these approaches to social policy neatly mapped onto the treaty models. Although the liberal capitalist model of economic integration lies at the heart of the process of Community integration as set out in the Treaty of Rome, the treaty also calls for higher standards of living for workers, thereby emphasizing the role of redistribution in the new arrangements. Additionally, even though the treaty did not establish the framework for a comprehensive European welfare state – there being no mention of health care, education, or minimum standards of social benefits – social policy was not totally absent from the integration project. However, the precise relationship between (national) social policy and the creation of a common market remained unclear. The debate, as it evolved, grappled with this question, repeatedly turning these models over and distorting their lines of configuration.

Debates on Harmonization in the 1980s

Significant pressures to develop a social dimension to the Community arose in the 1980s. Changes in employment practices, which, arguably, had their origin in the dramatic surge of technological developments in production processes, brought with them a fundamental transformation in labour markets. In particular, the era of "flexible" working had arrived, with employers restructuring their employment practices to create new types of atypical employment. In turn, this forced attention

upon the welfare systems in each of the member states, and on questions of whether and, if so, how these systems might be impeding the process of "labour market adjustment". Clearly, to the extent that individual countries responded differently to these new demands there was a likelihood that investment flows within the Community would be distorted as a direct result.

At the same time as labour markets were being transformed by technological change, forcing the Community to consider a harmonized response, other related social issues were arising. First, the incidence of structural or long-term unemployment was increasing rapidly, bringing with it the problem of economic disenfranchisement. Long-term unemployment – usually defined as a spell of unemployment lasting longer than one year – tends to persist. Individuals who have been unemployed long-term find themselves lacking the skills required by new industries, and retraining costs tend to be relatively high. Consequently, unemployed workers were being denied access to "the prosperity that one might expect in what [are] . . . still wealthy societies" (Krugman p. 20). Secondly, the technological changes were highlighting new problems surrounding the protection of flexible or atypical categories of workers, such as part-time, casual, temporary or seasonal employees, or the self-employed. These groups, growing in large numbers, were not covered by mainstream employment protection legislation and consequently many lost entitlement to basic social rights.

The challenge for the Community during the initial stages of such great societal reorganization was whether some of these issues should be addressed through the harmonization of social policy, on the basis of some basic welfare state principles that were yet to be defined. On the one hand, the failure of the common market to ensure sustained social progress in the 1970s led to the revival of "welfarist" arguments. Adopting a political reading of the treaty's social policy provisions, and in particular Article 117 EEC, the argument was made that it did in fact provide for social policy to set minimum social standards at the Community level. The majority of member states supported such a reading. On the other hand, the counterclaim made by the proponents of a deregulated labour market was that social regulations were harmful to the free functioning of market forces and were having adverse consequences on industrial competitiveness in what was becoming an ever more global market. This position was increasingly being championed by successive Conservative governments in Britain in the 1980s and 1990s. Such political readings of the treaty fuelled ideological arguments, as each side "recognized" its own position in treaty provisions.

However, not all arguments in support of a Community social policy were based on the traditional welfarist position. Adopting "social dumping" arguments, the Commission developed an economic as well as a political reading of the social provisions of the Treaty of Rome. Social policy was now considered in the light of the arguments about costs raised in the Spaak Report (Boch p. 4, Gold p. 14). The economic reading held that the treaty was very precise on its enactment of social policy at the Community level, in that certain social conditions were necessary for the functioning of free markets. "Social dumping" arguments now dominated debates.

According to Teague (pp. 78–79), there were two fears that social dumping gave rise to in a truly liberated market. The first fear was that a divergence in social standards might lead to "trade distortions and price wars", as peripheral member states with slow economic growth "restrain[ed] artificially the future growth of wages and other social changes so as either to increase exports or [to] reduce the penetration of their home market". Faced with the prospect of increased unemployment, member states with higher average wages would reduce their labour costs. This might "trigger cost and price reducing battles", as competitive advantage was sought through cost reductions. This in turn would result in a general lowering of social standards throughout the Community. The second fear was that firms would be motivated in their location decisions by differential social charges (Adnett p. 2). This might lead to the entrenchment of a dual Community labour market, with firms locating "complex and technical production tasks" in northern countries,

but at the same time locating "labour-intensive and low-skilled functions" in southern countries (see Teague). This would mean that a member state with a weakly regulated labour market and a low level of social provision would gain unfair competitive advantage within the Community (Adnett pp. 2–3).

The debate quickly came to be focused on "social dumping", rather than on social welfare. The free marketeers, led by the UK government, were quick to assert that social dumping was nothing more than an ill-grounded misconception. First, it simply would not happen; secondly, different levels of social protection were inevitable and not problematic. Differences in national provisions with regard to social protection would not give rise to distortions in the free functioning of the market. To quote from comments made by one British Conservative MP Eric Forth, to a select committee of the House of Lords that was considering the proposed Community directives on atypical employment protection (House of Lords p. 23):

> the argument behind the assertion of distortion has simply not been there . . . There are many elements . . . which can be seen, if you like, as distorting competition, such as climate, or geography, or peripherality . . . fuel taxes, transport costs. . . . These can be seen on the one hand as allegedly [sic] distortions of competition, or they can be seen as elements of competition.

Others agreed with this view, notably the Union of Industrial and Employers Confederations of Europe (UNICE), which, as the select committee noted, "utterly rejects any argument based on distortion of competition" (House of Lords p. 107 at point 6).

The academic debate also engaged with the phenomenon of social dumping. Some authors argued that social dumping was not a convincing economic justification for extending decision-making at Community level to the area of social security (see Petersen). Others held that fears of social dumping were unwarranted and supported their arguments by the failure to find evidence of significant social dumping effects, based on assessments of differences in employers' social security expenditure over a measured period of time (see Adnett). Evidence was collected indicating that factors other than social costs, for example, infrastructure and workers' productivity, were more significant in the motivation and direction of foreign investment (Majone p. 160). Other more plausible economic reasons were offered for the extension of social policy: for example, it was possible that tax harmonization might hold some repercussions for social security policy (see Petersen), or that levelling up in the social policy area might be important in order to sustain Economic and Monetary Union (see Adnett).

Political and economic arguments of this nature dominated intergovernmental discussions within the Council of Ministers throughout the 1980s, as UK ministers consistently blocked moves to inaugurate social policy. A key development during this time – the signing of the Charter of Fundamental Social Rights (1989) by all the then member states except Britain – had little impact, as the Charter was not fully implemented. The Commission proposed legislation to apply a number of the social rights contained in the Charter, but the proposal stagnated in meetings of the Social Affairs Council as the arguments ended in stalemate. Although, by the end of the 1980s, Community legislation had been enacted in three areas related to employment: gender equality, protection of workers' interests, and health and safety (see Gold, as well as Hoskyns) – the eventual lack of agreement on the necessity to establish common social conditions for economic exigencies meant that social harmonization at Community level would no longer feature as a viable approach to policy delivery. From then on, new approaches would be adopted to the question of the regulation of social policy (see Teague and Grahl).

Maastricht, Amsterdam, and Nice

During the Maastricht summit (1991), which brought together heads of state and government for the final negotiations on the content of the Treaty on European Union (TEU), social policy was raised to a position of "high politics" within the debate over the future configuration of "Europe". Late into the negotiations, the UK government threatened to jeopardize the overall process of constitutional reform if an extension of Community competence in the area of social policy was inaugurated by amendment to the original provisions of the Treaty of Rome. However, a newly constituted EU without a strengthened social policy at its core was not acceptable to other member states. To break the deadlock, a solution was found in an opt-out scenario, whereby all member states except the UK adopted a "Social Policy Agreement", which established new procedures for social policy delivery (see Barnard).

The new "twin-track Social Europe" (as Jo Shaw has called it) continued for six years, until the signing of the Amsterdam Treaty in 1997. At that time a changed political environment in Britain, with a new Labour government committed to ending the previous government's "opt-out", altered the dynamics of treaty negotiations. The resultant Amsterdam Treaty created a new Social Chapter (within Title XI, Articles 136–45 TEC) by integrating the original articles of the Treaty of Rome with the provisions of the Social Policy Agreement and making some additional amendments. The Treaty of Amsterdam also introduced a Title on Employment Policy (Title VIII), which sets out new provisions for coordination of national employment policies (see Burrows). Since the Amsterdam Treaty entered into force in 1999, all member states have been subject to common treaty provisions.

The main social policy article (Article 136 TEC, formerly Article 117, described above) now contains the following objectives: the promotion of employment, improved living and working conditions, proper social protection, and dialogue between management and labour; the development of human resources with a view to lasting high employment; and the combating of exclusion. Any measures adopted in pursuance of these objectives must take account of the diverse forms of national practices, the need to maintain the competitiveness of the Community economy, and the need to keep in mind fundamental social rights such as those set out in the Charter of Rights of 1989 (referred to above). Community competence is granted to support and complement member states' activities in a number of listed areas, including social security and social protection of workers, subject to unanimity in the Council of Ministers.

The quality of such competence has been specified by new amendments proposed at Nice in December 2000. Importantly, no licence is given to any harmonization of social security systems. The Nice provisions (not in force at the time of writing) explicitly state that the Council may adopt measures to encourage cooperation between member states in the above areas "excluding any harmonization of the laws and regulations of the member states" (new Article 137 (2) (a) TEC). The development of a common response at the EU level refers to exchanges of information and best practice, promotion of innovative approaches, and adoption of directives that set minimum requirements for gradual implementation but "shall not affect the right of the member states to define the fundamental principles of their social security systems and must not significantly affect the financial equilibrium thereof" (new Article 137 (4) TEC).

What we can conclude is that the original constitutional settlement, which assigned market-building policies to the supranational level and market-correcting policies to the national level (Streeck p. 72) appears to remain unaltered. Yet, even though no clear competence is granted for harmonization of social systems, this does not mean that national social systems remain untouched by these treaty provisions. On the contrary, the introduction of the need to maintain "competitiveness" as a stated goal of social policy implies an acceptance of the argument (explored above) that national measures for social protection do indeed have an impact on the functioning of markets. Treaty reform expressly injects Community economic norms into national coordination strategies, constraining the "modernization" of social security and social protection measures within a system of economic priorities laid down at Community level. The implication this holds for social policy is discussed below.

Arguably, the main development of the social policy provisions, retained from the Social Policy Agreement, is institutional rather than substantive in nature. One of the key principles

of Community governance – subsidiarity – is applied through the granting of consultation and negotiation rights to management and labour, the "social partners". This had been a longstanding objective of the Commission, which can be traced via such initiatives as the Social Action Programme (1974), the Val Duchesse dialogue, and the provisions of the Single European Act. Treaty provisions now enable a transfer of policy negotiation from the national level to a collective bargaining process at the level of the EU. Two new tracks for involving social partners co-exist: a consultation track, which gives powers to the Commission to consult widely with employers' and employees' organizations in the drafting of proposals that are then subject to co-decision; and a negotiation track, which applies the process of collective bargaining to policy-making, with negotiation taking place between the employers' group, UNICE (as mentioned above), the European Trade Union Confederation (ETUC), and the European Centre of Enterprises with Public Participation (CEEP). Collective agreements reached following the negotiation track can be enacted as directives by the Council and take on the full force of Community law, binding member states as to the result to be achieved. According to the *European Industrial Relations Review* (no. 240, p. 25) "the use of the new procedures represents perhaps the most radical development in Community social policy for many years, not least because of . . . important new responsibilities now wielded by the European-level organisations representing employers and trade unions." As Gerda Falkner has pointed out, the involvement of social partners in the making of employment law and policy "[does] not yet represent a longstanding tradition", but ETUC, UNICE, and CEEP can now be classified as formal co-actors in the process (Falkner 2000 p. 706). A notable consequence of treaty reform has thus been an increase in the number of transnational actors involved in the policy process.

The treaty provisions thus provide an altered institutional framework for policy delivery: directives covering atypical employment and parental leave have been adopted following these new routes (see Falkner 1998).

Nevertheless, this new environment has in fact met with some criticism of its ability to deliver. For example, Catharine Barnard argues that the social policy provisions have been used modestly for legislative purposes (see Barnard). Similarly, Erika Szyszczak states that, "despite optimism in some quarters, the Social Policy Agreement did not introduce a broad set of Community-level employment measures" (Szyszczak p. 201). Noreen Burrows concurs, pointing to a "lack of outstanding success of the Agreement itself since the adoption of the TEU" (Burrows p. 100). A further initiative to change the mechanisms for delivery of social policy is now contained in the Nice amendments. Interestingly, it stresses the role for national governments. The proposed new Article 144 TEC establishes a new Social Protection Committee, composed predominantly of senior officials from member states and with advisory status, to monitor the social situation and promote cooperation on social protection policies, including social exclusion and "modernization" of social protection systems. In fact, this committee was established in 2000, before the Treaty of Nice was negotiated. The significance of this initiative can only be measured by reference to developments that have taken place outside the treaties. It is to these that we now turn.

Developments Outside the Treaties

The "European Social Model"

The history of treaty reform described above suggests that member states have generally resisted the harmonization of social policies. What is detectable is an assertion of national governments' claims to control in these areas. This does not necessarily imply, however, that there are no problems with national social systems. Indeed, since the 1970s discussion of national social policy in all the member states has itself been dominated by controversy, to the extent that discussions at the Community level have increasingly been conducted in the shadow of of an intellectual critique whose proponents question the role of the national welfare state in the economic process (see O'Connor, Habermas, Offe). This critique, as it first emerged in the 1970s, argued that there was now an accumulating body of evidence suggesting that the provision of social welfare greatly distorts the operation of labour markets, thus explaining in part the sharp rise in unemployment throughout the Community. In particular, the social benefits available to the unemployed were excessively generous and, consequently, acted as disincentives to the seeking of work. This distorted the supply side of the labour market. On the demand side too, the welfare state was, they claimed, having a similar effect. The combination of the high taxation required to finance the welfare system and the high social costs directly associated with employing additional labour acted as a major disincentive to firms to hire more workers. This argument revealed a false assumption in ideal-type positions on the relation of social welfare to economic competitive goals, namely that the relation of the economic to the social was uni-directional – that economic functioning would have consequences for social outcomes, rather than the other way round: "economic policy would be concerned with increasing output as smoothly as possible; social policy would follow along and focus on redistributing that output so as to compensate for those left behind" (Heclo pp. 398–99).

A central policy question that now emerged at national level was whether, in seeking to alleviate poverty and promote a more equal distribution of income, the welfare state in all its manifestations, including the empowering of organized labour in negotiations with employers, was in fact having precisely the opposite effect.

The neoliberal reaction to this debate was to advocate a policy of deregulation to secure a minimal level of state intervention, on the view that social inequalities are desirable and necessary features of competitive free-functioning markets (Marsland p. 212). Although this extreme approach was favoured by successive British Conservative governments in the 1980s and 1990s, it was not supported in the political rhetoric either of other member states or of the Community institutions (the European Commission and the European Parliament). For most, there still remained an underlying commitment to the principle of the welfare state, with its critique of liberal capitalism, even if the structuring of social systems was under review (Heclo pp. 383–404). In the academic literature too, a number of authorities attacked the deregulatory position as a policy response, pointing in particular to the negative long-term effects that a deregulatory approach could have on the single European market. Critiques of the deregulatory model took issue with a policy that, they argued, obtained competitiveness through cost-cutting alone, rather than through intervening in other employment factors. According to this position there were negative effects of such strategies (Teague and Grahl p. 173):

Since fully fledged flexibility strategies tend to build up a reliance on low pay and casualized work, the result could actually be the discouragement of competition between firms on the basis of more positive improvements in areas such as technology, production methods and marketing.

For the most part, such views were offered in relation to investment, productivity, and competitiveness.

For the majority of social democratic parties across the Community, what was required was a reformulation of social democratic principles that stressed the positive relational aspect of social to economic policy. A significant example of this was the Basic Programme launched by the SPD in Germany, in 1989. This programme aimed to reconcile both "liberal" and "socialist" positions: "The Basic Programme spoke of the need 'to reconcile economic performance with social security' and stressed that 'individuality and solidarity should not be counterposed as opposites'" (Giddens p. 20). In this manner, what became known as "third way" arguments took hold of the policy debate. Denouncing the "trade off" between equality and efficiency, the politics of the "third way" was consistently expressed within domestic forums, and the French, Italian, and German governments all moved in this direction, as did the British "New Labour" government elected in 1997 under the leadership of Tony Blair. Advocates of the "third way" approach claimed

to be seeking to adjust the European model of welfare capitalism to the needs of a globally competitive economy, without sacrificing the security aspect of social welfare provision.

At the EU level this debate was brought under the banner of the "European social model", a strategy heavily influenced by the Commission, which "began a process of persuading member states to consider a radical and coordinated rethinking of their national social policies" (Szyszczak p. 201). Principles of the model were set down in a Commission White Paper on European Social Policy (1994), demonstrating a desire among member states to rethink the welfare state system in the light of the changing economic and technological environment, and, within that, to rethink the role of social policy in an increasingly global industrial system. The White Paper stated that both "competitiveness" and "solidarity" had to be taken into account in the building of a successful Europe (p. 9), and that "the pursuit of high social standards should not only be seen as a cost but also a key element in the competitive formula" (p. 10). Another Commission White Paper, on economic growth, competitiveness, and employment, published in the same year, echoed such sentiments. A new attempt at fostering a collective approach to social policy was now on the agenda. This time the method was to be, not harmonization, with a transfer of competence to Community level, but coordination of the reorganization of national social systems, which would be pursued outside the treaties.

The European Social Agenda 2000

The political context at the turn of the millennium, as described above, was one in which member states and the Commission claimed to be struggling to find effective means of regulating economic, employment, and social fields so that policy objectives in one area did not undermine policy goals in another. In a situation where member states were under pressure to forge a collective approach, yet to be defined, to the delivery of national social policy, but where the reassignment of policy to the supranational level was not a realistic option, the member states and the Commission established a new process of decision-making on social policy. This process, which has been referred to as the "Luxembourg process", introduces a form of policy transfer known as the "open method of coordination", described by the Commission as "a new and path-breaking method of EU policy-making" (see Lonnroth).

The Luxembourg process emerged at the Extraordinary European Council in Luxembourg in November 1997 and was first applied to employment policy in the European Employment Strategy. Subsequently, the European Council meeting in Lisbon in March 2000 agreed an overall economic, employment, and social strategy to implement the Luxembourg process at all levels. Under European Council instruction, the Commission published a proposed social agenda to this end – the Commission's Communication June 2000 (COM (2000)379 final) and the Commission proposal to combat social exclusion (COM(2000)368 final). Finally, meeting at Nice in December 2000, the heads of state and government negotiated a text, the "European Social Agenda", which applies the Luxembourg process to social policy. (The text is contained in Annex I of the Presidency Conclusions to the Nice European Council Meeting, December 2000.)

The central aim of the European Social Agenda is the renewal and improvement of the "European social model". In accordance with the Luxembourg process, this is to be achieved through the application of the open method of coordination to strengthen cooperation between member states. The Agenda sets out six policy guidelines, including "modernizing social protection". These very broad orientations, one of which, for example, is "more and better jobs", are accompanied by a mixture of both direct and indirect instructions to actors. Accordingly, there is considerable scope for policy development in the implementation of the Agenda.

Arguably, there are three distinctive features of the Luxembourg process as it is applied to social policy. First, an emphasis is placed on the developmental dimension of policy coordination and implementation: "It is an innovative way to combine the action of Community institutions, the intergovernmental action of the

member states, their contribution at national level, and beyond that, also the contribution of the various other actors to the process" (Lonnroth p. 1).

The Agenda aims to coordinate and encourage convergence in social systems in line with certain benchmarks, such as "quality" and "social as productive". Alongside benchmarking, peer review and exchange of "best practice" are anticipated. Outputs are in the form of "soft law": compliance is based on the self-interests of the member states rather than on the courts. Core incentives for implementation are premised either on a form of social legitimacy, as opposed to a legal obligation enforced via the judicial system, or on a "name and shame" strategy. Sanctions for nonimplementation are self-imposed, in the sense that rewards for developing and implementing coordinated polices consist of the anticipated increased "political legitimacy and market confidence ... where outcomes are seen as increased well-being of the citizens" (Lonnroth p. 1). This does not mean that legislation cannot be used. Along with the open method, the Agenda can be implemented in a variety of other ways: legislation, social dialogue, the structural funds, the support programmes, the integrated policy approach, analysis, and research. Thus the Agenda endorses a mixture of political and legal incentives for complying with recommendations and benchmarks. Legislation and directives are viewed as buttressing the process once it has got under way. The onus is placed on the member states to meet agreed EU benchmarks: how this is achieved is a matter for national, regional, or local policies.

The second distinctive feature of the process is the aim of including multiple actors in the implementation arrangements. The Agenda lists the following actors as having roles to play: Community institutions, the member states, local and regional authorities, the social partners, civil society, and business. On the face of it, and following the Luxembourg process as applied to employment policy, the Agenda adopts a participatory approach to policy development. A question can be raised, however, over the nature of the actors' roles. An examination of the evolution of the Agenda reveals a difference of approach as between the member states and the Commission concerning the governance arrangements for implementation. According to Commission documents and speeches in late 2000, the Agenda was intended to give birth to an improved form of governance. The Commission's position was premised on the developmental role as a dynamic and interactive process: "This means providing a clear and active role to all stakeholders and actors, enabling them to participate in managing the policies associated with this new Agenda" (Social Policy Agenda point 3.2). This position is echoed in the proposals on implementation (COM(2000)368 final, Article 5 on Implementation Arrangements):

> The Commission shall . . . have a regular exchange of views with representatives of nongovernmental organizations and the social partners . . . on the design, implementation and follow-up of the programme; [and] promote active partnership and dialogue between all the partners involved in the programme to encourage an integrated and coordinated approach.

However, the Agenda, which reflects the member states' interests, views national governments as key players and expressly instructs the Council of Ministers to implement the Agenda. The Council is constituted as the forum for the "open method", and is to take responsibility for formulating and updating common objectives, and for establishing qualitative and quantitative indicators and benchmarks. Moreover, new institution-building at ministerial level, in the form of the Social Protection Committee, has taken place to enable the Council to discharge this function, and has been given a legal basis in the Nice Treaty amendments (not yet ratified at the time of writing). The amount of wider consultation now envisaged is unclear. The Agenda anticipates that the Council will "[favour] contributions from the social partners and, as regards social exclusion, from nongovernmental organizations". In the main, the "Europeanization" of social policy is manifested here as a top-down process, with the European Council and the member states setting the benchmarks, either in an intergovern-

mental framework outside the treaties, or in the form of the Council and its new committee. Indeed, the Lisbon Council expressly stated that for social policy, as distinct from the employment policy, the "open method of cooperation" would be "complemented by a stronger guiding and coordinating role for the European Council" (see europa.eu.int/comm../employment_social. . ./newsagenda_en.ht).

Member states and national governments have claimed the position of "gatekeepers" of the implementation strategy. The extent to which national parliaments, local and regional authorities, social partners, civil society, and businesses will play active rather than passive roles will depend first, on relations within each member state and, secondly, on the ability of the Commission to organize the developmental aspect of the implementation arrangements (for example, through its choice of implementing instruments) and to shift the locus of the "politics" of social policy.

The third distinctive feature of the Luxembourg process is its adoption of an integrated approach to policy development. The Agenda promotes a mixture of social, economic, and employment initiatives premised on the acknowledgement of the "indissoluble link between economic performance and social progress" (European Social Agenda point 13). The exploitation of crosscutting possibilities is intended to create a "competitive" and "cohesive" Europe: here, as elsewhere, "third way" language dominates the Agenda (see also Kenner). In considering whether the integrated approach will protect the social dimension of the "third way", we note that the Agenda is presented against the background of a free market EU economy governed by the rule of Community law. Also, national social policy objectives have been subject to policy erosion, which derives in part from the economic aspects of integration enforced through strong *communautaire* legal processes (see Streeck, Leibfried and Pierson, and Scharpf, both 1988 and 1996). The integrated approach posits "soft law" in social policy against substantive EC law. Recent research by Simon Deakin and Hannah Reed on the European Employment Strategy, which also adopts the Luxembourg process, explores this question and concludes that "rather than forming a coherent whole of the kind which could represent a viable 'Third Way', the employment strategy remains riven by conflicts which may yet prove to be irreconcilable" (Deakin and Reed p. 99).

Deakin and Reed's study reveals that the social aspects of employment policy remain subordinated to the economic objectives of Economic and Monetary Union, and that, in the absence of a macroeconomic framework, the European Employment Strategy does not give rise to an integrated approach which protects social policy objectives. In a similar vein, Erika Szyszczak's evaluation of the Strategy concludes that "the dominant methodology of . . . the Commission's analysis. . . is an economic one" (Szyszczak p. 215). Further, the kinds of positive incentives envisaged under the open method to ensure implementation by the member states appear tenuous in the light of the ill-defined methods for meeting policy targets. Whether the Agenda's integrated approach is sufficient to anchor social policy is a moot point, particularly as we move into the next phase of enlargement of the EU.

Although admittedly the integrated approach is still in its early days (and, as mentioned above, much remains unratified at the time of writing), analysis conducted thus far does little to alleviate fears expressed elsewhere that the "third way" approach can and does drift towards the neoliberal, deregulatory position. Undoubtedly the "third way" produces a form of "ideological confusion" (Giddens p. 24). This concern has been voiced by critics of the White Paper on economic growth referred to above, who view this document as containing all the hallmarks of a deregulatory strategy. Bernd-Otto Kuper, for example, has pointed out that the White Paper makes many references to US and Japanese models as exemplars of the future "European social model", suggesting that the Commission hopes to encourage a reorganization of social security provisions, privatization of pension schemes, and the cutting back of expenditure in the social field. Similar fears have been expressed over the Commission's recent assessment of the implementation of the European Employment Strategy. This has been explored at length by

Erika Szyszczak, who illustrates how, in its evaluation of member states' performance in meeting stated targets (as expressed in "National Action Plans"), the Commission drew up a pecking order of member states: "a league table in which the USA and Japan are in the 'super league', both states performing comfortably in comparison with the 'top three' EU member states on each indicator" (Szyszczak p. 214). Member states with long histories of support for the European social model in a "reregulatory" sense (such as France and Belgium) "never feature in a top three ranking". It thus remains unclear whether the "third way" of the European social model is being upheld by contrast to competing models, or whether these models are being upheld as paradigms for the delivery of social policy. The continued lack of certainty on the appropriate and acceptable methods for achieving policy goals means that the substantive trajectory of EU social policy remains unpredictable.

Conclusions

While the debates on social policy in the European Community/EU have often been presented as being based on an ideological rift between liberal capitalists and social welfarists, this characterization, although existing at the level of political rhetoric, serves to camouflage the *realpolitik*, which involves an intricate set of arguments on the relationship between social policy and economic processes. In this policy area, as in so many others within the orbit of EU activities, the practice of negotiation, mediation, policy initiatives, and revisions dominates, with little space available to accommodate deep-seated ideological differences between member states.

A study of the evolution of the debates on social policy cannot but highlight the collapse of the traditional ideological models of liberal capitalism and social welfarism. What emerged was a growing realization that economic and social policy operated in the same sphere, both acting on the demand and supply side of the labour market. This realization gave birth to the "third way" politics of the 1990s, a policy shift that has now been "institutionalized" in the European Social Agenda 2000. Arguably, whether the "third way" is the "best" response in meeting the social challenges facing the EU will be determined by the extent to which it can resist sliding into a deregulatory approach and harnesses instead a viable solution to the delivery of social policy.

Much thus depends on the strategies adopted by the main actors in formulating and implementing social policy. Member states' governments have generally aimed to keep a tight rein on policy developments and have jealously guarded their competence over national social systems. Recent institution-building, in the form of the new intergovernmental Social Protection Committee, bears witness to this desire. However, the developments of the 1990s and early 2000, resulting in both treaty reform and the formulation of social strategies at the EU level, have now created a complex set of institutional arrangements for policy delivery, bringing new political actors into the frame. While this general trend is to be welcomed, it is too early to assess the impact that new positions and organizations will have on policy development. In a context where both policy choices and institutional arrangements are in a state of flux, the ability of any policy agreed at the EU level to adapt to a changing global order, while still preserving the security of individuals living and working within the EU, cannot merely be assumed.

Further Reading

Adnett, Nick, "Social Dumping and European Economic Integration", in *Journal of European Social Policy*, 5/1, 1995

Barnard, Catharine, "The UK, the 'Social Chapter' and the Amsterdam Treaty", in *The Industrial Law Journal*, 26/3, 1997

A discussion of the British "opt-out" during the 1990s

Boch, Christine, "The European Community and Sex Equality: Why and How?" in H. Queen (editor), *Sex Equality: Law and Economics*, Hume Papers on Public Policy 1/1, Edinburgh: Edinburgh University Press, 1993

An examination of the inclusion of Article 119 in the original EEC Treaty

Burrows, Noreen, "The New Employment Chapter and Social Policy Provisions of the Amsterdam Treaty", in John Usher (editor), *The State of the European Union: Structure, Enlargement and Economic Union*, London and New York: Longman, 2000

A comprehensive explanation for the limited use of these provisions, and full discussion of the potential use of sectoral dialogue as the way forward in employment policy

Carter, Caitríona A., "The European Social Model: Framework or Fallacy?", in John Usher (editor), as cited above under Burrows

Collins, Doreen, *The European Communities: The Social Policy of the First Phase*, Volume 2, *The European Economic Community 1958–72*, London: Martin Robertson, 1975

Collins, Doreen, "Social Policies", in Ali M. El-Agraa (editor), *Economics of the European Community*, fourth edition, Hemel Hempstead and New York: Harvester Wheatsheaf, 1994

Deakin, Simon, and Hannah Reed, "The Contested Meaning of Labour Market Flexibility: Economic Theory and the Discourse of European Integration", in Jo Shaw (editor), *Social Law and Policy in an Evolving European Union*, Oxford and Portland, OR: Hart Publishing, 2000

A study of the European Employment Strategy from the policy perspective of labour market flexibility

European Commission, *European Social Policy: A Way Forward for the Union*, White Paper Com (94) 333, Luxembourg, 1994

Falkner, Gerda, *EU Social Policy in the 1990s: Towards a Corporatist Policy Community*, London and New York: Routledge, 1998

An examination of the operation of the Social Policy Agreement throughout the 1990s

Falkner, Gerda, "The Council or the Social Partners? EC Social Policy between Diplomacy and Collective Bargaining", in *Journal of European Public Policy*, 7/5, 2000

An analysis of the institutional framework for social policy delivery after the Treaty of Amsterdam

Giddens, Anthony, *The Third Way: The Renewal of Social Democracy*, Cambridge and Malden, MA: Polity Press, 1998

An influential interpretation of the "third way" as a modernized centre–left position

Gold, Michael (editor), *The Social Dimension: Employment Policy in the European Community*, London: Macmillan, 1993

An examination of the substantive development of the Community's social policy from the 1950s to early 1990s

Habermas, Jürgen, *Legitimation Crisis*, Boston, MA: Beacon Press, 1975; London: Heinemann, 1976

Heclo, Hugh, "Towards a New Welfare State?", in Peter Flora and Arnold J. Heidenheimer (editors), *The Development of Welfare States in Europe and America*, New Brunswick, NJ: Transaction, 1981

A discussion of questions of welfare state politics

Hervey, Tamara, *European Social Law and Policy*, London and New York: Longman, 1998

A monograph on social policy with a focus on the role of Community law and the European Court of Justice in policy development

Hoskyns, Catherine, *Integrating Gender: Women, Law and Politics in the European Union*, London and New York: Verso, 1996

A key study on the evolution of the Community's gender equality policy

House of Lords Select Committee on the European Communities, Second Report on Part-time and Temporary Employment (Com (90) 228 final), London: Her Majesty's Stationery Office, 1991

Kenner, Jeff, "The EC Employment Title and the 'Third Way': Making Soft Law Work?", in *International Journal of Comparative Labour Law and Industrial Relations*, 15/1, 1999, pp. 33–60

Kenner adopts a "third way" reading of the employment provisions of the Treaty on European Union following the changes under the Treaty of Amsterdam, and provides analysis of the provisions in this light.

Krugman, Paul, "Europe Jobless, America Penniless?", in *Foreign Policy*, 95, Summer 1994, pp. 19–34

An essay on the distinction between the US and "European" economic and social models

Kuper, Bernd-Otto, "The Green and White Papers of the EU: The Apparent Goal of Reduced Social Benefits", in *Journal of European Social Policy*, 4/2, 1994

A critique of EU documents

Leibfried, Stephan, and Paul Pierson (editors), *European Social Policy: Between Fragmentation and Integration*, Washington, DC: Brookings Institution, 1995

A collection of essays on all aspects of European social and employment policy, and a critique of European social policy from the perspective of multilevel governance

Lonnroth, Juhani, "The European Employment Strategy: a Model for Open Coordination and the Role of the Social Partners", Paper presented to Conference on the Legal Dimensions of the European Employment Strategy, Brussels 9–10 October 2000, organized by the SALTSA/ Swedish National Institute for Working Life

Majone, Giandominico, "The EC between Social Policy and Social Regulation", in *Journal of Common Market Studies*, 31/2, 1993

A presentation of a regulatory approach to social policy

Marsland, David, *Welfare or Welfare State?*, London: Macmillan, and New York: St Martin's Press, 1996

A neoliberal analysis of the welfare state

O'Connor, James, *The Fiscal Crisis of the State*, New York: St Martin's Press, 1973; London: St James Press, 1974

A critique of the welfare state

Offe, Claus, *Contradictions of the Welfare State*, London: Hutchinson, and Cambridge, MA: MIT Press, 1984

Another critique of the welfare state

Petersen, Jorn Henrik, "Harmonisation of Social Security in the EC Revisited", in *Journal of Common Market Studies*, 29/5, 1991, pp. 505–26

Peterson, John, and Bomberg, Elizabeth, *Decision-making in the European Union*, London: Macmillan, and New York: St Martin's Press, 1999

Scharpf, Fritz W., "The Joint-Decision Trap: Lessons from German Federalism and European Integration", in *Public Administration*, 66/3, 1988

Scharpf, Fritz W., "Negative and Positive Integration in the Political Economy of European Welfare States", in Gary Marks *et al.*, *Governance in the European Union*, London: Sage, 1996

Shaw, Jo, "Twin-Track Social Europe – The Inside Track", in David O'Keeffe and Patrick M. Twomey (editors), *Legal Issues of the Maastricht Treaty*, London: Chancery Law, 1994

An analysis of the legal implications of the British opt-out from social policy at Maastricht

Spaak, Paul-Henri, *Spaak Report 1956 Comité Intergouvernemental Créé par la Conférence de Messine. Rapport des Chefs de Délégation aux Ministres des Affaires Etrangères*, Brussels: Secretariat, 1956

Streeck, Wolfgang, "Neo-voluntarism: A New European Social Policy Regime?", in Gary Marks *et al.*, as cited above under Scharpf 1996

Szyszczak, Erika, "The Evolving European Employment Strategy" in Jo Shaw (editor), as cited above under Deakin and Reed

A legal critique of "benchmarking" as a method of policy-making, as deployed in employment policy

Teague, Paul, *The European Community: The Social Dimension*, London: Kogan Page, 1989

A good introductory text on developments in social policy from the 1950s to the late 1980s

Teague, Paul and John Grahl, *Industrial Relations and European Integration*, London: Lawrence and Wishart, 1992

A description and analysis of the regime approach to the regulation of social policy adopted by the European Community in the late 1980s

Dr Caitríona Carter is a lecturer at the Europa Institute, University of Edinburgh. She is the author of work published in the areas of EU social policy, and on the role of national and subnational parliaments within the EU's multilevel system of governance. Her current research activities, conducted in collaboration with colleagues, and with funding from the Economic and Social Research Council, are to assess the impact of devolution in the UK on governance arrangements between the UK and the EU across a number of areas of public policy.

Chapter Sixteen

Environmental Policy

Pamela M. Barnes

Over the past 30 years the European Community and the EU have developed an impressive array of environmental policy instruments, so that, at first sight, the policy appears to be a highly successful example of cooperation and integration. Environmental policy is now firmly embedded into the treaties and enjoys widespread public support. There have been policy successes, yet the EU's European Environmental Agency, along with many others, believes that environmental progress overall has been poor.

One of the main reasons for the rather disappointing record of the policy is the tension that exists between the national and supranational tiers of government in the evolution of the policy. In particular, it is clear that as long as the national governments fail to implement effectively the agreed policy measures, then the environmental impact will be undermined. There are many vested interests involved in the development of environmental policy within the multilevelled and complex system of governance of the EU. The number of national and sectoral interests will increase with the accession of the states from central and eastern Europe and the Mediterranean region. Strengthening the implementation and enforcement of environmental policy is crucial if its effectiveness is not to be further undermined.

The First Three Environmental Action Programmes (1972–87)

Three important milestones may be identified in the development of the Community's policy on the environment:

- the adoption of the First Environmental Action Programme (EAP) in 1972;
- the inclusion of a chapter on the environment in the Single European Act in 1987; and
- the clarification of statements on the objectives of sustainable development and the integration of environmental objectives into the sectoral policies of the EU made in the Treaty of Amsterdam, which came into force in May 1999

Environmental action was not included in the original Treaty of Rome that established the European Economic Community (EEC) in 1957, but nine directives and one regulation were introduced before the adoption of the First EAP. Some of this legislation was adopted using Article 100 of the Treaty of Rome, which was concerned with the harmonization of national legislation to ensure the proper functioning of the internal market, or using the very broad Article 235. Other early directives concerned agricultural developments and were therefore adopted using either Articles 42 or 43 of the Treaty.

The First EAP marked the beginning of a more proactive and coherent approach to environmental protection within the European Community. However, it was not accompanied by a revision of the treaty itself. Environmental protection legislation continued to be introduced by reference to the terms of Articles 100 or 235 of the Treaty until the Single European Act of 1987.

For the introduction of any new policy three questions have to be asked: is it politically acceptable and compatible with the policies of the member states, can it be resourced, and is it necessary? In the case of environmental policy, the governments of the member states in 1972 responded to domestic pressures, in addition to pressure from the global community, to introduce measures to protect the European environment. Community funding was not an issue, as the Action Programme was concerned with the harmonization of national environmental policies. Supranational action would be taken only if effective action could not be achieved at the national or regional level.

The Treaty of Rome contained a commitment to improving the living and working conditions of the European population, and evidence had been amassing throughout the 1960s that environmental conditions were deteriorating and having an impact on the health of the populations. However, the economic imperative for the development of an environmental policy was clear in the First EAP. The central concern was to ensure that differences in the environmental policies being adopted by member states in response to domestic political pressures did not impose restrictions on the operation of the market and economic development within the Community. This continues to be an underlying dilemma for the EU's environmental policy-makers today: how to reconcile economic growth and the operation of the single market with the protection of the environment.

The First EAP identified the principles that have continued to form the basis of environmental action in the Community/EU. Of these the most important are that action should be taken at the most appropriate level of government; that prevention of pollution is better than trying to cure the problem after it has emerged; that the "polluter pays", putting the onus on the polluter to pay for measures to control pollution and clean up its effects; and that problems should be remedied at the source of the pollution (the "end of the pipe" approach).

The Second EAP (1977–81) and the Third EAP (1982–87) were intended to provide continuity for the measures that had been begun in 1972. The Third EAP was particularly concerned with ensuring that national environmental policies did not distort the operation of the single market. In addition, it also contained a new focus and commitment to making the most economic use possible of the natural resources of the environment.

The Single European Act and the Fourth Environmental Action Programme (1987–92)

The implementation of the measures of the Third EAP and the development of the Fourth (1987–92) took place against the background of the completion of the internal market. Concerns were raised about the impact that the opportunities for increased economic development and integration, through the liberalization of transport and energy in particular, might have on the environment. The outcome of this concern was pressure, led by the Danish government, to ensure that a chapter on the environment was included in the Single European Act in 1987. This was arguably the most important of the three milestones for the development of the environmental policy, as it provided a legal basis for Community action on environmental protection.

The basic principles identified in the First EAP were incorporated into the Treaty establishing the European Community (TEC) as Articles 174 and 175 (formerly 130r and 130s). Article 174 provided a very broad policy framework:

> Community policy on the environment shall contribute to pursuit of the following objectives:
> – preserving, protecting, and improving the quality of the environment;
> – protecting human health;
> – prudent and rational utilization of natural resources;
> – promoting measures at international level to deal with regional or worldwide environmental problems.

This provided the opportunity to introduce a very broad-ranging policy that encompassed the concepts of conservation as well as pollution control. The environmental chapter in the Single European Act also contained the first treaty articulation of the principle of subsidiarity, which was later to become the key political principle on which all decisions are to be taken within the EU. Environmental policy was therefore based firmly on the possibility of supranational action if the objectives could be achieved more effectively than by national action alone.

It was recognized that the Community is a very diverse geographical region but that nevertheless the member states should aim for a high level of environmental protection. In order to avoid waiting for absolute scientific proof, the Community has always advocated the "precautionary principle": that it is better to tackle environmental problems early rather than allowing the environmental degradation to continue. This has been particularly relevant in the development of legislation in areas such as chemicals, transport, and energy usage. In addition, a commitment was made to integrate environmental objectives into other EU policies.

The Fourth EAP addressed the failure of implementation of policy in a number of proposals, including one for a general directive on the freedom of access to information on the environment, introduced in 1990 (Dir. 90/313/EEC). This directive is a crucial element in the provision of opportunities for the public to participate in the process of decision-making and implementation and. It was reviewed and revised in 2000 to take account of problems that had emerged in the practical application of the directive and the technology developments that were changing the way in which information was created, stored, and transmitted (see European Commission 2000a).

The Fifth Environmental Action Programme (1992–2000): Towards Sustainability

The Fifth EAP (1992–2000) was very different from the earlier ones, in both tone and content. It was originally conceived as a long-term strategy for sustainable development and initially was not time-limited, as the earlier programmes had been. The primary objective of the Fifth EAP was the creation of an environmental policy that would contribute to sustainable development as it had been defined in the Brundtland Report for the World Commission

on Environment and Development in 1987.

Any assessment of the strategy that the EU has adopted depends on understanding this primary objective. The definition of sustainable development as "development that meets the needs of the present without compromising the ability of future generations to meet their own needs ..." (World Commission on Environment and Development p. 43) has become well-known to the general public and policy-makers alike. Unfortunately, that does not necessarily mean that its implications are understood. Sustainable development remains open to considerable controversy and debate.

There are three underlying principles. First, environmental protection is needed to enable us to have use of natural resources while also preserving them. Secondly, economic development is required in order to meet the aspirations of people to satisfy their needs. Thirdly, there must be equity or social justice to ensure that there is an appropriate distribution of resources and of the benefits of economic development, now and in the future. In addition, there are two objectives that underpin the concept: the public should participate in the policy process, and present actions should not constrain future development

Gro Harlem Brundtland, chair of the World Commission, stressed in the Report that her brief had been to formulate a global agenda for change. A development strategy that involved progressive change to the global economy and society was required to address the problems of poverty and of meeting people's needs without further degrading the environment and wasting natural resources. For the policy-makers of the EU, accepting Brundtland's definition meant that a long-term strategy had to be sought for what is a dynamic process. Action therefore had to be based on flexible policy instruments. A balance had to be found between economic development and environmental protection. In order to achieve this, some trade-off has to be made between the economic, environmental, and social dimensions that underlie the concept.

In the Fifth EAP, five sectors of economic activity were identified that have the potential to create high levels of environmental damage: agriculture, energy, manufacturing industry, transport, and tourism. Measures were identified and targets set for each of these areas, with provisions also for the management of environmental risks and accidents. Seven environmental priorities were identified for action within each of the sectors: climate change, acidification, biodiversity, water, the urban environment, coastal zones, and waste.

In order to enhance the effectiveness of the measures proposed in the EAP, the Commission advocated that the responsibility for environmental protection should be shared between all tiers of government and involve all the stakeholders. Three networks were established to facilitate the participation of interested groups in the policy. These were the European Consultative Forum on the Environment and Sustainable Development (the "Green Forum"); the Network for Implementation and Enforcement of Community Law (IMPEL); and the Environment Policy Review Group. Access to information and transparency in decision-making were highlighted as being essential to enable wide participation in the making of environmental policy.

It became apparent as the strategy in the Fifth EAP unfolded during the 1990s that, although it was the starting point for the development of policy leading to sustainable development, it could not be viewed as definitive. There was clear evidence that aspects of the EU's environment had deteriorated during the decade. The European Environmental Agency reported an unfavourable situation on eight of 15 environmental indicators that it had reviewed: climate change, ozone depletion, soil degradation, waste, human health, coastal and marine areas, rural areas, and mountainous areas. In six other cases – hazardous waste substances, transboundary air pollution, water stress, natural and technological hazards, biodiversity, and urban areas – there was evidence of some improvement. The issue of genetically modified organisms was seen as being beset by scientific problems and political controversies (see European Environmental Agency).

The Fifth EAP had been an ambitious and far-reaching programme when it was introduced, and it provided a positive foundation that could be built upon from 2000. Much of what had been advocated in the EAP involved changes in behaviour. This included measures as diverse as eco-labelling, environmental auditing and management schemes, and the use of economic instruments such as environmental taxes and tradable permits. Accordingly, some of the shortcomings of the programme may be due to the need for more time for the effectiveness of the strategy to be seen. The basic strategy of integrating environmental concerns into the other policies of the EU, sharing the responsibility, and the use of a broad mixture of policy instruments, in addition to legislation, remains the most valid approach to take for the future.

However, the Fifth EAP was a relative failure to the extent that it failed to provide a path to sustainable development (see Council of Ministers 1998, European Commission 1999a, and Economic and Social Committee). Some of the problems are those of society in general. There is increased demand for environmentally damaging products and services, as witnessed by the rise in private car ownership, demand for passenger air transport, and domestic air conditioning systems. Yet popular interest in, and support for, EU action to protect the environment has continued. Eurobarometer (no. 51) reported in 1999 that 83% of the people surveyed consider that protection of the environment is a priority for the EU and that 53% of them believe that decisions relating to the protection of the environment should be made at the EU level. Sustainable development will require changes to people's behaviour and, despite this evidence of continued popular support for environmental protection, there has been criticism of the lack of visibility of the EU's action and, and of the lack of accountability of the institutions to the citizens of the EU.

Changes Under the Maastricht Treaty

At the same time as the Fifth EAP was being developed, in 1991 and 1992, an intergovernmental conference was considering treaty revisions. However, the resulting Maastricht Treaty (the TEU) made only minimal changes to the articles relating to environmental policy, and they brought mixed results. On the one hand, the European Parliament gained power in the policy process. As it is considered to be the most environmentally concerned of the institutions, this was seen as a positive step forward. The use of qualified majority voting in the Council of Ministers was also extended to more decisions about environmental legislation. On the other hand, disappointingly for some environmentalists, decisions relating to the national choice of energy sources and the introduction of fiscal instruments to protect the environment remained subject to unanimity.

It was also feared that the strategy of the Fifth EAP would be undermined by the lack of clarity in the relevant treaty articles in relation to providing the legal basis for policy development. While a commitment to sustainable development was implied in the treaty, the phraseology used was that of a commitment to "sustainable and noninflationary growth respecting the environment". A somewhat weakened basis for the introduction of the necessary measures was thus provided. Also, the principle of subsidiarity was removed from the articles relating specifically to the environment and applied generally to all areas of EU policy. This in turn led to calls for clarification of the implications of the principle, as some national governments saw it as providing an opportunity to "claw back" competence for environmental policy.

The problem of ineffective implementation of policy was not dealt with in the treaty, as this is an issue that has to be resolved by national governments in collaboration with the Commission and the European Court of Justice. What the treaty revisions could have included was increased power of scrutiny for the European Parliament and/or more power over monitoring of the policy for the Commission. Unfortunately, it did neither.

Strengthening the Commitment to Sustainable Development

The third milestone in the development of the EU's environmental policy came with the ratification of the Amsterdam Treaty in 1999. This Treaty introduced a clear statement of commitment to "a harmonious, balanced and sustainable development" (Article 2 TEC), and laid down that "environmental protection requirements must be integrated into the definition and implementation of the Community's policies and activities . . . in particular with a view to promoting sustainable development" (Article 6 TEC (formerly 3c)). Protection of the environment has thus been put onto the same basis as economic development, as a core goal, giving the EU the opportunity significantly to strengthen its environmental policy. The introduction of more radical measures may be possible in the future, in addition to the strengthening of implementation and enforcement.

At the same time, an amendment was made to Article 95 TEC (formerly 100) introducing the "environmental guarantee", which enables national governments to maintain or introduce higher environmental standards even after harmonization measures have been adopted. In order to justify doing so, member states have to provide new scientific evidence relating to the problem. This carries with it the potential to undermine the coherence of the EU's environmental policy unless the accompanying safeguards of Commission review, careful management, and scrutiny are effective.

Implementation of Environmental Policy

As the EU's environmental policy has been developed through the adoption of a large number of laws, the implementation process concentrates in the first instance on ensuring that there is legal compliance with the legislation. The most frequently used form of legislation in the environmental area is a directive, which sets the objectives to be achieved but leaves the choice of means of implementation to the national governments. The first stage in the implementation process is the transposition of the directive into the different bodies of national legislation. The implementation process also includes ensuring that the infrastructure is in place to enable the national authorities to introduce the measures or procedures needed for practical compliance with the legislation. Enforcement by the national authorities includes the process of monitoring, imposition of national sanctions, and "on the spot" investigations and controls.

Each national government has a different approach to environmental protection. The potential for a large number of actors from both the public and the private sectors to be involved in the implementation and enforcement of policy has therefore increased with each enlargement of the EU, making the task more difficult.

The main problems of implementation of the legislation are delays in notifying national implementing measures; doubts about conformity with the legislation; poorly drafted legislation; uneven or weak application of the legislation at the national level; and failure to take into account the diversity of conditions at the national level.

The Commission publishes annual reports on the application of EU legislation. The statistics that are included in these reports on environmental legislation do not give a report on the state of the environment in the individual nation states but do give a measure of the political commitment to the policy (see Table 16.1). In addition, specific issues of failure of implementation, and the outcomes of actions taken by the European Court of Justice, are highlighted in the reports.

Alberta Sbragia has grouped the national governments of the EU into "leaders" and "laggards" on environmental issues (see Sbragia). It is possible to see this pattern reflected in the reports on the application of EU legislation. States such as the Netherlands and Denmark, along with Austria, Finland, and Sweden, are seen to be more environmentally progressive than many of the states of the Mediterranean region. Germany, which is often seen as a prime mover on many environmental issues within the EU, has faced the cost of environmental degradation in the five new *Länder* (states) since unification in 1990. This altered the German approach to environmental issues in the late 1990s (see Sbragia). Directives that proved to be particularly problematic for the German government to implement on time have included those "on the freedom of access to information on the environment" (Dir 90/323/EEC) and "on the assessment of the effects of certain public and private projects on the environment" (Dir 971/11/EC).

The Commission's reports do not address the issue of the way in which national policies come to influence policy development at the supranational level (highlighted by Sbragia, Andersen and Liefferink, and Zito). As a result, there is concern that policy measures that are appropriate in one national context, but not in another, may be adopted. Allegations are made that national governments are supporting measures that benefit their own industrial and economic development. These arguments provide support for supranational action to ensure that market distortion does not occur, and for more openness and transparency within the policy-making process, so that all interests may be seen to be consulted in the development of policy measures.

At the end of 1996 the Commission undertook a review of the implementation of environmental legislation (COM(1996)500). One of the main conclusions of the review was that more information about environmental policy could be obtained by preparing annual reports specifically directed towards environmental legislation and its implementation. The first report on environmental legislation was published as a Commission working document in 1999, covering the period October 1996 to December 1997. It highlighted the importance of increasing public awareness of environmental issues and of transparency in the policy process. An important aspect of the development of a policy of sustainability is enabling the public to participate in the policy process. It is essential for the EU to fulfil the commitments that have been made to involve all the stakeholders in the development of environmental policy in the future.

A further conclusion of the review was that implementation should be regarded as part of a process or "regulatory chain" that begins by considering the requirements of implementation at the earliest stages of drafting legislation. The transfer of information, and the easing of access to it, were highlighted as being crucial to the success of this more holistic approach. The role of the European Environment Agency, which is based in Copenhagen, has gained in importance during the 1990s as part of this strategy. It was established in 1990 to provide an accurate view of environmental degradation to assist in the legislative process (Council Regulation 1210/90): it therefore has no direct role in policy-making or implementation. It is not part of the Commission, but its remit is to provide information and alternative scenarios for the policy makers.

The implementation of policy has been significantly strengthened by Article 6 TEC. During the Cardiff summit in June 1998 the European Council asked the national governments and the European Commission to prepare strategies for integration of environmental requirements into sectoral policies, with indicators to monitor progress and inform the public. During 1998 and 1999 various reports in compliance with this request were submitted to the successive meetings of the European Council, culminating in a report at the Helsinki summit in December 1999 (see European Commission 1999c). One of the main conclusions of this report was that more detailed timetables of action and indicators were needed so that progress could be monitored. This implied a strengthened role for the informal network known as IMPEL (mentioned above). It was also recommended that more emphasis should be given to cross-sectoral issues, such as climate change, and to the contribution that environmental policy could make to employment creation.

The primary responsibility for the implementation of environmental policy rests with the national governments of the member states, but the Commission was given the competence to ensure the proper functioning of the policy. It is able to perform this role because of the procedures and penalties established in the treaty, which are supported by the judgements of the European Court of Justice. Important changes were made to Article 228 TEC (formerly 171) at Maastricht. This article provides the basis for action to be taken against a national government that fails to comply with any judgement of the Court as a result of noncompliance with legislation.

In the first instance, the Commission reports to the Court on the failure to comply, and the Court issues a "reasoned opinion" specifying the main points that have to be remedied. The Maastricht Treaty added the possibility of a fine if infringements continued after the national government had received the reasoned opinion. The first time the penalty was applied concerned a number of cases of infringement of environmental legislation. The amount of the fine is based on a uniform flat-rate payment for a member state that is then weighted against a number of criteria, including the state's ability to pay, the seriousness of the infringement, and the length of time the legislation has been ignored.

Although the first cases were begun in 1997 against a number of national governments, including those of France, Germany, and Italy, it was not until July 2000 that the first fine was actually imposed, on Greece. The Greek government was faced with a penalty payment of €20,000 per day from the date of the judgement (4 July) for failing to halt the discharge of toxic and dangerous waste into the River Kouroupitos in Crete. The funds were paid into the "own resources" account of the EU budget. In its report in 2000 on monitoring the success of the application of the law, the Commission highlighted the effectiveness of this measure as no new cases were brought to the European Court of Justice using these provisions in 1999 (see European Commission 2000b; see also Table 16.2 for details of the number and type of cases referred to the Court).

Our Future, Our Choice

The Sixth EAP, entitled *Our Future, Our Choice*, and covering the period 2001–10, was presented to the Council of Ministers at the end of 2000. The strategy of combining a mixture of legislation and policy instruments, such as voluntary agreements, the advocacy of the use of eco-taxes, use of tradable permits, and increased funding opportunities, had been introduced in the Fifth EAP, and had enabled a more flexible policy approach to be adopted during the 1990s. The Sixth EAP is based on the same approach and was therefore presented as a short strategy document, but with clearly established objectives to be met in the following decade. It was accompanied by thematic action programmes to target specific problems, such as the continuing concerns about the quality of water within the EU.

Two priorities were identified for the Sixth EAP: the search for solutions for the continuing problems associated with implementation and enforcement of policy; and the targeting of issues where existing policy appeared to have failed. Issues of particular concern were climate change, biodiversity, the efficient use and management of natural resources, waste management, the reduction of risks to the environment and human health from chemicals and genetically modified organisms, and soil degradation and desertification.

A number of underlying principles provided the framework and context for action. They included emphasis on the health-related aspects of environmental issues; the environmental challenges from the process of enlargement; the EU's contribution to the search for effective solutions to global environmental problems; the nature of the relationship between trade liberalization and environmental protection in the context of the EU's relationship with the developing world; the requirement to achieve coherence across environmental and other policies; setting qualitative and quantitative targets and timetables for action; better analysis of, and research into, environmental problems; and the use of a range of policy instruments in order to ensure that the link between economic growth and environmental pressure was broken and the objectives of sustainable development achieved.

The Challenge of Enlargement

Enormous problems have been left as a legacy of practices during the Communist period in the ten candidate states of central and eastern Europe. Many of the environmental problems caused by heavy manufacturing industry and accompanying polluting practices are being resolved as the privatization of industry and the restructuring of economic activity continue. However, many of the old industrial sites present problems with regard to the responsibility for the "clean up" that is required. New problems of air quality have emerged with increased ownership and use of cars. Disposal of household waste and water quality have also been highlighted as areas of concern. The generation and use of energy also present problems because of the major contribution that they make to pollution of the atmosphere. Concerns about the safety of nuclear installations and the disposal of nuclear waste have proved

to be particularly difficult to resolve. Given the lack of willingness of the national governments of the member states to pick up the bill for enlargement, the EU faces a dilemma: to what extent should resolving environmental problems be allowed to slow enlargement to central and eastern Europe?

The approach that has been adopted represents a compromise to ensure that enlargement should not be delayed. All candidate states for membership of the EU are required to accept all the existing EU legislation, the *acquis communautaire*. The enlargement strategies agreed by the candidate states and the European Commission have focused on the transposition of environmental legislation into national legislation as one of the prerequisites for accession. Questions of implementation will be resolved once the states have become members of the EU. However, key objectives that must be fulfilled by the time of accession have also been identified. It is likely that derogations will be required in specific areas, such as air quality and waste treatment, lasting between three and 13 years. Such an approach is not without precedent in accession procedures, but it will undoubtedly be controversial in the more environmentally progressive EU states, such as Austria, Denmark, Finland, and Sweden.

The dilemma for the candidate states is how to fund measures to implement and comply with EU legislation. It has been estimated that the costs of doing so will be in the region of €120 billion to €140 billion. The view of the EU has been that the new states must deal with the costs involved themselves, but it is apparent that a lot of financial support is required. Some assistance has been made available to the candidate states for their reviews of national legislation involving the transposition and compliance with EU legislation. However, transposition of the legislation is only the beginning of the process of extending the EU's environmental policy to the candidate states. Support will be necessary to develop the appropriate administrative support mechanisms for implementation, in addition to the necessary environmental infrastructure and monitoring procedures.

Limited support for funding for large-scale infrastructure needs in the sectors of transport and the environment has been made available through the creation of an Instrument for Structural Policies for Pre-Accession (ISPA), which has provided pre-accession aid of €1 billion a year from 2000. This support is subject to certain conditions and will be reduced if account is not taken of the "polluter pays" principle. Funding is also available from other sources, such as the PHARE programme (established in July 1989 to support the economic reconstruction of Poland and Hungary, and subsequently extended in both territorial and financial scope) or the Financial Instrument for the Environment (LIFE), set up in 1992. After 2000 the PHARE structural funds are to help industry with the environmental clean-up of old sites, such as waste heaps and mining spoils. In 1999 21 projects received LIFE funds. However, overall the resources are limited. As a result, the governments of the candidate states have adopted a strategy concentrating on the investments needed to implement the directives to improve the quality of drinking water and air quality, waste-water treatment, and waste management. These are considered to be the most environmentally beneficial, but they are also amongst the most expensive to implement.

Conclusion: the Future

The early history of the development of environmental policy in the European Community was characterized by fragmented and reactive measures designed to provide solutions to specific problems. The primary concern was to harmonize national environmental policies in order to prevent trade distortion. Despite these constraints, the policy area saw significant activity. The introduction of the environmental chapter into the Single European Act in 1987 enabled major steps forward in the development of a more holistic approach to environmental policy, in association with the completion of the internal market. The result was that by the beginning of the 1990s more than 200 pieces of Community legislation were in place and approximately 200 other measures had been introduced.

The Treaty revisions made at Maastricht (ratified 1993) and Amsterdam (ratified 1999) have given a firmer legal basis to the policy.

The Fifth EAP introduced a new direction to the policy. As a result, an increasingly proactive environmental policy was developed during the 1990s. Among the achievements of the decade the EU made a contribution to sustainable development and global environmental issues; adopted a more targeted approach to policy development; introduced a wider variety of policy instruments, and more rigorous assessment and review of the effectiveness of policy measures; and initiated strategies to take environmental requirements into account in its sectoral policies.

The EU's environmental policy is now firmly established around the main axes of subsidiarity and sharing of responsibility, consultation and involvement of the stakeholders, and sustainable development. The policy has thus achieved the goal of greater flexibility. The Treaty of Amsterdam introduced a commitment to the use of framework directives where it was possible to do so (in the Protocol on Subsidiarity). This approach has been used in the development of the EU's water policy. It is based on a framework directive designed to replace seven old directives, and to simplify and rationalize the protection of water quality within the EU (see European Commission 1997). However, the problems of implementation and enforcement that have been discussed in this chapter have become more urgent. Monitoring and management of the policy developments are key priorities for the future.

What is the way forward? The participation of the public in all stages of the policy process is an important dimension of any policy that is designed to lead to sustainable development. It has been and continues to be an important aspect of the development of the EU's environmental policy, for two reasons. First, the most effective means of dealing with environmental problems lies in balancing the interests of the various groups that will be affected. The emphasis on the introduction of economic and environmental indicators for proposed measures in the Sixth EAP provides a more rational basis for the development of future policy. This will be reinforced through more openness and opportunities for scrutiny of the policy measures. Secondly, more openness will help enforcement as the policy objectives are widely publicized and more people become more aware of the means by which they can complain about shortcomings.

Further Reading

Andersen, Mikael S., and Duncan Liefferink (editors), *European Environmental Policy: The Pioneers,* Manchester: Manchester University Press, and New York: St Martin's Press, 1997

Barnes, Pamela M., *The Evolution of the EU's Environmental Policy,* 1998, Academic Commentary available on the EUROTEXT website http://eurotext.ulst.ac.uk, sponsored by the European Commission

A useful summary of the main developments and issues

Barnes, Pamela M., and Ian G. Barnes, *Environmental Policy in the EU,* Cheltenham: Edward Elgar, 1999

A comprehensive and systematic analysis of the effectiveness of EU environmental policy

Council of Ministers 1990: "Council Regulation 1210/90 EEC on the Establishment of the European Environment Agency and the European Information and Observation Network", *Official Journal,* L 120, 11 May 1990

Council of Ministers 1998: "Decision no. 2179/98/EC on the Review of the EC Programme of Policy and Action in Relation to the Environment", *Official Journal,* L 275, 10 October 1998

Council of Ministers 2000: General Secretariat Information Note to National Delegations on the "Global Assessment" of the Fifth Environmental Action Programme, no. 8072/00, 28 April 2000

Economic and Social Committee, Opinion on the Global Assessment, NAT/061, May 2000

EU website at www.europa.int

This is an invaluable source of up-to-date information, including the full text of the Sixth Environmental Action Programme 2001–10, *Our Future, Our Choice,* as well as the official documents used in the preparation of this chapter and cited elsewhere in this list.

Eurobarometer, *Survey of Public Opinion in the EU,* 51, July 1999

European Commission 1997: Proposal for a Framework for Action in the Field of Water Policy, COM(1997)614, 1997

European Commission 1999a: *Europe's Environment: What Directions for the Future? (The Global Assessment of the Fifth Environmental Action Programme),* COM(1999)543 Final, 1999

European Commission 1999b: *Key Developments in the Implementation of the Fifth Environmental Action Programme,* Interservice/sept/ISCTABLE, 27 September 1999

European Commission 1999c: *From Cardiff to Helsinki and Beyond,* SEC (1999) 1941

European Commission 1999d: *Report on the Implementation of Community Waste Legislation,* COM(99) 752, 1999

European Commission 2000a: *Proposal for a Directive on Public Access to Environmental Information,* COM(2000)402

European Commission 2000b: *Seventeenth Annual Report on the Monitoring of the Application of Community Law,* COM(2000)92, Brussels

European Environmental Agency, *Environment in the European Union at the Turn of the Century,* Copenhagen: European Environmental Agency, 1999

Jordan, A. (editor), *Environment and Plannning C: Government and Policy,* 17/2, 1999

This "theme issue" on "EU Environmental Policy at 25" contains some interesting articles on a number of important issues.

Sbragia, Alberta, "Environmental Policy: Economic Constraints and External Pressures", in Helen Wallace and William Wallace (editors), *Policy-making in the EU,* fourth edition, Oxford and New York: Oxford University Press, 2000

World Commission on Environment and Development, *Our Common Future – the Brundtland Report,* Oxford and New York: Oxford University Press, 1987

The landmark report that had a major influence on environmental policy and put sustainable development on the global policy agenda

Zito, Anthony R., *Creating Environmental Policy in the European Union,* London: Macmillan, and New York: St Martin's Press, 2000

A study focusing on the role of the other actors in the policy process, institutions, ideas, and interests, as well as the national governments

---

Pamela M. Barnes is Jean Monnet Principal Lecturer in European Political Integration at the University of Lincolnshire and Humberside. In addition to the items cited above, her publications include *The Enlarged European Union* (with Ian G. Barnes), 1995.

Table 16.1   Implementation of Environmental Directives as of 31 December 1999

Member state	Directives applicable on 31 December 1999	Directives for which national implementing measures had been notified to the European Commission	Proportion notified (%)
Austria	150	143	95.3
Belgium	150	144	96.0
Denmark	150	148	98.6
Finland	150	145	96.6
France	150	145	96.6
Germany	150	142	94.6
Greece	155	147	94.8
Ireland	150	145	96.6
Italy	150	148	98.6
Luxembourg	150	145	96.6
Netherlands	150	149	99.3
Portugal	154	150	97.4
Spain	153	149	97.3
Sweden	150	148	98.6
UK	150	144	96.0

Source: Adapted from European Commission, *Seventeenth Annual Report on Monitoring the Application of Community Law,* COM(2000)92 Final, Volume V, Annex 1, p. 3

Table 16.2   Cases under Examination by the European Court of Justice as of 31 December 1999, by stage of proceedings

	Total cases	Cases under proceedings	Cases for which reasoned opinion had been sent to national government	Cases brought to the Court	Cases for which the procedure of Article 228 TEC has been opened[1]
Cases in the environmental sector	870	317	165	72	14
All cases	3,050	1,646	816	293	31

1 Article 228 TEC (formerly 171) paragraph 2 contains as the ultimate sanction "If the Member State concerned fails to take the necessary measures to comply with the Court's judgement within the time limit laid down by the Commission, the latter may bring the case before the Court of Justice. In doing so it shall specify the amount of the lump sum or the penalty payment to be paid by the Member State concerned."

Source: Adapted from European Commission, *Seventeenth Annual Report on Monitoring the Application of Community Law,* COM(2000)92 Final, Volume II, Annex 2, p. 24

Law
and
Society

Chapter Seventeen

The Legal System of the EU

Jo Hunt

For an explanation of the way in which cases and legislation are referred to, please consult the Guide to Citation at the end of this chapter.

While each member state of the EU has its own legal system, the creation of the European Community gave rise to a new legal order, both separate from and intimately linked to the national legal systems. For example, the EU's institutions have their own law-making powers, and there are detailed rules and principles guiding the use of these powers. There is a system of courts, designed to ensure that the law is made in accordance with these rules, and that the member states and the EU's institutions are abiding by their legal obligations. However, the Community legal system is heavily reliant on the national legal orders, since national authorities are responsible for the implementation and application of the law made at the supranational level. As the European Court of Justice (ECJ) declared in the landmark case of *Costa*, "the EEC Treaty has created its own legal system, which, on the entry into force of the Treaty, became an integral part of the legal system of the member states and which their courts are bound to apply" (Case 6/64 Costa v ENEL [1964] ECR 585 at p. 593).

Since its creation this new legal order has been in a state of dynamic evolution. Its contours are constantly shifting, new principles are emerging, and its relationship with national legal systems is being redefined. While the member states have a role to play in this process, it is generally agreed that the ECJ's own role has been determinative. Through its deci-

sions the Court has developed key principles that structure the relationship between the Community legal order and the national legal orders. Before the interface of the national and Community legal orders is examined (in Chapter 18), this Chapter will provide an overview of the constituent elements of the Community legal order. In turn, there will be an examination of the sources of law, the rules governing law making, and the role of the ECJ.

The discussion thus far has used the terms "Community law" and "Community legal order". These are used in place of the term European *Union* legal order. It is a contested point among legal scholars whether one can speak of the legal order of the EU. This is because the way in which decisions are made and the legal quality of these decisions differ significantly between each of the three pillars upon which the EU is constructed. The Community method of law-making, the one that occurs within the most well-established and central pillar of the EU, and which will be detailed below, is not as a rule employed in the two other pillars (the Common Foreign and Security Policy, and Police and Judicial Cooperation). Nor has the ECJ been allowed to play as central a role in the other pillars as it does in the Community pillar: indeed, it remains completely absent from the Common Foreign and Security Policy pillar. This has led some to claim that there are in fact three legal systems at the level of the EU, although their outer limits are blurred, and there is some overlap particularly between the Community pillar, on the one hand, and Police and Judicial Cooperation, on the other.

Sources of Law

Treaties

The Treaty establishing the European Communities (TEC) and appended protocols form the basic primary law of the European Community. The treaty has been amended on a number of occasions since it first came into force, as the Treaty of Rome, on 1 January 1958. For example, the Merger Treaty of 1965 brought together the previously separate institutions of the European Atomic Energy Community (Euratom), the European Coal and Steel Community (ECSC), and the European Economic Community (EEC). The Acts of Accession of 1972 extended Community membership to Denmark, Ireland, and the United Kingdom. Greece acceded under an Act of Accession of 1979, followed by Spain and Portugal in 1985, and Austria, Finland, and Sweden in 1995.

New areas of policy competence, new decision-making procedures, and increased powers for the European Parliament were incorporated into the TEC through the Single European Act, which entered into force on 1 July 1987. Subsequently, a new superstructure, with the Community at its heart, was formed when the Treaty on European Union (TEU, the Maastricht Treaty) came into force on 1 November 1993. In addition to setting up the three pillars of the EU, this treaty also made changes to the content of the core TEC. Again, new areas of Community policy competence were recognized and changes were made to the decision-making process. Structures for the administration of Economic and Monetary Union were also established.

In turn, both the TEC and the TEU have been amended by the Treaty of Amsterdam, which came into force on 1 May 1999. Significant changes brought about by this treaty include the transfer of part of the third pillar (formerly Justice and Home Affairs, regulated under the TEU, now Police and Judicial Cooperation) into the body of the TEC (Title IV, Visas, Asylum and Immigration); and the renumbering of existing treaty articles. In December 2000 political agreement was reached on another amending treaty, the Treaty of Nice. This treaty was the result of negotiations that had been opened with the objective of securing changes to the institutional structure of the EU in order to prepare it for the imminent accession of new member states.

Its amendments to the EC and EU treaties will come into effect following ratification. This is in accordance with the standard treaty amendment process, which is detailed at Article 48 of the TEU. Proposals for treaty amendment may come from any member state government, or from the Commission, and must be forwarded to the Council. If the Council, having taken advice from the other Community institutions, chooses to proceed, it must launch an intergovernmental conference (IGC), at which the representatives of the member states' governments enter into negotiations and reach agreement by common accord. Amendments take effect once each member state has ratified the changes in accordance with its own constitutional provisions (see Chapter 4 for a discussion of recent IGCs). The Treaty of Nice had not yet been ratified when this book went to press.

The TEC itself, which the ECJ has described as the "constitutional charter" of the European Community (Case 294/83 *Parti Ecologiste 'Les Verts'* v *European Parliament* [1986] ECR 1339 at p. 1365), sets out the basic framework within which Community action takes place. It identifies the Community's objectives, its areas of competence, its principal policy obligations, and the powers granted to the institutions.

Secondary Legislation

The treaties themselves may be seen as a skeleton framework: the EU's institutions must adopt secondary legislation to flesh it out. Article 249 of the TEC identifies and sets out the characteristics of the five basic forms of secondary legislation that may be adopted under the TEC: regulations, directives, decisions, recommendations, and opinions. These different tools serve different purposes.

A regulation is used when the institutions want to ensure that there is complete uniformity across the EU on a particular matter. This is because regulations have general application, they are binding in their entirety, and they are directly applicable, which means that they enter into force without the need for intervening legislation on the part of the member states. Regulations are most commonly used in policy areas such as agriculture, transport, and economic and monetary union (for example, Council Regulation 1466/97/EC on the strengthening of the surveillance of budgetary positions, and the surveillance and coordination of economic policies; *Official Journal* (usually cited as *OJ*) 1997, No. L209/1).

Directives offer the member states more flexibility, in that they are binding only as to the result to be achieved. The member states may therefore choose their own methods of achieving the objective set out in the directive. This will usually be done through the introduction of a piece of national legislation. If a member state fails to transpose the directive into national law, it can be brought before the ECJ for breach of the Community law obligations (see below). The directive is the tool most commonly used when the Community is seeking to achieve the harmonization or approximation of national laws, for example in the areas of environmental and social policy (e.g., Council Directive 93/104 concerning certain aspects of the organisation of working time, *OJ* 1993, No. L307/18).

Decisions, like directives, may be addressed to one or more of the member states, and may also be addressed to private undertakings, for example, in the area of competition law (e.g., Decision 94/815/EC, *OJ* 1994 L343/1, in which the Commission fined an undertaking ECU248 million for breach of Community competition law).

These three tools – regulations, directives, and decisions – are all legally binding. Regulations and decisions are binding in their entirety; directives are binding as to their objectives. The remaining tools set out in Article 249 do not have this binding quality. Instead, recommendations and opinions have only persuasive or "moral" force.

There are, in addition, a number of other nonbinding tools that are employed by the Community's institutions but are not formally recognized in Article 249 of the TEC. These include resolutions, guidelines, and interinstitutional agreements. Together with recommendations and opinions, these may be characterized as "soft law." While such soft law does not create legally enforceable rights and obligations, it may direct the institutions and member states to a particular course of action. These more informal methods of developing policy are becoming increasingly significant in the present era of subsidiarity (see below). In some instances, soft law is a precursor to the later adoption of hard law.

According to Article 254 of the TEC, all regulations must be published in the *Official Journal of the European Communities* (to be renamed the *Official Journal of the European Union* under the Treaty of Nice), as must those directives that are addressed to all member states, as well as all legal acts adopted under the codecision procedure (see below). Legal acts come into effect either on the date specified in their text, or on the 20th day after publication in the *OJ*. Legal acts that do not require publication come into effect upon notification of the parties involved.

The discussion above relates to the legal tools used in the central, Community pillar of the EU. The second and third pillars have their own sets of instruments, which do not accord with this fivefold categorization. In relation to the Police and Judicial Cooperation pillar, for example, Article 34(2) of the TEU sets out four instruments that may be adopted by the Council: common positions, conventions, decisions, and harmonizing framework decisions. In relation to the Common Foreign and Security Policy pillar, Articles 12–15 of the TEU detail an array of instruments: guidelines, common positions, joint actions, common strategies, and implementing decisions.

International Agreements

As a general rule, the EU has no independent legal personality of its own, which means that it is not recognized as competent to enter into legal obligations with other parties (however, see Article 24 of the TEU for an exception to this principle). The European Community does have legal personality, and thus the power to enter into legal agreements with international organizations and with states that are not members of the EU. Such treaties constitute a source of Community law. The procedure for concluding treaties with third parties is set out in Article 300 of the TEC. The Community does not have an unfettered power to enter into international agreements, however. They may only be concluded where the Community has either express powers (for example, in the area of the Common Commercial Policy, such as the World Trade Organization agreements) or implied powers so to do (on the latter point, see Case 22/70 *Commission* v *Council* (ERTA) [1971] ECR 263).

General Principles of Law

In addition to the written sources of law set out above, the ECJ has recognized the existence of a set of unwritten general principles of law that underpin the treaties and are binding on all parties. Such general principles include:

- respect for fundamental human rights (e.g. Case 11/70 *Internationale Handelsgesellschaft mbH* [1970] ECR 1125);
- the principles of equality and nondiscrimination;
- the principle of legal certainty, encompassing the principles of legitimate expectations and nonretroactivity (see, for example, Case 112/77 *August Töpfer & Co. GmbH* v *Commission* [1978] ECR 1019); and
- procedural rights, such as the right to due process and to be informed of the reasons behind a decision (e.g. Case 222/86 *UNECTEF* v *Heylens* [1987] ECR 4097).

These general principles are used in a variety of ways. For example, the Court may have recourse to them when interpreting primary and secondary Community law, or it may use them as yardsticks against which to test the legality of the acts of the institutions. General principles are derived from a variety of sources, a key source being the constitutional traditions of the member states.

Community Competence

As has been stated above, the treaties provide a basic framework for action. To enable the objectives of the Community to be met, the European Community and its institutions are empowered to adopt secondary legislation. It should be recognized, however, that there are limits on what the Community can do: it does not have a completely free hand to decide how, and on what, it will legislate. As Article 5 of the TEC clearly states: "the Community shall act within the limits of the powers conferred upon it by this Treaty and of the objectives assigned to it therein". The starting point for an understanding of Community competence is therefore that the Community operates in accordance with this principle of conferred or attributed powers: it can do only what a treaty empowers it to do and, where powers have been handed to it, it must work within those powers.

Express and Implied Competence

Where the Community is given an objective to achieve under the treaty, it is generally accorded express powers to adopt measures in furtherance of this objective. Within the treaty there are enabling provisions that detail the type of measure that can be used and indicate the process that must be followed. These differ from one policy area to another. Sometimes, however, the Community institutions may find themselves wanting to introduce a measure for which they can find no express legislative power. This absence could be due to any one of a number of factors. The member states may have decided not to hand over competence to the Community on a particular matter, or the absence may be due to an oversight when the treaty was being drafted. Alternatively, the need for Community action may simply not have been foreseen at the time that the treaty was concluded. The Court of Justice has recognized that, in addition to its express powers, the Community also has implied legislative powers that may be inferred from its objectives. According to the Court, where a specific task has been conferred on the institutions, they have the implied power to take such measures as are necessary to carry out that task (Cases 281, 283-5, 287/85 *Germany and others* v *Commission* [1987] ECR 3203).

It should also be noted that the drafters of the treaties themselves foresaw that there would not be specific express legislative powers in place to cover all eventualities. Thus, the TEC includes, at Article 308 a "catch all" provision enabling the Community to adopt measures when "action by the Community [is] necessary to attain, in the course of the operation of the common market, one of the objectives of the Community and this Treaty has not provided the necessary powers". Article 94 of the TEC also provides the Community with a general power to issue directives approximating such national measures as "directly affect the establishment or functioning of the common market".

The existence of such potentially wide-ranging powers may generate concerns about the Community's institutions escaping member state control, and leading the Community in directions that do not accord with the wishes of member states. There is, however, some inbuilt protection for member states against such a development, in that law-making under both Articles 94 and 308 of the TEC may be stalled by a negative opinion by any of the member states' governments, which are represented in the Council. Further, the ECJ has made it clear that Article 308 may not be used to adopt measures that would be of "constitutional significance" to the Community system (Opinion 2/94 *ECHR Case* [1996] ECR I-1759). That said, over the years the theory of implied powers and the existence of the general law-making powers has provided the legal context for a steady accretion of Community competences and the adoption of measures not necessarily foreseen by the treaties. The ECJ has been involved in determining the legality of such developments through the channel of the judicial review of Community legal acts. Some, however, have questioned whether in fact the Court has what is, in effect, the power to endorse such extensions of Community competence. To date, the most notable and outspoken opponent of the Court's *Kompetenz-kompetenz* has been the German Constitutional Court, the Bundesverfassungsgericht, in its Maastricht decision (see *Brunner* [1994] 1 CMLR 57, and further the discussion in Chapter 18 of this book). For an example of a case where the Court has refused to see competence extended, see the judgement in the Tobacco Advertising Directive case, Case C-

376/98 *Germany v Parliament and Council*, 5 October 2000.

Exclusive and Concurrent Competence, and the Principle of Subsidiarity

The attainment of certain policy objectives falls within the exclusive competence of the European Community. In such areas the Community is recognized as having the sole responsibility to act, and member states are therefore restricted in adopting measures either at the national level or by way of international agreements. Outside the area of exclusive competence lies the area of concurrent competence, where both member states and the Community share policy responsibility. It is important to distinguish between areas of exclusive and concurrent competence, as actions envisaged in areas of concurrent competence are subject to the operation of the principle of subsidiarity. This is significant for, even where the Community has been granted express powers in a policy area, it may be precluded from exercising those powers if to do so would contravene subsidiarity.

The principle of subsidiarity was introduced as a constitutional principle by the Maastricht Treaty. It is now set out at Article 5 of the TEC, and further guidance on its application is contained in the Protocol on the Application of the Principles of Subsidiarity and Proportionality, adopted at Amsterdam. In essence the principle erects a set of hurdles that the Community must overcome before it is permitted to legislate. The Community is required to establish that the objectives of its envisaged action cannot be sufficiently achieved by the member states or at any other level "closer to the citizen", and that they can be better met by the Community. As the Protocol suggests, action in conformity with the principle of subsidiarity is most often of a transnational nature, and where it can be shown that Community-level action presents clear benefits in comparison to action by member states.

No clear guidance is provided by the treaties on where the dividing line between exclusive and concurrent competence falls. Perhaps not surprisingly, the Commission itself lays claim to a wide zone of exclusive Community competence, which it sees as incorporating such policy areas as are essential to the full establishment of the single internal market. Others consider the exclusive zone to be very narrow, thus recognizing much greater scope for the application of the subsidiarity principle. The Court has a role to play both in demarcating areas of exclusive and concurrent competence, and, within the latter, assessing the conformity of legislation with the principle of subsidiarity (for example, see Case C-84/94 *UK* v *Council* (*Working Time Directive*) [1996] ECR I-5755]). Both tasks are politically contentious, and in particular doubts have arisen over the justiciability of subsidiarity, for some argue that it is too opaque and subjective a principle against which to perform a review of legislation.

Legal Base

All validly enacted Community legislation must be introduced under the correct legal base. As was mentioned above, these enabling provisions, which may be policy-specific (e.g., the law-making power in the area of the environment contained in Article 175 of the TEC), or more general (such as Articles 94 and 308 of the TEC, discussed above), indicate which of the law-making procedures is to be followed. The choice of legal base therefore determines who is involved in law-making and their relative powers in this process. It is often not clear which legal base should be used for the introduction of a particular measure and the Commission's choice may therefore be a strategic one, as it seeks to select the constellation of actors and powers most sympathetic to its policy objectives. Other institutions of the Community, and/or member state governments that believe that an incorrect legal base has been selected, may challenge the legality of the resultant Community act before the ECJ (as with the UK government's action in the *Working Time Directive case*, or the German government's action in relation to the Tobacco Advertising Directive, above). The Commission itself has brought actions challenging directives when the Council has substituted an alternative legal base to that used by the Commission (e.g., Case 300/89 *Commission* v *Council* (*Titanium*

Dioxide) [1991] ECR I-2867). Where more than one legal base is potentially available, the ECJ has declared that the choice is to be determined by the measure's predominant aim and content (Case C-155/91 *Commission* v *Council* [1993] ECR I-939).

Legislative Processes

Under the original Treaty of Rome, the standard law-making process was the one now referred to as the "consultation" process, according to which the Commission adopts a legislative proposal, which is then passed to the European Parliament for its opinion, and which then proceeds to the Council of Ministers. It is here that the final decision on the adoption of the legislation is taken, in accordance with a requirement of either unanimous agreement or a weighted qualified majority. Over the years variations upon this standard process have been introduced, most notably through an expansion in the formal powers of the directly elected European Parliament. Most legislation is now introduced through one of three routes: consultation, cooperation (set out at Article 252 of the TEC) or co-decision route (Article 251 of the TEC). Each affords the Parliament an increasingly significant voice in the process, to the extent that under the co-decision procedure the Parliament may, after a long-drawn-out and convoluted process, ultimately veto a piece of legislation. In exceptional cases, such as a decision to allow a new member state to accede, an assent procedure affords the Parliament this right at a first reading.

Article 253 of the TEC establishes that the legally binding acts of the legislative institutions must state the reasons on which they were based. Nonconformity with this duty to give reasons may amount to an infringement of an essential procedural requirement, and on this basis the measure may be overturned before the ECJ (see, for example, Case 45/86 *Commission* v *Council* (*Tariff Preferences*) [1987] ECR 1493). The enunciation of clear reasons also facilitates the Court's task in adjudging whether the measure in question properly respects the principles of subsidiarity and proportionality.

Article 249 recognizes that legally binding measures may be enacted through the European Parliament acting with the Council, as in the co-decision procedure; through the Council acting alone, as in the consultation procedure; or by the Commission acting alone. In a small number of areas, such as competition policy, the Commission has the power to enact legislation of its own motion (such as the power to adopt directives and decisions under Article 86(3) of the TEC). More commonly, however, the Commission has legislative powers delegated to it by the Council (see Article 202(3) of the TEC). These powers enable the Commission to adopt detailed regulations under parent measures adopted by the Council, or indeed, by the Council and the Parliament. The Commission exercises these powers through a system of committees, in which the member states' governments are represented and over which the Council retains some measure of control. The most tightly controlled of the committees is the so-called regulatory committee, while the management committee and the advisory committee afford the Commission greater independence in the decisions it takes. This system of decision-making through committees, the so called "comitology" regime, is used extensively and, while it enables decisions to be reached swiftly and efficiently, some – not least in the European Parliament – have expressed concern about the limited role that the Parliament has played in the process. Some improvement to this situation has recently been made through Council Decision 1999/468/EC *OJ* 1999, No. L184/23, which updates and amends the comitology system and designates a formal role for the Parliament.

The European Court of Justice and the Court of First Instance

Under Article 220 of the TEC the European Court of Justice is given the task of ensuring that "in the interpretation and application of this Treaty, the law is observed". More particularly, the ECJ's key functions are threefold:

- it polices the use of the law-making powers of the Community institutions, ensuring that the institutions are playing by the rules, through annulment actions;
- it seeks to ensure that member states abide by their legal obligations under Community law, through enforcement actions; and
- it offers interpretative assistance and advice to national courts on the meaning of Community law, by means of the preliminary ruling procedure.

Through the decisions it has handed down in the exercise of these functions the Court has played a central role in the development of some of the main principles upon which the Community legal order is based, such as the supremacy and direct effect of Community law (see Chapter 18), and issues relating to competence and the division of powers. In this way, the ECJ has animated the text of the treaties and brought the legal order to life. However, the ECJ has needed the active support, or at least the acquiescence, of a wide range of other actors in the formation of this legal order. Why such support has been forthcoming is a matter of intense academic debate.

Structure and Composition of the Courts

The European Court of Justice, which sits in Luxembourg, is currently composed of 15 judges, with one from each member state. This convention of one judge from each member state will be formalized by the Treaty of Nice. Appointed for renewable six-year terms, the judges are required to be qualified for "appointment to the highest judicial offices in their respective countries" or "jurisconsults of recognised competence" (Article 223 of the TEC). Among the current ranks of ECJ judges are many who have combined legal practice and judicial appointments with academic positions. There are also two women judges, the first having been appointed in October 1999. The Court is assisted in its work by eight advocates general, who have the task of making "independent and impartial submissions" in all cases before the ECJ (Article 222 of the TEC).

In addition, the Community judicature also includes a second court, the Court of First

Instance. This too is composed of 15 judges, but there are no advocates general assigned to it. Established in 1988, with a view to taking some of the pressure off the increasingly over-loaded ECJ, the Court of First Instance has jurisdiction to hear certain categories of cases, from which there lies an appeal in law to the ECJ. The categories of cases that can come before the Court of First Instance are to be expanded further after the coming into force of the Treaty of Nice. This development is seen as necessary in order to ease pressures on what is a vastly overloaded system. In a related move intended to ease the pressure on the system, the Treaty of Nice also introduces the possi-bility of a third level of Community court, the judicial panel. Such panels will have the juris-diction to deal with legal questions arising in certain clearly defined areas, such as in relation to staff cases.

Procedure of the Courts

It is rare to find all 15 judges of the ECJ sitting together to hear a case. In fact, it is far more common to find the Court sitting in chambers of either three or five judges. The full Court is reserved for only the most significant of cases, usually those involving a member state's gov-ernment or one of the Community's institu-tions, although such cases may also be heard by a Grand Chamber of nine or 11 judges. The Court of First Instance also generally sits in chambers and, since 1999, it has been able to hear cases using a single judge.

The standard procedure before the ECJ involves, first, the appointment to the case of an advocate general, as well as a judge-rapporteur, from within the ranks of the Court's judges. Following the submission of written pleadings by all parties to the action, the judge-rapporteur presents a report for hearing, summarizing the main facts and issues. On completion of this written round, the parties may present oral submissions before the Court. After the public delivery of the advocate gen-eral's opinion, the Court will meet in private to decide the case, with a draft judgement pre-pared by the judge-rapporteur as the start-ing point. Once agreement has been reached by a majority, a single collegiate judgement is delivered in open court. According to figures available for the year 2000, the average length of time for completion of this procedure is a little under two years – and that does not include the translation of cases into all the Community's languages, which in some cases may not take place until many months after the judgement has been delivered.

Actions in Annulment

As discussed above, when exercising their law-making powers under the treaties the Com-munity's institutions must comply with a number of conditions. For example, the insti-tutions must not operate outside the limits of their competence, they must, where necessary, respect the principle of subsidiarity, and their actions must conform with the necessary pro-cedural requirements. Under Article 230 of the TEC, the ECJ is given the power to review the legality of acts of the institutions and, where it is found that the necessary legal conditions have not been met, the Court has the author-ity to annul the act in question (Article 232 of the TEC). This power of review extends only to those acts of the institutions that have legally binding effects, recommendations and opinions being excluded under Article 230. The origi-nal version of this article appeared to limit review to the acts of the Council and Com-mission, no mention being made of the Parliament. In Case 294/84 *Parti Ecologiste 'Les Verts'* v *European Parliament* [1986] ECR 1339, however, the ECJ read into Article 230 the availability of an action in annulment against the Parliament. Similarly, in relation to the issue of who may bring actions, the Court extended the scope of the original article by adding the European Parliament to the list. The Treaty of Nice will further strengthen the role of the Parliament, granting it the same standing as the Council, the Commission, and the member states, which have open access to the Court. Until the Treaty of Nice is ratified, however, the Parliament's rights continue to be more restricted, as it can bring an action only in order to protect its own prerogatives (see Case C-70/88 *European Parliament* v *Council (Chernobyl)* [1990] ECR 2041). The ability of private indi-viduals, companies, and the like to bring actions is yet more circumscribed. These actors, whose challenges are brought before the Court of First Instance, must show that they have a direct and individual concern in the act complained of – a test that few succeed in passing (see the restrictive formula established in Case 25/62 *Plaumann & Co* v *Commission* [1963] ECR 95). The "individual" leg of the test makes it all but impossible for groups acting in the general public interest to mount a successful action (see for example Case T-585/93 *Stichting Greenpeace Council* v *Commission* [1995] ECR II-2205, and, on appeal from the Court of First Instance to the ECJ, Case C-321/95 P [1998] ECR I-1651].

Enforcement Actions

Article 10 of the TEC imposes upon member states the duty to "take all appropriate measures, whether general or particular, to ensure the fulfilment of the obligations" arising under Community law. The Commission has the role, as the "guardian of the treaties", of policing the member states' compliance with Community law. When an infringement of the law on the part of a member state comes to the Commission's attention, it may commence enforcement proceedings under Article 226 of the TEC. If there is no resolution under the administrative phase of this process, the case is passed to the ECJ. Enforcement actions can also reach the Court under Article 227, which gives member states the power to instigate actions against each other, although this power has been used exceedingly rarely (see, however, Case C-388/95, *Belgium* v *Spain*, judgement of 16 May 2000). In both situations, if the Court finds that there has been a breach of Community law it issues a declaratory judgement with which the member state must comply. Failure to do so may lead to the imposition of a fine (Article 228 of the TEC). The Court used the power to fine for the first time in Case 387/97 *Commission* v *Greece*, judgement of 4 July 2000, following Greece's continued infringement of environmental law.

Preliminary Rulings

Article 234 of the TEC provides an "organic connection" between the national courts and the European Court of Justice (see Shaw, cited in the Further Reading list at the end of Chapter 18). Through the preliminary rulings procedure, national courts may seek interpretative guidance from the ECJ on matters of Community law coming before them, including the validity of legal acts of the institutions. For the ECJ, this procedure "is essential for the preservation of the Community character of the law … and has the object of ensuring that in all circumstances the law is the same in all States" (Case 166/73 *Rheinmuhlen-Dusseldorf* [1974] ECR 33 at p. 43). Its significance has been immense: almost all of the "constitutionalizing" decisions to be considered in Chapter 18 were brought before the Court under Article 234. As a general rule, any court or tribunal may bring an action, and courts of last resort are under an obligation to do so (for exceptions to this rule, see Case 283/81 *CILFIT* [1982] ECR 3415). However, in the politically contentious area covered by Title IV of the TEC (visas, asylum, and immigration), Article 68(1) limits the power to make preliminary references to national courts of last resort only. While some have seen this as an unjustified restriction of the Court's jurisdiction, its introduction under the Amsterdam Treaty was accompanied by an extension of the ECJ's jurisdiction beyond the Community pillar, so that it now has a restricted power in relation to certain aspects of Police and Judicial Cooperation, subject to a member state's acceptance of its jurisdiction (see Article 35 of the TEU).

The Article 234 process is heavily used, and the average length of time taken to complete a reference is regarded by many as unacceptable. In an attempt to ease the increasing congestion, the member states have agreed in principle to extend the jurisdiction of the Court of First Instance, and to give it the opportunity to hear Article 234 references as well. Such a sharing of responsibility between the two Community courts had been opposed for some time by the ECJ itself, which has been fearful of seeing its authority challenged. At the very least, the sharing of this role raises the possibility of divergent interpretations of the law arising. There are safeguards against this, however: the ECJ has the power to intervene and review judgements of the Court of First Instance where it is felt that they threaten the unity and consistency of Community law.

Conclusion

The legal order of the European Community has been in a constant state of flux. The Court of Justice has traditionally played a crucial role in moulding the shape of this order. The Court could never stand accused of rendering mechanistic, value-free judgements. The Court is seen by some as an heroic institution, pushing forward the goal of further integration, sometimes in the face of recalcitrance on the part of member states. For others, however, the "success" of the Court has been achieved through unacceptable means: they see it as having ascribed itself powers, and established rules of constitutional significance, even though, in

their view, it is not authorized, and is ill-suited, to do either of these things. This wariness of the Court may prevent it from becoming a real force in the areas beyond the central Community pillar, as the member states refuse to extend its jurisdiction. The variation in styles of governance in the place accorded to the role of law as between the different pillars may make it difficult to define a coherent legal order for the EU as a whole, as opposed to the established Community legal order.

Further Reading

Please see Further Reading list at the end of Chapter 18.

Dr Jo Hunt is Lecturer in Law in the Centre for the Study of Law in Europe at the University of Leeds. She has contributed articles to journals and edited collections focusing on European Community law, the governance of the EU and its policy processes, and Community employment law and policy.

Guide to Citation

Legislation

The *Official Journal of the European Communities* (*OJ*), to be renamed the *Official Journal of the European Union* by the Treaty of Nice, is the authoritative source of Treaty (primary) and secondary legislation. It is published in three sections, the most important of which are the L series (adopted legislation) and the C series (non-binding acts, information, and notices). The S series contains details of contracts for public work and supplies.

Primary Legislation

The core Treaties are the Treaty establishing the European Communities (TEC) and the Treaty on European Union (TEU). These were amended by the Treaty of Amsterdam, which also introduced a renumbering of all treaty articles. Since 1997 consolidated versions of the TEC and the TEU have been published with their articles renumbered. As many people are familiar with the former numbering, the usual practice is to cite the new number of the article with the old number in brackets, followed by the abbreviation for the relevant Treaty, TEC or TEU, e.g., Article 11 (formerly J1) TEU on the Common Foreign and Security Policy; Article 5 (formerly 3b) TEC on subsidiarity.

Secondary Legislation

Secondary legislation may be cited by number, short title, and *OJ* reference.

For regulations, the legislation number is followed by the year, e.g., Council Regulation 888/92/EEC on a Community ecolabel award scheme, OJ 1992 L99/1.

For directives and decisions, the year precedes the legislation number, e.g., Council Directive 90/314/EEC on package holidays, *OJ* 1990 L158/59.

Case Law

Since the establishment of the Court of First Instance, a letter prefix has been used to indicate which of the two Courts the case is before – C indicates the ECJ, and T the Court of First Instance. This is followed by the case number and the year in which it was lodged. There may be more than one number, as cases dealing with essentially the same point may be joined. The number is followed by the name of the parties and a reference to its publication in the European Court Reports (year, part, and page number; ECJ judgements appear in Part I, those of the Court of First Instance in Part II). Where a case has yet to be published the date of judgement is given. Thus, for example, Case C-415/93, *Union Royale Belge des Sociétés de Football Association ASBL* v *Bosman* [1995] ECR I-4921; Case T-105/95, *WWF UK* v *Commission* [1997] ECR II-313.

Appeals to the ECJ from the CFI are indicated by the letter P, e.g., Joined Cases C-174/98 P and C-198/98 P, *Netherlands and van der Wal* v *Commission* [2000] ECR I-0001.

Chapter Eighteen

Enforcing Community Law in the Member States

Tamara K. Hervey

For an explanation of the way in which cases and legislation are referred to, please consult the Guide to Citation at the end of Chapter 17.

The key to an understanding of the effect of Community law in the member states, and consequently its enforcement at the suit of individuals, is the relationship between Community law and national law. Although the Treaty of Rome gives indications as to the relationship between Community law and national law, the corpus of law governing this question emanates largely from the European Court of Justice. To this end, the Court has elaborated two core legal principles, describing the "constitutional qualities" (see Shaw) of Community law: "direct applicability" and "supremacy".

Direct Applicability and Supremacy of Community Law

Unlike ordinary international law, Community law automatically becomes part of national legal orders, without the need for specific implementation. This has implications for national parliaments, which are thereby excluded from the Community's legislative process. The principle of direct applicability also imposes duties on national courts, which are obliged to apply measures of Community law as if they were part of the national legal order. As the Court put it in Case 106/77 *Simmenthal II* [1978] ECR 629, "every national court must, in a case within its jurisdiction, apply Community law in its entirety and protect rights which the latter confers on individuals".

Moreover, the Court has held that Community law is "supreme", or enjoys precedence over conflicting national law. The Treaty of Rome is silent on the question of priority of norms; the concept of supremacy of Community law is judge-made. The seminal case is Case 26/62 *Van Gend en Loos* [1963] ECR 1, in which the Court described Community law as a "new legal order", within which member states have limited their sovereign rights. The concept was developed in Case 6/64 *Costa v ENEL* [1964] ECR 585, where the Court explained that Community law, "an independent source of law, could not, because of its special and original nature, be overridden by domestic legal provisions ... without being deprived of its character as Community law and without the legal basis of the Community itself being called into question". Supremacy of Community law is thus regarded by the Court as essential to the legal basis of the Community itself.

Binding Community law automatically takes precedence over *all* provisions of national law, even those enacted subsequently to the Community measure. For instance, in Case 106/77 *Simmenthal II*, it was held that national laws providing for the payment of fees by importers for public health inspections of imported goods were inapplicable, as they were inconsistent with the provisions of the Treaty of Rome on free movement of goods. Whether the national rules were enacted before or after the Community provisions was irrelevant. Even a putative right in Community law takes precedence over conflicting national provisions. In Case

C-213/89 *Factortame I* [1990] ECR I-2433, the Court held that a national court must grant interim relief to a party suffering loss caused by an alleged breach of Community law. The effect of that ruling was that a British Act of Parliament was set aside, while the substantive issue was decided. Even where the breach of Community law has not yet been established, the principle of supremacy of Community law may apply, in order that individuals may enjoy interim protection by national courts.

Giving Effect to the Constitutional Qualities of Community Law

The principles of direct applicability and supremacy do not in themselves guarantee that they are put into effect in practice. To this end, the Court has developed three techniques or processes that ensure that Community law takes effect in the member states, and is applicable in priority over conflicting national norms. These are "direct effect" (justiciability), "state liability" (responsibility), and "indirect effect" (interpretation) (see Shaw). Moreover, the Court requires the use of "effective" remedies in national law to enforce Community law rights.

Direct Effect

Certain provisions of Community law are enforceable in national courts by individuals, either against the state or against other individuals. Not all provisions of Community law are directly effective. Some provisions may be enforced only by the state; some lack the necessary precision to form the basis of individual rights; some need to be filled out with measures of implementation before they can be relied on by individuals. The direct effect of a provision depends on its justiciability, that is, on whether national courts can apply it, as it is, to the facts of a case in national proceedings, without any further action either by the Community or by the authorities of a member state.

In order to have direct effect, a provision of Community law must meet three preconditions. First, it must be sufficiently clear, precise and unambiguous: in other words, it must be specific and not general. For example, Article 10 TEC, which provides that "Member States shall take all appropriate measures ... to ensure fulfilment of the obligations arising out of this Treaty ..." is not directly effective as it is too general.

Secondly, the provision must be unconditional. Although a strict application of this precondition would lead to the position that any rule of Community law to which exceptions were made could not have direct effect, the Court has been generous in its interpretation of this second precondition. For example, Article 39 TEC, concerning free movement of workers, has direct effect, in spite of its exclusion provisions, such as those providing exemptions on the grounds of public policy, public security, and public health (see Case 41/74 *Van Duyn* v *Home Office* [1974] ECR 1337).

Thirdly, the provision must not be dependent upon an action or decision within the control of an independent authority, either of a member state or of the Community itself. If a provision leaves discretion to a member state, or another body, to determine its precise implications, it is not directly effective. For example, a measure requiring member states to establish a system of protection for employees in the event of the insolvency of their employer, but leaving considerable discretion as to the organization and financing of that system, is not directly effective (Cases C-6 & 9/90 *Francovich* v *Italian State* [1991] ECR I-5357).

The European Court of Justice has held, in a series of important decisions, that provisions of the main sources of Community law may be directly effective. The Court first held that articles of the Treaty of Rome could have direct effect in Case 26/62 *Van Gend en Loos*. The case concerned the question of whether a Dutch importer could lawfully be charged an import duty that had been increased since the Treaty of Rome entered into force. The treaty specifically provided in Article 12 (now 25) TEC that no new duties be introduced on goods moving between member states. In reaching its decision that Van Gend en Loos was not required to pay the duty, the Court relied upon "the spirit, the general scheme, and the wording" of the treaty. The objective of the treaty was the establishment of a common market, which was of direct concern to individuals of the member states. The Court also referred to the institutional structure of the Community, in particular the preliminary rulings procedure, the function of which is to secure uniform interpretation of Community law by the national courts. Therefore, the Court concluded, the treaty is more than an agreement creating mutual obligations between the member states. The Community constitutes a "new legal order . . . the subjects of which comprise not only member states, but also their nationals".

In addition to imposing obligations upon nationals of member states, Community law confers upon them "rights which become part of their legal heritage". Since 1962 the Court has found that very many treaty articles are directly effective, including the main provisions on the free movement of goods, many of those concerned with the free movement of workers, the competition provisions, and the provision concerning equal pay for women and men.

In the *Van Gend en Loos* case, the individual concerned invoked a provision of Community law in an action against a state authority, the Dutch customs and excise service. The Court was subsequently required to decide whether treaty articles could also have direct effect in actions brought against individuals. It is customary to refer to these two concepts as "vertical" direct effect (between an individual and the state) and "horizontal" direct effect (between individual and individual). The Court held in Case 43/75 *Defrenne* v *SABENA II* [1978] ECR 1365 that treaty provisions could be horizontally directly effective. The case concerned Article 119 (now 141) TEC, the equal pay provision. The Court relied upon the nature of the provision concerned, its aim, and its place in the scheme of the treaty. The Court concluded that "since Article 119 is mandatory in nature, the prohibition on discrimination between men and women applies not only to the action of public authorities, but also extends to . . . contracts between individuals".

A regulation, according to Article 249 TEC, is "binding in its entirety and directly applicable in the member states". In general, provisions of regulations, as long as they meet the preconditions, enjoy direct effect. A decision, according to Article 249 TEC, is "binding in its entirety upon the person to whom it is addressed". A decision addressed to an individual has direct effect provided that the preconditions are fulfilled (Case 9/70 *Grad* v *Finanzamt Traustein* [1970] ECR 825). It is logical that decisions, which impose binding obligations upon their addressees, should be capable of being invoked against their addressees by another individual before a national court.

A directive, according to Article 249 TEC, is "binding as to the result to be achieved, on each member state to which it is addressed, but shall leave to the national authorities the choice of form and methods" of implementation. It was originally thought that, since the treaty does not describe directives as directly applicable, directives could not produce direct effect. The Court thought otherwise in Case 41/74 *Van Duyn* v *Home Office* [1974] ECR 1337. The Court reasoned that simply because the treaty provides that regulations are directly applicable, and can therefore have direct effect, this does not necessarily mean that other measures can never have direct effect. The Court explained that it would be "incompatible with the binding effect attributed to a directive by Article 189 to exclude, in principle, the possibility that the obligation which it imposes may be invoked by those concerned".

In order to be directly effective, directives must also meet the preconditions. Since directives always give discretion to the member states as regards form and method of implementation, they do not become directly effective immediately upon enactment. However, after the end of the time limit by which implementation is to be effected, the obligation upon the member state becomes absolute and the directive may be relied upon directly by individuals before a national court (Case 148/78 *Pubblico Ministero* v *Ratti* [1979] ECR 1629). Even where a member state has implemented a directive, if that implementation is inadequate, or allegedly inadequate, the directive itself may be invoked before a national court (Case 51/76 VNO [1977] ECR 113). The direct effect of directives does not relieve member states of the obligation to implement directives (Case 102/79 *EC Commission* v *Belgium (Vehicles Directives)* [1980] ECR 1473).

The question of whether directives enjoy horizontal direct effect, that is, whether they are enforceable against an individual as opposed to a state authority, was not settled until 1986. The principal argument against a horizontal direct effect is that the obligation in a directive is a state obligation: directives are directly effective against the state because the state is not entitled, in an action against it, to rely upon its own failure to implement the directive. An individual has not failed to implement the directive, so the argument does not extend to horizontal direct effect (see Opinion of Advocate General Slynn in Case 8/81 *Becker* [1982] ECR 53). The principal argument for horizontal direct effect of directives is based on equality: if directives are not enforceable against individuals, but only against state authorities, then the rights of individuals in similar situations will differ. The inequality is particularly stark where employment law directives are concerned; there, an individual employee's rights will depend upon whether the employer is public or private. The Court expressly rejected the concept of horizontal direct effect for directives in Case 152/84 *Marshall I* [1986] ECR 723, holding that the direct effect of directives exists only in relation to member states and that a directive may not of itself impose obligations upon individuals. However, the Court gave a broad definition to the concept of the state, holding that the capacity in which the state was acting was irrelevant for the purposes of direct effect. In Case 152/84 *Marshall I* the directive was enforceable against a health authority (an "emanation of the state") acting as employer. The Court gave further guidance concerning the concept of "emanation of the state" for the purposes of direct effect of directives in Case C-188/89 *Foster* v *British Gas* [1990] ECR 3313. A directive may be enforced against "a body, whatever its legal form, which has been made responsible, pursuant to a measure adopted by the state, for providing a public service under the control of the state, and has for that purpose special powers beyond those which result from the normal rules applicable in relations

between individuals". This is potentially a very broad test, allowing individuals to rely upon the provisions of directives against many public and quasipublic authorities.

The Court has been invited by its advocates general on several occasions to reconsider its ruling in Case 152/84 *Marshall I* that directives are not horizontally directly effective, but on each occasion the Court has either avoided the issue (Case C-271/91 *Marshall II* [1993] ECR I-4367; Case C-316/93 *Vaneetveld* v *SA Le Foyer* [1994] ECR I-763) or confirmed its previous ruling (Case C-91/92 *Faccini Dori* [1994] ECR I-3325). In a few more recent decisions, the effect of the Court's ruling has been the "incidental" horizontal direct effect of a directive: however, it is not generally felt that these decisions affect the established position (see, e.g., Case C-194/94 *CIA Security* [1996] ECR I-2201).

State Liability

Where an individual suffers loss through a breach of Community law on the part of a member state, the state may be liable to that individual in damages. This principle of state liability was established in Cases C-6 & 9/90 *Francovich* v *Italian State* [1991] ECR I-5357, and elaborated in a number of subsequent rulings, including those in Cases C-46 and 48/93 *Brasserie du Pêcheur* and *Factortame III* [1996] ECR 1029, in which the Court confirmed that it applies to all breaches of Community law, not only the failure to implement a directive correctly.

State liability under this mechanism depends upon the nature of the breach of Community law that gave rise to the loss or damage. The Court has held that the rule of law infringed must have intended to confer rights on individuals, and that there must be a direct causal link between the breach and the damage. In addition, the breach must be "sufficiently serious". This final condition is difficult to satisfy. The Court has held that the actions of the member state must constitute a "manifest and grave" breach, amounting to a flagrant disregard of its obligations in Community law. Thus, in Cases C-6 and 9/90 *Francovich* this condition was satisfied, as there had been a ruling against the member state, Italy, establishing its breach, and Italy had failed to rectify the situation. In contrast, the condition was not satisfied in, for instance, Cases C-283 & 291/94 *Denkavit* [1996] ECR I-5063. Germany, the defendant member state, in common with almost all the other member states, had adopted a particular interpretation of a complex taxation directive. That interpretation turned out to be incorrect. The Court pointed out that "those member states took the view, following discussions in Council, that they were entitled to adopt such an interpretation". This was the first occasion on which the Court had pronounced on the correct interpretation of the directive. In these circumstances, the Court held that a "sufficiently serious breach" had not been established.

Indirect Effect

A third process for guaranteeing the applicability and supremacy of Community law within national legal orders is that of "indirect effect". This rule of interpretation was introduced by the Court in Case 14/83 *Von Colson* v *Land Nordrheinwestfalen* [1984] ECR 1891 and Case 79/83 *Harz* v *Deutsche Tradax* [1984] ECR 1921. These cases concerned the same directive (Directive 76/207/EEC), but in one case the employer was a prison – an "emanation of the state" – and in the other the employer was a private company. Rather than highlight the inequality arising from its ruling in Case 152/84 *Marshall I* on horizontal direct effect of directives, the Court concentrated upon Articles 5 (now 10) and 189 (now 249) TEC, explaining that the duty of member states to take all appropriate measures to comply with Community obligations is incumbent upon all authorities of the member states, including the courts. Therefore, national courts are under a duty in Community law to interpret national law in the light of the objectives of a relevant directive, in order to give effect to that directive. This rule of interpretation is a significant alternative to direct effect of directives, as it is unaffected by the distinction between public and private defendants.

The Court confirmed in Case C-106/89 *Marleasing* [1990] ECR I-4135 that the obligation extends to interpretation of *all* national law, not only national law introduced in order to implement the directive. However, national courts are required only to do "everything possible" to give effect to directives. It is not "possible" to provide a consistent interpretation that involves a breach of a general principle of Community law, such as that of legal certainty (Case 80/96 *Kolpinghuis Nijmegen* [1987] ECR 3969; Case C-168/95 *Arcaro* [1996] ECR I-4705). Nor is it "possible" for a national court to go beyond its national canons of interpretation (Case C-334/92 *Wagner Miret* [1993] ECR I-6911; Case C-192/94 *El Corte Inglès* [1996] ECR I-1281). This final caveat is potentially a significant restriction on the indirect effect process of enforcement of Community law.

Effective Remedies

The general rule is that provisions of Community law are enforceable by individuals, in the national courts, by means of the remedies provided for by national law (Case 33/76 *Rewe-Zentralfinanz* v *Saarland* [1976] ECR 1989). There are no special "European Community law remedies", apart from that of state liability, and there are no treaty provisions specifying which remedies should be available. However, the Court has refined this position by developing a number of principles concerning national remedies for Community rights.

The remedy available for a breach of Community law must be equivalent to the remedy that would be available for a comparable breach of national law. Every type of action available in national law must be available to enforce directly effective Community provisions: this is the "nondiscrimination" or "comparability" principle. Further, the remedy must not make it impossible in practice to exercise Community rights – the "effectiveness" principle (Case 45/76 *Comet* [1976] ECR 203; Case 158/80 *Rewe Handelsgesellschaft* [1981] ECR 1805). Remedies available must be real and effective, having a "real deterrent effect" in discouraging breaches of Community law (Case 79/83 *Harz* v *Deutsche Tradax*). These principles apply to the amount of compensation available (Case C-271/91 *Marshall II*) and to enforcement procedures, including limitation periods (Case C-208/90 *Emmott* [1991] ECR I-4269). However, more recent cases suggest that Case C-208/90 *Emmott* must be regarded as a "high water mark" ruling. The principle of effective remedies depends a great deal upon the details of the case in hand, and in particular the nature of the Community law rights being enforced (see, e.g. Case C-338/91 *Steenhorst Neerings* [1993] ECR I-5475; Case C-410/92 *Johnson II* [1994] ECR I-5483; Case C-66/95 *Sutton* [1997] ECR I-2163). This element of the way in which Community law takes effect in the member states thus remains the least developed to date.

The ability of individual citizens to enforce provisions of Community law before national judicial and administrative forums for the resolution of disputes has proved crucial to the development of Community law as an independent and unique legal order. Supremacy and direct applicability of Community law, instrumentalized through direct effect, state liability, indirect effect, and the principles of comparable and effective remedies, have ensured not only that individuals are the beneficiaries of Community rights, but also that the aims of Community law are carried out in the member states. The European Court of Justice claims to be the ultimate authority on the relationship between Community law and national law.

Some Examples of Response of National Courts

It is one thing for the European Court of Justice to pronounce upon the "constitutional status" of Community law and its relationship with national legal orders. It is quite another for these norms to be accepted by judicial authorities within the member states. The extent to which such norms have been so accepted may be regarded as testimony to the existence of the Community's legal order as a unique system that is neither of the species of international law, nor of domestic law, but has elements of both.

An account of the relationship between Community and national law based only on

the perspective of the Court would be hopelessly incomplete, and would present the evolution of the Community's "constitution" as merely a Court-led juristic exercise. A more complete, but nonetheless still unashamedly legal, perspective would be to include consideration of the responses of national judiciaries, in particular national constitutional courts, to the emerging doctrines of Community "constitutional law" discussed above. This perspective constructs the Community legal order as one that operates on a "multilevel" basis, and holds that "every national court is a Community court". The interactions and discourse between national courts and the Court are an essential element of the process of constitutionalization.

The Treaty of Rome envisages national authorities as the primary means of enforcement of provisions of Community law in the member states. Member states are obliged by their membership of the EU (Article 10 TEC) to make constitutional provision in order to guarantee the supremacy and direct applicability of Community law within their national legal orders. However, in a number of member states, respect for principles of democracy, as expressed through the "sovereignty" of national legislatures, and the separation of powers between the legislature and the judiciary, and for the guarantees of fundamental human rights led to a reluctance on the part of some national courts to give full effect to the principles of supremacy and direct effect of Community law.

Sovereignty

A reluctance to accept supremacy of Community law over a subsequent national law is evident even in the founder member states, as, for example, in the attitude of the Conseil d'Etat, the superior court of administrative law in France. In the eyes of the Conseil d'Etat, the national legislature was sovereign, so if national law conflicting with pre-existing Community law was enacted, effect would be given to the will of the legislature and not to the Community provision *(Semoules* 1 March 1968; *Cohn Bendit* [1980] 1 CMLR 543). More recently, however, the Conseil d'Etat has softened its position and it is now prepared to give priority to provisions of the treaties (*Nicolo* [1990] 1 CMLR 17), regulations (*Boisdet* [1991] 1 CMLR 3), and directives (*Philip Morris* [1993] 1 CMLR 253). Following the *Judgement of the Conseil Constitutionnel* (Constitutional Court) [1993] 3 CMLR 345, concerning the compatibility of the Maastricht amendments to the Treaty of Rome with the French Constitution, the Constitution was amended (almost 30 years after Case 6/64 *Costa* v *ENEL*) to include an explicit reference to transfer (or pooling) of sovereign powers to the EU (French Constitution, Title XV, Article 88–1).

In the United Kingdom, the reluctance of the courts to alter their longstanding deference to the doctrine of the sovereignty of Parliament inevitably led to difficulties over British compliance with Community law. Originally, the British courts were adamant that the source of the legal effect of Community provisions in national law was not the Treaty of Rome, as interpreted by the European Court of Justice, but the European Communities Act 1972, enacted by the British Parliament. The relevant sections of the Act provide that rights and duties that, according to Community law, are directly applicable or directly effective, are to be given legal effect in the UK, and that any existing or future measures of national law are to be interpreted and have effect subject to this provision. Judicial notice is to be taken of the rulings of the European Court of Justice concerning questions of interpretation and effect of Community law. The wording of the Act left it open to the British courts to give effect to directly effective provisions of Community law over contradictory national provisions not solely by virtue of the supremacy of Community law, but by means of a national statutory rule of interpretation. The European Communities Act 1972 requires that national law be interpreted in order to give effect to Community law (*Macarthys* v *Smith* [1979] 3 All ER 325; *Garland* v *BREL* [1982] 2 All ER 402; *Pickstone* v *Freemans* [1988] 2 All ER 803; *Litster* v *Forth Dry Dock Engineering* [1989] 1 All ER 1134). Parliamentary sovereignty is thus preserved, while effect is given to Community law in the United Kingdom.

However, the rule of interpretation approach is satisfactory only where the national law lends itself to the desired interpretation. It is not appropriate for resolving cases where an interpretation consistent with Community obligations cannot be sustained by the national provision. The House of Lords in the UK was faced with this situation in *Factortame* [1990] 3 CMLR 375, where the UK Merchant Shipping Act 1988 was contrary to provisions of the Treaty of Rome and, taking account of Parliament's purpose in enacting the legislation, could not be interpreted to comply with Community law. The judgement of Lord Bridge that "it has always been clear that it was the duty of a United Kingdom court . . . to override any rule of national law found to be in conflict with any directly enforceable rule of Community law", is evidence that, in some circumstances, the British courts will now recognize the supremacy of Community law explicitly and directly.

There are also examples of national courts embracing the doctrine of supremacy of Community law. For example, the courts in Ireland have accepted the principles of supremacy and direct effect of Community law from the beginning of that country's membership of the Community, in 1973. In *Pigs and Bacon Commission*, 30 June 1978, [1978] *Journal of the Irish Society of European Law* 87, it was held that Community law takes legal effect in the Irish system in the manner in which Community law itself provides. So, since Community law provides for supremacy of Community provisions over national provisions, Irish courts must give effect to that rule. Where Community law provides for direct applicability or direct effect of Community provisions in national law, Irish courts must ensure their application or effect. This is an example of a particularly "Community-minded" approach from national courts.

Fundamental Human Rights

The constitutions of several member states provide explicit guarantees of fundamental human rights. Fundamental rights are higher legal norms than all others applicable in the national legal system and so provisions of law conflicting with fundamental rights provisions may be set aside as unconstitutional. This position is potentially in conflict with the principle of supremacy of Community law, since a national court finding that a directly applicable measure of Community law infringed a national constitutional fundamental rights provision would be obliged to set aside the Community law.

The German Bundesverfassungsgericht (Constitutional Court) originally adopted a position that where there is a conflict between guarantees of fundamental rights in the German Grundgesetz (Basic Law, or Constitution) and in Community law, the fundamental rights prevail, so long as the European institutions have not resolved the conflict (So *Lange I* [1974] 2 CMLR 540). In other words, the Bundesverfassungsgericht reserved to itself the right, so long as the EU has no system of human rights, to supervise the application of Community law in Germany with respect to its conflict with fundamental rights. The European Court of Justice responded to this position with the assurance that fundamental rights were already protected in Community law, as general principles of law (Case 11/70 *Internationale Handelsgesellschaft* [1970] ECR 1125). The Bundesverfassungsgericht has subsequently modified its position by confirming that, so long as the European institutions, and in particular the European Court of Justice in its case law, generally ensure effective protection of fundamental rights similar to that guaranteed under the Basic Law of the Federal Republic, then the Bundesverfassungsgericht will no longer examine the compatibility of Community legislation with fundamental rights (So *Lange II* 3 CMLR 225). However, in *Brunner* [1994] 1 CMLR 57, the Bundesverfassungsgericht enunciated some potentially fundamental reservations about the Court's constitutional construct of Community law. The Bundesverfassungsgericht expressed the view that the transfer of sovereign powers to the EU was permissible only as far as it is compatible with the central tenets of German constitutional law: democracy, the rule of law, the essential content of the protection of fundamental rights, and

Germany's federal structure. Even more significantly, the Bundesverfassungsgericht held that competence to determine the scope of the Community's competence (*Kompetenz-Kompetenz*) remains ultimately at the seat of national constitutional courts. This perspective is fundamentally opposed to the Court's account of supremacy and its own view of its place in the Community's constitutional order.

Similarly, in Italy the national courts had some reservations about the concept of supremacy of Community law, in particular supremacy over national fundamental rights provisions. In *Frontini* [1974] 2 CMLR 372 the Corte Costituzionale (Constitutional Court), while confirming that, in general, provisions of Community law have "full compulsory efficacy and direct application" in Italy, held that if a Community provision violated fundamental constitutional principles or principles of human rights the Corte Costituzionale would ensure that Community law was compatible with those principles. In the subsequent case of *Granital* No 170 of 8 June 1984 (see *Common Market Law Review*, 21, 1984, p. 765) the Corte Costituzionale expressly affirmed the principle of supremacy of Community law, but reiterated its caveat from *Frontini* concerning review of Community provisions in terms of their consistency with the protection of fundamental rights.

In Ireland, the conflict between the protection of fundamental human rights and Community law has been particularly difficult. Although, in general, Irish courts respect the approach of the European Court of Justice to the principle of supremacy of Community law, this fidelity was tested to its limit in litigation over the distribution of information about abortion, which remains illegal in the Republic. The conflict here seemed to be between the provision of the Irish Constitution prohibiting abortion and the Community provisions concerning freedom to provide services, including medical services. In *SPUC* v *Grogan* [1990] 1 CMLR 689, the Irish Supreme Court refused to grant interim relief while the substantive issue was referred to the European Court of Justice, a course of action that Community law seems to require (see Case

C-213/89 *Factortame*). The Irish Supreme
Court further hinted that it would be prepared
to deny supremacy to Community law in the
event of a direct conflict with a national constitutional provision concerning fundamental
rights. However, this situation did not arise, as
the European Court of Justice held on the facts
of this particular case that, as an "economic
nexus" between the students advertising the
abortion service and the clinics providing it was
absent, no entitlement in Community law had
been breached (Case C-159/90 *SPUC* v *Grogan*
[1991] ECR I-4685). What the position would
be if a true conflict arose between Community law and such a provision of the Irish
Constitution remains unresolved.

Conclusion

It seems that any conflict between the
approach of the Court and that of the national
courts concerning supremacy and direct
applicability may be increasingly regarded as
being merely of historical interest. However,
the related question of *Kompetenz-Kompetenz* (see
Chapter 17, and above) remains very much a
live issue. National judiciaries may accept
Community law as supreme and directly
applicable, but this applies only to *validly enacted*
Community law. Moreover, the issue of the
extent to which national courts applying Community law are obliged to alter national procedures and remedies remains incomplete in its
resolution. Thus, the details of the instrumen-
talization of Community law's constitutional
qualities in practice are still being elaborated, through a continuing dialogue between
national courts and the European Court of
Justice.

Further Reading (also for Chapter 17)

Arnull, Anthony, *The European Union and Its Court of
  Justice*, Oxford and New York: Oxford University
  Press, 1999

  A detailed legal account of the contribution that
  the Court has made to the integration process
  and to specific policy fields

Bogdandy, A. von, "The Legal Case for Unity: The
  European Union as a Single Organisation with

a Single Legal System", *Common Market Law
  Review*, 36, 1999, pp. 887–910

  An alternative view of the coherence and cohesiveness of the EU legal order after the Treaty
  of Maastricht

Chalmers, Damian, *European Union Law*, Volume 1,
  Law and EU Government, Aldershot: Dartmouth, 1998

  A detailed contextual analysis of the relevant
  principles of Community law, with a great deal
  of theoretical and other background information
  and comment

Craig, Paul, and Gráinne de Búrca, *EU Law: Text,
  Cases and Materials*, second edition, Oxford and
  New York: Oxford University Press, 1998

  This text covers Community "constitutional" and
  "substantive" law, which makes it very long. It is
  an authoritative discussion and analysis by two
  distinguished scholars, with an accessible style
  and detailed content.

Curtin, D., "The Constitutional Structure of the
  Union: A Europe of Bits and Pieces", *Common
  Market Law Review*, 30, 1993, pp. 17–69

  A classic work on the fragmented nature of the
  legal order after the ratification of the Maastricht
  Treaty

Dehousse, Renaud, *The European Court of Justice: The
  Politics of Judicial Integration*, London: Macmillan,
  and New York: St Martin's Press, 1998

  An important work that places the Court and its
  actions within the framework of political actors
  and pressures

Hartley, Trevor C., *The Foundations of European
  Community Law*, fourth edition, Oxford and New
  York: Oxford University Press, 1998

  The leading "doctrinal" textbook on the "constitutional" aspect of Community law, as opposed
  to the substantive law, with detailed scholarly
  analysis of all relevant provisions and principles.
  This is law for lawyers, so it tends to lack political context.

Mancini, G.F., *Democracy and Constitutionalism in the
  European Union*, Oxford: Hart, 2000

  A collection of thought-provoking and enlight-
  ening essays written from an insider's perspective, Mancini having been both an Advocate
  General and a Judge of the European Court of
  Justice

Mancini, G.F., "The Making of a Constitution for Europe", *Common Market Law Review*, 26, 1989, pp. 595–614

The story of the "constitutionalization" of the Treaty of Rome by the ECJ, from a respected former Advocate General and Judge of the ECJ.

Shaw, Jo, *Law of the European Union*, third edition, London: Macmillan, 2000

This is the best short introduction to the "constitutional" elements of Community law. It contains incisive analysis and, with its contextual presentation, is well structured, with a view to introducing the central concepts of Community constitutional law.

Slaughter, Anne-Marie, Alec Stone Sweet and J.H.H. Weiler, (editors), *The European Court and National Courts: Doctrine and Jurisprudence*, Oxford: Hart, 1998

A collection of detailed national reports on the reception of Community law in national legal orders, with a number of comparative essays considering concerns of legal theory arising from comparative analysis of the reports

Weiler, J.H.H., *The Constitution of Europe*, Cambridge and New York: Cambridge University Press, 1999

A collection of Professor Weiler's scholarly, contextual, critical, normative, even at times impassioned essays, spanning ten years

---

Tamara K. Hervey is Professor of Law at the University of Nottingham. She is the author of *European Social Law and Policy* (1998), and has contributed articles and chapters to journals and edited collections, focusing on sex discrimination, labour and social welfare law, and European Community "constitutional" law. She is currently working, under a Leverhulme Fellowship, on a book about European health law and policy.

Chapter Nineteen

Cooperation on Justice and Home Affairs

Helen Xanthaki

For an explanation of the way in which cases and legislation are referred to, please consult the Guide to Citation at the end of Chapter 17.

Historical Background and Legal Basis

Although the field of justice and home affairs is widely regarded as one of the newer areas of Community policy, its seeds can be traced to the Naples Convention of 1967 on cooperation and mutual assistance between customs administrations. This provided the first framework for exchanges between the national authorities of member states in the field of security and justice. It opened the way for further collaboration, organized in schemes such as the Trevi Group, which coordinated initiatives to combat terrorism and international crime, or the Schengen Convention of 1985 on the abolition of internal border controls and the harmonization of measures on visas, asylum, and police and judicial cooperation.

After the Single European Act of 1987 defined the internal market as "an area without internal frontiers" that included the free movement of people as well as goods, services and capital, it was recognized that a formalized framework of cooperation in aspects of justice and home affairs was needed. Title VI (Articles K1-K9) of the Maastricht Treaty of 1993 – the Treaty on European Union (TEU) – introduced a third pillar covering asylum policy, the crossing of external borders, customs, immigration, drugs, international fraud, judicial cooperation in civil and criminal matters, and police

cooperation. The decision-making processes on justice and home affairs were to be similar to those used in decision-making on the common foreign and security policy. Three types of legal instruments were available: joint positions, incorporating the common position of member states on a particular topic or point; joint decisions, furthering collaboration in cases where a common approach would achieve better results compared to national measures from individual member states; and conventions, resembling the relevant sources of international law and requiring a lengthy process of ratification.

Some of the problems deriving from the TEU were detrimental to the advancement of cooperation: for example, the Commission's right of initiative was limited and shared with the member states, the paucity of information passed on to the European Parliament restricted its ability to take part in the legislative process, the jurisdiction of the European Court of Justice (ECJ) was limited to only those third-pillar instruments that expressly subjected themselves to it, and the Council was bound by the unanimity requirement.

These problems were partially resolved by the Treaty of Amsterdam (signed in 1997 and ratified in 1999), which in Articles 61–69 (formerly Articles 73i–73q) established "an area of freedom, security and justice", incorporated the Schengen Convention into the EU's *acquis*, although with opt-outs for Ireland and the United Kingdom, and set a five-year deadline for the adoption of measures to prevent and combat organized crime and terrorism. The Treaty of Amsterdam also transferred external border controls, asylum, immigration, and judicial cooperation in civil matters into the first pillar, while maintaining – at least for the first five years – unanimity for Council decisions, shared power of initiative between the Commission and member states, and mere consultation of the European Parliament. The third pillar now includes police and judicial cooperation on criminal matters, racism, and xenophobia. The Commission has been given the power of initiative, albeit still shared with member states, and the Parliament has a clearer advisory role. The ECJ has jurisdiction to hear preliminary rulings on the interpretation of third-pillar instruments, actions for annulment of framework decisions or decisions by the Commission or member states, and disputes between member states on the application or interpretation of third-pillar instruments, so long as the six-month deadline for the resolution of the dispute by the Council has expired. Conventions now enter into force subject to ratification by only half of the signatory states. Joint actions have been abolished as third-pillar instruments and replaced by framework decisions, equivalent to directives setting out goals to be achieved by the most suitable measures within each member state, and decisions, equivalent to the implementing measures of framework decisions.

Assuming that the Treaty of Nice, signed in 2001, is eventually ratified and enters into force, it will introduce qualified majority voting (QMV) for cooperation in the field of civil matters, with the exception of family law. Unanimity for police and judicial cooperation in criminal matters will be removed. In the area of asylum and immigration, QMV will apply only after 2004, and will not cover either the conditions of entry and residence for third-country nationals or the "sharing of the burden" of receiving refugees. The Treaty will also incorporate the conclusions of the Tampere summit on Eurojust, a chamber of magistrates of national courts, as a means of enhancing cooperation between judicial and other relevant national authorities, and facilitating the fight against international crime.

Free Movement of Persons

The Treaty of Rome had as one of its objectives the "free movement of persons", and this right was extended in the Maastricht Treaty to give the EU's citizens the right to travel, live, and work in any member state under the same conditions – that is, with the same rights and obligations – as nationals of the host state. These conditions include guarantees of the right to participate in elections for both the European Parliament and the local authorities in the host country; the right to seek diplomatic protection by the authorities of any member state; access to judicial and quasijudicial authorities of the host state under the conditions introduced for nationals of that state; and the same employment rights as nationals of the state.

Free movement, however, is primarily understood to mean the abolition of controls on the internal frontiers of the EU and the harmonization of entry rules for third-country nationals. In 1985 five member states decided to try to realize this goal by signing the Schengen Convention, an intergovernmental agreement outside the legal framework of the Community. Additional member states followed and when it entered into force in 1995 the Convention covered Belgium, France, Germany, Luxembourg, the Netherlands, Portugal, and Spain. Following the Treaty of Amsterdam, the Schengen Convention became part of EU law on 1 May 1999, and it now extends to all member states except the United Kingdom and Ireland which have not yet decided to sign the agreement (*OJ* 1999 L119). Denmark has signed the Convention but has retained the option to decide whether subsequent measures agreed under it will be applicable to its territory or not. Iceland and Norway, members of the longstanding Nordic passport union with three EU member states (Denmark, Finland, and Sweden), take part in an extra-EU Committee (*OJ* 1999 C211), deciding on the application of Schengen measures to their territories (*OJ* 2000 L15). On 1 December 2000 the Council adopted a decision applying the Schengen *acquis* to Denmark, Finland, Iceland, Norway, and Sweden (Decision 2000/777/EC, *OJ* 2000 L309). The Commission has also accepted a request from Ireland to participate in the part of Schengen related to police and judicial cooperation on criminal matters, drugs, and the Schengen Information System (SEC (2000) 1439).

The Schengen Convention abolishes all internal borders and creates a single area with external borders that are subject to common rules on passport control, visas, and asylum. Separate air terminals and ports for people travelling within the Schengen area are being created. For third-country travellers, entry and short-stay visas are awarded under harmonized rules, all third-country nationals must declare their movements between the Schengen countries, rules for asylum-seekers are harmonized, and the right of surveillance and nonpursuit has been introduced. The roles and tasks of border administrators are coordinated, and they have automatic access to information on persons and vehicles stored on the Schengen Information System. In 2001 the new network, which includes information on immigration, unified the data available to all national border authorities, thus, it was hoped, guaranteeing security within the EU.

Immigration and Asylum

The Treaty of Amsterdam set out a number of objectives aimed at creating a common approach in the area of immigration and asylum. Articles 61, 62, and 63 TEC cover the main points of policy in this area. They include the removal of controls for all persons crossing internal EU frontiers, common rules for the crossing of external EU frontiers, and harmonized conditions for the free circulation within the EU of third-country nationals for a maximum period of three months. There will also be standardized criteria for judging requests for asylum, minimum standards of treatment for refugees and displaced persons from third countries, measures against illegal immigration, a common definition of residence rights for third-country nationals, and common measures on entry and stay for third-country nationals and members of their families.

The majority of these objectives must be met within five years from the Treaty's entry into force, under the framework set in the conclu-

sions of the meeting of the European Council in Tampere in 1999. The task of introducing legislation for the achievement of these aims lies with both the Commission and the member states until 2004, when the Commission will acquire sole power of initiative. All proposals require unanimity in the Council. Despite the fact that the provisions on the free movement of persons come under the first pillar, the jurisdiction of the ECJ on issues of immigration and asylum is restricted by Article 68 TEC. Preliminary rulings are admissible only on three conditions: that national courts of last resort have referred to the Court; that the issue for which clarification is sought does not form part of a national judgment, having become *res judicata*; and that the issue is not related to the manner in which law and order are maintained in the member state concerned. However, quite unusually in EU law, the Council and the Commission have the same right to request a preliminary ruling as member states have.

The Treaty of Nice (again, assuming ratification) will amend Article 67 TEC by introducing a partial and deferred switch to QMV by means of protocols or political declarations. However, QMV will begin only from 1 May 2004, or after the adoption of Community legislation on the common rules and basic principles of immigration and asylum policy. Even when the new voting regime is applied, it will not concern the central elements of the policy on asylum and immigration, such as the conditions for entry and residence of third-country nationals in Article 63(3)a TEC, or the "sharing of the burden" in Article 63(2)b TEC. The opt-outs for the United Kingdom, Ireland, and Denmark will be maintained.

Measures taken to attain the EU's goals in the area of asylum and immigration include Council Decision 2000/596/EC, on the creation of a European Refugee Fund, and a number of resolutions of the Council, predating the Treaty of Amsterdam, on the strict conditions for family reunion for third-country nationals with an expectation for long-term residence (SN 2828/93), on the exceptional nature of admission for temporary employment (*OJ* 1996 C274/3), on the conditions of entry for the self-employed (*OJ* 1996 C274/4), on the expiry of student visas after the end of studies (*OJ* 1996 C274/10), on the principles to be taken into account before the review of national immigration laws (*OJ* 1996 C80/2), and on "marriages of convenience" (*OJ* 1997 C382/1). The Joint Action on resident permit formats (*OJ* 1997 L7/1) and the Joint Action on the annual exchange of information on repatriation (11903/96 of 22 November 1996) are measures for the protection of the EU, rather than means to aid immigrants.

The Dublin Convention of 1990 established the important principle that an application for asylum should be considered by only one EU member state, and established the guidelines for determining which state is responsible for examining it. Current proposals include a regulation on the criteria to be used in assessing applications for asylum within the framework of the Convention and a regulation on EURODAC, a system for the computerized comparison of asylum-seekers' fingerprints to guard against multiple applications for asylum status. Other initiatives include proposals for a directive on minimum standards of granting and withdrawing refugee status, a communication on a common asylum policy, and a directive on the conditions for the reception of asylum-seekers.

For those who reach the EU and manage to apply to the appropriate country under the Dublin Convention, an asylum application may be rejected on the basis of the seeker's opportunity to seek asylum in a safe third country, which would render the application "manifestly unfounded" under the London Resolution of 1992. Only those who overcome these hurdles may have the opportunity to have their case heard, but only provided that they fall within the scope of application of the Geneva Convention of 1951 or the New York Protocol of 1967, as enshrined in the Joint Position of 1996 on the concept of refugees (*OJ* 1996 L63/2).

The United Kingdom and Ireland have opted out of Title IV (ex IIIa) TEC introduced by the Treaty of Amsterdam, thus acquiring the right to refrain from applying any measures falling within the scope of asylum and immigration, while exempting themselves from the duty to finance EU policy in these areas.

Similarly, Denmark has decided to opt out of this policy; however, the relevant Danish Protocol awards Denmark the right to opt into the policy as a package, rather than on a selective basis, as is the case with the British and Irish Protocol.

The parallel existence of two legal regimes in the areas of asylum and immigration within the territory of the EU creates obvious dangers of discrimination for both EU nationals and third-country immigrants or asylum seekers. The prospect of an influx of refugees and immigrants into the most lenient country of the EU, and its use as a common first and, under the Dublin Convention, only port of call, is accentuated by the apparent lack of tangible harmonization of rules even among the Schengen states. The situation will continue even under the Treaty of Nice and it is an indication of the huge diversities among member states that the intergovernmental conference in 2000 made little progress towards greater harmonization.

Judicial Cooperation in Civil Matters

The issue of judicial cooperation in civil matters is addressed by Articles 65 and 293 (formerly Article 220) TEC. Civil cooperation began with Article 220 of the original Treaty of Rome, which provided the legal basis for negotiations among member states on the simplification of formalities for the reciprocal recognition and enforcement of court judgements.

This Article, and subsequent Articles K.1(6) and K.3(2)(c) TEU, served as the legal basis for a number of conventions, including the Brussels Convention of 1968 and the Lugano Convention of 1988, which dealt with judicial powers and the enforcement of judgements in civil and commercial matters; the Convention of 1995 on insolvency proceedings; the Rome Convention of 1980 on the law applicable to contractual obligations; and the second Brussels Convention of 1998 on the country in which divorce applications must be filed, and on the conditions for the recognition and enforcement of judgements reached in other member states, which has now been replaced, except for

Denmark, by Council Regulation 1347/2000 (*OJ* 2000 L160).

However, in view of the ineffectiveness of conventions as instruments for implementing legislation, the intergovernmental conference in 1996 was faced with the task of achieving cooperation between national authorities to ensure complete free movement for EU citizens (natural and legal persons) who suffer from the intricacies of crossborder litigation, especially in the fields of divorce, matrimony, inheritance, and arbitration. The Treaty of Amsterdam transferred cooperation in civil matters into the first pillar. Article 65 (formerly Article 73m) TEC sets out the goals of the EU in the area of judicial cooperation in civil matters: improvement and simplification of crossborder service of legal documents, collection of evidence, and recognition and enforcement of judicial decisions in civil and commercial cases; promotion of compatible rules on the conflict of laws and on jurisdiction; and elimination of obstacles to the good functioning of civil proceedings.

The conclusions of the meeting of the European Council in Tampere in 1999 outlined the future for EU policy in the area of collaboration in civil law. Three main areas of action were identified as the immediate priorities: allowing easy and direct access to justice; enhancing the mutual recognition of civil judgements; and enabling convergence in the area of procedural law.

Access to justice for EU citizens is to be achieved through the gradual introduction of the European Judicial Network in civil and commercial matters, with a mandate to improve judicial cooperation in these fields while providing nonlawyers with information facilitating access to justice in cases of crossborder litigation (COM(2000)592). The Commission's Green Paper on legal aid in civil matters (COM/2000/0051/final) contained proposals for the provision of legal aid to all citizens, including those resident in countries other than that of origin and those involved in crossborder litigation.

Mutual recognition is to be achieved on the basis of the "Programme of Measures for Implementation of the Principle of Mutual Recognition of Decisions in Civil and Com-

mercial Matters" (*OJ* 2001 C12) adopted by the Justice and Home Affairs Council on 30 November 2000. The programme eliminates obstacles in the enforcement of civil judgement on crossborder disputes for small claims, noncontested claims, and family law disputes. Council Regulation 44/2001/EC introduces common standards on jurisdiction, and on recognition and enforcement of civil and commercial judicial decisions (*OJ* 2001 L12), whereas Council Regulation 1347/2000/EC refers to the same issues albeit in relation to divorce, separation, annulment of marriage, and parental responsibility for children of both spouses (*OJ* 2000 L160). Regulation 1346/2000/EC resolves the problems of insolvency proceedings (*OJ* 2000 L160), while Regulation 1348/2000/EC has been unsuccessful in attempting to introduce a simplified and brief common method of service of judicial and extrajudicial documents (*OJ* 2000 L160).

Little success has been achieved in realizing the third priority of the Treaty of Amsterdam, the standardization of procedural rules. The issue is neglected in the Treaty of Nice, which does not refer to judicial cooperation in the field of civil law.

Police and Customs Cooperation

The seeds of customs cooperation, which was a priority for the European Economic Community in its early years, can be found in the Naples Convention of 1967 on cooperation and mutual assistance between customs administrations. In 1995 the Customs Information System (CIS) for the exchange of data on drug-trafficking and military material was established.

The seeds of police cooperation can be traced in the first Trevi groups on terrorism and the organization of police departments, which began their work in 1976. By 1989 the mandate of what by then were four Trevi groups was to act as "think tanks" for the Council of Ministers in the areas of police cooperation, organized crime, the free movement of persons, and terrorism.

The Schengen system established a corps of liaison officers within each of the signatory states responsible for the exchange of information on organized crime, illegal immigration, drugs, and terrorism. Under Schengen, police officers may pursue a suspect in the territory of other member states, while multinational patrols carry out checks within the Schengen territory.

Article K.1(9) of the Maastricht Treaty provided the basis for greater police and customs cooperation as a means of preventing and combating terrorism, unlawful drug-trafficking, and other serious forms of international crime. It also proposed the establishment of an EU-wide system for exchanging information within a European Police Office (Europol).

The Treaty of Amsterdam in Article 29 (formerly K1) identifies "closer cooperation between police forces, customs authorities, and other competent authorities in the Member States" as one of the key means of creating an area of security and justice. Article 30 determines police cooperation as operational collaboration for the prevention, detection, and investigation of criminal offences; collaboration on, and exchange of, information and data, mainly though Europol; cooperation and joint activities in the areas of training, exchange of personnel and equipment, and forensic research; and common evaluation of investigative techniques used for the prevention and combat of organized crime.

The creation of Europol was first raised in 1991, at a meeting of the European Council in Luxembourg. The Europol Convention was signed in 1995 but entered into force as late as 1998. However, from as early as 1995 a temporary Europol Drugs Unit was set up to promote cooperation in the areas of drug-trafficking and money-laundering. Its terms of reference were subsequently extended to cover measures to combat trafficking in radioactive and nuclear substances, clandestine immigration networks, vehicle-trafficking, and money-laundering associated with these criminal activities. The fight against trade in human beings was also added later. In January 1999 Europol was awarded additional powers to combat terrorism and the counterfeiting of currency.

Article 30.2 TEC authorizes the Council to adopt measures enabling Europol to facilitate, support, and coordinate specific investigative operations by the competent authorities of the member states; to ask the competent authorities of the member states to conduct their investigations and to develop specific expertise that may be put at the disposal of other member states to assist them in investigating cases of organized crime; and to promote close cooperation between prosecuting/investigating officials specializing in the fight against organized crime.

Current initiatives in the area of police and customs cooperation include the new European Police College, offering, from 2001 onwards, training courses for national police personnel; the establishment of a task force of European police chiefs; and the creation of joint police/customs command centres. The Council is also engaged in negotiations over football hooliganism, exchanging information and experience on the subject, and defining common rules on stadium bans and media attitudes.

The Fight against Organized Crime

The free movement of persons, goods, and capital within the EU has the unfortunate side-effect of creating unique opportunities for organized crime. Following the enhancement of police and juridical cooperation in the 1990s, the European Council, at its meeting in Tampere in 1999, called for an efficient and comprehensive approach to the fight against all forms of transnational crime leading (it was hoped) to a balanced development of EU-wide measures against crime while protecting the freedom and legal rights of individuals and economic operators. Thus, the fight against organized crime consists of crime prevention, punishment of criminals, and deprivation of the rewards of their crime. The main focus of EU policy in this respect is on trafficking in human beings, the sexual exploitation of women and children, cybercrime, terrorism, drug-trafficking, economic crime, and environmental crime.

Probably the most successful Commission initiative in this area concerns money-laundering. Despite the considerable diversity within the national legal orders of member states, the Money-laundering Directive (91/308/EEC), as amended, is now in force. The directive had been criticized as inadequate because it lacked provision on joint indictments for some of the most serious crimes, and because it limited the definition of money-laundering to cover the proceeds of certain crimes only. The amended directive defines money-laundering as the intentional conversion, transfer, concealment, use, possession or acquisition of any type of property originating from any type of criminal activity, thus exclusively defining the precise actions or omissions that fall within the scope of the legislation. The new directive clarifies the particular obligations imposed on financial institutions, credit institutions, and vulnerable professions as a means of combating organized crime. Indeed, the sectors covered by these obligations have been extended to include not only financial and credit institutions, now clearly defined, but also professions engaged in types of activity that render them vulnerable to criminals.

In response to the request of the European Council, meeting in Vienna, for measures to enhance the fight against organized crime within the framework of the Treaty of Amsterdam, on 27 March 2000 the Council adopted an action programme entitled "The Prevention and Control of Organized Crime: A European Strategy for the Beginning of the New Millennium" (*OJ* 2000 C124). This puts forward a large number of recommendations for such measures. The focus remains on the policy against drug dependency, and on the need for cooperation among national judicial and police authorities of the member states and third countries.

The future of the fight against organized crime within the EU seems to be linked to the creation of an EU-wide crime prevention network. Although a relevant measure has not yet been taken, the Council has decided that this would be a positive step. The Commission seems to share this approach (COM(2000)786).

Judicial Cooperation in Criminal Matters

Reaching agreement on any form of common legal text in the area of judicial cooperation in criminal matters has proved to be extremely difficult for the member states of the EU.

Despite the binding force of the Strasbourg European Convention on Mutual Assistance (1958), the Strasbourg Additional Protocol on Mutual Assistance (1978), Chapter 2 of the Benelux Treaty of 1962, and the Schengen Implementation Convention of 1990, and notwithstanding the declarations of the need for a European system of effective judicial cooperation in criminal matters, repeated both in the TEU and in the Treaty of Amsterdam, effective cooperation on criminal matters has so far eluded the EU. Although Council resolutions have been adopted in this area, they refer to sporadic specialized and technical issues, as in the convention on simplified extradition procedure between the member states of the EU, agreed in 1995 (*OJ* 1995 C78), the Council resolution of 1995 on the lawful interception of telecommunications (*OJ* 1996 C329), or the Joint Action of 1998 on the European Image Archiving System (FADO) (*OJ* 1998 L351), or the Council resolution of 1999 on the introduction of penal sanctions against counterfeiting in connection with the introduction of the euro (*OJ* 1999 C171).

More generalized measures have proved to be ineffective. In fact, notwithstanding their political value as expressions of common agreement on the need for them, most instruments intended to promote general cooperation have been widely criticized for having little practical value, as, for example, was the case with the Joint Action of 1996 on a framework of exchange of liaison magistrates (*OJ* 1996 L105), or the Joint Action of 1998 on good practice in mutual legal assistance in criminal matters (*OJ* 1998 L191). One of the more successful initiatives in this field has been the European Judicial Network, which was introduced in September 1998 as a unit aiming to encourage and facilitate mutual assistance by establishing direct contact between law practitioners responsible for judicial cooperation in criminal matters. As a result of this contact, law practitioners acquire information on the international and European instruments applicable to individual cases.

At Tampere the European Council introduced a list of priorities for the enhancement of judicial cooperation in criminal matters between member states. These include facilitating and accelerating cooperation between competent ministries and judicial or equivalent authorities of the member states in relation to proceedings and the enforcement of decisions; facilitating extradition between member states; ensuring compatibility of rules applicable in the member states, as may be necessary to improve such cooperation; preventing conflicts of jurisdiction between member states; and progressively adopting measures establishing minimum rules relating to the constituent elements of criminal acts and penalties in the fields of organized crime, terrorism, and illicit drug-trafficking. The Council also introduced Eurojust, a team of national experts and magistrates that aims to facilitate judicial cooperation on cases of serious organized crime.

The possibility of achieving effective judicial cooperation in criminal matters seems less remote after the Council Act of 29 May 2000 establishing the Convention on Mutual Assistance in Criminal Matters between the Member States of the EU (*OJ* 2000 C197). This identifies various routes for making progress on criminal judicial cooperation, mainly by facilitating specific forms of mutual assistance, by establishing minimum standards for the lawful interception of communication, and by guaranteeing uniform data protection. The European Parliament endorsed the Convention, subject to amendments, on 14 November 2000. In particular, the Parliament amended the initial draft in order to ensure that a member state refusing a request for mutual assistance, on the basis that such a request amounted to a circumvention of the fundamental guarantees enshrined in its national law, provided a written reply to that request within a maximum period of two months. The Parliament was also eager to establish that the principle of confidentiality, particularly with respect to the confidentiality of members of the legal professions, cannot be used as a means of refusing mutual assistance under the Convention.

The Treaty of Nice (if ratified) will amend Article 29 TEC by emphasizing the role of Eurojust as a means of achieving effective cooperation in criminal matters. Under Article 31 TEC, as amended by the Treaty of Nice, Eurojust will acquire a clear and extensive mandate to facilitate "proper" coordination of national prosecuting authorities, to support criminal investigations in cases of serious cross-border crime through the use of analyses carried out by Europol, and to facilitate letters rogatory and extradition requests in collaboration with the European Judicial Network.

The Future

EU activity in the field of justice and home affairs has suffered from its fragmentation into pillars 1 and 2 as a result of the Treaty of Amsterdam. Although the eagerness of a number of member states to proceed towards greater collaboration must be noted, the resistance of others to taking part in most of the initiatives intended to advance common action in this area cannot be underestimated. Although the transfer of almost half of this field into the first pillar guarantees further integration in the areas of free movement of persons, fundamental rights, and cooperation on civil matters, the parallel introduction of different clusters of collaboration, through Schengen and other Conventions, seems likely to create divergent standards of free movement for EU citizens, thus, perhaps, circumventing the principle of nondiscrimination due to nationality. The Treaty of Nice attempts to rationalize this fragmentation through the abolition of unanimity in the first pillar and the introduction of a more flexible ratification process for Conventions in the third pillar. It remains to be seen whether this attempt will bear fruit. Nevertheless, most commentators expect that justice and home affairs will continue to offer examples of applied integration of variable speeds for the foreseeable future.

Further Reading

European Commission, *Memorandum to the Members of the Commission: Summary of the Treaty of Nice SEC (2001)* 99

The best brief yet complete analysis to date of the effect of the Treaty of Nice on EU law

Glöckler, Gabriel, Lee Junius, Gioia Scappucci, Simon Usherwood, and Julian Vassallo, *Guide to EU Policies*, London: Blackstone Press, 1998

An excellent, albeit brief, overview of justice and home affairs under the Treaty of Amsterdam, with an exceptional diagram showing the roles of EU institutions in this area

Hailbronner, Kay, and Patrick Weil, *From Schengen to Amsterdam: Towards a European Immigration and Asylum Legislation*, Trier: Academy of European Law Trier, 1999

A collection of essays (in English, French, and German) on immigration and asylum policy at the EU and national levels before the signing of the Treaty of Nice, including an interesting part on refugee law within the EU and international perspectives

Monar, Jörg, "Justice and Home Affairs in the Treaty of Amsterdam: Reform at the Price of Fragmentation", *European Law Review*, 23, 1998, pp. 320–35

One of the best discussions of the effect of fragmentation of legal norms in the area of justice and home affairs

Peers, Steve, *EU Justice and Home Affairs Law*, London: Longman, 2000

The most recent and comprehensive book on Justice and Home Affairs before the signing of the Treaty of Nice, this provides authoritative analysis of all main aspects of the topic, including primary sources and case law. It is essential reading for students and lawyers.

Peers, Steve, "Justice and Home Affairs: Decision-Making after Amsterdam", *European Law Review*, 25, 2000, pp. 183–91

An interesting piece on the history of justice and home affairs, with particular reference to the impact of the Treaty of Amsterdam. It includes an interesting approach to the "flexible" yet complex relationship between the law applicable to countries within Schengen and that of the two member states that opted out.

Stefanou, Constantin, and Helen Xanthaki, "The EU Draft Money-laundering Directive: A Case of Interinstitutional Synergy", *Journal of Money-laundering Control*, 3, 2000, pp. 325–35

An analysis of the text and the synergistic work of the EU institutions for the compromises that led to the new Money-laundering Directive

---

Dr Helen Xanthaki is Senior Research Fellow in Legislative Studies and Academic Director of the Sir William Dale Centre for Legislative Studies of the Institute of Advanced Legal Studies, University of London. She has contributed articles and chapters to books and journals, in Britain and elsewhere, in the areas of EU law, comparative law, and legislative drafting.

Chapter Twenty

The EU Charter of Fundamental Rights

Mike Meehan

The recognition and protection of human rights at the international level has taken on an increased importance in recent years, in legal discourse as in public debate. The empowering nature of this discourse has led to an accumulation of competing rights claims, with ever-wider scope and application. The Pinochet case and the justifications for intervention in Kosovo are high-profile examples of how the importance of the notion of the protection of rights and their promotion has come to symbolize the present *Zeitgeist* of legal and political discourse. Indeed, one could legitimately ask if human rights have become the principle of the age.

In recent years, and to an even greater extent, the EU and its development as a polity have also become sources for this discourse. In its external dealings, the European Community has long demanded conformity with internationally established standards of human rights in return for trade agreements, through the inclusion of "human rights clauses", and more recently the EU has begun developing a foreign and security policy that, it is claimed, is based on particular values that respect human rights, as, for instance, in Article 11(1) of the Treaty on European Union, or TEU. Internally, treaty provisions, declarations of the institutions, and the case law of the European Court of Justice (ECJ) have made loud claims that rights are being protected. However, the exposed faultline at the heart of these claims has been the fact that the acts of the EU's institutions, or of their agents – as when member states act on behalf of the institutions in imple-

menting EU law – are not subject to direct supervision of their respect for human rights, or lack of it, in relation to some legally enforceable set of principles or rights. Respect for fundamental rights is ensured only in that they can be shown to be general principles of Community law that are consistent with the objectives of the Community and the EU. Since the accession of the Community to the European Convention on Human Rights (ECHR) has been rejected unless by treaty amendment (*Opinion 2/94* [1996] ECR I-1759), there has been no guarantee for the EU's citizens that their rights will be protected in the same way that they are protected under domestic law, whether through statutory provisions or through constitutional bills of rights, or under international law, through conventions and other agreements on rights.

These concerns have been among the main sources of inspiration behind the expansion of a discourse on human rights within the Community legal order, culminating in the decision of the European Council, meeting in Cologne in June 1999, to establish an EU Charter of Fundamental Rights.

The Background to the Charter

The Role of the European Court of Justice

One might expect that the driving force behind promoting the discourse of rights to a position of prominence and influence within the EU would have been some or all of the political institutions – the Council, the European Parliament, and the Commission. Nothing could be further from reality. Rather, the development of rights protection within the EU has been characterized by judicial activity.

No specific reference to a commitment to protect human rights was made in the founding treaties. The most obvious explanation for this was that the original function of the treaties was to provide a framework for the development of an economic space guided by liberal free market principles. Constitutional or legislative provisions at the national level were considered the appropriate mechanisms for protecting rights, while instruments such as the ECHR obliged states to meet certain standards at the international level. However, the continual increase in the scope of Community law and competences, together with the incremental development of the notions of supremacy and direct effect by the ECJ, led to rising fears that the potential for violations of human rights by the Community institutions, or by member states implementing Community law, was becoming a palpable reality. In building its own judicial precedents over time the Court took the initiative over other institutions in opening the potential for a discourse on rights within the Community order, in response to arguments presented by applicants in litigation.

In fact, the ECJ originally refused to entertain the possibility of finding acts of the Community institutions to be unlawful on the grounds of a violation of fundamental rights, as epitomized by its decisions in Case 1/58 *Stork* [1959] ECR 17 and Joined Cases 16 and 17/59 *Geitling* [1959] ECR 17. These decisions reflect the mainly functional and economic interpretation of Community law that prevailed at the time, and indicate the Court's concern with establishing the parameters of Community competences, of which fundamental rights were not considered to be a part. Following the consolidation of the principle of the supremacy of Community law over inconsistent national law of any level, including constitutional law, in a series of cases starting with the seminal decision in Case 6/64 *Costa* v *ENEL* [1964] ECR 585, it appeared that no clear protection was afforded to human rights in the supervision of Community law by the ECJ.

The ECJ then responded by introducing the notion of human rights as being a part of the general principles of Community law (see Chapter 18) that it was responsible for applying. In Case 29/69 *Stauder* [1969] ECR 419, the Court made its first reference to human rights. The flexible and imprecise nature of general principles of Community law created its own difficulties. The difficulty now was how to develop this discourse on rights in a logical and coherent fashion. The landmark supremacy Case 11/70 *Internationale Handelsgesellschaft* [1970] ECR 1125 pitted the ECJ against the German constitutional order over the issue of protection of fundamental rights. The ECJ did attempt, at p. 1,134, to reassure the German Federal Court that

> in fact, respect for fundamental rights forms an integral part of the general principles of Community law protected by the Court of Justice. The protection of such rights, while inspired by the constitutional traditions common to the Member States, must be ensured within the framework of the structure and objectives of the Community.

The repercussions of this decision took years to work through the German courts.

The main challenge now facing the ECJ was to convince those national courts charged with the task of protecting rights under national constitutions that it was also in the business of protecting rights in just as consistent and effective a manner. It thus sought a certain source of legal stability for the future development of its jurisprudence in relation to rights. The fundamental rights mentioned in the *Internationale Handelsgesellschaft* case were said to have been inspired by the constitutional traditions common to the member states. Yet this source soon proved to be problematic. Serious problems would have resulted if the Community judges had decided to define rights that they recognized as representing a common constitutional tradition by reference to a particular standard of one particular state (see Weiler). A particular fundamental right that is given protection in one member state may express the meeting point of competing rights claims (e.g., individual interests versus state interests), indicating a balance based on the values of the society in question. If this is then considered a "constitutional tradition" of that particular state, its transposition to the EU level imposes an understanding of values that may be at odds with arrangements in other states. The most graphic illustration of this dilemma was the issue of the competing rights claims in the Irish reference case of Case 159/90 *SPUC* v *Grogan* [1991] ECR I-4685, involving the distribution of information on abortion services in other member states. How did the Court proceed?

In Case 4/73 *Nold* v *Commission* [1974] ECR 491 the ECJ stated (at para. 13) that, in safeguarding fundamental rights

> the Court is bound to draw inspiration from constitutional traditions common to the Member States, and it cannot therefore uphold measures which are incompatible with fundamental rights recognized and protected by the Constitutions of those States. Similarly, international treaties for the protection of human rights on which the Member States have collaborated, or of which they are signatories, can supply guidelines which should be followed within the framework of Community law.

A second source of rights was identified in the form of international treaties on human rights, representing a fixed set of standards for the protection of rights, as well as a more coherent and consistent point of reference. The ECHR was the obvious regional instrument that might serve as a guide for the ECJ. It contains a series of rights that are widely considered to be of universal value and that transcend the national variations resulting from common constitutional traditions. However, it also represents only a minimum standard of protection below which signatory states are not allowed to permit their protection to fall. These sources became the roots of the formula used in the case law of the ECJ and in the treaty amendments as part of the expansion of the discourse on rights within the EU.

The Role of the Other Institutions

The first specific reference by the other institutions to human rights is contained in the Joint Declaration on Fundamental Rights made by the European Parliament, the Council, and the Commission in 1977, in which they stressed "the prime importance they attach to the protection of fundamental rights", derived from the two sources already discussed: the constitutions of the member states and the ECHR. The latter was said to represent a common source of commitment to protecting human rights for the nine member states at the time.

Since the mid-1970s the Commission has gradually come to play a more significant role in the process of developing a discourse on human rights within the framework of European integration. After first rejecting the need for accession to the ECHR, it later changed its view and advocated accession. This did not meet with much favour, and other issues, such as the progressive moves towards increased economic integration, came to dominate the business of the Council and the Commission during the 1980s. The Commission renewed its proposal for accession in 1990 and the road was open to *Opinion 2/94* issued by the ECJ in 1996 (see below).

The European Parliament has identified the promotion and protection of human rights as one of its primary concerns as a representative assembly. The strongest expressions of this commitment have been the Declaration of Fundamental Rights and Freedoms that it issued in 1989, and the incorporation of this declaration into a draft constitution for the EU adopted by the Parliament by resolution in 1994 (the Herman Report). The Declaration lists a series of rights that go beyond those listed in the European Convention to include those already addressed in the Community treaties, as well as innovative notions such as enshrining the principles of democracy, protection of the environment, and consumer protection.

However, it has been at the summit meetings of the European Council that the most important steps have been taken by amending the treaties in response to the development of the discourse on human rights within the EU. The Single European Act of 1987, which amended the Treaty of Rome 30 years after it was signed, introduced in its Preamble the first direct reference to the notion of protecting human rights. Article F of the TEU, signed in 1992, took a more concrete step forward. It provided that "the Union shall respect fundamental rights as guaranteed by the European Convention for the Protection of Human Rights and Fundamental Freedoms ... and as they result from the constitutional traditions common to the Member States, as general principles of Community law". This amendment recognized the particular importance and place of the ECHR in the development of the discourse on rights, and reflected the tried and tested formula adopted by the ECJ in its decisions. The TEU also created particular rights resulting from the new status of EU citizenship.

A setback occurred with *Opinion 2/94*, delivered by the ECJ following a request by the Council to establish whether the Community had the competence, as the treaties stood, to accede to the ECHR and whether any basis could be found in the treaties explicitly or implicitly giving a general power to the Community's institutions to legislate in the area of fundamental rights. The Court found that there was no such existing basis, and that such a power could be brought about only by amending the treaties.

Although treaty changes were to follow, there was no consensus at the intergovernmental conference that was concluded in Amsterdam in 1997 to provide the EU with the competence to enact rules relating to human rights. Instead, a new Article 6 TEU was formed from the old Article F. Its first section now reads: "The Union is founded on the principles of liberty, democracy, respect for human rights and fundamental freedoms, and the rule of law, principles which are common to the Member States". Article 6(2) reaffirms the formula provided for in the old Article F.

"Serious and persistent" breaches of the above principles can now result in the possibility of suspending a member state's voting rights within the Council under Article 7. The political difficulties of taking such action were illustrated by the reaction of other member states' governments to the controversial inclusion in the Austrian government of Jörg

Haider's Freedom Party, which has espoused political views that clearly contradict the spirit of Article 6. Article 46 TEU now empowers the ECJ to oversee the compatibility of acts of the institutions taken under the treaties by reference to Article 6(2).

The Path to the Charter

For those who advocated accession by the EU to the ECHR or an EU Bill of Rights, the results of the negotiations in Amsterdam were disappointing. However, a particular impetus had been created. During 1999, against the backdrop of the Commission resigning following accusations of corruption, and of low turnouts for the European Parliament elections, compounding the continuing debate about a "democratic deficit" within the EU polity, the issue of the protection of rights within the EU again came to the fore. Several reports were commissioned that investigated issues of the protection of rights within the EU. On the occasion of the 50th anniversary of the adoption of the Universal Declaration of Human Rights in December 1998, the European Council, meeting in Vienna, formally issued a declaration of its own, affirming the "primary importance" that it attached to the Universal Declaration. The Council's belief in the universality and indivisibility of human rights was also emphasized, and it committed itself to their protection and support in the future. The publication of an annual Human Rights Report was called for and an interim report was submitted for consideration to the Cologne summit in June 1999. In their concluding remarks, the authors of this document stated that it was "an effort to make the EU's human rights policies more consistent and more transparent".

The Process and Procedure

The most important result of this interim report was a Council decision to establish a body to draw up an EU Charter of Fundamental Rights. The language of the decision reflects a recognition of the concerns mentioned above by stating (at para. 1) that "there appears to be a need, at the present stage of the Union's development, to establish a Charter of

Fundamental Rights in order to make their overriding importance and relevance more visible to the Union's citizens". No new powers to make law in this area were envisaged in the decision. Indeed, the fact that the decision included an acknowledgement that respect for fundamental rights had "been confirmed and defined by the jurisprudence of the European Court of Justice" supports the view that the primary motivation for adopting this decision was to bring about a kind of compilation of those rights already applicable at the Community/EU level, to present them in an understandable and accessible form, and thus to attempt to assuage claims that the EU as a polity lacks a coherent form of democratic legitimacy.

The Council envisaged the creation of a drafting body that would be made up of representatives from the various EU institutions as well as members of national parliaments, with other institutions providing observers (para. 3). A solemn proclamation of a Charter of Fundamental Rights based on the draft presented to and then approved by the Council would then be made by the three main political institutions. Whether and how the Charter would then become part of the treaties' framework would be considered later (para. 4).

At Tampere in October 1999 the European Council established the rules concerning the composition, method of work, and practical arrangements for the body to draft the Charter. It was to be made up of 62 members: 15 representatives of the heads of state or government of the member states; one representative of the Commission; 16 designated members of the European Parliament; and two designates from each of the parliaments of the member states. It thus constituted a unique body in the history of European integration, in that its members were drawn from four different sources, two national and two supranational. Two observers from the ECJ as well as two from the Council of Europe (the non-EU body ultimately responsible for the European Convention on Human Rights) were also selected. EU institutions were to be given hearings, and there was also a possibility that "other bodies, social groups, and experts" would be invited to give their views.

Between its first meeting, on 17 December 1999, and to the presentation of its draft Charter to the European Council, in Biarritz on 13 October 2000, the "Convention", as the drafting body voted to call itself, heard and received the views of a multitude of institutions, groups, and individuals, by way of public hearings or written submissions. In a commendable spirit of openness, the body published all written submissions received on a specially created website, in order to promote and further debate on the subject. The framework for the working method of the body was provided by the Tampere conclusions, with the executive body of the Convention, the Praesidium, being responsible for the actual drafting of the document. Proposals were then discussed by the members and the Convention agreed early in its proceedings that progress would be made by way of consensus rather than by vote.

A series of issues were raised by the decision to create and use such a body in drafting an EU Charter. On a positive note, the body may arguably be counted a success, at least to the extent that it fulfilled its mandate of producing a draft Charter that was then approved by the European Council without amendment and proclaimed at the beginning of the Nice summit. The Convention also completed its task on time, in the face of considerable drafting difficulties and considerable scepticism. Indeed, the body's success has led to discussion about using the same kind of organizational structure for possible future tasks, such as drawing up an EU constitution. From a more negative perspective, the Convention seemed in some ways to confirm the already prevalent view that the EU is dominated by elitist and technocratic decision-making. Although up to three quarters of the members of the Convention were politicians, it is not clear to what extent, if at all, civil society had any influence or effect on the drafting of the Charter. Civil society was, of course, invited to submit and make its views known, yet there was no sign at all of a dialogue, which seemed strange in relation to such an important process. The reality was, of course, that very few citizens of the EU were actually aware of what was taking place on their behalf.

The Content of the Charter

The Charter (*OJ* 2000 C364/01), which was adopted as a political declaration on 7 December 2000, consists of a preamble and 54 articles grouped into seven chapters (see Table 20.1). The mandate entrusted to the Convention by the Cologne decision had stated (at para. 2) that

> The European Council believes that this Charter should contain the fundamental rights and freedoms as well as basic procedural rights, guaranteed by the European Convention for the Protection of Human Rights and Fundamental Freedoms, and derived from the constitutional traditions common to the Member States, as general principles of Community law. The Charter should also include the fundamental rights that pertain only to the Union's citizens. In drawing up such a Charter account should furthermore be taken of economic and social rights as contained in the European Social Charter and the Community Charter of the Fundamental Social Rights of Workers (Article 136 TEC), insofar as they do not merely establish objectives for action by the Union.

The first point to note is that the aspiration of drafting a document that formally recognized the universality and indivisibility of fundamental rights was realized. The Charter contains rights that bridge the division between civil and political rights, on the one hand, and economic and social rights on the other. Indeed, it goes beyond this division by including rights that stem from citizenship of the EU while also recognizing the existence of rights that result from the new challenges being faced at the beginning of the 21st century, such as those in the areas of bioethics, asylum, and environmental protection.

Secondly, the Charter is unique in its formulation and presentation. The Preamble maintains that the indivisible and universal rights listed in the Charter are based on a series of "common values" of the "peoples of Europe". These shared values of human dignity, freedom, equality, and solidarity, along with justice and citizens' rights, provide the headings for the six chapters of rights listed. The focus of the declaration of rights in the Charter is thus different in form from that of other such declarations. Thus, the chapter on "dignity" calls for respect of the right to life and the prohibition of torture; the chapter on "freedom" calls for the right to liberty and freedom of expression; and so on.

Charter Rights and the ECHR

The influence of the ECHR is clearly evident. The Cologne decision mentioned the Convention as the first source for rights to be included in the Charter and the prominent place given to it reflects the strong influence the Convention has had on the development of a consciousness of human rights within the EU. At least 20 of the articles listing rights to be protected rely heavily on or are inspired by the ECHR and its protocols, a fact reinforced by the commentaries given to the Charter rights (Charter 4473/00). The challenge was to formulate a means whereby the Charter rights were at least of a standard equal to these Convention rights and to ensure that there was only the minimal possibility of divergence between the protections offered by the two jurisdictions.

What then is the relation to be between the ECHR rights and those in the Charter? Article 52 allows for the limitation of guaranteed rights. Such action can only be provided for by law and the actual essence of the rights must be respected in doing so. The limitation must also be proportionate to the "limits necessary for the protection of legitimate interests in a democratic society". If the right to be limited corresponds with a Convention right, then "the meaning and scope of those rights shall be the same as those laid down by the Convention".

Article 53 relates to the level of protection to be attained for rights to be protected under the Charter. It states that

> Nothing in this Charter shall be interpreted as restricting or adversely affecting human rights and fundamental freedoms as recognized, in their respective fields of application, by Union law and international law, and by international agreements to which the

Union, the Community or all the Member States are a party, including the European Convention on Human Rights, and by the Member States' constitutions.

The explicit reference to the European Convention indicates a recognition that it constitutes a minimum standard in all cases. This article is also intended to allow current and future developments in the case law of the European Court of Human Rights (based in Strasbourg) to be taken into account when examining the rights provisions related to the ECHR in the Charter.

Other Rights

The Charter also includes rights that pertain only to the EU's citizens. These rights mainly concern those created by the introduction of citizenship of the EU in the TEU. The draft Charter contains eight rights that are restricted to those holding the status of citizenship of the EU or legal residency of the EU, such as the right to petition the European Parliament, the right to complain to an Ombudsman, a general right to freedom of movement within the EU, and the right to stand for and vote in local and European Parliament elections in the place where citizens reside. Although this may appear to be an affront to the principle of the universality of human rights – a principle endorsed by the Preamble – citizens' rights result from the application of a particular status, whereas human rights are considered to be inherent to all human beings.

Finally, economic and social rights may be included in the Charter insofar as they are more substantial than just "objectives for action by the Union". The two sources for such rights are listed as the Council of Europe's Social Charter and the Community's own provisions. A large debate within the field of the general theory of human rights concerns the feasibility and potential for such rights to be made justiciable. A distinction is often made between "binding rights", which are legally justiciable, and "programmatic rights", which are political objectives. These latter rights depend on the implementation of political programmes based on appropriate policies and measures to ensure

their promotion, access, enforcement, and effectiveness. The chapters of the Charter on "equality" and "solidarity" contain provisions protecting what can be classified as social and economic rights. Examples include the right to collective bargaining and action, and the principle of equality between men and women.

At first sight, proponents of economic and social rights would be likely to be disappointed with the level of protection to be afforded to these rights in the Charter. The language used in the chapter on solidarity especially is quite vague. Moreover, most of these rights are to be exercised only "in accordance with Community law and national laws and practices." This appears to refer these rights back to the differing levels of protection that may exist in the various member states, where national laws may dilute the right in question. Intense lobbying took place over the summer of 2000 as these rights were continuously amended, following the expression of reservations by various interested parties. For example, in September an interim draft of these specific rights included a right to take collective action "at all levels". The Confederation of British Industry, supported by the UK government, strongly opposed such a formulation and the final approved draft saw this wording eliminated. However, trade unions and other social partners may still have some reason to be optimistic, since the Charter has formally recognized that "solidarity" rights are fundamental and are indivisible from other protected rights. Moreover, a wide variety of social rights are listed, so that the Charter could, perhaps, serve as a springboard for greater protection of such rights. The Preamble specifically refers to other international treaties, such as the Council of Europe's Social Charter, and other "international obligations", which can of course include conventions of the International Labour Organization. The vague language of the "solidarity" chapter, while it has disappointed some, also means that there is much that might potentially be built upon. This cross-referencing to other international agreements is also reflected in Article 53, establishing the level of protection of the Charter rights.

Other innovations of the Charter are the inclusion of a right to asylum, the prohibition of the trafficking of human beings, and the right to respect for an individual's physical and mental integrity.

The Scope of the Charter

The Cologne decision to establish the Charter made no specific reference to what the Council's views were of the intended scope to be given to the Charter, but a closer reading of the text offers some clues. The decision states in its first paragraph that "the obligation of the Union to respect fundamental rights has been confirmed and defined by the jurisprudence of the European Court of Justice". The Court has in its case law subjected the acts of the Community institutions to its own form of human rights review and has then extended this review to cover two situations. First, where the member state acts as an agent of the Community in implementing a Community measure or takes measures itself commensurate with an executive discretion provided for in a sphere of activity generally regulated by European law (Case 5/88 *Wachauf* v *Germany* [1989] ECR 2609), the Court will supervise the acts for possible violations of the general principles of fundamental rights. Secondly, the Court has also increased the exercise of its rights review jurisdiction over situations where a member state claims the possibility of derogating from the treaty-based freedoms of movement (Case 260/89 *ERT* v *DEP* [1991] ECR I-292). These judicial advances on the part of the Court have touched on sensitive questions of national interest and sovereignty, and the judges have had to tread carefully. Logical though this extension of rights review may be, in the light of the Court's developing jurisprudence since the mid-1970s, the potential for conflict is high, as it is in these very areas that the incremental and imprecise nature of the development of general principles of fundamental rights by the Court can come up against stubborn resistance, in the form of more precise national constitutional or legislative measures.

Article 51 of the Charter seeks to establish the parameters of its scope: "The provisions of this Charter are addressed to the institutions and bodies of the Union, with due regard for the principle of subsidiarity, and to the Member States only when they are implementing Union law". This reflects the case law of the ECJ. The reference to subsidiarity was a late amendment to this article and highlights member states' concerns to impose strict limits on the application of the Charter's provisions. This concern is reflected again later in the same article, where it is stated that the Charter is not to create any new tasks or powers for the Union, nor modify any existing ones (Article 51(2)).

Although the drafters of the document appear to have been very conscious of being seen not to extend the existing competences of the Union, they have clearly made the "institutions and bodies of the Union" subject to the Charter's provisions. It will therefore be difficult for the Council to justify allowing the more shadowy bodies created under the second and third pillars to avoid being subject to its provisions. At the present moment these latter bodies are subject to very little scrutiny. It is clear that the increased activities of the recently created EU agencies will also be subject to the Charter's provisions. The effectiveness of this scrutiny will obviously depend on the status to be given to it.

The Status of the Charter

Indeed, the question of what status the Charter would have was the subject of considerable debate and discussion over the period of the drafting of the Charter. The Cologne decision in its fourth paragraph seemed to give a specific mandate to the drafting body with regard to this point:

> The European Council will propose to the European Parliament and the Commission that, together with the Council, they should solemnly proclaim on the basis of the draft document a European Charter of Fundamental Rights. It will then have to be considered whether and, if so, how the Charter should be integrated into the Treaties.

It seems, then, that the European Council favoured a political proclamation of rights adopted with the other two institutions. This would be consistent with the approach taken in the Joint Declaration on Fundamental Rights in 1977. The Charter's provisions would not be legally justiciable before the Court, and the question of its status would thus be one for future discussion. The Commission succinctly described the Convention's task as one "of revelation rather than creation, of compilation rather than innovation" (Commission Communication COM(2000)559).

Despite these directions from the European Council, the Convention soon indicated a desire to treat the issue more seriously. At the first meeting of the drafting body its newly elected President, Roman Herzog, suggested that the body approach its task in seeking to "constantly keep the objective in mind that the Charter that we are drafting must one day, in the not too distant future, become legally binding". Indeed, the Convention's subsequent work was premised on the understanding that the actual drafting of the Charter would have to permit the eventual legal assimilation of the document into the treaties, if so decided by the European Council.

Support for adopting a legally binding Charter of Fundamental Rights came from a variety of sources. The European Parliament's delegation to the Convention was mandated to take a strong position on the final status to be given to the Charter (by EP Resolution A5-0064/2000). The same support for an eventual legally binding set of rights is found in a Commission Communication (COM(2000) 644) on the final draft produced in September 2000, in which it stated that:

> it is . . . preferable, for the sake of visibility and certainty as to the law, for the Charter to be made mandatory in its own right and not just through its judicial interpretation. In practice, the real question is when and how it should be incorporated in[to] the Treaties.

Such support was also forthcoming from the great majority of groups that made submissions to the Convention's work, as well as from a number of member states' governments.

This demand has considerable theoretical value. Because the protection of rights within the EU is primarily based on jurisprudence developed by the ECJ in a piecemeal fashion, it is subject to certain difficulties and weak-

nesses, some mentioned above. The ECJ's ability to protect rights in the absence of specific provisions is weakened by the Council's not wanting to grant jurisdiction to the Court (such as in many aspects of the second and third pillars), or by the possibility of overriding interests with a clear legal status in the treaties (such as the common objectives of the Community), or most notably by a lack of political will to include provisions on human rights in the treaties. A legally binding charter would greatly improve and legitimate the ECJ's jurisdiction in relation to the review of fundamental rights. It would reinforce a "rights culture" at a crucial time, as the EU undergoes enlargement, and provide a much more useful supervision of the law-making powers of the institutions.

However, there was no consensus among the national governments during the intergovernmental conference in 2000 on the final status of the Charter. Indeed, Keith Vaz, the British Minister for Europe, made his government's opposition to a binding charter clear by describing its function as being "a showcase of rights", which would have no more legal effect than the Beano comic book. The essence of this point of view is that it seeks to reinforce the idea that the purpose of the Charter is only to make rights visible to the EU's citizens and, where it can, also serve as a guide to both the EU's institutions and its citizens in identifying their rights and obligations. Indeed, it has been argued that the very visibility of rights can have an educative and empowering effect, and should not be underestimated. The rights protected within the EU are scattered across the founding treaties themselves, in the legislative acts of the Community, and among the general principles recognized by the ECJ. The Charter in such a form has the potential to bring them together in a clearer and more consistent way. It may also serve as an important guideline and source of reference that the Court can use for refining its general principles, and for giving substance to Article 6 TEU, for which it now has an interpretative jurisdiction. In a somewhat ironic fashion, it would then be the task of the judicial body to interpret and apply a political declaration proclaimed by the other EU institutions. A charter in the form of a proclamation could also be seen as an exercise in legitimacy, where an aspect of European integration that has a real effect on citizens' lives, the protection of their fundamental rights, is clearly shown as being at the heart of the EU's development.

The Future

The Charter should not been seen in isolation from other issues. Legal certainty, consistency, and even propriety in relation to civil and political rights would be achieved if the EU was given the legal competence to accede directly to the ECHR. This would mean that the Court of Human Rights in Strasbourg, established by the Council of Europe with the specific goal of promoting the protection of human rights in Europe, would have the ultimate say over the compatibility of acts of the Community and EU institutions with the standards set in the provisions of the Convention. This logic would also extend to its eventual accession to other human rights instruments, such as the revised Social Charter of the Council of Europe, the International Covenant on Civil and Political Rights, and others to which the member states are already parties.

A particular problem is the lack of a focus on rights and the restricted jurisdiction given to the ECJ under the second and, in particular the third, pillars of the EU (see Chapter 19). Since the TEU was ratified a great deal of development has taken place in these areas without a parallel development of rights and limitations to complement them. The decision-making process is mainly intergovernmental in character, and is subject to very little effective scrutiny or transparency. Of perhaps greater concern is the lack of accountability of the bodies that execute decisions under these pillars. The decisions relating to police and judicial cooperation in criminal matters have, and will have, serious consequences for fundamental rights. Even the absorption of the provisions on asylum and immigration into the EC Treaty seems to favour executive power over individual rights. The Court's jurisdiction here is expressly restricted under Article 68 of Title IV.

The call for an effective charter of rights must also be seen in the light of the continuing process of "constitutionalization" of the EU.

This process can be seen in liberal democratic terms as subjecting a polity to the rule of law, where the latter is given political legitimacy by the fact that its existence is founded by and clearly defined through law. It can also be seen as a means of simplifying the EU's complex legal and political framework. The draft treaty produced by the European University Institute on the Commission's request is a good illustration of this process. Of the eight titles proposed, one is given over specifically to "fundamental rights". The Commission has expressed its approval of the findings of this report and stated that it believes that "there is a very close link between reorganization of the Treaties and the incorporation of the Charter in them" (Commission Communication COM (2000)434). This process is also being strongly advocated on the political level by the European Parliament (see the reports of its Committee on Constitutional Affairs, listed under Further Reading below), and by the German, Italian, and Belgian governments.

Indeed, a broad debate has followed the speech in May 2000 by Germany's Foreign Minister, Joschka Fischer, setting out his views on the finality of European integration. In envisaging the creation of a European Executive and a reformed European Parliament, Fischer foresees the need for a "European Constituent Treaty" that would clearly define the division of competences between the reformed institutions of the EU and the member states. This treaty would be part of a constitutional framework "centred around basic human and civil rights", the best expression of which is now the adopted Charter (see Fischer). French President Jacques Chirac, following Fischer's call for an existential debate on the future of the EU, calls the period to follow the signing of the Nice Treaty *la grande transition*, during which the institutional questions to be addressed, in order to facilitate enlargement to the East and a "deepening" of EU policies, will have to include the question of the final status to be given to the Charter (see Chirac).

As has been mentioned, the apparent success of the drafting body has prompted claims that this might be a suitable structure for the eventual drafting of an EU constitution. The relative transparency and accessibility of the

Convention's work, as well as its unique representativeness, suggest that it could be an appropriate model to engage in such a task if so required. A Council decision would be required to make this a reality, however.

Article 6 TEU now lists the rights and values upon which the Union is founded. Although Article 7 TEU (as amended by the Treaty of Amsterdam) introduced the possibility of suspending a member state's voting rights in the Council for a serious and persistent violation of the fundamental rights referred to in Article 6, no mechanism was elaborated for preventing such violations. The new Treaty of Nice has sought to address this anomaly. Upon receiving the assent of the European Parliament and after hearing the representations of the member state concerned, the Council, acting by a majority of four fifths of its members, can make a declaration stating that a clear danger exists of a member state committing a serious breach of such rights. The Council can then issue such recommendations as it sees fit to the member state in question. The right of initiative to trigger such a serious political sanction lies with the Commission, the Parliament, or at least one third of the member states under the new Treaty amendments agreed in December 2000.

The Treaty of Nice also contains an annexed declaration on the future of the Union. It was formally recognized at Nice that there was a need for a deeper and wider debate on the future direction and identity of the EU. The two EU presidencies of 2001 (Sweden and Belgium) are charged with the task of promoting a general debate on this very subject in consultation with the EU institutions, national parliaments, civil society, business, the academic community, and the candidates for future accession to the EU. The issues to be considered include the question of simplifying the treaties to render them clearer and more accessible; the identification of a clear division of powers between Community competencies and the powers of member states; the role of national parliaments in the institutional framework of the EU; and the future status and role of the Charter. The two presidencies will be responsible for the preparation and presentation of two progress reports to the European

Council on the findings of this public debate and consultation, and another intergovernmental conference, in 2004, will examine what changes to the treaties will be considered necessary.

Conclusion

The solemn proclamation of this Charter of Fundamental Rights at the Nice summit on 7 December 2000, following its drafting by the Convention and its approval by the EU heads of state and government at the special Biarritz summit in October, means that the EU stands, yet again, at a turning point in its development as a polity. Even if the mood of solemnity at the signing session that winter's afternoon in Nice owed more to the simmering tensions over the tough negotiations to follow than to the perceived effect of the instrument, the subject of a legally binding charter and its role in the general debate about the future shape of the EU has been referred to the next intergovernmental conference. Although debate and controversy have accompanied the drafting and approval of the Charter, the significance of its adoption as a political declaration and the momentum generated by the drafting process may well have a fundamental effect on the future constitutional development and identity of the Union.

Further Reading

Alston, Philip (editor), *The EU and Human Rights*, Oxford and New York: Oxford University Press, 1999

> A wideranging collection of articles on the issue of the protection of human rights and the EU. The very influential article by Philip Alston and Joseph Weiler, which opens the book, is essential reading for its depth of analysis.

Chirac, Jacques, *Our Europe*, Speech given at the Bundestag, 27 June 2000, London: The Federal Trust, 2000

Clapham, Andrew, *Human Rights and the European Community: A Critical Overview*, Baden-Baden: Nomos, 1991

> This book is a little dated now, yet it is still a comprehensive review of the area.

Comité des Sages, *Leading by Example: A Human Rights Agenda for the EU for the Year 2000*, October 1998

Committee on Constitutional Affairs of the European Parliament, *Report on the Drafting of an EU Charter of Rights* (Duff/Voggenhuber Report), A5-0064/2000

Committee on Constitutional Affairs of the European Parliament, *Report on the Constitutionalization of the Treaties* (Duhamel Report), A5-0289/2000

European Parliament, Resolution (Herman Report) A3-0064/94 on an EU Constitution, 10 February 1994

Expert Group on Fundamental Rights, "Affirming Fundamental Rights in the EU: Time to Act", in *Report of the Expert Group on Fundamental Rights*, Brussels: European Commission, February 1999

Feus, Kim (editor) *The EU Charter of Fundamental Rights: Text and Commentaries*, London: The Federal Trust 2000

This is the first book on the Charter in English. It comprises a series of wideranging articles written by members of the "Convention", academics, lawyers, political scientists, and politicians. The contributions emphasize the broad impact that the Charter is likely to have.

First EU Annual Report on Human Rights, final version, Document 11350/99, 1 October 1999

Fischer, Joschka, *From Confederation to Federation: Thoughts on the Finality of European Integration*, London: The Federal Trust, 2000

House of Lords Select Committee on the European Union, *Eighth Report on the EU Charter of Fundamental Rights*, 16 May 2000

Shaw, Jo, *Law of the European Union*, third edition, London: Palgrave, 2000

The most accessible, well-written and up-to-date textbook on the constitutional law of the EU

Weiler, Joseph, and N. Lockhart, "'Taking Rights Seriously' Seriously: The European Court and its Fundamental Rights Jurisprudence", two parts, *Common Market Law Review*, 32, pp. 51–94 and 579–637

Aimed mainly at a legal readership, this is an in-depth examination of the role of the European Court of Justice in the area of human rights.

Weiler, J.H.H., *The Constitution of Europe*, Cambridge and New York: Cambridge University Press 1999

A wonderfully erudite collection of essays on the development of the "European polity". The article on fundamental rights is particularly relevant.

Mike Meehan is a lecturer in law at Liverpool John Moores University. He previously taught UK public law at the University of Bordeaux, France. He is presently researching a PhD on the Charter, entitled "Ethics, Rights, and the EU Polity", at Birkbeck College, University of London.

Table 20.1   The EU Charter of Fundamental Rights at a Glance

Preamble	Common values of the peoples of Europe
	Indivisible and universal values that, along with the principles of democracy and the Rule of Law, found the Union
	Union respects cultures and traditions of the peoples of Europe
	Need to make rights visible
	Rights protected by various constitutional traditions and international obligations reaffirmed in accordance with the principle of subsidiarity
	Responsibilities and duties come with these rights
Dignity (Articles 1–5)	Right to respect and protection of human dignity
	Right to integrity of the person
	Prohibition of torture and inhuman or degrading treatment or punishment
	Prohibition of slavery and forced labour
Freedoms (Articles 6–19)	Right to liberty and security
	Respect for private and family life
	Protection of personal data
	Right to marry and found a family
	Freedom of expression and information
	Freedom of assembly and association
	Freedom of the arts and sciences
	Right to education
	Freedom to choose an occupation and right to engage in work
	Freedom to conduct a business
	Right to property
	Right to asylum
	Protection in the event of removal, expulsion or extradition
Equality (Articles 20–26)	Equality before the law
	Nondiscrimination on a series of grounds
	Respect for cultural, religious and linguistic diversity
	Equality between men and women
	Rights of the child
	Rights of the elderly
	Integration of persons with disabilities
Solidarity (Articles 27–38)	Workers' right to information and consultation
	Right of collective bargaining and action
	Right of access to placement services
	Protection in the event of unjustified dismissal
	Fair and just working decisions
	Prohibition of child labour and protection of young people at work
	Protection of family and professional life
	Right to social security and assistance
	Right of access to health care
	Access to services of general economic interest
	Protection of the environment
	Consumer protection
Citizens' Rights (Articles 39–46)	Right to vote and stand as candidate in European Parliament elections
	Right to vote and stand as candidate in local elections
	Right to good administration
	Right of access to documents
	Right to refer cases of maladministration to the European Ombudsman
	Right to petition the European Parliament
	Freedom of movement and of residence within the EU
	Right to diplomatic and consular protection
Justice (Articles 47–50)	Right to an effective remedy and a fair trial
	Presumption of innocence and right of defence
	Principles of proportionality and legality
	Double jeopardy rule
General Provisions (Articles 51–54)	Scope of Charter rights
	Scope of limitations of Charter rights
	Level of protection
	Prohibition of abuse of rights

Chapter Twenty-One

Cultural Issues, Debate, and Programmes

Terry Sandell

Policies, issues, and activities related to culture in the EU cannot be understood at a theoretical or practical level outside the wider context of the EU's development and transition from a trading community to an as-yet ill-defined fledgling federal state, a process in which the Single European Act was of fundamental and unambiguous importance, and the Maastricht Treaty on European Union its logical extension.

The foundation on which the Community has been built, the Treaty of Rome (1957), contained only two fleeting references to culture: in connection, first, with nondiscrimination and, secondly, with exceptions to free movement of goods, where a special case is made for "the protection of national treasures possessing artistic, historic or archaeological value" (Articles 7 and 36 respectively).

Until Maastricht, culture was, from a strictly legalistic point of view, not a sphere of Community competence. Some have maintained that there was indeed never any intention that it should be. As the British Conservative educationalist Lord Vaizey, for example, argued in 1979

It is, I think, not an accident that neither culture nor art is mentioned in this exceptionally long and detailed Treaty [of Rome]. It is extremely detailed . . . for example . . . it refers to unwrought lead, zinc spelter, unwrought zinc, tungsten unwrought in powder, molybdenum unwrought, tantalum unwrought. It cannot be by accident that the words art, music, culture and so on do not appear in a Treaty as detailed as that . . .

The absence of any legal base for culture as an area of competence did not, however, impede substantial Community involvement, by design and by default, in cultural matters and cultural spending. A Directorate-General of the European Commission, DG X, was set up to cover audiovisual, information, communication, and culture matters. Specialized committees had also appeared that were related to culture – for example, the Youth, Culture, Education, Media, and Sport Committees of the European Parliament. The European Parliament and the Commission pronounced on culture, the Economic and Social Committee (ESC) gave opinions on it, and, later, ministers of culture met within the Council of Ministers and issued resolutions on it. That these institutions had no brief to do so was underlined, it could be argued, by the fact that in the Single European Act culture is not mentioned once.

This fundamental lack of legality and legitimacy until Maastricht created serious distortions in the way cultural activity was carried out. It also caused tensions between member states. The United Kingdom, for example, showed a marked reluctance to see culture become an area of Community competence and consistently adopted a "minimalist" position, in clear contrast to the line taken by enthusiastic "maximalists" such as France. Denmark had also taken a robust line against culture being an area of competence, not least because of its obligations and commitments within the Nordic Council. Germany, for constitutional reasons, because culture is the responsibility of each *Land* (state) not the *Bund* (the federation), was also cautious. The field of culture in fact offers a very interesting case study of the contentious, deliberate, and inexorable extension of the Community beyond its narrower and earlier goals as outlined in the original Treaty of Rome.

Although there was no legal basis for Community action in the cultural field, there had in many quarters always been vague and unchallenged cultural assumptions related to the "European idea". The claim that Jean Monnet wished that, if he could have started again, he would have begun with culture, whether true or not, has certainly reflected the views of many others, particularly when there has been a problem with the economic or political dimension of the Community's development. Edward Heath, who took the United Kingdom into the Community, commented that it "wasn't just formed to look after fish", and it is easy to understand that those who had a vision for "Europe" wished neither to confine it to matters related to herrings and molybdenum unwrought, nor to see either of those commodities as the symbol of the great unifying European ideal.

Development of Cultural Policy

Cultural yearnings first came to the bureaucratic surface in the 1970s when the European Parliament voted budget lines specifically for culture, with the funding directed mainly towards heritage matters. The budget grew, but remained small by Community standards. The European Parliament's generosity, however, gave the Commission an opportunity to create a small cultural affairs unit, in 1973, and an incentive to prise open a path into cultural activity. The Commission used its initial activity to justify further activity, which was then rationalized *post facto* by the Commission's Communications on culture, and by other means, to look as though by the late 1980s there had always been a widely agreed strategy for cultural action. The reality was different.

The Commission attempted to rewrite the history of its direct involvement in culture. For example, in its Communication (*New Prospects for Community Cultural Action*), issued in 1992, it claims to identify particular periods in which specific objectives were achieved. A less ideal-ized overview of the history of the Community's cultural involvement, however, would be as follows.

First, between 1977 and 1982 there was a disingenuous attempt by the Commission to justify direct Community involvement in culture by putting forward bureaucratic, quasi-Marxist definitions of culture in order to shoehorn it into the framework of the Treaty of Rome. The timing (Five-Year Plans) and the definitions used in the Communications on culture appear to betray a strong indirect influence from traditions of state socialism. Culture and the arts become the "Cultural Sector" and the "Cultural Sector" becomes "the socio-economic whole formed by persons and enterprises dedicated to the production and distribution of cultural goods and services".

Next, between 1982 and 1985 the Commission exploited these new definitions to engage further in ad hoc symbolic cultural activities and made an attempt to give the impression that the expanded activity was taking place within a coordinated, agreed framework that had clear boundaries. This was done against the background of the split between the member states supporting Community cultural activity and those that were not.

Thirdly, between 1985 and 1991 there was something of a coming to terms with the "created facts" of Community action in culture, on the one hand, and, on the other, the unavoidable reality that some countries were refusing to be manipulated further into new levels of activity. A process began of establishing recognizable structures and imposing some controls over DG X, including ministerial ones, through the regular meetings of ministers of culture, which began in 1985 in the context of the Council of Ministers.

Fourthly, between 1991 and the late 1990s moves were made towards creating a legally based, consistent, and structured framework for cultural action, reflected in the Maastricht Treaty (Article 151 TEC, formerly 128), with explicit constraints on direct Community activity extending too far or too fast. The bureaucratic definitions of culture had become unfashionable, partly at least because of the collapse of Communism in central and eastern Europe in 1989, and the collapse of the Soviet

Union in 1991. The Commission now began to use rhetoric about culture in a more honest, relatively transparent, and more accountable way. Culture was being transformed into a "crosscutting" issue, relevant to several of the Community's areas of interest and jurisdiction, and, it was said, should be promoted and nurtured through conscious exploitation of the Community's noncultural legislation, schemes, and funds.

Finally, since the late 1990s culture has continued to develop as a "crosscutting" issue, further benefiting from structural funds, in particular the European Regional Development Fund and the European Social Fund. An attempt was made to legitimize further and to tidy up "direct" Commission activity through the introduction of the Culture 2000 programme, adopted in February 2000, which absorbed various existing programmes. MEDIA Plus, a five-year programme (2000–04) with a budget of €400 million, has replaced MEDIA 2. The Prodi reforms in 1999 saw DG X and DG XXII merged into a single Directorate-General for Education and Culture (EAC).

The Maastricht Treaty

Over the earlier period, up to the early 1990s, the Commission issued four Communications on culture: *Community Action in the Cultural Sector* (1977); *Stronger Community Action in the Cultural Sector* (1982); *A Fresh Boost for Culture in the European Community* (1987); and *New Prospects for Community Cultural Action* (1992).

It was, however, the Maastricht Treaty, establishing the EU, that put culture *de jure* on the agenda. It thus retrospectively legitimized the Commission's and the European Parliament's substantial cultural activity and interests, and made some sense of the otherwise random resolutions of the Council of Ministers. After Maastricht, this widespread activity was re-examined, redefined, and quantified as the basis for developing future cultural policy and programmes.

The provisions on culture agreed at Maastricht were very much a compromise between member states with quite seriously differing positions. While the broader and historically

more significant principle that culture is a legitimate area of Community competence was secured by the countries that took a maximalist approach, the minimalist countries built into the drafting various restraining, defensive elements, including a requirement for unanimity.

The period of debate and argument leading up to Maastricht was significant, as it created the opportunity for a "repositioning" of culture as a crosscutting issue. This has suited everyone involved, minimalists and maximalists alike, as well as the vested interests of the arts and culture lobby, which is small in comparison to other lobbies at the EU level but is growing. Thus, culture was not only modestly put on the agenda in its own right, but came to be seen as a legitimate subheading or issue on several of the other established EU agenda items, such as social development, employment, tourism, training, education, and so on. It also brought unambiguously to the fore the fact that several directorates-general other than the old DG X (Audiovisual, Information, Communication, Culture) have an impact on cultural matters.

Only a relatively small number of the 61,351 words of the Maastricht Treaty on European Union were devoted to culture, but they marked a significant new development. In particular, Title IX (now XII) of the treaty was symbolically important as it gave "Culture" its own section. Article 151 (formerly 128) has five clauses:

(1) The Community shall contribute to the flowering of the cultures of the Member States, while respecting their national and regional diversity, and at the same time bringing the common cultural heritage to the fore.

(2) Action by the Community shall be aimed at encouraging cooperation between Member States and, if necessary, supporting and supplementing their action in the following areas:

  – improvement of the knowledge and dissemination of the culture and history of the European peoples;

  – conservation and safeguarding of the cultural heritage of European significance;

  – noncommercial cultural exchanges;

– artistic and literary creation, including in the audiovisual sector.

(3) The Community and the Member States shall foster cooperation with third countries and the competent international organizations in the sphere of culture, in particular the Council of Europe.

(4) The Community shall take cultural aspects into account in its action under other provisions of the Treaty. [The Treaty of Amsterdam added "in particular in order to respect and promote the diversity of its cultures".]

(5) In order to contribute to the achievement of the objectives referred to in this Article, the Council:

– acting in accordance with the procedure referred to in Article 251 and after consulting the Committee of the Regions, shall adopt incentive measures, excluding any harmonization of the laws and regulations of the Member States. The Council shall act unanimously throughout the procedures referred to in Article 251;

– acting unanimously on a proposal from the Commission, shall adopt recommendations.

There were two other references elsewhere in the Maastricht Treaty to culture, at Article 92 (3)(d) under Title V (now Title VI, Art. 87) on Common Rules on Competition, Taxation, and Approximation of Laws, and in Article 3. The latter is a résumé of main points in the Treaty and mentions again the contribution to the "flowering of the cultures of the member states". The other reference, related to permitting state aids under certain circumstances, specifically allowed "aid to promote culture and heritage and conservation where such aid does not affect trading conditions and competition in the Community to an extent that is contrary to common interest". It was an important exemption, as well as significant, as it implicitly accepts that culture is a special case.

A close reading of Article 151 reveals a certain amount of "padding", presumably to justify culture having a separate heading. Furthermore, three significant restraining clauses were embedded in it. The first control on action

was that it must be taken after consulting the Committee of the Regions. This represented a new layer of consultation and, in the case of Germany, for example, where culture is constitutionally the responsibility of the *Länder*, it meant something more than a rubber stamp. The second was the specific reference to excluding any harmonization of the laws and regulations of the member states, which effectively prevents the Commission from forcing through legislation on the basis of Article 151. The third constraint on action was that the Council of Ministers will act unanimously throughout the procedures referred to in Article 251 (co-decision by the Council and European Parliament), and the result of this will be not only that legislation under Article 151 will be impossible, but that even any incentive measures proposed will require unanimity in the Council.

The clear focus of Article 151, therefore, was on member states cooperating bilaterally and multilaterally in the field of culture. The role of the EU was to encourage such cooperation and, if necessary, support and supplement their action in limited specific areas. Legally speaking, it is not for the EU to take the lead or to control, nor for it to operate even in a supporting role in all areas of culture. The only explicit cultural brief for direct action that the EU was given by the Maastricht Treaty was to contribute to "the flowering of the cultures of the member states", which, if it has any meaning at all, can only be understood in the context of past suspicion of the Commission and in particular fears that it was working towards a centrally planned Community cultural policy, based on a supranational conception of the Community and an artificial conception of what constitutes "European culture". The unambiguous reference to fostering cooperation with, in particular, the Council of Europe, was an oblique reference to the previous lack of cooperation – sometimes to the point of hostility – between the Commission's DG X and the Council of Europe (representing a much larger "Europe" than the EU does) where their areas of interest and responsibility clearly overlapped.

It is, however, the fourth clause of Article 151 that, in many respects, has had the greatest impact on the EU's involvement in culture, as it is stipulated that the EU should take cultural aspects into account in its actions under other treaty provisions. It thus turned cultural matters into a crosscutting issue, not dissimilar from environmental matters, allowing culture to take a greater share of resources within existing programmes even where their objectives are not specifically cultural.

Financial Support for the Cultural Sector

Quite independently of the direct interest in cultural matters through DG X, which involved only a relatively modest budget, it became evident by the early 1990s that, without the Community institutions being conscious of it, and beyond the wildest proposals of the most ardent propagandists for Community involvement in culture, the Community, through other directorates-general of the Commission, had indirectly channelled approximately ECU2.47 billion into the cultural sector in the period 1989–93, an average of ECU494 million a year (Bates and Wacker p. iii). This represented approximately 0.8% of the total Community budget – ironically, not far short of the 1% target for expenditure on culture once demanded by the European Parliament.

Directorates-general that were involved indirectly with culture and spending on culture included DG XXII, which was involving itself in higher education arts training; DG XXIII, in connection with tourism-related heritage projects; DG I, in areas of cultural diplomacy (for example, a Central American cultural festival that it organized in Brussels); DG V, in the field of arts education and cultural training; DG XVI, for some capital projects; DG III in relation to intellectual property matters; and DG VI, with, for example, social initiatives in rural areas.

The figures given above need, however, to be broken down to be fully understood. Spending with a direct and conscious cultural objective – that is, funding handled primarily by the then DG X – for the period 1989–93 represented only 0.06% of the Community budget and significantly less if one broke down the figures further and removed the audiovisual

initiatives. Without the Measures to Encourage the Development of the Audiovisual Industry (MEDIA) programme and some other related activity in the audiovisual field, direct cultural spending fell to 0.014% of the total Community budget.

Using these same figures shows, however, that 82.7% of the funding benefiting culture came from the structural funds (see Chapter 14), which have economic and social objectives, not direct cultural ones. While representing the bulk of the funding of Community involvement in culture, such spending represented only 2.8% of the total structural funds budget at that period. Thus, DG X, the battleground on which the maximalists and minimalists had focused, was in reality a sideshow to the real Community cultural action, which came from other directorates-general indirectly (see Table 21.1).

In the case of the United Kingdom, for example, it has been estimated that funding for cultural projects from structural funds in the period 1994–99 was £25 million in Objective 1 regions, £199 million in Objective 2 regions, and £52.5 million in Objective 5b regions. Apart from cultural tourism projects, mainstream arts projects that received funding included the new Dundee Arts Centre (more than £1 million), the Glasgow Gallery of Modern Art (more than £3 million), the National Centre for Literature in Swansea (more than £1 million), the Burns Bicentenary Festival, and various theatres.

Cultural funding is also coming through other, apparently unlikely, programmes under the European Regional Development Fund, such as Interreg II (crossborder cooperation), Konver (support for areas of military industrial decline), Rechar II (conversion of former coal-mining areas), Resider II (conversion of steel areas) and Retex (support for declining clothing and textile industry areas). In the case of Interreg II, for example, the county of Kent has received £1.5 million and its neighbour East Sussex £1.6 million, while in England alone £52.5 million has gone to cultural projects under Konver, £5 million under Rechar II, and £500,000 under Resider II. Apart from drawing on these Community initiatives, the cultural sector has also benefited from "innovative actions", special allocations from structural funds that were given for eight areas of local and regional development, one of which was culture and heritage. Thirty-two pilot projects to develop local heritage and establish cultural networks between regions and towns in the EU have been supported in this way, with the United Kingdom being involved in 12.

Audiovisual, Television, and Broadcasting

Audiovisual, television, and broadcasting have been the major focus of Community attention, for three main reasons. First, these are economically significant activities and, in the field of broadcasting there is strong competition from Japanese hardware and US program software. Secondly, they clearly have a mass impact. Thirdly, they bring out nationalist sentiments, since many people see cinema, for example, as a barometer of cultural virility, and television and cinema together as the primary battlefields on which to fight the cultural imperialism of "Americanization". Indeed, the Community's involvement in media policy and activity is so extensive and complex that it warrants a study in its own right. It is appropriate, however, to sketch a little of the background.

From the early 1980s the European Parliament had been calling for a comprehensive Community policy on broadcasting. It even set up its own pressure group, both to pursue the elimination of technical barriers for transfrontier broadcasting through the adoption of common standards for direct broadcasting satellites (DBS), telecommunications, programme production, and reception technology – specifically, high-definition television (HDTV) – and also to promote and support the programme-making industry within the Community.

It was so strongly motivated because of the negative experience of the 1960s, when there were different and incompatible technical standards for colour television in different member states (PAL and SECAM). It also realized that the proliferation of broadcasting by cable and satellite, in the wake of deregulation at national level, could see the end of the fragmented European broadcasting market, which would then lead to a greatly increased demand for programmes. This represented both an opportunity, by way of a large and economically promising market for the development of European production skills, and a threat, in the form of the potential gap between demand and supply that would then be met by US programme-makers.

There have been important Council directives in this area, notably the directive on Television Without Frontiers (Dir. 89/552/EEC) of 3 October 1989, which grew out of a 350-page Commission Green Paper on the establishment of a common market for broadcasting, especially by satellite and cable (COM(84)200 final), published five years earlier. The directive forbade the restricting or hindering of broadcasts from other member states, put limits on, and set standards for, advertising (for instance, it should not exceed 15% of daily transmission time and not constitute more than 20% of broadcasting within a given one-hour period), and set targets concerning programming and content (a majority of the broadcasting time to be for European programmes and 10% of the time for "independent European productions").

The Community has also involved itself in technical standards relating to telecommunication services and equipment, notably its adoption of MAC transmission standards for satellite television and a strategy for the introduction of HDTV. This complex and contentious area led to support, beginning in 1986, for Eureka-95, a project to develop HDTV equipment, and to the setting up of Vision 1250, a "European economic interest grouping", to manage the introduction of HDTV facilities in the Community.

In 1990, Community calculations gave an estimated turnover of ECU25 billion for the audiovisual sector, which was expected to rise to ECU35 billion by 2000. Yet European interests were, and still are, in a weak position. It was estimated that in 1989 only 11% of what the Commission called fiction programmes broadcast in Europe were of European origin. It was estimated that in 1990 demand in Europe for such programmes would be in the order of 500,000 hours, but European production capacity was put at between 10,000 and 15,000 hours only. Meanwhile, in the United States and Japan, European programmes represented less than 2% of the programmes and films shown on television. Distribution of films in Europe was 60% controlled by US companies; the situation with the distribution of videos was better but there was still a very large proportion of non-European control.

These structural and historical weaknesses fuelled the demands for a Community approach, particularly from the French, and this led to measures that were unquestionably interventionist and protectionist. It led both to the MEDIA programmes and to an Audiovisual Eureka (that is, a European Research and Coordination Agency). MEDIA I covered the production, distribution, and financing of both television programmes and films through various schemes. It started in 1987 with pilot experiments; a five-year programme running to 1995 was then approved by the Council of Ministers in 1990. It consisted of various programmes underpinned by a strategy to encourage professional synergies in a "European audiovisual area" through seed money and balancing market forces. It covered all areas, including production, which the Commission was explicitly instructed should not be part of its brief. The Audiovisual Eureka, meanwhile, had been launched in 1989. Although Community funds went into it, 26 countries signed the original charter of participation.

The MEDIA II programme, covering 1996–2000, was originally costed at ECU400 million, although under pressure from the United Kingdom, Germany, and the Netherlands this was cut to ECU310 million. However, even this reduced figure represented an increase of more than 50% over the previous MEDIA programme. MEDIA II was followed by MEDIA Plus, covering the period 2000–04. Some argue that MEDIA II was a considerable success, citing statistics that suggested that the proportion of European films distributed outside their country of origin had increased from 14% in 1996 to more than 22% in 1999, and that more than 60% of such films had been supported by the MEDIA programme.

The degree to which all these measures have helped to overcome the problem of the fragmentation of the production and distribution of European programmes and films remains to be seen. New problems continued to arise, for

example, in relation to HDTV. In the context of the World Trade Organization, US threats based on the argument that the EU is discriminating against the United States and other non-European countries illustrate how complex this area is. In response to the Americans, the EU has argued – perhaps inconsistently, since its involvement in broadcasting was supposedly not a cultural policy but a response to the needs of a service industry – that this is a special case because there are cultural considerations.

The Current Agenda

There are six broad issues that are central to the culture area: EU policy on state aids, nondiscrimination, and competition law; intellectual property rights; the mobility and social conditions (for example, remuneration, training, social security, and pensions) of "cultural workers"; the movement of works of art and heritage; the free movement of the products of the cultural industries; and questions of taxation.

On the subject of state aids, nondiscrimination, and competition law, Article 87 (3)(d) TEC has helped to clarify what was an unclear position, with wording suggesting that, although not wholly excluded from the rules, culture is being treated liberally and as a special case. Discrimination on the grounds of nationality is, however, no longer acceptable in relation to state aids or national subsidy schemes operated by member states, as several cases have shown. For example, following action by the Commission, the German government had to drop the adjective "German" from its criteria for a film producers' fund, in order to rebuff the accusation that it was violating four EC Treaty Articles, these being 12 (formerly 7) on nondiscrimination, 39 (formerly 48) on free movement of persons, 43 (formerly 52) on right of establishment, and 49 (formerly 59) on free movement of services. The Dutch had opened up their film fund to foreigners, but ran into trouble as they insisted that they should meet a residence requirement not applied to Dutch applicants, who did not have to be resident in the Netherlands. They similarly opened up their literature fund to Flemish-speaking Belgians. It remains generally true, however, that discrimination on the grounds of residence or language or quality, or a combination of these, can represent a reasonable defence to protect national schemes from intra-EU exploitation or distortion.

Harmonization relating to copyright and intellectual property (known in Roman law as author's rights and neighbouring rights) is complicated, but is being pushed through. The Commission's attempt to introduce the principle of rights for 70 years after the death of the author (similar to the practice in Germany, rather than the 50 years that has been the practice in some other countries) has been accepted, and *droit de suite* – a royalty payment to artists each time one of their works is sold, that is, each time it changes hands by commericial transaction, a practice already operating in some countries – has also made headway.

On the question of mobility and the socio-economic conditions of "cultural workers", one of the main areas of debate had been how to include those in central and eastern Europe. The other main area of debate concerns extending the social security and pensions provisions operating in one or two countries for artists and performers, which imaginatively take account of their special needs and the often irregular nature of their employment.

The movement of works of art and heritage is a contentious issue with a tendency for there to be a North–South divide, reflecting fundamentally different perspectives. Italy, for example, is concerned that some of its cultural heritage is disappearing Northwards, both through the art markets and through theft. EU legislation has tried to deal with the question of theft, but progress depends on much closer practical cooperation among customs officers, police, and museums, rather than on what are probably unrealistic proposals to catalogue all works of art of national significance, favoured by some countries.

The free movement of the products of the "cultural industries", as well as of television and broadcasting, is made more complex by the tendency towards protectionism and regulation among member states. They want to defend diversity and resist the trend of these industries towards concentration, globalization, and dom-

ination by US and Japanese interests. They fear that real opportunities for competition are difficult to find in markets dominated by a small number of multinational companies. Americanization of European culture, "Dallasification" of European television, and the "mediamorphosis" of minorities remain real sources of concern.

The approximation and harmonization of tax provisions in member states form another important area where progress has been made, but where there are complex practical problems. Value-added tax (VAT) is a good example. The EU's attempts to make cultural organizations exempt from VAT would have meant that in the United Kingdom, for example, many organizations would be worse off. British charitable organizations have the right to reclaim VAT in important high-cost areas, for example, related to the maintenance of buildings, which they would lose if they were VAT-exempt (in which case a cultural organization would be unable to reclaim VAT on its costs, the value of which could be greater than any savings from not paying VAT). Defining which cultural organizations qualify for VAT exemption, without substantial loss to the Treasury, has been another difficult matter to resolve. The United Kingdom's nonconformity on VAT with other European countries and its past refusal to accept *droit de suite* have contributed to London's becoming the key international art market, and British interested parties have expressed fears that, if the British government falls into line, the market will move to Switzerland or the United States. There are, however, areas where taxation could easily and helpfully be harmonized. The varying levels of withholding tax are unnecessarily confusing. This is a tax that a promoter must deduct from fees paid to foreign performers to meet local income tax requirements.

Since Maastricht the cultural sector has had to be taken into account when apparently non-relevant legislation is being drafted, regarding, for example, health and safety in the workplace, or data protection. The proposed distance-selling directives could have bankrupted many small (as well as large) theatres, concert halls, and arts organizations and centres, both by imposing constraints on their exploitation of computerized box-office data, which in many countries is central to their marketing, and by legal restrictions on telephone credit card sales of tickets.

Cultural Programmes

In the directly cultural sphere – that is, activity carried out by DG X – a Communication issued by the Commission in 1994, *European Community Action in Support of Culture*, set out its views for action up to the year 2000, including rationalization of incentive measures into two draft arts and literature programmes, covering 1996–2000.

The first was a general arts programme, Kaleidoscope 2000, intended to supersede the existing Kaleidoscope programme. Started in 1990 and replacing the Platform Europe programme, Kaleidoscope was refocused in 1993 to cover three areas: cultural events involving three or more member states; action encouraging the mobility or training of creative artists; and support for crossfrontier cultural networks. In 1995 the budget was ECU3,747,000 and the programme covered 132 projects. The Kaleidoscope 2000 programme, with a proposed budget of ECU68 million, was scaled down by culture ministers to cover only 1995–98, and the budget was cut to ECU26.5 million.

The other programme, in support of translation, was Ariane, with a proposed budget of ECU34 million. Member states disagreed on the details of this programme and, as unanimity was required, it took time to reach a common position.

Other DG X initiatives included a museum-twinning programme, with a budget for 1995 of ECU1 million, aimed at mainstream museums in southern European countries.

In the heritage field, the Commission launched the Raphael programme for the period 1996–2000, covering five areas: development and promotion of cultural heritage; networks and partnerships; access to heritage; innovation, training, and professional mobility; and cooperation with third countries and international organizations. The total budget proposed was ECU70 million.

Geographical extension of EU cultural activity has also been a significant trend. In 1994 it was agreed that the associated countries of central and eastern Europe should participate in particular EU Councils, including Culture, as part of the preparation for accession. Protocol 31 of the European Economic Area (EEA) Agreement has been modified to include culture so that EEA countries that are not EU member states (Norway, Liechtenstein, Iceland) have access to EU cultural programmes, but participation is at their own expense. In addition, the EU's PHARE programme funded major projects aimed at promoting change in the cultural sector in Bulgaria and Romania, and culture-related projects have also been supported under TACIS, which covers the countries of the former Soviet Union and Mongolia. Geographical "creep" has now extended to the non-EU Mediterranean countries. A Med-Media programme was established for networks and projects with media professionals and institutions in the Mediterranean non-member countries, and was followed in the late 1990s by other cultural sector activity, particularly heritage, open to Algeria, Cyprus, Egypt, Israel, Jordan, Lebanon, Malta, Morocco, Syria, Tunisia, Turkey, and the Palestine National Authority.

The Culture 2000 Programme

The Education and Culture Directorate-General's Culture 2000 programme, adopted early in 2000, replaced the existing "direct" cultural programmes mentioned earlier. Open to 28 countries – the 15 EU member states, the three EEA/EFTA countries, the three Baltic states, Bulgaria, the Czech Republic, Hungary, Poland, Romania, Slovakia, and Slovenia – the budget for the period January 2000 to December 2004 was set at €167 million (originally proposed as €450 million). Although the replacement of several programmes by one was intended to ensure control and more transparency, some believe that the effect has been to jeopardize projects that would otherwise have prospered. There is also cynicism among many in the cultural sector who feel that the Culture 2000 programme simply does not recognize how projects are developed in the real world: what is being given are "cash prizes" for managing to complete a 56-page application form demanding baroque financial arrangements, rather than project development grants. This view was given further credence when decisions on the first round of successful projects (those taking place in 2000) were not forthcoming until well into 2001. It reinforced an image of bureaucratic incompetence and lack of clear procedures, not helped by allegedly cavalier assessment of applications. The EU's own rule that it cannot announce in one calendar year funding for the next means that the earliest it can announce the annual programme is after mid-January of the year in which the activity is to take place, which allows too short a lead time for most projects and organizations.

On the positive side, for its first year €32 million was given to 219 projects, out of 1,023 applications, in three categories: projects involving partners from at least three member states (197 projects); structural and multiannual projects involving partners from at least five member states (19 projects); and three special activities, namely, two European "heritage laboratories", a European prize for contemporary architecture, and the European Cities of Culture programme. Culture 2000 was intended to be a framework programme, but the Commission still could not resist stumbling into what appeared to be totally random areas of detail, such as offering funding for Verdi centenary events after the centenary year had already started.

The Future

Although no longer implacably hostile to cultural activity by the EU, the "minimalist" countries continue to uphold the principles of unanimity, subsidiarity, and complementarity, and, in the case of the United Kingdom, the Department of Culture, Media, and Sport insists that there is no "additionality", that is, that the costs of any new EU activity must be met from the relevant existing domestic budgets. For the maximalists, meanwhile, there is enough on the agenda to keep them content, and less danger than in the past of serious EU divisions on culture, even if, with the widening of the EU, outdated concepts such as "graduated integration" or initiatives similar to the French Blue Book of 1987 may reappear. (The

Blue Book, a prospectus produced by France to coincide with the 30th anniversary of the Treaty of Rome and reflecting French frustration at the time, contained a menu of cultural and educational activity that could have gone ahead without all Community member states participating: a "Europe *à la carte*".)

Over the coming decade it is likely that four areas in particular will witness interesting developments. The first is the debate about "European cultural identity", an issue that will become increasingly prominent and in which protectionist arguments about the dangers of cultural globalization will no doubt feature as prominently as ever. The second is the accession of a number of new countries, which will probably tend to be sympathetic to the ambitions of the current maximalists. The third is the shape of the stuctural funds: the current round ends in 2006 and accounts for more than 80% of the EU's cultural funding, but any further funds after that may be redirected to central and eastern Europe, possibly creating pressure from countries in western Europe for new "direct" cultural funding to compensate. The fourth area concerns the promotion of the cultural diversity of the "old Europe" and the problem of how the cultural diversity of the urbanized minority groups that originated from outside Europe will be handled by the EU's institutions, especially on over-stretched budgets.

Further Reading

Bates and Wacker, *Community Support for Culture: A Study Carried out for the Commission of the European Community*, Brussels: Directorate General X of the European Commission, June 1993

Delgado-Moreira, Juan, "Cohesion and Citizenship in EU Cultural Policy", *Journal of Common Market Studies*, 38/3, 2000

One of the few examples of academic literature on the EU's cultural policy

Directorate-General for Education and Culture, website at www.europa.eu.int/comm/dgs/education_ culture/index_en.html

European Commission, Communication, *New Prospects for Community Cultural Action* (COM(92)149 final), 1992

European Commission, Communication, *European Community Action in Support of Culture*, (COM(94) 356 final), 1994

European Commission, webpages at europa.eu.int/comm/avpolicy/mediapro/media_en.htm

This provides access to information on the MEDIA programme.

European Commission, webpages at www.europa.eu.int/comm/culture/index_en.html

This provides access to an overview of cultural policy and the relevant legal texts.

Harrison, Jackie, and Lorna Woods, "European Citizenship: Can Audio-Visual Policy Make a Difference?", *Journal of Common Market Studies*, 38/3, 2000

Another rare foray into the field by two scholars

Informal European Theatre Meeting, *Information Box 2 – Bread and Circuses*, Brussels, 1992

MEDIA programme for the United Kingdom, website at www.mediadesk.co.uk

Vaizey, John, Lord, speech at a conference, "The Arts and the EC", at the Institute of Contemporary Arts, London, 11 May 1979

Terry Sandell OBE FRSA is Director of the Visiting Arts, an international arts agency. He has been Director of the British Council in Vienna, Cultural Attaché in the British Embassy in Moscow, and, from 1989 to 1992, Director of the British Council in the former Soviet Union. He also lectures and acts as a consultant, and has led Council of Europe cultural policy reviews of the Russian Federation, Romania, Azerbaijan, and Georgia.

Table 21.1   Categories of EU Involvement in Cultural Activities

Category	*Scope and examples*
Political and bureaucratic activity	production of policy research, reports, communications, resolutions, and recommendations
Institution-building and -strengthening	support for organizations or establishments with a Community profile or with the potential to project a positive Community image, such as the European Community Youth Orchestra, formally proposed by the European Parliament in 1976 and patronized by the Commission ever since
Support for one-off events, visits, and exchanges	both ad hoc and through DG X programmes, such as Platform Europe and Kaleidoscope, and the current Culture 2000 programme
Support for regular events	for example, the European City of Culture initiative and the proliferating Community culture prizes, such as the European Prize for Contemporary Architecture, the European Literary Prize, and the European Translation Prize
Support for cultural heritage	with a strong emphasis on conservation and tourism-related projects
Training	both directly on a small scale through DG X (examples included grants for arts administrators, instrument-makers, choreographers, composers, painters, conservation specialists, and gardeners), and indirectly through, for example, DG V and the European Social Fund (one European Social Fund project in Spain alone trained 60,000 people in restoration skills and crafts) or schemes such as Erasmus, Tempus, Force, and Petra
Information	
Extensive support for the "audiovisual sector"	films, television programmes, and broadcasting more generally
Miscellaneous support for books, reading, and translation	now absorbed into the Culture 2000 programme
Support for capital and infrastructure projects	indirectly through structural funds
Activities related to third countries	through cultural clauses in cooperation treaties with developing countries in the Africa, Caribbean, and Pacific group; with candidate countries in central and eastern Europe; and with other countries that have relevant association or cooperation agreements

Source: Author's analysis of official sources, some cited in the Further Reading list

External Relations

Chapter Twenty-Two

The Common Foreign and Security Policy

David Allen

In retrospect it seems precipitate of the framers of the Treaty on European Union (Maastricht Treaty, or TEU) to have declared in Article J that "a common foreign and security policy is hereby established". The existence of such a policy – generally referred to as the CFSP – as a separate pillar indicates that the member states of the European Community (EC) were not able to agree, in 1991, to integrate European Political Cooperation (EPC), their well-established intergovernmental procedure for coordinating national foreign policies, into the formal law-making procedures of the Community. Those states that would have liked to have gone further down the road of legally based supranational integration, involving law-making procedures and the taking of qualified majority votes, reluctantly accepted the Maastricht compromise arrangements, but only on the condition that they be reviewed five years later at another intergovernmental conference (IGC). However, neither at Amsterdam in 1997 nor at Nice in 2000 were the member states' governments prepared to overturn the "intergovernmental" basis of the CFSP, although, as we shall see, they were prepared to allow the European foreign policy process to become more and more centred on Brussels, rather than on national capitals.

The EU itself has no legal standing in the international system: only the European Community and its member states have legal standing. Further, the CFSP covers only one aspect of its role in the world, for the external economic activities of the EU, involving mainly trade, aid, and development policies, but also the external aspects of all internal EU business, take place within the first pillar of the TEU, that of the EC, and create, and are governed by, Community law. The TEU has several references to the need to ensure consistency between the three pillars, and its establishment of a common institutional framework is designed to achieve this, most especially between the EU's external economic activities and the CFSP.

The EPC Inheritance

Many people see the CFSP as simply a continuation of the practices established over 20 years within EPC. The system of regular meetings at a variety of levels between officials and ministers from national foreign ministries was established under the Luxembourg Report in 1970, and gradually expanded and consolidated until 1987, when it was given a treaty basis within the Single European Act (SEA). However, the original intention to keep EPC distinct from Community structures and procedures was maintained in the SEA. Thus, although Title III, in which the Community's member states agreed to "endeavour jointly to formulate and implement a European foreign policy", represents a legally binding agreement (between "high contracting parties" rather than member states), it is just like any other international treaty, but it is not part of the EC treaty process. However the fact that the separate EC and EPC titles were combined in a *Single* European Act indicated that a majority of the member states hoped eventually to bring EPC into the Community proper, under the auspices of a European Union.

The EPC system essentially involved regular multilevel contacts among the foreign ministries of the Community's member states. Until the SEA provided for the establishment of a small secretariat in Brussels, EPC had no central institutions and was managed exclusively by the member state that held the presidency of the Council of Ministers (which rotates on a six-monthly basis), albeit often in partnership with the other two members of the presidency "troika", consisting of representatives of the incumbent, preceding and succeeding presidencies. Although both the Commission and the European Parliament gradually developed roles within the EPC process, after initially being deliberately excluded, these were essentially subsidiary, as the member states' governments continued to guard jealously their sovereign rights over the sensitive area of foreign policy. Significantly, there was no initial role for the European Court of Justice, nor did one develop, because its competence is rigidly tied to matters covered by the EC Treaty.

Under EPC, regular meetings of foreign ministers, both separately and in the margins of the Council, were prepared by the political directors meeting in the Political Committee – these political directors being officials of a broadly similar status to the ambassadors who participate in the Committee of Permanent Representatives (Coreper), but based at home, in their national foreign ministries. Below the meetings of the political directors there developed a proliferation of regular and *ad hoc* working groups of officials at departmental and desk officer level. The system was further lubricated by a telex system, Coreu, that directly connected the foreign ministries of the member states, and, after a few years, the Commission. In non-member third countries, EPC meetings of representatives of the Community's member states were organized by the presidency ambassador, who also represented the collection of member states (known over time as the Six, the Nine, the Ten, the 12, and now the 15). At the UN and in other international organizations a collective Community position was often put forward alongside the various national stances of the member states.

The EC too, as we noted above, had its external activities and procedures. Within the General Agreement on Tariffs and Trade (GATT), for instance, the Commission negotiated on behalf of the Community, within the confines of a mandate laid down by the Council of Ministers (see Chapter 24). Inevitably, the two procedures came into contact with one another. The fact that the Commission came to participate in EPC deliberations reflected the fact that it remained difficult to maintain a neat distinction between economic and political matters. While the EC system was in constant need of political guidance in its conduct of external relations, it was also the case that many EPC objectives could be achieved only by using Community instruments, such as aid or other economic rewards and sanctions including, of course, the possibility of EC membership.

The EPC system was often accused of being more about procedures than substance and of being essentially reactive – a cosy club of national diplomats interested only in the preservation of national interests rather than the articulation of the "European" interest. It was argued that the procedures were designed to facilitate consultation and to generate common declarations, but that the need for consensus, and the member states' concern to preserve their national foreign policies and positions, prevented progress towards significant joint action, other than the diplomatic presentation of common positions that were usually bland in the extreme and failed to rise above the lowest common denominator. Nevertheless, some substantive progress was made and by the 1980s the member states had positions on the Middle East conflict, the "new Cold War", Central America, and other situations that differed significantly from the positions advanced by the United States. Under EPC they had begun to develop a Community identity, such that they could be described as presenting a "second" western view of international relations. Of course, this limited development disappointed those who felt that the EC would not become a proper union until it had a fully fledged foreign and defence policy administered by central institutions. It was also the case that the limited degree of consensus on foreign policy matters, combined with the defence taboo, meant that the ECs weak foreign policy and political presence stood in marked contrast to its growing and already formidable presence in the international political economy. Nevertheless, it was argued by some that, given time, the EPC socialization process would facilitate the development of a foreign policy of greater substance. However, the end of the Cold War presented a new set of more formidable challenges to the EPC system with an expectation, both within and outside the EC, that it would play a leading role in the evolution of a "new European order".

The Impact of Political Transformation in Europe

With the end of Communism in central and eastern Europe, and eventually in the Soviet Union, and with the unification of Germany, many felt that the EC's hour had come. While institutions such as Comecon, the Warsaw Pact, and perhaps even NATO seemed to have lost their *raisons d'être*, the EC found itself in the spotlight. Now it seemed that obstacles to enlargement of the EC were greatly reduced, with two distinct groupings seeking membership of the Community and thus of EPC. The member states of the European Free Trade Area (EFTA), which had wanted to join the Community ever since the single market programme was instituted, but were inhibited by their neutrality from joining an institution with foreign policy and security pretensions, now abandoned the European Economic Area (EEA) and sought full membership. Similarly, the former Communist states of central and eastern Europe, liberated from the control of the Soviet Union, now saw the EC as the framework for their future prosperity and security.

Within the Community there were some member states, such as Britain, that argued for immediate enlargement, while others, such as France, feared that "widening" would lead to weakening and therefore advocated a further "deepening" of the Community before new members were considered. The result was a decision to deepen first, initially by formalizing the commitment to Economic and Monetary Union (EMU) but also, at German insistence,

by making progress towards political union – by which was meant, in the first instance, developing the Community's institutions, and its foreign and security policy apparatus. The two IGCs that led up to the Maastricht agreements thus represented the Community's initial response to the new situation in Europe. On the foreign policy side, it was clear that the Community and its member states faced a whole new series of challenges and expectations in the "new Europe", and there were doubts about whether the EPC process was capable of bearing the weight of these new responsibilities.

Even though we have suggested that during the Cold War the Community's member states within EPC had moved towards creating a separate international identity for themselves, this was very much within the parameters laid down by the confrontation between the superpowers. Although there had been constant discussions about enhancing the security and defence identity of western Europe, as long as the Soviet Union was represented as the major threat it was unlikely that there would be enthusiasm for moving away from or risking undermining the protective umbrella of the US-dominated NATO. Even the common foreign policy stances that the Community's member states had managed to cobble together under EPC were conditioned by the influences of the superpowers and many felt that the member states were in a rather luxurious position: they were able to dabble in collective foreign policy-making without having to take ultimate responsibility and stood safe in the knowledge that the two superpowers, both individually and together (because of their shared concern to avoid war with one another), provided a kind of safety net.

Regardless of their competing ideas about the ideal development of the Community, the member states now found themselves facing a "new European order" that was extremely uncertain. The nature of the security threat had clearly altered, as had the position, potential, and expectations of the Community. While the Soviet Union broke up and its major successor state, Russia, became increasingly internally focused, the United States too seemed to be in retreat from Europe, its major objectives there having now, it appeared, been achieved. What was left was the EC – the object of interest of every non-member state in Europe, with the potential to build on its role as a major trading power and become a more complete international actor.

The TEU and the CFSP

The TEU represented a compromise among the various ambitions of the then 12 member states of the Community. Although the notion of an all-embracing European Union was established, it was to involve the continuation of the well-established distinction between the supranational activities of the Community and the intergovernmental habits developed within the EPC process. The TEU provided for three pillars, dealing with, respectively, the EC, the newly named CFSP (the old EPC), and a new third pillar covering cooperation in the field of justice and home affairs. There were some innovations in the second, CFSP pillar, with the introduction of the long-term objective of creating a common defence policy and eventually a common defence (see Chapter 23), and with the provision, against the logic of an intergovernmental pillar, for the limited application of qualified majority voting (see below).

Although the CFSP was to remain as a separate pillar and was thus not integrated into the Community's decision-making processes under the Treaty of Rome, the TEU seeks to ensure consistency in the EU's external positions by providing for a common institutional framework. Consistency and coherence present a particular problem for the EU, where the overlap between the external policy of the Community (within pillar 1) and the CFSP (pillar 2) is obvious. Further, the establishment of a similar form of intergovernmental cooperation in the field of justice and home affairs (pillar 3) meant that the EU was now concerning itself with such matters as immigration, asylum, terrorism, major crime, and drug-trafficking, which are related to its internal security but clearly also have a major external dimension. Any true common foreign and security policy would clearly require the harmonious coordination and joint management of cooperative activity in all three pillars.

To this end the TEU gives formal roles to both the Commission and the European Parliament within the CFSP process. The Commission is to be "associated with all aspects of the CFSP" and shares the right of initiative with the member states, unlike in the first, Community pillar, where the Commission has the sole right of initiative. Thus, while the Commission has the legal right to be involved in the CFSP process it does not have the exclusive role of defining the "European" interest. The European Parliament is to be "kept informed" of all CFSP developments and has, of course, taken a keen interest in the arrangements, which were unclear when the TEU was signed, for financing the CFSP. The lack of legislative provision means that there was no role envisaged for the European Court of Justice. The establishment of a common institutional framework meant that the Community's Council of Ministers became the Council of the Union and, like the European Council, was given the task of considering all aspects of external relations, foreign policy, and security within the same forum, regardless of which pillar they might originate in.

At official level the TEU suggested that in time Coreper (the member states' ambassadors based in Brussels) and the Political Committee (the member states' political directors based in national capitals) might be fused together, along with the various working groups of the Council and EPC that had previously been kept separate, even though they had all developed the habit of meeting mainly in Brussels. The small secretariat established by the SEA was to be expanded and fully integrated into the Council secretariat. During the last years of Jacques Delors's presidency of the Commission, a new Directorate-General, DG1A, was established to handle the Commission's input into the CFSP, but in his Commission Jacques Santer sought to bring the political and economic aspects of the Commission's external relations together so as to match the developments in the Council discussed above. The result was that there were now four Commissioners with direct external relations portfolios (CFSP, Trade, Lomé, and Development Aid for the rest of the world), and several more whose portfolios had external aspects (Agriculture, Single

Market, Competition, and so on). Under the Maastricht arrangements, therefore, there were at least three centres of foreign policy activity within the EU, all loosely connected and bound by the objective of consistency, but also, in a sense, all rivals with one another. First of all there were the 12 (and, after 1995, 15) member states, all of which continued to shape and implement their own national foreign and defence policies. Second, there was the CFSP – the framework within which the member states and the EU's institutions sought to coordinate their foreign policy and defence activities. Finally, there was the European Commission, a participant in the CFSP process, but with its own extensive "first pillar" responsibilities. While the member states insisted on retaining their own foreign ministries and diplomatic services, the Commission could be seen as having ambitions to emulate them and, perhaps, eventually to replace them with DG 1A, along with its extensive network of overseas posts and representations, of which there were more than 100 at the time of the Maastricht Treaty and 125 in 2001. The CFSP, nevertheless, lacked central institutions, other than the expanded secretariat, and relied heavily on the Council Presidency and the troika for representative duties.

As far as the work of the CFSP is concerned, the TEU requires the member states to "inform and consult one another", on "any matter of foreign and security policy", in order to ensure that their "combined influence is exerted as effectively as possible by means of concerted and convergent action". Provision is made for the Council to establish a common position (much as had been the case with EPC) and it is the member states' duty to ensure that their national policies conform with these common positions. The TEU extends the member states' degree of commitment, however, by its provisions for the establishment of joint actions. Here, the Council of Ministers takes general guidance from the European Council in deciding whether a matter should be the subject of a joint action. When adopting a joint action and as part of the provisions for implementation, the Council can choose to define certain matters relating to implementation that will be decided in the future by

qualified majority vote. This represents only a limited movement away from the basic principle that governs both of the intergovernmental pillars, of seeking consensus or acting only by unanimity. A unanimous vote is required to establish a joint action and another unanimous vote is required to decide that qualified majority voting may take place with regard to subsequent implementation. Article J3 also provided a further safeguard, in that "any change of circumstances" could lead to further review and a reversion to consensus decision-making.

Despite all these limitations, joint actions did represent an evolution from the old EPC process, which had been limited to consultation, as they were meant to "commit the member states in the positions they adopt and in their conduct of activity". The idea was to move from common declarations to common actions, and perhaps also from reaction to initiative and action. Further, member states were required to inform one another in advance of any proposal to adopt a national position or take national action with regard to a matter covered by a joint action. In this way, the member states agreed to limit the scope of their own unilateral action, even though they continued to claim the right to pursue national foreign policies.

The TEU came into operation only towards the end of 1993 and since then the 12 original signatories have been joined by three new members – Austria, Sweden, and Finland. These three new members were required to accept not just the *acquis communautaire* of the Community but also the *acquis politique* that represented all the achievements of EPC and the CFSP to date. This they managed to do with little apparent difficulty (although they did not become full members of the Western European Union – see Chapter 23), even though their previous foreign policy experience as neutral states had been rather different from that of the 11 – that is, the 12 excluding Ireland, which is also a neutral state.

In the period between the ratification of the TEU and the signing of the Treaty of Amsterdam, as well as carrying on the EPC practice of facilitating agreement on literally hundreds of common positions, the CFSP procedures led to the establishment of more than 50 joint actions dealing mainly with events in the former Yugoslavia, Africa, and the Middle East, but also with certain other matters. Thus, for example, the "European order" was addressed in the Balladur Pact; concern over the proliferation of both nuclear and conventional weapons was expressed in the EU's support for the renewal of the Nuclear Nonproliferation Treaty, the Korean Peninsular Energy Development Organization (KEDO), the campaign against land mines, and the "code of conduct" for arms suppliers; and the EU also took action over political aspects of trade relations, as in its response to the Helms–Burton legislation enacted by the US Congress. It was, however, symptomatic of the need for consistency between the EU pillars that while the decision to establish these joint actions was a political one, taken within the CFSP pillar, the means to achieve the agreed objectives usually lay within the first, EC pillar. Thus, the initial success of a joint action such as the Balladur Pact owed much to the fact that the EU was able to exploit the desire of the states of central and east Europe to enjoy better economic relations with the Community and, eventually, to become full members of the EU.

As we noted above, the TEU provided for a further IGC to begin in 1996 with a specific commitment for the member states to review progress on the CFSP. While some argued that this was too soon, since the TEU was after all ratified only in late 1993, others felt that the EU's disastrous performance on Slovenia, Croatia, and Bosnia–Herzegovina – which had begun with the Luxembourg Presidency declaring in 1991 that "this is the hour of Europe not the United States" and had ended in late 1995 with the EU being sidelined by the United States as it brokered the Dayton Accords – more than justified a substantial overhaul of the CFSP process. Thus, the British government argued that the experience with the collapse of Yugoslavia demonstrated the impossibility of attaining a supranational, "European" foreign policy, while others argued that, on the contrary, it demonstrated the urgent need for just such a policy.

As the IGC opened in 1996 it was difficult to argue with the assessment that the CFSP had to date done little to bring about progress from the old EPC system and many maintained that

the new procedures in fact diminished the socialization process that was such a marked feature of EPC. The common declarations remained innocuous and indicative of the lowest common denominator by which the member states operate; the joint actions were numerous but did not amount to anything very substantive. There was a host of proposals for improving the CFSP procedures, many of which revisited arguments and positions that had remained unresolved after the negotiations in 1991.

The Treaties of Amsterdam and Nice

The IGC that preceded the Treaty of Amsterdam was a lengthy process that was soured in 1996 by a serious dispute between the United Kingdom and the rest of the EU over the question of BSE. The British government's position, which, for a brief period during the Italian Presidency, involved a policy of noncooperation in the Council, was not made any easier by a conflict within the ruling Conservative Party that effectively prevented John Major's government from playing anything other than a negative role in the IGC process. When it was completed, after a British election that saw the Labour Party elected on a commitment to reverse the negativity towards the EU that had characterized the previous government, the Treaty of Amsterdam made few formal changes to the CFSP process and did little to meet the expectations of those who sought to develop the defence role of the EU (see Chapter 23).

The fundamental principle of unanimity was preserved, albeit with one or two variations that at least had the potential for further development. Article 23 of the new consolidated treaty (see Document 22.1) provided for the notion of "constructive abstention", which allows member states, provided that they do not represent in total more than one third of the EU by weighted vote in the Council, to abstain from a vote, and thus avoid being bound by that vote while nevertheless accepting that it still commits the Union. This form of flexibility, which some have nevertheless condemned as "destructive" abstention, might enable the member states to break the dead-lock of unanimity such as was caused by Greece's refusal to approve the joint recognition of Macedonia. By 2001, however, no such abstention had been recorded in the CFSP.

The new treaty also introduced the idea of a "common strategy" (Article 13.2) to be decided upon unanimously by the European Council on the basis of a recommendation by the Council. Once a common strategy has been agreed the treaty provides for the Council to implement it "in particular by adopting joint actions and common positions" (Article 13.3), and these decisions, along with those implementing them, can be taken by a qualified majority (Article 23.2). However, it should also be noted that the ever-cautious member states also inserted a clause (Article 23.2) that allows any one of them to oppose the adoption of any CFSP decision by a qualified majority on the grounds of "important and stated reasons of national policy". This is, in effect, the old Luxembourg Compromise, given legal status for the first time. Further evidence of a renewed intergovernmentalism was illustrated by the fact that the member states decided at the last moment not to give the EU, as opposed to the European Community, legal personality. Instead, it was decided to give the Council the power, on an *ad hoc* basis, to authorize the Presidency to negotiate and conclude agreements on matters outside the Community's competence – i.e., on the CFSP – or to do so with the Commission on matters of mixed competence. Even then the member states reserved the right to complete national ratification procedures before being bound by a "Union" agreement.

The major institutional innovation in the Amsterdam Treaty is the creation of the post of High Representative for the CFSP and the establishment (via a Declaration) of a policy planning and early warning unit. The High Representative was also to be the Secretary General of the Council. At the European Council in Cologne in 1999 Javier Solana, then Secretary General of NATO, was appointed to the post and then, later in that year, also to the post of Secretary General of the Western European Union (WEU), in order to preside over its incorporation into the EU and thus the CFSP (see Chapter 23). At the same time, the Policy Planning and Early Warning Unit was established within the Council Secretariat and, under the direction of its first head, Christoph Heusgen, became known more simply as the Policy Unit. The Policy Unit initially consisted of 20 A-grade officials, 15 of whom were drawn from the member states, three from the Council Secretariat (although the Council Secretariat retained its own Directorate dealing with the CFSP), and one each from the Commission and the WEU. The Policy Unit was further expanded as a result of the decisions taken in the context of the Common European Security and Defence Policy (CESDP), with members of the newly established Military Staff also taking up their posts in 2000 and 2001.

The appointment of Solana and the establishment of the Policy Unit, both based in Brussels, were indicative of a further "Brussels-ization" of the CFSP. This tendency for the Council to expand in Brussels potentially challenges the role of the rotating Presidency of the Council, as well as the role of diplomats based in national capitals. The CESDP institutional arrangements agreed at the European Council in Helsinki at the end of 1999 provided for the eventual establishment of a Military Committee and a Military Staff, but the most significant innovation as far as the CFSP was concerned was to be the creation of a Political and Security Committee, based in Brussels and staffed by CFSP "ambassadors" themselves based in the permanent representations of the member states.

The eventual implementation of the Treaty of Nice (which had yet to be ratified when this book went to press) will make four changes in these arrangements. Two are rather technical: Article 24 of this treaty enables the Council to act by a qualified majority when concluding CFSP agreements for which a qualified majority is required for internal decisions; and a small addition to Article 23(2) makes it possible for the Council to use a qualified majority to appoint a special representative in accordance with Article 18(5) to the CFSP that does not relate to the CESDP. Next, a modification of Article 25 makes it clear that the Political and Security Committee will, in effect, replace the Political Committee. The question can therefore be asked as to whether the CFSP "ambassadors", who are also effectively deputy political directors, will replace their nominal bosses and in practice meet in semipermanent session in Brussels (rather like Coreper) – a significant change from the previous system that had political directors travelling, albeit on a regular basis, from national capitals and one that adds more weight to the argument that the CFSP is becoming "Brussels-ized". Finally, the member states have also agreed that, where they deem it appropriate, the High Representative may chair the Political and Security Committee instead of the Presidency.

The Role of the Commission

The significant increase in the power of the Council over CFSP matters raises a number of questions about the evolving role of the Commission in relation to the CFSP. At the time of the Amsterdam Treaty a separate Declaration was appended noting the Commission's intention to reorganize its directorates-general and to bring external relations under the overall responsibility of a Vice President (a match for the High Representative?) instead of under the collective authority of four Commissioners. In the event, Romano Prodi, after being appointed President of the Commission in 1999, decided to give his two Vice Presidents responsibility for reforming the Commission and liaising with the European Parliament (understandable in view of the context of Prodi's appointment), and, as his predecessors had, appointed four external relations Commissioners, changing their portfolios from the geographic to the functional. Nevertheless, it was made clear that *primus inter pares* among the four would be Chris Patten (of the United Kingdom), who was given the External Relations portfolio – the crucial post for coordinating foreign policy. The other three portfolios cover trade, enlargement, and development aid. Patten's responsibilities thus include responsibility for the CFSP and the management of the Commission's external services. Patten is not a Vice President but he is clearly meant to be the Commission's foreign minister. Inevitably, given the nature of their respective jobs, Patten and Solana have been seen as rivals, despite their apparent determi-

nation to work together on cross-pillar issues, such as the EU's policy towards the Western Balkans. While Solana has been kept busy driving the CESDP forward, Patten has been under considerable pressure within the Commission to seize the initiative over the development of civilian crisis management systems and to lay claim to a role for the Commission in the many nonmilitary aspects of the "Petersberg" tasks that were written into the Amsterdam Treaty (Article 17(2)).

At the time of writing the relationship between Patten and Solana remains controversial. Solana worries about the openness and insecurity of Community procedures, and has sought to insulate his own operations, not just from the Commission but from the rest of the Council Secretariat. Meanwhile, Patten complains, with some justification, that, while CFSP decisions are increasingly being taken in isolation by the Council, the responsibility for implementing those decisions usually falls upon the Commission, and other Community institutions and bodies. For Romano Prodi the essential link between decision and implementation would be best made by making the High Representative the permanent chair of the Political and Security Committee, if not the Council itself, and by making him also a member of the Commission. However, this is not necessarily likely to appeal to the larger member states, which see Solana as "their" man.

Whatever the ultimate role of the High Representative and the fate of the CESDP, the European Commission has an important role to play in relation to the CFSP, if only to demand coherent and realistic political guidance from the Council. Most aspects of Community business, whether nominally internal or external, have an international dimension, and are likely either to produce "political" responses from the outside world or to be used by the EU to underpin its own "political" stance towards the outside world. Indeed, one might argue that the EU's policies on enlargement, trade, and development aid, all of which represent major responsibilities for the Commission, are in reality at the heart of any "EU foreign policy", and require responsible political direction from the CFSP process. One of the negative features of the period since the

Franco–British Declaration of St Malo and all that flowed from it (see Chapter 23) has been the relative neglect of the CFSP itself, as well as other aspects of Community external relations. While Solana has attempted to maintain a high profile over a range of portfolios and has undoubtedly sought, where possible, to work with the Commission in the new "troika" consisting of the Presidency, the High Representative, and the External Relations Commissioner, most of his time since taking up office has been devoted to the CESDP, and in particular to resolving the many problems that arise in bringing the WEU into the EU and establishing a working relationship between the EU and NATO. The sidelining of the CFSP and the obsession with the CESDP in recent years has meant that it has been difficult for the Commission to play a full part in a set of procedures that are also becoming more rather than less intergovernmental. Meanwhile, Solana has neither a large staff nor significant resources, relying as he does on the small Policy Unit and the various special envoys that have been appointed in recent years to cover the Middle East, the Western Balkans, Central Africa, and Cyprus. If a more sensible balance between the civilian and the military aspects of the CFSP is restored, then the Commission, with its relatively large staff and resources may well have a significant role to play in the CFSP. However, if present trends continue, it is more likely to be a supportive and implementative role, rather than a leadership role.

Conclusion

The CFSP is clearly in a state of flux. Many of the recently introduced procedural innovations, such as constructive abstention and limited qualified majority voting, have either not been used or have been overshadowed by the absolute determination of the member states to maintain unanimity, and thus a veto, on all matters to do with defence. While the ever-growing list of joint actions and common positions continues to be more significant quantitatively than qualitatively, the more recent introduction of "common strategies" also seems to have failed to make much difference to the EU's relations with either Russia, Ukraine or the

Mediterranean, the targets of the first three common strategies, which were introduced in 2000 and 2001. Indeed, in early 2001 Javier Solana sent a highly critical report to the Council, arguing that in all three of these cases the EU's policies and procedures were already well-established, and that the lengthy and long-winded common strategies added little value. He also noted that, in the case of Russia, despite its wordiness the common strategy had not proved useful in framing the EU's response to the very important issue of Chechnya and that it was an appreciation of the nonutility of common strategies that had led to the abandonment of the proposed fourth strategy aimed at the Western Balkans. Further, Solana noted that none of the available qualified voting procedures had been used. He concluded that, as they had developed to date, common strategies had become a largely bureaucratic exercise, burdening each presidency with a perceived need to introduce a new work plan and handicapped by the fact that they were public documents. Solana made some procedural suggestions, in particular making a plea that common strategies should become internal and confidential EU policy documents, but his criticisms seem to suggest that procedural innovations developed during IGCs are not the best way of making progress on the CFSP. The same point can be made about the evolution of the CESDP (as outlined in Chapter 23), where all significant progress has occurred in between IGCs and has been formalized in the more obscure Presidency Reports, rather than in treaty amendments.

The CFSP, like EPC before it, is thus most likely to evolve through the *ad hoc* experience of dealing with real situations than through the detailed consideration of IGC papers, Presidency Conclusions, and treaty texts. At the time of writing the French Presidency Report on the CESDP, which is more than 40 pages long, appears to constitute a sort of manual for dealing with the civilian and military aspects of an international crisis. The wording is elegant and balanced, but one doubts whether the complex procedures it elaborates would survive a real crisis intact. Since it was established in 1991, the CFSP has failed to serve the EU's interests in the succession of crises in former Yugoslavia;

most of its other activities pale into insignificance alongside this major trauma in the "new European order". However, while some have noted a constant gap between the expectations for, and the capabilities of, the CFSP in the 1990s (see Hill 1993, for example), others have perceived a gradual narrowing of the gap, and a slow but steady evolution of the CFSP. Whether one is optimistic or pessimistic about the current state of affairs, it is clearly going to be some time before the CFSP provides the basis for a European foreign policy.

Further Reading

Cameron, Fraser, *The Foreign and Security Policy of the EU: Past, Present and Future*, Sheffield: Sheffield Academic Press/UACES, 1999

A clear guide written by a practitioner and seasoned observer of the CFSP

Eliassen, Kjell (editor), *Foreign and Security Policy in the European Union*, London: Sage, 1998

A useful collection of articles written by both academics and insiders

Forster, Anthony, and Wallace, William, "Common Foreign and Security Policy: from Shadow to Substance?", in Helen Wallace and William Wallace (editors), *Policy-making in the European Union*, fourth edition, Oxford and New York: Oxford University Press, 2000

A reliable and well-written analysis of the evolution of EPC and the CFSP

Hill, Christopher, "The Capability–Expectations Gap, or Conceptualizing Europe's International Role", in *Journal of Common Market Studies*, 31/3, September 1993

A groundbreaking analysis of the CFSP and the EU's role in the world

Hill, Christopher (editor), *The Actors in Europe's Foreign Policy*, London and New York: Routledge, 1996

A survey of the impact of the CFSP on the foreign policies of the EU's member states

Hoffman, Stanley, "Towards a Common Foreign and Security Policy", in *Journal of Common Market Studies*, 38/2, June 2000

A recent survey by one of the leading commentators on the EU and its role in the world

Nuttall, Simon, *European Political Cooperation*, Oxford: Clarendon Press, and New York: Oxford University Press, 1992

The definitive book on EPC by an ex-practitioner – as close to an official history as it is possible to get

Nuttall, Simon, *European Foreign Policy*, Oxford and New York: Oxford University Press, 2000

The story of the origins and early days of the CFSP

Peterson, John, and Helene Sjursen (editors), *A Common Foreign Policy for Europe?: Competing Visions of the CFSP*, London and New York: Routledge, 1998

This collection contains chapters by most of the leading commentators on the CFSP, including a "revisiting" by Christopher Hill of his article cited above.

Regelsberger, Elfriede, Philippe de Schoutheete de Tervarent, and Wolfgang Wessels (editors), *Foreign Policy of the European Union: From EPC to CFSP and Beyond*, Boulder, CO: L. Rienner, 1997

A collection of articles by a large group of European observers of the CFSP in the mid-1990s

Smith, Michael, "The Common Foreign and Security Policy", Chapter 10 in Simon Bromley (editor), *Governing the European Union*, London: Sage and the Open University, 2001

An analysis of the CFSP by a leading UK specialist, which includes a useful case study of the CFSP and the conflict in the former Yugoslavia

---

David Allen is Jean Monnet Senior Lecturer in European Studies and Deputy Director of the East Midlands EU Centre at Loughborough University. He is the author of numerous articles and chapters on the foreign policy of the EU and on policy-making within the EU.

Document 22.1 Key Treaty Articles on the Common Foreign and Security Policy

[Consolidated text of the TEU as amended by the Treaties of Amsterdam and Nice. Revisions agreed at the Nice Council in December 2000 are in italics: as indicated, in some cases they involve deletions and in others new words or paragraphs to be added when the Treaty of Nice comes into force. Articles covering the Common European Security and Defence Policy can be found in Document 23.1.]

TITLE V

PROVISIONS ON A COMMON FOREIGN AND SECURITY POLICY

Article 11

1. The Union shall define and implement a common foreign and security policy covering all areas of foreign and security policy, the objectives of which shall be:
    - to safeguard the common values, fundamental interests, independence and integrity of the Union in conformity with the principles of the United Nations Charter;
    - to strengthen the security of the Union in all ways;
    - to preserve peace and strengthen international security, in accordance with the principles of the United Nations Charter, as well as the principles of the Helsinki Final Act and the objectives of the Paris Charter, including those on external borders;
    - to promote international cooperation;
    - to develop and consolidate democracy and the rule of law, and respect for human rights and fundamental freedoms.
2. The Member States shall support the Union's external and security policy actively and unreservedly in a spirit of loyalty and mutual solidarity.

    The Member States shall work together to enhance and develop their mutual political solidarity. They shall refrain from any action which is contrary to the interests of the Union or likely to impair its effectiveness as a cohesive force in international relations.

    The Council shall ensure that these principles are complied with.

Article 12

The Union shall pursue the objectives set out in Article 11 by:

- defining the principles of and general guidelines for the common foreign and security policy;
- deciding on common strategies;
- adopting joint actions;
- adopting common positions;
- strengthening systematic cooperation between Member States in the conduct of policy.

Article 13

1. The European Council shall define the principles of and general guidelines for the common foreign and security policy, including for matters with defence implications.
2. The European Council shall decide on common strategies to be implemented by the Union in areas where the Member States have important interests in common.

Common strategies shall set out their objectives, duration and the means to be made available by the Union and the Member States.

3. The Council shall take the decisions necessary for defining and implementing the common foreign and security policy on the basis of the general guidelines defined by the European Council.

    The Council shall recommend common strategies to the European Council and shall implement them, in particular by adopting joint actions and common positions.

    The Council shall ensure the unity, consistency and effectiveness of action by the Union.

Article 18

1. The Presidency shall represent the Union in matters coming within the common foreign and security policy.
2. The Presidency shall be responsible for the implementation of decisions taken under this Title; in that capacity it shall in principle express the position of the Union in international organisations and international conferences.
3. The Presidency shall be assisted by the Secretary-General of the Council who shall exercise the function of High Representative for the common foreign and security policy.
4. The Commission shall be fully associated in the tasks referred to in paragraphs 1 and 2. The Presidency shall be assisted in those tasks if need be by the next Member State to hold the Presidency.
5. The Council may, whenever it deems it necessary, appoint a special representative with a mandate in relation to particular policy issues.

Article 19

1. Member States shall coordinate their action in international organisations and at international conferences. They shall uphold the common positions in such fora.
    In international organisations and at international conferences where not all the Member States participate, those which do take part shall uphold the common positions.
2. Without prejudice to paragraph 1 and Article 14(3), Member States represented in international organisations or international conferences where not all the Member States participate shall keep the latter informed of any matter of common interest. Member States which are also members of the United Nations Security Council will concert and keep the other Member States fully informed. Member States which are permanent members of the Security Council will, in the execution of their functions, ensure the defence of the positions and the interests of the Union, without prejudice to their responsibilities under the provisions of the United Nations Charter.

Article 21

The Presidency shall consult the European Parliament on the main aspects and the basic choices of the common foreign and security policy and shall ensure that the views of the European Parliament are duly taken into consideration. The European Parliament shall be kept regularly informed by the Presidency and the Commission of the development of the Union's foreign and security policy.

The European Parliament may ask questions of the Council or make recommendations to it. It shall hold an annual debate on progress in implementing the common foreign and security policy.

Article 23

1. Decisions under this Title shall be taken by the Council acting unanimously. Abstentions by members present in person or represented shall not prevent the adoption of such decisions.

    When abstaining in a vote, any member of the Council may qualify its abstention by making a formal declaration under the present subparagraph. In that case, it shall not be obliged to apply the decision, but shall accept that the decision commits the Union. In a spirit of mutual solidarity, the Member State concerned shall refrain from any action likely to conflict with or impede Union action based on that decision and the other Member States shall respect its position. If the members of the Council qualifying their abstention in this way represent more than one third of the votes weighted in accordance with Article 205(2) of the Treaty establishing the European Community, the decision shall not be adopted.

2. By derogation from the provisions of paragraph 1, the Council shall act by qualified majority:
    −   when adopting joint actions, common positions or taking any other decision on the basis of a common strategy;
    −   when adopting any decision implementing a joint action or a common position.
    −   *when appointing a special representative in accordance with Article 18(5)* **(to be added)**.
    If a member of the Council declares that, for important and stated reasons of national policy, it intends to oppose the adoption of a decision to be taken by qualified majority, a vote shall not be taken. The Council may, acting by a qualified majority, request that the matter be referred to the European Council for decision by unanimity.

    The votes of the members of the Council shall be weighted in accordance with Article 205(2) of the Treaty establishing the European Community. For their adoption, decisions shall require at least 62 votes in favour, cast by at least 10 members.

    This paragraph shall not apply to decisions having military or defence implications.

3. For procedural questions, the Council shall act by a majority of its members.

Article 24

1. When it is necessary to conclude an agreement with one or more States or international organisations in implementation of this Title, the Council, *acting unanimously* **(to be deleted)** may authorise the Presidency, assisted by the Commission as appropriate, to open negotiations to that effect. Such agreements shall be concluded by the Council *acting unanimously* **(to be deleted)** on a recommendation from the Presidency.

2. *The Council shall act unanimously when this agreement covers an issue for which unanimity is required for the adoption of internal decisions* **(to be added)**.

3. *When the agreement is envisaged to implement a joint action or common position, the Council shall act by a qualified majority in accordance with Article 23(2)* **(to be added)**.

4. The provisions of this Article shall also apply to matters falling under Title VI. *When the agreement covers an issue for which a qualified majority applies for the adoption of internal decisions or measures, the Council shall act by a qualified majority in accordance with Article 34(3)* **(to be added)**.

5. No agreement shall be binding on a Member State whose representative in the Council states that it has to comply with the requirements of its own constitutional procedure; the other members of the Council may agree that the agreement shall *nevertheless* **(to be added)** apply provisionally to them.

6. *Agreements concluded under the conditions set out in this Article shall be binding on the institutions of the Union* **(to be added)**.

Article 25

Without prejudice to Article 207 of the Treaty establishing the European Community, a Political *and Security* **(to be added)** Committee shall monitor the international situation in the areas covered by the common foreign and security policy and contribute to the definition of policies by delivering opinions to the Council at the request of the Council or on its own initiative. It shall also monitor the implementation of agreed policies, without prejudice to the responsibility of the Presidency and the Commission.

Within the scope of this Title this Committee shall exercise, under the responsibility of the Council, political control and strategic direction of crisis management operations **(to be added)**.

The Council may authorise the Committee, for the purpose and for the duration of a crisis management operation as determined by the Council, to take the relevant decisions concerning the political control and strategic direction of the operation without prejudice to Article 47 **(to be added)**.

Article 26

The Secretary-General of the Council, High Representative for the common foreign and security policy, shall assist the Council in matters coming within the scope of the common foreign and security policy, in particular through contributing to the formulation, preparation and implementation of policy decisions, and, when appropriate and acting on behalf of the Council at the request of the Presidency, through conducting political dialogue with third parties.

Article 27

The Commission shall be fully associated with the work carried out in the common foreign and security policy field.

Chapter Twenty-Three

The Development of the Common European Security and Defence Policy

Richard Whitman

Since 1997 a remarkable change has taken place in the Common Foreign and Security Policy (CFSP) with the development by the EU of a Common European Security and Defence Policy (CESDP).

In 1991 Article J.4 of the Treaty on European Union (TEU), or Maastricht Treaty, which created the CFSP, introduced defence and military security as a component of the policy area. This represented the breaking of a taboo, in that questions of European military security had previously been regarded as being under the purview of NATO, with a limited role for the Western European Union (WEU). However, until 1997 there was a very slow realization of the aspiration in the TEU's provisions for the CFSP to "include all questions related to the security of the Union, including the eventual framing of a common defence policy, which might in time lead to a common defence".

The slow development of the CESDP can be explained through the significant differences of view between the member states as to what the military security role of the EU should be. There have been differences of opinion between those member states that envisage the EU supplanting NATO in this area; those that wish to develop a defence role for the EU only to complement the work of NATO; and those that are uncomfortable with the EU developing a defence dimension at all. All 15 member states are, however, in agreement that this policy area should remain intergovernmental rather than become supranational.

The formal launch of the CESDP at the European Council held in Helsinki in December 1999 was not driven by treaty amendments such as those concluded in the Treaty of Amsterdam in 1997. Much more significant factors have been the recent conflicts in south-eastern Europe and a reassessment by the government of the United Kingdom, one of the more significant military powers among the EU's member states, of its previously hostile attitude towards a deepening of policy in this area. The EU's objectives in the defence domain do, however, remain limited. The current intention is to create a Rapid Reaction Force (RRF) to undertake crisis prevention and crisis management missions. These are understood as including peacekeeping tasks, humanitarian and rescue tasks, and tasks for combat forces in crisis management (to include peacemaking).

Historical Background

Defence remained off the agenda of European integration for many years from the mid-1950s onwards. The high point of integration proposals in the defence domain had been the French proposal for a supranational European Defence Community (EDC). It was made against the backdrop of the outbreak of the Korean War in 1950 and the fear that an attack on western Europe by the Soviet Union might follow. The objective of the French proposal was to facilitate the rearmament of West Germany, which aroused fears of a revival of German militarism, by subsuming the German armed forces within a 100,000-strong integrated European army. The EDC Treaty provided for the creation of this force, and for the appointment of a European Minister of Defence to control a common budget and procurement system and report to a Council of Ministers. It was signed by the founding six member states of the European Coal and Steel Community (Belgium, France, West Germany, Italy, Luxembourg, and the Netherlands) in May 1952. However, the treaty failed to gain ratification in the French National Assembly in August 1954. From this failure onwards the defence arrangements for western Europe have remained firmly and resolutely intergovernmental.

The founding six member states of the European Economic Community, as well as those that joined in the 1970s and 1980s, were all content to retain NATO as the primary organization through which they arranged their collective defence and military security, with the single exception of Ireland, which remained neutral. This is not to say that tensions between the European members of NATO and the United States, the "hegemon" of the alliance, were not present. Periodically, the transatlantic relationship was in crisis, for example as a result of the French decision to leave the integrated military command structure of NATO in 1966 and the decisions by the Reagan Administration to deploy intermediate-range nuclear forces in Europe in the early 1980s and to build a strategic missile defence system ("Star Wars").

The European members of NATO retained membership of their own collective military security organization, the WEU, which had been created in March 1948 with the signing of the Treaty of Economic, Social and Cultural Collaboration and Collective Self-Defence (the Brussels Treaty) by the United Kingdom, France, Belgium, Luxembourg, and the Netherlands. Under Article V of the Brussels Treaty there was a mutual defence guarantee between the signatories. A Western European Defence Organization was created at that time to enact the collective defence provisions of the treaty. The creation of NATO in April 1949 altered this situation. NATO represented a firm US commitment to guarantee the security of western Europe and those states in western Europe that joined NATO clearly valued this more than their own collective efforts

to provide for their security. The Western European Defence Organization was duly merged with NATO, and the collective defence of western Europe became inseparable from the Atlantic alliance. The WEU remained in existence, for the Brussels Treaty had been signed with a 50-year lifespan, but subsequent efforts by states in western Europe to increase their capabilities collectively were pursued within this transatlantic relationship and through NATO until the 1990s.

As the WEU was supplanted by NATO, it sought to carve out a different role for itself. In 1954, in the aftermath of the collapse of the proposed EDC, the WEU was overhauled. Its military functions continued to be undertaken by NATO but it was expanded to include West Germany and Italy. The WEU undertook the task of monitoring the rearmament of West Germany, and the prohibitions on that country's developing biological, chemical or nuclear weapons. For this purpose the member states created an Agency for the Control of Armaments, and this activity remained a core function of the WEU throughout the 1950s and 1960s. The WEU was, therefore, not a military alliance: it possessed no means to direct military forces, as it lacked a military command structure for use in time of conflict, and NATO provided the means of guaranteeing the collective defence of its members. The WEU's real function was to provide a venue in which government ministers and (through the WEU Assembly) parliamentarians from NATO member states in western Europe were able to meet collectively. This was especially important until 1973, when the United Kingdom joined the European Community; thereafter ministerial meetings, which had taken place three times a year, ceased.

Until the mid-1980s, then, the WEU was in hibernation. The Brussels Treaty remained in force and the collective defence guarantee remained in place, but the WEU had no public profile except for the meetings of its Assembly. However, in the early 1980s the member states of the European Community were encouraged to seek a forum for the discussion of defence issues by their concern about the aggressive policy of Ronald Reagan's administration towards the Soviet Union The discussion of defence within the confines of the Community was not acceptable to a number of member states, as was demonstrated by the failure of the Genscher–Colombo plan of 1981, which proposed adding defence to the process of foreign policy coordination known as European Political Cooperation (EPC) undertaken by the member states (see Chapter 22). They therefore looked for an alternative forum.

Meeting in Rome in October 1984, on the 30th anniversary of the signing of the amended version of the Brussels Treaty, the WEU Council, composed of foreign and defence ministers, agreed to breathe some life back into the organization. It was agreed to create a "presidency" for the WEU, rotating every year, and for the Council to meet twice a year. Concerns about the conduct of US policy towards the Soviet Union were to push the member states of the WEU to take matters further. Meeting in October 1986, Reagan and Mikhail Gorbachev came close to agreeing to eliminate intermediate-range nuclear forces in Europe. This position had been taken by the United States without consultation with its allies in western Europe, even though the deployment of these missiles in the early 1980s had caused them to have to face down considerable domestic opposition. The allies accordingly became concerned that they should be in a position to balance the US position and to be able to convey their collective interests more effectively. In October 1987 WEU ministers approved a Platform on European Security Interests that included an objective to develop a "European defence identity" as a part of a strengthened "European pillar" of NATO.

The Platform provided the launching pad for an expanded role for the WEU. In the summer of 1987 the WEU had deployed naval forces to maintain freedom of shipping in the Persian Gulf, threatened by the war between Iran and Iraq. The operation was a genuinely collective effort: Belgium, France, Italy, the Netherlands, and the United Kingdom deployed minesweepers for 18 months in the Gulf; West Germany replaced vessels removed by these states from the Atlantic and the Mediterranean; and Luxembourg assisted in the financing of the operation. However, the European Community and the WEU remained separate and

separable. The Single European Act of 1987, which introduced the process of EPC into the Treaty of Rome, permitted the discussion of the political and economic aspects of security but not military security. Denmark, Greece, and Ireland remained outside the WEU, but Spain and Portugal joined it in 1988 following their accession to the Community in 1986 and in tandem with their accession to NATO. This was the first enlargement of the organization since 1954 and had some symbolic importance as a reflection of its revival.

Breaking the Taboo on Military Security

The end of the Cold War altered the geopolitical landscape of Europe with German unification and the demise of the Soviet Union. These events generated a debate about the role of the European Community in the transformed international relations of Europe. The demise of the Soviet Union altered the security environment and raised questions as to whether NATO continued to have a *raison d'être*. A debate took place about a new European security architecture and how the Community should respond to this situation. It was decided to discuss deepening integration among the member states through two intergovernmental conferences (IGCs), one on Economic and Monetary Union (EMU) and a second on Political Union. The then 12 member states were in agreement that the Community faced new foreign policy challenges and acknowledged that there were increased expectations from third parties that it should enhance its role in international relations. In the Treaty on European Union (the Maastricht Treaty, or TEU) the member states sought to enhance their ability to harmonize their foreign policy on an intergovernmental basis by transforming the process of EPC into the Common Foreign and Security Policy (CFSP – see Chapter 22 for further details).

The TEU was an important landmark, in that for the first time issues of military security and defence were to be discussed within the confines of the EU. The treaty established the CFSP and widened efforts at foreign policy harmonization to include "the eventual framing of a common defence policy, which might in time lead to a common defence", and designated the WEU as the body that would "elaborate and implement decisions and actions of the Union which have defence implications" (then Articles J4.1 and J4.2. of the TEU). The WEU provided a readymade mechanism for the member states to exploit. It also had several advantages. First, the implementation of the defence provisions would be kept at arm's length: this suited Ireland and Denmark in particular, for reasons of public sensitivity about defence becoming a component of the EU. Secondly, the WEU had been developed as a complement, rather than as an alternative, to NATO: this suited the Atlanticist members of the EU. Thirdly, it was an intergovernmental rather than a supranational organization and the notion that national sovereignty was preserved could be maintained. Finally, the European Commission was not a member of the WEU and was excluded from a role in this area: this suited the United Kingdom and France.

The use of the WEU as the vehicle for an EU defence policy did raise two substantive issues that have dogged subsequent discussions on defence by the EU member states. The first was "variable geometry": the memberships of the EU, the WEU, and NATO are not identical (see Table 23.1). Greece joined the WEU in 1993 but Denmark ruled itself out of a commitment to future membership of the WEU, and participation in the "elaboration and the implementation of decisions and actions of the Union which have defence implications". This was a part of the settlement with other EU member states designed to address the Danish public's concerns on the TEU, as manifested in the "no" vote in the first referendum on the TEU in June 1992. The intention was to ensure that there would be a "yes" majority in favour of ratification in Denmark's second referendum on the Treaty. Since the enlargement of the EU in 1995, there have also been four states – Austria, Finland, Ireland and Sweden – that were neutral during the Cold War and are still not members of either the WEU or NATO.

The second issue was the relationship between NATO and the EU/WEU. In a Declaration attached to the TEU the then nine members of the WEU spelled out their proposals for the future. The relationship between the EU and the WEU was to be developed so that the WEU would be the defence component of the EU while remaining a means to strengthen the European pillar of the Atlantic alliance, the "European Security and Defence Identity" (ESDI). The relationship between the EU and the WEU was not to be envisaged as something separate from NATO. However, the working out of the relationship between the EU, the WEU, and NATO to facilitate the developments envisaged in the TEU was to prove a difficult and drawn-out process.

The Council of Ministers of the WEU meeting in Petersberg, Germany, in June 1992 issued a Declaration in response to the TEU. The Petersberg Declaration signalled the intention of the WEU to expand its operations to encompass "humanitarian and rescue tasks, peacekeeping tasks, and tasks of combat forces in crisis management", thereafter known as the "Petersberg tasks". Further, the WEU agreed to create different categories of membership: "observer", "associate", and "partner".

The WEU slowly created institutions to undertake the Petersberg tasks. A WEU Planning Cell was created in 1993: it developed an inventory of Forces Answerable to the WEU (FAWEU) to identify those forces available to carry out WEU tasks and created a framework for the development of a WEU Maritime Force. In addition, the post of Director of Military Staff was created with responsibility for the Planning Cell and the WEU Situation Centre, and the WEU Military Committee was activated. A commitment was also made to create an independent European satellite system and to develop further the WEU's capability to use satellite imagery for security purposes by developing a Satellite Centre at Torrejon in Spain.

However, all these developments were insignificant when compared to the capabilities of NATO. At the NATO summit in January 1994 the principle that NATO assets and capabilities could be made available for WEU operations was endorsed, in particular through the concept of "combined joint task forces" (CJTFs). The CJTF concept created the possibility of military structures to run military operations that may not include the United

States and was a key strand of the development of an ESDI within NATO. However, slow progress was made on working out the practicalities of the WEU having recourse to NATO capabilities. It was not until May 1997 that NATO's Military Committee designated the Deputy Supreme Allied Commander for Europe (DSACEUR) as the principal point of contact between the NATO Strategic Commands and the WEU, and, most importantly, as the preferred operation commander for WEU-led operations. Work was much slower on a NATO–WEU Framework Agreement to facilitate the actual use of NATO assets by the WEU. The continuing separation between NATO and the EU was illustrated by the fact that the first ever visit by the EU Presidency to the NATO Secretary General took place only in December 1998.

The operational activities of the WEU during this period were negligible. In particular, the WEU's involvement in the Yugoslav conflicts and their aftermath was minor. There was assistance in the enforcement of the UN-mandated embargo on goods and arms, through an Adriatic task force and a presence on the Danube. In addition, the WEU provided a police force for the town of Mostar in Bosnia–Herzegovina between the summer of 1994 and the autumn of 1996. The first use of Article J4.2 of the TEU was in June 1996, when the WEU was asked by the EU to undertake preparatory work for the evacuation of nationals of member states when their safety was threatened in third countries. The EU also requested the WEU to prepare a military response to the crisis in the Great Lakes region of Africa in May 1997, although the rapid changes of events on the ground resulted in this action not being undertaken. In the latter part of 1998 the EU tasked the WEU to undertake three activities: to monitor the situation in Kosovo via the Satellite Centre; to assist with landmine-clearing in Croatia; and to study the feasibility of international police operations to assist the government in Albania, and then to implement them.

By the late 1990s the WEU was carrying out the majority of its activities "at 21" – that is, involving all its full members, observers, and associate members – and was thus blurring the legal distinctions between the different categories of membership (see Table 23.1). Observer status was accorded to the five EU states that are not members of the WEU: Austria, Denmark, Finland, Ireland, and Sweden. Associate membership was accepted by the European members of NATO that were not members of the EU: Turkey, Norway, Iceland, Poland, Hungary, and the Czech Republic. These associate members, by their nomination of assets to FAWEU, became entitled to participate in WEU operations on the same basis as full members and to be involved in the institutions of the WEU. The WEU also created an "associate partner" status, which was offered to the seven states in central Europe and on the Baltic that had Europe Agreements with the EU. Associate partner status also offered involvement in the WEU's operations and institutions.

Under the TEU the relationship that developed between the EU and the WEU was evolutionary. The EU had very limited recourse to the WEU and the latter focused upon the development of an operational capability to facilitate its aspirations. The desire of some member states to deepen the relationship was manifested in the debates surrounding the intergovernmental conference called in 1996 to consider the future development of the EU, which resulted in the Treaty of Amsterdam.

The TEU had provided for an IGC in 1996 to review the functioning of the EU and had specifically included the evaluation of progress on the provisions on defence as part of the agenda. The slow development of the defence provisions within the TEU and the general unhappiness over the performance of the CFSP process, in particular in the face of events in the Balkans, ensured that the discussions on defence in 1996 were extensive. Indeed, the greatest dispute within the discussions on the CFSP that year centred on the future of the relationship between the EU and the WEU. The eventual formula agreed upon in the text of the Treaty of Amsterdam (in June 1997) was a strengthening of the commitment in the TEU from the "eventual" framing of a common defence policy to a "progressive" framing "should the European Council so decide", and the "fostering of closer institutional relations with the WEU with a view to the possibility of the integration of the WEU into the Union" (Article 17.1, formerly J7.1 – see Document 23.1 for full text). This possible integration of the WEU into the EU was to be on the basis of a decision by the European Council. The essentially unchanged relationship between the EU and the WEU was largely due to unwillingness on the part of the UK government to accept any significant change, although a new government under Prime Minister Tony Blair had been elected the previous month.

A substantive development was the acceptance by the neutral states (Finland, Sweden, Ireland, and Austria) of the inclusion of the humanitarian and peacekeeping elements of the Petersberg tasks of the WEU in the text of the Treaty of Amsterdam (Article17.2, formerly J7.2), along with an entitlement for non-WEU members to participate fully in these tasks (17.3, formerly J7.3). The Finnish and Swedish governments in particular did express some disquiet at the inclusion of military security within the competencies of the EU, and were keen to promote crisis management as the most important practical task that the EU could undertake; the Petersberg tasks were included in the Treaty of Amsterdam on their initiative.

The WEU signalled its willingness to respond to the commitment of the member states under the Treaty of Amsterdam, and a Protocol provided for the EU and the WEU to draw up arrangements for enhanced cooperation within one year of the treaty's coming into force. The appointment of Javier Solana as the first High Representative of the CFSP, in June 1999, was significant in placing a former NATO Secretary General as the public face of the CFSP. In November 1999 Solana also became Secretary General of the WEU and "double-hatted" the two roles. The provisions of Article 17 were to be reviewed at a further intergovernmental conference.

New Initiatives on Defence

The Treaty of Amsterdam did not come into force until May 1999 (following ratification) and, by that date, its provisions on defence had been somewhat overtaken by events. The

agreement that had been forged in June 1997 reflected a compromise between those states that wanted to deepen cooperation in the defence domain and those states that were unwilling to accept further developments at that time. The United Kingdom fell into the latter group and when, in the autumn of 1998, Prime Minister Tony Blair publicly made clear that the UK government was rethinking its attitude towards defence within the EU, the debate on the defence provisions of the Treaty of Amsterdam was reopened.

The UK government's alternative to what was agreed at Amsterdam was not clear. It was proposing that the EU needed to have a better intergovernmental decision-making system for military operations involving only European states and that there needed to be a genuine military operational capacity available to the EU, complementary to that of NATO. In part, this was motivated by the British experience during its Presidency of the EU, when the outbreak of fighting in Kosovo had confronted Blair with the labyrinthine procedures to be navigated if the member states had wished to intervene in the conflict. The UK government maintained that it had no fixed proposal or blueprint as to how to achieve its goals. What is clear is that the aim of the reopening of the debate on defence was to maximize the potential of Britain's influence in Europe. This was of crucial importance to the government in the context of the forthcoming move to Economic and Monetary Union on 1 January 1999, with the United Kingdom remaining outside and therefore at risk of being marginalized.

Two successive events provided the opportunity for the British government to clarify its position to other EU governments: the informal meeting of the EU's heads of state and government at Pörtschach on 24 and 25 October 1998; and the first informal meeting of the EU's defence ministers, in Vienna on 4 November 1998. At both of these events it became clear that the British government wanted to see fresh thinking on European foreign and defence policy, and it appeared that its leading members were approaching reform with relatively open minds. Subsequently, at their summit on 2 December 1998, the French and German governments reaffirmed their shared position of seeking the integration of the WEU into the EU, which had been their view during the inter-governmental conference in 1996.

The Declaration of St Malo

The debate moved on apace with the British and French governments affirming their joint willingness to move the discussion forward on the development of an EU military capacity at a summit meeting in St Malo on 3 and 4 December 1998. The two governments' joint Declaration on European Defence (see Document 23.2) represented a profound recon-figuration of the position that the British government had taken in negotiating what was to become the Treaty of Amsterdam. The Declaration represents the first time that the two governments have agreed such a bilat-eral statement, highlighting Franco–British common ground on five main points:

- The EU must have the capacity to decide to act, to be able to act autonomously, and to be ready to do so in international crises requiring military force.
- NATO remains the foundation of collec-tive defence for Europeans through Arti-cle 5 of the Washington Treaty, but a collective defence commitment must be maintained as currently through Article V of the Brussels Treaty.
- The institutional arrangements for decision-making by the EU on defence matters are to remain intergovernmental and to take place through the European Council, the General Affairs Council, and a forum for the meeting of defence min-isters. Defence is not to be "commun-itarized", that is, subjected to the decision-making procedures of Pillar 1.
- The EU will need to have the capabilities to analyze, have access to sources of intel-ligence, and plan to facilitate the decision-making and approval of eventualities in which military action is to be undertaken without the involvement of the whole Atlantic alliance.
- The member states of the EU need to cre-ate armed forces that are capable of undertaking the military tasks that may

be required without the involvement of the whole Atlantic alliance.

The Declaration of St Malo somewhat over-shadowed the decision of the WEU Ministerial Council meeting in Rome on 16 and 17 Nov-ember 1998 that a process of informal reflec-tion on Europe's security and defence should be undertaken. The EU's heads of state and government, meeting in Vienna on 11 and 12 December 1998, gave the incoming German Presidency of the EU the task of developing the debate on defence and committed them-selves to re-examining the issue at their meet-ing in Cologne in June 1999. All of this activity was taking place against the backdrop of the preparations for the NATO summit in Wash-ington, DC, in April 1999, at which the alliance was scheduled to launch its new Strategic Concept.

The Washington Summit

The communiqué issued by the Washington Summit in April 1999 went much further than earlier NATO positions on the ESDI, not least because it referred to the EU rather than the WEU and therefore took for granted that the EU had displaced the WEU. NATO had accepted the notion that the EU would have an autonomous capability. There were four key elements in the declaration:

- The EU was to be given assured access to NATO planning for EU-led operations.
- Previously identified NATO capabilities and assets would be available for use in EU-led operations.
- Command options for EU-led operations would be identified.
- NATO's planning system would be adapted to incorporate the availability of forces for EU-led operations.

The reconciliation of the EU's aspirations for operational capability with the continuing centrality of NATO was not the sole concern of the United States at the Washington summit. The Defence Capabilities Initiative (DCI), also launched at the summit, was spurred by the so-called "revolution in military affairs". It has been argued that the difference in US and European forces' technological capabilities is most likely to drive the United States and other NATO member states apart: the gap between the more advanced US military technology and that possessed by Europeans means that functioning together is increasingly difficult. This was clearly demonstrated during the 11-week air campaign against the Federal Republic of Yugoslavia. The modest contribution of European states to the air campaign (24 March to 10 June 1999) highlighted their lack of key capabilities. The differing responses of the EU's member states to the crisis also suggested that differences of opinion on the appropriateness of the use of military force for the resolution of political problems is likely to be a key issue when deployment decisions are taken.

The Cologne Council

However, events in Kosovo did not deflect the EU's member states from developing the details of an EU defence policy. In Cologne in June 1999 the European Council, in a declaration entitled Strengthening the Common European Policy on Security and Defence, formally committed itself to the position taken by the French and the British at St Malo: that the EU should have the "capacity for autonomous action, backed up by credible military forces, the means to decide to use them, and a readiness to do so . . .". This declaration represented the crossing of a Rubicon. None of the member states refused to sign it, although Denmark retained its formal reservation.

The Cologne declaration restated the assertion made at St Malo that the EU's desire to have a capacity for autonomous action created the need for capabilities. The declaration foresaw two possible means of implementing EU-led operations:

- EU-led operations using NATO assets and capabilities, as foreseen in the declaration issued by the Washington summit; or
- EU-led operations without recourse to NATO assets and capabilities

The question that still remains open is just how much capability the EU needs to possess,

independently from NATO, to guarantee its freedom for autonomous action, especially for EU-led operations without recourse to NATO assets and capabilities. A key phrase at Cologne was the need to avoid "unnecessary duplication". As some commentators have suggested, this presumably means that there will be some, apparently "necessary" duplication.

The operational capabilities identified in the declaration issued at Cologne were threefold:

- European military capabilities for conflict prevention and crisis management, (envisaged on the basis of existing national, binational and multinational forces;
- The development of suitable intelligence, strategic transport, and command and control capabilities; and
- The restructuring of European defence industries and more efficient defence collaboration.

The declaration set a particular design brief that has informed EU conceptions of the future relationship between the EU and NATO. A timetable was also set at Cologne to take the necessary decisions by the end of 2000 to attain these objectives. In part this was to be achieved by folding the WEU into the EU.

Creating Headline Goals

The European Council meeting in Helsinki in December 1999 formally launched the CESDP envisaged at Cologne (see the Presidency Conclusions in Document 23.3). The guiding notion remained that set at Cologne: that the EU should have the autonomous capacity to take decisions and, where NATO as a whole is not engaged, to launch and then to conduct EU-led military operations in response to international crises in support of the CFSP.

At Helsinki a "headline goal" was set for a military force that could be deployed rapidly and would be capable of carrying out the full range of Petersberg tasks. This force would be made up of 60,000 troops that would be ready for operations in 2003 and be capable of staying in the field for at least one year. This will mean that the member states would have to provide 200,000 military personnel, because of the need to rotate troops on active service. This military force would consist of readily deployable military capabilities. The necessary collective capabilities in the fields of command and control, intelligence, and strategic transport would need to be developed rapidly, to be achieved through voluntary coordinated national and multinational efforts. It was recognized that this determination to carry out Petersberg tasks would require the member states to improve national and multinational military capabilities.

To support this force, important decisions were taken at Helsinki to create "new political and military bodies . . . to enable the Union to take decisions on EU-led Petersberg operations and to ensure, under the authority of the Council, the necessary political control and strategic direction of such operations". The new bodies created were an interim Political and Security Committee (generally known by its French acronym of COPS), which was to meet once a week; an interim Military Body, forerunner of a Military Committee (MC) composed of representatives of the member states' commanders in chief; and a Military Staff, the precursor of a European staff headquarters. These latter two bodies were installed in the General Secretariat of the Council to provide military expertise to the Interim Military Committee and the Secretary General/High Representative. These bodies began functioning on 1 March 2000, with permanent arrangements envisaged as taking place as soon as possible after the meeting of the European Council in Nice in December 2000.

The European Council in Helsinki also set out that "modalities will be developed for full consultation, cooperation, and transparency between the EU and NATO, taking into account the needs of all EU member states". Four *ad hoc* NATO–EU working groups were established by the European Council meeting in Santa Maria da Feira in June 2000 to facilitate the development of an EU–NATO "interface"; all four are now in operation. They are working on security issues; the EU's military capabilities; EU access to NATO assets and capabilities; and the definitive arrangements to be concluded between the EU and NATO. The group responsible for permanent EU–NATO

arrangements is a joint meeting at ambassadorial level of the interim Political and Security Committee and the NATO Council; it first met in September 2000.

Getting the relationship between the EU and NATO correct is a crucial concern for the United States and was expressed in a succinct manner by the then US Secretary of State, Madeline Albright, in an article published in the *Financial Times* on 7 December 1998. Albright expressed concerns about "decoupling" the transatlantic link, "duplicating" defence resources, and "discrimination" against European members of NATO that are not in the EU (Turkey, Iceland, Norway, and since April 1999 also the Czech Republic, Hungary, and Poland). The European Council in Helsinki set out to address "discrimination" by making it clear that there was an aspiration to create principles for cooperation with these three countries, and other European partners, in EU-led military crisis management operations, but without prejudicing the EU's ability to take autonomous decisions. This was taken further at the European Council in Santa Maria da Feira in June 2000, which made a commitment to create a "single institutional framework" with distinctive consultative arrangements for the non-EU European members of NATO ("EU+6") and for candidates for EU accession ("EU+13"). This did not adequately address concerns about "discrimination" and the government of Turkey reacted by stating publicly that, on the basis of these proposals, it could not accept automatic EU access to NATO assets and capabilities, and it remains hostile to the CESDP.

Another feature of the decisions taken at Helsinki that was then taken further at Feira was the commitment to develop the civilian aspects of crisis management. A headline goal was set for a nonmilitary Rapid Reaction Facility, which had been proposed by the European Commission. The Facility is designed to focus on re-establishing the civilian structures necessary to ensure political, social and economic stability, and to give a civilian capacity to the rapid reaction military force by mobilising nonmilitary personnel such as police officers, customs officials, and judges. Headline goals have also been set in this area: to have up to

5,000 police officers available by 2003 and to be able to deploy 1,000 within 30 days.

The Helsinki Council created a route map for the EU to follow to realize its CESDP objectives. It also left the WEU as an organization without a major role. The WEU Council meeting in Porto (15 and 16 May 2000) gave the WEU Permanent Council the task of looking at what future was left for the WEU. Meeting in Marseilles on 13 November 2000 the Council adopted a transition plan to transform itself into a residual organization. The WEU will continue to exist, essentially to oversee Article V of the amended Brussels Treaty, but with a much reduced Secretariat, the WEU Assembly, and the Western European Armaments Group. The WEU Institute for Security Studies and the Satellite Centre in Torrejon are to be integrated into the EU. Despite the fact that the WEU member states long ago decided to leave guarantees under Article V to NATO – and despite the fact that the guarantees have not been tested to date – it is unlikely that it will be ignored in future discussions on reform. For a number of EU member states, most notably France, Article V is politically important and a commitment to collective defence is deemed too important to drop.

From December 1999 onwards considerable work went into finding the mechanisms to realize the operational objectives set at Helsinki. The European Council at Feira rubberstamped agreements, forged by the EU's foreign and defence ministers in March, to hold a Capabilities Commitment Conference at the end of November 2000. The Interim Military Body drew up a catalogue on the ground, air, and naval components needed for the Helsinki headline goal. This catalogue of forces contained four basic scenarios for Petersberg missions, and the land, air, and maritime forces that would be needed. Member states were asked to specify the unit, number and size, detail, and duration of forces that they could be counted on to supply. The Capabilities Commitment Conference met on 20 November and the member states officially announced their commitments, which were sufficient to meet the headline goal. The following day the member states met with the EU candidate members and then a separate

meeting took place between the member states and the non-EU European NATO allies to take note of these states' possible contributions.

Deepening European armaments cooperation is likely to prove one of the more difficult tasks set by the member states. This longer-term aspiration was expressed in a new clause in the Treaty of Amsterdam that provided for cooperation between member states in the field of armaments, and it was reiterated at St Malo, Cologne, and Helsinki. Despite the existence of the Western European Armaments Group (WEAG) and the Western European Armaments Organisation (WEAO) as subsidiary bodies of the WEU, progress has been slow. The participants include all ten full members of the WEU, Denmark, Norway, Turkey, the Czech Republic, Poland, and Hungary. Austria and Finland have both submitted applications to join. However, it is noteworthy that France, Germany, Italy, and the United Kingdom – four key players in European armaments cooperation that had become impatient with the slow progress of the WEAG – have formed a new Organisation Conjointe de Coopération pour L'Armament (OCCAR). Collaborative projects have had a poor recent history: for example, the "Horizon" frigate project collapsed in May 1999 when the United Kingdom dropped out of it and France left the Multi-Role Armoured Vehicle (MRAV) programme to pursue a national solution for this capability.

More significant developments have taken place outside these organizations. In October 1999 the German company Dasa and the French company Aerospatiale Matra agreed to merge their aerospace and defence activities into the European Aeronautic, Defence, and Space Company (EADS), which is now the world's third largest aerospace company. British Aerospace (BAe Systems) remained outside this merger but merged with the defence business components of GEC Marconi (see also Chapter 9).

The Treaty of Nice

The developments in the field of the CESDP in 1999 and 2000 took place alongside the work of another intergovernmental conference (see Chapter 4). Defence did not feature significantly on the agenda, but some changes were made to the TEU at Nice to reflect developments in the defence field since the Treaty of Amsterdam had been signed.

The Treaty of Nice makes two main changes to the TEU articles dealing with defence. Firstly, the provisions referring to the WEU as the provider of the operational capability of the common defence policy were removed from Article 1 (see Document 23.1). This was an acknowledgement of the agreement at the Helsinki European Council that the member states are collectively to develop the military security provisions of the CFSP within the EU, rather than at arm's length through the WEU. A second change was that Article 25 of the TEU was amended to change references to the "Political Committee" to the "Political and Security Committee" (known under its French acronym COPS). The amendment confirmed that COPS will be responsible for both the CFSP and CEDSP. The important new role of COPS as the centrepiece of the CESDP is recognized in the Nice amendments that state that "this Committee shall exercise, under the responsibility of the Council, political control and strategic direction of crisis management operations". The Treaty of Nice also explicitly rules out enhanced cooperation provisions of the treaty as not applying to matters having military or defence implications.

In a Declaration on the European Security and Defence Policy attached to the Treaty it was made clear that its ratification is not a precondition for the CESDP to become operational. Rather, it was agreed that this should happen as soon as possible and no later than the second half of 2001, under the Belgian Presidency. The crucial document in this regard is the Presidency Report on the European Security and Defence Policy, which forms an appendix to the Conclusions that are normally agreed as the outcome of European Council meetings. The report details all that had been agreed by the member states on the CESDP over the previous two years and outlines the work still to be undertaken to realize the objectives in this policy area. The document represents a useful summary of the developments, and the challenges to be overcome, in this field.

Conclusion

The CESDP is a very new policy domain for the EU and further developments are to be expected in the future. The crucial question is whether the member states will be able to realize the objectives that they have set for themselves. The obstacles to be faced should not be underestimated, as questions of national sovereignty remain acute in relation to defence. The CESDP remains firmly intergovernmental and no move to a "supranationalization" of the process is likely to occur in the foreseeable future.

The EU needs to achieve success in four aspects if it is to realize its aspirations for the CESDP and to have this force fully operational by the 2003 deadline: developing the military capabilities; ensuring that its decision-making mechanisms enable the force to be used; developing the relationship between the EU and NATO to facilitate the use of force by the EU; and creating structures that attract the participation of non-EU European members of NATO. This is a considerable agenda. Further, focusing on institutional arrangements sidesteps the question as to what the CESDP might actually become in the future. Up till now the CESDP has been developed in terms that are intended to make it intertwined with NATO and not to undermine the Atlantic alliance. Therefore, of crucial significance for the future development of the CESDP is the relationship that is developed with George W. Bush's administration and its emerging attitude towards this area.

Further Reading

Angréani, Gilles, Christoph Bertram, and Charles Grant, *Europe's Military Revolution*, London: Centre for European Reform, 2001

This set of proposals for the future enhancement of the CESDP is of particular interest because the Centre for European Reform was an important source of ideas for the British government as it shifted its thinking on European defence in 1998.

Deighton, Anne (editor), *Western European Union 1954–1997: Defence, Security, Integration*, Oxford: St Anthony's College, 1997

A comprehensive analysis of the WEU's historical development, institutions, and operational activity to 1997

Fursdon, Edward, *The European Defence Community: A History*, London: Macmillan, and New York: St Martin's Press, 1980

A full history of this failed proposal

Heisbourg, François, *et al.*, *European Defence: Making it Work*, Chaillot Papers 42, Paris: Western European Union Institute for Security Studies, 2000

An extremely useful compilation of issues to be faced in developing a CESDP, and a very useful source of comparative statistical information on the defence expenditure and capabilities of the EU's member states

Howorth, Jolyon, "Britain, NATO, and CESDP: Fixed Strategy, Changing Tactics", in *European Foreign Affairs Review*, 5/3, 2000, pp. 377–96

An examination of the shifting British attitudes to European defence in the late 1990s

Howorth, Jolyon, *European Integration and Defence: The Ultimate Challenge*, Chaillot Papers 43, Paris: Western European Union Institute for Security Studies, 2000

A useful study placing developments in the CESDP in the context of European integration

International Institute for Strategic Studies, *European Defence Autonomy?*, special issue of *Survival*, 42/2, 2000

A set of six articles examining different dimensions of the possibility of an autonomous European defence capability

The Military Balance 2000–2001, London: Oxford University Press for the International Institute for Strategic Studies, 2000

An annual publication assessing the military capabilities and the defence economics of countries around the world, including the member states of the EU

Presidency Report on the European Security and Defence Policy, 2000, at europa.eu.int/council/off/conclu/index.htm)

Rees, G. Wyn, *The Western European Union at the Crossroads*, Boulder, CO: Westview Press, 1998

A definitive history of the WEU

Roper, John, "Keynote Article: Two Cheers for Mr Blair? The Political Realities of European Defence Cooperation", in *The European Union: Annual Review 1999–2000, Journal of Common Market Studies*, 8, 2000, pp. 7–23

A useful analysis of the creation of the CESDP and the problems still to be resolved

Yost, David, "The NATO Capabilities Gap and the European Union", *Survival*, Vol. 42/4, 2000–01, pp. 97–128

An analysis of the gap in operational capabilities between the United States and the European members of the Atlantic alliance

Internet Sources

Western European Union: http://www.weu.int/

Western European Union Assembly: http://assembly.weu.int/

North Atlantic Treaty Organization: http://www.nato.int/

Council Secretariat of the Council of the European Union (location of the CESDP institutions): http://ue.eu.int/pesc/

Dr Richard Whitman is the Director of the Centre for the Study of Democracy at the University of Westminster. He has previously published on the external relations of the EU, and on its Common Foreign and Security Policy. His most recent publication is *The Foreign Policies of European Union Member States* (coedited with Ian Manners), 2000.

Table 23.1 The "Variable Geometry" of EU, WEU, and NATO Membership, 2001

Country	EU Member State	WEU Full Member	WEU Observer	WEU Associate Member	WEU Associate Partner	NATO Member
Austria	Yes		Yes			
Belgium	Yes	Yes				Yes
Denmark	Yes		Yes			Yes
Finland	Yes		Yes			
France	Yes	Yes				Yes
Germany	Yes	Yes				Yes
Greece	Yes	Yes				Yes
Ireland	Yes		Yes			
Italy	Yes	Yes				Yes
Luxembourg	Yes	Yes				Yes
Netherlands	Yes	Yes				Yes
Portugal	Yes	Yes				Yes
Spain	Yes	Yes				Yes
Sweden	Yes		Yes			
UK	Yes	Yes				Yes
Czech Republic				Yes		Yes
Hungary				Yes		Yes
Iceland				Yes		Yes
Norway				Yes		Yes
Poland				Yes		Yes
Turkey				Yes		Yes
Bulgaria					Yes	
Estonia					Yes	
Latvia					Yes	
Lithuania					Yes	
Romania					Yes	
Slovakia					Yes	
Slovenia					Yes	
Canada						Yes
USA						Yes

Document 23.1 Key Treaty Provisions on the EU's Security and Defence Policy

[The amendments to the Treaty on European Union agreed at the Nice Council in December 2000 are in italics: as indicated, in some cases they involve deletions and in others new words or paragraphs to be added when the Treaty of Nice comes into force.]

Article 17

1. The common foreign and security policy shall include all questions relating to the security of the Union, including the progressive framing of a common defence policy, in accordance with the second subparagraph, which might lead to a common defence, should the European Council so decide. It shall in that case recommend to the Member States the adoption of such a decision in accordance with their respective constitutional requirements.

    The Western European Union (WEU) is an integral part of the development of the Union providing the Union with access to an operational capability notably in the context of paragraph 2. It supports the Union in framing the defence aspects of the common foreign and security policy as set out in this Article. The Union shall accordingly foster closer institutional relations with the WEU with a view to the possibility of the integration of the WEU into the Union, should the European Council so decide. It shall in that case recommend to the Member States the adoption of such a decision in accordance with their respective constitutional requirements. (**To be deleted.**)

    The policy of the Union in accordance with this Article shall not prejudice the specific character of the security and defence policy of certain Member States and shall respect the obligations of certain Member States, which see their common defence realized in the North Atlantic Treaty Organisation (NATO), under the North Atlantic Treaty and be compatible with the common security and defence policy established within that framework.

    The progressive framing of a common defence policy will be supported, as Member States consider appropriate, by cooperation between them in the field of armaments.
2. Questions referred to in this Article shall include humanitarian and rescue tasks, peacekeeping tasks and tasks of combat forces in crisis management, including peacemaking.
3. *The Union will avail itself of the WEU to elaborate and implement decisions and actions of the Union which have defence implications.*

    The competence of the European Council to establish guidelines in accordance with Article 13 shall also obtain in respect of the WEU for those matters for which the Union avails itself of the WEU.

    When the Union avails itself of the WEU to elaborate and implement decisions of the Union on the tasks referred to in paragraph 2 all Member States of the Union shall be entitled to participate fully in the tasks in question. The Council, in agreement with the institutions of the WEU, shall adopt the necessary practical arrangements to allow all Member States contributing to the tasks in question to participate fully and on an equal footing in planning and decision-taking in the WEU. (**These three paragraphs to be deleted.**)

    Decisions having defence implications dealt with under this Article shall be taken without prejudice to the policies and obligations referred to in paragraph 1, second subparagraph.
4. The provisions of this Article shall not prevent the development of closer cooperation between two or more Member States on a bilateral level, in the framework of the WEU and the Atlantic Alliance, provided such cooperation does not run counter to or impede that provided for in this Title.
5. With a view to furthering the objectives of this Article, the provisions of this Article will be reviewed in accordance with Article 48.

Article 25

Without prejudice to Article 207 of the Treaty establishing the European Community, a Political *and Security* (**to be added**) Committee shall monitor the international situation in the areas covered by the common foreign and security policy and contribute to the definition of policies by delivering opinions to the Council at the request of the Council or on its own initiative. It shall also monitor the implementation of agreed policies, without prejudice to the responsibility of the Presidency and the Commission.

Within the scope of this Title this Committee shall exercise, under the responsibility of the Council, political control and strategic direction of crisis management operations (**to be added**).

The Council may authorise the Committee, for the purpose and for the duration of a crisis management operation as determined by the Council, to take the relevant decisions concerning the political control and strategic direction of the operation without prejudice to Article 47 (**to be added**)

Document 23.2 Franco–British Joint Declaration on European Defence, St Malo, 4 December 1998

The Heads of State and Government of France and the United Kingdom are agreed that:

1. The European Union needs to be in a position to play its full role on the international stage. This means making a reality of the Treaty of Amsterdam, which will provide the essential basis for action by the Union. It will be important to achieve full and rapid implementation of the Amsterdam provisions on CFSP. This includes the responsibility of the European Council to decide on the progressive framing of a common defence policy in the framework of CFSP. The Council must be able to take decisions on an intergovernmental basis, covering the whole range of activity set out in Title V of the Treaty of European Union.
2. To this end, the Union must have the capacity for autonomous action, backed up by credible military forces, the means to decide to use them and a readiness to do so, in order to respond to international crises.

    In pursuing our objective, the collective defence commitments to which member states subscribe (set out in Article 5 of the Washington Treaty, Article V of the Brussels Treaty) must be maintained. In strengthening the solidarity between the member states of the European Union, in order that Europe can make its voice heard in world affairs, while acting in conformity with our respective obligations in NATO, we are contributing to the vitality of a modernised Atlantic Alliance which is the foundation of the collective defence of its members.

    Europeans will operate within the institutional framework of the European Union (European Council, General Affairs Council and meetings of Defence Ministers).

    The reinforcement of European solidarity must take into account the various positions of European states.

    The different situations of countries in relation to NATO must be respected.
3. In order for the European Union to take decisions and approve military action where the Alliance as a whole is not engaged, the Union must be given appropriate structures and a capacity for analysis of situations, sources of intelligence and a capability for relevant strategic planning, without unnecessary duplication, taking account of the existing assets of the WEU and the evolution of its relations with the EU. In this regard, the European Union will also need to have recourse to suitable military means (European capabilities pre-designated within NATO's European pillar or national or multinational European means outside the NATO framework).
4. Europe needs strengthened armed forces that can react rapidly to the new risks, and which are supported by a strong and competitive European defence industry and technology.
5. We are determined to unite in our efforts to enable the European Union to give concrete expression to these objectives.

Document 23.3   Extracts from the Presidency Conclusions of the European Council in Helsinki, 10 and 11 December 1999, Concerning the Development of the CESDP

II.   Common European Policy On Security And Defence

25. The European Council adopts the two Presidency progress reports on developing the Union's military and non-military crisis management capability as part of a strengthened common European policy on security and defence.

26. The Union will contribute to international peace and security in accordance with the principles of the United Nations Charter. The Union recognises the primary responsibility of the United Nations Security Council for the maintenance of international peace and security.

27. The European Council underlines its determination to develop an autonomous capacity to take decisions and, where NATO as a whole is not engaged, to launch and conduct EU-led military operations in response to international crises. This process will avoid unnecessary duplication and does not imply the creation of a European army.

28. Building on the guidelines established at the Cologne European Council and on the basis of the Presidency's reports, the European Council has agreed in particular the following:
    - cooperating voluntarily in EU-led operations, Member States must be able, by 2003, to deploy within 60 days and sustain for at least 1 year military forces of up to 50,000–60,000 persons capable of the full range of Petersberg tasks;
    - new political and military bodies and structures will be established within the Council to enable the Union to ensure the necessary political guidance and strategic direction to such operations, while respecting the single institutional framework;
    - modalities will be developed for full consultation, cooperation and transparency between the EU and NATO, taking into account the needs of all EU Member States;
    - appropriate arrangements will be defined that would allow, while respecting the Union's decision-making autonomy, non-EU European NATO members and other interested States to contribute to EU military crisis management;
    - a non-military crisis management mechanism will be established to coordinate and make more effective the various civilian means and resources, in parallel with the military ones, at the disposal of the Union and the Member States.

29. The European Council asks the incoming Presidency, together with the Secretary-General/High Representative, to carry work forward in the General Affairs Council on all aspects of the reports as a matter of priority, including conflict prevention and a committee for civilian crisis management. The incoming Presidency is invited to draw up a first progress report to the Lisbon European Council and an overall report to be presented to the Feira European Council containing appropriate recommendations and proposals, as well as an indication of whether or not Treaty amendment is judged necessary. The General Affairs Council is invited to begin implementing these decisions by establishing as of March 2000 the agreed interim bodies and arrangements within the Council, in accordance with the current Treaty provisions.

Chapter Twenty-Four

The EU and the World Trading System

Nigel Grimwade

The EU constitutes one of the key players in the global economy. In 1999 it accounted for an estimated 40% of world merchandise exports if intra-EU exports are included and 14.6% if extra-EU exports only are taken. This was a larger share than that of any single country, even the United States. EU exports of commercial services accounted for 42% of world exports (including intra-EU exports), a higher share than for any other region of the world. So far, deepening internal integration has not been at the expense of wider external integration. In line with other advanced industrialized regions and countries, trade between the EU and the rest of the world has grown at a faster rate than output of goods and services, implying growing international economic interdependence.

Structure of the EU's External Trade

In 1999, the EU exported US$2,176 billion-worth of merchandise exports, of which 63% went to other member states (in "intra-EU" trade). The remaining 27% ("extra-EU" trade) went to the rest of the world. Table 24.1 sets out the geographic structure of the EU's trade with the rest of the world. Nearly 22% of EU exports went to the United States, which accounted for an equivalent share of EU imports. The North American Free Trade Area (NAFTA), comprising the United States, Canada, and Mexico, was the EU's most important regional trading partner. Japan was the EU's second largest trading partner, although

the EU's imports from Japan were considerably more than its exports to it. Much the same was true of the EU's trade with the whole of the Asian region. The EU's imports from the member states of the Association of Southeast Asian Nations (ASEAN) exceeded the EU's exports to them. The same was true of the EU's trade with China and South Korea, although not of its trade with Hong Kong. By way of contrast, its trade balances with Latin America and the oil-producing states of the Middle East were positive. Not surprisingly, a significant proportion of the EU's trade takes place with its neighbours to the East and to the South (the Mediterranean countries), with which it has special trading relationships. Some of these are candidate countries hoping to join the EU in the next five years. In total, the 13 candidate countries accounted for almost 16% of the EU's exports and just under 12% of its imports. Trade with the developing countries that have been signatories of the Lomé Convention – the African, Caribbean and Pacific (ACP) states – accounted for a relatively small proportion of the EU's trade.

The Common Commercial Policy

The EU's trading policy towards the rest of the world is governed by the Common Commercial Policy (CCP) provided for by Articles 131–35 of the Treaty establishing the European Community (formerly 110–16). Article 133 states that the basis of the CCP is the principle of uniformity as applied particularly, but not exclusively, to the following: changes in tariff rates; the conclusion of tariff and trade agreements; the achievement of uniformity in measures of liberalization; and export policy and measures to protect trade, such as those taken in the event of dumping or subsidies. Article 132 states that the CCP also requires countries to harmonize their systems for granting export aid to third countries "to the extent necessary to ensure that competition between undertakings of the Community is not distorted".

The procedure for implementing the CCP is also set out in Article 133. Responsibility for implementing the CCP resides with both the European Commission and the Council of Ministers. It is the task of the Commission to submit proposals to the Council, which is to act by qualified majority voting (QMV). Where the Community is seeking to negotiate trading agreements with other countries or organizations, the Council authorizes the Commission to open the negotiations. The Commission conducts the negotiations in consultation with a special committee appointed by the Council and within a framework laid down by the Council. When negotiations have been completed, they are concluded by the Council acting under QMV.

An important amendment was added when the Treaty on European Union was agreed at Maastricht in 1991, giving any member state's government, the Council, or the Commission the right to refer any tariff or trade agreement to the European Court of Justice to ensure that it is compatible with the EC Treaty. This became important following the completion of the Uruguay Round of negotiations under the General Agreement on Tariffs and Trade (GATT) in December 1993 and temporarily threatened to delay ratification of the final agreement. A dispute arose between the Council and the Commission as to the authority of the Commission to negotiate an agreement covering services and intellectual property rights. The Commission referred the matter to the European Court of Justice for clarification. In November 1994 the Court ruled that trade in goods and crossborder services, such as telecommunications, audiovisual services, or financial services that are transmitted electronically, falls exclusively within the jurisdiction of the Commission. However, other types of services were declared to be a shared responsibility of the Council and the Commission, while jurisdiction for intellectual property rights, other than cases involving counterfeit goods crossing borders, was said to remain with member states.

Changes in Tariff Rates

A key principle stipulated in Article 133 is that the power to change any tariff resides with the EU and not with individual member states. Because the EU is a customs union, it operates a common customs tariff and therefore any amendment to it can only be effected by the EU. This means that the EU negotiates new tariff or trading agreements with other countries as a collective entity. Thus, when the EU participates in multilateral trade negotiations, such as the GATT Uruguay Round, it bargains as a bloc. It is often argued that this gives the member states much greater negotiating power than would be the case if they were to bargain individually. Likewise, when the member states enter into bilateral trading agreements with other countries, they do so collectively.

An important element in the EU's CCP has been its programme of bilateral trading agreements entered into with certain of its trading partners. Although the terms of these agreements vary greatly, each provides partners with preferential access to the EU market, whether on a unilateral basis or on a reciprocal basis. An example of a nonreciprocal preferential trading agreement is the Lomé Convention, first signed in 1975 between the European Community and a group of African, Caribbean, and Pacific (ACP) countries. These countries now enjoy duty-free access to the EU market for more than 90% of their exports, but are not required to offer the EU anything equivalent in return. The Lomé Convention is, however, soon to be replaced by the Cotonou Convention, which will eventually result in the creation of a series of regional free trade areas between the EU and these countries. At the other extreme, the EU has, since 1996, operated a customs union with Turkey that includes internal free trade for industrial goods and a common customs tariff. Between these two extremes, the EU has signed free trade agreements with a diverse group of countries providing for preferential access on a reciprocal basis. Since 1994 the EU has operated the European Economic Area (EEA) with three members of the European Free Trade Area (EFTA), Norway, Liechtenstein, and Iceland (the fourth member of EFTA, Switzerland, never ratified the treaty). The EEA has created single market conditions for industrial goods, while it excludes most agricultural products, and it has liberalized the movement of capital, services, and labour. Free trade agreements have also been negotiated with Israel, certain of the Mediterranean countries, South Africa, Mexico, Russia and other CIS states, and Mercosur (the Southern Cone Common Market, comprising Argentina, Brazil, Paraguay, and Uruguay). A more limited trade facilitation and cooperation agreement also exists between the EU and members of ASEAN.

At the same time as entering into these preferential trading agreements, the EU has cut its tariff on a multilateral basis through GATT. As a result the EU's external tariff has become much less important as a weapon of trade policy. As of 1 July 1995 the simple average tariff across all products stood at 9.6%. However, in the Uruguay Round of GATT the EU agreed to further reductions in the EU's common customs tariff to be implemented over five years to 1 July 2000. When the cuts have been fully implemented, the EU's unweighted average tariff on industrial goods will be only 3.7%, although tariffs will remain higher on agricultural goods. High tariffs will also continue to exist on certain "sensitive" manufactured products such as textiles and clothing, footwear, certain types of motor vehicles, and radio and television sets. Further, when the Uruguay Round agreements are fully implemented, all EU tariffs will be fully bound, including tariffs on agricultural goods. Today, a more important role is played in trade policy by nontariff measures than by tariffs.

Anti-dumping Policy

One of the major ways in which the EU protects its producers from foreign competition is through the use of its anti-dumping policy.

Article VI of GATT allows countries to introduce anti-dumping measures where it can be demonstrated that imports of a particular product have been dumped and that the dumping is causing "material injury" to domestic producers. Dumping is defined as a situation where the export price of a good is below its "normal value". In many cases the latter is taken to be the domestic price of the good "at an equivalent level of trade". However, where insufficient domestic sales have taken place during the period in question, countries are allowed to construct a "normal value" using costs of production plus some reasonable mark-up for selling costs and profits, or to use the export price in some third country as a proxy.

The European Community first introduced anti-dumping regulations in July 1968, although they were not implemented until 1976. Since then, the Community has made considerable use of these provisions. The Commission is required to act on any complaint of dumping brought by domestic producers. If the Commission decides that there is sufficient evidence for an investigation, provisional anti-dumping duties may be imposed for a period not exceeding four months, which may be extended for a further two months. These are repayable if subsequently no case is found to exist. If, however, the investigation provides evidence of dumping and of injury, or the threat of injury, to EU producers, the Council may impose definitive duties on a proposal from the Commission. Under the rules of GATT and its successor, the World Trade Organization (WTO), the anti-dumping duty must not exceed the margin of dumping. Alternatively, the Commission may accept undertakings offered by the exporters in the form of a revision of prices that serve to eliminate the margin of dumping. The EU's anti-dumping policy places a time limit of five years on any measures introduced, although they may be extended if an interested party can show that their removal would again lead to injury or the threat of injury.

In 1987 the Community introduced a highly controversial addition to its anti-dumping armoury in the form of the "screwdriver plant" regulation (Council Regulation 1761/87). Under this provision, where foreign producers set up assembly plants inside the Community following the imposition of anti-dumping measures, the same duties may be imposed on these products as on those imported directly, that is, without assembly, from the country in question. Community rules require that the value of imported parts and materials must exceed the value of all other parts and materials by at least 50%. The Commission has interpreted this to mean that parts and materials coming from a source other than the dumping country must amount to more than 40% of the total value of all parts and materials. Subsequently, this regulation was used against Japanese producers of electronic typewriters and photocopiers. This led to a Japanese complaint to GATT that the Community's anti-circumvention measures were illegal under GATT's rules. In March 1990 a GATT panel did indeed confirm that the measures were incompatible with GATT provisions, a decision that was bitterly contested by the Community. The right of countries to take anti-circumvention measures became an issue in the Uruguay Round negotiations concerned with anti-dumping, but countries were unable to reach agreement. It therefore remains unclear whether or not, in the future, the EU will be able to employ this particular addition to its anti-dumping policy.

The Final Act of GATT's Uruguay Round introduced a new code to govern the use of anti-dumping, which replaced those introduced in earlier rounds. This necessitated the EU making certain changes to its anti-dumping policy (see Council Regulation 3283/94). In some respects the EU's new anti-dumping regulation makes it easier for the EU to impose anti-dumping measures, due to an important change in the decision-making procedures for anti-dumping cases. In future, preliminary decisions by the Commission to use anti-dumping measures can become definitive on the basis of a simple majority vote of the Council rather than the QMV required until now. Under the old rules, it was possible for two large member states plus one small one to veto proposals by the Commission. This gave the more liberally minded member states the power to block the imposition of anti-dumping measures. The removal of this veto has meant

that, for a measure to take effect, it is sufficient for eight member states (in the current EU of 15) to support a proposal from the Commission. In other respects, however, the use of anti-dumping policy has become more difficult. There are more detailed rules governing the calculation of the dumping margin, stricter time limits on anti-dumping procedures, and an enhanced role for users and consumers' associations to make representations in anti-dumping investigations.

Safeguards

Another method by which the EU may grant domestic producers protection is that of safeguards. Under Article XIX of GATT, still in force under the WTO, countries may introduce emergency measures against imports if, as a result of "unforeseen developments", a product is being imported in such quantities as to cause or threaten "serious injury". For many years the Commission was unsuccessful in its attempts to wrest this aspect of trade policy from the control of the member states' governments. Until 1985 member states retained the right to introduce emergency quotas, although the Commission had the right subsequently to revoke or amend the measures. Even then, member states could refer the matter to the Council for adjudication on the basis of QMV. In 1985, however, this right was abolished except where a safeguard clause was contained in a bilateral agreement between a member state and some third country. Competence for safeguards now resides with the Commission, which is empowered to impose quantitative restrictions on imports to prevent serious injury or the threat of serious injury. The EU's rules also provide for "surveillance measures" where imports cause or threaten serious injury. These involve monitoring the quantity of imports for a fixed period of time through the use of import licences.

In the past, rather than impose quotas the EU has sometimes preferred to negotiate an agreement on "voluntary export restraint" (VER) with the exporting country. In this case, the exporting country undertakes to limit exports of the product causing injury to the market of the importing country for a given period of time. The first Community-wide VER was negotiated by the Commission with Japan in 1983, to regulate exports of video cassette recorders into the Community. In 1991 the Commission negotiated a similar agreement with Japan governing automobiles. This replaced a series of national VERs that several member states already operated with Japan, as well as quotas applied by some of the others. Under the agreement Japan undertook to monitor the growth of its exports to the EU on the assumption that they would not exceed 1.23 million units in 1999 in a total EU market forecast at 15.1 million units. As part of the agreement the EU undertook to complete the liberalization of the European car market by the end of 1999. However, most VERs have now been ended under an agreement reached in the Uruguay Round to eliminate all existing "grey area measures", including VERs, by the end of the 1990s.

The New Commercial Policy Instrument

In 1984 the Community added a further measure to its trade policy armoury, in the form of the "new commercial policy instrument" (NCPI) (Council Regulation 2641/84). This empowers the Council, on the recommendation of the Commission and following a proper investigation, to retaliate against any country that is engaging in "illicit trading practices" injurious to Community exporters in third-country markets. Proceedings are initiated on the complaint of either a Community producer or a member state. Retaliatory measures may take the form of any measure deemed appropriate providing that it is compatible with the Community's international obligations and procedures. The measure closely resembles the controversial Section 301 measures contained in US trade law, which provide for similar retaliation against countries applying "unfair treatment" to US exports. In November 1994 the Commission submitted proposals to the Council intended to make the NCPI more effective. These proposals were subsequently embodied in the New Trade Barriers Regulation (Council Regulation 3286/94) adopted by the Council of Ministers. Specifically, the changes enable

EU exporters to obtain quicker investigations of cases where they confront illegal trading practices in foreign markets. A new committee, made up of representatives from the member states and chaired by a representative of the Commission, considers complaints or requests for action and decides whether the evidence is sufficient to initiate a fuller examination. If so, the matter goes before the Council of Ministers for a decision based on QMV. However, where this involves another member of the WTO, no measures can be taken until authorized by the WTO's Dispute Settlements Board (see below). Perhaps not surprisingly, given its controversial nature, the EU has used this policy instrument sparingly since its introduction.

The EU and GATT

At the time when the European Economic Community was set up, all six founder member states were signatories of GATT. Although GATT is based on the principle of nondiscrimination – the "most favoured nation" (MFN) principle – Article XXIV specifically allows contracting parties to set up customs unions or free trade areas subject to certain conditions:

- tariffs must be eliminated on "substantially all the trade" between the countries involved;
- the level of the common external tariff should be no higher than the average levels of tariffs imposed on the same imports by the member states before the formation of the union; and
- third countries should be compensated for any loss of trade brought about by the formation of the union.

In effect, GATT treats customs unions such as the EU as a single customs territory.

As a signatory of GATT the European Community was required to abide by its rules, which included a willingness to participate actively in multilateral negotiations to bring about a progressive reduction in the levels of tariffs and other barriers to trade. As we have seen, these negotiations took place in "rounds" at intervals dictated by the willingness of GATT signatories to engage in trade liberalization. In each round, countries were expected to offer other countries "concessions", in the form of tariff cuts or the binding of tariffs at agreed levels, in return for receiving other equivalent concessions from their trading partners: this became known as the principle of reciprocity. Because of the MFN rule, any concession granted by one GATT country to another in the course of negotiation was automatically extended to all other contracting parties.

There have been no fewer than eight rounds of multilateral negotiation conducted under the auspices of GATT. In the four rounds since its formation, the Community has played a major role, offering cuts in its common customs tariff in exchange for concessions received from its major trading partners. This resulted in a gradual reduction of the common customs tariff as applied to industrial goods, although agricultural goods remained subject to a high level of external protection under the Common Agricultural Policy (CAP). In return, the Community gained improved access for its exports to overseas markets. However, because GATT was mainly concerned with tariff liberalization, the Community's imports from the rest of the world remained subject to nontariff forms of protection, as did its exports to the rest of the world. Only in the seventh round, known as the Tokyo Round, was a serious attempt made to tackle nontariff barriers.

The latest GATT round, the Uruguay Round, took place between 1986 and 1993, the final agreement being signed in April 1994. It was both bigger than any of the previous rounds, involving 117 countries, and more complex. Further, it was not concerned simply with negotiating lower tariffs, although that remained an important objective. At the insistence of the United States and other exporters of agricultural goods, it was agreed that some progress should be made on opening up trade in agriculture, which had previously been unaffected by the liberalization process under GATT. This created a problem for the Community because its agriculture remained heavily protected under the CAP. In order to convince developing countries of the desirability of another round, it was also agreed that an attempt should be made to eliminate the non-

tariff restrictions on trade in textile products under the Multi-fibre Arrangement (MFA), first negotiated in 1973. The MFA allowed the developed countries to treat imports of textiles differently from other products for a period of time, in order to allow their textile industries the space to adjust. In addition to these "old issues", and again largely at the insistence of the United States, it was agreed to add three "new issues" to the agenda of the Uruguay Round: trade in services, trade-related aspects of intellectual property rights (TRIPs), and trade-related investment measures (TRIMs).

Then, too, there was the need to build on the progress made in the preceding Tokyo Round in tackling the problem of nontariff barriers. This had worked mainly through developing a series of side codes to the main agreement designed to regulate the use of nontariff measures. There was a need, however, to strengthen and extend these codes, as well as to tackle the problem of the spread of "grey area measures". Linked to this was the need to reform GATT's safeguards clause, which had not worked well and which had contributed to the spread of extralegal measures such as the VERs discussed above. Other GATT rules, such as those regulating the creation of regional trading agreements, were also seen to be in need of reform in the light of new developments in the world trading system. Finally, there was an urgent need for GATT countries to examine ways of making the mechanism for settling disputes between them work more swiftly and effectively.

Despite the complexity of the agenda and the fact that negotiations nearly broke down on several occasions, an agreement was eventually reached towards the end of 1993. This was signed at Marrakesh in Morocco in 1994 and took effect on 1 January 1995. On agriculture, the EU was forced to make concessions on the level of domestic protection it could continue to grant to its farmers and the level of subsidies that could be paid to exporters. Under pressure from the United States and the Cairns Group of countries exporting agricultural goods, it was agreed to lower levels of import protection in two ways. First, all existing nontariff barriers were to be replaced with tariffs, in a process known as "tariffication", and tariffs were to be gradually reduced by an average of 36% over six years, but by 24% over ten years for developing countries. Secondly, the level of domestic support granted to farmers, whether through price support or domestic subsidy, was to be cut by 20% over six years, but by 13.3% for developing countries. In addition, countries agreed to reduce the value of subsidies paid to agricultural exporters by 36% over six years and to reduce the volume of subsidized exports by 21% over the same period. These measures fell a long way short of what the United States and the Cairns Group were seeking, but they represented the first attempt made under GATT to liberalize agricultural trade.

On industrial products, further progress was made on reducing and, in some cases, eliminating tariffs. On average, the EU cut tariffs on industrial goods by 37%, in line with the average reduction for developed countries as a whole. These were to be staged over six years. In addition, agreement was reached to eliminate tariffs altogether on a wide range of goods, including pharmaceuticals, construction equipment, medical equipment, steel, beer, spirits, furniture, farm equipment, wood and paper products, toys, and some fish products. Finally, the EU, along with other industrialized countries, agreed to bind all remaining tariff rates.

As a major exporter of services the EU also stood to gain greatly from an agreement to extend GATT disciplines to this area of trade. One of the major achievements of the Uruguay Round was to secure a new General Agreement on Trade in Services (GATS). GATS has three major parts. First, it includes a framework agreement that lists a set of general obligations and disciplines. These include an unconditional MFN rule, requiring countries to provide equal treatment for the service suppliers of other countries, although they can request temporary exemption for particular sectors. Secondly, it incorporates a list of specific commitments that countries have agreed to apply to service industries listed in their schedules. These include measures to improve market access and commitments to provide foreign service providers with "national treatment", that is, treating them no less favourably than domestic service providers. Thirdly, GATS

contains a number of special annexes covering industries that are subject to special provisions. Industry-specific annexes are included for financial services, telecommunications, air transport services, basic telecommunications, and maritime transport services.

GATS failed to live up to the ambitious goals set by the United States at the beginning of the negotiations and came closer to the "softer" approach being advocated by the Community. Nevertheless, it did provide a framework for future negotiations, beginning the process of liberalizing trade in services. Important new agreements on liberalizing trade in financial services and telecommunications were negotiated after the Uruguay Round had been completed.

With regard to the other major new issues, namely TRIPs and TRIMs, the EU also made significant gains. A new TRIPs agreement provided European firms with increased protection for their intellectual property, including copyright, trademarks, industrial designs, patents, and so on, in other GATT countries where this was not already in existence. All countries were required to introduce laws protecting firms from an infringement of intellectual property rights within a transitional period of five years, but 11 years in the case of the least developed countries. The TRIMs agreement required countries to eliminate all foreign investment measures that distort trade, such as "local content" requirements, which stipulate particular levels of local procurement that foreign investors must adopt, or "trade balancing" requirements, which restrict the volume or value of imports to an amount related to the level of the product that foreign investors export.

In return for these agreements, the developed countries were required to make major concessions on products of interest to developing countries. In this respect, the agreement on textiles was especially important. This provided for the phasing out, over ten years, of the Multifibre Arrangement, which, as mentioned above, had governed trade in textiles since 1975. The Uruguay Round provided for the gradual reintegration of textile products into GATT beginning on 1 January 1995, with products amounting to at least 16% of total imports.

Countries, however, were free to choose which textile products to include. This did not prevent countries from introducing new restrictions on products, once they have been reintegrated, if they should be causing or threatening serious injury to domestic producers. In this case, however, any measures introduced are subject to the conditions specified in GATT's new safeguards clause (see next paragraph) governing any form of emergency protection.

Finally, the Uruguay Round introduced some major changes in GATT rules. First, a new GATT safeguards clause (Article XIX) was agreed placing certain limits on the use of emergency protection. This included an undertaking by countries to get rid of VERs and all other "grey area" measures within four years, although they were each allowed to retain one VER for a further 12 months beyond this deadline. A key issue in the negotiations over the reform of Article XIX concerned whether countries could impose selective and thus discriminatory measures on countries where emergency protection was granted. Although the EU favoured a selective approach, the new clause precluded this. However, an important loophole within the agreement does allow the use of selective measures in special circumstances.

Secondly, a new code was agreed for the use of anti-dumping measures. This tightened up some of the rules and procedures governing the use of anti-dumping, to prevent some of the misuses that had become widespread. Few of the changes did anything to limit significantly the ability of the EU to use anti-dumping measures in the future. However, the EU was unsuccessful in its attempt to change the rules to permit countries to apply duties on goods where exporters had circumvented measures imposed by setting up screwdriver plants in the importing country (see above).

Thirdly, the agreement contained a new code on subsidies that went much further than the code negotiated as part of the Tokyo Round in regulating the use of subsidies that distort trade. In particular, for the first time ever, there was a prohibition placed on domestic subsidies, not just on export subsidies, that distort trade: these became known as "actionable subsidies". In the past, GATT rules had sought only to outlaw

export subsidies that directly distorted trade. However, as in the past, agricultural subsidies remain outside the scope of the new code.

The EU and the WTO

One of the major weaknesses of GATT had been that it lacked sufficient powers to enforce the various rules and agreements that the contracting parties had entered into. In part this was due to the fact that GATT was never anything more than a treaty, which signatories agreed to apply on a provisional basis only. At the time when it was signed, it was the intention to replace GATT within a few years with a new International Trade Organization (ITO) that would have had a permanent existence. However, the charter for an ITO was never ratified by the US Congress and the proposal remained a dead letter. As a result, GATT continued in existence for longer than was ever intended. The provisional nature of GATT contributed towards its ineffectiveness, in particular in the area of enforcement. One aspect of this was that countries could avoid abiding by rules that were in conflict with laws passed before the time of accession, by invoking "grandfather rights". Thus, the United Kingdom was allowed to continue granting imperial preference to Commonwealth countries, despite the fact that GATT rules established the principle of nondiscrimination. A further problem arose if it was decided to add new rules to GATT, as any country could choose not to apply these rules. One way of dealing with this was for those countries wanting to apply new rules to a particular area of trade to negotiate special side agreements that would be binding only on those countries that signed up. This approach was used in the Tokyo Round to develop special codes to prevent non-tariff distortions to trade, such as subsidies.

A further difficulty concerned the procedures existing within GATT for settling disputes between parties. A key provision of GATT was that, wherever possible, countries should settle their disputes by consultation rather than by retaliation. Only when this procedure had been fully exhausted would retaliation be allowed. Under GATT's mechanism for settling disputes, any country could bring a complaint against another country that it considered to be "nullifying or impairing" its rights under GATT. If necessary, an independent panel of experts would be appointed to investigate the case and make a recommendation. If the complaint was upheld and the recommendations of the panel were subsequently adopted by the GATT Council, the country at fault was expected to respond by making the necessary changes. In practice, however, this mechanism did not work well. As there were no time limits set for any of the stages involved, cases could drag on for a very long time. Moreover, because GATT operated on the basis of consensus, any country could block the adoption of a report with which it disagreed, thereby ensuring that its recommendations never became enforceable. Where a report was adopted but the country found to be at fault refused to implement its findings, the other contracting parties were generally unprepared to authorize any sanctions against the country in question, leaving it free to continue with the measures that had caused the dispute in the first place.

In the course of the Uruguay Round it was widely acknowledged that the time had come to make major constitutional changes to the legal framework on which the postwar rules-based system of trade rested. It was decided that a new multilateral trading organization was needed to take the place of GATT, with greater powers to compel countries to abide by the rules embodied in GATT and other agreements. As a result, on 1 January 1995 the WTO came into being. The WTO brings together a number of different agreements: the General Agreement relating to Goods (GATT 1994), the General Agreement on Services (GATS), and the Agreement on Trade-related Aspects of Intellectual Property Rights (TRIPs). In addition, it has responsibility for the trade policy review mechanism developed under GATT to monitor member states' trade policies as well as for a new improved dispute settlement mechanism. An important aspect of the WTO is that countries that join are required to abide by all of the agreements and cannot select those to which they wish to adhere. The old GATT mechanism for settling disputes has been replaced by a new procedure that pro-

vides for a much more rapid resolution of disputes. All WTO countries have an automatic right to a panel enquiry and there are strict time limits on each stage of the investigation. Although a country can appeal against any panel report with which it disagrees, if the appeals body comes out in favour of the original report, it can be blocked only if all countries are in favour of doing so. Finally, if a country fails to comply with the findings of a panel report the WTO may authorize any country to introduce sanctions against that country. Moreover, these can be applied to any aspect of the trade of the offending country and need not be confined to the specific industry in which the offending measures have been applied.

The EU has been an active user of the new disputes settlement mechanism, making no fewer than 47 complaints in the first four years following the establishment of the WTO. This was exceeded only by the United States, which made 60 complaints over the same period. At the same time the EU has been the object of another 28 complaints by other members of the WTO. In most cases these disputes have been resolved by the country in question removing or altering the measure causing the dispute. In several cases, however, the dispute has dragged on for longer without any resolution of the problem. In two cases, both involving a complaint by the United States against the EU, this has resulted in the WTO authorizing other countries to introduce sanctions against the EU. The first concerned the EU's import regime for bananas, which granted preferential treatment to bananas imported from producers in the Caribbean that were signatories of the Lomé Convention. Although the granting of tariff preferences was permitted under a special "waiver" granted to the EU by the WTO, the EU's system of import quotas and licensing was found by a WTO panel to be contrary to WTO rules. The complaint was brought by the United States, although the countries most adversely affected by the EU's import regime were the "dollar" banana-producing countries, such as Guatemala, Honduras, and Ecuador, which are able to grow bananas at much lower cost than the ACP countries can. Although the EU made several attempts to alter its import regime to make it more acceptable to these countries, a further WTO panel found that the changes were inadequate in several respects. In April 1999, after bilateral negotiations between the EU and the United States broke down, the WTO authorized the United States to impose sanctions worth US$191 million to cover the losses incurred as a result of the EU's banana import regime. The United States announced 100% tariffs to be imposed on nine EU products exported mainly by France and the United Kingdom, the two countries considered to be most influential in maintaining the EU's banana import regime.

A second dispute involving hormone-treated meat was also the subject of a US complaint to the WTO. Since 1987 the European Community had operated a ban on the import of beef produced using artificial hormones that were regarded as creating a risk of cancer. Although the WTO's rules do allow countries to block imports of products that are dangerous to public health, they must provide the scientific evidence to show that there is such a risk. In 1997 a WTO panel set up to investigate the US complaint maintained that, according to most scientific studies carried out on the health risk from using artificial hormones in producing beef, there was no discernible danger to human health. The EU lodged an appeal against the findings of the panel, but the appeal body upheld the original ruling. The EU refused to remove its import ban, arguing that it needed longer to carry out its own risk assessment. In 1999, after a further complaint to the WTO by the United States, the WTO finally authorized the United States and Canada to impose sanctions on imports from the EU.

The banana and beef disputes were the first cases under the new dispute settlement mechanism in which the WTO authorized any of its member states to impose sanctions on imports from other member states that had failed to implement the findings of a WTO panel. Other disputes, involving genetically modified food, aircraft subsidies, and trade marks for Cuban rum, have also arisen in relation to recent US complaints to the WTO against the EU. However, it should be pointed out that the EU has also been active in lodging complaints with the WTO against practices operated by the United States that were said to have had an adverse effect on the EU's exports. Thus, in February 2000, following a complaint from the EU, a WTO panel ruled that a system for granting tax exemption for US companies selling their goods through overseas subsidiaries set up for this purpose amounted to an illegal export subsidy. On the one hand, the active use made by WTO members of the new dispute settlement mechanism may be regarded as a measure of its success: it is presumably far better that countries settle their disputes at a multilateral level, in accordance with agreed rules and procedures, and after an independent investigation, than by acting unilaterally. Unilateral retaliation always favours the big and the powerful over the small and insignificant. On the other hand, it is disconcerting that the two largest members of the WTO have found themselves almost continuously at odds with each other over trade and unable to reach agreement on a solution to disputes between them extending over relatively long periods.

Differences between the EU and United States also surfaced at a special WTO ministerial conference convened in Seattle in November 1999 to discuss the agenda for another round of multilateral trade negotiations. The impetus for a further round of trade negotiations, following so soon after the completion of the Uruguay Round, arose in part from the perceived need to address issues left unresolved in the previous round. The Final Act of the Uruguay Round had specifically provided for further negotiations in the year 2000 in two areas where only limited progress was achieved in the Uruguay Round, namely, agriculture and services. Whereas the United States and the EU shared a desire to bring about further liberalization in the market for services, they remained at odds over the desirability of further subsidy reductions affecting agriculture. At Seattle the United States made it clear that it favoured a new round of trade negotiations, but with a narrow agenda concerned mainly with issues such as agriculture and services. The EU, on the other hand, favoured a broader agenda, covering a variety of issues, such as trade and the environment, trade and labour standards, trade and competition policy, and foreign direct investment, that had not been addressed in the Uruguay Round. The Seattle conference ended without agreement on any agenda for a new round – and, notoriously, amid large-scale antiglobalization protests that hampered the ministers' work – but both the United States and the EU remain committed in principle to the goal of launching a new round.

A major cause of the breakdown was the failure of the EU, and other industrialized regions and countries, to win the support of the developing countries, which account for two thirds of the WTO's membership, for a fresh round of negotiations. First, the developing countries complained that developed countries had done too little to implement the commitments that they had entered into as part of the Uruguay Round. In particular, they had dragged their feet on textiles and increased rather than reduced protection in relation to agriculture. Secondly, developing countries were suspicious of the motives of both the United States and the EU in calling for the issue of labour standards to be introduced into trade rules. The developed countries wanted the rules changed to allow restrictions to be placed on goods produced using unacceptable employment methods. Some of the developing countries saw this as an attempt by the developed countries to introduce protectionism through the back door. It remains to be seen whether sufficient agreement can be reached between developed and developing countries on the desirability of a ninth round of multilateral trade negotiations, and, if so, what issues this should address.

Conclusion

Not only does the EU account, as we have seen, for a sizeable proportion of world trade, it is also able through its Common Commercial Policy to exert considerable bargaining power and trading strength. On the whole it has done so in a way that has facilitated rather than hindered the expansion of world trade. Through its participation in GATT and its membership of the WTO, the EU has progressively reduced its common customs tariff. An important exception has been agriculture,

where the EU has continued to operate a protectionist policy and where it has shown a reluctance to eliminate trade-distorting subsidies. Tariffs, however, are no longer the most important impediment to free trade, even in industrial goods. Under its Common Commercial Policy, the EU possesses some powerful nontariff means for restricting trade and, from time to time, it has shown a willingness to employ these, sometimes for protectionist ends. On occasions this has brought the EU into conflict with its major trading partners. In recent years, in particular, the EU has become embroiled in a series of disputes with the United States, its major trading partner, which have threatened to undermine the workings of the newly established WTO. Nevertheless, the EU remains firmly committed to the goal of multilateral free trade and has made clear its wish to see this objective furthered through the launching of a new round of trade negotiations.

Further Reading

European Commission, *European Economy* 52, *The European Community as a World Trading Partner*, Luxembourg: Office for Official Publications of the European Communities, 1993

A valuable official publication on trade policy

European Commission, *The Single Market Review: Impact on Trade and Investment – External Access to European Markets*, Subseries IV, Volume 4, Luxembourg: Office for Official Publications of the European Communities, and London: Kogan Page, 1997

European Parliament, *The Economic Impact of Dumping and the Community's Anti-dumping Policy*, Working Papers, Economic Series, Luxembourg: Office for Official Publications of the European Communities, 1993

GATT, *Trade Policy Review – The European Communities*, Geneva: GATT, 1991 and 1993; and WTO, *Trade Policy Review – The European Union*, Geneva: WTO, 1995, 1997, and 2000

The most comprehensive and detailed accounts of the external trade policy of the Community and the EU

GATT, "Final Act of the Uruguay Round – Press Summary", in *The World Economy*, 17/3, May 1994

GATT, *The World Economy*, 22/9 Bonus Issue, *Towards the Millennium Round – Views from Europe*, December 1999

Grimwade, Nigel, *Consumer Electronics and the EC's Anti-dumping Policy*, London: National Consumer Council, 1991

Grimwade, Nigel, "The External Impact of the EU's Internal Market Programme", in *European Business Journal*, 10/2, 1998

Holmes, P., and J. Kempton, "EU Anti-dumping Policy: A Regulatory Perspective", in G. Majone (editor), *Regulating Europe*, London and New York: Routledge, 1996

Memedovic, Olga, Arie Kuyvenhoven, and William T.M. Molle (editors), *Multilateralism and Regionalism in the Post-Uruguay Round Era: What Role for the EU?*, Boston, MA, Dordrecht, and London: Kluwer, 1999

Sapir, André, "Trade Regionalism in Europe: Towards an Integrated Approach", in *Journal of Common Market Studies*, 38/1, March 2000

Schott, Jeffrey J., *The Uruguay Round: An Assessment*, Washington, DC: Institute for International Economics, 1994

Nigel Grimwade is Principal Lecturer and Head of the Economics and Finance Division at South Bank University, London. His recent publications include *International Trade Policy and the Uruguay Round* (1997) and *International Trade* (2000).

Table 24.1   The EU's Merchandise Trade with the Rest of the World, 1998 (ECU billions and %)

	Exports		Imports	
	ECU billions	%	ECU billions	%
United States	160.65	21.96	151.65	21.29
Canada	14.88	2.03	12.74	1.79
Japan	31.53	4.31	65.78	9.23
Candidate countries (13)	116.45	15.92	82.78	11.62
CIS[1]	28.94	3.96	27.87	3.91
Mediterranean countries	67.73	9.26	42.38	5.95
Latin America	49.46	6.76	35.53	4.99
China	17.38	2.36	41.81	5.87
Hong Kong	17.30	2.36	9.71	1.36
South Korea	9.10	1.24	15.59	2.19
ASEAN[2]	30.49	4.17	52.17	7.32
South Asia	12.65	1.73	15.43	2.17
Australia and New Zealand	14.75	2.02	9.79	1.37
NAFTA[3]	184.81	25.26	168.41	23.64
ACP[4]	22.58	3.09	21.40	3.00
Gulf countries	27.84	3.81	13.78	1.93
OPEC[5]	48.60	6.64	44.60	6.26
World	731.58		712.37	

1 Commonwealth of Independent States
2 Association of Southeast Asian Nations
3 North American Free Trade Area
4 African, Caribbean, and Pacific countries
5 Organization of Petroleum-exporting Countries

Source: EUROSTAT-COMEXT, *External Trade Yearbook*, 1999

Chapter Twenty-Five

The EU and the United States

Michael Smith

Since World War II, the integration of western Europe has been strongly influenced by the United States, and the United States in turn has posed some of the most challenging policy problems for the European Community and now the EU. The EU and the United States between them account for a large proportion of world trade and investment; they play central roles in the operation of international economic institutions; they are at the core of the development of new technologies; and they are also at the core of the western security system, which has in many ways provided an "umbrella" under which the industrial countries of the North Atlantic area have prospered since the late 1940s.

The total value of bilateral trade in goods and services between the EU and the United States amounted to around US$343 billion in 1999, with the United States running a US$45 billion deficit in that year. In 1999, the United States accounted for around 24% of exports from the EU and 21% of imports into it, while the EU accounted for 22% of US exports and 19% of imports into the United States (see Figure 25.1). The EU is by a long way the largest source of direct investment in the US economy, with about US$372 billion of accumulated investment stock in 1996, or 59% of all foreign direct investment in the United States. In its turn, the EU hosted around US$348 billion of accumulated US direct investment in the same year, or 48% of all US direct investment abroad. (See Tables 25.2 and 25.3.) Between them, the EU and the United States account for around 30% of world trade and 60% of the world's aggregate GDP.

The relationship between the EU and the United States is thus intimate and at the same time problematic. The link is not entirely a technical economic one; it is also strongly influenced by cultural, political, and security concerns. Nor is the relationship one in which the two sides keep at arm's length from each other; through the mechanisms of trade, technology, investment, and industrial development, as well as those of popular and elite contacts, the two entities have been subject to processes of interpenetration that often make it seem hard to know where "Europe" stops and "the United States" begins. For example, in areas such as office equipment and in many service industries, it is often difficult to distinguish European from US products or European firms from US ones. Policies made in the EU are both directly affected by, and directly affect, a wide range of US interests and groupings; the challenge for policy is thus to be aware of these and to respond to them without neglecting the interests of the EU itself.

The Relationship to the Late 1980s: Partnership or Rivalry?

The postwar history of relations between the European Community/EU and the United States can be divided for the purposes of analysis into six key phases: foundation, consolidation, fragmentation, disintegration, rebuilding, and transformation. These were not, of course, hermetically sealed and separated from each other, and a brief review of each will give an understanding of the continuity and change in the relationship.

Foundation, 1945–50

The origins of US concern with the process of integration in western Europe lie deep in attempts to stabilize Europe after World War II, and in the structures of the Cold War. The United States gave aid to western Europe through the Marshall Plan, with the twin aims of stabilizing political and economic structures in an increasingly divided Europe, and of encouraging economic cooperation in the western half of the continent. In many ways, therefore, the United States could be seen as a major driving force in the establishment of the European Coal and Steel Community. In addition, the establishment of NATO, in 1949, as the main means to guard collective western security, and the US guarantee to defend western Europe provided an essential securing buttress to the process of economic integration. It should be noted, however, that there were those in the United States who feared the rise of a protectionist western Europe; equally, there were those in western Europe, particularly in the United Kingdom, who resisted the temptations of integration. The United States could certainly provide the context and shape the direction of specific initiatives, but it could not determine the results.

Consolidation, 1950–58

During the first great period of postwar "European construction", Americans were a constant presence and source of support in western Europe, either through their power in the economic sphere or through their ability to provide security. The Treaty of Rome, which founded the European Economic Community (EEC) in 1957, can thus be seen in some ways as one of the most important pieces in the jigsaw of the transatlantic alliance, for it set up the basis for a partnership between the United States and a uniting western Europe. However, this was not the whole of the story. In 1952–54, the United States had supported the establishment of a European Defence Community, which had failed as the result of opposition in France and elsewhere. The French, who had originally proposed the Defence Community, were unable to achieve ratification of the agreement in their National Assembly because of fears about national sovereignty and the impact on colonial involvements in Southeast Asia and North Africa. They could, however, accept the intergovernmental agreement on which the Western European Union (WEU) was based. The rearmament of West Germany thus had to be achieved through the device of the WEU, which was set up in 1955.

In 1956, the British and the French invaded the Suez Canal Zone in an attempt to overthrow President Gamal Nasser of Egypt, acting in collusion with Israel, an operation that led to severe transatlantic recriminations. The setting up of the EEC was thus to take place within an atmosphere of some tension between the founding members and the United States, compounded by the fact that some sectors of the US economy, particularly agriculture and steel, were directly threatened by increasing integration in western Europe. By 1958, when the currencies of the major western countries became fully convertible under the Bretton Woods system (of which the core institution was the IMF), it could be said that the "western economic alliance" was complete. Alternatively, it could be said that the stage had been set for further disputes.

Fragmentation, 1958–71

Three features dominated the EEC–US relationship during the 1960s. First, President John F. Kennedy proclaimed the need for an Atlantic partnership based on the economic and security links between the United States and a uniting western Europe. Secondly, the process of uniting western Europe proved to be time-consuming and a source of tensions among those Europeans involved. Thirdly, as the 1960s wore on the previous dominance of the US economy was eroded and became subject to open challenge. These three trends were interconnected: the US pressure for "Atlantic partnership" created resentments, especially in France; the process of integration led to increasing frictions between the French and their partners; and the uncertainty of US economic performance meant that the French and others could mount an offensive designed to destabilize the US dollar. The French in particular resented the dominance of the dollar and argued for a return to the gold standard. Other countries in western Europe, such as West Germany, resisted US pressures to effectively devalue the dollar. The result was a series of crises based on unstable flows of dollars into and out of western Europe.

Against this background, the considerable achievements in EEC–US cooperation during the 1960s, particularly in the field of trade negotiations within the so-called "Kennedy Round" of the General Agreement on Tariffs and Trade (GATT) from 1963 to 1966, were overshadowed by recriminations about currencies and economic performance. These in turn led to an increasing tendency towards unilateral actions. The US military intervention in Vietnam and the movement towards *détente* in Europe also meant that issues of an essentially political nature were bound to find their way onto the agenda during the 1970s.

Disintegration, 1971–75

From the early 1970s onwards, it becomes quite difficult to identify dominant trends in the relationship between the European Community (EC) and the United States, since the chief feature of the relationship at this time was the coexistence of apparently contradictory tendencies. There is no doubt, however, that in the early 1970s a series of crises led to a near-disintegration of the relationship. The starting point can be placed in August 1971, when US President Richard Nixon proclaimed what came to be called his "New Economic Policy". This was designed to deal with the consequences of the Vietnam War, and the increasing deficits in both the US federal budget and the US balance of payments. One of its chief features was an effective devaluation of the dollar, accompanied by a series of trade measures designed to give the United States more control over its own fate. The net effect was to undermine the set of rules that had governed the development of the world economy since the 1940s and to increase tensions with the country's dominant trading partner, the EC.

These tensions were exacerbated by the Yom Kippur War between Israel and its neighbours, and the subsequent oil price crisis, as well as by events in the EC itself, where inflation and recession were accompanied by the introspection caused by the work involved in the entry of the United Kingdom, Denmark, and Ireland). The increasing political activity of the EC, through the growth of "European political cooperation" (known as EPC) meant that such issues also had an inescapable link to US political leadership, both as it directly affected the EC and more broadly, and this too resulted in frictions.

Rebuilding, 1975–85

As noted above, the coexistence of trends towards disintegration and cooperation was characteristic especially of the late 1970s and early 1980s. On the one side, there was the continuing threat of inflation and recession. In the EC this exacerbated the trends towards economic divergence and "Eurosclerosis", the stagnation of the integration process and inability to achieve further reform of the EC institutions. In the United States, it gave rise to strident calls for protectionism. On the other side, there was the inevitability of the attempt to cooperate, given the growth of interdependence and the need to regulate economies that were increasingly closely connected. Thus, the series of western economic summits, which began in 1975, and the increasingly close consultation over trade and monetary relations, began to rebuild the institutions of EC–US cooperation – the IMF, GATT, the OECD, and the Group of Seven (G7) from the middle of the 1970s – which increasingly involved Japan, both as a partner and as a source of problems.

The onset of the "new Cold War" in the late 1970s, and the ascendancy of President Ronald Reagan in the United States, created new tensions. "Reaganism", with its emphasis on US power, and the unilateral use of both economic and military weapons, implied both confrontation in the security sphere and conflicts in the transatlantic economy. All of these tendencies could be observed in the recriminations over policies in Afghanistan, Poland, and elsewhere, with the United States unilaterally imposing economic and diplomatic sanctions, and then pressuring its allies in western Europe to follow suit. They often resisted US pressures, for example over participation in the Moscow Olympic Games in 1980, or over the sanctions imposed on the Soviet Union after the declaration of martial law in Poland in December 1981.

Nevertheless, the mechanisms of collaboration between the United States and the EC were not destroyed. They continued to provide the infrastructure for the management of increasing interdependence and interpenetration, which were to reach new heights in the late 1980s, even while political tensions were at their peak.

Transformation, 1985–99

Up to 1985, it could be argued that the changes and challenges faced in EC-US relations had been contained within the "western system" of economic and security institutions. Even the Gaullist challenge of the late 1960s and the Reaganite impact on the 1980s had essentially been managed within the established order. During the mid-1980s, however, a series of fundamental changes began to make themselves felt, and these came to a dramatic head in the early 1990s. Within the EC, the member states became involved in the process that became known by the shorthand slogan "1992": the attempt, through the completion of the single European market, to boost the competitiveness of the EC's industries, and to provide the basis for new levels of economic and even political integration. A direct contributing factor to this effort was the perception in western Europe that there was a need for new measures to boost competitiveness, both with the United States and with Japan, in an increasingly global economy. The Uruguay Round of trade negotiations within GATT, which began in 1986, provided a further focus for competition between the EC and the United States, particularly over issues such as agriculture.

At the same time, the economic consequences of Reaganism began to make themselves felt in massive US budget and trade deficits, while the military assertiveness of the United States seemed to create the need for a more organized EC voice in foreign policy. Events in the Soviet Union, and the increasingly radical impact of "Gorbachevism", created a new focus on the future of Europe as a

whole, which in turn gave a different complexion to the Atlantic alliance. These seeds were sown several years before the dramatic events of 1989–91. At one and the same time, they underlined both the continuing importance of the EC and the United States to each other, and the fundamental nature of new challenges and opportunities.

The Impact of the End of the Cold War

It is clear that major processes of change were under way in EC–US relations from the early 1980s onwards. The collapse of the Soviet bloc and then the Soviet Union itself between 1989 and 1991 created a fundamentally new context for the evolution of transatlantic economic and political relations, and irrevocably shifted the EC–US balance. The most obvious cause of this shift was the disappearance of the division of Europe, which had been a constant factor in the period 1945–89. This was accompanied by the unification of Germany within the EC, which promised to change the balance both within the Community, and between the Community and the outside world. The EC itself could be seen as one of the most obvious sources of stability in a new and uncertain world, and thus became a magnet for those elsewhere in Europe who wished to shelter under its wing. Meanwhile, the status of the United States and its long-established security presence in western Europe became open to question: was there any continuing rationale for the presence of 300,000 US troops in Western Europe, or for that matter, for NATO itself? While the intense economic relationship between the two sides of the Atlantic could not be reversed, and was indeed growing all the time, the institutional, political, and security context was transformed. Not only this, but the growing awareness of processes of globalization in the economic and technological spheres brought the possibility of another dimension of profound change.

In these circumstances, it was inevitable that there would be questioning of the EC–US relationship. One dimension of the debate resolved itself into two linked questions: what kind of "Europe" would be created by the many changes taking place?; and what kind of United

States would emerge from the inevitable questioning of the post-Cold War era? To the first question, there were a number of possible answers. Many Americans, and not a few Europeans, feared the emergence of a "fortress Europe", based around the protection of the single market, and of the social and economic provisions made in the previous decade. Such a European Community would not be a responsive partner; more likely, it would be confrontational in both the world economy and the world security system. By contrast, there were those in the EC itself, particularly in the European Commission, where they were led by two External Relations Commissioners, Hans van den Broek (to 1989) and then Leon Brittan (1990–99), who wished the EC to be seen as a "world partner", playing its part in the opening up of world trade and other global processes, and contributing vitally to the emergence of a new European order based on negotiation and the establishment of new institutions. This view was complementary to those held by a number of groupings in the United States, in particular the State Department, which saw the EC as the indispensable means through which Europe would be stabilized and thus the key to the reduction of US commitments in the post-Cold War environment.

On the US side, fraught debate had started in the later 1980s, when it began to appear that the United States was entering a period of long-term decline because of the erosion of its economic base and the burdens imposed by the excesses of Reaganism. However, the debate was oddly divided. On the one hand, there were the "declinists", in particular Paul Kennedy and Lester Thurow, who emphasized the need for the United States to adjust to its "loss of empire" and to defend itself against nimbler competitors, especially in the EC and Japan. On the other hand, there were the "triumphalists", who regarded the collapse of the Soviet bloc – not to mention the defeat of Saddam Hussein and Iraq in the Gulf War of 1991 – as evidence that the US was now the only true superpower. The "triumphalists" were actually divided between those who saw the United States as being able to impose its will abroad and those who wanted to maintain

a sort of isolation based on strength. As was to be expected, US policies were an uneasy mixture of triumphalism and insecurity, glorying in military strength and achievement at the same time as fearing that the economy was being taken over, particularly by the Japanese (not so much by Europeans). From the point of view of the EC, the resulting uncertainty created a rather volatile atmosphere for transatlantic relations.

As a result, the early 1990s witnessed what might be termed an "experimental" period in EC–US relations. Many of the long-term features of the relationship were still to be observed: the GATT Uruguay Round was only the latest, if the most ambitious, of a series of trade negotiations that had begun in the 1950s; there was continuing close consultation about the implementation of the European single market; and there was an intense two-way flow of investment between the United States and the EC. At the same time, however, there were important new beginnings, best exemplified in the EC–US Transatlantic Declaration of November 1990. This established a set of common interests and procedures around which it was hoped that a new and more securely founded relationship could grow. From the US point of view, it expressed both the view that the EC was essential to the new "European architecture" and the need to keep some kind of control over the future development of the EC. From the EC's perspective, it expressed the acceptance of relative equality between the partners, and also held out the promise of an infrastructure for the handling of relations in new areas of economic and political concern. Central to both points of view was the perception that essentially political processes had created a new reality, in which the EC–US relationship could never be the same again.

Maastricht, the Clinton Administration, and the "New World Order"

The context for the Maastricht negotiations and the Treaty on European Union was thus intimately linked to the end of the Cold War, and less directly to the whole issue of relations in the post-Maastricht world between the

United States and what the Treaty created: the EU. The context for this new departure was also linked to the continuing need for intense EU–US interaction in such international economic and security organizations as GATT. An implicit question for all of the participants at Maastricht was whether the Treaty would make the EU a more capable partner for the United States in the management of international order and, more particularly, European order, and, in turn, whether the United States was interested in, or even capable of, devolving significant power to the EU in the political and security domains. There were indeed those who argued that the United States was "leaking power" in any case, and thus that the EU was being thrust into a position of shared leadership.

Just as the single market programme had convinced many Americans that the EC was becoming a more potent economic competitor, so the negotiations leading up to the Treaty on European Union either promised or threatened a more capable EU in two specific areas. First, the establishment of a timetable for Economic and Monetary Union (EMU) gave at least the distant prospect that an EU currency could become a competitor with the US dollar in the international financial system. Secondly, the provisions for a "common foreign and security policy" (CFSP), although not fully integrated into the EU structure, could be seen as strengthening the capacity of the EU to contribute to decision-making on security issues, in Europe or beyond, at a time when the established North Atlantic institutions, such as NATO, were under challenge. To a certain extent, it could appear that the new EU was equipping itself to become a vital contributor to the stabilization of post-Cold War Europe. During the 1950s, its precursor, the European Coal and Steel Community, had performed a role of this kind, but only in a divided continent dominated by the US and Soviet superpowers, and in the relatively restricted sphere of economic and social stability. Now it was being called upon to perform a more comprehensive and active role. Already, the EC was leading the provision of assistance to the states of the former Soviet bloc and conducting wideranging negotiations for the construction of new relationships

with countries all over the "new Europe". Maastricht promised to consolidate these roles and to give the EU a new basis for partnership with the United States.

At the same time, the United States was itself going through a process of change and potential renewal. The excesses of Reaganism and the intense debates about the country's role in the post-Cold War world led in 1992 to a presidential election campaign in which the victory of Bill Clinton promised a series of new beginnings. Based primarily on the urgency of domestic economic and social renewal, Clinton's programme paid little initial attention to the international scene, and viewed the EU as both an economic competitor and a political support for a policy of "selective engagement" in European conflicts. The implication was that trade and other disputes with the EU would be pursued in a hardnosed way, and that the EU would also be expected to take responsibility for the management of conflict in the "new Europe". Many in the EU were quite willing to take on this latter task, but were to be found wanting in certain crucial respects, in particular because of the gap between the EU's diplomatic and economic influence, on the one hand, and, on the other, its lack of any military capacity.

The potential policy problems for the EU in this situation can be illustrated from a number of angles. In the first place, the US stance on economic competitiveness made for some extremely difficult negotiations in the later stages of the GATT Uruguay Round, with agriculture as the key, but not the only, area of intense EC–US friction. Not only this, but the US attempt to open EU markets, such as those for public procurement, worth several billion dollars a year, gave rise to continuing and highly political disputes in areas where there was also a high level of technical complexity. In the political and security spheres, the problems were concentrated in the affairs of the former Yugoslavia and the former Soviet Union. During the years 1992–94 the problem of what action to take in the former Yugoslavia became a running sore in relations between western Europe and the United States. While both sides wanted a peaceful resolution to the Bosnian war, each had its own distinct set of policy preferences and policy constraints to which it responded. The Soviet situation was also a matter of considerable anxiety, given the Clinton administration's overwhelming concern with the survival of Boris Yeltsin's government in Russia and with the politics of nuclear weapons, in contrast to the more civilian priorities of the EC/EU, which focused on aid and investment.

The Changing Agenda of the Late 1990s

Between the mid-1980s and the late 1990s the EU–US agenda was in many respects transformed to include a host of new political and social issues, but these did not replace the established economic, political and security concerns.

The "Established Agenda"

The longstanding concern of the EU and the United States with their mutual economic relations has created a substantial continuing agenda of policy concerns. On the one side, there are what could be termed "systemic issues", focused on the operation of the world economy, and the roles of the EU and the United States therein. The major focus of these issues in the early 1990s was the GATT Uruguay Round of world trade negotiations, which eventually led to the creation of the permanent World Trade Organization (WTO) in 1995 to replace GATT. Throughout the negotiations, the EC/EU and the United States took central roles. In many respects they agreed on the desirability of stronger rules for trade and exchange, but there was equally a concern on both sides to establish positions and to gain more effective access to growing markets, for example those in audiovisual products and financial services. While differences over the latter were at least partly resolved by an agreement in 1997, the former remained a focus of tensions, especially between France and the United States. By the late 1990s there was increasing pressure to proclaim a new "millennium round" of WTO negotiations, but the attempt to do so led to failure and acrimony during and after the WTO's ministerial meeting in Seattle in December 1999.

Another significant focus of EC/EU–US interaction has been the G7, the grouping of the world's seven largest economic powers, which is best expressed in the annual western economic summits. In both the GATT and the G7, the positions of the EU and the United States are challenged by the growth of new economic centres, particularly Japan and Southeast Asia, but in the longer term, arguably, China and other large developing economies, such as India and Brazil. The G7 and several of the global financial institutions, such as the IMF and the World Bank, have been the focus of tensions between the EU and the United States in the aftermath of the establishment of the euro and EMU in January 1999. Many American observers and decision-makers argue that "Euroland" should be represented by a single delegation, rather than those of separate EU member states.

The underlying problem for the EU and the United States is that, although they share an interest in the multilateral regulation of world trade and exchange, they also differ sharply on specific sectoral issues. During the GATT Uruguay Round, this was particularly clear in the case of agriculture (new negotiations on which were being prepared in 2000), but there are also long-running and unresolved disputes in a variety of other areas: steel, with US accusations of dumping and unfair trade by the EC/EU; civil aircraft, with the two sides exchanging accusations about the European Airbus and other projects that, according to the United States, have received unfair subsidies; trade with developing countries, with both sides being concerned to establish their own "spheres of influence" while retaining open access elsewhere; and cars, with the EU being greatly concerned both by the growth of Japanese "transplant" production in the United States and by the confrontational tactics adopted by Washington in US bilateral talks with the Japanese. The picture in many of these areas in the mid-1990s would be broadly recognizable to observers from the mid-1960s.

There is an established agenda of EU–US interaction in the field of politics and security. For more than 20 years, there has been interaction, consultation, and, frequently, some friction over areas such as the Middle East and

Central America, and over trade with the (now former) Soviet bloc and related matters. The events of the mid-1990s could in some respects be seen as a continuation of these longer-term trends, now in the new framework of the Transatlantic Declaration, with its procedures for consultation and exchange of policy proposals, but in the late 1990s the development of a "European security and defence identity" (ESDI), and of concrete EU collaboration in the military field, threatened to create new tensions over the "division of labour" between the two sides of the Atlantic.

The "New Agenda"

Although there is a great deal of continuity in EC/EU–US relations, it is clear that in the new century there are novel elements in the relationship arising from the changes in the EU, the United States, and the broader international arena already outlined. At the "systemic" level, both the international economy and the international security system are in a state of profound flux. Globalization and the interpenetration of economic processes have created a world in which questioning of old groupings is ever more frequent. Significantly, the WTO has found itself dealing not only with "traditional" trade issues, but also with problems of trade in services, intellectual property rights, investment and competition, and national or international standards. In the aftermath of the GATT agreement of 1993–94, a number of other systemic issues came to the fore, including the links between trade and the environment, and those between trade and workers' rights. On both of these issues the EC and the United States broadly share positions, but there have been important differences of opinion on the ways in which regulation at the national or the international level should occur, specifically, the extent to which the free market should be the key, or whether government action is necessary. The problem is that for the EU and the United States national regulations, national markets, and national companies are no longer always relevant units to work with, given the increasing role of multinational companies, and the globalization of ownership and production.

The transformation of the international security system and the halting emergence of a "new world order" have also challenged EU–US policy processes. Whereas both the EC/EU and the United States wished to re-establish a form of international order in the aftermath of the collapse of the Soviet bloc, they have differed significantly on some of the ways in which this might be done and the institutions through which it could be channelled. The key initial test – though not the only one – was over the former Yugoslavia, both in relation to Bosnia–Herzegovina (1991–95) and later in relation to Kosovo (1999). Although the EU had a dominant "local" role, and major resources to aid reconstruction or political stabilization, the United States alone – whether independently or acting through NATO – possessed the material capabilities that were essential to a security settlement. Both the EU and the United States are surrounded by a host of other institutional frameworks – the UN, the Organization for Security and Cooperation in Europe, NATO, the WEU – which offer possibilities, but also pose challenges of coordination and linkage.

At the "sectoral" level, there are also new challenges for policy-making in the EU and the United States. Economic and social problems are now not easily confined within national or regional borders, and the result is that a "new agenda" has arisen in which apparently "domestic" issues have international ramifications. In the late 1990s, EU–US relations thus included attention to transport policy, particularly air routes and proposals for "open skies" agreements; competition policy and the treatment of national companies in overseas markets; taxation policies in relation to multinational companies; employment, unemployment, and social security; and information technology, e-commerce, and the "information society". For both the EU and the United States, these issues bring together internal and external policy-making, and challenge political leaders to develop new mechanisms of coordination and conflict resolution. When these are added to the political and security challenges arising in central and eastern Europe or the former Soviet Union, and to the "widening" and "deepening" of the EU itself, it can be seen that the relationship has in many ways entered a new and uncertain era.

Towards a New Atlantic Partnership?

Throughout its history, the relationship between the EC/EU and the United States has been characterized by expectations of North Atlantic partnership, which have often been disappointed. At times, these expectations have taken the form of "grand designs", usually promulgated by Washington, such as those proposed by President Kennedy in 1962 for "Atlantic Partnership", or by Henry Kissinger in 1973 for a "new Atlantic Charter". These have usually been undermined, almost immediately, by specific events and the general untidiness of the real world. In many ways, there is an extremely strong partnership between the EU and the United States, brought about by the growth of interdependence and interpenetration, and the inescapable need for the two sides to work together at both the governmental and the corporate level, for example on high-technology products, multinational products such as cars and consumer electronics, and financial services. The networks of cooperation are intensive, whether they emerge from markets, from the interaction of policy elites, or from the procedures of the New Transatlantic Agenda or other shared institutional commitments.

Nevertheless, the growth of instrumental partnerships and networks may not be enough to fulfil the political need for partnership and symbolic commitment. Thus, during the mid- and late 1990s there emerged from both Washington and Brussels a demand for new negotiations, first centred on a "Transatlantic Free Trade Area" (TAFTA) and later on the idea of a "New Transatlantic Marketplace". Both proposals would have taken advantage of the infrastructure of cooperation already assembled through the 1970s, 1980s, and 1990s, and would have led, over a period of anything up to 20 years, to a wideranging free trade area with mechanisms for dispute settlement and joint policy initiatives. As ever in EU–US relations, the implications intersected with the development of the EU itself (through the intergovernmental conferences of 1996–97 and 2000, the launch of the euro and the CFSP/ESDI processes, and future enlargement to the East); with the changing nature of administrations in Washington, notably the possibility that the "second Bush administration", from 2001 onwards, would constitute a newly "nationalist" successor to Bill Clinton's presidency; and with the broader development of the world economy and the international security system. To that extent, the first years of the new century show a good deal of continuity with the previous 50 and more years of EC/EU–US relations, even while the world around both has changed profoundly.

Further Reading

Baldwin, Robert E., Carl B. Hamilton, and André Sapir (editors), *Issues in US–EC Trade Relations*, Chicago: University of Chicago Press, 1988

   A major collection on the economics of US–EC relations in the mid-1980s

Buchan, David, *Europe: The Strange Superpower*, Aldershot: Dartmouth, 1993

   Chapter 10 deals with the EU/US/Japan "triangle".

Calingaert, Michael, *European Integration Revisited: Progress, Prospects, and US Interests*, Boulder, CO: Westview Press, 1996

   Orientated especially towards the needs of US business, but an acute analysis nonetheless

Directorate-General on External Economic Relations, *Progress Report on EU–US Relations*, quarterly publication

   A collection of very useful data and reports on particular disputes or areas of collaboration

Eichengreen, Barry (editor), *Transatlantic Economic Relations in the Post-Cold War Era*. New York: Council on Foreign Relations, 1998

   A good collection covering trade, monetary relations, and migration, as well as providing general analysis

Europe, Washington, DC: Delegation of the European Commission, monthly publication

   This official publication is useful not only for what the Europeans want to tell the Americans, but also for articles on US responses at both national and state level.

European Commission, *Report on United States Barriers to Trade and Investment*, annual publication

A collection of very detailed data on problems for EU trade and investment

European Commission, website at www.europa.eu.int

Featherstone, Kevin, and Roy H. Ginsberg, *The United States and the European Community in the 1990s: Partners in Transition*, second edition, London: Macmillan, and New York: St Martin's Press, 1996

A detailed treatment of issue areas, particularly economic cooperation, and competition and foreign and security policies

Gompert, David, and Stephen Larrabee (editors), *America and Europe: A Partnership for a New Era*, Cambridge and New York: Cambridge University Press, 1997

An excellent collection of policy-relevant pieces, especially on political and security issues

Guay, Terrence, *The United States and the European Union: The Political Economy of a Relationship*, Sheffield: Sheffield Academic Press/UACES, 1999; London and Chicago: Fitzroy Dearborn, 2001

A good study of the international political economy, with history and current policy issues

Harrison, Glennon (editor), *Europe and the United States: Competition and Cooperation in the 1990s*, Armonk, NY: M.E. Sharpe, 1994

A wide-ranging collection originally produced as a study for the US Congressional Research Service

Hocking, Brian, and Michael Smith, *Beyond Foreign Economic Policy: The United States, the Single European Market and the Changing World Economy*, London and Washington, DC: Pinter, 1997

A detailed analysis of the US response to the European single market at different levels of policy-making

Hufbauer, Gary C. (editor), *Europe 1992: An American Perspective*, Washington, DC: Brookings Institution, 1990

One of the most authoritative collections of US views on the single market programme

Kahler, Miles, and Werner Link, *Europe and America: A Return to History*, New York: Council on Foreign Relations Press, 1996

A strong historical treatment of transatlantic relationships

Krause, Lawrence, *European Economic Integration and the United States*, Washington, DC: Brookings Institution, 1968

The best early treatment of the issues, from an economic perspective

Lundestad, Geir, *"Empire" by Integration: The United States and European Integration, 1945–1997*, Oxford and New York: Oxford University Press, 1998

An excellent short historical treatment, generally from a US perspective

Peterson, John, *Europe and America in the 1990s: Prospects for Partnership*, second edition, London and New York: Routledge, 1996

A perceptive treatment of the history, with a detailed study of the "new Atlanticism" of the 1990s

Smith, Michael, *Western Europe and the United States: The Uncertain Alliance*, London and Boston: Allen and Unwin, 1984

An evaluation of the key components and policy processes in the transatlantic relationship

Smith, Michael, "The United States and 1992: Responses to a Changing European Community", in John Redmond (editor), *The External Relations of the European Community: The International Response to 1992*, London: Macmillan, and New York: St Martin's Press, 1992

An assessment of the responses of different groups in the United States, particularly government and business

Smith, Michael, and Stephen Woolcock, *The United States and the European Community in a Transformed World*, London: Pinter, for the Royal Institute of International Affairs, 1993

This study has a particular focus on the dimensions of change and the implications for the European order.

Tsoukalis, Loukas (editor), *Europe, America and the World Economy*, Oxford and New York: Blackwell, 1986

A very strong collection of essays on major areas of dispute, with comments by leading scholars and policy-makers

US Mission to the EU, website at www.useu.be

Woolcock, Stephen, Jeffrey Hart, and Hans van der Ven, *Interdependence in the Post-multilateral Era*,

Lanham, MD: University Press of America/ Center for International Affairs, Harvard University, 1985

A study that is strong on theories of multilateralism and trade, with case-studies of EC–US policies

Woolcock, Stephen, *Market Access Issues in EC–US Relations: Trading Partners or Trading Blows?*, London: Pinter, for the Royal Institute of International Affairs, 1991

This study focuses strongly on new issues in the GATT Uruguay Round negotiations.

Michael Smith is Professor of European Politics at Loughborough University. He is a former Chair of the University Association for Contemporary European Studies and a member of the Editorial Board of the *Journal of Common Market Studies*. He has contributed numerous articles to journals such as the *Review of International Studies*, the *International Journal*, and *International Affairs*.

Table 25.1   US Trade with Major partners (US$ billions)

	1994	1995	1996	1997	1998	1999
US Exports to:						
World	512.4	583.9	622.8	688.9	683.0	683.0
EU-12/EU-15	102.8	123.6	127.5	139.0	146.1	148.9
United Kingdom	26.8	28.8	30.9	36.4	39.1	38.3
Germany	19.2	22.4	23.5	24.5	26.6	26.8
France	13.6	14.2	14.4	16.0	17.7	18.8
Italy	7.2	8.9	8.8	9.0	9.0	10.1
Netherlands	13.6	16.6	16.6	19.8	19.0	19.4
Belgium/Luxembourg	10.9	12.5	12.5	13.4	13.9	12.4
Japan	53.5	64.3	67.5	64.6	56.6	56.4
US Imports from:						
World	663.1	743.4	791.4	870.7	913.8	1030.2
EU-12/EU-15	110.8	131.9	142.7	160.1	176.1	194.5
United Kingdom	25.1	26.9	28.9	32.7	34.8	39.2
Germany	31.8	36.8	38.9	43.1	49.8	55.1
France	16.8	17.2	18.6	20.7	24.1	25.9
Italy	14.7	16.5	18.2	19.4	21.0	22.4
Netherlands	6.0	6.4	6.6	7.3	7.6	8.5
Belgium/Luxembourg	6.3	6.1	6.8	7.9	8.4	9.2
Japan	119.1	123.6	115.2	121.7	121.9	130.9
Balance with:						
World	−151.4	−159.6	−168.6	−181.8	−230.9	−347.1
EU-12/EU-15	−8.1	−8.3	−15.2	−21.1	−30.0	−45.6
United Kingdom	1.8	1.9	2.0	3.8	4.3	−0.9
Germany	−12.5	−14.5	−15.5	−18.6	−23.2	−28.3
France	−3.2	−2.9	−4.2	−4.8	−6.4	−7.1
Italy	−7.5	−7.6	−9.4	−10.4	−12.0	−12.3
Netherlands	7.6	10.2	10.0	12.5	11.4	10.9
Belgium/Luxembourg	4.6	6.4	5.8	5.5	5.5	3.2
Japan	−65.7	−59.3	−47.7	−57.1	−65.3	−74.5

Sources: OECD; Department of Commerce, July 2000

Table 25.2   US Direct Investment Position Abroad on a Historical-Cost Basis at Yearend (US$ billions)

Year	World	EU-12/EU-15	United Kingdom	Canada	Japan
1987	314.3	124.0	57.8	44.5	15.7
1988	335.9	131.1	62.7	49.5	18.0
1989	372.4	149.5	63.9	61.2	18.8
1990	430.5	180.5	69.5	72.7	22.6
1991	467.8	199.4	70.7	79.8	25.4
1992	499.0	210.2	85.2	68.7	26.6
1993	559.7	235.4	104.3	69.6	31.2
1994	621.0	260.8	111.3	75.0	36.7
1995 (EU-15)	717.6	315.1	122.8	85.4	38.4
1996 (EU-15)	796.5	348.4	142.6	91.6	39.6

Source: Department of Commerce, Survey of Current Business, July 1997

Table 25.3   Foreign Direct Investment Position in the US on a Historical-Cost Basis at Yearend (US$ billions)

Year	World	EU-12/EU-15	United Kingdom	Canada	Japan
1987	271.8	165.4	79.7	24.0	35.2
1988	314.7	188.3	95.7	26.6	51.1
1989	373.7	216.1	105.5	28.7	67.3
1990	396.7	224.4	102.8	30.0	81.8
1991	418.8	224.1	98.2	36.3	93.8
1992	425.6	220.6	89.1	37.8	97.5
1993	464.1	253.1	102.4	40.1	99.2
1994	502.4	272.2	111.1	42.1	104.5
1995 (EU-15)	560.9	319.0	126.2	48.3	107.9
1996 (EU-15)	630.0	372.2	142.6	53.8	118.1

Source: Department of Commerce, Survey of Current Business, July 1997

Figure 25.1   Principal Trading Partners of the US and EU

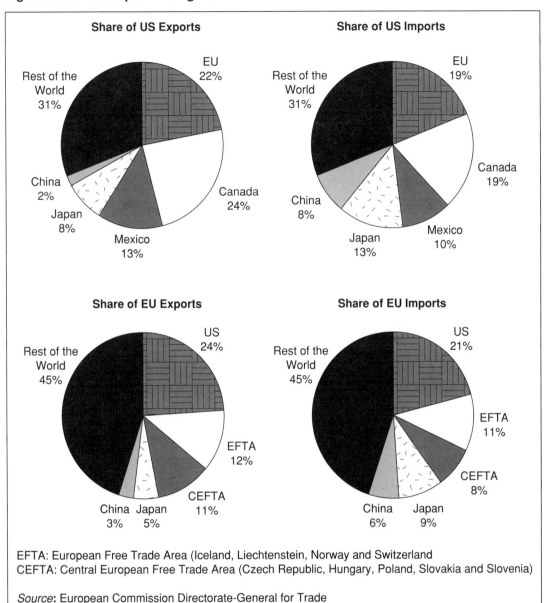

EFTA: European Free Trade Area (Iceland, Liechtenstein, Norway and Switzerland
CEFTA: Central European Free Trade Area (Czech Republic, Hungary, Poland, Slovakia and Slovenia)

Source: European Commission Directorate-General for Trade

Chapter Twenty-Six

The EU and Russia

Jackie Gower

The European Community had no official relationship with the Soviet Union until the late 1980s and trade relations were based on bilateral agreements with individual member states. This was largely a result both of the Soviet government's negative perception of the Community as the economic arm of the western alliance and the Community's reluctance to afford recognition to the Council for Mutual Economic Assistance (CMEA, or Comecon) as an international institution comparable to itself.

In 1986 Mikhail Gorbachev signalled a major shift in Soviet policy towards western Europe, and negotiations were opened between the Community and Comecon, leading to a joint declaration two years later that established mutual recognition. This paved the way for the conclusion in 1989 of a trade and cooperation agreement between the Soviet Union and the Community similar to those that had recently been agreed with Hungary and Poland. The agreement normalized trading relations between the Community and the Soviet Union by providing for "most favoured nation" (MFN) treatment, in accordance with the rules of the General Agreement on Tariffs and Trade (GATT), but it did not offer any significant preferential access to the single market and provided only quite limited technical assistance. After the Soviet Union disintegrated in 1991, the terms of the agreement were extended to all the individual successor states, including Russia, and a much more extensive aid programme of "technical assistance for the Commonwealth of Independent States" (TACIS) was introduced.

The dramatically new political situation in central and eastern Europe in the early 1990s presented the EU with a major policy challenge. Most of the former Communist states, including the three Baltic states, indicated their determination to secure membership of the EU as soon as possible and so enlargement has dominated the EU's agenda for the past decade (see Chapter 7). However, quite as big a challenge has been for the EU to develop its policy towards states such as Russia that have not expressed a desire for membership and yet clearly need to be integrated into the mainstream of European political, social, and economic life, in order to avoid establishing a new dividing line across the continent.

The Partnership and Cooperation Agreement

The decision taken by the Community in October 1992 to open negotiations with Russia on a Partnership and Cooperation Agreement (PCA), rather than an association or "Europe" agreement like those it was offering to states in central and eastern Europe, indicated that even so soon after the end of the Cold War it was differentiating between those states that were expected to become EU members and those that were not. There is therefore no mention of future membership in the PCA but only a reference to the agreement "favouring a gradual rapprochement between Russia and a wider area of cooperation in Europe, and neighbouring regions, and Russia's progressive integration into the open trading system". However, the scope of the political and economic cooperation that it envisages indicates that the intention was to provide the legal framework for a significant upgrading of relations from the earlier trade and cooperation agreement.

After two years of tough negotiations the new agreement was finally signed in Corfu in June 1994. However, its ratification was delayed because of opposition within the EU to Russia's policy in Chechnya and it only came into effect in December 1997.

Political Provisions

The preamble to the agreement stresses the importance of the "common values" shared by the EU and Russia, and makes it explicit that the agreement is conditional on both parties continuing to respect the principles of democracy, respect for human rights, the rule of law, and the market economy. One of the EU's main objectives is to support Russia's reforms by providing incentives to maintain progress towards a stable democratic system and a functioning market economy, and, conversely, disincentives to deviate from the path of reform. Article 107 provides the basis for the unilateral suspension of the agreement if either party fails to fulfil their obligations, while a joint declaration appended to the agreement makes it clear that "respect for human rights constitutes an essential element of the Agreement". This has enabled the EU to insist that the situation in Chechnya is a legitimate item to be included on the agenda of the regular meetings held within the framework of the PCA although pressure from some quarters to suspend the agreement altogether has been resisted.

The institutionalization of "political dialogue" in these regular meetings constitutes potentially one of the most significant elements of the PCA. EU–Russia summits are held every six months (usually in May and October), and bring together the Prime Minister of the country holding the Presidency of the EU Council, the President of the EU Commission, the EU's Secretary General/High Representative for the Common Foreign and Security Policy, and the President of Russia and other senior Russian ministers. They provide the opportunity for a regular exchange of views at the highest

possible political level on a wide range of economic, political, and security issues of mutual concern, and in particular they provide a channel for raising matters that have the potential to cause tensions within the relationship. Typically the agenda includes reports from both the EU and Russia on major internal developments; a review of the work being undertaken within the PCA framework; and a discussion of current international questions, such as the Middle East or the Western Balkans.

A "joint statement" issued at the end of each meeting sets the broad agenda for the work of the Cooperation Council (ministers), the Cooperation Committee (senior officials), and the Parliamentary Cooperation Council (members of the European Parliament and of the Russian State Duma) that have been created under the PCA. These bodies in turn have set up numerous subcommittees and working groups to look at specific technical and policy issues. It is this continuous interaction between Russian and EU politicians and officials that is probably the most significant outcome of the PCA. The cooperation institutions also provide the framework for dialogue on the wide range of issues envisaged in the EU's "Common Strategy on Russia", including cooperation on foreign policy, security and defence, justice and home affairs, and the environment (see below).

Economic Provisions

Although the majority of the articles of the PCA concern economic and trade matters, they are actually fairly modest in their scope and fell considerably below the Russian negotiators' hopes of achieving terms of trade with the EU similar to those obtained by states in central and eastern Europe under their Europe Agreements. In the short term the PCA with Russia amounts to a modest extension of the terms of the trade and cooperation agreement of 1989, with most-favoured nation status still covering trade in goods, which is the lowest form of trade preference. In practice at the moment this is not a major obstacle to trade, as the bulk of Russian exports to the EU are raw materials, especially natural gas and oil, on which no tariffs are levied. However, Russia is very keen to diversify its exports and fears that its manufactured goods are at a competitive disadvantage compared with those produced in central and eastern Europe.

Therefore, in the longer term, the most significant provision of the PCA will probably turn out to have been the undertaking, in Article 3, to examine in 1998 "whether circumstances allow the beginning of negotiations on the establishment of a free trade area", which provides the possibility for a significant evolution of the economic relationship. The Russian financial crisis in August 1998 inevitably meant that the discussions were suspended and further progress towards the goal of free trade is dependent on the recovery of the Russian economy. It remains the long-term goal for both parties, however, and is potentially the best way of ensuring that Russian economic interests are protected in the context of EU enlargement. There is also a commitment from the EU's member states to give active support to Russia's attempt to join the World Trade Organization (WTO), which would greatly facilitate Russia's full integration into the global economy.

In the short term, the Russian government is anxious to hold the EU to its commitment to eliminate nontariff barriers and quantitative restrictions (quotas), especially on "sensitive" goods such as textiles, steel, and nuclear materials, which are subject to special restrictive agreements. The underlying problem has arisen from the EU's scepticism about the extent to which the Russian economy has moved away from its former practice of "dumping" heavily state-subsidized goods on western markets and become a genuine market economy. Although there have been gradual moves to greater liberalization, allegations of unwarranted restrictions on competitively priced Russian exports continue to attract a great deal of negative coverage in the Russian media, and complaints are regularly raised at the cooperation councils and committees, and even the summits.

In the longer term, nontariff barriers, such as product specifications, health and safety standards, and other legal provisions governing the single market, present the greatest obstacles to an expansion of EU–Russian trade in both goods and services. Article 55 of the PCA commits Russia "to ensure that its legislation shall be gradually made compatible with that of the Community" in respect of most of the single market *acquis*, including company and banking law, company accounts and taxes, health and safety, competition, public procurement, consumer protection, the environment, technical rules and standards, and customs laws. The candidate states of central and eastern Europe are of course required to harmonize their legislation as a prerequisite for EU membership, but it seems uncertain whether the Russian authorities will in practice be able and willing to adopt so much of the EU's *acquis* in the absence of the incentive of eventual membership. However, if Russia did so the effect would be to create something close to the European Economic Area in respect of free movement of goods, services, and capital (but not labour) across most of the European continent, covering a combined market of more than 600 million people. In the long term this would provide the best guarantee that Russia would be fully integrated into a common European economic and social space, which is one of the main objectives of both the EU and Russian strategies.

The EU's Common Strategy on Russia

The PCA provides a legal framework for the development of political and economic cooperation with Russia, but it gives little indication as to the kind of long-term relationship that the EU hopes will evolve from it. This was not surprising in the context of the political uncertainty prevailing when the agreement was negotiated, but by the late 1990s the EU was beginning to have a clearer idea about its objectives in relation to its largest and most important neighbour. Indeed, both Russia and the EU had come to recognize each other as the two key powers on the continent, and there was a growing shared appreciation of the importance of their relationship, both for themselves and for Europe as a whole. It is therefore not surprising that the EU decided to make its first use of the new policy instrument of "common strategies", provided in the Treaty of Amsterdam, by adopting a "Common Strategy on Russia" at the European Council in Cologne in June 1999.

The EU's Objectives

The "Common Strategy" contains the clearest indication so far of what it calls "the vision of the EU for its partnership with Russia":

A stable, democratic and prosperous Russia, firmly anchored in a united Europe free of new dividing lines, is essential to lasting peace on the continent. The issues that the whole continent faces can be resolved only through ever closer cooperation between Russia and the European Union. The European Union welcomes Russia's return to its rightful place in the European family in a spirit of friendship, cooperation, fair accommodation of interests, and on the foundations of shared values enshrined in the common heritage of European civilization (*OJ* L157, 1999).

The reference to "ever closer cooperation" indicates that the relationship is expected to be evolutionary, but it is worth noting that there is no suggestion that future membership of the EU is even the long-term goal. Instead, the strategy develops the concept of "partnership", which is now described as "strategic", and identifies a long list of areas in which the EU and Russia have a shared interest in working together, including those that come under the EU's second and third pillars – foreign and security policy, and police and judicial cooperation.

The Common Strategy identifies the EU's two "clear strategic goals":

– a stable, open and pluralistic democracy in Russia, governed by the rule of law and underpinning a prosperous market economy, benefiting alike the people of Russia and of the European Union;
– maintaining European stability, promoting global security, and responding to the common challenges of the continent through intensified cooperation with Russia.

Although the PCA is still described as "the core of the relationship between the Union and Russia", the "Common Strategy" is intended to expand the cooperation into more overtly political areas, and clearly marks a commitment to more intensive interaction beyond the earlier emphasis on trade and aid.

The "Common Strategy" identifies four principal objectives, and contains numerous examples of the initiatives and projects that might be undertaken in the short to medium term in order to realize them.

First comes "consolidation of democracy, the rule of law, and public institutions in Russia". The EU's decision-makers continue to be concerned at the fragility of the democratic order in Russia and therefore propose to offer support for institutional reform, for example by promoting contacts between judicial authorities and law enforcement bodies in EU member states and Russia, to encourage the development of an independent judiciary and accountable police and prison services. The EU also hopes to contribute to the strengthening of Russia's civic society by encouraging greater contact between Russian and EU politicians, at both national and local levels, promoting cultural and educational exchanges, and supporting independent nongovernmental organizations. For example, at the EU–Russia summit in May 2001 the European Trade Union Confederation and the Federation of Independent Trade Unions of Russia signed a cooperation agreement pledging that they would work together to promote social rights in the context of the EU–Russia partnership.

Secondly, the strategy envisages the "integration of Russia into a common European economic and social area". There is already a considerable measure of economic interdependence: the EU is the most important of Russia's trading partners and Russia supplies a significant proportion of the EU's energy, mainly in the form of natural gas and oil. This interdependence is seen as a positive development that will provide the foundations for pan-European peace, stability, and prosperity. As already discussed, the PCA contains a large number of measures that are intended to facilitate increased trade and other commercial activity, including provision for the development of a free trade area. The "added value" of the "Common Strategy" therefore lies mainly in identifying a large number of areas in which the EU should offer support to Russia's efforts to develop a stable market economy. These mainly take the form of specialist advice, training opportunities, and increased scientific and technical cooperation, financed under the TACIS programme (considered in more detail below). Clearly, the stabilization of the Russian economy is the most immediate priority, but in the longer term it is envisaged that there should be a much deeper economic relationship that goes beyond simply trade. It was therefore agreed at the EU–Russia summit in May 2001 that a high-level experts group should be established to consider what the concept of a common economic area, or "space" as it is often called, might entail, and to identify measures needed to achieve it. The President of the European Commission, Romano Prodi, also proposed that EU–Russian trade might in future be denominated in euros, as both a practical and symbolic move toward closer economic relations.

Thirdly, the "Common Strategy" focuses on "cooperation to strengthen stability and security in Europe and beyond". This objective and the kind of cooperation it envisages clearly reflect the much greater role the EU is now seeking to play in regional security with the development of the Common European Security and Defence Policy (discussed in Chapter 23). It is obviously important to reassure Russia that the EU's new activism in the security field does not present any kind of threat to her interests, and the most effective way to do so is by actively engaging Russia in both enhanced political dialogue and joint initiatives. The most interesting and potentially most important proposal is to create a "permanent policy and security dialogue", in which the Secretary General of the European Council, who is also the High Representative for the Common Foreign and Security Policy (currently Javiar Solano), would play a key role. It is also proposed that Russia could be invited to contribute to any future EU "Petersberg mission" involving crisis management and peacekeeping forces.

Finally, the "Common Strategy" addresses "common challenges on the European continent". It is widely recognized that the main threats to security in Europe following the end of the Cold War lie not in direct military threats but in social and environmental dangers, such as those presented by nuclear power,

pollution, and other environmental hazards; organized crime, such as moneylaundering and trafficking in drugs and people; illegal immigration; and terrorism. Clearly, there is enormous scope for cooperation in meeting these challenges and Russia has indicated its interest in working closely with the EU in seeking solutions. There is a joint action plan to fight organized crime, involving cooperation between EU and Russian law enforcement agencies, and several important environmental projects, especially in northwestern Russia under the "Northern Dimension" initiative.

The main purpose of the "Common Strategy" was to clarify what the EU was trying to achieve in relation to Russia, and to enhance the effectiveness of its policy by bringing together all the various initiatives already being undertaken, by the EU collectively and bilaterally by the member states, into a comprehensive cross-pillar programme. Responsibility for its implementation is entrusted to the member state holding the Council Presidency, which draws up a work-plan for its six-month term and sets the priorities. This was intended to create a sense of momentum, but experience so far suggests that some member states have regarded it as largely a bureaucratic exercise and it is difficult to identify many concrete "value-added" outcomes from the adoption of the Strategy.

One unexpected but highly significant consequence of the EU's adopting the "Common Strategy on Russia" is that it seems to have contributed to the Russian government's affording a higher priority to its relationship with the EU and publicly issuing its first substantial policy statement on the EU. Although there was no formal consultation with Russia during the drafting of the strategy, there was considerable informal discussion, particularly with some individual member states, and a draft paper outlining Russia's own views on the future development of the relationship was circulated. This was later formalized into the "Medium-term Strategy for Relations between the Russian Federation and the European Union (2000–2010)", and was presented by the then Prime Minister Vladimir Putin at the EU–Russia summit at Helsinki in October 1999. Although there are clear differences in emphasis, there is a striking commonality in both the objectives and the specific areas identified for further cooperation in the two strategy documents, which augurs well for further development of the relationship.

TACIS

The EU clearly has a strong interest in encouraging Russia to continue along the path of political and economic reform, and the TACIS programme is its main policy instrument of support for the transition process. TACIS operates in all 12 member states of the Commonwealth of Independent States (CIS) and is roughly comparable to the PHARE programme developed for (most of) central and eastern Europe, although, at about €1.50 per capita each year, the level of aid has been substantially lower than that given in the candidate states. Nevertheless, TACIS is the largest technical assistance programme in Russia: more than €2 billion were allocated between 1991 and 2000, either under Russia's national TACIS programme or through multilateral initiatives involving crossborder projects (see the TACIS Annual Report). The indicative budget for the TACIS national programme for the Russian Federation over the period 2000–03 is €300–360 million, supplemented by further assistance under other TACIS programmes such as the Nuclear Safety Programme, the Regional Cooperation and Crossborder Programmes, and the TACIS Cooperation Programme with the European Bank for Reconstruction and Development (see the TACIS Indicative Programme 2000–03).

The main purpose of TACIS is to provide financial and technical assistance for specific projects in a wide range of areas (see Tables 26.1 and 26.2 for the allocation 1997–2000). It is intended to facilitate the transfer of western "knowhow" and expertise to assist in the development of the institutions, legal and administrative systems, and management skills essential for a stable democracy and a properly functioning market economy. An "indicative programme", covering four years at a time, provides the policy framework for the operation of TACIS in Russia, and identifies the main priorities for funding and other forms of cooper-

ation. The Indicative Programme for 2000–03 proposes that support should be concentrated on projects falling within three crucial areas: support for institutional, legal, and administrative reform; support to the private sector and assistance for economic development; and support in addressing the social consequences of transition. Annual "action programmes" are then drawn up detailing specific projects that have been selected for support within the guidelines of the Indicative Programme. These programmes are now meant to be "dialogue-driven", based on extensive consultation and cooperation with the Russian authorities, and there is a close relationship between the EU delegation based in Moscow and the TACIS Coordinating Unit responsible to the Russian government. There are also TACIS Technical Offices in a number of major cities, and the intention is to increase the efficiency of project management by increased decentralisation and cooperation with regional authorities and other local bodies.

Although in the early years much of the money went to western consultants who provided advice, there has been increasing recognition that the key to the success of Russia's transformation and modernization lies in developing the necessary skills and values among her own population. One of the largest and most successful projects has been the Managers' Training Programme, initiated at the request of former President Boris Yeltsin to help to equip the younger generation with the managerial and business skills needed to turn Russian enterprises into internationally competitive companies. It is organized by a consortium of business schools from eight EU countries, and involves seminars, and internships lasting two to three months, for young managers in EU host companies to experience at first hand western business culture and management practices. Other training projects have been targeted at civil servants and local government officials, judicial and law-enforcement personnel, and discharged military officers needing to adapt to new civilian careers. Twinning projects that facilitate the exchange of experience and the encouragement of networking are increasingly seen as vital parts of many TACIS initiatives, and also help to develop a sense of partnership and greater mutual understanding. The TACIS Tempus programme has encouraged universities in EU member states to form partnerships with their counterparts in Russia, in order to stimulate reform in higher education, and to facilitate the mobility of staff and students.

Significant funding has also gone into projects to support the conversion of industries from military to civilian production, as at the International Science and Technology Centre in Moscow. Numerous other projects have provided advice and technical assistance to tackle environmental problems, modernize infrastructure, improve border crossings, and develop new health and social security systems. There is also a special fund called Bistro (the Russian word for "quick") that can be used to support small-scale projects to meet locally-perceived needs: it has helped to short-cut what is often seen to be the excessive bureaucracy involved in the TACIS programme generally.

There has also been a distinct TACIS Democracy Programme to promote democratic values and practices throughout Russian society, and to support efforts to create a strong civil society. This is clearly an area where other international institutions, such as the Council of Europe, the UN Committee for Europe, and the Organization for Security and Cooperation in Europe, are also active, and the EU has often worked alongside them, for example in monitoring elections. In the light of concern about Russian policy in Chechnya, the new TACIS Regulation covering 2000–06 has made the promotion of democracy, respect for human rights, and the rule of law higher priorities for TACIS funding, and has made it clear that support for other projects is dependent on Russia's respecting democratic norms (Council Regulation 99/2000).

It is difficult to evaluate how effective the TACIS programme has been in promoting the EU's objectives in relation to Russia. One of the problems is that, although the total sums involved seem quite large from the EU's perspective, they are actually miniscule as a proportion of Russia's GDP, and so have little direct impact on its economy. Russia is a vast country with enormous needs for investment to modernize and restructure almost all aspects of its economic and social infrastructure. In the early years after the collapse of the Communist system Russia hoped for an aid package from the West equivalent to the Marshall Plan that helped to rebuild western Europe after World War II. There has therefore been disappointment and considerable bitterness at what many Russians see as the meagre response from their affluent western neighbours. However, on a more positive note, the TACIS programmes have not only funded a number of useful projects but, above all, have brought a wide range of people and institutions from EU member states into partnership, dialogue, and cooperation with their counterparts in Russia, and helped to end Russia's isolation from the rest of Europe.

The Northern Dimension

Although it is not exclusively directed at Russia, the "Northern Dimension" provides further opportunities for constructive engagement and, as most of the other states in the region that it addresses are preparing for accession to the EU, Russia is increasingly seen as its main focus. It is the result of an initiative in 1997, sponsored by Finland, to encourage greater cooperation among all the states in northern Europe, irrespective of whether they are EU members or not. The Northern Dimension was approved in principle at the European Council in Vienna in December 1998 and formally launched the following year at the Council in Helsinki. It brings together the 15 member states of the EU, the four northern candidate states (Poland, Estonia, Latvia, and Lithuania), the two northern members of the European Economic Area that are not in the EU (Iceland and Norway), and Russia. In the context of the future enlargement of the EU, the overriding objective is to encourage people and institutions in northwestern Russia to feel that their homeland forms an integral part of the region, rather than being isolated and potentially therefore alienated.

The Northern Dimension is a concept rather than an organizational entity and it does not involve either new institutions or financial instruments. It is based on the recognition that there is already a large degree of interdependence among the states in the region, and that their long-term security, stability, and sustainable development rest on coordinated action to resolve common problems. One of the most frequently iterated principles is "positive interdependency" between the EU, the Baltic Sea region, and Russia, and the objective is to ensure "win–win" outcomes from concrete projects that bring clear benefits both to Russia and to its regional neighbours.

An "Action Plan" for 2000–03, adopted at the European Council in Santa Maria da Feira in June 2000, identified a large number of areas in which crossborder cooperation on concrete projects would be beneficial. These include transport, energy, nuclear safety, the environment, public health, trade, international crime, and Kaliningrad, the detached region of Russia that is destined to become an enclave surrounded by member states of the EU once enlargement to the East has been completed. However, although this action plan is likely to serve as a useful reference point in identifying priorities and goals, all specific action, especially if it involves finance, has to be undertaken through existing legal and financial instruments (PHARE, TACIS, and Interreg) or with the support of other international financial institutions, such as the European Bank for Reconstruction and Development or the Nordic Investment Bank.

The Northern Dimension initiative has been received positively by the Russian government, while the subnational authorities in the northwestern region of Russia, including the Leningrad and Novgorod *oblasts*, have shown considerable interest in the opportunities that it offers for greater contact and cooperation with neighbouring regions. Examples of projects that have been undertaken within the framework of the programme include schemes, funded by TACIS, to improve the management and clean-up of the Krasny Bor hazardous waste disposal site near St Petersburg; support for the Sortavala sewage treatment plant near the Russian–Finnish border; and joint Finnish–Russian efforts to improve the quality of water in towns in Karelia (a province now in Russia that used to be part of Finland). There has also been considerable action in relation to nuclear safety, especially concerning the disposal of

radioactive waste into the sea, which is clearly of concern to all the states in the region. Other projects have improved border crossing facilities between Finland and Russia, and between Kaliningrad, Lithuania, and Poland. Kaliningrad is seen by both Russia and the EU as the test case for the effectiveness of the Northern Dimension (see below).

Prospects for the EU-Russia Partnership

The EU sets a high priority on developing good relations with Russia and, as has been discussed, it now has not only a strategy but a set of policy instruments through which it hopes to establish a strategic partnership with its important neighbour. The prospects of that goal being achieved depend crucially on Russia's successfully making the transition to a stable democracy, based on respect for human rights and the rule of law, and also to a stable market economy capable of being fully integrated not only into the European trading system but also into the global economy. At the time of writing the prospects look reasonably encouraging, with signs of economic recovery in Russia after the disastrous crash in 1998 and a strong President who seems to want stronger political as well as economic relations with the EU as part of his strategy of encouraging a multipolar world order.

Two developments are making the relationship between the EU and Russia increasingly important for both parties: growing economic interdependence and the fairly imminent prospect of EU enlargement, involving many of Russia's neighbours and former allies. Clearly, in both cases there is the potential for the consequences to be positive, encouraging a deeper and stronger relationship between the EU and Russia, but also, probably inevitably, a number of problems and tensions are expected to arise.

Growing Economic Interdependence

The EU is now Russia's most important trading partner: in 1999 it accounted for 33.2% of its exports and 36.7% of its imports (see Table 26.3). It is widely predicted that, after the EU has enlarged to take in the candidate states of central and eastern Europe, more than 50% of Russia's trade will be with EU member states. Statistically, trade with Russia is much less important to the EU, accounting for only 4.4% of imports and 2.1% of exports in 2000 (see Table 26.4). However, the figures belie the true importance of trade with Russia, as it supplies 15% of the EU's imported fuel, mainly oil and natural gas.

Both Russia and the EU predict a steady increase in the levels of trade between them in the next decade, and see more intensive economic relations as the firmest foundation for their political partnership. It is expected that the demand for imports from the EU will rise significantly as the Russian economy grows, and the provisions for trade liberalization in the PCA are implemented. At the moment Russia has a large and growing trade surplus with the EU (see Table 26.5): this is partly due to the recent rise in energy prices, but it is also a result of the financial crisis and the devaluation of the rouble in 1998. It is widely assumed in the EU that as the Russian economy stabilizes, and incomes begin to rise, its market of nearly 150 million people will offer great promise of increased activity. If a stable legal framework for commercial activities is established in Russia, foreign direct investment and trade in services are also likely to rise from their current low levels (see Tables 26.6 and 26.7). Similarly, the more entrepreneurial and outward-looking business people in Russia see the enlarged EU market as offering very attractive opportunities. As President Putin is quoted as having said in his opening speech at the EU–Russia summit in May 2001, the political will for the development of bilateral cooperation "is now buttressed by a real interest in cooperation both from national governments as well as from broad business quarters and entrepreneurs" (Itar-Tass 17 May 2001).

However, there are a number of difficult issues to be resolved if economic interdependence is to deepen. One is the different perspective of the two parties on the place of energy and other raw materials in their future trading relationship. On the EU side, one of the key goals is to establish an energy partnership with Russia to enhance the reliability

of energy supplies and reduce dependence on the volatile Middle East. An "energy dialogue" has been established within the framework of the PCA to develop ways of encouraging EU investment in, and technology transfer to, Russia's energy industries. Although the Russian government officially welcomes such initiatives, there is concern that an overemphasis on energy on the EU side will only reinforce what is seen as Russia's "third world" trading position as a supplier of raw materials and importer of manufactured goods (see Table 26.8). The Russians are therefore anxious to encourage what they regard as a more balanced trading relationship with the EU, and are pressing hard for the removal of the remaining restrictions on exports of goods, especially those in the high-technology field, such as arms, nuclear reactors, and aircraft, where, they believe, EU protectionism is obstructing market access.

Russia is also anxious to ensure that the EU is sensitive and sympathetic to the possible negative implications for trade with Russia of its enlargement to include countries in central and eastern Europe. Although since the end of the Cold War there has been a dramatic shift in the central and eastern European states' trade from Russia and towards the EU, the level of interaction with Russia is still quite significant. Russia is nervous that it might suffer the consequences of trade diversion as a result of the accession of these states to the EU, as happened when Finland joined in 1995. Russia is also concerned that its own exports of manufactured goods to the present 15 EU member states might be undercut by the new member states in central and eastern Europe when they enjoy the full benefits of integration into the single market. There is a special working group within the PCA framework analysing the likely trade implications of EU enlargement and it is expected to be an important item on the agendas of EU–Russia meetings over the coming years. In the long term, if Russia joins the WTO and also makes progress on harmonizing its laws with those of the EU's single market, many of the anticipated problems would be overcome and the free trade area envisaged by the PCA would become a realistic option.

EU Enlargement and Russia's Neighbours

So far Russia has been much more relaxed in its attitude towards the enlargement of the EU than it has been over that of NATO. Generally, Russia expects to benefit from the extension of the EU's stability and prosperity to the states close to its borders, and sees it as enhancing security rather than threatening it. It is an obvious but important point that enlargement will physically bring Russia and the EU closer to each other, with a common border not only with Finland but also with Estonia, Latvia, Lithuania, and Poland (the latter two with Kaliningrad). This geographical proximity will inevitably enhance shared perceptions of the importance of the relationship, and, as enlargement has become both more certain and more immediate, the meetings held under the PCA have assumed a higher priority in both Moscow and Brussels. Both sides are determined to ensure that their future much-extended common border will not become a new dividing line across Europe, but there are a number of significant problems to be resolved if Russia is not going to feel excluded and disadvantaged when most of its western neighbours accede to the EU. The economic impact has already been discussed so this final section will consider some of the other potential problems arising from EU enlargement.

One of the most difficult issues will directly concern those borders: how the EU can safeguard what will be its new external border without imposing new restrictions on the legitimate movement of goods and people between Russia and neighbouring states. There is already resentment in Russia at the measures being taken by the candidate states to tighten border controls, in line with the EU's *acquis*, and to adopt the common visa regime. This is an understandably sensitive issue, particularly in relation to the Baltic states, where there are large Russian-speaking minorities. It is also a major issue in relation to Kaliningrad, which has enjoyed relatively free transit rights for both goods and people through Lithuania and Poland to the rest of the Russian Federation. The EU Commission hopes that if border facilities and procedures can be improved to ensure that the formalities required are carried out quickly and efficiently, it will be possible to mitigate the negative impact on business and tourist travel and the transport of goods. This is one area where TACIS funding has already been put to good effect. In relation to Kaliningrad, where, it is estimated, 9 million border crossings take place each year, the Commission has proposed using the flexibility permitted by the EU's rules "imaginatively", for example by offering multiple-entry, transit, and short-term visas, and making it easier and cheaper to obtain them.

Kaliningrad has officially been recognized by both the Russians and the EU as the "test case" of their partnership. In view of Russia's long-standing determination to reject any external attempt to interfere in its domestic affairs, it is interesting that it has been willing to put the future development of Kaliningrad on the shared agenda of the PCA and of the Northern Dimension. In large measure this is a reflection of the scale of the problems presented by the region. All reports on the situation in Kaliningrad paint a grim picture of industrial decay, social deprivation, appalling pollution, serious public health problems, corruption, and organized crime. Clearly, there are major transborder implications and the EU is anxious to find ways to work with Russia in transforming Kaliningrad into a thriving, prosperous, and well-run region that could play a valuable role as a bridge between the enlarged EU and Russia itself. The Commission published a major report on the situation of Kaliningrad in the context of EU enlargement in January 2001, not only outlining the problems but also putting forward some ideas and options for discussion with Russia. Inevitably Kaliningrad will be a major agenda item at EU–Russia meetings for many years and will continue to provide a real test of the concept of a "strategic partnership".

In conclusion, relations between the EU and Russia have been substantially transformed, in a little over ten years, from virtually no official contact to a comprehensive and institutionalized relationship that is valued by both sides. There will undoubtedly be many problems and tensions between them as the relationship develops, but that is also true of the EU's relations with, for example, the United States. What will be important, not just for the EU and Russia but for Europe as a whole, is that both sides remain committed to working together to find solutions and remain convinced that cooperation is the best way forward. Only then would there be any realistic hope that the "strategic partnership" to which they both aspire could become a reality.

Further Reading

Agreement on Partnership and Cooperation between the European Communities and their Member States and Russia, in *Official Journal of the European Communities*, L327, 28 November 1997

Baranovsky, Vladimir (editor), *Russia and Europe: the Emerging Security Agenda*, Oxford and New York: Oxford University Press, 1997

An interesting collection of essays on the general question of Russia's place in Europe after the Cold War

Baxendale, James, Stephen Dewar, and David Gowan (editors), *The EU and Kaliningrad: Kaliningrad and the Impact of EU Enlargement*, London: The Federal Trust, 2000

A useful collection of papers presented at a Round Table in Brussels in March 2000, with participants from all the countries in the Baltic Sea region

BBC Monitoring Service, "Participants in Russia–EU Summit Pleased with Results of Talks", text of report in English by Russian news agency Itar-Tass, 17 May 2001

A Russian press report on this meeting, containing extensive quotations from President Putin's opening speech

Borko, Youri, "The New Intra-European Relations and Russia", in Marc Maresceau (editor), *Enlarging the European Union: Relations between the EU and Central and Eastern Europe*, London and New York: Longman, 1997

An early analysis of the prospects for the partnership and cooperation agreement between Russia and the EU, by one of the few Russian academic experts on the EU

Directorate-General for External Relations of the European Commission, website at www.europa.eu.int/comm/external_relations/index/htm

All of the official documents cited and a great deal of other useful material can be obtained here

European Commission, *Russian Federation TACIS Indicative Programme 2000–2003*, Brussels, 2000

European Commission, *TACIS 2000 Action Programme: Russian Federation*, Brussels, 20 October 2000

European Commission, *The TACIS Programme Annual Report 1999*, Brussels, COM(2000)835 Final, 2000

European Commission, *Communication from the Commission to the Council: The EU and Kaliningrad*, Brussels, COM(2001)26 Final, 2001

European Parliament, Task Force Enlargement Briefing no. 22, *Statistical Annex*, March 2001

This contains useful trade data for the EU and Russia. It can be obtained at www.europarl.eu.int/enlargement/briefings/index_en.htm

Gower, Jackie, "EU–Russian Relations and the Eastern Enlargement: Integration or Isolation", in *Perspectives on European Politics and Society*, 1/1, 2000

A more extensive discussion of the issues raised in the final section of this chapter

Gower, Jackie, "Russia and the European Union", in Mark Webber (editor), *Russia and Europe: Conflict or Cooperation?*, London: Palgrave, and New York: St Martin's Press, 2000

An analysis of the development of the relationship between the EU and Russia, with particular consideration of Russia's views and objectives

Gower, Jackie, "The EU and Russia: The Challenge of Integration without Accession", in Jackie Gower and John Redmond (editors), *Enlarging the European Union: The Way Forward*, Aldershot: Ashgate, 2000

A discussion as to why it is assumed that Russia will not become a member of the EU, and the conceptual and practical problems that this assumption poses for European integration

Leshoukov, Igor, *Beyond Satisfaction: Russia's Perspectives on European Integration*, Bonn: Zentrum für Europäische Integrationsforschung, 1998

A provocative discussion of the partnership and cooperation agreement, with many important insights into the debate within Russia on its future relationship with the EU

"Medium-Term Strategy for the Development of Relations between the Russian Federation and the EU (2000–2006)"

This official document of the Russian government is available in Russian, in *Diplomatichesky Vestnik* (Moscow), 11, 1999, or in English, on the Finnish EU Presidency site at www.presidency.finland.fi

"The European Union's Common Strategy on Russia", in *Official Journal of the European Communities*, L157, 24 June 1999

Timmermann, Heinz, "European–Russian Partnership: What Future?", in *European Foreign Affairs Review*, 5/2, 2000

A good discussion of the EU's "Common Strategy on Russia" and Russia's "Medium-Term Strategy on the EU", with some useful references to Russian sources

---

Jackie Gower is Honorary Senior Lecturer in European Politics at the University of Kent at Canterbury and Review Editor (with Brian Ardy) of the *Journal of Common Market Studies*. She has written and advised extensively on EU enlargement and EU–Russian relations, including serving as the specialist adviser to the European Communities Committee of the House of Lords for its report on *Enlargement of the EU: Progress and Problems* in 1999.

Table 26.1   Allocations under TACIS Action Programmes for the Russian Federation, 1997–2000 (€ millions)

	1997	*1998*	*1999*	*2000*
Institutional, legal, and administrative reform	16	30	15	28
Private sector support and economic development	29	32	18	14
Alleviation of social consequences of transition	11	3	5	6
Development of infrastructure networks	24	20	11	0
Environmental protection and natural resources management	5	10	8	4
Rural economic development	13	9	5	0
Policy advice and small project programmes	31	28	23	39
Other	4	10	8	7
Total	133	140	92	98

Source: Directorate-General for External Relations, *The EU's Relations with Russia; An Overview*, atwww. europa.eu.int/comm/external_relations/index/htm

Table 26.2   Estimated Allocations to Russia under other TACIS Programmes, 1997–2000 (€ millions)

	1997	*1998*	*1999*	*2000*
Regional programmes	21	22	16	15
Nuclear safety	34	17	12	33
Donor coordination	27	29	29	32
Programme implementation support	17	16	19	18
Other	6	5	5	2
Total	105	88	80	100

Source: Directorate-General for External Relations, *The EU's Relations with Russia; An Overview*, at www. europa.eu.int/comm/external_relations/index/htm

Table 26.3   External Trade of Russia 1992–99 (€ millions and %)

	Exports			Imports		
	Total	of which EU	%	Total	of which EU	%
1992	32,386	15,582	48.1	28,491	12,289	43.1
1993	37,615	16,799	44.7	22,845	9,563	41.9
1994	53,028	18,840	35.5	32,450	12,929	39.8
1995	59,323	19,917	33.6	35,473	13,763	38.8
1996	66,138	21,413	32.4	35,050	12,413	35.4
1997	75,022	24,689	32.9	46,209	17,264	37.4
1998	63,679	20,581	32.3	38,301	13,861	36.2
1999	67,982	22,540	33.2	28,416	10,416	36.7

Sources: Direction of Trade Statistics, Yearbooks, IMF, COMEXT, Eurostat, European Parliament Task Force Enlargement Briefing 22

Table 26.4   Trade with Russia in Relation to Total EU Trade (€ millions and %)

Rank		1993	1995	2000
6	Imports	17,412	22,112	44,979
%		3.7	4.1	4.4
12	Exports	12,642	16,081	19,749
%		2.7	2.8	2.1

Source: Directorate-General for Trade, European Commission

Table 26.5   Trade of the EU with Russia, 1992–2000 (€ millions)

	Imports from Russia	Exports to Russia	Balance
1992	10,746	6,927	–3,819
1993	17,089	12,699	–4,390
1994	21,498	14,385	–7,113
1995	21,491	16,128	–5,363
1996	23,298	19,093	–4,205
1997	26,591	25,179	–1,412
1998	23,090	21,046	–2,044
1999	25,926	14,727	–11,192
2000	44,979	19,749	–25,230

Sources: COMEXT database, Eurostat, European Parliament Task Force Enlargement Briefing 22

Table 26.6   Direct Investment Between the EU and Russia, 1997–99
(€ millions and %)

	1997	1998	1999
Inflows	293	34	566
share of EU total (%)	0.6	0.03	0.5
Inward Stocks	2,456	1,984	2,550
Russian share of total EU inward stock (%)	0.5	0.3	0.4
Outflows	1,723	435	342
share of EU total (%)	1.6	0.2	0.1
Outward stocks	2,419	2,803	3,145
Russian share of total EU outward stock (%)	0.4	0.3	0.3

Source: Directorate-General for Trade, European Commission

Table 26.7   EU Trade in Services with Russia, 1997–99 (€ millions and %)

	1997	1998	1999
Imports	3,681	3,730	3,164
share of EU total (%)	1.8	1.7	1.4
Exports	4,216	3,694	3,123
share of EU total (%)	1.9	1.6	1.3

Source: Directorate-General for Trade, European Commission

Table 26.8   Main Products in EU–Russia Trade, by value, 2000
(€ millions and %)

	EU Imports		EU Exports	
	Value	Russia share (%)	Value	Russia share (%)
Agricultural	1,977	2.5	2,684	4.5
Energy	22,512	15.4	97	0.3
Machinery	365	0.1	6,067	2.1
Transport	144	0.1	1,454	1.0
Chemicals	2,018	2.9	2,674	2.1
Textiles, clothing	291	0.4	1,164	3.0

Source: Directorate-General for Trade, European Commission

Chapter Twenty-Seven

The EU and the Mediterranean

Ricardo Gomez

The 1990s saw the EU's relations with non-member states around the Mediterranean basin absorbed into a new and comprehensive policy framework: the Euro–Mediterranean Partnership. This new package was based on the negotiation of new bilateral Euro–Mediterranean association agreements between the EU and the 12 "partners" – Algeria, Cyprus, Egypt, Israel, Jordan, Lebanon, Malta, Morocco, the Palestinian Authority, Syria, Tunisia, and Turkey – and the signing of a wideranging multilateral declaration and work programme, the Barcelona Process. The main aims of the new partnership were to foster "security and stability" in the Mediterranean by increasing the prosperity of the partner states and by enhancing regional cooperation at both governmental and societal levels.

The Historical Setting

A Patchwork of Associated States, 1957–72

The first phase of Mediterranean policy was largely commercial in orientation, accomplishing little more than the enshrining of existing trading patterns between the Community and third countries, many of which were former colonies of member states. Lacking the instruments to pursue a comprehensive policy in the region, the Community adopted an approach to relations with Mediterranean third countries that appeared rather haphazard. The Treaty of Rome gave only vague directions as to how relations with the region should evolve and it proved relatively easy for the Community to avoid making substantive commitments.

As the Mediterranean states lined up to establish formal relations with the Community, it responded with a mixture of association agreements for Greece, Malta and Turkey, special preferential commercial arrangements for France's former colonies in North Africa, and a series of commercial accords with the remainder of the Mediterranean non-member countries. The result was a hierarchy of agreements based on differentiated commercial and political privileges, indicating a lack of any clear strategic direction on the Community's part.

A Global Mediterranean Policy, 1972–90

At their summit meeting in Paris in 1972 the Community's heads of state and government resolved to ensure "an overall and balanced handling" of the Community's relations with the Mediterranean third countries, and instructed the European Commission to look at reformulating the association agreements. The Commission responded by submitting proposals to the Council of Ministers for a new policy framework, the "Global Mediterranean Policy" (GMP) – centring on new cooperation agreements that covered financial, technical, and social matters, and the expansion of the geographical scope of the associative network.

One of the long-term objectives of the GMP was the creation of a Mediterranean free trade area. The Commission attempted to persuade the member states to accept the idea that the economic development of the Mediterranean, an explicit long-term objective of the GMP – was a natural extension of European integration. It also argued that the free circulation of goods alone would not promote development in the region, and that the GMP should also include provisions on capital movements, technology transfers, technical cooperation, labour, and environmental and financial cooperation.

One of the main commitments included in the new policy was to the removal of barriers to trade in industrial products, with the exception of textiles and refined petroleum, by 1 July 1977. There was also a commitment to improve access to the Community for Maghrebi agricultural exports, "without endangering the legitimate interests of the member states", and the reduction of customs duties by 20–80% according to the product and time of year. Development aid, described as financial and technical cooperation, was attached to each agreement in financial protocols, and was supplemented by loans and grants from the Community budget and the European Investment Bank (EIB). Cooperation councils and committees were set up under each agreement to bring together representatives from the Commission, member states, and individual non-member governments.

A cursory glance suggests that the GMP fulfilled many of the Community's promises. The agreements included provisions for cooperation between the EU and the governments of the associate states in a variety of fields, including the environment, industry, business investment, and science. On the particularly sensitive subject of labour policy, existing bilateral arrangements on the treatment and status of foreign workers in the Community were supplemented by a new agreement on nondiscrimination and the equal treatment of workers. The creation of ministerial cooperation councils gave the agreements institutional structures to facilitate political exchanges between the Community and associates, and to deal with implementation problems when they arose.

However, while the new agreements were undoubtedly more comprehensive than the earlier commercial agreements, the underlying pattern of the Community's relations with the Mediterranean nonmembers remained one of qualified and limited assistance. Community member states continued to insist on deroga-

tions and protective measures, particularly on the sensitive subject of agricultural imports, wherever the interests of their own domestic producers were perceived to be threatened. The idea of a free trade zone foundered in the face of irreconcilable differences among the member states about the Community's stance on preferential market access and liberalization. From the associates' point of view, the agreements failed adequately to take into account the commercial, cultural, and historical specificities of their relationships with the Community. Put simply, the accords merely perpetuated their economic dependence on western Europe.

Redefining the EU's Mediterranean Policy

The end of the 1980s saw a clearer strategic direction begin to emerge in the Community's Mediterranean policy. Opinion among key actors within the Community, and in western Europe more generally, converged around the view that the Mediterranean region posed both immediate and longer-term security problems for Europe. The sudden geopolitical transformation of Europe in 1989–91 had a profound impact on both the Community's external environment and its internal order. Its reaction was to turn to its eastern boundary and begin considering ways to bring former Soviet-bloc states back into the "European fold". Nevertheless, awareness of the vulnerability of the Community's southern flank was also growing. With the uneasy balancing effect of US–Soviet competition in the region removed, the challenges and complexities of Mediterranean security became increasingly apparent. In this dramatically different geostrategic context, the Community, and then the EU, was expected to assume a much larger share of the responsibility for security in its own backyard.

The Community was forced to act in any case because of the weaknesses of its "Global Mediterranean Policy". By 1989 the economic positions of several Mediterranean associates had deteriorated to the point of crisis. External debts had risen throughout the 1980s following dramatic falls in oil revenues, the global collapse of commodity prices, and the failure of domestic economic policies. Violent antigovernment riots in Algeria during 1988, principally over rising food prices and declining living standards, drove home the relatively fragile nature of many of the region's economies and political systems.

The Community's trade relationship with the Mediterranean states was an obvious target for criticism. Despite the association and cooperation agreements, trade with the Community had failed to act as an effective motor for economic growth in most of the associate countries. The nonmembers' share of total Community imports declined from 11% in 1980 to 8.2% by 1988, as western Europe's trade with Asia gained ground. As European economies slipped into recession in 1990, a further contraction of trade was expected, and the old issue of improving market access assumed even greater significance.

With a former Spanish parliamentarian, Abel Matutes, in charge of the Community's relations with the Mediterranean region, the subsequent reevaluation of Mediterranean policy was very much led by the Commission. Exploratory proposals for an upgraded policy were presented to the heads of state and government at the European Council in Strasbourg in 1989. The Commission's paper containing these proposals acknowledged the poor economic performance of the majority of Mediterranean associates and highlighted their failure to meet the growing demand for jobs by rapidly expanding populations as a major threat to social stability.

The outcome of Matutes's policy review was the "Redirected Mediterranean Policy", a mixture of promises to improve the terms of the bilateral agreements, additional funding from both the Community budget and the EIB, and new financial instruments. There was a commitment to improve market access in a number of "sensitive" sectors, including agricultural products and textiles. There was a further increase in the funds made available from the Community budget and the EIB to Mediterranean third countries in the fourth generation of financial protocols (1991–96 – see Table 27.1). A new Regulation provided ECU2.3 billion for "decentralized, horizontal or regional cooperation", as, for example, through interuniversity programmes, assistance for small and medium-sized enterprises, joint local authority ventures, environmental projects, and "the cultural dimension of development".

In hindsight, the "redirected" policy did little more than act as a legitimating device for increased aid to the Mediterranean. As a strategy it was afflicted with the same faults that had impaired its "global" predecessor: the gap between the Commission's policy prescriptions and what the member states would sanction; the ineffectiveness of policy in addressing the structural asymmetry of Euro–Mediterranean economic relations; and the reliance on existing policy instruments that were clearly failing to stimulate trade. However, the redirected policy at least ensured that relations with the Mediterranean stayed on the Community's external relations agenda during the early 1990s, at a time when it was preoccupied with its own internal development, as well as with the rapidly evolving situation in central and eastern Europe.

Mediterranean Policy After the Gulf War

Even before negotiations on the redirected policy were completed a combination of factors galvanized the Community into a further evaluation of its Mediterranean strategy. The Gulf War (1990–91) left exposed a gaping hole between the Community and the Arab world, as pent-up frustration with Europe, and the West in general, was released in many Arab states. Antiwestern demonstrations, particularly those that took place in European capitals, alarmed European governments, which feared a backlash against their commercial interests in the region and hostility from Moslem citizens in Europe. One French *député* even called for a "Marshall Plan" for the Mediterranean. The Community's failure to project a unified political position on the conflict or to take into account the cultural implications of European involvement in the US-led coalition undoubtedly damaged its credibility in the eyes of the Arab world, and made the "Redirected Mediterranean Policy" appear largely irrelevant.

The same period saw attempts by a number of the region's governments to build new multilateral, intergovernmental forums for dialogue without the Community's involvement. A proposed Conference on Security and Cooperation in the Mediterranean did not take-off, while a "5+5" Group, comprising France, Italy, Portugal, Spain, Malta, Algeria, Libya, Mauritania, Morocco, and Tunisia, was created in October 1990, but stalled following the imposition of sanctions on Libya and the political crisis in Algeria. The failure of both these proposals persuaded the Mediterranean member states, led by Spain, that policy change should be pursued through the new EU.

The Mediterranean member states were assisted by the creation of the EU's common foreign and security policy (CFSP) under the Maastricht Treaty. One effect of the CFSP was to galvanize the EU's governments into more thorough consideration of their common foreign policy interests, and in the aftermath of the Gulf War the Mediterranean was widely regarded as a priority area for common foreign policy actions. A report on the CFSP presented to the European Council in Lisbon in 1992, divided the Mediterranean into two geographical areas for strategic actions in favour of economic development, security, and stability: the Maghreb and the Middle East. While the definition of these common interests was imprecise, the Lisbon text nevertheless listed the broad objectives that the EU should pursue.

Consistent with the Lisbon text, the Commission initially continued to focus on the Maghreb. By the end of 1992 several months of exchanges between the Commission and the Moroccan and Tunisian governments had established the need for new agreements with the EU, based on three distinct lines of action. First, both sides agreed to further renegotiation of the terms of trade in the agreements, with Morocco and Tunisia pressing for full free trade in all sectors. Secondly, provisions would be included in each agreement covering rights of establishment, rules on the movement of services and capital, technical cooperation, and the possibility of joint research and development projects. Thirdly, the new agreements would include provisions for "social cooperation", essentially ministerial dialogue on issues such as migration, and living and working conditions for Maghrebi citizens in the EU. At

a meeting of EU foreign ministers in December 1992 the Commission's recommendations were given the green light by the member states and work began on mandates for the Commission to begin negotiations.

However, in view of the rapidly evolving Middle East peace process, the Commission saw the partnership as a means to stimulate "post-conflict" economic cooperation between Arab states and Israel. There was also a sense among the other Mediterranean third countries that too much of the EU's attention was being devoted to the Maghreb. When it appeared during 1993 that Israel and the Palestine Liberation Organization (PLO) might be coming close to concluding a lasting peace settlement, the partnership proposals were duly extended to embrace the Mashreq, and to take in the EU's relationships with Cyprus, Malta, and Turkey. By 1994 the EU's relationships with the Mediterranean nonmember countries had been subsumed under a single policy framework: the Euro–Mediterranean Partnership.

The Euro–Mediterranean Agreements

The principal policy instrument attached to the Euro–Mediterranean Partnership (EMP) took the form of upgraded association agreements, also known as "Euro–Mediterranean agreements". Echoing the GMP, its purpose was to facilitate gradual liberalization of trade over a transitional period of up to 12 years. Some sectors were excluded – most notably trade in services – and the Council of Ministers again ruled out the unconditional liberalization of agricultural trade, although, after strong diplomatic pressure from the Maghrebi governments, the EU promised to review the market situation for Mediterranean agricultural products by the end of the 1990s. Nevertheless, the scope of the agreements was far wider than before. All the new agreements were to include provisions for cooperation on issues such as energy policy, crime, and immigration. Formalized political dialogue, superseding the system of cooperation councils and committees, gave the agreements stronger institutional structures. Regular dialogue would take place at levels ranging from ministers to senior foreign office officials.

The precise provisions of the trade component of the Euro–Mediterranean agreements varied from one partner country to another, but they all contained certain common features.

- customs duties on EU exports of industrial products to the partner were to be eliminated gradually during the transitional period (while partners' exports of these products already had duty-free access to the EU);
- the gradual liberalization of trade in agricultural products was to proceed through the application of preferential access to the market on a reciprocal basis, taking traditional trade flows as a starting point; and
- the extension of trade preferences would be based on the existing arrangements, while the Mediterranean partners were to extend more limited preferences to EU exports, although this situation was to be reviewed after 1 January 2000.

The Euro–Mediterranean agreements were essential to the long-term success of the EMP. The economic centrepiece of the partnerships, a free trade area, implied the complete removal of barriers to trade across all sectors. For the majority of the Mediterranean partners, their commitment to the EMP depended on their seeing tangible economic benefits well before the deadline for the completion of the free trade area, which was to be 2010. Free trade presented significant risks for states that have few resources at their disposal to alleviate the negative effects of increased competition on domestic producers.

In the event, the EU again proved disappointingly defensive. Full liberalization of trade in manufactured products posed few problems for negotiators. The Mediterranean partner countries accepted that their markets would have to be fully opened to manufactured goods from the EU, while the member states saw little danger of increased competition following full liberalization. However, the EU's firm line on traditional trade flows in agriculture left little scope for more generous import quotas, even where the partners demonstrated that they had

the production capacity to take up their full quotas.

Having been promised free trade, the Mediterranean partners' negotiating demands were inevitably far in excess of the levels prevailing under existing import quotas. Most intractable of all were the negotiations with Egypt, which stalled in 1996 over the quota offered on potatoes and failed to move for over a year. By the beginning of 2001 the EU was still to conclude its negotiations with Algeria, Lebanon, and Syria (see Table 27.3 for the status of the negotiations). The EU was forced to admit that the completion date for the free trade area would be pushed back by at least five years, to 2015.

The Barcelona Process

The seeds of the Barcelona process also germinated in the vacant ground left by the aborted Conference on Security and Cooperation in the Mediterranean and the "5+5" project. The attempts to create these two regional forums had demonstrated the high level of support around the Mediterranean for multidimensional, functional cooperation, underpinned by strong institutional architecture. The keyword was "interdependence", reflecting the recognition that common Mediterranean problems, ranging from crime to environmental pollution, should be managed at the regional level. Consistent with its own long-established advocacy of enhanced regional organization, the Commission's proposals for a Euro-Maghreb partnership, set out in 1992, called for the bilateral track of the EU's new Mediterranean strategy to be complemented by dialogue on "all matters of common interest" between the Community and Algeria, Morocco, and Tunisia. By 1993 the Community had been participating constructively in the multilateral track of the Middle East peace process for two years, following the Madrid conference of 1991. The Commission became convinced that the scope of the Euro–Mediterranean Partnership should be extended to Israel and the Mashreq countries. Such a move would provide another channel for the normalization of governmental relations between Arabs and Israelis, as well as providing the basis for strategic action across the region. In a follow-up communication to the Council, the Commission argued that multi-sectoral, functional cooperation between governments and private actors was essential to the consolidation of the peace process in the long term, and mentioned the possibility of establishing "joint institutions".

The idea of convening a conference was first put forward at the EU's summit in Corfu in June 1994, after the Spanish government had offered to host the event at the end of its Council Presidency in 1995. However, the real watershed for the Barcelona process was the European Council at Essen in December 1994. The agreement to hold the conference formed part of an intergovernmental package, in which the Mediterranean member states accepted that eastern enlargement of the EU had to be its main priority in exchange for a clear signal that a significant gesture would be made towards the South.

In the context of the EU's Mediterranean policy, a multilateral conference served a number of purposes. First, it offered the EU a high-profile platform from which to "sell" the EMP to the partners themselves and to the wider world. It was the kind of grand political gesture called for by Jacques Delors, who argued that the EU needed to send "powerful messages to its neighbours" in the East and the South alike. Secondly, given the economic disruption likely to arise from the "Euro–Med" free trade initiative, the conference also amounted to a form of political compensation. It would create a facade of diplomatic equality and elevated political status for the partners in relation to the EU, at least in the short term. Thirdly, it was also expected that the conference would help to kick-start the negotiation of Euro–Mediterranean agreements with Morocco and Tunisia, which had stalled during 1994. The assumption was that all parties would want to conclude the negotiations before the event, as a sign that the EMP was making tangible progress.

Leaving aside its utility as a political signal, the conference also presented the EU with an opportunity to set out the principles of the EMP in a multilateral framework that was expected to generate foreign policy actions in its own right. The "multilateralization" of Mediterranean policy would equip the EU with an additional foreign policy tool, designed to facilitate the "boundary management" objectives of its Mediterranean policy by drawing together the various functional cooperation programmes under a single heading. Given the anticipated participation of the vast majority of the Mediterranean littoral states, the conference would be a step forward in the EU's attempt to construct a regional identity to underpin the EMP.

The Barcelona Declaration and Work Programme were negotiated between the EU and the Mediterranean partners over the course of 1995. It was structured into three chapters:

- a political and security chapter, including measures designed to promote regional political stability, the nonproliferation of weapons, respect for democratization and human rights, and specific "confidence-building" measures;

- an economic and financial chapter, including another restatement of the commitment to establish a free trade area by 2010, as well as commitments to increased economic, financial, and technical cooperation, and other forms of support for the economic development of the partners' economies; and

- a "social and human" chapter, covering such matters as dialogue between social organizations, cultural exchanges (between schools and universities, for instance), and other forms of nongovernmental cooperation.

Despite a host of problems over the text of the final declaration, the participation of Libya, and the granting of observer status to the United States, the Barcelona conference was widely heralded as a success. Pictures of Israeli, Lebanese, Palestinian, and Syrian representatives standing together in the Catalan sunshine seemed to some observers to capture the very essence of the "Barcelona spirit".

Work on implementation of the Declaration and Work Programme immediately began in the various ministerial and diplomatic committees and forums spawned by the Barcelona meeting. The Commission was given the role of overall coordinator of the follow-up process. A senior officials committee, comprising ambassadors and other high-ranking foreign ministry personnel, was established to oversee the political and security partnership. The other two chapters were to be overseen by the Euro–Med Committee, in which the member states were represented only by the Troika (the outgoing, current, and incoming presidencies). The Commission and all 12 partners were to be represented on both these committees.

The Political and Security Partnership

The language of the political and security chapter was ambitious, committing the signatories to "establishing a common area of peace and stability", and to upholding principles of human rights and fundamental freedoms, self-determination, and territorial integrity. Drawing on principles established in such international agreements as the charters of the UN and the Conference on (now Organization for) Security and Cooperation in Europe, the chapter was intended to subject Mediterranean security to internationally accepted standards and rules of interstate conduct. The signatories agreed to promote confidence- and security-building measures, to ensure the nonproliferation of nuclear weapons, and to cooperate in the "fight against terrorism". An undertaking was also made to examine the possibility of a "peace and stability charter", although it was expressly identified in the text as a long-term goal.

Not surprisingly, it proved difficult to make headway in this politically sensitive area. The breakdown of the Middle East peace process rendered Arab–Israeli cooperation on the first chapter virtually impossible. Nevertheless, by late 2000 several measures had been agreed and were at various stages of implementation, including:

- regular training and information seminars for diplomats;
- a network of foreign policy institutes (EuroMesco);
- a system for voluntary cooperation among civil protection services on disasters, focusing on the sharing of expertise and training;

- a register of bilateral agreements between signatories; and
- the exchange of information on international conventions on human rights, disarmament, and other humanitarian issues.

Work on the "peace and stability charter" also fell hostage to the fortunes of the peace process in the Middle East. The problems over agreeing on a mutually acceptable form and content for the charter were reflected in the decisions that it should be politically rather than legally binding, and should operate by consensus only. The signatories had been aiming to adopt a text by the end of 2000, but at their ministerial meeting in Marseilles in November 2000 it was agreed that the renewed tension in the Middle East meant that further delay was unavoidable.

The Economic and Financial Partnership

The economic and financial chapter, the centrepiece of the Barcelona process, became the "engine" of the EMP, committing the signatories to establishing one of the world's largest free trade zones by 2010, with a potential market of 800 million people. The measures set out in the Barcelona Work Programme were designed to complement the Euro–Mediterranean agreements by stimulating regional economic integration, inward investment, and infrastructural development, and by setting out guidelines for the management of common resources.

As an integral component of the EU's regional strategy, the second chapter laid down the methods by which a framework of economic governance would be extended to the region, and underscored the neoliberal orthodoxy inherent in the partnership. The Work Programme earmarked the harmonization of import/export procedures, rules, and standards as the priority for implementation. Provisions relating to the extension of existing cooperation in fields such as energy, rural development, technology transfer, technical assistance for business cooperation, and investment were all directed towards readying the partners for the shock of a rapid transition to free trade.

Laced with a heavy dose of the EU's own economic self-interest, the second chapter was premised on a selective externalization of the EU's single market model, using methods already employed in the EU's eastern enlargement strategy. The Work Programme added up to a wish list of issues on which the EU's objectives could best be met through multilateral action. For instance, the rapidly expanding presence of European investors in the natural gas industry in North Africa would clearly benefit from the extra protection afforded by international agreements. At a relatively low cost to the EU – grants and EIB loans, more "dialogue", and the exchange of technical expertise – it could obtain security of supply and a more welcoming economic climate for investors.

The rather peripheral role of the Mediterranean partners in the preparation of the Barcelona process, coupled with their relatively weak bargaining power, left them little alternative other than to accept what was a flawed package from their point of view. Most criticisms from the partners were targeted at areas left out of the Declaration and Work Programme, and at the use of bilateral negotiations to set the terms of the free trade area, a method that enabled the EU to deal with each partner individually and thus rule out any possibility of collective bargaining. Capital and goods would move increasingly freely throughout the region; labour would not. The Declaration made a brief reference to the liberalization of trade in services, but no provisions for it were included in the Work Programme. On foreign investment, regarded as a crucial determinant of the partnership's success, the Work Programme included only a vague pledge to "help create a climate favourable to the removal of obstacles to investment, by giving greater thought to the definition of such obstacles".

As in relation to the first chapter, the implementation of the economic and financial chapter started with meetings to agree common principles as the basis for the alignment of policies in the sectors concerned. Follow-up conferences were organized to cover a bewildering range of sectors, many of which simply spawned further meetings.

As was the case with the first chapter, the principal benefit of the second chapter was its

construction of networks of actors – principally businesses and consultancies – from all the partner countries. Getting private business interests on board was essential to the free trade initiative. The Mediterranean region accounted for only 2% of total overseas investment by EU businesses, limiting the assumed stabilizing effect of economic integration. Much of the work undertaken after Barcelona therefore focused on increasing incentives for capital investment. Investors' guides, funded by the Commission, were compiled for each of the partners. Networks of chambers of commerce and economic institutes were mandated to improve the flow of business information and increase awareness of investment opportunities. Funds from MEDA, the financial instrument for the Barcelona process, were provided for European consultancies to advise small and medium-sized enterprises in the partner countries, and to oversee the implementation of joint projects between EU and third-country businesses. While there were some problems starting up business development projects in partner countries with comparatively underdeveloped investment regimes, the emergence of an ethos of joint participation was nevertheless taken to be a sign of progress.

The Human Chapter

The third chapter of the Barcelona Declaration was intended to integrate "civil society" into the process, and to instigate "cultural dialogue" and "exchanges at human, scientific and technological levels". The range of subjects covered in the Declaration and Work Programme was impressive, identifying numerous new avenues of cooperation in areas such as education, human health, democratic practices, migration, terrorism, drug trafficking, international crime, corruption, and racism.

On the face of it, the incorporation of a sociocultural dimension was a laudable objective, lacking in previous versions of Community and EU Mediterranean policy. At the same time, however, it was fraught with difficulties, opening up the EU to accusations of "neocolonialism" through the imposition of its cultural and social values on the developing world. The Work Programme struck an uneasy balance between progressive language on cultural and social issues, and tough passages on crime, drug trafficking, migration, and terrorism, issues that were, arguably, the EU's real priorities.

The principal benefits of the third chapter were, arguably, felt outside the Barcelona process itself. A "Euro–Med Civil Forum" had been established on the fringes of the conference, organized and funded by the Communidad Autonoma (regional government) of Catalonia, the European Commission, the EU's Economic and Social Committee, the Spanish Foreign Ministry, and Unesco. Around 1,200 representatives from 700 "social bodies" participated in the first forum, which discussed issues ranging from cooperation between small and medium-sized enterprises to religious dialogue and intercultural exchanges. Less visible, though potentially more politically significant, was the "Alternative Mediterranean Conference" attended by 2,000 delegates from 300 associations including antiracist movements, trade unions, and other nongovernmental organizations. It challenged the state-led nature of the Barcelona process, singling out the dominance of trade liberalization and the involvement of authoritarian governments in the process.

By the time of the Euro–Med foreign ministers' meeting in Malta in 1998 the number of initiatives under the third chapter had mushroomed. At the second meeting of the Euro–Med Forum some delegates complained that it had become difficult to keep track of developments. The fact that appraising the third chapter was so problematic suggested that at least one of the aims of the exercise – to stimulate decentralized cooperation between nongovernmental actors – was under way.

A "Common Strategy" for the Mediterranean

Five years after the Barcelona conference it was clear that the EMP had fallen short of expectations, from both the EU's and the partners' perspectives. The External Relations Commissioner, Chris Patten, described his "frustration" with the Barcelona process, citing delays in the disbursement of aid, the failure to stimulate intraregional trade, and the thorny question of agricultural trade as areas of concern. Patten also sought to bolster cooperation on justice and home affairs. The Arab Mediterranean states were particularly critical of the failure to exert pressure on Israel over the Palestinian territories and of the problems with the implementation of the MEDA financial package. Ahead of the fourth meeting of the Euro–Med foreign ministers, scheduled to take place in Marseilles in November 2000, the Commission called for a "reinvigoration of the Barcelona process", and put forward proposals for speeding up the conclusion of the Euro–Mediterranean association agreements, examining the steps required to liberalize agricultural trade in the region, procedural improvements to the MEDA programme, the conclusion of the "Euro–Mediterranean Charter for Peace and Stability", and a new "Information and Communication Programme" to improve the visibility of the EMP.

The Commission's call for the EMP to be "reinvigorated" coincided with the European Council's elaboration of a "Common Strategy for the Mediterranean", which made the region one of the first subjects for a common strategy, the new CFSP instrument introduced under the Treaty of Amsterdam (Article 13). Formally adopted at the European Council in Santa Maria da Feira in June 2000, much of the strategy merely restated the goals set out in the Barcelona Declaration, albeit in stronger language. Its main purposes appeared to be to improve the consistency of Mediterranean policy with other EU policies and to boost the EU's credentials as a political actor in the Middle East. Provisions were also included for the EU's monitoring of the results of activities in relation to the Mediterranean to be improved.

Two features of the strategy were particularly noteworthy. First, the document made a more explicit link between the Middle East peace process and the partnership activities. While the EU had previously been cautious about overlap between the two, the strategy represented an unequivocal acknowledgement of their perceived inseparability. The EU offered its "good offices and assistance to the core parties of the peace process", and suggested that the "stability charter" might be used to reinforce security in the Middle East. Greater emphasis was placed on the coordination of actions instigated under the EMP with those under the CFSP. For instance, the text included a request for the EU's High Representative and Special Envoy to the Middle East to suggest ways in which the Barcelona process could be used to promote stability in the Middle East once peace had been established.

Secondly, the document went some way to integrating into the Mediterranean policy the conclusions of the European Council in Tampere in 1999 on justice and home affairs. In particular, the strategy contained a paragraph on the status of nationals from the partner countries who were legally residing in the EU. That issue had been a point of contention between the EU and Mediterranean nonmember states ever since the days of the Global Mediterranean Policy. By the same token, its inclusion was a measure of the EU's growing concern about the perceived security implications of migration from the region.

The adoption of the strategy may go some way to enhancing the strategic coherence of the EU's Mediterranean policy. It should facilitate improved linkages between "first pillar" actions, the CFSP, and justice and home affairs (now known as police and judicial cooperation). It should also act as a reference point for the member states' own Mediterranean policies. Nevertheless, without sustained and durable peace in the Middle East, the effectiveness of the Euro–Mediterranean Partnership in inducing economic, social, and political change in the region is likely to remain limited.

Conclusions

The EU's Mediterranean policy has developed in fits and starts, with new elements being periodically added to the overall policy package over four decades. At the outset the foundation for the policy was the management of trade relations with Mediterranean third countries. To the extent that objectives existed, they were initially driven by the commercial interests of the member states and, in the cases of Greece and Turkey, by Cold War strategic considerations. When the first set of agreements was absorbed into the Global Mediterranean Policy, the Community's ambitious rhetoric far

exceeded the reality of the deals that it offered to the Mediterranean non-member countries. The label "policy" might therefore be seen as a convenient disguise for a disparate collection of trade and association agreements.

From the late 1980s onwards, perceptions among key actors within the Community converged around the view that European states had to carry a bigger share of the burden of security in the Mediterranean following the ending of the Cold War. The Community was seen as the most appropriate "framework" to put in place the prescribed policy measures after experimentation with the "5+5" dialogue and other subregional forums had failed. A considerable volume of analysis and research pointed to the need for policy change. While previous incarnations of Mediterranean policy had lacked a clear set of objectives, the 1990s saw the EU set about identifying its long-term goals for the region, culminating in the creation of the Euro–Mediterranean Partnership.

The word "strategy" appears throughout the policy documents that set out the EU's proposals for the partnership. The question then arises as to whether the EU's Mediterranean policy is a genuine example of strategic foreign policy in action. The acid tests of effective strategic action must surely be, first, the attainment of long-term objectives and, secondly, the achievement of a genuinely transformative impact. The Partnership falls some way short in both respects. On the trade component of the Euro–Med package, the EU remains open to accusations of protectionism. The EU's financial aid to the region, despite the substantial increases of the 1990s, is still far below the level that would represent an effective redistribution of resources from North to South. In political terms, the Partnership is handicapped both by the shortcomings of the EU's own foreign and security policy mechanism, and by the conflict in the Middle East. In a region whose fragile stability will become increasingly vital to European security, partnership is unlikely to be enough.

Further Reading

Aliboni, Roberto, *European Security Across the Mediterranean*, Chaillot Papers, No. 2, Paris: Institute for Security Studies, 1991

A detailed analysis of various regional and national security challenges in the Mediterranean region, and a useful analysis of specific European interests

Barbé, Esther, "Balancing Europe's Eastern and Southern Dimensions", in R. Zielonka (editor), *Paradoxes of European Foreign Policy*, The Hague: Kluwer Law International, 1998

A concise analysis of the pull on the EU's foreign policy from central and eastern Europe, and, particularly, the Mediterranean region

Brauch, Hans Günter, Antonio Marquina, and Abdelwahab Biad, *Euro–Mediterranean Partnership for the 21st Century*, London: Macmillan, and New York: St Martin's Press, 2000

A good analysis of the current policy issues

Calleya, Stephen, *Navigating Regional Dynamics in the Post-Cold War World: Patterns of Relations in the Mediterranean Area*, Aldershot: Dartmouth, 1997

An original analysis of international relations in and around the Mediterranean

Djankov, Simeon, and Bernard Hoekman, *Catching Up With Eastern Europe? The Union's Free Trade Initiative*, Washington, DC: International Bank for Reconstruction and Development (World Bank), January 1996

A systematic analysis of progress towards free trade in the Mediterranean region, by two economists

European Commission, *Strengthening the Mediterranean Policy of the European Union: Establishing a Euro–Mediterranean Partnership*, Brussels, COM(94)427 Final, 19 April 1994

The document that sets out the main elements of the "Euro–Med" Partnership

European Commission, *The Role of the European Union in the Peace Process and its Future Assistance to the Middle East*, Brussels, COM(97)715 Final, January 1998

A presentation of the EU's contribution to the peace process, including discussion of how its role might change in the event of a settlement

European Commission, *Reinvigorating the Barcelona Process*, Brussels, COM(2000)497 Final, October 2000

The Commission's report to the Council and European Parliament in preparation for the fourth meeting of Euro–Mediterranean foreign ministers in October 2000

European Parliament Committee on Foreign Affairs, Defence, and Security Policy, *Report on the Joint Report by the Presidency of the Council and the*

Commission on Mediterranean Policy – Follow-up to the Barcelona Conference, Brussels, A4-0027/97, February 1997

An influential committee's view of the Partnership

Hakura, Fadi, "The Euro–Mediterranean Policy: The Implications of the Barcelona Declaration", in *Common Market Law Review*, 34/2, 1997

A good mixture of legal and political analysis of the Barcelona process

Joffé, George, "The European Union and the Maghreb", in Richard Gillespie (editor), *Mediterranean Politics*, Volume 1, London: Pinter, 1994

A critical analysis of the earlier phases of the Community's Mediterranean policy

Joffé, George (editor), "Special Issue: The Barcelona Process: Building a Euro–Mediterranean Regional Community", *Mediterranean Politics*, 5/1, 2000

This special issue of a scholarly journal contains a range of articles on political, security and economic issues in the Mediterranean region.

Khader, Bichara, *Le Partenariat Euro–Méditerranéen*, Louvain-la-Neuve: Centre d'Études et de Recherches sur le Monde Arabe Contemporain (CERMAC), 1996

A comprehensive account of the partnership, including some useful statistical information as well as incisive political commentary

Pierros, Filippos, Jacob Meunier, and Stan Abrams, *Bridges and Barriers: The European Union's Mediterranean policy, 1961–1998*, Aldershot: Ashgate, 1999

A clearly structured history of the topic

Pomfret, Richard, "The European Community's Relations with the Mediterranean Countries", in John Redmond (editor), *The External Relations of the European Community: The International Response to 1992*, London: Macmillan, and New York: St Martin's Press, 1992

A good overview of the development of Mediterranean policy

Rhein, Eberhard, "Europe and the Mediterranean", in *European Foreign Affairs Review*, 1/1, 1996

A good summary of the EU's Mediterranean policy by a practitioner

Spencer, Claire, "Building Confidence in the Mediterranean", in *Mediterranean Politics*, 2/2, 1997

A thoughtful analysis of one of the key principles of the Barcelona process

Tovias, Alfred, "The EU's Mediterranean Policies under Pressure", in Richard Gillespie (editor), *Mediterranean Politics*, Volume 2, London: Pinter, 1996

An assessment of the pressure for reform on EU Mediterranean policy, particularly strong on the economic dimension of "Euro–Med" relations

Tovias, Alfred, and Jordi Bacaria, "Free Trade and the Mediterranean", in *Mediterranean Politics*, 4/2, 1999

An examination of intraregional trade among the partner countries, with some proposals for reform. The same issue of *Mediterranean Politics* contains other useful articles on Mediterranean regionalism.

Internet sources

In addition to the printed sources listed above, there are numerous websites that cover all dimensions of the Euro–Mediterranean Partnership.

A good starting point is the *Euromed Internet Forum* (www.euromed.net) hosted by the Mediterranean Academy of Dipomatic Studies. It contains a wide range of official documents and other sources of information.

The European Commission's website for Mediterranean and Middle East policies is also impressive (europa.eu.int/comm/external_relations/med_mideast/intro/index.htm).

Euromesco, the network of foreign policy institutes attached to the Barcelona process has its own website at www.euromesco.net

---

Ricardo Gomez is a lecturer in EU politics at the University of Strathclyde. He is writing a book on the Euro–Mediterranean Partnership and also working on EU foreign economic policy.

Table 27.1 Financial Aid from the European Community/EU to Mediterranean Partners, 1978–96 (Ecu/€ millions)

	First Protocol (1978–81)	Second Protocol (1981–86)	Third Protocol (1986–91)	Fourth Protocol (1991–96)
Algeria				
Community budget grants	44	44	56	70
EIB loans	70	107	183	280
Total	114	151	239	350
Cyprus				
Community budget grants	10	16	18	24
EIB loans	20	28	44	50
Total	30	44	62	74
Egypt				
Community budget grants	77	126	200	258
EIB loans	93	150	249	310
Total	170	276	449	568
Israel				
Community budget grants	–	–	–	–
EIB loans	30	40	63	82
Total	30	40	63	82
Jordan				
Community budget grants	22	26	37	46
EIB loans	18	37	63	80
Total	40	63	100	126
Lebanon				
Community budget grants	10	16	20	24
EIB loans	20	34	53	45
Total	30	50	73	69
Morocco				
Community budget grants	74	109	173	218
EIB loans	56	90	151	220
Total	130	199	324	438
Syria				
Community budget grants	26	33	36	43
EIB loans	34	64	110	115
Total	60	97	146	158
Tunisia				
Community budget grants	54	61	93	116
EIB loans	71	78	131	168
Total	95	139	224	224
Total	699	1,059	1,680	2,089

Source: europa.eu.int/comm/external_relations/med_mideast/intro/index.htm

Table 27.2   Distribution of Commitments under the MEDA Programme, 1995–99
(€ millions)

	1995	1996	1997	1998	1999	1995-1999
Bilateral						
Morocco	30		235	219	172	656
Algeria			41	95	28	164
Tunisia	20	120	138	19	131	428
Egypt		75	203	397	11	686
Jordan	7	100	10	8	129	254
Lebanon		10	86		86	182
Syria		13	42		44	99
West Bank/Gaza	3	20	41	5	42	111
Turkey		33	70	132	140	375
Total bilateral	60	370	866	875	783	2,954
Regional	113	33	93	46	133	418
Technical assistance			22	20	21	63
Total	173	403	981	941	937	3,435

Source: European Commission, *Reinvigorating the Barcelona Process*, COM(2000)497 Final, October 2000

Table 27.3   Progress on Negotiations on Euro–Mediterranean Association
Agreements as of January 2001

	Negotiations Opened	Negotiations Concluded	Agreement Signed	Entry into Force
Morocco	1993	November 1995	February 1996	March 2000
Tunisia	1993	June 1995	July 1995	March 1998
Israel	1994	September 1995	November 1995	June 2000
Jordan	1996	April 1997	November 1997	–
Egypt	1996	June 1999	–*	–
PalestinianAuthority	1996	December 1996	February 1997	July 1997
Algeria	1997	[not yet]	–	–
Lebanon	1997	[not yet]	–	–
Syria	1998	[not yet]	–	–

Note: * The agreement with Egypt was initialled in January 2001 and may therefore be considered to be close to formal signature.

Source: European Commission, *Reinvigorating the Barcelona Process*, COM(2000)497 Final (updated)

Figure 27.1 The EU and its Mediterranean Partners

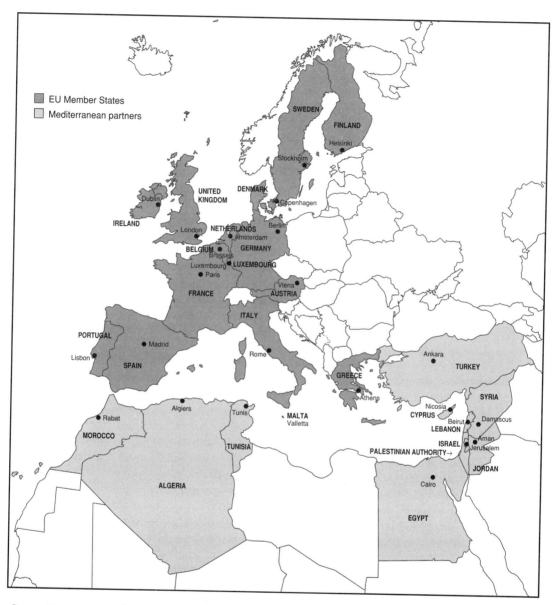

Source: European Commission, *The Barcelona Process, Five Years On*, Luxembourg: Office for Official Publications of the European Communities, 2000

Chapter Twenty-Eight

The EU's Relations with Developing States

Marjorie Lister

The literature on European integration and even on the EU's foreign policy is often surprisingly light on the subject of relations with developing countries. This is true for a variety of reasons, including the general inward-looking tendency of the EU, as evidenced in the agenda of the intergovernmental conference in 2000, which focused almost entirely on its own internal reform. As is too often the case in constituent policy-making for the EU, foreign and development policy took a back seat in the deliberations.

Another reason for the relative neglect of development policy in EU theory has been its relegation to the area of postcolonial relations. Developing countries, which are often poor and weak, can be interpreted as having more to do with the member states' rather chequered past as colonial powers (at least in the cases of Germany, France, Belgium, the United Kingdom, Italy, and the Netherlands) rather than their future, which can be variously conceived of as "European", "transatlantic" or even global. In its *Green Paper on Relations between the European Union and the ACP Countries on the Eve of the 21st Century* (1996) the European Commission tried, albeit unconvincingly, to distance itself from this colonial past by claiming that its development policy for the 21st century had to be restarted from scratch, since the colonial and postcolonial periods were now over. Even the contention that the colonial age is over might come as a surprise to the inhabitants of the 20 remaining colonial possessions of the EU member states.

A further reason why EU development policy, which has a substantial literature dating back to the 1970s, has not received much attention is the relative failure of the postwar development project in general and the Community/EU's development project in particular. Development aid is widely considered a "sunset industry". Neither substantial financial transfers, trade preferences for poor countries nor food and humanitarian aid have brought about the elimination of global poverty that the international development community has sought. One of the most notable strands in development literature directly poses the question of whether aid works or not. The answers often appear inconclusive or dependent upon the political preconceptions of the authors. Scholars who study aid frequently note the limited funds available and the frequent cases of aid failure. Aid receipts and economic growth are not always positively correlated. Since aid is not unquestionably successful, they conclude that improving trade, which after all involves much greater sums than aid, must be the key to progress for developing countries. Similarly, there is a common tendency among scholars who study trade policy and development to take the view that trade prospects for developing countries are limited; the ability of many to compete in the global marketplace is doubtful. Therefore the answer to their development problems must be aid. Thus, there seems to be no short answer to the development problems of the poorest countries; both aid and trade preferences remain imperfect but necessary instruments for the task of development cooperation.

What is particularly noticeable in the European Community's development policy since the end of the 1980s is the deterioration of the distinct policy identity created by successive development commissioners, such as Claude Cheysson or Edgard Pisani. In the 1990s policy seldom veered far from the policies of what the EU calls the "principal donors", the World Bank and the IMF. Further, the policies of the IMF and the World Bank are not unchanging, but vary considerably: the user charges for primary education and health care which were prescribed in the 1980s, for instance, were no longer seen as valid in the 1990s. Each successive annual report of the World Bank seems to focus on a new key element to bring into development thinking and practice: the environment, gender, the "East Asian model", poverty focus, the role of the state – but none of this new thinking has so far solved the international development problem. Indeed, the latest thinking of the World Bank, which today is the intellectual leader of the development community, is to focus on bringing all these elements into a coordinated donor framework, that is, doing them all together at once. This "Comprehensive Development Framework" may produce future benefits, but has so far failed to capture the intellectual high ground of development theory.

If the record of public international development aid is difficult to "sell" to the political elites, to the public at large, or to specific institutions, such as the US Congress, the record of Community/EU development aid is, if anything, even more awkward. Many academic and consultants' studies have concluded that EU aid programmes have problems, and that their results have been "mixed", "patchy" or "could do better". Even the European Commission's own Green Paper, mentioned above, has accepted this verdict of limited success in its development cooperation policy.

Not only the rightwing lobby opposed to aid and state intervention and the leftist lobby opposed to aid and global capitalism, but even the EU's External Affairs Commissioner, Chris Patten, and the British Secretary of State for International Development, Clare Short, have echoed the severest criticisms of EU aid. Short charged in mid-2000 that the EU is "the worst development agency in the world", being slow and inefficient, not focused on poverty alleviation, and bureaucratically overstretched.

She argued that if the next two years did not see a big improvement in EU aid performance, the member states should consider downsizing the EU development programme in favour of more effective aid agencies. Patten has clearly found the backlog of undisbursed EU aid, which reached US$18.7 billion in 2000, and the delays in payments of six and a half years for Latin America to eight and a half years for the Mediterranean, unacceptable.

The pro-development vision of "association" between overseas territories and the Community that was set out in Part IV of the Treaty of Rome, and reiterated in the four successive Lomé Conventions, the first of which was signed in 1975, is widely recognized by the international development community as no longer sufficient. Whether the new Cotonou Convention signed in June 2000 with 77 developing countries will succeed in bridging the gap between the EU's vision and its competence, in both trade and development aid policy, remains to be seen. To be successful in the future, the EU's development policy may well have to aim at doing fewer things, but doing them more effectively.

Towards a New Development Policy

The EU is grappling with a range of issues that will affect its relations with developing countries in the 21st century. Development policy, along with trade policy and political concerns, forms a central part of the EU's external actions. The EU has constructed a complex set of interregional "partnerships" with widely varying groups of developing countries. From the African, Caribbean, and Pacific (ACP) group to the developing countries of the Mediterranean basin and the Southern Cone of Latin America, the few constants in the EU's relations with developing countries seem to be that they are elaborate, are differentiated, vary in priority according to the politics of the day, and can make sense only in terms of the unique historical and geopolitical contexts that engendered them. At the same time, the EU aspires to be a global player, with concerns over poverty, gender inequalities, environmental problems, and violent conflicts throughout the developing world.

Despite the problems mentioned above, European development cooperation could have a number of advantages. The proponents of EU aid cite:

- potential economies of scale – if the aid programmes of the EU and the member states could be combined, there would be savings and efficiency gains. The EU's critical mass in political, economic, and financial terms would give it a leading global role for coordination and consistency in development policies. At the moment the EU's influence within the international donor community and the international financial institutions, such as the IMF or the World Bank, is smaller than its economic input.
- spreading the special, fundamental values of Europe – these are generally argued to include democracy and good governance, respect for human rights, and the rule of law.
- building on the EU's presence – the EU has political and trade relations with almost all developing countries, as well as a large representation through its delegations "on the ground". These existing networks provide a sound basis for future expansions of relations.
- the experience of integration – the EU, as the world's most successful example of regional integration, may have a model to export to developing countries. Regional integration could help developing countries in enhancing their economic development and their participation in global markets, and in dealing with problems of regional conflict and social inequalities.
- access to the world's largest single market – in the opinion of the EU, developing countries need to be gradually integrated into the world economy. In this view, negotiating reciprocal free trade areas between the EU and individual developing countries, such as Mexico, or regional groupings of developing countries, such as the Southern Africa Development Community, is a positive step.
- the supposed "political neutrality" of the Community/EU – this characteristic was particularly emphasized during the Cold War, and derived primarily from the desire of successive French governments to convince developing countries that an alliance with the Community offered a middle way between the two competing superpowers, the United States and the Soviet Union. The European Community of the 1970s and 1980s was supposed to be a civilian power, an economic rather than a political entity, and a new organization untainted by the stains of colonialism. Today the EU is much more open about its political interests and objectives, and has plans to build a military capability for peacekeeping and crisis management. Nevertheless, in speeches and EU documents, the EU's alleged political neutrality in development terms is still regularly invoked.

As a development aid donor, the EU is extremely important. Taken together with its 15 member states, it is the world's largest giver of aid, furnishing some 55% of total official development assistance and more than two thirds of the international aid that is in the form of grants. The EU is also the largest single donor of humanitarian (emergency) aid. But the EU's record is marred by a number of failings, chief among these being slow disbursement and excessively bureaucratic procedures; poor coordination between the EU, on the one hand, and the member states on the other; the tying of much aid to EU purchases; the failure to prioritize and thereby have a significant effect in any sector (see Table 28.1); the failure to integrate development policy with commercial or agricultural policy; poor evaluation and dissemination of information; and the lack of a coherent overall strategy.

In "The European Community's Development Policy", a Communication from the European Commission to the Council of Ministers and the European Parliament in April 2000, the Commission agreed to take the initiative in coordinating member states' development activities in six priority sectors where it believes that the Community has a comparative advantage over other donor agencies. The Commission has set out these extremely broad sectors, not in any order of priority, as follows:

- trade and development, including trade and investment policies, technical assistance, capacity-building, and increasing the competitiveness of the private sector;
- regional integration and cooperation, including addressing economic, social, and environmental problems;
- support for macroeconomic policies, linking them to poverty reduction and especially to sectoral programmes for health and education;
- transport, including both the creation and maintenance of infrastructure – this has been seen as very outdated by those who argue that what is really needed is information and communications technology, as recognized in the Fourth Lomé Convention;
- food security and sustainable rural development programmes; and
- building institutional capacity, good governance, and the rule of law.

Along with these six priority areas, the Commission designated the crosscutting principles of good governance, respect for human rights and the rule of law, poverty reduction, institution- and capacity-building, gender equality, and environmental sustainability, which are to inform all its development actions. In addition, the Commission will try to refocus the activities of its humanitarian assistance arm, the European Community Humanitarian Office (ECHO), and better integrate its activities with long-term development programmes.

As well as new sectoral priorities, important administrative reforms are on the EU's development policy agenda. These include improving project cycle management and using multiannual programming of aid. However, these reforms may not succeed in simplifying procedures. The EU's delegations in developing countries, and those countries' own authorities, are to be given greater roles in project management in order to speed and improve project implementation. Improvements in structures and communications with the European Parliament, member states, and the working groups and committees of the Council of Ministers are also envisaged. Less time should be taken by member states

in approving individual projects and more effort devoted to strategic and "upstream" decisions.

The distribution of development policy responsibilities within the European Commission has always been less than optimal, owing more to politicking by member states than to strict considerations of efficiency. This, unfortunately, is a situation that continues under the Prodi Commission. The Development Directorate-General, under Poul Nielson, ostensibly has chief responsibility for development, but it actually shares this brief with the Directorates-General for Trade and for External Affairs. The Development Directorate-General has responsibility for humanitarian aid, but not for non-ACP programmes, general implementation, or evaluation. Chris Patten, as External Affairs Commissioner, has responsibility for these areas, as well as for the Common Service (SCR) for aid programming and implementation. Trade policy, including its development aspects, falls under the directorate of Pascal Lamy.

The EU wants to deconcentrate and decentralize its instruments of cooperation in order to deliver more effective results. The existence of more than 60 separate development-related budget lines, along with the European Development Fund (EDF), which is separate from the EU's general budget, makes reorganization a priority. The Commission would like the EDF to be brought into the general EU budget, but this proposal remains controversial. Whether it would guarantee a suitable level of funding and improve the efficiency of aid management is still debatable. Bringing the EDF into the normal budgetary process would reduce member states' direct control over their contributions, as well as eliminating the EDF's special status as a negotiated rather than "granted" aid instrument.

The blunt instrument of "conditionality" – putting aid on a stop/go basis according to the recipients' performance on issues such as human rights and democracy – is to be refined into an instrument of "selectivity", linking disbursements to results in a smoother continuum. However, this risks the EU becoming involved only in sectors or countries where its interventions seem likely to produce quick and quantifiable results.

The development of appropriate intervention methods for countries in conflict or post-conflict situations is a further goal set by the Commission. The EU's systems of programming, monitoring, and evaluating projects, and then feeding results back into policy formulation, are to be enhanced. Another long overdue proposal is for the Commission to produce annual reports on the whole range of the EU's development actions, reviewing the priorities for strategic actions, adapting policy priorities and objectives, and reporting on the implementation of the policies.

The EU is presently trying to steer its way through a number of conflicting objectives. It wants to increase the poverty focus of its aid, while not abandoning its friends among middle-income developing countries in areas such as the Caribbean. The EU wants to increase the effectiveness of its aid, but without greatly increasing the resources devoted to this sector. Compared to other aid agencies, the European Commission is also significantly understaffed, which has a negative impact on its ability to make and carry out policies (see Figure 28.2). The EU expects developing countries to accept primary responsibility for managing their own development, but EU development support is to be conditional on whether developing countries adopt the priorities and methods approved by the EU for their development processes.

The EU also hopes to address the problem of preventing the "new internal wars" in developing countries, the violent and often apparently purposeless conflicts that have mushroomed since the end of the Cold War in such countries as Rwanda, Congo (the former Zaïre), Liberia, and Sierra Leone, but without allocating the extensive financial resources or long-term military commitments that this might require. It wants to put similar policy frameworks in place for its relations for all developing countries, but it seeks to differentiate among them by offering different policy instruments to different countries and regions. While it aspires to a global development policy, the EU gives priority to developing countries with greater proximity to the EU or with particular salient problems or crises. The EU wishes to have a development policy that is newly minted, but rests on the *acquis* built up with groups of developing countries over the previous 40 years.

From the Lomé Conventions to the Cotonou Agreement

Up to the 1990s the series of Lomé Conventions represented the brightest star in the EU's firmament of development policies. They were supposed to provide the finest model of cooperation between the states of the North and South, and to express the pinnacle of international development thinking.

The Lomé system was more elaborate and institutionalized than the Franco–African summits, and had more aid funds and development instruments than the Commonwealth. It also had a longer track record than any of the "Pan-American" development initiatives involving the United States and Latin America. The Conventions even had more impressive texts than any other development agreement, with references to alleviating poverty, protecting the environment, recognizing the role of women, and promoting all human rights and the dignity, well-being and self-fulfilment of individuals.

Nevertheless, the concrete results of the Community's cooperation with the (eventually) 77 signatory developing countries in Africa, the Caribbean, and Pacific were modest. The Lomé aid and trade regime did not amount to an "engine of growth" for them. They remained largely poor and powerless, with 39 of the 77 falling into the category of "least developed" despite, in many cases, decades of partnership with the Community. This failure, along with the changes in the international political situation after 1989, led to considerable uncertainty in the mid-1990s about whether a successor agreement should or would be negotiated when the effectiveness of the fourth Lomé Convention expired at the end of February 2000. In the 1990s the Community/EU's interests wandered away from its old Lomé partners and towards the closer and economically more promising regions of the former Warsaw Pact countries and the southern Mediterranean (North Africa).

This loss of attention caused serious concern among ACP policy-makers, not least because their much-vaunted Lomé partnership seemed to be slipping away, with nothing on offer to replace it. The European Commission's Green Paper of 1996, mentioned above, launched a valuable debate about the future of the ACP–EU partnership. Although the Green Paper expressed a great deal of postmodernist angst and uncertainty about the future of the Convention, it elicited a surprising amount of support for the principles of Lomé from a variety of "stakeholders", ranging from ACP heads of state to nongovernmental organizations and academics.

Negotiations for the Cotonou Agreement commenced in September 1998. Agreement was reached in February 2000, notwithstanding a last-minute attempt by the EU to open discussions on migration, which almost brought about the collapse of the agreement. The relative unity of the ACP negotiators was apparent, as was their inability to get many of their key demands accepted by the EU. These included an increase in aid in real terms, and the continuation of the mineral support scheme, Sysmin, and the commodities support scheme, Stabex. Stabex and Sysmin had been much vaunted as the EU's progressive answer to the ACP countries' economic development problems in the 1970s and 1980s, especially under Lomé I and II respectively. However, although they were popular with the recipients, these complicated aid programmes failed to live up to expectations and disappeared from the Cotonou text, although some elements of the Stabex scheme were incorporated into discretionary provisions to support export earnings from the long-term assistance allocation to the ACP states.

The signing of the Cotonou Agreement was battered by external events. On the one hand the disruption of the World Trade Organization's summit in Seattle by a variety of anti-capitalist, antiglobalization, pro-environment, and other activists helped to concentrate the minds of the decision-makers of industrialized countries, and encouraged them to exert their full efforts to reach a satisfactory agreement with the ACP states before they could be deluged with unwanted protestors. Yet external events also had a delaying impact on the final signing ceremony. The ceremony was to have been held in Fiji in May 2000, but a coup on the island caused the move to Cotonou in Benin and a month's delay. Uncertainty about the EU's attitude towards Cuba's possible sign-ing of the Cotonou Agreement, a prospect supported by the ACP states, also marred the run-up to the signing.

New Features

The new features of the Cotonou Agreement include a 20-year duration (double the length of Lomé IV), with reviews every five years. The goal of simplifying the complicated text was to be met by placing reference texts, including political and economic guidelines and priorities, separate from the main agreement. Nevertheless, the main partnership agreement remained as long and complex as ever, with greater detail on a number of subjects and demanding new issue areas, such as the conflict-related actions discussed below.

Another change in Cotonou was the explicit addition of non-state actors to the partnership. These are to include subnational units of government, private sector business entities, and "civil society" actors, although exactly which actors are to be involved in which circumstances is left unclear. The elimination of poverty has been made the central objective of the partnership, with the parties accepting an obligation to take appropriate actions to meet this goal. The donor community's global poverty reduction target of 50% by 2015 is cited in the text, but no specific performance targets are established for the EU–ACP partnership.

The Cotonou Agreement emphasizes the importance of the political dialogue among the signatories. Political dialogue, which has always been a key part of cooperation between the Community/EU and the ACP group, is now more explicitly described. All subjects of common, regional, or subregional interest can be discussed, from issues of peace and stability to development strategies and sectoral policies. Dialogue can take place formally or informally, inside or outside the institutional edifice, at regional, subregional, or national level. Representatives of regional, subregional and civil society organizations, as well as governments, can be associated with the dialogue.

For the first time, "peace building", "conflict prevention", and "conflict resolution" appear in the text. Article 11 of the Cotonou Agreement obliges the parties to take active roles in these fields within the framework of the partnership. The focus of the cooperation activities is to encompass capacity-building for conflict prevention, strengthening democratic legitimacy and good governance, establishing mechanisms for the peaceful conciliation of group interests, supporting civil society, and effectively managing natural resources. Other activities envisaged for support include the demobilizaton and reintegration of former combatants into society (including child soldiers); limiting military expenditure by the ACP states; removing landmines; preventing development aid from being diverted to military uses; preventing and limiting the spread of violence; seeking the peaceful resolution of existing disputes; and restoring post-conflict societies to self-sustaining development. The challenge for the Cotonou partners will be to carry out these new and ambitious activities successfully within the existing development budget, and to link them where necessary without recourse to military assistance, the use of which is not specified in the Agreement.

The Fourth Lomé Convention introduced controversial "essential elements", namely principles the nonobservance of which could result in the suspension of a state from the Convention. To the essential elements of respect for human rights, democratic principles, and the rule of law, as established in Lomé IV, the Cotonou Agreement adds "good governance", meaning transparent and accountable management, and the absence of serious corruption. The problems of applying standards of "good governance" to the ACP countries – and the question of whether the EU itself meets these standards of transparency, accountability, and noncorruption – remain to be addressed.

The amount of aid allocated to the EDF is often a very contentious issue for the ACP–EU partnership, but in the case of this new agreement there was little controversy over the EU's offer. As noted above, the ACP states did not succeed in getting the EU to offer a real increase in the aid package for the Cotonou Agreement (see Table 28.2). The European Commission argued that although, at a value of €15.2 billion, the aid package was not a real increase, efficiency gains would be achieved through quicker disbursement mechanisms. Administrative changes provided for within the

agreement are meant to simplify and thereby speed up project planning and implementation. The Commission also drew attention to the €9.9 billion left unspent from previous rounds as a handy addition to the resources available for 2000–07, rather than as an embarrassing sign of previously poor aid management. Welcome new provisions of the Cotonou Agreement provide for better integration of humanitarian or disaster relief aid, which is mainly allocated under the Community's budget, with the long-term development aid allocated under the EDF. This process should be facilitated because both EDF (development) aid and ECHO (humanitarian) aid now fall under the directorate of the European Commission.

The ACP group had succeeded in having provisions on their debt problems inserted in Lomé IV in 1990. The Community had previously argued that ACP states' debts were the province of the member states and not of the Community. The Lomé IV provisions on debt principally involved Community technical assistance for debt management, speeding up aid disbursements to debt-affected states, and awarding finance in the form of grants so as not to increase the debt burden. At the mid-term review of Lomé IV, in 1995, there had been little enthusiasm from the EU for discussing further the problem of debts. By contrast, the Cotonou Agreement explicitly allows the resources of the EDF to be used case by case directly for debt relief.

Another important area of improvement in the Cotonou Agreement is in its treatment of gender. While Lomé IV referred to "man, the main protagonist and beneficiary of development", Cotonou recognizes "development centred on the human person, who is the main protagonist and beneficiary of development". Lomé IV mentioned the importance of women as participants in, and beneficiaries of, development (Article 13), but it failed to make gender awareness a mainstream concern in many fields of development where women's contributions are vital. The Cotonou Agreement established a new standard for the partnership to take systematic account of gender and women's interests in all fields, political, economic, and social. Nevertheless, explicit references to gender or women's issues have not been incorporated into central areas of the agreement such as the political dialogue, references to civil society, provisions on agricultural development, food security, or trade.

Trade

The trade provisions of the Cotonou Agreement differ significantly from those of the successive Lomé Conventions. The bedrock of the Lomé system was the granting of nonreciprocal trade preferences for the developing countries. That is, manufactured goods and some noncompeting agricultural products from ACP countries were to have duty-free access to the Community's market, but, in recognition of their weaker economic status, the ACP states were not compelled to give Community products such preferential treatment. Some tropical products on which ACP economies were highly dependent, such as sugar or bananas, received special favourable treatment under protocols to the Lomé Conventions.

The problems with this system were numerous. On the one hand, trade preferences for developing countries in general are perceived not to have worked, partly because, as global tariff levels declined from an average of almost 40% in 1947 to less than 5% on manufactured goods by 1994, the margin of preference that developing countries could receive was greatly diminished. Moreover, Lomé trade preferences benefited or advantaged only about one third of total ACP exports. The main source of ACP export earnings, primary commodities, benefited relatively little from tariff preferences, because they tended to enter industrialized markets at low rates of duty in any case. Although the preferences for the ACP states were generous, at least as compared to the treatment of other countries, the ACP group's share of Community/EU trade fell rather than rose.

The objective of the Cotonou Agreement is not mainly to give developing countries special treatment, but to foster their gradual and seamless incorporation into the world economy, by helping them to expand their trade and meet the challenges of globalization. The agreement obliges the parties to move away from the Lomé system of nonreciprocal preferences and towards new trading arrangements compatible with the rules of the WTO. Trade barriers on both sides are to be progressively removed, and the rules of origin and cumulation are to be simplified for all least developed countries. The special commodity protocols for sugar, beef and veal, and bananas are to be reviewed, with the objective of safeguarding their benefits for the ACP countries but not necessarily the protocols themselves.

The main new characteristic of the Cotonou trade regime will be the gradual creation of reciprocal "economic partnership agreements" between the EU and groups of ACP countries, or in some cases single countries. Negotiations for the new arrangements will begin in 2002, with new agreements being instituted in 2008. Present ACP countries that fail to negotiate terms with the EU by 2008 risk having to fall back on the EU's Generalised System of Preferences for developing countries, a trade arrangement less favourable to their financial interests than the Lomé system was. Only the 39 least developed ACP countries will have the option of free, nonreciprocal access for almost all of their exports to the EU market by 2005, instead of negotiating economic partnership agreements.

Conclusion

The Treaty of Maastricht set out broad common objectives for the EU's development policy, including sustainable social and economic development, the integration of developing countries into the world economy, and the eradication of poverty. In practice, however, the EU is still struggling with difficult issues of aid administration and coordinating the policies of the member states. The EU confronts the challenge of turning its vision of being a global actor and a leading development policy-maker into an area of unquestioned competence.

The development priorities of the EU changed rapidly at the end of the 20th century. The end of the Cold War in particular precipitated significant new development thinking. In the mid-1990s the EU attempted to raise the profile of its relations with the Mediterranean region and Latin America. It sought to establish free trade areas in the Mediterranean, with Mercosur (the Southern Cone Common Market in South America), and with South Africa. Developing countries in Asia have received a high priority in speeches by EU decision-makers, but have received less attention in practice. Central America, which rose to an elevated level on the European Community's political agenda in the 1980s, became of less concern following the formal establishment of peace in the region.

During much of the 1990s the Lomé policy towards the EU's closest developing country partners, the now 77 ACP countries, drifted downwards on the EU's agenda. The Cotonou Agreement of 2000, which replaced Lomé, is almost universally described as possessing the potential to reinvigorate the partnership, but the EU now faces the task of proving the worth of the new arrangements in practice.

Further Reading

Babarinde, Olufemi, "The European Union's Relations with the South: A Commitment to Development?", in Carolyn Rhodes (editor), *The European Union in the World Community*, Boulder, CO: L. Rienner, 1998

A good overview of the EU's development policy and a critical assessment of its effectiveness

Cosgrove-Sacks, Carole (editor), *The European Union and Developing Countries: The Challenges of Globalization*, London: Macmillan, and New York: St Martin's Press, 1999

A large collection of studies by an international team of authors covering the forces shaping EU development policy and relations with the ACP states in the Mediterranean, Asia, and Latin America. The focus is on the way the policy is adapting to the new challenges of globalization and the end of the Cold War.

Directorate-General for Development, European Commission, website at www.europa.eu.int/comm/dgs/development/index_en.htm

This electronic source offers a great deal of useful material, including the text of the ACP–EU Partnership Agreement signed at Cotonou on 23 June 2000

European Commission, *Green Paper on Relations between the European Union and the ACP Countries on the Eve of the 21st Century*, Brussels, COM(96)570, November 1996

A useful survey of the EU's policy under the successive Lomé Conventions, with the Commission's proposals for its reform

European Commission, "The European Community's Development Policy", Communication from the Commission to the Council and the European Parliament, Brussels, COM(2000) 212 Final, 26 April 2000

The Commission's explanation of its proposals for a new approach to development policy in relation to the ACP states

European Parliament Working Group on the Future of ACP–EU Relations (rapporteur: Glenys Kinnock), *Final Report on the Future of ACP–EU Relations*, Strasbourg, AP/2880/B/Fin 2000

A critical assessment of the new partnership agreement that also provides interesting insights into the negotiations that led to it

Lister, Marjorie (editor), *New Perspectives on European Union Development Cooperation*, Boulder CO: Westview Press, 1999

A useful collection of chapters by an international team of scholars and development experts assessing the record of the EU's development policy under the Lomé Conventions and the prospect for the new partnership agreement with the ACP states. It includes discussion of issues that are often rather neglected in the development literature, such as gender, human rights, and democracy.

Lister, Marjorie, *The European Union and the South: Relations with Developing Countries*, London and New York: Routledge, 1997

A good introduction to the subject that places the EU policy in the context of the common foreign and security policy and Europe's colonial history. The main focus is on Lomé IV but it also includes a chapter on the EU's relations with its southern neighbours in the Mediterranean.

Overseas Development Institute, "The Effectiveness of EC Aid", London: Overseas Development Institute, June 2000

The text of a submission to an enquiry into the effectiveness of the European Community's development policy undertaken by the House of Commons Select Committee on International Development

---

Dr Marjorie Lister is Senior Lecturer in Politics in the Department of European Studies at the University of Bradford. She has lectured and written widely on the EU's external relations in general and its development policy in particular.

Table 28.1   EU Aid, by Sectoral Commitments, 1986 and 1998 (€ millions and %)

	1986 (€ millions)	1986 (% of total)	1998 (€ millions)	1998 (% of total)
Programme aid (Stabex, Sysmin)	159	6.2	974	11.3
Food aid	655	26.0	690	8.0
Humanitarian aid	80	3.1	936	10.9
Aid through nongovernmental organizations	49	1.9	204	2.4
Natural resources	163	6.4	437	5.1
Other productive sectors	214	8.4	592	6.9
Economic infrastructure and services	249	9.8	1850	21.5
transport and communications	130	5.1	928	10.8
energy	112	4.4	434	5.0
banking and finance	8	0.3	488	5.7
Social infrastructure and services	86	3.4	1291	15.0
education	13	0.5	450	5.2
health and population	24	0.9	313	3.6
water supply	49	1.9	293	3.4
other social	1	–	235	2.7
Governance and civil society	3	0.1	525	6.1
Crosscutting	89	3.5	481	5.6
environment	4	0.1	146	1.7
gender	0	0	13	0.2
rural development	7	0.3	215	2.5
other	78	3.1	107	1.2
Not attributable by sector	796	31.2	632	7.3
Total	2,553		8,614	

Source: European Commission, "The European Community's Development Policy", Communication from the Commission to the Council and the European Parliament, COM(2000)212 Final, Brussels, 26 April 2000

Table 28.2   EU Aid to the ACP States under the Cotonou Agreement, 2000–07 (€ millions)

Total new money (Ninth European Development Fund)	15,200
grants and risk capital	13,500
European Investment Bank loans	1,700
Unspent balances from previous EDFs	9,900
Total funds available	25,100

Source: ACP–EU Partnership Agreement, signed at Cotonou on 23 June 2000

Figure 28.1   The African, Caribbean, and Pacific States

The African	Congo (Brazzaville)	Liberia	Seychelles
Countries	Congo (Kinshasha)	Madagascar	Sierra Leone
Angola	Côte d'Ivoire	Malawi	Somalia
Benin	Djibouti	Mali	South Africa
Botswana	Equatorial Guinea	Mauritania	Sudan
Burkina Faso	Eritrea	Mauritius	Swaziland
Burundi	Ethiopia	Mozambique	Tanzania
Cameroun	Gabon	Namibia	Togo
Cape Verde	Gambia	Niger	Uganda
Central African	Ghana	Nigeria	Zambia
Republic	Guinea	Rwanda	Zimbabwe
Chad	Guinea-Bissau	Sao Tome and	
Comoros	Kenya	Principe	
	Lesotho	Senegal	

The Caribbean

Antigua and Barbuda	Dominican Republic	Saint Kitts and Nevis
The Bahamas	Grenada	Saint Lucia
Barbados	Guyana	Saint Vincent and the Grenadines
Belize	Haiti	Suriname
Dominica	Jamaica	Trinidad and Tobago

The Islands of the Pacific

Fiji	Samoa	Vanuatu
Kiribati	Solomon Islands	Wallis and Futuna
New Caledonia	Tonga	
Papua-New Guinea	Tuvalu	

Figure 28.2   Personnel in EU Bilateral Agencies, European Commission, and World Bank

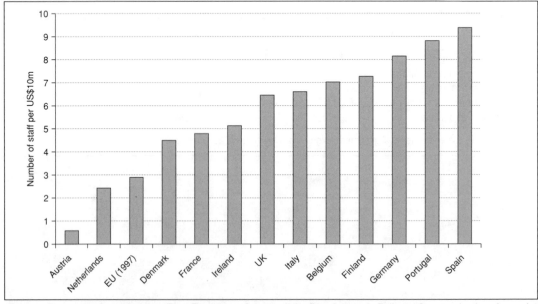

Source: European Commission, "The European Community's Development Policy", Communication from the Commission to the Council and the European Parliament, COM(2000)212 Final, Brussels, 26 April 2000

Future

Chapter Twenty-Nine

The EU of the Future: Federal or Intergovernmental?

John Pinder

European nation-states have become intensely interdependent. They can no longer discharge their responsibilities with respect to the economy, security, or ecology except by working together. Their citizens need a large, open economy in which the new technologies can flourish; they need effective control over cross-border pollution; and they need a stable European system that minimizes threats to security. The EU will stand or fall by its contribution to fulfilling these conditions of citizens' well-being.

The Union's success will depend on its political structure. There are two opposing views as to the structure most apt to succeed: federal institutions, providing a new, EU layer of democratic government for those matters that interdependence has placed beyond the reach of the states acting separately; or cooperation among the governments of the several states, an intergovernmental system. Between a federal and an intergovernmental system there is a spectrum of arrangements, within which the Union now stands. A comparison of the federal and intergovernmental alternatives may help to clarify the prospects for the Union's development in one or the other direction.

A Federal Polity

There are already many federal elements in the powers and institutions of the EU; and the federal idea remains an important influence on the Union's development. Yet that idea has been obscured by political controversy. A clear definition is needed.

A federal polity divides public powers between at least two levels of government. The federal powers normally include at least trade, currency, security, and some elements of taxation; and powers not attributed to the federal level remain with the member states. Each level of government has its own democratic institutions. There is a federal legislature, comprising a house of the people and a house of the states, which enacts the laws and to which the federal executive, or government, is responsible, except in presidential systems, where the executive is responsible directly to the citizens. The rule of federal law is ensured by a federal judiciary. The citizens relate directly to the federal institutions, not just indirectly, through the governments of the member states; nor are the federal institutions subordinate to those governments, although the governments may be represented in the house of the states, as in the German Bundesrat.

The idea of a European federal constitution was strongly promoted by British federalists in the years up to 1940 and constitutions were drafted by distinguished jurists such as W. Ivor Jennings in *A Federation for Western Europe* (see Jennings, Mackay, and Pinder 1986 pp. 26–155). Their thinking was transmitted to the postwar European federalist movement, in particular by the Italian federalist leader Altiero Spinelli (see Mayne and Pinder 1990 pp. 83–85). Following the first direct elections to the European Parliament in 1979, Spinelli secured the Parliament's approval in 1984 of a draft Treaty on European Union, which amounted to a federal constitution; and the Parliament produced a second draft in 1994 (see European Parliament 1984, 1994). The idea of a federal constitution remains influential in several member states, but some governments have resisted it, so many federalists have resorted to proceeding by a succession of federal steps.

Proceeding by Federal Steps

The Declaration by the French Foreign Minister Robert Schuman on 9 May 1950, which launched the creation of the European Coal and Steel Community, described it as "a first step in the federation of Europe" and as "the first concrete foundation of European federation, which is indispensable to the preservation of peace". The idea of proceeding by a series of steps, or building blocks, came from the principal founder of the Community, the Frenchman Jean Monnet, who was responsible for the Schuman Declaration; and the Community has indeed developed in that way. Successive building blocks have included the Treaties of Rome, the direct elections to the European Parliament, the Single European Act, the Treaty on European Union (the Maastricht Treaty), and the Amsterdam Treaty, each block putting in place powers or institutional elements that could eventually become part of a federal structure (see Pinder 1993 pp. 45–47).

The Treaties have by now given the Union substantial elements of a federal system (see Pinder 1998 Chapter 10). It has powers in the fields of trade, currency, the environment, and the budget, together with advancing cooperation on internal and external security. Its institutions include what amounts to a federal judiciary; a two-house legislature, in which the European Parliament, representing the citizens, has growing legislative power, although the Council, representing the states, is still the more powerful legislative body and dominates policy on internal and external security; and an executive, the European Commission, which has considerable federal competences, although here again the Council has maintained close control. The Maastricht Treaty has recognized a form of citizenship and citizens have direct relations with the Union's institutions, apart from the Council.

The Union still falls short of being a federal polity, however, since it lacks a number of essential elements. Although the European Parliament has equal legislative power with the Council for more than half the volume of legislation, it is only consulted, and in some cases is ignored, regarding the rest. The Council votes by a qualified majority for some four fifths of the legislation, but unanimity prevails on matters such as taxation and predominates in the field of foreign and security policy. The Commission, while having significant executive powers and being increasingly accountable to the Parliament, is still dominated by the Council. In short, before the Union's institutions could properly be called federal, it would have to go further towards making qualified majority voting in the Council the general rule, giving the Parliament equal legislative power with the Council, and giving the Commission full executive competences. As regards the Union's powers, completion of Economic and Monetary Union should, despite current weaknesses such as the British opt-out, provide it with the principal remaining powers required to make it a federal system in fields other than security, where it is as yet far short of approaching federal powers and likely to remain so for a considerable time to come.

The forces that have impelled the Community to incorporate these federal elements are still influential. They include powerful economic interests that have promoted the customs union, the single market, and the single currency, in order to create an economic base in which Community business can be internationally competitive. The strongest political interests are the drives of both France and Germany to establish a framework within which member states can be sure of having stable relationships with each other, and with Germany in particular. This motive is shared by most of the other states, whose leaders are conscious of the dangers that could arise from instability. Support for developing the political framework as a federal parliamentary democracy has been strongest in those states, in particular Germany, Italy, Belgium, and the Netherlands, which may be described as institutionally federalist.

A number of leading statesmen have promoted federal steps. Among Monnet's generation were Konrad Adenauer, Alcide De Gasperi, Robert Schuman, and Paul-Henri Spaak. Later came Valéry Giscard d'Estaing, Roy Jenkins, Jacques Delors, François Mitterrand, and Helmut Kohl. Leading German Christian Democrats have consistently favoured reform of the Union's institutions "to make its structures and procedures more democratic and federal" (Schäuble and Lamers p. 15), and in May 2000 Joschka Fischer, Foreign Minister in Germany's Centre Left government, affirmed his aim of "transition from a union of states to full parliamentarization as a European Federation" (Fischer p. 16), thus linking his ideas with those of the constitutional federalists.

There is a substantial literature that views the development of the Union in this light (see, for example, Baròn, Burgess, and Pinder 1998 and 2001), but these ideas are opposed by those who prefer intergovernmental cooperation to federal integration.

Intergovernmentalist Critique of Federalism

"There is and can be no Europe other than a Europe of the states – except of course for myths, fictions and pageants": thus the French President, Charles de Gaulle, expressed his opposition to Community federalism in May 1962 (see de Gaulle). In more mundane language, the former British Prime Minister Margaret Thatcher criticized the federalists in a speech in Bruges in 1988 as wanting a "remote, centralized, bureaucratic organization" that would "suppress nationhood", and insisted that instead "we should keep power at the national level" (see Thatcher 1988 p. 4 and Thatcher 1993 p. 23). She saw the European Parliament as a "remote, multilingual parliament, accountable to no real European public opinion and thus increasingly subordinate to a powerful bureaucracy" (Thatcher 1993 p. 27). Following Thatcher's lead, there has been a flow of antifederalist literature in Britain since the early 1990s. The Commission has been criticized as a bureaucratic, unelected body, usurping the rights of the member states' governments; and the European Court of Justice has been called an "activist" court, which "decides the extent of the Community's pow-

ers" and "displays the basic features of a federal state". It has been suggested that there is no need for a "Community legal order": the Treaties and the member states' courts should suffice (Howe 1993 p. 105). Power should remain with the member states, and their representatives in the Council should as far as possible proceed by unanimity, thus retaining the veto to prevent decisions unwelcome to any single one.

The competences of the Union are criticized by many intergovernmentalists as too far-reaching. They oppose the single currency, not only as an economic straitjacket but also on the grounds that it "predetermines the creation of a federal political union and the abolition of the nation state" (Spicer p. 187; see also Redwood). Conservative intergovernmentalists tend to regard the drift of Union policy as corporatist, *dirigiste*, and protectionist, and to resent what they see as the "collectivist economic and social philosophy" of the Commission and European Court of Justice (Harris p. 129). Against that view, there have been left-wing attacks on the integration process as capitalist and subservient to the multinational companies (see, for example, Holland). Both rightwing and leftwing critics of federalism insist that internal and external security must remain the preserve of intergovernmental cooperation.

A federal Europe has also been criticized as subjecting other Europeans to German domination. Thatcher believed that Europe without the United States "will still find the question of German power insoluble". For her, in so far as Europeans themselves have to counter German power, they should do so through coalitions of nation-states, not within federal institutions (Thatcher 1993 pp. 20–21). A more federal, or "deeper", Union is also criticized as making the accession of states in central and eastern Europe more difficult. Intergovernmentalists tend to want a looser and more flexible Union, reaching, in the view of some, as far as Belarus and Ukraine (Brunner p. 46), or even Russia (Séguin p. 54), or, echoing de Gaulle's rhetoric, stretching from the Atlantic to the Urals (Hill p. 232), although most would not include members of the Commonwealth of Independent States (CIS).

Mainstream intergovernmentalism envisages, then, a Union based on cooperation among governments. There is a tendency to seek to reduce the scope of the Union in favour of international organizations such as the UN, the IMF, the World Bank, NATO, and the Organization for Security and Cooperation in Europe (Thatcher 1993 p. 30). Federalism is held to lead, in Thatcher's words, to "a European superstate exercising a new dominance from Brussels" (Thatcher 1988 p. 4); or, in a formulation by Philippe Séguin, a leading Gaullist Eurosceptic, the Maastricht Treaty was intended to lead "implacably to the emergence of a federal superstate" (Séguin p. 51).

Proposals for Intergovernmental Reform

There are radical intergovernmentalists who wish to convert the EU into an international organization in which each member state would be free to choose which policies to adopt, or who would even scrap the Union altogether. More influential are those who prefer to retain the single market and the institutions required to make it work, while allowing member states to opt into or out of intergovernmental cooperation in other fields. Among these is a group that drafted a European constitution along such lines (see European Constitutional Group).

This group's constitution would both vest executive power in the European Council of Heads of State or Government and the Council of Ministers, and reinforce the Council's domination of the legislative process. The European Parliament, renamed the Union Chamber, would be joined by a Chamber of Parliamentarians containing representatives from the member states' parliaments. The Union Chamber would have the power to reject bills by a majority of 80% of its members, which would be extremely difficult to attain; it would otherwise be consultative. The Chamber of Parliamentarians could reject bills by a simple majority, on the grounds either that they would go beyond the scope of the constitution or that the aim could be secured by the member states without action by the Union.

The Commission's executive role would be reduced and its exclusive right to initiate legislation would be removed. Cases concerning the extent of the Union's powers would be judged, not by the European Court of Justice, but by a court of judges from the supreme courts of member states. Union law would, however, prevail, in order to enable the single market to be effectively applied, in contrast with the demand of more radical intergovernmentalists for the primacy of national law (see Séguin p. 53 and Spicer p. 195).

For matters other than the single market or the constitution, any member state could opt out of the application of any or all Union laws, and simple majorities of the Council and the Chamber of Parliamentarians could repatriate any power from the Union. A neoliberal policy of minimal regulation, protection, and public expenditure at Union level would be entrenched in the constitution and existing Union regulations could be abolished by simple majority vote. Agricultural protection would be sharply restricted and the aim would be to lower progressively, and ultimately to prohibit, all protection of any kind. There would be an overwhelming bias towards reduction of the Union's expenditure, with approval of the budget requiring a qualified majority of 80% in the Council, including each of the five largest states, and with any net contributor entitled to veto either the total budget or any individual item.

This intergovernmentalist constitution offers a coherent and logical outline of a minimalist Union, with federal elements in the institutions removed as far as is compatible with a plausible single market; with the right for member states to opt out of all powers and laws save those required for the single market; and with entrenched policies for deregulation, free trade, and minimal expenditure. This responds in many respects to Thatcher's call for "a Community of sovereign states committed to voluntary cooperation, a lightly regulated free market, and international free trade" (Thatcher 1993 p. 23), although it sets greater store on underpinning the single market by the rule of law.

The draft constitution was followed by a book providing a theoretical basis for its orientation (see Vibert). The pattern of representative government prevailing in member states was rejected as unsuitable for a multinational union. The Council would become the European government, the Commission its civil service, and the European "assembly" would be mainly consultative, with a new chamber, representing member states' parliaments, empowered to vote down legislation, as had been proposed in the group's draft constitution. The book was followed by a study group on reforming the Union, whose report, while it contained a number of the earlier group's ideas, presented them alongside more integrationist proposals, to provide a wideranging set of options for reform (see ICRI).

Federalist Critique of Intergovernmentalism

From a federalist viewpoint, the intergovernmentalist proposals are undemocratic, ineffective, too narrow to meet the needs of citizens, and apt to lead eventually to disintegration of the Union.

Federalists criticize the Council as it stands today for legislating in an undemocratic way, with no public access to its legislative sessions. Since the ministers cannot spend much time together, the task of reaching agreement on the laws falls heavily on the committees of member states' officials that prepare the Council's work for it. Given the way in which a multinational committee of officials works, the proceedings are opaque and byzantine; and the larger the number of member states, the more byzantine they are likely to become. The intergovernmentalist reassertion of the power of the Council would shift the Union yet further away from normal democratic principles of legislation.

Federalists also criticize the Council because it exercises executive powers along with its legislative role, without being accountable to any parliamentary chamber, whereas the draft intergovernmentalist constitution would reinforce the Council's dominance in both fields together.

Federalists see intergovernmental cooperation as not only undemocratic but also ineffective in taking decisions and applying the rule of law. They fear that a weakening of the Court of Justice would undermine the effectiveness of the rule of law, which has done much to civilize power relationships within the Union. They also doubt that committees of 15 member states' officials, and soon more, all responsible to their respective ministers, can act as efficiently as the Commission in ensuring the execution of Union policy. Nor would federalists regard it as feasible to entrench particular policy orientations constitutionally, as that draft constitution proposed. A Union constitution should be seen, rather, as defining the institutional framework within which policies would be determined.

Federalists also doubt whether a Union could be sustained if its only solid field of policy, free from opting out, would be the single market. Cohesion policy is seen as necessary to temper the pain that the market may inflict on the weaker parts of the Union's economy. Economic and monetary union is seen as the completion of the single market, and as a consequence of the interdependence of financial markets. The development of a federal system is also seen as an essential response to the growing interdependence in matters of security: internal, external, and environmental.

If political power is to be exercised jointly to deal with the problems of interdependence in these fields, federalists argue that it must be exercised by an effective executive, or government, accountable to elected representatives and subject to the rule of law. They see the intergovernmental method as inadequate to meet Europe's needs. They fear that failure to deal with pressing common problems will lead to disillusion about the Union; that the more powerful member states will lose interest in the Union and resort to more traditional diplomatic methods; that opting out will become the general rule; and that, as the number of member states increases, the Union's capacity for decision and action will decline. They fear that the Union will eventually disintegrate if the intergovernmental approach prevails.

The Future: Federal or Intergovernmental?

The easiest prediction is a straight-line projection. If the Union is static, it will continue more or less unchanged. Forecasts along these lines were made for the 1970s, following the blockage of the Community's development by France under de Gaulle, and were again made for the 1990s after Britain had played a similar role (see Lindberg and Scheingold Chapter 9, and Milward p. 439). Following the development of the Union in the 1990s, it may be tempting to predict that such progress will continue or, following some recent trends, that the Union will remain as it stands at the dawn of the 21st century. However, beyond the medium term, member states and their citizens are not likely to support a Union that fails to respond to their common interests with an effective and democratic form of government.

As interdependence and the problems arising from it continue to grow; it will become increasingly evident that effective government is needed to deal with them; and for democratic European countries, government has to be democratically responsible. A Union with the present mix of intergovernmental and federal elements will inhibit member states from acting decisively with their own institutions and powers, while remaining unable itself to cope with some of the most critical problems. The further the Union is enlarged into central and eastern Europe, the more inadequate the present mixture will become. If a sufficiently effective and democratic government does not emerge for the Union, member states, and the larger ones in particular, will insist on taking independent action themselves.

Some, particularly in Britain, do not want to wait before shifting the Union in that direction. The more extreme rejectionists would disrupt the Union or resort to secession. Closer to the mainstream are those who would retain the single market, recognizing that it requires qualified majority voting and the rule of law, but introduce "flexibility" for the rest of the Union's affairs, with the right for any member state to opt out of all laws or policies that are not approved by unanimity in the Council. The outstanding case at present is the refusal of Britain, Denmark, and Sweden to participate in the single currency, but there are other examples, and they could proliferate. It has been suggested that such flexibility would cause "a growing political and legal fragmentation"

of the Union, and hence "the risk of disintegration" (Monar pp. 32 and 40); and it is indeed doubtful whether the single market could survive as an island of integration in a sea of flexibility. Governments feeling their states to be losers would become reluctant to cooperate and even to fulfil their obligations. Support would ebb away as the Union disappointed citizens' expectations that it will deal with common problems in fields such as cohesion, the environment, crime, and general economic policy. The democratic processes within the states would be a centrifugal force if democracy remains underdeveloped at Union level.

Fear of this has led many, particularly among the six states that founded the Community, to advocate the creation of a core group to move ahead together towards further integration. One such proposal was made in June 2000 by the French President, Jacques Chirac, who suggested a "pioneer group" that would participate in "all the spheres of reinforced cooperation"; he mentioned in particular economic policy coordination, security and defence, and the fight against crime. The group would be open to all member states that wished to participate and would have a "flexible cooperation mechanism", serviced by a secretariat for "ensuring the consistency of [their] positions and policies" (Chirac p. 16).

Chirac launched his proposal in a speech to the German Bundestag, and clearly envisaged that the core group would be led by France and Germany. However, while such an informal intergovernmental arrangement might initiate the development of a more solid core within the Union, it would itself be too weak to ensure the "consistency of the positions and policies" of the group's members for any significant length of time. Hence there have been proposals to establish a federal core within the Union, such as that put forward in May 2000 by Germany's Foreign Minister, Joschka Fischer, to which Chirac's idea was an intergovernmentalist response.

Fischer's proposal was that a pioneer group should construct a federation within the Union (Fischer pp. 16–25). The group would create a "centre of gravity" for the EU with "a new European framework treaty, the nucleus of a constitution of the Federation". The group would have its own institutions, establishing "a government which within the EU would speak with one voice on behalf of the members of the group on as many issues as possible" (Fischer p. 23). While the group would at first comprise those states that were ready and willing, the aim would be to lead the Union as a whole to become a federal polity. An alternative outcome might be that nonparticipating states would form a relationship with the federal core akin to the European Economic Area that now links Iceland, Liechtenstein, and Norway with the EU's single market. Alternatively, given the difficulty of establishing a federation as a separate entity within the Union, the project could fail, thus strengthening the forces of intergovernmentalism throughout. Nevertheless, whether by means of a successful core group or through reform of the EU itself, the Union is at least as likely to be converted into a federal system.

The central, Community pillar of the Union is not as far as is generally supposed from becoming an effective and democratic system of federal government. The rule of Community law is already ensured under the aegis of the Court of Justice. The extension of co-decision between Parliament and Council to virtually the whole of legislation, as in a federal system, is a realistic prospect. The Commission, accountable to the Parliament and the Council, has many of the powers of a federal executive, although the retention of some executive powers by the Council is a substantial element of intergovernmentalism that could frustrate the development of effective federal government. Without the completion of a democratic legislative process and of an effective federal executive, the Community could revert to a predominantly intergovernmental Community system; and the opt-outs from the single currency in particular remain a serious weakness. Even so, a federal Community remains a feasible prospect.

Giving federal institutions responsibility for the Union's common foreign and security policy (CFSP), and for the military aspects of security in particular, is a different matter. While a federal system for the Community pillar may not be far off, cooperation in the field of defence is at an early stage and still entirely intergovernmental. The integration of armed forces that would follow from Union responsibility for defence would convert the Union into a federal state; and this would have to be developed by a series of steps over what could be a long period. A resurgence of intergovernmentalism in the Community itself would, meanwhile, remain possible, but a successful federal Community at the heart of the Union would provide a pole of attraction for federal development in the field of security too.

Whatever the course of policy in the nearer future, it is not possible to predict whether the Union will, in the longer term, move towards a federal or an intergovernmental system from its present unstable equilibrium between the two. One cannot be confident that the forces that favour federal powers and institutions to deal with ever-growing interdependence will be stronger than the forces that seek to preserve the independence of the nation-states. However, what a federalist – and the reader will doubtless be aware by now that this writer is one – may confidently predict is that intergovernmental cooperation will fail to master the problems that come with interdependence, whereas a federal polity could offer the citizens of the EU a better prospect of economic well-being, a healthy environment, and freedom from threats to their security.

Further Reading

Baròn, Enrique, *Europe at the Dawn of the Millennium*, London: Macmillan, and New York: St Martin's Press, 1997

An illuminating and readable account of the EU by a former President of the European Parliament

An important contribution on this theme

Brunner, Manfred, "Functional Realities of Trade, Sovereignty and Democracy", in Stephen Hill (editor), as cited below

Burgess, Michael, *Federalism and European Union: The Building of Europe, 1950–2000*, London and New York: Routledge, 2000

Chirac, Jacques, *Our Europe*, speech given at the Bundestag, 27 June 2000, London: The Federal Trust, 2000

The President of France proposes a core group within the Union, organized intergovernmentally.

Duff, Andrew, John Pinder, and Roy Pryce (editors), *Maastricht and Beyond: Building the European Union*, London and New York: Routledge, 1994

A comprehensive study of the main elements of the Maastricht Treaty with implications for the Union's future development

European Constitutional Group, *A Proposal for a European Constitution*, London: European Policy Forum, 1993

A coherent proposal for an intergovernmentalist Union of neoliberal orientation, containing a draft constitution and an explanatory text

European Parliament, *Draft Treaty Establishing the European Union*, Luxembourg: European Parliament, February 1984

A pioneering proposal for a treaty of a federal type, inspired by Altiero Spinelli

European Parliament, *Second Report of the Institutional Committee on the Constitution of the European Union*, Rapporteur Fernand Herman, European Parliament A3-0064/94; and European Parliament, "Resolution on the Constitution of the European Union", *Minutes of the Sitting*, 10 February 1994

A successor to the draft treaty cited above

Fischer, Joschka, *From Confederation to Federation: Thoughts on the Finality of European Integration*, London: The Federal Trust, 2000

A bold speech by the German Foreign Minister, delivered on 12 May 2000 at the Humboldt University, Berlin, advocating action by a group of member states in order to develop the EU into a federation over the long term.

Gaulle, President Charles de, Press Conference, 15 May 1962

Harris, Ralph (Lord Harris of High Cross), "Alors, Delors! Deceiver or Dunce?" in Stephen Hill (editor), as cited below

Hill, Stephen (editor), *Visions of Europe: Summing up the Political Choices*, London: Duckworth, 1993

A collection of essays, mostly by anti-Maastricht politicians and academics advocating intergovernmental cooperation

Holland, Stuart, *UnCommon Market: Capital, Class and Power in the European Community*, London:

Macmillan, and New York: St Martin's Press, 1980

The title expresses the author's view at the time

Howe, Martin, "Justice and the European Superstate", in Stephen Hill (editor), as cited above

ICRI: Independent Commission for the Reform of the Institutions and Procedures of the Union, *Advancing the Union*, London: European Policy Forum, 1999

A wideranging review of proposals for reform of the Union.

Jennings, W. Ivor, *A Federation for Western Europe*, Cambridge: Cambridge University Press, and New York: Macmillan, 1940

Contains an elegant constitution drafted by an eminent jurist

Lamers, Karl, *A German Agenda for the European Union*, London: The Federal Trust and Konrad Adenauer Stiftung, 1994

This contains an English translation of the German CDU/CSU paper by Wolfgang Schäuble and Karl Lamers, which proposed the creation of a core group of member states as a step towards a federal EU.

Lindberg, Leon N., and Stuart A. Scheingold, *Europe's Would-be Polity: Patterns of Change in the European Community*, Hemel Hempstead and Englewood Cliffs, NJ: Prentice-Hall, 1970

A neofunctionalist text, predicting a largely static Community

Mackay, R.W.G., *Federal Europe*, London: Michael Joseph, 1940; reprinted Holmes Beach, FL: Gaunt, 1999

Mackay, who advocated a federation, presents a draft constitution.

Mayne, Richard, and John Pinder, with John C. de V. Roberts, *Federal Union: The Pioneers – A History of Federal Union*, London: Macmillan, and New York: St Martin's Press, 1990

The story of a British federalist movement

Milward, Alan S., *The European Rescue of the Nation-State*, London: Routledge, and Berkeley: University of California Press, 1992

Milward shows how the European Community provided a context for the preservation of national welfare states.

Monar, Jörg, "The Future of European Governance", in Otto von der Gablentz, Dieter Mahncke, Pier-Carlo Padoan, and Robert Picht (editors), *Europe 2020: Adapting to a Changing World*, Baden-Baden: Nomos Verlagsgesellschaft for the College of Europe, 2000

Pinder, John, "Federal Union 1939–41", in Walter Lipgens (editor), *Documents on the History of European Integration, Vol.2, Plans for European Union in Great Britain and in Exile 1939–1945*, Berlin and New York: de Gruyter, 1986

Pinder, John, "The New European Federalism: The Idea and the Achievements", in Michael Burgess and Alain-G. Gagnon (editors), *Comparative Federalism and Federation*, London: Harvester Wheatsheaf, and Toronto: University of Toronto Press, 1993

An explanation of a "stepwise" approach to a federal Europe

Pinder, John, *The Building of the European Union*, third edition, Oxford and New York: Oxford University Press, 1998

An account of the development of the EC/EU from a federalist perspective

Pinder, John, *The European Union: A Very Short Introduction*, Oxford and New York: Oxford University Press, 2001

Another account from a federalist perspective, but more concise and less academic

Redwood, John, *Our Currency, Our Country: The Dangers of European Monetary Union*, London and New York: Penguin, 1997

A leading British Conservative Eurosceptic's criticism of the EMU project

Schäuble, Wolfgang, and Karl Lamers, "Reflections on European Policy", report reproduced in English in Karl Lamers, as cited above

Séguin, Philippe, "*La politique autrement*: Reform it Altogether", in Stephen Hill (editor), as cited above

Spicer, Michael, *A Treaty Too Far: A New Policy for Europe*, London: Fourth Estate, 1992

A Eurosceptic view of Maastricht

Thatcher, Margaret, *Britain and Europe*, text of a speech delivered in Bruges by the British Prime Minister on 20 September 1988, London: Conservative Political Centre, 1988

Mrs (now Baroness) Thatcher warns against a centralized "superstate" and advocates intergovernmental cooperation.

Thatcher, Margaret, "Europe's Present Political Architecture", in Stephen Hill (editor), as cited above

Vibert, Frank, *Europe: A Constitution for the Millennium*, Aldershot: Dartmouth, 1995

A theoretical basis for an intergovernmentalist constitution

John Pinder is Honorary Professor of the College of Europe, Bruges, Chairman of the Federal Trust, and Honorary President of the Union of European Federalists. He was Director of the Policy Studies Institute, London, from 1964 to 1985. In addition to the publications cited above, he is the author of *Altiero Spinelli and the British Federalists: Writings by Beveridge, Robbins and Spinelli, 1937–1943* (1998) and editor of *Foundations of Democracy in the European Union: From the Genesis of Parliamentary Democracy to the European Parliament* (1999).

Appendices

Appendix 1

Chronology

1944	**July**	Representatives of Resistance movements meeting in Zürich issue a declaration calling for the creation of a European federal union once peace has been restored.
1947	**March**	The "Truman Doctrine" is announced by the US government, promising support for democratic governments that are under threat from Communism.
		The Treaty of Dunkirk is signed, creating a military alliance between France and the United Kingdom.
		Belgium, Luxembourg, and the Netherlands decide to establish a customs union.
	June	The US government launches the Marshall Plan for the economic reconstruction of Europe.
	October	The General Agreement on Tariffs and Trade (GATT) is established.
1948	**January**	The "Benelux" customs union between Belgium, the Netherlands, and Luxembourg comes into operation.
	March	The Treaty of Brussels, signed by France, the United Kingdom, and the three Benelux states, sets out their common aims of providing collective security and encouraging cooperation in economic, social, and cultural spheres.
	April	The Organization for European Economic Cooperation (OEEC) is established, with 16 founding member states, to act as the managing agency for US financial assistance given under the terms of the Marshall Plan.
	May	The Congress of Europe, attended by nearly 700 representatives from 16 European states, meets in the Hague and passes a resolution calling for the creation of "an economic and political union in order to assure security and social progress". Often seen as the high point of postwar European federalism, this ambitious proposal is subsequently modified as a result of pressure from governments opposed to the creation of supranational institutions.
1949	**April**	The Treaty of Washington, establishing the North Atlantic Treaty Organization (NATO), is signed by the United States, Canada and ten states in western Europe.
	May	The Council of Europe is founded in Strasbourg as an intergovernmental consultative forum on all matters other than defence. The advent of the Cold War effectively restricts membership of the Council of Europe to states in western Europe, although membership is formally open to all European states.
1950	**May**	The French Foreign Minister, Robert Schuman, calls for the coal and steel industries of France and West Germany to be placed under a common supranational authority, and for other European states to be invited to participate in the new organization. The date of the publication of what has since been known as the Schuman Plan, 9 May, is now celebrated as "Europe Day".
	June	A committee chaired by Jean Monnet begins work on the implementation of the Schuman Plan, and the establishment of the European Coal and Steel Community.

	October	The French Prime Minister, René Pleven, calls for the creation of a European Defence Community in a document now known as the Pleven Plan.
	November	The European Convention on the Protection of Human Rights and Fundamental Freedoms is agreed by the Council of Europe.
1951	**April**	The Treaty of Paris establishes the European Coal and Steel Community (ECSC) with six member states: Belgium, France, Italy, Luxembourg, the Netherlands, and West Germany.
1952	**May**	The founding treaty of the European Defence Community (EDC) is signed in Paris by the six member states of the ECSC.
	July	The ECSC comes into operation.
1953	**March**	A draft treaty on a European Political Community is agreed by the member states of the ECSC.
1954	**August**	The French National Assembly rejects the EDC treaty. Both the EDC and the European Political Community projects collapse.
	October	The Treaty of Brussels (March 1948) is modified and extended to include Italy and West Germany, and the Brussels Treaty Organization is transformed into the Western European Union.
1955	**June**	A conference of ECSC foreign ministers is convened at Messina to consider the next steps towards European integration.
	July	The Spaak Committee is set up to consider proposals for further integration.
1956	**June**	The member states of the ECSC open discussions on the creation of a European Economic Community and a European Atomic Energy Community.
1957	**February**	The United Kingdom proposes a European free trade association.
	March	The Treaties of Rome, establishing the European Economic Community (EEC) and the European Atomic Energy Community (Euratom), are signed by six founding states that are already members of the ECSC: Belgium, France, Italy, Luxembourg, the Netherlands, and West Germany.
	October	The OEEC establishes a committee to try to secure agreement on a free trade area for the whole of western Europe, in the hope of avoiding an economic rift between the founding states of the EEC and the non-EEC states.
1958	**January**	The Treaties of Rome establishing the EEC and Euratom come into effect.
1960	**January**	The Stockholm Convention, establishing the European Free Trade Association (EFTA), is signed by seven founding member states: Denmark, Sweden, Norway, Austria, Portugal, Switzerland, and the United Kingdom.
	May	The Stockholm Convention comes into effect.
	December	The OEEC is reorganized, and renamed the Organization for Economic Cooperation and Development (OECD), following failure to agree on a free trade area for the whole of western Europe.
1961	**July**	The Fouchet Plan is proposed for a "union of states" that accords with the preference, expressed by President Charles de Gaulle of France among others, for an approach to integration focused on nation-states rather than federalism.
		An Association Agreement signed between the EEC and Greece.
		Ireland applies to join the EEC.
	August	The United Kingdom and Denmark apply for membership of the EEC.
	October	Enlargement negotiations begin between the EEC and the United Kingdom, Ireland, and Denmark.

1962	**January**	The EEC adopts the first regulations to create a common agricultural policy (CAP).
	April	Norway applies for membership of the EEC.
1963	**January**	Charles de Gaulle, President of France, vetoes British membership of the EEC. Ireland and Denmark withdraw their applications.
		A Treaty of Friendship and Cooperation is signed between France and West Germany.
	July	The first Yaoundé Convention is signed between the EEC and 18 African states.
	September	An Association Agreement is signed between the EEC and Turkey.
1964	**May**	The "Kennedy Round" of GATT negotiations opens. A single delegation, led by the Commission, negotiates on behalf of the member states of the EEC .
	June	The Yaoundé Convention comes into force.
1965	**April**	A Merger Treaty is signed creating a single Council of Ministers and a single Commission for the three Communities (ECSC, EEC, and Euratom). The term "European Communities" (abbreviated as "EC") comes into use from this time.
	June	President Charles de Gaulle instigates a French boycott of EC institutions to try to prevent any further "supranational" developments.
1966	**January**	The member states of the EC agree the "Luxembourg compromise", which enables France to resume its participation in EC institutions but preserves the use of the national veto in the Council of Ministers.
1967	**May**	Denmark, Ireland, and the United Kingdom apply again for EC membership.
	July	The Merger Treaty signed in April 1965 comes into effect.
		Norway applies for EC membership.
	November	President de Gaulle vetoes British membership of the EC for the second time.
	December	The Council of Ministers continues to be deeply divided over enlargement and cannot reach agreement on the opening of accession negotiations.
1968	**July**	The EC customs union is completed with the abolition of all customs duties and quotas on intra-EC trade, and the adoption of the common external tariff.
1969	**April**	Resignation of President de Gaulle
	July	Georges Pompidou, the new President of France, declares that he has no objection in principle to British membership of the EC.
		The second Yaoundé Convention is signed.
	December	At a summit meeting in the Hague the heads of state and government of the EC agree on a set of major initiatives covering enlargement, institutional reform, cooperation on foreign policy (known as European Political Cooperation, or EPC), and the establishment of economic and monetary union by 1980.
1970	**April**	The EC's member states agree a new system for financing its activities through its "own resources", rather than direct national contributions.
		A Treaty Amending Certain Budgetary Provisions provides the EC with a new financial structure and increases the budgetary powers of the European Parliament.
	June	The EC opens membership negotiations with Ireland, Denmark, Norway, and the United Kingdom.
		A preferential trade agreement is signed with Spain.

	October	Two influential reports are published: the Werner Report on Economic and Monetary Union, and the Davignon Report on European Political Cooperation.
		The preferential trade agreement with Spain comes into effect.
1971	**January**	The second Yaoundé Convention comes into force.
	December	The EC opens negotiations on special trade agreements with those EFTA member states that have not applied to join the EC.
1972	**January**	Denmark, Ireland, Norway, and the United Kingdom conclude membership negotiations with the EC and sign treaties of accession.
	March	EC states establish the "snake" mechanism, which is intended to stabilize currency fluctuations.
	May	In Ireland, a majority voting in a referendum supports entry to the EC.
	July	Special Relations Agreements are concluded between the EC and the remaining member states of EFTA.
	September	In Norway, a majority voting in a referendum rejects EC membership.
	October	In Denmark, a majority voting in a referendum accepts EC membership.
		A summit meeting of EC heads of state and government in Paris agrees guidelines on the future development of the EC, and restates the goal of achieving economic and monetary union by 1980.
1973	**January**	The United Kingdom, Denmark, and Ireland accede to the Community.
	May	A Special Relations Agreement is signed between Norway and the EC.
1974	**April**	In the United Kingdom, the newly elected Labour government, under Harold Wilson, begins to seek renegotiation of the terms of the United Kingdom's accession treaty.
	December	Another summit meeting in Paris agrees to institutionalize summit meetings, in the form of a European Council, and to establish a European Regional Development Fund (ERDF). It also agrees on the principle that the European Parliament should be directly elected.
1975	**February**	The first Lomé Convention is signed by the EC and 46 African, Caribbean, and Pacific (ACP) states.
	March	Membership renegotiations between the EC and the United Kingdom are concluded.
		The first meeting of the newly instituted European Council is held in Dublin.
	June	In the United Kingdom, a large majority voting in the country's first ever national referendum approves the renegotiated terms for continued membership of the EC.
		Greece applies for EC membership.
	August	The Conference on Security and Cooperation in Europe closes with the signing of the Helsinki Final Act, a nonbinding general agreement dealing with the three broad themes of security, economics, and technological cooperation between the 35 signatory states.
1976	**January**	The Tindemans Report on European union is published.
	July	Negotiations open on Greek membership of the EC.
1977	**March**	Portugal applies for EC membership.
	July	Spain applies for EC membership.
	October	The Court of Auditors is established as a formal EC institution, replacing the original Board of Audit.

1978	**October**	The EC opens membership negotiations with Portugal.
	December	The European Council agrees to set up a European Monetary System (EMS) based on a European currency unit (Ecu).
1979	**February**	The EC opens membership negotiations with Spain.
	March	The EMS comes into operation. The United Kingdom decides to remain outside the exchange rate mechanism (ERM) that is established as part of the EMS.
	May	A Treaty of Accession is signed by the EC and Greece.
	June	The first direct elections to the European Parliament are held; they have been at five-yearly intervals ever since.
	October	The second Lomé Convention is signed by the EC and 58 ACP states.
	November	Margaret Thatcher, Conservative Prime Minister of the United Kingdom since May, demands a reduction in the country's contributions to the EC's budget.
	December	The European Parliament exercises its budgetary powers and rejects the EC budget for the first time.
1981	**January**	Greece becomes the EC's tenth member state.
	October	The London Report on closer European Political Cooperation is accepted by the EC's foreign ministers.
1983	**January**	A common fisheries policy (CFP) is agreed after six years of negotiations.
	June	A "Solemn Declaration on European Union" is signed by the members of the European Council, meeting in Stuttgart.
1984	**January**	A free trade area is created between the EC and EFTA.
	February	The European Parliament approves by a large majority a Draft Treaty Establishing the European Union, an ambitious blueprint proposed by its Committee on Institutional Affairs.
	June	The European Council, meeting at Fontainebleau, agrees measures to reduce the United Kingdom's net contributions to the EC budget.
		The French government proposes that the WEU be revived as a European security forum.
	December	The third Lomé Convention is signed by the EC and 66 ACP states.
1985	**June**	Treaties of accession are signed between Spain and Portugal and the EC.
		The Commission publishes its white paper, *Completing the Internal Market*, outlining the measures that, in its view, need to be taken to remove the remaining physical, technical, and fiscal barriers between member states.
		The European Council, meeting in Milan, agrees to convene an intergovernmental conference to revise the Treaty of Rome.
		The report of the Adonnino Committee on a "People's Europe" is published.
	September	The intergovernmental conference on institutional reform of the Community begins work.
	December	The European Council, meeting in Luxembourg, agrees the text of the Single European Act, which will revise the Treaty of Rome. It incorporates commitments to complete the internal market by 31 December 1992, and to carry out other institutional and policy reforms, including establishing a treaty basis for cooperation on foreign policy.
1986	**January**	Spain and Portugal become the 11th and 12th member states of the EC.

1987	**April**	Turkey applies for EC membership.
	July	The Single European Act comes into effect.
1988	**February**	The European Council accepts the "Delors I" package on Community budgetary reform, prepared by Jacques Delors, President of the Commission. It also agrees to reduce expenditure on the CAP, and to increase expenditure on the regional and social funds.
	June	The EC signs an agreement with the Council for Mutual Economic Assistance (Comecon), establishing mutual recognition and opening the way to closer relations with the Soviet Union and most countries in central and eastern Europe.
		At a meeting of the European Council in Hanover, Jacques Delors is asked to chair a committee investigating how EMU can be achieved.
	September	The British Prime Minister, Margaret Thatcher, delivers a robustly Eurosceptic speech at the College of Europe in Bruges.
1989	**April**	The Delors Committee presents its proposals for a three-stage progression to EMU.
	May	An EC Charter of Fundamental Social Rights is proposed.
	June	The European Council, meeting in Madrid, agrees that the first phase of EMU will begin in July 1990.
	July	Austria applies for EC membership.
	September	The Court of First Instance is established to reduce the workload of the European Court of Justice.
	November	The Berlin Wall is opened, precipitating the final stage in the collapse of the Communist regimes of central and eastern Europe.
		An extraordinary meeting of the European Council is called to discuss the dramatic developments in central and eastern Europe, and the possible unification of Germany.
	December	The European Council, meeting in Strasbourg, decides to convene an intergovernmental conference at the end of 1990 to agree the treaty changes necessary for EMU and to adopt the Social Charter. The United Kingdom dissents from both decisions.
		The fourth Lomé Convention is signed by the EC and 68 ACP states.
		The EC signs a trade and cooperation agreement with the Soviet Union.
1990	**April**	A special meeting of the European Council in Dublin confirms the EC's commitment to political union.
	June	The European Council, meeting in Dublin, agrees that an intergovernmental conference on political union should work alongside the one planned on EMU.
	July	Cyprus and Malta apply to join the EC.
	October	With the unification of Germany the five *Länder* that had constituted the German Democratic Republic (East Germany) since 1949 become part of the EC.
		At a special meeting of the European Council in Rome all the EC's member states except the United Kingdom agree that the second stage of EMU should begin on 1 January 1994.
	December	The intergovernmental conferences on political union and EMU are opened in Rome.
1991	**July**	Sweden applies for EC membership.

	August	Following the failure of an attempted coup d'état against President Mikhail Gorbachev, the Soviet Union begins to break up into independent states.
	December	The European Council, meeting at Maastricht, agrees the Treaty on European Union, based on three pillars: the reformed European Communities, the Common Foreign and Security Policy, and Cooperation on Justice and Home Affairs.
		The EC signs association (Europe) agreements with Poland, Hungary, and Czechoslovakia.
1992	**February**	The Treaty on European Union is signed at Maastricht.
	March	Finland applies to join the EC.
	May	The member states of the EC and EFTA sign an agreement to create a European Economic Area (EEA).
		Switzerland applies to join the EC.
	June	A majority voting in a referendum in Denmark rejects the Treaty on European Union (51% against, 49% for)
	September	The pound sterling and the Italian lira are withdrawn from the ERM.
		A majority voting in a referendum in France accepts the Treaty on European Union by a slim majority (51% for, 49% against)
	November	Norway applies to join the EC.
	December	A majority voting in a referendum in Switzerland rejects EEA membership (50.3% against, 49.7% for). Switzerland's application for EC membership is suspended.
		The European Council, meeting in Edinburgh, agrees to Danish opt-outs from those parts of the Treaty on European Union that led to the rejection of the treaty in the Danish referendum. The Council also agrees to open accession negotiations with Finland, Sweden, and Norway in early 1993, and adopts the financial perspective for 1993–99.
1993	**February**	The EC opens accession negotiations with Austria, Finland, and Sweden.
	April	The EC opens accession negotiations with Norway.
	May	In Denmark, a majority of those voting in a second referendum accept the Treaty on European Union on a vote of 57% for and 43% against.
	June	The European Council, meeting in Copenhagen, agrees that the associated countries of central and eastern Europe should become EU members as soon as they meet certain political and economic criteria for accession.
	August	The ERM plunges into crisis as a result of uncertainty in international currency markets.
	October	The German Constitutional Court rules that the Treaty on European Union is compatible with the German Basic Law and therefore can be ratified.
	November	The Treaty on European Union comes into force.
	December	GATT negotiations are concluded after delays caused by disagreements between the EU and the United States.
1994	**January**	Stage 2 of EMU commences and the European Monetary Institute is established.
		The agreement on the EEA comes into effect.
	March	The Committee of the Regions, established by the Treaty on European Union, meets for the first time in Brussels.
		Austria, Finland, Sweden, and Norway accept the EU's membership terms.
		Hungary applies for EU membership.

	April	Poland applies for EU membership.
	June	A Partnership and Cooperation Agreement between the EU and Russia is signed at the European Council in Corfu.
	November	In Norway, a majority voting in a referendum rejects EU membership (52% against, 48% for).
1995	**January**	Austria, Finland, and Sweden become members of the EU, taking its membership to 15.
	May	The Commission publishes a white paper on preparation of the associated countries of central and eastern Europe for integration into the internal market of the EU.
	June	Romania and Slovakia apply for EU membership.
	October	Latvia applies for EU membership.
	November	Estonia applies for EU membership.
		The Barcelona Declaration is adopted by the EU member states and 12 states in the Mediterranean region, with the goal of creating a Mediterranean free trade area by 2010.
	December	Lithuania and Bulgaria apply for EU membership.
1996	**January**	The Czech Republic applies for EU membership.
	March	A new intergovernmental conference opens at a special meeting of the European Council in Turin.
	June	Slovenia applies for EU membership.
	December	The European Council, meeting in Dublin, agrees the Stability and Growth Pact to ensure strict budgetary discipline in the future euro zone.
1997	**June**	A draft version of the Treaty of Amsterdam is agreed, but decisions on the most difficult issues, concerning institutional reform for enlargement, are postponed until the next intergovernmental conference. The Labour government elected in May withdraws the United Kingdom's objections to the Social Protocol and it is agreed that it will be incorporated into the treaty.
	July	The Commission publishes *Agenda 2000*, a document containing its recommendations on the strategy for enlargement, including the reform of CAP and structural policies. It also issues its opinions on the ten applicant states in central and eastern Europe, identifying five of them as meeting the Copenhagen criteria for EU membership: the Czech Republic, Estonia, Hungary, Poland, and Slovenia.
	December	The European Council, meeting in Luxembourg, agrees to open accession negotiations in the spring of 1998 with the five states identified by the Commission in July (see above), as well as with Cyprus.
		The EU's Partnership and Cooperation Agreement with Russia comes into force
1998	**March**	The first meeting of the European Conference, held in London, is attended by all the EU's member states and candidate states except Turkey.
		Accession negotiations are opened with Cyprus, the Czech Republic, Estonia, Hungary, Poland, and Slovenia.
	May	A special meeting of the European Council in Brussels agrees that 11 member states of the EU meet the Maastricht convergence criteria and therefore can participate in Stage 3 of EMU when it is launched on 1 January 1999.
	June	The European Central Bank is established in Frankfurt, with Wim Duisenberg as its first President.

	September	The new government in Malta reactivates its membership application following the victory of the Nationalist Party in the general election.
	December	A joint declaration on European defence, agreed by the British and French governments at a summit in St Malo, proposes that the EU should develop a limited military capability.
1999	**January**	Stage 3 of EMU is launched as 11 of the EU's 15 member states irrevocably fix their exchange rates to the euro and the European Central Bank assumes responsibility for monetary policy. Denmark, Sweden, and the United Kingdom choose not to participate, while Greece does not yet meet the convergence criteria set out in the Treaty on European Union.
	March	Jacques Santer, President of the Commission, resigns, along with all the other members of the College of Commissioners, following the publication of a very critical report by the Committee of Independent Experts, alleging corruption and mismanagement.
		The European Council, meeting in Berlin, agrees the financial perspective for 2000–06, including reform of the CAP and structural funds, so that the first wave of enlargement can go ahead. It also endorses the nomination of Romano Prodi as the President of the new Commission that is to take office in September.
	May	The Treaty of Amsterdam comes into force.
	June	In the fifth set of direct elections to the European Parliament, the turnout falls to its lowest level so far: 50.2% of the electorate do not participate.
		The European Council, meeting in Cologne, agrees the Common Strategy on Russia and the Employment Pact.
	October	A special meeting of the European Council is held in Tampere to discuss new initiatives on cooperation in justice and home affairs.
	December	The European Council, meeting in Helsinki, agrees to open accession negotiations with Bulgaria, Latvia, Lithuania, Malta, Slovakia, and Romania, and confirms that Turkey is a candidate for EU membership but does not yet meet the Copenhagen criteria. The Council also agrees on the agenda for a new intergovernmental conference, and on plans to develop a rapid reaction force for crisis-management and peacekeeping operations.
2000	**February**	The intergovernmental conference opens with its agenda mainly limited to the institutional issues left over from the negotiations on the Treaty of Amsterdam.
		Accession negotiations are opened with the six states approved by the European Council in Helsinki (see December 1999).
	June	The Cotonou Agreement is signed by the EU and 77 ACP states, replacing the Lomé Conventions.
	September	A majority voting in a referendum in Denmark rejects adoption of the euro (53% against, 47% for).
	October	At a special meeting in Biarritz the European Council approves the draft Charter of Fundamental Rights.
	December	The European Council agrees the Treaty of Nice, including the institutional arrangements for enlargement of the EU up to 27 member states. It also adopts the Charter of Fundamental Rights as a general statement of political principles, without legal force.
2001	**January**	Greece adopts the euro.

	February	The Treaty of Nice is signed.
	June	A majority voting in a referendum in Ireland rejects the Treaty of Nice (54% against, 46% for)
		The European Council, meeting in Göteborg, agrees that it should be possible for those candidate countries that are ready to do so to complete accession negotiations by 2002. The Council also adopts the Sixth Environmental Action Programme and a strategy for sustainable development.
	July	Belgium assumes the Presidency of the European Council.
2002	**January**	Euro notes and coins become legal tender in the 12 countries in the euro zone.
		Spain assumes the Presidency of the European Council.
	July	Denmark assumes the Presidency of the European Council.
	December	Accession negotiations with those applicant states that are ready for EU membership are due to be completed.
2003	**January**	Greece assumes the Presidency of the European Council.
2004	**January**	A new intergovernmental conference scheduled to begin its work.
	June	The sixth round of direct elections to the European Parliament is due to be held, with those states that have agreed accession treaties taking part.
2005	**January**	A new Commission takes office.

Appendix 2

Glossary

à la carte: an extreme form of differentiated or flexible integration, in which member states can choose as if from a menu the new policies and other forms of cooperation in which they participate. While overcoming the problem of finding a consensus on every new initiative, the concept of integration *à la carte* is generally seen as undermining the established philosophy and practice of the EU.

accession: the legal process of becoming a member of the EU. It involves agreement on an accession treaty, setting out the terms and conditions of membership, which then has to be approved unanimously by the Council, by a majority in the European Parliament, by all the existing member states' parliaments, and by the candidate state itself through its own ratification process, which may require the holding of a referendum to endorse membership.

accession criteria: the criteria used to assess whether a state meets the political and economic conditions set for EU membership by the European Council in Copenhagen in June 1993: see Copenhagen criteria

accession partnership: an agreement between the EU and each state applying for EU membership, which is designed to enable the candidate state to align itself as far as possible with the acquis communautaire (see below) prior to its accession. It involves agreement each year on the priorities to be followed by the candidate state, based on the Commission's annual report on its progress in meeting the accession criteria, and the provision by the EU of resources to help it to do so.

ACP states: the African, Caribbean, and Pacific states, now numbering 77 and mostly former colonies or dependent territories of EU member states, that have been associated with the EU through the four Lomé Conventions and, most recently, their successor, the Cotonou Agreement, signed in 2000. The agreements have given the ACP states preferential access to the EU's market and financial support through the European Development Fund.

acquis communautaire: the entire body of legal and political obligations that comprises the EU's heritage and that all members must accept. The *acquis* today runs to more than 80,000 pages and includes the treaties, the extensive body of secondary EC legislation, the case law of the European Court of Justice, and international agreements. It is one of the conditions of membership that a candidate state must not only accept the *acquis* in its entirety, but be in a position to implement and enforce it properly

acquis politique: a less commonly used term, referring to the corpus of political agreements, resolutions, and decisions on foreign policy issues derived within the European Political Cooperation process up to 1993 and then through the CFSP procedures introduced by the Treaty on European Union

additionality: the principle that money allocated from the structural funds to support projects in the EU's regions should be used in addition to member states' funds allocated for regional development, not instead of them

Advocate General: a senior legal officer of the European Court of Justice who advises and assists the judges. There are nine advocates general and their main duty is to submit in open court a "reasoned submission", known as the Opinion, setting out the main facts of the case and the relevant case law, which is then used by the judges as the basis for their decision.

Agenda 2000: an important set of documents published by the Commission in July 1997 under the full title *Agenda 2000: For a Stronger and Wider Union*. It contains the Commission's Opinions on the applications from ten states in central and eastern Europe, proposals for the future financing of the EU for the period 2000–06, and a strategy for enlargement, including proposals for reform of the Common Agricultural Policy and the structural funds.

approximation of laws: the term used in the Treaty of Rome for the process of harmonizing or standardizing laws affecting the operation of the single market

assent procedure: one of the European Parliament's decision-making procedures, first introduced under the Single European Act, giving it the power to veto but not amend a proposal previously agreed, usually unanimously, by the European Council. The procedure is used for major political decisions, such as the approval of the accession of a new member state, most international agreements, the adoption of a uniform procedure for elections to the European Parliament, the organization and objectives of the structural funds, and the imposition of sanctions under Article 7 of the Treaty on European Union on a member state for a serious and persistent breach of fundamental human rights.

association agreement: a treaty establishing reciprocal rights and obligations between the Community (not, strictly speaking, the EU) and a state or group of states, typically providing for reciprocal market access and other forms of economic and political cooperation. A number of different forms of association agreement have been developed, ranging from the "Europe agreements" with states in central and eastern Europe, which recognize that the associated state's goal is full EU membership, to the agreements with the ACP and Euro-Med states, which are focused on providing support for their economic and political development.

avis: a widely used term for the official opinions that the Commission prepares when a state submits an application for EU membership, assessing whether it meets the accession criteria and recommending whether accession negotiations should be opened with it

Barcelona process: the continuous dialogue and cooperation between the EU and 12 states in the southern Mediterranean region that takes place within the framework of the work programme of the Euro-Mediterranean Partnership (see below) agreed in Barcelona in November 1995

Benelux: the customs union established by Belgium, the Netherlands, and Luxembourg in 1948. The term is also used as an acronym for the three states.

blocking minority: the number of votes required to reject a proposal under the rules for qualified majority voting in the Council of Ministers. The size of the required total, and therefore the number of member states that would have to contribute their votes to it, have always been highly contentious questions.

Brussels: as well as being the capital city of Belgium, it is the site of many of the EU's institutions, including the Commission and the Council, and also the headquarters of the WEU and NATO. The term "Brussels" is also used, often pejoratively, to refer to the EU institutions established and functioning from there, as in "Brussels bureaucracy".

Bundesbank: the German central bank, a powerful independent institution that has been obliged under the Basic Law of 1949 to make price stability its main priority for its monetary policy. It served as the model for the European Central Bank (ECB). Both the Bundesbank and the ECB have their headquarters in Frankfurt am Main.

Bundesrat: upper house of the German Federal Parliament, which represents the governments of the *Länder* (regions)

Bundestag: lower house of the German Federal Parliament

cabinet: the private office of a Commissioner, usually consisting of six to eight people personally chosen by him/her to offer advice and coordinate specific policy areas. The most senior member is known as the *chef de cabinet*.

CAP: see Common Agricultural Policy

CESDP: see Common European Security and Defence Policy

CET: see Common External Tariff

CFI: see Court of First Instance

CFSP: see Common Foreign and Security Policy

chapters: the 31 sections into which the *acquis communautaire* (see above) has been divided for the purpose of accession negotiations with candidate states, e.g. the agriculture and budget chapters

Charter of Fundamental Rights: a political document proclaimed by the European Council, meeting in Nice, in December 2000, containing a comprehensive list of political, social and economic rights that the EU's citizens are entitled to expect the EU's institutions to respect in their dealings with them. The future status of the Charter, particularly whether it should be incorporated into the treaties and thus become part of the EU's legal order, is one of the key items on the agenda for the next intergovernmental conference.

CIS: see Commonwealth of Independent States

CJTF: see Combined Joint Task Force

closer cooperation: the term used in the Treaty of Amsterdam to refer to a group, consisting of at least a majority of the member states, establishing closer links with one another in a new policy area when other states are unwilling to do so. Examples in the past have included the Social Protocol (attached to the Treaty on European Union) and the Schengen Convention. Closer cooperation is closely associated with the concepts of flexible integration and variable geometry (see below). It has always been seen as a "last resort" outcome when it has proved impossible to secure consensus on new initiatives. Special procedures are applied to protect both the integrity of the *acquis communautaire* and the interests and rights of other members. In the Treaty of Nice (not yet ratified when this book went to press), the term "enhanced cooperation" is used instead and the rigour of the procedures is slightly eased.

CMEA: Council for Mutual Economic Assistance: see Comecon

codecision procedure: now the most commonly used legislative procedure, it ensures that new legislation is subject to joint decision by the European Parliament and the Council of Ministers. It was introduced in the Treaty on European Union and its use has been extended by the Treaty of Amsterdam and (assuming that it is ratified) the Treaty of Nice. When the Parliament and the Council disagree on a proposal, a conciliation committee is convened to try to resolve the issue. If it is unsuccessful, the proposal cannot become law, so the Parliament can in practice exercise a veto. Codecision has been seen by some as one way of increasing the democratic legitimacy of the EU, but its complexity is a major disadvantage.

cohesion: the principle of solidarity among the member states of the EU, particularly in relation to reducing the disparities between richer and poorer regions. It was introduced into the Single European Act as one of the objectives of the Community, largely as a result of pressure from the poorer states. The main policy instruments in cohesion policy are the structural funds and, since 1994, the Cohesion Fund.

Cohesion Fund: a new fund set up in 1994, under the terms of the Treaty on European Union, to provide financial support for environmental and infrastructure projects in what were then the four poorest EU member states, Greece, Ireland, Portugal, and Spain. Its original purpose was to help the less developed states meet the economic criteria for participation in EMU. However, even after qualifying for EMU, they have been reluctant to accept that they no longer need the generous aid they have become accustomed to receive.

College of Commissioners: the collective term for the President and other Commissioners, signifying that they work as a collegiate body, taking decisions collectively and sharing responsibility, rather than acting as individuals. The most significant consequence of their collegiality is that the European Parliament cannot censure individual Commissioners.

Combined Joint Task Force (CJTF): an operational principle approved by NATO in January 1994 whereby its military assets and capabilities could be made available to the WEU for specific tasks or missions. The operational significance of the concept is that European NATO members could engage in limited military action without the participation of the United States, although clearly only with its approval.

Comecon: the most widely used (originally journalistic) name for the Council for Mutual Economic Assistance (CMEA). It was established by the Soviet Union in 1949 in order to coordinate, and in practice control, economic relations among the Communist states in the Soviet bloc. There was no official mutual recognition between the EC and Comecon until after Mikhail Gorbachev came to power, and it was only in 1988 that a joint declaration was signed signalling the beginning of the development of a relationship. In the wake of the collapse of the Communist regimes in the following year, Comecon was formally dissolved in 1991.

Commission: see European Commission

Committee of Agricultural Organizations in the European Union (Comité des Organisations Professionnelles Agricoles, or COPA): an umbrella organization of farming unions and associations (known, like many other such bodies, by its French acronym rather than its English one), which lobbies the EU in defence of farming interests.

Committee of Permanent Representatives (Comité des Représentatifs Permanents, or Coreper): the French acronym Coreper is widely used to refer both to the powerful committee composed of the heads of the permanent delegations retained in Brussels by each EU member state and to the totality of the dense substructure of committees through which these delegations work. The heads of the permanent delegations hold ambassadorial rank and represent their governments in the day-to-day workings of the Council of Ministers outside Council meetings. Their staff sit on numerous working groups and committees dealing with the whole range of EU business. Coreper is central to the intergovernmental decision-making and policy-making processes: a substantial proportion of EU business is agreed at this level and then endorsed at meetings of the Council.

Committee of the Regions: established under the terms of the Treaty on European Union, the Committee is composed of 222 representatives of regional and local authorities. Its establishment was recognition of the increasingly important role played by regional governments in many member states and of the fact that many regional political authorities had established offices in Brussels to represent their interests. The Committee of the Regions has to be consulted by the Commission and Council on a wide range of matters affecting local and regional interests, including education, culture, cohesion policy, the environment, transport, and crossborder cooperation. However, its opinions have only advisory status.

Common Agricultural Policy (CAP): a protectionist policy for EU agriculture, based on a system of price support and still accounting for nearly half of the EU budget. It has been criticized for many years on both financial and environmental grounds, but reform has proved extremely difficult due to the continuing importance of the farm lobby in many member states.

Common European Security and Defence Policy (CESDP): formally launched by the European Council in Helsinki in December 1999, with a commitment to develop for the first time an EU military capability in the form of a rapid reaction force to be used for humanitarian and rescue tasks, peacekeeping, and crisis management (the "Petersberg tasks"). It also involves the creation of new political and military bodies, including a Political and Security Committee (widely known by its French acronym, COPS), a Military Committee, and a Military Staff.

Common External Tariff (CET): it is a defining feature of a customs union that member states are committed to apply a common customs tariff on all goods entering from outside the union.

Common Foreign and Security Policy (CFSP): building on the experience of European Political Cooperation, the Treaty on European Union provides for cooperation in foreign policy and the possibility of developing a role for the EU in defence through the WEU. The CFSP is the second pillar of the EU, meaning that action in these highly sensitive political areas is on the basis of intergovernmental cooperation, usually requiring unanimity, with only limited roles for the Commission or the European Parliament.

Common Market: a popular term for the EEC and, later, the EC. Its original usage reflected the economic nature of the EEC, but for some it has retained political currency, expressing a hostile reaction to, or even denial of, the growing political and social competency of the EU. "Common market" is also a concept used in the analysis of economic integration, meaning that there is free movement of goods, services, capital, and labour within the given area.

Commonwealth of Independent States (CIS): a rather loose association of 12 of the former Soviet republics (all except the three Baltic states), in which the Russian Federation plays a leading but not dominant role. Established in December 1991, it provides a framework for cooperation on a range of political, economic, and security issues.

Community Support Framework (CSF): one of the requirements in the operation of the EU's cohesion policy is that a member state should agree with the Commission a CSF, a comprehensive plan for the region that includes a series of linked programmes, before it can obtain support from the structural funds.

competence: a term used to describe the authority of the EU to undertake a specific action or propose legislation in a particular policy area, based on articles in the relevant EU treaties. In practice, the legal position is often complex and subject to dispute, as in most policy areas competence is shared between the EU and the member states. The European Court of Justice ultimately determines where competence lies.

Conference on Security and Cooperation in Europe (CSCE): see Organization for Security and Cooperation in Europe

consultation procedure: the legislative procedure prescribed in the Treaty of Rome and used exclusively until the introduction of the cooperation and assent procedures by the Single European Act. It is still used in certain policy areas, most notably in relation to the Common Agricultural Policy. Under the consultation procedure the Council is legally obliged to consult the Parliament but is not required to accept its opinion.

convergence criteria: the five economic conditions, stipulated in the Treaty on European Union, which must be met before a member state can take part in the third stage of EMU involving the adoption of the single currency. They cover the ratio of government deficit and debt to GDP, price stability, the level of interest rates, and exchange rate stability. They are intended to ensure that the economies of the states have converged sufficiently so that economic development within the euro zone is balanced and does not give rise to tensions between the participating member states.

Cooperation in Justice and Home Affairs: the original title of the third pillar of the TEU. See Justice and Home Affairs.

COPA: see Committee of Agricultural Organizations in the European Union

Copenhagen criteria: the criteria set out by the European Council in June 1993 to assess the eligibility of states for EU membership. The criteria are that a candidate country must have achieved stability of institutions guaranteeing democracy, the rule of law, human rights, and respect for and protection of minorities; that it must have a functioning market economy, as well as the capacity to cope with competitive pressure and market forces within the EU; and that it must have the ability to take on the obligations of membership, including adherence to the aims of political, economic, and monetary union. The last criterion is interpreted as meaning that the state must have the institutional and administrative capacity to implement and enforce the *acquis communautaire* (see above) in full.

COPS: the widely used French acronym for the Political and Security Committee - in French, the Comité politique et de sécurité – responsible for the management of the CFSP and the CESDP.

Coreper: see Committee of Permanent Representatives

Council: the name used in the treaties for the Council of Ministers

Council for Mutual Economic Assistance: see Comecon

Council of Europe: established in 1949 as a result of a decision taken at the Congress of Europe held in the Hague the previous year that a European union or federation should be created. Disagreements between the proponents of federalism and those favouring a purely intergovernmental form of cooperation meant that the Council of Europe was given only limited powers. It was largely eclipsed by the more ambitious projects for integration, the ECSC and EEC. Its main achievement has been agreement on the European Convention on Human Rights and the establishment of a Court of Human Rights to provide legal redress for citizens who believe that their rights have been violated. It has always had a much wider membership than the EC/EU and now includes virtually all the states in Europe, including Russia. Based in Strasbourg, it is commonly confused with the EU, with which it shared its assembly building until recently, and which has adopted the same blue and gold flag.

Council of Ministers: the Council of Ministers represents the national interests of the member states and remains the most important decision-making institution in the EU. Its composition changes according to the policy area under discussion, with the appropriate national ministers attending meetings concerning their responsibilities, for example agriculture, energy or environment. Although it is rare for formal votes to be taken in the Council, the question whether decisions are taken on the basis of consensus or by a qualified majority has always been extremely contentious. See also Luxembourg Compromise and qualified majority voting.

Court of Auditors: the Court of Auditors was established in 1977, replacing the Audit Board. The Court of Auditors is responsible for financial probity within the EU, and has the power to scrutinize revenue and expenditure accounts. It publishes an extremely detailed annual report, usually containing strong criticism of the financial management of EU policies. It is a highly respected institution and, particularly since the resignation of the Santer Commission in 1999, its role in ensuring that the EU puts its house in order has been widely seen as crucial.

Court of First Instance (CFI): established under the terms of the Single European Act (1986), the Court of First Instance came into operation in 1989 to ease the burdens on the European Court of Justice. It has jurisdiction over the ECSC, competition policy, and administrative disputes in the EU institutions. The Treaty of Nice (assuming that it is ratified) will expand its role further.

CSF: see Community Support Frameworks

CSCE: Conference on Security and Cooperation in Europe. See Organization for Security and Cooperation in Europe

customs union: a free trade area in which agreement has been reached on a common external tariff to apply to all trade with nonmembers as the central feature of a common commercial policy

deepening: a term used to describe the process by which the degree of integration within the EU is increased by expanding the scope of its policy competence and moving decisively in the direction of supranational decision-making, for example by accepting qualified majority voting as the norm in the Council of Ministers. There has been considerable debate as to the relationship between the aims of deepening and widening (the enlargement of the EU). Some people believe that deepening must accompany widening if the EU is to survive enlargement on the unprecedented scale now envisaged, while others believe that a larger EU would inevitably be able to do less, and therefore integration would be shallower.

democratic deficit: a term used to summarize the view that the EU lacks effective parliamentary supervision and democratic accountability. The argument is that the transfer of powers from national authorities to the EU level means that national parliaments have lost their control over a significant amount of legislation and public expenditure, while the European Parliament has not been given adequate powers to ensure that it is able to exercise effective scrutiny instead. The result is a "democratic deficit", with the Council of Ministers and Commission seemingly escaping the normal process of democratic accountability. It is regarded as a problem because it arguably undermines the legitimacy of the EU in the eyes of its citizens, from whom it seems to be increasingly remote.

differentiated integration: the most neutral term used to describe a situation in which cooperation in a particular policy area either does not involve all EU members or involves them at different levels of intensity or at a different pace. It therefore breaks with the tradition of European integration that all members move together at the same speed towards a shared goal, although in practice there always has been some recognition that objective differences between member states might justify some special consideration. Various models of differentiated integration have been proposed and in some cases adopted in recent years. See *à la carte*, closer cooperation, flexibility, multispeed Europe, variable geometry.

direct election: the election of the Members of the European Parliament (MEPs) every five years by the voters in each member state. Although provision for direct election was made in the Treaty of Rome, it was not until 1979 that the member states agreed to implement it. Until then, MEPs had been drawn from national parliaments. It was hoped that direct election would increase the legitimacy of the European Parliament and strengthen its case for more powers, but repeatedly low turnouts at the elections have threatened to undermine its democratic credibility.

directive: the most common form of Community law, the directive is binding on each member state as to the result to be achieved, but leaves the national authorities some discretion over the precise form and methods to be used. Each national government has to transpose the directive into national law by a date specified in the directive.

Directorate-General (DG): the main administrative unit within the Commission, each DG being responsible for specific functional areas such as agriculture, trade, external relations or enlargement. They are therefore rather like ministries or government departments in a state. A Commissioner is responsible for the overall direction of policy within each DG.

EAGGF: see European Agricultural Guidance and Guarantee Fund

EAP: see Environmental Action Programme

EBRD: see European Bank for Reconstruction and Development

EC: see European Community and European Communities

ECB: see European Central Bank

ECHR: see European Convention on the Protection of Human Rights and Fundamental Freedoms and European Court of Human Rights

ECJ: see European Court of Justice

Ecofin: the name commonly used for the Council meetings of the economic and finance ministers of the EU member states

Economic and Financial Committee: a new institution established to help coordinate economic and financial policy after EMU was launched in January 1999. Its membership includes two senior officials from the Commission, two from the European Central Bank, and two from each of the member states. It is an advisory body to Ecofin and has established itself as a key player in EMU policy-making.

Economic and Monetary Union (EMU): a significantly higher form of economic integration involving the adoption of a single currency for use by its members. It had been a longstanding objective of the EC and the Treaty on European Union committed member states to achieve it in three stages by 1 January 1999. It was launched on schedule with 11 states participating; Greece joined in January 2001. Euro notes and coins will replace national currencies from 1 January 2002. The operation of a common currency involves the member states in much more intensive coordination of their economic policies, including, potentially, fiscal policy. The degree of pooling of economic sovereignty involved in EMU has made it one of the most politically contentious issues in some member states, and Denmark, Sweden, and the United Kingdom had not decided to join as of June 2001.

Economic and Social Committee (ESC or Ecosoc): established under the terms of the Treaty of Rome, the Economic and Social Committee acts as an advisory body to both the Commission and the Council of Ministers. It has to be consulted before legislation is agreed on a wide range of issues. Its membership is drawn from national interest groups representing employers, workers, and other groups, such as farmers and consumers. Its reports are quite authoritative but it is one of the less important of the EU's institutions and some doubts have been raised about its future.

Ecosoc: see Economic and Social Committee

ECSC: see European Coal and Steel Community

ECU: see European Currency Unit

EDC: see European Defence Community

EDF: see European Development Fund

EEA: see European Economic Area, European Environmental Agency

EEC: see European Economic Community

EFTA: see European Free Trade Association

EIB: see European Investment Bank

EMI: see European Monetary Institute

EMP: see Euro-Mediterranean Partnership

EMS: see European Monetary System

EMU: see Economic and Monetary Union

enhanced cooperation: the term used in the Treaty of Nice instead of closer cooperation (see above)

enlargement: the expansion of the EU to include new member states. There have been four enlargements in the EC/EU's history: in 1973, when Denmark, Ireland, and the United Kingdom joined the Community; in 1981, when Greece joined; in 1986, when Spain and Portugal joined; and in 1995, when Austria, Finland, and Sweden became EU members. The EU is expected to enlarge again in 2004–05, possibly with as many as ten new members, and then to continue to enlarge over the following years until it reaches a total membership of more than 30 states.

EP: see European Parliament

EPC: see European Political Cooperation

Erasmus: see European Community Action Scheme for the Mobility of University Students

ERDF: see European Regional Development Fund

ERM: see Exchange Rate Mechanism

ESCB: see European System of Central Banks

ESDI: see European Security and Defence Initiative

ESF: see European Social Fund

ETUC: see European Trade Union Confederation

EU: see European Union

EU 15: the present 15 member states of the EU – Austria, Belgium, Denmark, Finland, France, Germany, Greece, Ireland, Italy, Luxembourg, Netherlands, Portugal, Spain, Sweden, and the United Kingdom

Euratom: see European Atomic Energy Community

euro: the name adopted in 1995 for the single currency to be used in the Economic and Monetary Union. It was introduced at the rate of one Ecu to one euro on 1 January 1999, when 11 member states irrevocably locked their national currencies into the new system. Greece did so on 1 January 2001. Euro coins and notes will replace national currencies in those states participating in EMU from 1 January 2002.

euro zone: a collective term for the economies of the member states that have adopted the euro. See also "Euroland".

"Euroland": a term in popular use, particularly in the media, to signify the area in which the single currency has been introduced. It is at least as often called the "euro zone".

Euro–Mediterranean Partnership: a new policy framework adopted at the Barcelona Conference in November 1995 for the development of a comprehensive political and economic relationship between the EU and 11 Mediterranean states – Algeria, Cyprus, Egypt, Israel, Jordan, Lebanon, Malta, Morocco, Syria, Tunisia, Turkey – along with the Palestinian Authority. The main policy instrument is an upgraded association agreement, the Euro-Mediterranean Agreement, providing for the progressive liberalization of trade with the objective of creating a free trade area between the states in the region and the EU by 2010. There are also numerous other initiatives in the political, security, economic, environmental, cultural, and educational fields being undertaken within the framework of the work programme agreed at Barcelona. See also MEDA.

Europe Agreements: the name commonly used for the association agreements signed by the EU and countries in central and eastern Europe during the 1990s. Their economic provisions helped to integrate the economies of these countries into the wider European market in advance of their full accession to the EU. See also association agreement.

European Agricultural Guidance and Guarantee Fund (EAGGF): the fund established in 1962 to finance the Common Agricultural Policy (CAP). It consists of two parts: a guarantee section, which provides the money for the CAP's price support policy; and a guidance section, which provides support for restructuring and modernization of agriculture.

European Atomic Energy Community (Euratom): established in 1957 at the same time as the European Economic Community. Its objectives were to promote research and development in the field of atomic (nuclear) energy, to establish safety standards, to ensure the peaceful use of nuclear energy, and to prevent the improper use of fissile materials. When the Communities were amalgamated in 1967, Euratom lost its independent identity. It has sometimes been viewed as the poor relation of the EC.

European Bank for Reconstruction and Development (EBRD): set up on the initiative of François Mitterrand, President of France, in 1991, as an international financial institution specifically designed to assist the states of central and eastern Europe to make a successful transition from planned to market economies. It is a precondition for access to the EBRD's financial support that a state has a stable democratic system of government.

European Central Bank (ECB): an independent body established in June 1998 under the terms of the Treaty on European Union and based in Frankfurt am Main. It is the successor to the European Monetary Institute, which managed the former European Monetary System. Its main responsibilities are for the monetary policy of the euro zone, and for the management of the foreign exchange operations and reserves of the states participating in EMU.

European Coal and Steel Community (ECSC): established in 1952 under the terms of the Treaty of Paris, the ECSC was the first of the three European Communities, and thus the model for the EEC and Euratom. The ECSC was proposed by the French Foreign Minister, Robert Schuman, who believed that economic cooperation was essential to securing peace in Europe. He argued that supranational control of coal and steel would reduce the ability of individual European states to develop a military industrial capacity to wage war. See also neofunctionalism.

European Commission: one of the key EU institutions, combining some features of a European government with others of a bureaucracy or civil service. It plays a central role in policy-making, initiating proposals and consulting or negotiating with pressure groups, national officials, and the other EU institutions. However, it is the Council of Ministers that takes the final decisions, increasingly together with the European Parliament. The Commission is also responsible for the implementation of EU policy, although national administrations undertake most of the practical work. One of its most important functions is to act as a "watchdog" over respect for Community law: it can refer suspected infringements to the European Court of Justice.

European Communities: the term refers to the three European Communities of the 1950s, the European Economic Community (EEC), the European Coal and Steel Community (ECSC), and the European Atomic Energy Community (Euratom), which were brought together by the Merger Treaty of 1967.

European Community (EC): the term was commonly used to refer to the European Economic Community and to the combined European Communities after 1967. It is now officially used as the collective name of the three European Communities, which constitute the first pillar of the European Union. See also European Communities.

European Community Action Scheme for the Mobility of University Students (Erasmus): a Community-funded programme established in 1987 to encourage university students to study in other EC member states than their own, in the belief that the experience would not only benefit individuals but also encourage the development of a "European identity" among the younger generation. The programme was extended in 1991 to include students from the EFTA states. In 1995 Erasmus was brought within a broader educational scheme called Socrates. It has also been extended to students from states applying for EU membership.

European Convention on the Protection of Human Rights and Fundamental Freedoms (ECHR): more usually referred to simply as the European Convention on Human Rights. The Convention, signed in 1950, was the first initiative taken by the newly established Council of Europe.

It has acquired significant moral authority throughout Europe as the benchmark for human rights observance and the Treaty on European Union makes explicit reference to it as one of the sources of its core principles.

European Council: originally an informal meeting of the heads of state and government of the member states, the European Council has evolved into one of the most important and influential of the EU's institutional structures, with responsibility across all three of its pillars. The European Council is required to meet at least twice a year, and in practice usually meets twice during each Presidency semester. Its decisions often mark major turning points for the EU and are published as the Presidency Conclusions.

European Court of Human Rights (ECHR): an agency of the Council of Europe with responsibility for upholding the Convention on Human Rights (with which, confusingly, it shares an acronym). It is based in Strasbourg and its work is often confused in the media with that of the EU's court, the European Court of Justice.

European Court of Justice (ECJ): based in Luxembourg, the ECJ is the EU's highest court and its decisions are enforced through the courts of the EU member states. The ECJ is charged with ensuring that EC law is interpreted and applied in the same way throughout the EU; that member states fulfil their obligations under the treaties; and that the EU's own institutions act according to the law. The ECJ has no jurisdiction within member states over national laws unless they are deemed to be in conflict with EC law or treaty provisions, where it has ruled that Community law takes precedence. The ECJ has 15 judges and nine advocates general, and they act independently of national control. Judicial appointments are made by the Council of Ministers on recommendations from national governments.

European currency unit (Ecu): introduced in 1979 as a key component of the European Monetary System, the Ecu was the precursor to the euro, although there were never any Ecu notes or coins in circulation. The value of the Ecu was based on a "basket" of member states' currencies, weighted according to their respective strengths.

European Defence Community (EDC): an ambitious initiative launched by the French Prime Minister, René Pleven, in 1950, at the height of the Cold War and soon after the outbreak of war in Korea, with the aim of creating a (west) European army under a supranational political authority. One of the main objectives of the Pleven Plan was to prevent West Germany from creating an independent military capability by permitting its rearmament within an international framework. The EDC was also conceived as part of the strategy for European integration being pursued by Robert Schuman and Jean Monnet with the ECSC. An EDC treaty was agreed in 1952 by the same six member states as were involved in the ECSC, but it was rejected by the French National Assembly and the project collapsed in 1954.

European Development Fund (EDF): established under the terms of the first Yaoundé Convention, the EDF has provided development assistance to the ACP states within the framework of the Lomé Conventions and, since 2001, the Cotonou Convention.

European Economic Area (EEA): created in 1994 as a result of a comprehensive agreement between the EU and the EFTA states, with the exception of Switzerland, which did not ratify the treaty after the EEA had been rejected in a referendum. The EEA has effectively extended the EU's single market across most of western Europe, with free movement of goods, services, capital, and people. It involved the EFTA states accepting most of the single market *acquis*. Austria, Finland, and Sweden subsequently decided that they would apply to become EU members. The EEA continues to operate with just three remaining EFTA states: Iceland, Norway, and Liechtenstein.

European Economic Community (EEC): one of the original three European Communities of the 1950s, founded in 1957 with the signing of the Treaty of Rome. The six founding member states ("the Six") were France, West Germany, Belgium, the Netherlands, Luxembourg, and Italy. Although one of the key objectives was to create a common market, the Treaty of Rome also had political goals, including preserving peace and liberty, and laying the foundations of an "ever closer union among the peoples of Europe".

European Environmental Agency (EEA): established in 1993 in Copenhagen, the main function of the agency is to collect and collate detailed environmental data.

European Free Trade Association (EFTA): established in 1960 under the terms of the Stockholm Convention, EFTA was created as an alternative to the European Economic Community. It initially consisted of seven member states: Austria, Denmark, Norway, Portugal, Sweden, Switzerland, and the United Kingdom. Iceland and Liechtenstein later became members, and Finland obtained associate membership. The main attraction of EFTA was the fact that it was only a free trade area, with none of the political aspirations of the EEC. It was thus a very suitable organization for those states that were concerned to preserve their neutrality and/or their national sovereignty. All but four of EFTA's member states have since become EU members, and Iceland, Norway, and Liechtenstein form part of the European Economic Area.

European Investment Bank (EIB): established under the terms of the Treaty of Rome to finance capital investment within the Community that would benefit Community development. Member states subscribe capital on a pro-rata percentage basis. The EIB is headed by a board of governors composed of the finance ministers of the member states. It has played a leading role in helping to finance major investment projects aimed at improving infrastructure, such as the Trans-European Networks and the Channel Tunnel.

European Monetary Institute (EMI): an agency, now defunct, established under the terms of the Treaty on European Union to promote closer collaboration between the member states on the development of a single European currency, to monitor the European Monetary System, and to advise the European Council on monetary matters. The EMI was based in Frankfurt am Main. It has been replaced by the European Central Bank, which is also based in Frankfurt.

European Monetary System (EMS): established in 1979, the EMS represented the second attempt by the Community to establish monetary stability within its boundaries by maintaining a system of fixed but adjustable exchange rates, the Exchange Rate Mechanism (ERM). It paved the way for the launch of EMU and the single currency.

European Parliament: composed of directly elected representatives from each of the EU member states, the Parliament aspires to be the democratic voice of the EU's citizens. Most of its plenary sessions are held in Strasbourg, the city that is said to symbolize Franco–German reconciliation, although it also meets in Brussels, where meetings of party groups and parliamentary committees are also held. The Treaty of Rome gave the Parliament, then known as the Assembly, only consultative and supervisory powers, but successive revisions to the treaty have considerably expanded its legislative and budgetary powers.

European Police Office (Europol): originating in the Europol Drugs Unit set up in 1995, the European Police Office became operational on 1 July 1999, with its headquarters in the Hague. It is a coordinating agency responsible for promoting police cooperation across the member states in joint areas of concern, particularly fraud, money laundering, drugs trafficking, illegal immigration, and terrorism.

European Political Cooperation (EPC): a process of foreign policy cooperation between EC member states, introduced informally in 1970 as a consequence of the Davignon Report and then formally recognized by the Single European Act in 1987. EPC was superceded by the more ambitious provisions of the Treaty on European Union for the development of the Common Foreign and Security Policy. See Common Foreign and Security Policy.

European Recovery Programme: see Marshall Plan

European Regional Development Fund (ERDF): The ERDF is one of the EU's structural funds, specifically targeted at projects designed to reduce the disparities between the regions of the EU. See Cohesion and Structural Funds.

European Security and Defence Identity (ESDI): the term used to signify strengthening the coherence and effectiveness of the group of European member states of NATO. It is sometimes also called the "European pillar" of the alliance.

European Social Fund (ESF): one of the EU's original structural funds, the ESF was established in 1960, under the terms of the Treaty of Rome, to promote employment opportunities, to raise living standards, and to make employment easier, particularly by helping to enhance geographic and occupational mobility. Finance from the ESF has been used to retrain the unemployed and to offer training to workers in need of re-employment or new skills. Particular attention has been paid to the long-term unemployed, to women, and to those under 25 years of age.

European System of Central Banks (ESCB): composed of the European Central Bank (ECB) and the national central banks of all the EU member states. The national central banks of those states that have not adopted the euro, and therefore conduct their own monetary policies, do not take part in the decision-making with regard to the single monetary policy for the euro zone. The term "Eurosystem" (see below) is used to describe the situation when the ECB and the national central banks that are in the euro zone are carrying out the treaty responsibilities of the ESCB with regard to the management of the single currency.

European Trade Union Confederation (ETUC): an umbrella organization for European trade unions and federations, recognized as one of the "social partners" that the Commission is obliged to consult before submitting any proposals in the social field

European Union (EU): created by the Treaty on European Union when it came into force in November 1993, the EU rests on three pillars: the European Communities (EC), the Common Foreign and Security Policy (CFSP), and Cooperation in Justice and Home Affairs (renamed Police and Judicial Cooperation in Criminal Matters by the Treaty of Amsterdam). The decision-making procedures and powers of the institutions differ between the pillars, with the second and third pillars relying on intergovernmental cooperation, in which national officials play a greater role than in the first pillar.

Europol: see European Police Office

Euroscepticism: the term commonly used to describe a wide spectrum of critical opinion on the EU, ranging from doubt and distrust of European integration through to implacable hostility to it. Euroscepticism is a growing phenomenon across the EU, reflecting popular dissatisfaction with many aspects of it, including specific policies such as EMU and enlargement, and the way in which the EU's institutions operate.

Eurosystem: the collective term used to refer to the European Central Bank and the national central banks of the EU member states that have adopted the euro. Its main tasks are to define and implement the monetary policy of the euro zone, for example setting interest rates; to conduct foreign exchange operations; to promote the smooth operation of payment systems; and to advise the EU and national authorities on matters within its field of competence.

Exchange Rate Mechanism (ERM): in association with the Ecu (see above), the ERM was a core element of the European Monetary System, established in 1979 to try to create currency stability between the EC's member states. The ERM was the central mechanism that regulated the fluctuating values of the currencies that were tied to the Ecu. If the exchange value of a currency fluctuated outside the set parameters, the central banks of the member states intervened in the international money markets, buying or selling in order to restore currency values.

federalism: a system of government in which powers are divided on a constitutional basis between a central government and provincial or regional units of government. Each level of government has its own policy competencies and institutional framework, and is considered to be "sovereign" within its own spheres of jurisdiction. Within western Europe, Austria, Belgium, Germany, and Switzerland are all federal states. In the context of the EU, there have been influential people since before World War II who have believed that the long-term goal of European integration should be the creation of a federal union, with policy competencies shared between federal or supranational institutions and the member states. Others, however, have rejected the concept of a federal union, especially as related to the future of the EU, and sought to preserve national sovereignty within a looser framework of intergovernmental cooperation. See also intergovernmentalism.

FEOGA: see European Agricultural Guidance and Guarantee Fund, for which this is the French acronym

financial perspective: an agreement by all three of the EU's budgetary authorities (Commission, Council, and European Parliament) on a financial plan for the next seven years, detailing projected expenditure under the main budget headings. The financial perspective then forms the framework for the preparation of the detailed annual budgets. It was introduced as a result of the Interinstitutional Agreement on Budgetary Discipline and Improvement of the Budgetary Procedure in 1988 in order to provide greater stability and efficiency in the budget decision-making process.

flexibility: the principle that, if some EU member states want to integrate more closely or in different policy areas than other members, they can do so. It is a term seen to have generally positive connotations by both the proponents and opponents of deeper integration and so is relatively neutral in the debates about the future direction of the EU. The principle of flexibility was incorporated into the Treaty of Amsterdam as "provisions for closer cooperation". In the Treaty of Nice (not yet ratified) the strict conditions for its use are eased slightly and it is renamed "enhanced cooperation". See also closer cooperation.

four freedoms: the free movement of goods, services, capital, and labour across national borders, crucial to the functioning of the single market. The four freedoms involve not just the removal of physical barriers, such as tariffs and border controls, but also agreement on such matters as health and safety standards for goods, and professional qualifications and social security rights for workers.

free trade area: the lowest form of economic integration, in which the barriers to trade in goods and services between participating member states are removed

G7/ G8: see Group of Seven/Eight

GATT: General Agreement on Tariffs and Trade, the international forum through which multilateral trade negotiations were conducted from 1947 onwards. At the close of the Uruguay Round of negotiations in 1995 the GATT was institutionalized and renamed the World Trade Organization (WTO).

Group of Seven/Eight: an informal association of the seven major industrial states (now eight, including Russia): Canada, Germany, France, Italy, Japan, Russia, the United Kingdom, and the United States. Summits began between finance ministers in 1977, and have since involved heads of state and government meeting annually to discuss broad economic themes. As trade policy is an exclusive EU competence, the President of the Commission also attends to represent the EU as a whole. In recent years the meetings have become the focus of violent anti-globalization protests.

hard core: a group of EU member states that is willing to move towards closer integration, either as a vanguard group going ahead to show the way for other states to follow (see multispeed Europe) or as a semipermanent separate entity (see variable geometry)

High Representative for the CFSP: a new title and function of the Secretary-General of the Council, introduced under the terms of the Treaty of Amsterdam. The role of the High Representative is to assist the member state holding the Council Presidency in the conduct of the CFSP. Javier Solana was appointed the first High Representative in 1999.

IGC: see intergovernmental conference

Implementation and Enforcement of Environmental Law (IMPEL): an informal network that encourages cooperation among the national agencies responsible for implementation and enforcement of EU law concerning the environment

Instrument for Structural Policies for Pre-Accession (ISPA): a new EU fund introduced in 2000 for pre-accession aid, particularly for improvements in transport and the environment, to enable applicant states to meet EU standards

Intergovernmental: a model of collective decision-making that does not involve any loss of sovereignty to supranational institutions. In the context of the EU, the term means policy-making and decision-making by the officials and ministers of member states, usually requiring unanimity, rather than by the usual "Community method", established by the Treaty of Rome, in which the Commission, European Parliament and Court of Justice have significant roles. The second and third pillars of the TEU are "intergovernmental", in contrast to the "supranational" first pillar based on the EC. See also supranational.

intergovernmental conference (IGC): the formal term for the process whereby member states negotiate amendments to the founding treaties, now according to Article 48 of the Treaty on European Union. An IGC takes the form of a series of meetings, often over a period of several months, of representatives of the governments of the member states, at both official and ministerial level. An IGC is usually concluded at a meeting of the European Council where the heads of state and government hammer out an agreement on a draft treaty, which then has to be ratified by all the member states before it can come into force.

intergovernmentalism: a theoretical explanation, often used in contrast to "neofunctionalism" (see below), of the process and character of European integration that suggests that national governments and nation states continue to play a central role. Major steps towards greater integration are best accounted for by bargains struck by the largest member states to further their own national interests.

internal market: an alternative term used to describe the single market

justice and home affairs (JHA): "Cooperation in Justice and Home Affairs" was the title of the third pillar of the Treaty on European Union, providing for intergovernmental cooperation on such matters as asylum, immigration, border controls, combating international crime, and judicial cooperation. The Treaty of Amsterdam transferred responsibility for asylum, visa, and immigration policy, and for external border controls, to the first pillar, and the third pillar was renamed "Police and Judicial Cooperation in Criminal Matters" to reflect its new focus.

Lomé Conventions: the first Convention was signed in 1975 and three further Conventions were subsequently agreed before it was superseded by the Cotonou Agreement in 2000. Lomé was the keystone of the EC/EU's development policy towards those African, Pacific, and Caribbean (ACP) states with which the EU member states have historical ties, mostly as former colonies. See ACP.

Luxembourg Compromise: an agreement in 1966 between the then six member states that resolved the political crisis caused by France's boycott of EC meetings in protest at a number of developments, including the scheduled introduction of qualified majority voting in the Council of Ministers. The compromise involved maintaining the principle of majority voting but agreeing that "when very important issues are at stake discussions must be continued until unanimous agreement is reached". In practice, this meant that the national veto was retained until agreement was reached in the Single European Act to move towards the use of qualified majority voting in limited circumstances. See qualified majority voting.

Marshall Plan: the Marshall Plan, or European Recovery Programme, was established and funded by the US government to stimulate the economic recovery of Europe (in practice, western Europe) after World War II. The financial assistance given under the Marshall Plan was managed by the Organization for European Economic Cooperation (OEEC), which encouraged economic cooperation on an intergovernmental basis.

MEDA: the financial instrument of assistance introduced as part of the Euro-Mediterranean Partnership launched in 1995 with the EU's 12 southern Mediterranean neighbours to support economic development, political stability, and social cohesion. See Euro-Mediterranean Partnership.

MEDIA II: a programme of measures to encourage the audiovisual industry in EU member states

MEP: Member of the European Parliament (see above)

most favoured nation (MFN): a principle of international trade policy whereby a signatory of a multilateral trade agreement agrees to extend to all other signatories the same treatment with respect to tariffs and quotas that it extends to its most favoured trading partner. It is one of the lowest forms of trade preference, and is therefore not particularly generous.

multilevel governance: a concept that is increasingly used to analyse the complex sharing of decision-making powers and responsibilities between different levels of government (local, regional, national, and supranational) in what is seen as the evolving EU "polity". A good example of multilevel governance is the EU's structural policies, which involve the Commission, Parliament, national ministries, and regional and local authorities in a process that is interactive rather than dominated by any one level.

multispeed Europe: one of the various models of differentiated integration, in which the member states proceed towards closer integration at different speeds but towards the same final destination. Typically it involves a group of "avant-garde" states going ahead at a faster pace while others lag behind, either from necessity or through choice. The operation of the European Monetary System and the convergence criteria for EMU are often cited as examples where it has been accepted that not all the member states might be able to participate from the beginning. The prospect of enlargement to include the much poorer and less economically developed states in central and eastern Europe has put the possibility of variable speeds in the integration process on the EU's agenda, and the Treaties of Amsterdam and Nice have included procedural and institutional mechanisms whereby new proposals could be agreed. See also closer cooperation, flexibility.

NATO: see North Atlantic Treaty Organization

neofunctionalism: for many years the dominant theory of European political and economic integration. Neofunctionalism purports to explain the process by which political integration would be achieved by incremental economic integration in specific sectors. The central concept is "spillover", referring to the pressure for integration in one sector to lead to integration in related sectors, gradually binding member states into closer political as well as economic relationships. Neofunctionalism was very influential in the early years of postwar European integration, reflecting Jean Monnet and Robert Schuman's strategy of starting with coal and steel (the ECSC) and then moving on to the common market and atomic energy (the EEC and Euratom). Although neofunctionalism has been rejected by most later theorists, it continues to influence study and debate about the future of the EU. See also intergovernmentalism.

Nordic Council: an intergovernmental and interparliamentary association established by Denmark, Finland, Sweden, Norway, and Iceland, in 1952. The Nordic Council is a consultative body with a limited institutional framework, but many important initiatives have been taken within its framework, contributing to a strong sense of regional solidarity. Three of its members are now also members of the EU and special steps have been taken to ensure that close cooperation among the Nordic states continues.

North Atlantic Treaty Organization (NATO): a collective defence organization, set up in 1949, through which the US and Canada committed themselves to defend western Europe. It has had some difficulty in defining its role in the new European context after the end of the Cold War, and Russia has called for it to be disbanded, like its erstwhile counterpart, the Warsaw Pact. All the new democracies in central and eastern Europe have been keen to become NATO members. The Czech Republic, Hungary, and Poland did so in 1999, while other ex-Communist states, including Russia, have established close relationships with NATO on the basis of "Partnership for Peace" agreements.

NUTS: an acronym of the French title of the system used to classify the EU regions, the Nomenclature of Territorial Units for Statistics. It is a hierarchical system based loosely on the size of the region, with level 1 regions corresponding to the standard regions in the United Kingdom or the *Länder* in Germany. The system is used for statistical purposes and as the basis of the operation of the EU's cohesion policy.

OCCAR: Organization Conjointe de Coopération pour l'Armament, an agency set up by France, Germany, Italy, and the United Kingdom to encourage cooperation on the production of armaments

OECD: see Organization for Economic Cooperation and Development

OEEC: see Organization for European Economic Cooperation

Official Journal (OJ): the customary short title for the *Official Journal of the European Communities*, the authoritative record of the EC/EU, published continuously in all the official languages by the Office for Official Publications of the EC in Luxembourg. It is published in three sections: the L series, containing a record of agreed legislation; the C series, containing draft legislation, information, and notices; and the S series, with notices and calls for tender for contracts for public works and supplies. Proceedings of the European Parliament are recorded in the Annex. Once the Treaty of Nice has been ratified its full title is to be changed to the *Official Journal of the European Union*.

OLAF: the acronym of the European Anti-Fraud Office, set up in June 1999 to take responsibility for combating fraud against the EU budget. It has the power to investigate the management and financing of all the EU's institutions and bodies. It has total operational independence.

opt-out: a potentially permanent exemption from a treaty provision granted to a member state, usually to avoid a stalemate when the other member states wish to go ahead with cooperation in a new field, as, for example, when the United Kingdom's two opt-outs, on the Social Chapter and on participation in the third stage of EMU, were agreed at Maastricht.

Organization for Economic Cooperation and Development (OECD): established in 1961, on the initiative of the United States, to replace the OEEC (see next entry), the OECD now has a membership extending beyond Europe and North America. It has developed into an international economic forum for the major industrial countries of the world, publishing authoritative reports on a wide range of economic issues from its headquarters in Paris.

Organization for European Economic Cooperation (OEEC): established in 1948 to manage and administer US aid under the Marshall Plan, intended to stimulate the economic recovery of western Europe. The OEEC was replaced by the OECD (see previous entry) in 1961.

Organization for Security and Cooperation in Europe (OSCE): created in 1994 as a result of the decision to institutionalize the series of Conferences on Security and Cooperation in Europe that had helped to reduce tensions during the Cold War. The OSCE is a pan-European security forum that promotes dialogue on important issues, such as human rights and respect for minorities, but does not have the resources to play as active a role in security as some of its members, most notably Russia, would like it to.

own resources: the EU's budget revenue, which is derived from four elements: agricultural duties and sugar and isoglucose levies; customs duties on imports from third countries; a proportion of national revenues from value-added tax (VAT); and an additional resource based on the GNP of each member state.

Partnership and Cooperation Agreement (PCA): a treaty establishing a comprehensive economic and political relationship between the EU and a member state of the CIS. The PCAs agreed with Russia and Ukraine include provision for the future development of a free trade area between them and the EU.

Petersberg tasks: humanitarian and rescue tasks, peacekeeping, and crisis management were identified in 1992 at a ministerial meeting of the WEU in Petersberg, Germany, as appropriate missions for the WEU. They were adopted as the tasks that the EU should assume responsibility for in the expanded role of the CFSP, as outlined in the Treaty of Amsterdam, and for which the EU has developed a limited military capability (see CESDP).

PHARE: a financial assistance programme established in 1989 to assist in the economic and political transition of Poland and Hungary – hence its acronym, which originally stood for "Pologne et Hongrie Assistance pour la Restructuration Economique". Since 1991–92, however, the programme has been extended to all of the candidate states.

pillar(s): a metaphor for the institutional structure of the EU created by the Treaty on European Union. The pillar structure was the result of a compromise by which major new areas of policy competence were included in the treaty but made subject to intergovernmental decision-making procedures rather than the normal Community method. The first pillar comprises the three European Communities, and includes the single market, EMU, and the other economic and social policies. Pillar two is the Common Foreign and Security Policy. Pillar three was known as Cooperation in Justice and Home Affairs, as agreed at Maastricht, but it was reorganized under the Treaty of Amersterdam and its name was changed to Police and Judicial Cooperation in Criminal Matters.

Policy Planning and Early Warning Unit (PPEWU): established in the General Secretariat of the Council to provide expert analysis and advice on external developments coming within the remit of the Common Foreign and Security Policy

Presidency: within the EU this term usually refers to the Council Presidency, the system whereby each member state in turn, for six months at a time, assumes the responsibility for chairing all meetings at ministerial and official level, managing the Common Foreign and Security Policy, and representing the EU in external forums. There are also Presidents of the Commission, of the European Parliament, and of the European Court of Justice, but as these are positions held by specific individuals, rather than collectively by a member state, the term "Presidency" is hardly ever applied.

Protocol on Social Policy: also known as the Social Chapter, the Protocol contained many of the provisions of the Social Charter. It was annexed to the Treaty on European Union because the Conservative government of the United Kingdom refused to agree to its being incorporated into the treaty itself. One of the first actions of the Labour Government elected in May 1997 was to agree that the protocol should be incorporated into the Treaty of Amsterdam. See also Social Charter.

qualified majority voting (QMV): QMV is a method of voting used within the Council of Ministers that allows decisions to be taken even when there is not a consensus. Each member state is allocated an agreed number of votes, which is loosely based on the size of its population but favours the smaller states. Until the Treaty of Nice comes into operation, a minimum of 62 votes out of the 87 available is required for a legislative proposal to be approved. Which areas of policy may be decided by QMV, the number of votes cast by each state, and the number of total votes required for a decision have always been among the most politically sensitive issues ever since the Luxembourg Compromise (see above). QMV was a major issue on the agenda at the intergovernmental conference preceding the Treaty of Nice, as the EU prepared itself for a probable enlargement to a membership of up to 27 states.

SAPARD: the standard acronym for the Special Accession Programme for Agriculture and Rural Development, a programme to support the rural economies of the applicant states in central and eastern Europe until they become EU members and thus eligible for aid from the structural funds

Schengen Convention: an agreement signed in 1985 by Belgium, France, Germany, Luxembourg, and the Netherlands, under which they would gradually remove their common border controls. It was inspired by the goal of the single market to abolish all internal border controls but the agreement itself was concluded outside the EC's legal framework. Its implementation was delayed until a second convention had been signed in 1990. Since then all the other EU member states have become parties to it, except Ireland and the United Kingdom. The European Council decided at Amsterdam in June 1997 to incorporate the Schengen *acquis* into the EU from May 1999. Ireland and the United Kingdom secured opt-outs, whereas Norway and Iceland, which do not belong to the EU but do belong to the Nordic Passport Union (along with Denmark, Finland, and Sweden), signed special agreements allowing them to participate in the free movement area of the EU.

single currency: the common currency, known as the euro, of the Economic and Monetary Union, established on 1 January 1999. Euro notes and coins will be in circulation in all the EU member states, except Denmark, Sweden, and the United Kingdom, from 1 January 2002.

single European market or **single market**: terms used since the mid-1980s to signify the common market that was one of the main objectives of the Treaty of Rome but which had still not been fully achieved. The Single European Act set a target date of 31 December 1992 for the completion of the single market and the term "1992" was adopted as a shorthand way of referring to the completion of the Community's single market programme. It involved the removal of the remaining physical, technical, and fiscal barriers to the free movement of goods, services, capital, and labour within the Community to create a "Europe without frontiers".

Social Charter: the name most commonly used for the Charter of Fundamental Social Rights of Workers, which was signed by all the EU's member states, except the United Kingdom, in 1989. It was only a political declaration without any legal force, but it led directly to the Protocol on Social Policy (see above).

Social Chapter: a term commonly used to refer to the Protocol on Social Policy.

sovereignty: a principle originating in political theory and now customary in international law, meaning that the ultimate legal authority to take and enforce decisions in a state rests with its national political authorities. Membership of the EU requires a state to transfer powers, and thus some of that authority, in those areas covered by the treaties, to the EU's institutions, in which it participates but over which it cannot exercise unilateral control. Those who support European integration interpret such transfer of powers as a matter of pooling or sharing sovereignty; Eurosceptics regard it as involving a loss of sovereignty.

System of Stabilization of Export Earnings: see Stabex

Stability and Growth Pact: an agreement that commits the states participating in EMU to continue to pursue budgetary discipline, in an attempt to strengthen the euro on international money markets. The Commission monitors the performance of the euro zone states and significant financial penalties can be imposed on any participating state that has a budget deficit exceeding 3% of its GDP.

Strasbourg: the site of one of the European Parliament's main buildings, in which most of its plenary sessions are held, despite pressure to hold more, if not all, of them in its equally large building in Brussels. The city is also the home of the Council of Europe and its Court of Human Rights.

Structural Funds: the financial instruments of the EU's cohesion policy, designed to provide support for projects directed at the economic development or regeneration of the poorer regions of the EU, in order to reduce regional disparities in employment and standards of living. The funds are the European Regional Development Fund, the Social Fund, and the "guidance" component of the European Agricultural Guidance and Guarantee Fund. Although not strictly one of the structural funds, the Cohesion Fund has a similar purpose, although it is targeted at the poorer member states rather than at specific regions.

subsidiarity: an important concept incorporated into the Treaty on European Union as one of the guiding principles of the EU. Subsidiarity refers to the principle that decisions should be taken at the lowest level of government, and as close to the citizen as possible, consistent with effective action. It is the usual basis for deciding on the allocation of policy competences to the respective levels of government in a federal system, but it is seen by opponents of federalism as a powerful check against the further encroachment of the EU's institutions on national competences. These very different perceptions of the role of subsidiarity in the EU illustrate the ambiguity of the principle and suggest the practical difficulty in applying it.

supranational: a model of collective decision-making in which an individual nation state may sometimes find itself obliged to accept an outcome that it would not have chosen. It involves the roles of institutions and actors that are independent of the member states, such as the Commission, the European Parliament, the European Court of Justice, and EU-level pressure groups, in the policy-making process. It also involves decision-making by qualified majority voting rather than unanimity, which means that a member state cannot exercise a national veto over decisions that it dislikes. Opponents of supranational decision-making infer that it causes a loss of national sovereignty, but its proponents argue that it represents a "pooling" of sovereignty. See sovereignty.

supremacy of Community law: although the Treaty of Rome made no provision for resolving a conflict between Community and national law, the European Court of Justice has ruled in its case law that Community law must prevail. In practice, this means that a national law deemed to be in conflict with Community law must be either repealed or amended.

Sysmin: see System for Safeguarding and Developing Mineral Production

System of Stabilization of Export Earnings (Stabex): a system designed to safeguard the export earnings of the Lomé Convention states against fluctuations in the world market prices of certain commodities. Stabex gives assistance in the form of both grants and low-interest loans.

System for Safeguarding and Developing Mineral Production (Sysmin): a system similar to Stabex (see previous entry) that protects the minimum price for mineral exports from Lomé Convention states to EU states during periods of economic downturn. Assistance is given in the form of long-term low-interest loans. Oil and gas production are excluded from this system.

TACIS: see Technical Assistance for the Commonwealth of Independent States

TCA: see Trade and Cooperation Agreement

TEC: see Treaty Establishing the European Communities

Technical Assistance for the Commonwealth of Independent States (TACIS): an aid programme for the successor states of the Soviet Union, with the exception of the Baltic states, which are eligible for funding from PHARE (see above). It provides finance for projects to support their transition to market economies and the consolidation of their democratic political systems.

Tempus: see Trans-European Mobility Programme for University Studies

TENS: See Trans-European Networks

TEU: see Treaty on European Union

Trade and Cooperation Agreement (TCA): A fairly limited economic agreement that the EU concludes with third countries when it wants to encourage the development of greater trade and economic cooperation with them. They have often been upgraded later into more substantial economic and political agreements, for example the Europe Agreements with the central and eastern European states and the Partnership and Cooperation Agreements with Russia and the other members of the CIS.

Trans-European Mobility Programme for University Studies (Tempus): a programme established in 1990 to provide financial assistance for the reform of university education in central and eastern Europe. The scheme also promotes staff and student exchanges between universities in that region and their counterparts in the EU.

Trans-European Networks (TENs): an integrated EU-wide system of transport, energy, and communications networks, developed with the support of EU finance from the cohesion and structural funds. The objectives are to contribute to social and economic cohesion, and to stimulate growth in the single market.

transparency: a concept meaning openness, and particularly applied to the way in which the EU's institutions operate, or are seen by critics to fail to operate, effectively and democratically. It involves opening some meetings to the public, making more information available about the contents of decisions and how they were taken, and trying to simplify the decision-making procedures so that ordinary citizens can follow what is happening. The objective is to make the EU more understandable and therefore, it is hoped, more legitimate in the eyes of its citizens.

Treaty Establishing the European Community: the name now more commonly used for the revised Treaty of Rome. It covers all the economic and social policies of the EU, its institutions, and its decision-making processes.

Treaty on European Union (TEU): the treaty that created the EU, frequently called the Maastricht Treaty after the Dutch city where it was agreed in 1991

Treaty of Paris: the founding treaty of the European Coal and Steel Community, signed in April 1951

Treaty of Rome: the founding treaty of the European Economic Community, signed in March 1957

UNICE: see Union of Industrial and Employers Confederations of Europe

Union: a name commonly now used to refer to the EU both in official documents and in more general usage

Union of Industrial and Employers' Confederations of Europe (UNICE): one of the most powerful interest groups operating in the EU system, defending the interests of big business and employers. It is an umbrella organization of the main employers' associations in the member states and is one of the "social partners" that the Commission has to consult before proposing legislation on social or economic matters.

variable geometry: a form of differentiated integration in which the membership of various policy groupings, either informal or based on formal institutions, differs from one group to another. It does not necessarily depend on there being a "hard core" of pro-integration states, as some states may favour closer integration in some policy areas while being cautious in others. There are already several examples of variable geometry within the EU, as in the slight but significant differences in the membership of the groups participating in the Schengen arrangements for the removal of border controls, the single currency, and the planned military capability under the CESDP. In addition, not all EU states are members of NATO and, of those that are, not all are members of the WEU.

Warsaw Treaty Organization (WTO): commonly referred to as the Warsaw Pact. This organization was established in 1955 by the Soviet Union in response to West Germany's admission to NATO.

Membership was limited to the Soviet Union and those states in central and eastern Europe that had fallen into its sphere of influence in the late 1940s. Dominated by the Soviet Union, the Warsaw Pact collapsed in 1990 and was abolished in 1991.

Western European Union (WEU): an organization for collective defence that was developed from the Brussels Treaty Organization of 1948 but was completely overshadowed by NATO throughout most of the Cold War. It was revived in the 1980s, on the initiative of France, which found its exclusively European membership attractive. As a result of Franco–German agreement, the WEU became the security arm of the EU under the terms of the Treaty on European Union, and there was speculation that it might become an EU institution. However, following the decision to develop a military capability within the EU, the WEU may well be disbanded.

widening: a term frequently used to signify the enlargement of the EU by the accession of new members. Its relationship to the deepening of integration is controversial, but on all previous occasions when the EU has been widened there have been pressures for policy and institutional reform. See also deepening, enlargement.

World Trade Organization (WTO): founded in 1994, the WTO became operational in early 1995 to replace GATT as the mechanism for international trade negotiations. See GATT.

Appendix 3

Personalities

Presidents of the European Commission

1958–67	Walter Hallstein	Germany
1967–70	Jean Rey	Belgium
1970–72	Franco Maria Malfatti	Italy
1972–73	Sicco Mansholt	Netherlands
1973–77	François-Xavier Ortoli	France
1977–81	Roy Jenkins	United Kingdom
1981–85	Gaston Thorn	Luxembourg
1985–95	Jacques Delors	France
1995–99	Jacques Santer	Luxembourg
1999–	Romano Prodi	Italy

Secretaries General of the Commission

1958–87	Emile Noël	France
1987–97	David Williamson	United Kingdom
1997–2000	Carlo Trojan	Netherlands
2000–	David O'Sullivan	Ireland

Presidents of the European Parliament since direct elections began

1979–82	Simone Veil	France	Liberal Group
1982–84	Piete Dankert	Netherlands	Socialist Group
1984–87	Pierre Pflimlin	France	European People's Party
1987–89	Henry, Lord Plumb	United Kingdom	European Democratic Group
1989–92	Enrique, Barón Crespo	Spain	Socialist Group
1992–94	Egon Klepsch	Germany	European People's Party
1994–97	Klaus Hänsch	Germany	Party of European Socialists
1997–99	Jose Maria Gil-Robles	Spain	European People's Party
1999–	Nicole Fontaine	France	European People's Party

Secretary General of the Council and High Representative for the Common Foreign and Security Policy

1999–   Javiar Solana Madariaga   Spain

President of the European Central Bank

1998–   Willem Duisenberg   Netherlands

Members of the European Commission, 1999–2004

Romano Prodi	Italy	President
Neil Kinnock	United Kingdom	Vice President, Administrative Reform
Loyola de Palacio	Spain	Vice President, Relations with the European Parliament, Transport and Energy
Mario Monti	Italy	Competition
Franz Fischler	Austria	Agriculture, Rural Development and Fisheries
Erkki Liikanen	Finland	Enterprise and Information Society
Frits Bolkestein	Netherlands	Internal Market
Philippe Busquin	Belgium	Research
Pedro Solbes Mira	Spain	Economic and Monetary Affairs
Poul Nielson	Denmark	Development and Humanitarian Aid
Günter Verheugen	Germany	Enlargement
Chris Patten	United Kingdom	External Relations
Pascal Lamy	France	Trade
David Byrne	Ireland	Health and Consumer Protection
Michel Barnier	France	Regional Policy
Viviane Reding	Luxembourg	Education and Culture
Michaele Schreyer	Germany	Budget
Margot Wallström	Sweden	Environment
Antonio Vitorino	Portugal	Justice and Home Affairs
Anna Diamantopoulou	Greece	Employment and Social Affairs

The entries below describe briefly a number of significant people who have played a role in the development of the EC/EU and some of those who are expected to shape its future.

ACHESON, Dean (1893–1971): US Secretary of State from 1949 to 1953. Acheson was a keen advocate of European integration and a close friend of Jean Monnet, whom he had met in Washington, DC, when Monnet was an Allied economic planner there during World War II. Acheson was the author of US support for the European Coal and Steel Community and also gave support to the Franco–German rapprochement desired by Konrad Adenauer.

ADENAUER, Konrad (1876–1967): Chancellor of West Germany from 1949 to 1963. As a Christian Democrat, Adenauer was an ardent supporter of European integration, which, in his opinion, should be based on Franco–German reconciliation. He acted as his own foreign minister for the duration of his Chancellorship, and followed a policy designed to rehabilitate West Germany and to integrate it into western Europe. The objectives of his foreign policy were to ensure the security of his state and to work for German reunification. His friendship with Charles de Gaulle secured the desired Franco–German relationship, which has since shaped the process of European integration.

ANDREOTTI, Guilio (1919–   ): Prime Minister of Italy from 1972 to 1973, from 1976 to 1979, and from 1989, to 1991; Minister of Foreign Affairs from 1983 to 1989. Andreotti was an influential figure in the revival of European integration in the mid-1980s that was to culminate in the Maastricht Treaty. In particular, he is credited with outmanoeuvring British Prime Minister, Margaret Thatcher, at the Milan Council in June 1985, and securing the decision to launch the intergovernmental conference that led to the Single European Act.

AZNAR, José-Maria (1953–   ): Prime Minister of Spain since 1996. Aznar's centre–right government successfully ensured that Spain qualified to be among the first group of states to adopt the single currency. Although a committed supporter of European integration, he is determined to defend Spain's national interests, especially in relation to the structural and cohesion funds, from which Spain has benefited so much in the past.

BLAIR, Tony (1953–   ): Prime Minister of the United Kingdom since 1997. Blair is committed to a much more positive policy towards the EU than any British Prime Minister has pursued since Edward Heath (see below). Although he shares the preference that all his predecessors have shown for intergovernmental cooperation rather than federalism, he has taken a much more pragmatic approach to treaty reform than either Margaret Thatcher or John Major. Immediately after his party won the general election in 1997, he announced that Britain would no longer opt out of the social chapter, and he has indicated that he has no objection in principle to the single currency, once the economic conditions are right for its adoption. However, public opinion against the euro makes its adoption one of the most difficult challenges facing his second administration and he is constrained by his promise to hold a referendum on the issue. His fear that his ambition to play a leading role in EU affairs is undermined by Britain's exclusion form the euro zone has led him to take a lead in other major policy spheres such as enlargement and defence, surprising other government leaders in 1998 by proposing that an EU rapid reaction force should be developed. He has also tried to win support among social democratic leaders for the "third way" approach of New Labour to social and economic policy.

BRIAND, Aristide (1862–1932): Foreign Minister of France from 1925 to 1932 and Prime Minister 11 times. Briand was a prominent early supporter of European integration. In a memorandum issued in 1930 he advocated a form of European union to guarantee peace.

BRANDT, Willy (1913–92): Foreign Minister of West Germany from 1966 to 1969, and Chancellor from 1969 to 1974. An influential social democrat, Brandt is probably still best known as the architect of *Ostpolitik*, the policy of openness towards the Soviet Union and the states of central and eastern Europe, including the German Democratic Republic (East Germany). A series of agreements helped to establish more normal relations between West Germany and its neighbours, and contributed to détente between the western and eastern blocs. Brandt was also committed to European integration and strongly supported Britain's membership of the European Community, pressing the French to agree to enlargement. However, he was unwilling to accept that West Germany should be the paymaster for the Community, clashed with the French government over the Common Agricultural Policy, and opposed the creation of the Regional Development Fund.

BRITTAN, Sir Leon (1939–   ): Vice President of the European Commission from 1989 to 1999. A former British Conservative cabinet minister, Brittan joined the Commission as one of the two British Commissioners appointed by Margaret Thatcher's government. He was given responsibility for competition policy and financial institutions. His Commission portfolio placed him in a central role with regard to the completion of the single market, and caused friction between him and Thatcher as a result of his pro-European views. His belief in liberal economics also caused tensions between him and Jacques Delors, the President of the Commisssion, who objected to Brittan's emphasis on free trade. In 1993 Brittan became the Commissioner responsible for economic relations, successfully leading the EU's negotiations in the Uruguay Round of the GATT. He served on the Santer Commission with responsibility for external trade, but was obliged to resign in 1999 along with the rest of his colleagues, although no criticisms were made of him personally.

BROWN, Gordon (1951–); British Chancellor of the Exchequer since 1997, he has pursued a more cautious policy towards the EU than Prime Minister Tony Blair and some other members of the government. He transferred responsibility for interest rates to the Bank of England, so that the United Kingdom would meet the Maastricht requirement for national central banks to be independent but has insisted that the economic conditions must be right before the United Kingdom could adopt the euro. Although he has set five economic tests that must be satisfied before moving to the single currency, many people believe that the decision will inevitably have to be a political one.

CHIRAC, Jacques (1932–): Prime Minister of France from 1974 to 1976 and from 1986 to 1988; President since 1995. Chirac was the founder of the Rassemblement pour la République (RPR), one of the main centre-right parties in France, often known as the Gaullists. He prefers an intergovernmental rather than federal approach to European integration. However, he has been determined to maintain France's central role in the EU, and was prepared to pursue unpopular economic and social policies to ensure that France would meet the Maastricht criteria for participation in EMU. Since the victory of the Left in the general election in 1997, he has had to work with a Socialist Prime Minister, Lionel Jospin, under the difficult circumstances known in France as "cohabitation". During France's Presidency of the EU Chirac presided over the intergovernmental negotiations that were concluded at Nice in December 2000. In 2001 he was increasingly under pressure as a result of investigations into a number of corruption scandals alleged to have taken place during his long term of office as Mayor of Paris (1977–95).

COCKFIELD, Francis, Lord (1916–): European Commissioner, with responsibility for the internal market, from 1985 to 1989. Lord Cockfield is most widely known as the author of the White Paper issued in 1985 that set out the requirements and timetable for the completion of the single European market. Although he had been nominated by Margaret Thatcher as a trusted advocate of the free market, he became a committed integrationist, even suggesting that a single currency was the logical next step to the internal market. As a result, he was not renominated by her government for a second term on the Commission.

DE GASPERI, Alcide (1881–1954): Prime Minister of Italy from 1945 to 1954. De Gasperi set the tone for prevailing Italian attitudes towards European integration after World War II. He was an ardent supporter of European integration, seeing it as a means of assisting Italian economic development and of restraining political extremism in postwar Italy.

DE PALACIO DEL VALLE-LERSUNDI, Loyola (1950–): Vice-President of the European Commission since 1999 with responsibility for relations with the European Parliament, Transport, and Energy. A member of the Spanish centre-right People's Party, she was Minister for Agriculture, Fisheries, and Food 1996–99.

DELORS, Jacques (1925–): President of the European Commission from 1985 to 1994. Delors, a prominent French Socialist politician before his appointment to the Commission, was the most activist of recent Presidents, with a clear agenda for deeper political, economic, and monetary integration. The main achievements during the ten years of his leadership included the completion of the internal market, the Single European Act, the adoption of the Social Charter, agreement on budgetary reforms, and the development of detailed plans for Economic and Monetary Union, which were incorporated into the Treaty on European Union. In all these areas Delors made major contributions, and both the budget and the EMU proposals bear his name. However, in a number of significant cases he did not achieve his goals, and the compromise on the three "pillars" structure of the Maastricht Treaty was a major disappointment for him. He worked closely with François Mitterrand, although he also had good relations with Helmut Kohl and was sympathetic to German unification. Inevitably, his overtly integrationist ambitions also made him enemies, most notably Margaret Thatcher and the British tabloid press.

DUISENBERG, Willem (Wim) (1935–): Minister of Finance in the Netherlands from 1973 to 1977; Executive Director of De Nederlandsche Bank from 1981 to 1982 and then its President from 1982 to 1997; President of the European Monetary Institute from 1997 to 1998; President of the European Central Bank since 1998. At the time of Duisenberg's appointment as President of the European Central Bank, there was speculation that he had privately agreed, under pressure from the French government, to retire early so that Jean-Claude Trichet, the President of the Banc de France, can take over the position. Duisenberg oversaw the launch of Economic and Monetary Union on 1 January 1999, and the preparations for the introduction of euro notes and coins on 1 January 2002.

FISCHER, Joschka (1948–   ): Vice Chancellor and Minister of Foreign Affairs of Germany since 1998. Fischer is the most senior Green member of Germany's first Red–Green coalition at the federal level. As he had been a radical leftwing militant in the 1970s and a Green activist since 1982, his appointment aroused considerable interest throughout the EU. In fact, he has continued Germany's longstanding European policy of commitment to deeper political and economic integration, while also actively supporting enlargement to Germany's eastern neighbours. In an important speech at the Humboldt University in Berlin in May 2000 he outlined what he stressed was his personal vision for the future of the EU, which was clearly a federal model with a directly elected Commission. He came under considerable pressure from Green Party activists during the NATO bombing of Serbia in 1999, but he maintained his government's support for EU and NATO policy in the Balkans. He is also committed to the development of an EU military capability with full German participation.

FONTAINE, Nicole (1942–   ): Vice President of the European Parliament from 1989 to 1999, President since 1999. Fontaine was first elected as a French MEP in 1984 and is a member of the European People's Party group. She is particularly interested in issues related to "a citizen's Europe", including education, youth, culture, and women's rights.

GAULLE, Charles de (1890–1970): Leader of the Free French Forces from 1940 to 1945, President and Prime Minister of France from 1944 to 1946, Prime Minister from 1958 to 1959, President from 1959 to 1969. De Gaulle was responsible for the restoration of France as a European power with global influence in the aftermath of World War II. His foreign policy both projected and protected France's independence of action. De Gaulle did not reject European economic integration, but he insisted that it should not limit France's autonomy. He objected to the implied federalism of the Treaty of Rome and argued for a *Europe des patries*, a Europe of nation-states. De Gaulle's political blueprint for Europe was presented as the Fouchet Plan, but the Plan was rejected by the other member states of the Community. De Gaulle twice vetoed British membership of the European Economic Community (in 1963 and 1967), on the grounds that Britain would act as a conduit for US influence within the Community. He was responsible, with Konrad Adenauer, for the reconciliation between France and West Germany that was the cornerstone of postwar European integration.

GENSCHER, Hans-Dietrich (1927–   ): Foreign Minister of West Germany from 1974 to 1990 and of unified Germany from 1990 to 1992. During his exceptionally long period in office Genscher had a major influence on the development of the EC/EU, pressing for deeper political as well as economic integration. Genscher was the principal architect and co-author, with the Italian Foreign Minister, of the Genscher–Colombo Plan of 1981, which advocated political union and led indirectly to the Single European Act and the Treaty on European Union.

GISCARD D'ESTAING, Valéry (1926–   ): President of France from 1974 to 1981. Giscard formed a close personal and working relationship with Helmut Schmidt, the Chancellor of West Germany, and together they exercised strong leadership in the development of the European Community throughout the 1970s. They jointly initiated the European Monetary System and the Ecu, which were to pave the way to EMU and the single currency. Giscard was also responsible for the institutionalization of the summit meetings of heads of state and government, as the European Council, in order to provide more effective political leadership for the Community. After he lost the presidential election in 1981, he became a member of the European Parliament and leader of the Liberal Group. He also served as President of the European Movement. In later life he became a greater champion of deeper political integration than he had been when, as President of France, he had felt constrained by the legacy of de Gaulle.

GONZÁLEZ, Felipe (1942–   ): Prime Minister of Spain from 1982 to 1996. As the leader of Spain's first Socialist government since the death of the dictator Francisco Franco in 1975, González played a crucial role in the modernization of the country's society and economy, and the development of regional governments. He believed that membership of the European Community would bring both political stability and economic prosperity to Spain, and enable it to become once again an influential European state. After Spain joined the Community in 1986 he argued strongly in favour of the principle of "cohesion", whereby the poorer states would receive financial aid to help to narrow the economic disparities between them and the richer states. The inclusion of a "cohesion fund" in the Maastricht Treaty and the introduction of EU citizenship were both attributed to his negotiating skills. He was also successful in persuading other leaders to strengthen the EU's Mediterranean policy, to balance the support being given to the new democracies in central and eastern Europe. The Barcelona Conference in 1995 and the agreement to launch a new Euro–Mediterranean partnership were widely seen as the main achievements of Spain's EU Presidency, and as personal triumphs for González. He was defeated in the Spanish general election the following year, amid allegations of corruption and a secret assassination campaign against Basque terrorists, and has since withdrawn from public life.

HALLSTEIN, Walter (1901–82): President of the European Commission from 1958 to 1967. Hallstein had been West Germany's representative in the negotiations leading to the establishment of the European Coal and Steel Community, and also at the Messina Conference that drafted the Treaties of Rome. He worked closely with Jean Monnet and Robert Schuman, and shared their federalist ideals, believing that political and economic integration were inextricably linked. He was an activist President of the Commission and much of the credit for the success of the early years of the EEC is probably attributable to him. However, his belief that the Commission was an embryonic supranational government inevitably led him into a sharp conflict with President de Gaulle of France, which culminated in the "empty chair" crisis of 1965, when France boycotted the Community's institutions. Hallstein resigned in 1967 amid reports that de Gaulle would block his appointment to a further term as Commission President.

HEATH, Sir Edward (1916–   ): Prime Minister of the United Kingdom from 1970 to 1974. Heath, a Conservative member of the House of Commons from 1950 to 2001, led the British delegation that attempted to negotiate entry to the EEC in 1961–63 and was bitterly disappointed by de Gaulle's veto on UK membership. After his party's election victory in 1970, he reopened negotiations and successfully led Britain into the Communities in 1973, although the question of membership seriously divided his own party, as well as the opposition Labour Party. His government was defeated in a general election in February 1974, mainly on domestic issues, and Heath was replaced as the leader of the Conservative Party in 1975 by the strongly Eurosceptic Margaret Thatcher. Heath became increasingly more outspoken as a supporter of greater political and economic integration in Europe, and his apparent personal bitterness towards his successor was focused on opposition to her policy towards the Community. He has continued to be one of his party's leading advocates of European integration, sharply criticizing the policies of both John Major and William Hague, Thatcher's successors as leader of the Conservatives, from the backbenches of the House of Commons until his retirement.

JOSPIN, Lionel (1937–   ): Prime Minister of France since 1997. President Jacques Chirac was obliged to appoint Jospin, a political opponent, to the premiership after Jospin's Socialist Party and its allies won a majority in the National Assembly. In relation to policy towards the EU, there has been little tension during the period of "cohabitation" as Chirac and Jospin hold fairly similar views on European integration and France's role in it. Thus, although he advocates further integration to include the coordination of taxation and economic policies at the EU level, in what he has called a "European economic government", Jospin believes strongly that it should be on the basis of a "federation of nation states". He has explicitly rejected the German federal model, in which he believes France would have the same status as one of the *Länder*. Thus, although he remains committed to the traditional Franco–German alliance, it is clear that he has a very different vision of the final political shape of the EU than either Schröder or Fischer. Jospin also has rather more traditionally socialist views than some other social democratic leaders in the EU and has pressed strongly for policies to protect what he calls "the European social model".

KINNOCK, Neil (1942–   ): European Commissioner, with responsibility for transport, from 1995 to 1999, and Vice President of the Commission, with special responsibility for its reform, since 1999. Kinnock was the leader of the British Labour Party from 1983 to 1992, but resigned the post after failing to defeat the Conservatives at a general election. As Commissioner for transport he was particularly committed to the development of Trans-European Networks. He was promoted to his present post in the aftermath of the resignation of the Santer Commission on charges of corruption and maladministration. He headed a task force for administrative reform that in March 2000 produced a white paper outlining radical proposals designed to improve the efficiency, accountability, transparency, responsibility, and public service ethos of the Commission.

KOHL, Helmut (1930–): Chancellor of West Germany from 1982 to 1990 and of unified Germany from 1990 to 1998. Kohl has attributed his lifelong support for European federalism to his own experiences during and immediately after World War II, and he actively worked for political union. The unification of his country further strengthened his belief in the need for greater European integration, which he saw as the best way of reassuring Germany's neighbours that its unification presented no threat to their interests. He created an active partnership with President François Mitterrand of France, who shared his deep commitment to the Franco–German alliance as the bedrock of postwar European integration. He also worked closely with the Commission President, Jacques Delors, especially in relation to EMU, a cause close to both their hearts.

LAMY, Pascal (1947–): European Commissioner for Trade since 1999. A graduate of the prestigious Ecole Nationale d'Administration and a former civil servant, Lamy served as *chef de cabinet* to the Commission President, Jacques Delors, from 1984 to 1994 and as his special aide for G7 summits. He worked in the private sector from 1994 to 1999, notably on the restructuring of the French bank Crédit Lyonnais, before returning to Brussels. He is a firm believer in the liberalization of trade, and is leading the EU's bilateral trade negotiations with the United States and Japan, as well as the multinational negotiations within the World Trade Organization. Lamy believes that the west European experience of preferential regional trading arrangements should be used as a model for similar regional trading initiatives elsewhere in the world.

LUBBERS, Ruud (1939–): Prime Minister of the Netherlands from 1982 to 1986 and from 1989 to 1994. Lubbers is an ardent advocate of European integration. His most significant contribution to the process was to chair the Maastricht summit in 1991 and broker agreement on the Treaty on European Union. The other main achievement of the Dutch Presidency in 1991 was the signing of the European Energy Charter, which Lubbers had proposed as a way of offering practical support to the countries of central and eastern Europe.

MAJOR, John (1943–): Prime Minister of the United Kingdom from 1990 to 1997. When Major succeeded his fellow-Conservative Margaret Thatcher as Prime Minister he said that his goal was to place Britain "at the heart of Europe", and to end the self-imposed isolation that had characterized the final years of her administration. He claimed that the concessions that he secured at Maastricht in December 1991, including the removal of the word "federal" from the final draft of the treaty and agreement on the British opt-outs from both the social chapter and the single currency, demonstrated the success of his policy of "constructive engagement". However, the deep divisions within his own party on what came to be known simply as "Europe" made it increasingly difficult for him to play a positive role within the EU and his government came to be seen by many as a serious obstacle to further European integration.

MANSHOLT, Sicco (1908–1995): Commissioner responsible for agriculture from 1958 to 1972, Commission President in 1972. Mansholt came from a farming background and was Agriculture Minister in the Netherlands before being appointed to the new EEC Commission. He was the principal architect of the Common Agricultural Policy, which he had first advocated in 1950 in the Council of Europe. Although the policy has subsequently been widely criticized, Mansholt anticipated many of its excesses and had recommended that the policy of price support should be accompanied by plans for the radical rationalization and modernization of agriculture. His scheme was only partially adopted by the member states, as a result of bitter opposition from powerful farm lobbies, especially in France, and he retired from the Commission in disillusionment.

MITTERRAND, François (1916–96): President of France from 1981 to 1995. Mitterrand was generally more sympathetic to European integration than most of his predecessors and he played a leading role in the developments leading up to the agreement on the Treaty on European Union. European integration became increasingly central to his overall political strategy when he was forced to abandon much of the radical programme on which the parties of the left, under his leadership, had won their historic victory in 1981. He became convinced that France's economic prosperity and political ambitions could best be achieved within the framework of the Community. He established a close partnership with Helmut Kohl and together they exercised a decisive leadership during more than a decade of European integration, with the completion of the internal market, and the commitment to achieve Economic and Monetary Union, being their key achievements. Mitterrand's foreign policy was shaped by traditional French suspicions of the transatlantic alliance, and he took the initiative in proposing that the Western European Union should be revived in 1984 and provision made in the Maastricht Treaty for it to assume responsibility for the EU's new role in defence. Although Mitterrand was weakened by ill health and corruption scandals in his later years, his contribution to the creation of the EU is seen, even by some of his former enemies, as a significant legacy.

MONNET, Jean (1888–1979): President of the High Authority of the European Coal and Steel Community (ECSC) from 1952 to 1955. Monnet was a practitioner rather than a politician, and had extensive experience as an economist, businessman, and diplomat before he became the head of the new French Planning Commission in 1945. The early success of the ECSC, which he had persuaded the French Foreign Minister, Robert Schuman, would be the best first step towards their shared goal of European union, paved the way for the creation of the EEC and Euratom. He also drafted the Pleven Plan, which called for the creation of a European Defence Community, and was bitterly disappointed when it was rejected by the French National Assembly. He resigned from the ECSC in 1955 and devoted the rest of his life to promoting his federalist ideals through his Action Committee for the United States of Europe. His name continues to be associated with the "Community method", covering both the integration strategy (sectoral/neofunctionalist) and the supranational policy-making procedures developed in the ECSC, the EEC, and Euratom.

NOËL, Emile, (1922–1996): Secretary General of the European Commission from 1958 to 1987. Noël was a committed believer in European integration, and worked for the Consultative Assembly of the Council of Europe, and then for the ad hoc committee responsible for drafting proposals for a European Political Community, before starting work at the new Commission. He went on to become the most senior official during the first 30 years of the Community's development. He worked closely with six successive Presidents of the Commission, and provided invaluable experience and continuity, as well as vision. After he retired from the Commission he became President of the European University Institute in Florence.

PATTEN, Chris (1944–   ): External Relations Commissioner since 1999. Patten was a Conservative member of the British House of Commons from 1979 to 1992, and held several ministerial positions under Margaret Thatcher and John Major. He was the last Governor of Hong Kong, serving from 1992 until its transfer to Chinese sovereignty in 1997. Patten has found it difficult to define a clear role for himself, given the appointments of Javiar Solana as the Secretary General of the Council and High Representative for the Common Foreign and Security Policy, and of Commission colleagues responsible for trade, enlargement, and development.

PRODI, Romano (1939–   ): Prime Minister of Italy from 1996 to 1998, President of the European Commission since 1999. A former professor of economics, Prodi became chairman of the Ulivo (Olive Tree) centre-left coalition in 1995 and was elected to the Italian Parliament in 1996. His most notable achievement as Prime Minister was to ensure that Italy met the Maastricht criteria for participation in EMU, although the austerity measures his government imposed were very unpopular. He is an ardent federalist, and an ambitious and astute politician, but he has found it difficult to exercise the same authority as, for example, Jacques Delors. Prodi was bitterly disappointed not only by the outcome of the intergovernmental conference that produced the Treaty of Nice, but also at the way in which, he felt, he had been sidelined in the final negotiations. Reform of the Commission itself, to restore its tarnished image in the wake of the ignominious resignation of his predecessor Jacques Santer, is his greatest challenge and also, perhaps, his best hope of establishing his own credibility.

SANTER, Jacques (1937–   ): Prime Minister of Luxembourg from 1984 to 1995, President of the European Commission from 1995 to 1999. Santer was a compromise candidate for his Commission post, being chosen only after John Major had vetoed the nomination of the generally preferred candidate, Jean-Luc Dehaene of Belgium, because of his "federalist" convictions. Santer proved to be a greater advocate for political union than some had expected, but he was a much less effective leader than his predecessor, Jacques Delors. His Commission was forced to resign en bloc in March 1999, after fierce criticisms of their alleged mismanagement and corruption were aired in the European Parliament. Although Santer was not directly implicated in the scandals, he was criticized for his weak leadership in allowing such practices to continue.

SCHRÖDER, Gerhard (1944–): Chancellor of Germany since 1998. At the time of his Red–Green coalition's election victory, much was made of the fact that Schröder represented a new generation of German politicians whose views had not been shaped by the experience of World War II. In fact, however, his father had been killed in battle and his commitment to European integration, like that of his predecessors, is based on the belief that it is the best way to ensure peace. He has called for the transformation of the EU into a federation modelled on the German system, with the Commission becoming, in effect, the EU's government, the European Parliament's legislative powers extended and the Council of Ministers transformed into a second chamber like the Bundesrat. However, his commitment to deeper integration is combined with a greater assertion of Germany's interests within the EU and, in particular, a determination to ensure that the financial burden is more equitably shared by the other member states. Similarly, while strongly supporting enlargement, Schröder has also sought to ensure that Germany's interests are protected, for example in relation to transition periods for the free movement of people.

SCHUMAN, Robert (1886–1963): Prime Minister of France from 1947 to 1948 and Foreign Minister from 1948 to 1952. A firm believer in European integration and political union, Schuman was born in Luxembourg and grew up in Lorraine when it was part of Germany. He was convinced that European unity could only be based on Franco–German reconciliation and his greatest contribution to European integration was to devise a practical plan for achieving it. He was persuaded by Jean Monnet that the most viable approach to their goal of political integration would be one based on limited economic integration on a sectoral basis. The Schuman Plan, issued in 1950, proposed the pooling of the coal and steel industries of France and Germany under a common authority. Other states were invited to participate, and the European Coal and Steel Community, established in 1952, served as the model for the EEC in 1957. In 1986, in recognition of Schuman's contribution to European integration, the centenary of his birth was commemorated by declaring 9 May "Europe Day".

SOLANA MADARIAGA, Javier (1942–): Secretary General of the Council of the European Union, High Representative for the Common Foreign and Security Policy, and Secretary General of the Western European Union since 1999. Solana, served in the Socialist government of Spain from 1982 onwards, notably as Minister for Foreign Affairs from 1992 to 1995. He was Secretary General of NATO from 1995 to 1999, playing a key role during NATO's engagement in the Kosovo crisis. It is widely believed that he is therefore in a good position to negotiate the future relationship between the EU's new military bodies and those of the NATO alliance, one of the key tasks he has been engaged in since leaving NATO. He is also expected to be active in establishing a clearer international role for the EU, and to oversee the development of its military capability under the Common European Security and Defence Policy.

SPAAK, Paul-Henri (1899–1972): Foreign Minister or Prime Minister of Belgium on several occasions between 1936 and 1966; Secretary General of NATO from 1957 to 1961. Spaak was one of the leading figures in the postwar movement promoting European integration, chairing the newly created Organization for European Economic Cooperation in Europe in 1948 and serving as the first President of the Consultative Assembly of the Council of Europe. However, his most significant contribution to the development of European integration was his skilled chairmanship of the intergovernmental conference, set up after the Messina Conference in 1955, that drafted the Treaties of Rome establishing the European Economic Community and the European Atomic Energy Community (Euratom). He was subsequently bitterly disappointed by the setbacks to the development of the Communities in the 1960s, especially the use by President Charles de Gaulle of France's veto over enlargement and the outcome of the "empty chair" crisis of 1965.

SPINELLI, Altiero (1907–86): founder of the European Federalist Movement; member of the European Commission from 1970 to 1976. An ardent advocate of European federalism, Spinelli founded the European Federalist Movement in Italy during World War II and, with other Resistance leaders, issued a call for a federal union to be established. He remained extremely active in the European Movement, publishing several important documents on European federalism, and after his period on the Commission, was a Communist member of the European Parliament (MEP) from 1979. He believed that the directly elected European Parliament had a mandate to draft a federal constitution to replace the Treaty of Rome and joined a group of likeminded MEPs that met regularly in the Crocodile Restaurant in Strasbourg. The "Crocodile Club" provided the main inspiration behind the Draft

Treaty establishing the European Union that was adopted by the European Parliament by a large majority in 1984 and set the agenda for institutional reform in the 1980s and 1990s.

THATCHER, Margaret, Baroness (1925–): Prime Minister of the United Kingdom from 1979 to 1990. Although Thatcher agreed with the liberal economic thrust of the Community, which accorded with her own brand of Conservatism, she strongly objected to its political and social aspects. During the period 1979 to 1984 she was engaged in a running battle with the Community over the cost of British membership; her persistence led in 1984 to an agreement that Britain would receive an annual rebate on its contributions to the Community budget. She then enthusiastically endorsed the initiative to complete the single market by 31 December 1992 and was persuaded to accept limited institutional reform in the Single European Act to facilitate the necessary legislation. However, she became increasingly alarmed by the growing momentum of integration in the late 1980s, especially by proposals for a single currency and a charter of social rights. In a speech at the College of Europe in Bruges in 1988 she passionately rejected the federal model and put forward her own vision of European cooperation between sovereign nation states. As she became increasingly hostile to "Brussels" and isolated in European Council meetings, senior members of her own party decided that she had become a liability both to her party and to Britain's national interests, and she was forced to resign. She continues to be one of the most outspoken critics of the EU and an icon of the Eurosceptic movement.

VERHEUGEN, Günter (1944–): European Commissioner for Enlargement since 1999. Verheugen was a member of the German Free Democratic Party until 1982, when he joined the Social Democrats. He then served as a member of the Bundestag, from 1983 to 1999, and was Minister for European Affairs from 1998 to 1999. He now faces the enormous challenge of overseeing the negotiations with the applicant states and the implementation of the EU's pre-accession strategy, to pave the way for what is expected to be the EU's largest ever enlargement.

Appendix 4

Representation of Member States in the Institutions of the EU

The Treaty of Nice, assuming that it is ratified by the member states, will change the national representation in some EU institutions from 2004 (European Parliament) or 2005 (Commission, weighting of the votes in the Council), in anticipation of enlargement. In a Declaration on the Enlargement of the European Union included as Annex II to the Treaty of Nice, representation is specified for a EU of 27 members. Obviously, new member states will only be allocated these seats and votes when they have acceded to the Union. In the tables that follow, the figures are given for an EU of 15 member states before 2004/5 and for an EU of up to 27 members after 2005.

The European Commission

1999–2004 (15 Member States)

Austria	1	Italy	2
Belgium	1	Luxembourg	1
Denmark	1	Netherlands	1
Finland	1	Portugal	1
France	2	Spain	2
Germany	2	Sweden	1
Greece	1	United Kingdom	2
Ireland	1		

2005–2009 (up to 27 States)
The Commission will comprise one Commissioner from each member state.

From 2010 (27 or more Member States)

From the date on which the first Commission takes up its duties after the accession of the 27th member state, the number of members of the Commission will be less than the number of member states, but the final total has yet to be agreed. The members of the Commission will be chosen according to a rotation system based on the principle of equality and all states will take their turn in not having one of their nationals as a Commissioner.

The European Parliament

1999–2004 (15 Member States)

Germany	99	Portugal	25
United Kingdom	87	Sweden	22
France	87	Austria	21
Italy	87	Denmark	16
Spain	64	Finland	16
Netherlands	31	Ireland	15
Greece	25	Luxembourg	6
Belgium	25		
		Total	626

MEPs sit in multinational groups according to party, rather than by nationality (see Table 2.3)

2004–2009 (up to 27 Member States, Depending on Date of Accession of New Members)

Germany	99	Bulgaria	17
United Kingdom	72	Austria	17
France	72	Slovakia	13
Italy	72	Denmark	13
Spain	50	Finland	13
Poland	50	Ireland	12
Romania	33	Lithuania	12
Netherlands	25	Latvia	8
Greece	22	Slovenia	7
Belgium	22	Estonia	6
Portugal	22	Cyprus	6
Czech Republic	20	Luxembourg	6
Hungary	20	Malta	5
Sweden	18		
		Total	732

Allocation of Seats for European Parliament Election, June 2004

Seats will be allocated on the basis of the table above to those new member states that have signed accession treaties by 1 January 2004. If the total number of MEPs to be elected from existing and new member states is less than the 732 specified in the Treaty of Nice, a pro-rata correction will be made to the number of representatives to be elected in each country. It is therefore expected that the actual number of MEPs elected per member state in 2004 will be slightly higher than indicated in the table.

The European Court of Justice

Each member state nominates one Judge. There will no change after enlargement.

The Committee of the Regions and the Economic and Social Committee

15 Member States

Germany	24	Portugal	12
United Kingdom	24	Sweden	12
France	24	Austria	12
Italy	24	Denmark	9
Spain	21	Finland	9
Netherlands	12	Ireland	9
Greece	12	Luxembourg	6
Belgium	12		

27 Member States

Germany	24	Bulgaria	12
United Kingdom	24	Austria	12
France	24	Slovakia	9
Italy	24	Denmark	9
Spain	21	Finland	9
Poland	21	Ireland	9
Romania	15	Lithuania	9
Netherlands	12	Latvia	7
Greece	12	Slovenia	7
Czech Republic	12	Estonia	7
Belgium	12	Cyprus	6
Hungary	12	Luxembourg	6
Portugal	12	Malta	5
Sweden	12		

Weighting of Votes in the Council

For decisions taken on the basis of qualified majority voting (QMV), number of votes by country in order of size of population

Until 1 January 2005 (15 Member States)

Germany	10	Portugal	5
United Kingdom	10	Sweden	4
France	10	Austria	4
Italy	10	Denmark	4
Spain	8	Finland	3
Netherlands	5	Ireland	3
Greece	5	Luxembourg	2
Belgium	5		
		Total	87

At least 62 votes are required for a qualified majority.

From 1 January 2005 (up to 27 Member States)

Germany	29	Bulgaria	10
United Kingdom	29	Austria	10
France	29	Slovakia	7
Italy	29	Denmark	7
Spain	27	Finland	7
Poland	27	Ireland	7
Romania	14	Lithuania	7
Netherlands	13	Latvia	4
Greece	12	Slovenia	4
Czech Republic	12	Estonia	4
Belgium	12	Cyprus	4
Hungary	12	Luxembourg	4
Portugal	12	Malta	3
Sweden	10		

If there are still only 15 member states on 1 January 2005, 169 votes out of a possible total of 237 will be required for a qualified majority. When the total membership reaches 27, at least 258 votes out of a possible 345 will be required. For an intermediate number of member states, the threshold will need to be agreed. (See Chapter 2 for further details of the rules governing the use of qualified majority voting.)

Appendix 5

Bibliography

This bibliography is intended to draw the attention of readers to some of the most interesting and useful English-language books, journals, and websites on the EU. It makes no claim to be comprehensive: there is a vast and ever-growing literature on all aspects of European integration and the books listed here are only a small sample. The Further Reading list at the end of each chapter should be consulted for reading on specific topics covered in the book; books listed there have not been included in this bibliography except where they are of more general interest.

One of the greatest challenges in studying the EU is to keep up to date with changes both in its own institutions and policies and in the theories and methodologies used in the academic analysis of its development and operation. The review sections of the journals listed here are particularly useful as sources of information on the new books that will have been published since this book went to press.

Reference

Bainbridge, Timothy, *The Penguin Companion to the European Union*, second edition, London and New York: Penguin, 1998

A little outdated, but still useful for its short and authoritative explanations of key concepts and terminology

Dinan, Desmond (editor), *Encyclopedia of the European Union*, London: Macmillan, and Boulder, CO: L. Rienner, 2000

A widely respected and authoritative reference book, with more than 700 alphabetically listed entries covering acronyms, concepts, countries, institutions, personalities, and policies. Some of the entries are short essays by internationally renowned academic or professional experts, while others have a dictionary or glossary format with concise explanations.

Economist, Pocket Europe in Figures, fourth edition, London: Profile, 2000

Facts and figures on the geography, population, socioeconomic profiles, trade, and environment of the 48 countries in Europe

Edwards, Geoffrey, and Georg Wiessala (editors), *The European Union 2000/2001: Annual Review of Activities*, Oxford: Blackwell, 2001

This annual publication provides an invaluable survey and analysis of key political, economic and legal developments and issues in the EU by leading experts. It is published as a supplement to the *Journal of Common Market Studies*, but it is also available as a freestanding book.

European Communities/Union, *Who's Who in the European Union?*, Luxembourg: Office of Official Publications of the European Communities, 2001

Details of the locations and addresses of all the EU's buildings in Brussels, Luxembourg, and Strasbourg; an alphabetical list of MEPs and members of the Economic and Social Committee; and the organizational structure of all EU bodies and institutions, with the names and contact details of all staff down to heads of units

European Companion 2001–2002, The, 11th edition, London: The Stationery Office, 2001

An annual directory of the EU's institutions with the biographies and contact details (including e-mail) of more than 1,000 politicians and officials. It is too expensive for most people to buy, but it is an invaluable library resource.

Eurostat, *Eurostat Yearbook: 2001*, Luxembourg: Office of Official Publications of the European Communities, 2001

An annual publication containing an immense wealth of statistics on all aspects of the EU and its member states

Eurostat–European Commission, *Statistical Yearbook on Candidate and South-east European Countries: 2001*, Luxembourg: Office of Official Publications of the European Communities. 2001

An annual publication of statistics and data on the states that are current or future candidates for EU membership

Leach, Rodney, *A Concise Encyclopedia of the European Union from Aachen to Zollverein*, third edition, London: Profile, and Chicago: Fitzroy Dearborn, 2000

An exceptionally clear and helpful book aimed at the general reader who wishes to take part in an informed discussion on the EU, although it is equally valuable for students and professionals new to the field. The entries are selected on the basis of what such a readership might want to know about, and are concise, accurate, and interesting.

Leonard, Dick, *The Economist Guide to the European Union*, seventh edition, London: Economist Books, 2000

An annual survey of the main economic and political developments and issues, with some useful statistical data

Ramsey, Anne (editor), *Eurojargon: A Dictionary of European Union Acronyms, Abbreviations and Sobriquets*, sixth edition, Bruton: CPI, and Chicago: Fitzroy Dearborn, 2000

With over 4,000 entries, this book is not only outstanding in its comprehensiveness but also graphic evidence of the full extent of the problem of the "Eurojargon" that baffles and infuriates all but the inner circles of the EU's bureaucracy. It is an invaluable guide for all those working on EU projects, lobbying or otherwise interacting with the EU's institutions.

Roney, Alex, and Stanley Budd, *The European Union: A Guide through the EC/EU Maze*, sixth edition, London and Dover, NH: Kogan Page, 1998

A general overview of the development of the EU, its institutions, and its policy-making processes. The book is aimed more at practitioners than at academics. It contains useful details of EU-funded programmes and initiatives.

Urwin, Derek, *Dictionary of European History and Politics 1945–1995*, London and New York: Longman, 1996

Pan-European in its scope and very useful for the wider European context of personalities, organizations, countries, and events

General Texts

Archer, Clive, *The European Union: Structure and Process*, third edition, London and New York: Continuum, 2000

A popular text for undergraduate students of politics, covering the history of integration, and the EU's institutions and policies, including external relations

Bromley, Simon (editor), *Governing the European Union*, London: Sage in association with the Open University, 2001

Written as one of the core texts for the Open University's course *Governing Europe*, the book combines clarity and attractive presentation with a commitment to encourage students to engage in the academic debates about the nature of the EU as a polity and the key issues surrounding its future development.

Church, Clive, and David Phinnemore, *European Union and European Community: A Handbook and Commentary on the Post-Maastricht Treaties*, London and New York: Harvester Wheatsheaf, 1994

A detailed commentary on the provisions of the Treaty on European Union set within a broad historical and policy perspective. The book contains extensive extracts from the treaties and other related documents, making it an invaluable reference source for students and professionals.

Cram, Laura, Desmond Dinan, and Neill Nugent (editors), *Developments in the European Union*, London: Macmillan, and New York: St Martin's Press, 1999

A very useful set of chapters on key institutional and policy issues by a team of leading academic experts. Books in this series are regularly revised, so a second edition will soon update coverage of issues and developments.

Dinan, Desmond, *Ever Closer Union: An Introduction to European Integration*, second edition, London: Macmillan, and Boulder, CO: L. Rienner, 1999

A widely acclaimed survey and analysis of the history, institutions, and policies of the EC/EU. Although the title suggests that it is only an "introduction", this is a very comprehensive, detailed, and authoritative study that makes a significant contribution to the literature on European integration. It is also very readable, although its length may be rather offputting.

Galloway, David, *The Treaty of Nice and Beyond: Realities and Illusions of Power in the EU*, Sheffield: Sheffield Academic Press/UACES, 2001

A very comprehensive analysis of the outcome of the Nice negotiations and their implications for the future. Written by a senior adviser in the Council Secretariat, it also gives some fascinating insights into the politics of the negotiating process itself.

George, Stephen, and Ian Bache, *Politics in the European Union*, Oxford and New York: Oxford University Press, 2001

An attractively presented text for undergraduate students that combines a strong theoretical section with comprehensive coverage of the EU's history, member states, institutions, and key policy areas. The book is supported by a website of teaching resources.

McCormick, John, *Understanding the European Union: A Concise Introduction*, London: Macmillan, and New York: St Martin's Press, 1999

A very good general introduction to the history and institutions of the EU, with thematic chapters on the EU and its member states and its citizens, economic integration, and relations with the rest of the world. Boxed summaries provide a clear presentation of key facts and other useful information.

Nicoll, Sir William, and Trevor C. Salmon, *Understanding the European Union*, Harlow: Longman, 2001

A very accessible introduction to the history and institutions of the EU. It is particularly noted for its strong section on the attitudes of the EU's member states to integration in general and also to specific policies and issues.

Pinder, John, *The European Union: A Very Short Introduction*, Oxford and New York: Oxford University Press, 2001

Despite being exceptionally small and short (or perhaps precisely because of those qualities), this is a very valuable introduction to the EU for the general reader or busy professional. A great deal of useful information is presented extremely succinctly, with lots of charts and diagrams.

Usher, John (editor), *The State of the European Union: Structure, Enlargement and Economic Union*, Harlow and New York: Longman, 2000

An interdisciplinary perspective on the implications of the Treaty of Amsterdam and other key issues, such as monetary union and enlargement, although the majority of the contributors are legal scholars. It includes consideration of a generally rather neglected topic: the implications of UK devolution, especially the creation of the Scottish Parliament, for the conduct of British policy in the EU.

History and Development

Burgess, Michael, *Federalism and the European Union: The Building of Europe, 1950–2000*, London and New York: Routledge, 2000

An overtly federalist interpretation of postwar European integration, arguing that federal ideals have been a major influence at all stages of the EC/EU's development

Dedman, Martin, *The Origins and Development of the European Union 1945–1995*, London and New York: Routledge, 1996

A concise and very readable history of the origins of the EU, with the emphasis placed firmly on the early period of postwar integration, so that there is only a rather brief account of developments since the Treaty of Rome

Dyson, Kenneth, and Kevin Featherstone, *The Road to Maastricht: Negotiating Economic and Monetary Union*, Oxford and New York: Oxford University Press, 1999

Widely regarded as the definitive account of the negotiations leading to the historic agreement to move to Economic and Monetary Union. At nearly 900 pages, this is a book for the specialist rather than the general reader, but it does tell a fascinating story.

McCallister, Richard, *From EC to EU: An Historical and Political Survey*, London and New York: Routledge, 1997

A comprehensive history of the EC/EU that highlights some of the key turning points in its evolution

Milward, Alan S., *The European Rescue of the Nation-State*, second edition, London and New York: Routledge, 1999

A controversial but widely respected study of the motives behind the early moves towards integration in postwar Europe, this is an important contribution to academic debate, and essential reading for more advanced students of both history and politics.

Monar, Jörg, and Wolfgang Wessels (editors), *The European Union After the Treaty of Amsterdam*, London and New York: Continuum, 2000

A collection of chapters by a very distinguished international team of practitioners and academics on the impact of the Treaty of Amsterdam on key policy areas and the institutional system. Their analysis focuses on the need for further reforms if the challenges posed by enlargement are not to lead to the danger of fragmentation.

Moravcsik, Andrew, *The Choice for Europe: Social Purpose and State Power from Messina to Maastricht*, Ithaca, NY: Cornell University Press, 1998; London: UCL Press, 1999

A liberal–intergovernmentalist interpretation of the development of the EU from one of the leading EU specialists in the United States

Pinder, John, *European Community: The Building of a Union*, third edition, Oxford and New York: Oxford University Press, 1998

Offering a federalist perspective on the development of the EU and its policies, this is a very readable general introduction to the subject, without much explicit theory.

Salmon, Trevor, and William Nicoll (editors), *Building European Union: A Documentary History and Analysis*, Manchester: Manchester University Press, 1997

A collection of more than 100 documents that is unusual in that it includes material from as early as the 17th century. The editors provide a critical introduction to each document that places it in its historical context and explains its importance.

Stirk, Peter, *A History of European Integration since 1914*, London and New York: Pinter, 1996

A comprehensive, chronological study of the process of European integration from the violent instability that followed World War I through to the aftermath of the Cold War

Stirk, Peter, and David Weigall (editors), *The Origins and Development of European Integration: A Reader and Commentary*, London and New York: Pinter, 1999

A well-selected collection of extracts from treaties, speeches, and other documents that not only provides a valuable resource for the study of the major events in the history of European integration but also gives a flavour of the debates that surrounded them at the time. Each chapter is introduced by a substantial critical review that serves to put the documents that follow into their historical context.

Urwin, Derek W., *The Community of Europe: A History of European Integration since 1945*, second revised edition, London and New York: Longman, 1995

An introductory survey of European integration that sets the EC/EU into the broader context of early postwar European cooperation and then traces its internal development through to the mid-1990s. A popular student text that is both very readable and comprehensive.

Political Institutions and the Political Process

Cini, Michelle, *The European Commission: Leadership, Organisation and Culture in the EU Administration*, Manchester: Manchester University Press, 1996

A fascinating study that seeks to explain what the Commission does, how it does it, and why. Drawing on extensive research, the author uses the perspectives of leadership, organization and administrative culture to assess the legitimacy and effectiveness of this important institution.

Corbett, Richard, Francis Jacobs, and Michael Shackleton, *The European Parliament*, fourth edition, London: John Harper, 2000

An authoritative and very detailed study by three "insiders", an MEP and two of the Parliament's senior officials, this is widely considered to be the definitive reference source on the organisation, procedures, and powers of the Parliament.

Greenwood, Justin, *Representing Interests in the European Union*, London: Macmillan, and New York: St Martin's Press, 1997

A comprehensive assessment of the roles and importance of interest groups in the development and policies of the EU. It provides analysis and a great deal of useful data on professional, consumer, social, business, labour, and general interest groups that are active at the EU level.

Hayes-Renshaw, Fiona, and Helen Wallace, *The Council of Ministers*, London: Macmillan, and New York: St Martin's Press, 1997

One of the first full-length studies of the role and function of the EU's chief decision-making body, and its relationships to other EU institutions and the member states. Based on extensive research, it is rich in the empirical detail and perceptive analysis for which the authors are renowned.

Hix, Simon, *The Political System of the European Union*, London: Macmillan, and New York: St Martin's Press, 1999

An important book on account of its methodology and approach as much as its content. The author sets out to demonstrate that the EU can be analyzed like any other political system by the systematic application of political science concepts and theories. The result is a stimulating text for more advanced students, researchers, and teachers.

Holland, Martin, *European Community Integration*, London: Pinter and New York: St Martin's Press, 1993 (second edition forthcoming)

An interesting interpretation of the EU's evolution, exploring the tension between the intergovernmental and federal approaches. It assumes a certain amount of prior knowledge, so it is not a good introductory text.

Nugent, Neill, *The Government and Politics of the European Union*, fourth edition, London: Macmillan, and Durham, NC: Duke University Press, 1999

A very widely used and highly regarded undergraduate text providing a detailed analysis of the EU's institutions and policy processes. A very welcome new feature in this edition is the inclusion of a concluding chapter that critically surveys the main theoretical and conceptual tools that are used to analyze the EU's development and operation.

Nugent, Neill (editor), *At the Heart of the Union: Studies of the European Commission*, second edition, London: Macmillan, and New York: St Martin's Press, 2000

An important collection of studies reflecting the recent upsurge of interest in the Commission as a focus for research, after many years of relative neglect

Nugent, Neill, *The European Commission*, London and New York: Palgrave, 2001

A very comprehensive and detailed study of the Commission's organisation, functions, and relationships with other EU actors. It assumes a prior knowledge of the EU's system of governance and is intended for more advanced students or those who have some experience of working in or with the EU bureaucracy.

Sherrington, Philippa, *The Council of Ministers: Political Authority in the European Union*, London and New York: Pinter, 2000

A detailed account of the operation and role of what is undoubtedly both the most powerful and the most secretive of the EU's institutions. Based on extensive research and interviews, it provides important insights into the way the EU really works.

Smith, Julie, *Europe's Elected Parliament*, Sheffield: Sheffield Academic Press/UACES, 1999

A very readable and up-to-date study of the growing importance of the European Parliament's role in the EU's policy-making system, and the continuing debate about its future role and legitimacy

Warleigh, Alex (editor), *Understanding European Union Institutions*, London and New York: Routledge, forthcoming

A very clearly presented student text, with a good overview introduction on how the EU works and individual chapters explaining the functions of all the main institutions, including the less well-known ones such as the Court of Auditors, the Ombudsman, and the Committee of the Regions

Policies and Policy-Making

Please also see further reading recommended at the end of the chapters covering specific policy areas.

Andersen, Svein, and Kjell Eliassen (editors), *Making Policy in Europe: The Europeification of National Policy-making*, second edition, London and Thousand Oaks, CA: Sage, 2001

One of the first studies of the interaction between the EU and national policy-making, with the theoretical and conceptual analysis applied to a selection of case-studies; now extensively revised

Barnes, Ian G., and Pamela Barnes, *The Enlarged European Union*, London and New York: Longman, 1995

The title is somewhat misleading as this is not really a book on enlargement but rather a general student text covering all the main EU policies in an accessible and informative manner.

Cram, Laura, *Policy-making in the European Union: Conceptual Lenses and the Integration Process*, London and New York: Routledge, 1997

A strong theoretical introduction is applied to case studies, with a detailed examination of the development of social policy and of information and communication technology policy.

Glöckler, Gabriel, Lie Junius, Gioia Scappucci, Simon Usherwood, and Julian Vassallo, *Guide to EU Policies*, London: Blackstone Press, 1998

A structured survey of the EU's main policies, including the Common Foreign and Security Policy, and Justice and Home Affairs, identifying the rationale, legal bases, and policy instruments for each

Levy, Roger, *Implementing European Union Public Policy*, Cheltenham: Edward Elgar, 2000

Using data from the Court of Auditors' reports, this study provides an empirical analysis of the performance of EU programme management in the five main spending areas between 1977 and 1996.

Peterson, John, and Elizabeth Bomberg, *Decision-making in the European Union*, London: Macmillan, and New York: St Martin's Press, 1999

A theory-based introduction to decision-making in seven major policy areas, drawing on the authors' extensive research. It is an important contribution to the literature, but its clear and user-friendly style makes it also suitable for use as a student text.

Richardson, Jeremy (editor), *European Union: Power and Policy-making*, second edition, London and New York: Routledge, 2001

An impressive collection of authoritative studies of the way policy is made in the EU, drawing together the latest theoretical and empirical research on the role of institutions, lobbying, representation, and the nature of the supranational polity.

Wallace, Helen, and William Wallace (editors), *Policy-making in the European Union*, fourth edition, Oxford and New York: Oxford University Press, 2000

The latest edition of this ground-breaking book once again brings together an impressive array of academic experts. A very useful introduction provides the theoretical framework for a large number of policy case-studies informed by the latest research in the field.

Economics

Artis, Michael, and Frederick Nixon (editors), *The Economics of the European Union: Policy and Analysis*, second edition, Oxford and New York: Oxford University Press, 1997 (third edition forthcoming)

A comprehensive and accessible guide to the main social and economic policies of the EU, written by a team of experts. There is also a useful overview of the political structures and development of the EU, including consideration of the economics of its enlargement.

Begg, Iain, and Nigel Grimwade, *Paying for Europe*, Sheffield Academic Press/UACES, 1998

Based on a study commissioned by the European Parliament, this is an excellent and up-to-date survey of the "own resources" system of the EU's budget and possible new sources of revenue.

El-Agraa, Ali, *et al.*, *The European Union: History, Institutions, Economics and Policies*, sixth edition, London and New York: Prentice-Hall, 2000

A very popular text, long-established on economics courses, that includes chapters on the historical development of the EU and the role of its institutions, as well as coverage of all the major socioeconomic policy areas.

Grauwe, Paul de, *Economics of Monetary Union*, Oxford and New York: Oxford University Press, 2000

One of the best texts on EMU, it provides a balanced analysis of the issues together with very useful figures, tables, and other data.

Gros, Daniel, and Niels Thygesen, *European Monetary Integration: From the European Monetary System to European Monetary Union*, second edition, Harlow and New York: Longman, 1998

Excellent on the development of EMU and very comprehensive on the economics of EMU

Hitiris, Theo, *European Union Economics*, fourth edition, London and New York: Prentice-Hall, 1998

A clear and accessible introduction to the economics and policies of the EU

Laffan, Brigid, *The Finances of the European Union*,

London: Macmillan, and New York: St Martin's Press, 1997

A very comprehensive recent survey of the politics of the budgetary process

Pelkmans, Jacques, *European Integration: Methods and Economic Analysis*, Harlow and New York: Longman, and Heerlen: Open University of the Netherlands, 1997

A good student text that combines the economic analysis of integration with its application to policies and case studies. Although aimed particularly at undergraduate economics students, its clear style makes it suitable for a wider readership.

Swann, Dennis, *The Economics of Europe: From Common Market to European Union*, ninth edition, London: Penguin, 2000

This very readable and comprehensive book has been one of the most widely recommended introductory texts on the economics of European integration for more than 30 years.

Law

Arnull, Anthony, *The European Union and Its Court of Justice*, Oxford and New York: Oxford University Press, 1999

A detailed legal account of the contribution that the Court has made to the integration process and to specific policy fields

Chalmers, Damian, *European Union Law*, Volume 1, *Law and EU Government*, Aldershot: Dartmouth, 1998

A detailed contextual analysis of the relevant principles of Community law, with a great deal of theoretical and other background information and comment

Dehousse, Renaud, *The European Court of Justice: The Politics of Judicial Integration*, London: Macmillan, and New York: St Martin's Press, 1998

An important work that places the Court and its actions within the framework of political actors and pressures

Hartley, Trevor C., *The Foundations of European Community Law*, fourth edition, Oxford and New York: Oxford University Press, 1998

The leading "doctrinal" textbook on the "constitutional" aspect of Community law, as opposed to the substantive law, with detailed scholarly

analysis of all relevant provisions and principles

Kent, Penelope, *Law of the European Union*, third edition, Harlow and New York: Longman, 2001

This book offers a clear legal perspective on the institutions, decision-making processes, and general principles of Community law. Chapters cover specific areas such as competition law, and broader themes such as the social dimension and equal treatment. Although aimed mainly at lawyers, its clear presentation makes it accessible for students of other disciplines as well as for business people and other professionals.

Medhurst, David, *A Brief and Practical Guide to EU Law*, second edition, Oxford: Blackwell Science, 1994 (third edition forthcoming)

The title reflects the author's intention to provide a "quick guide" for practitioners "who are in a hurry to master the subject", and the admirably clear presentation suggests that he may have succeeded. The book also contains a guide to the relevant case law and other relevant documents for the use of those who need to go beyond the basics.

Shaw, Jo, *Law of the European Union*, third edition, London: Macmillan, 2000

Widely thought to be the best short introduction to the "constitutional" elements of Community law, the book is well-structured, and is notable for its clear and incisive analysis.

Weatherill, Stephen, and Paul Beaumont, *EU Law*, third edition, London: Penguin, 1999

A legal perspective on the institutions and an introduction to the main elements of EU law

Weiler, Joseph (editor), *The EU, the WTO and the NAFTA: Towards a Common Law of International Trade*, Oxford and New York: Oxford University Press, 2000

A useful collection of essays that puts the EU in the wider context of international trade developments

The External Role of the EU

Please see the further reading recommended at the end of the chapters in the section of the book on External Relations. The following books are recommended as useful general introductions to the EU's role in the world and include chapters on some of the topics not covered in this book as well as some of those that are.

Bretherton, Charlotte, and John Vogler, *The European Union as a Global Actor*, London and New York: Routledge, 1999

A good introduction to the concept of the EU as an "actor" in the world, with interesting and varied case studies of its role in relation to security, international environmental diplomacy, North–South relations, global trade issues, and relations with its own "near abroad"

Peterson, John, and Helene Sjursen (editors), *A Common Foreign Policy for Europe? Competing Visions of the CFSP*, London and New York: Routledge, 1998

A useful collection of chapters by some of the leading academic authorities in the field, covering theoretical issues in the analysis of the EU's external role, some of the practical problems involved in the development of the CFSP, and case studies of the EU's relations with Poland, the Mediterranean states, and Latin America

Piening, Christopher, *Global Europe: The European Union in World Affairs*, Boulder, CO: L. Rienner, 1997

This is a book written by an insider rather than an academic so it is more concerned with analyzing what the EU does and assessing its effectiveness than engaging in theoretical debates. It is very authoritative and packed with valuable information as well as interesting insights. The first chapter is on trade but all the others cover the EU's relations with particular regions, including central and eastern Europe, the Mediterranean, North America, Latin America, Asia, and the developing world.

Rhodes, Caroline (editor), *The European Union in the World Community*, Boulder, CO: L. Rienner, 1998

A very useful introduction, discussing the identity of the EU in international affairs, is followed by an interesting set of case studies on the EU's role in relation to particular states or regions and international issues such as the environment.

The EU and its Member States

Anderson, Jeffrey, *German Unification and the Union of Europe*, Cambridge and New York: Cambridge University Press, 1999

The author charts the sources of continuity and change in German policy towards the EU, and explores the dynamics of the relationship between the domestic politics of German unification and deeper integration in the EU. The focus is on political economy, with particular attention given to trade, the internal market, and energy.

Bulmer, Simon, Charlie Jeffery, and William Paterson, *Germany's European Diplomacy: Shaping the Regional Milieu*, Manchester: Manchester University Press, 2000

An analysis of Germany's role in the EU and its use of what the authors describe as "soft" power to further its interests through the encouragement of a milieu of multilateral cooperation. It includes an analysis of the dynamics of Germany's key relationships with France, the United Kingdom, and the Netherlands, and explores the interlinkages between internal and external factors in shaping policy. The focus of the book is on the impact of the new German government elected in 1998, and on continuity and change in Germany's EU policy.

George, Stephen, *An Awkward Partner: Britain in the European Community*, third edition, Oxford and New York: Oxford University Press, 1998

The title of this critical analysis of Britain's role in the postwar process of European integration itself became part of the debate about Britain's relationship with the EC/EU. The author expresses his hope that, as a result of the election of the "New Labour" government in 1997, this will be the last edition that he will produce under this title.

Goetz, Klaus, and Simon Hix (editors), *Europeanised Politics? European Integration and National Political Systems*, London and Portland, OR: Frank Cass, 2001

An examination of the impact of European integration on the politics and government of EU member states, including executive–legislative relations, pressure groups, parties, voting behaviour, and judicial politics.

Guyomarch, Alain, Howard Machin, and Ella Ritchie (editors), *France in the European Union*, London: Macmillan, and New York: St Martin's Press, 1998

Chapters by academic experts examine French governments' policies, and the attitudes of parties, interests, and the public towards European integration. The book considers both the influence that France has exerted on the development and policies of the EU, and the way that EU membership has in turn influenced and shaped French domestic institutions and policies.

Hooghe, Liesbet, and Gary Marks, *Multi-level Governance and European Integration*, Lanham, MD: Rowman and Littlefield, 2000

An interesting exploration of the dual process of centralization (to the EU) and decentralization (to subnational regions) that has characterized European politics in recent decades

Manners, Ian, and Richard Whitman (editors), *The Foreign Policies of European Union Member States*, Manchester: Manchester University Press, 2000

A very useful systematic comparison of the foreign policy processes of all the EU member states, identifying those aspects that have been "Europeanized" through EU membership and those that have been retained or excluded by national governments. It contains a good mixture of theoretical and empirical material by an international group of specialists.

Mény, Yves, Pierre Muller, and Jean-Louis Quermonne, *Adjusting to Europe: The Impact of the European Union on National Institutions and Policies*, London and New York: Routledge, 1996

This book explores the relationship between national and EU policy-making, and the ways in which member states have adapted their political institutions and policy processes as a result of their EU membership.

Young, John, *Britain and European Unity, 1945–1999*, second edition, London: Macmillan, and New York: St Martin's Press, 2000

A very comprehensive survey of British policy towards European integration up to and including the decision not to adopt the euro in 1999.

Journals

There are frequently articles published on the EU in the major political science, economics, and law journals but the journals listed below specialize in covering research on the EU and therefore are a good starting point for finding articles related to more specialized topics.

Common Market Law Review

As its title may suggest, this journal has been published for nearly 40 years and focuses almost exclusively on Community law. Apart from articles on particular issues and topics, it contains useful reviews and analysis of important recent cases in the European Court of Justice.

European Economic Review

A journal for economists rather than the general reader. Its articles can be fairly technical but it often includes useful articles on the EU.

European Economy: Reports and Studies

Published by the European Commission's Directorate-General for Trade and Economic Affairs, the *Reports and Studies* is a supplement to *European Economy*, which contains official Commission reports to the Council and Parliament. The *Reports and Studies* series contains research-based articles on aspects of the European economy, often covering topical macroeconomic issues.

European Law Review

This contains articles and shorter notes on legal issues and developments in both the European Court of Justice and the European Court of Human Rights. It also publishes tables of recent legislation and cases heard before both courts.

Journal of Common Market Studies

The title is rather misleading and reflects the fact that it has been the leading academic journal in the field for more than 30 years. It publishes research-based articles on important theoretical and empirical issues concerning the development of the EU, mainly from the perspectives of economics and political science.

Journal of European Integration

A bilingual multidisciplinary journal that aims to be pan-European in its scope but has a number of good articles on the EU

Journal of European Public Policy

As its title suggests, this is primarily a political science journal focussing on the policy-making process and specific public policy issues. Many of its articles concern the EU directly, but some also cover developments within European states.

Perspectives on European Politics and Society

Pan-European in scope but regularly includes articles on the EU. This journal is only available electronically by subscription. Details can be found at www.brill.nl

Websites

Compiled by *Ian Thomson*, Executive Editor of *Know Europe* and Manager of the European Documentation Centre at the University of Cardiff, Wales

European Union: General

EUROPA http://europa.eu.int

The entry point for information from the EU's institutions and agencies, including agendas, policies, and the debate on the future of Europe

Europe on the Internet: Web Directory http://www.knoweurope.net

A structured listing of free access websites of European information, broken down into "EU Databases", "Keeping up to date", "Institutions", "Policies", and "Miscellaneous"

European Commission: *General Report on the Activities of the European Union* http://europa.eu.int/abc/doc/off/rg/en/welcome.htm

A concise annual report on the activities of the EU that can often give leads for further information

European Commission: *Bulletin of the European Union* http://europa.eu.int/abc/doc/off/bull/en/welcome.htm

A concise monthly report on the activities of the EU

European Parliament Fact Sheets http://www.europarl.eu.int/factsheets/default_en.htm?redirected=1

An excellent source for introductory information on the EU's institutions and policies

European Commission: *Glossary: Institutions, Policies and Enlargement of the European Union* http://europa.eu.int/scadplus/leg/en/cig/g4000.htm

A useful listing of key concepts and terms, with explanations

Information on the legislative and judicial processes

European Parliament: *Legislative Observatory (OEIL)* http://wwwdb.europarl.eu.int/dors/oeil/en/search.shtm

A site allowing users to trace the progress of legislative proposals and initiatives, with useful summaries of each stage reached

European Commission: *PreLex* http://europa.eu.int/prelex/apcnet.cfm?CL=en

This site permits users to trace the progress of legislative proposals and initiatives, with many hyperlinks to full text sources.

European Commission: EUR-Lex http://europa.eu.int/eur-lex

A major free-access service of legislative and judicial information. It includes access to the full text of EU Treaties, judgements of the European Court of Justice, proposed, adopted and consolidated legislation, and the latest 45 days' issues of the *Official Journal* C and L series.

European Commission: *CELEX* http://europa.eu.int/celex

The main EU legislative and judicial database. It is a pay access site. It offers more powerful searching options and comprehensive coverage than EUR-Lex (listed above).

European Commission: *SCADPLUS: Union policies* http://europa.eu.int/scadplus/leg/en/l00000.htm

Summaries of key legislation in many policy areas

European Commission: Official Documents http://europa.eu.int/comm/off/index_en.htm

This is not a comprehensive site but it does allow convenient access to key Communications, Green Papers, White Papers, Work Programmes and Action Plans.

Current developments

European Commission: Press and Communication Service http://europa.eu.int/comm/press_room/about_en.htm

Access to a number of services, primarily aimed at the media, but useful for anyone wanting to keep up to date with events and initiatives. In particular, the Press Release database RAPID is a valuable source of concise information.

European Commission: Press and Communication Service: *RAPID: Latest Press Releases* http://europa.eu.int/rapid/start/lastdocs/guesten.htm

This takes you straight through to the Press Releases (and related material) added today.

EUROPA: *What's New* http://europa.eu.int/geninfo/whatsnew.htm

A day-by-day listing of new information on EUROPA. Note that the listing is highly selective. There are two subsections, in addition to the main listing: "What's new: EU Institutions and Agencies" takes you to the "What's new" pages of each individual institution and agency, and "What's new: Commission" takes you through to the "What's new" pages of individual Directorate's General of the European Commission.

EUROPA: *Agenda of the EU Institutions* http://europa.eu.int/news/cal-en.htm

Allows you to find out the detailed day-to-day imminent activities of each of the EU Institutions

European Commission: *Agenda of Weekly Meeting* http://europa.eu.int/comm/secretariat_general/meeting/index_en.htm

The detailed agenda of the weekly European Commission meeting (in French only)

Contact information

European Commission: *IDEA: Interinstitutional Directory* http://158.169.50.70/idea/en/index.htm

Names, addresses and contact details for persons working in all of the EU's instititions, including members of the European Parliament

European Commission: Secretariat General: *Directory of Special Interest Groups* http://europa.eu.int/comm/secretariat_general/sgc/lobbies/instruments/instruments_en.htm

Contact details for the pan-European special interest groups recognized by the European Commission

Sources of finance

European Commission: Secretariat General: *Grants and Loans from the EU* http://europa.eu.int/comm/secretariat_general/index_en.htm

Bibliographical information

European Commission: Library: *ECLAS* http://europa.eu.int/eclas

This is essentially the Commission's library catalogue. It provides bibliographical references to EC publications and documents, and externally published monographs and journal articles on European topics. Increasingly, it also offers links to full texts of EC sources on the web.

Information on EU policies

EUROPA: *European Union: Policies* http://europa.eu.int/pol/index-en.htm

Offers access to information on EU policies from all the EU Institutions

European Commission: Directorates-General http://europa.eu.int/comm/dgs_en.htm

The websites of the Directorates General of the European Commission are the key source of EU policy and background information

Miscellaneous EU sources of interest

Council of the European Union: *EU Presidency website* http://ue.eu.int/en/presid.htm

Every six months a Member State assumes the Presidency of the EU and creates a website of information for the period of the Presidency. The latest, and some of the earlier Presidency websites, can be found here.

European Commission: Treaty of Nice Portal http://europa.eu.int/comm/nice_treaty/index_en.htm

Text and background information, with documents associated with the intergovernmental conference of 2000

EUROPA: *The future of Europe debate* http://europa.eu.int/futurum/index_en.htm

A website set up to encourage debate about the longterm future of the EU leading up to the Intergovernmental Conference in 2004

European Commission: *The European Union in the World* http://europa.eu.int/comm/world

A portal that brings together links to EU information on external relations, trade, humanitarian affairs, development policies, enlargement, the Common Foreign and Security Policy, and relations with individual countries and regions in the world.

Other intergovernmental organizations active in Europe

Organization for Economic Cooperation and Development (OECD) http://www.oecd.org

Council of Europe http://www.coe.fr

European Free Trade Association (EFTA http://
www.efta.int/structure/main/index.html

IMF http://www.imf.org

North Atlantic Treaty Organisation (NATO)
http://www.nato.int

Organization for Security and Cooperation in
Europe (OSCE) http://www.osce.org

UN Economic Commission for Europe (ECE)
http://www.unece.org

World Trade Organization (WTO) http://www.
wto.org

National governments in Europe

European governments on the web http://www.
gksoft.com/govt/en/europa.html

Links to national, regional and local government
websites in all the countries of Europe

Newspapers and related sources for recent information

All the sites below are useful for obtaining information on current developments in the EU. They
are less useful for searching for information on
developments in the past.

BBC News: World: Europe http://news.bbc.co.uk/
hi/english/world/europe/default.stm

Euobserver http://euobserver.com

EurActiv http://www.euractiv.com/cgi-bin/eurb/
cgint.exe?l&1000=1&1001=65&tmpl=index7

European Voice http://www.european-voice.com

Financial Times: European stories http://news.ft.
com/news/worldnews/europe

Moreover.com: European integration http://www.
moreover.com/cgi-local/page?o=portal
&c=EU%20integration%20news

Public Information Europe http://www.publicinfo.
net/home.htm

Academic sources

European Research Papers Archive (ERPA) http://
eiop.or.at/erpa

A portal that offers access to papers from six

research organizations, in Europe and the
United States, dealing with European integration

Miscellaneous

Free Britain http://www.freebritain.co.uk

This Eurosceptic site includes links to likeminded
non-UK organizations.

European Foundation
http://www.europeanfoundation.org/index.html

The website of a prominent "Europhile" organization

House of Lords Select Committee on the European
Union: Reports   http://www.parliament.the-
stationery-office.co.uk/pa/ld/ldeucom.htm

A valuable series of reports on current issues
relating to the institutions and policies of the EU

New generation commercial European information services

eLEXtra (NOMOS) http://www.elextra.de

EU Aware (Ellis Publications/Thomson Legal and
Regulatory Group Europe) http://www.ellispub.
com/Online/euaware.htm

EU Direct (Butterworths) http://www.butterworths.
co.uk/about/index.htm

European Access Plus (Chadwyck-Healey/Bell and
Howell) http://www.europeanaccess.co.uk

KnowEurope (Chadwyck-Healey/Bell and Howell)
http://www.knoweurope.net

Lawtel EU (Lawtel) http://www.lawtel.com

Specialized indexes/portals to European-related material: general

ECLAS http://europa.eu.int/eclas (you can restrict
search for internet sources)

Europe on the Internet : Web Directory http://
www.knoweurope.net (click on "Web Directory")

Euroguide http://www.euroguide.org

European information http://www.uni-mannheim.
de/users/ddz/edz/net/enet.html

European information sources http://www.lib.

berkeley.edu/GSSI/eu.html

European integration information resources http://
eiop.or.at/euroint

European search engines, directories and lists
http://www.netmasters.co.uk/european_search_
engines

Specialized indexes/portals to European-related material: news

BBC News: Europe http://news.bbc.co.uk/hi/
english/world/europe/default.stm

EU Business http://www.EUbusiness.com

Euobserver http://euobserver.com

EurActiv http://www.euractiv.com

Financial Times: Europe http://news.ft.com/news/
worldnews/europe

Moreover.com http://www.moreover.com/cgi-local/
page?o=portal&c=EU%20integration%20news

Yahoo: European stories http://search.news.yahoo.
com/search/news/?p=%22European+Union

Specialized indexes/portals to European-related material: subject/category specific

Euro Portal http://www.crosswater-systems.com/
em0000.htm

Guide to European legal databases http://www.llrx.
com/features/europe.htm

Oneworld http://www.oneworld.org/europe/index.
html

Index

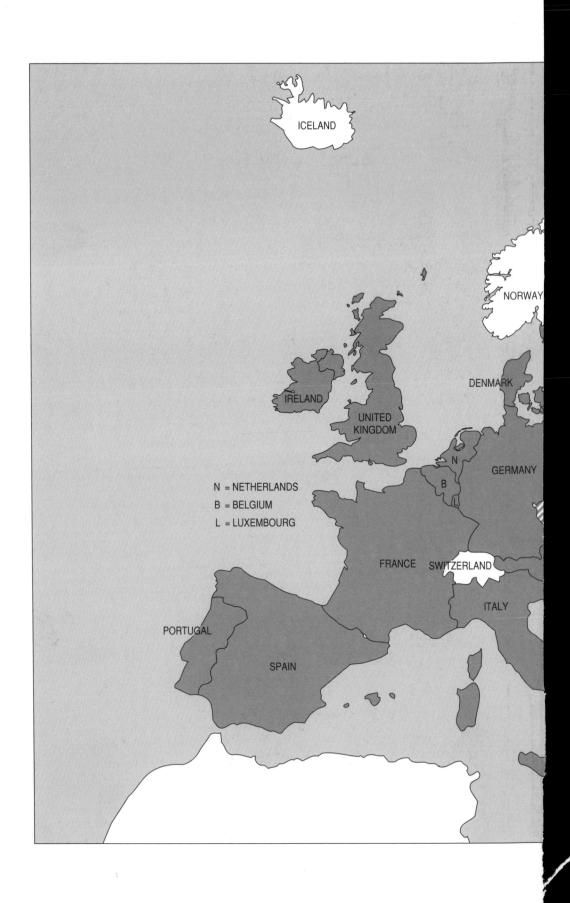